SCEPTICISM AND IRRELIGION
IN THE SEVENTEENTH AND
EIGHTEENTH CENTURIES

BRILL'S STUDIES IN INTELLECTUAL HISTORY

General Editor

A.J. VANDERJAGT, University of Groningen

Editorial Board

M. COLISH, Oberlin College
J.I. ISRAEL, University College, London
J.D. NORTH, University of Groningen
H.A. OBERMAN, University of Arizona, Tucson
R.H. POPKIN, Washington University, St. Louis-UCLA

VOLUME 37

SCEPTICISM AND IRRELIGION IN THE SEVENTEENTH AND EIGHTEENTH CENTURIES

EDITED BY

RICHARD H. POPKIN

AND

ARJO VANDERJAGT

E.J. BRILL

LEIDEN • NEW YORK • KÖLN

1993

The paper in this book meets the guidelines for permanence and durability of the Committee on Production Guidelines for Book Longevity of the Council on Library Resources.

B
837
.S285
1993

Library of Congress Cataloging-in-Publication Data

Scepticism and irreligion in the seventeenth and eighteenth centuries / edited by Richard H. Popkin and Arjo Vanderjagt.
    p.   cm.—(Brill's studies in intellectual history, ISSN 0920-8607; v. 37)
    English, French, and German.
    Proceedings of the Conference on Scepticism and Irreligion in the Seventeenth and Eighteenth Centuries, held July 31-Aug. 4, 1990, at the Netherlands Institute for Advanced Study in the Social Sciences and the Humanities.
    Includes index.
    ISBN 9004095969 (cloth)
    1. Skepticism—History—17th century—Congresses. 2. Skepticism—History—18th century—Congresses. 3. Irreligion—Europe—History—17th century—Congresses. 4. Irreligion—Europe—History—18th century—Congresses. I. Popkin, Richard Henry, 1923- . II. Vanderjagt, Arjo. III. Conference on Scepticism and Irreligion in the Seventeenth and Eighteenth Centuries (1990: Netherlands Institute for Advanced Study in the Social Sciences and the Humanities) IV. Series.
    B837.S285   1993
    211'.7'09032—dc20
                                            92-44598
                                            CIP
                                            r93

Die Deutsche Bibliothek – CIP-Einheitsaufnahme

Scepticism and irreligion in the seventeenth and eighteenth centuries / ed. by Richard H. Popkin and Arjo
Vanderjagt. — Leiden; New York; Köln: Brill, 1993
    (Brill's studies in intellectual history; Vol. 37)
    ISBN 90-04-09596-9
NE: Popkin, Richard H. [Hrsg.]; GT

                ISSN   0920-8607
                ISBN   90 04 09596 9

CONTENTS

PREFACE

The Conference on Scepticism and Irreligion in the Seventeenth and Eighteenth Centuries was held from 31 July to 4 August 1990 at the Netherlands Institute for Advanced Study in the Social Sciences and the Humanities in Wassenaar near The Hague, The Netherlands (NIAS), which is a research institute of the Royal Netherlands Academy of Arts and Sciences. We are grateful to NIAS Director Prof.dr D. van der Kaa for his hospitality and to the staff for their fine practical arrangements.

The papers presented here were read in whole or in part during the Conference; some authors changed their texts later, others did not. Their contributions form a heterogeneous collection. They derive from different areas of scholarly endeavour and present their topics in a variety of styles and languages. The editors saw fit to interfere as little as possible in the texts that they received: no attempt was made to bring into accord all ideas, facts and interpretations—or even spelling, like the word "scepticism" or "skepticism", each of which has strong defenders. Nonetheless, all papers were scrutinized carefully, especially with regard to quotations and translations from the sources. Footnotes were edited thoroughly; references were harmonized and sometimes shortened where appropriate; in view of the proliferation of publishers today, it seemed wise to follow a new trend by including their names in bibliographical references to modern books. The papers are here presented roughly in chronological order.

The publication of this volume was made possible through the considerable, generous financial support of the *Dr C. Louise Thijssen-Schoutestichting* (Utrecht) and the *Foundation for Intellectual History* (London, England). We thank Mrs Elisabeth Erdman-Visser of E.J. Brill Publishing, Leiden, for her interest in this project and the possibility of including this volume in Brill's Studies in Intellectual History.

Richard H. Popkin
Arjo Vanderjagt

CONTRIBUTORS

Dr SUSANNA ÅKERMAN (Uppsala University)
Artillerigaten 57 III, 11450 Stockholm, Sweden

Dr SILVIA BERTI (Dipartimento di Studi Storici, Università degli Studi "La Sapienza", Roma) Via della Fonte di Fauno, 15, 00153 Rome, Italy

Ms CONSTANCE BLACKWELL, Foundation for Intellectual History, 28 Gloucester Crescent, London NW1, England

Prof.dr OLIVIER BLOCH (University of Paris I – Panthéon – Sorbonne) 23, rue du Chemin Vert, 75011 Paris, France

Dr HARRY BRACKEN (University of Groningen)
Goeman Borgesiuslaan 125, 9722 RE Groningen, The Netherlands

Prof.dr JAMES E. FORCE, Department of Philosophy, University of Kentucky, Lexington, Kentucky 40506, USA

Prof.dr ALAN GABBEY, Department of Philosophy, Barnard College Columbia University, New York, New York 10027, USA

Dr SARAH HUTTON, School of Humanities and Education, University of Hertfordshire, Wall Hall Campus, Aldenham, Herts. WO2 8AT, England

Prof.dr DAVID S. KATZ, Department of History, Tel Aviv University, Tel Aviv, Israel

Prof.dr ALAN CHARLES KORS, Department of History, University of Pennsylvania, 207 College Hall, Philadelphia, Pennsylvania 19104–6379, USA

Dr LOTHAR KREIMENDAHL, Institut für Philosophie, Ruhr-Universität Bochum, Postfach 10 21 48, 4630 Bochum 1, Germany

Dr SYLVIA MURR (Bordeaux University)
51, rue de Caudran, 33000 Bordeaux, France

Prof.dr EZEQUIEL DE OLASO (Centro de Investigaciones Filosoficas) Minones 2073, 1420 Buenos Aires, Argentina

Prof.dr RICHARD H. POPKIN (Washington University and University of California—Los Angeles) 15340 Albright Street #204, Pacific Palisades, California 90272, USA

Dr Arjo Vanderjagt, Faculty of Philosophy, University of Groningen, A-weg 30, 9718 CW Groningen, The Netherlands

Prof.dr Theo Verbeek, Faculty of Philosophy, University of Utrecht, Postbus 80.126, 3508 TC Utrecht, The Netherlands

Prof.dr Ernestine van der Wall, Faculty of Theology, University of Leiden, Postbus 9515, 2300 RA Leiden, The Netherlands

Prof.dr Richard A. Watson, Department of Philosophy, Washington University, St. Louis, Missouri 63130, USA

Dr Ruth Whelan, Department of French, Trinity College, University of Dublin, Dublin 2, Ireland

Richard H. Popkin

INTRODUCTION

SCEPTICISM AND IRRELIGION IN THE SEVENTEENTH AND EIGHTEENTH CENTURIES

The conference on scepticism and irreligion in the seventeenth and eighteenth centuries held at the Netherlands Institute for Advanced Study (NIAS) at Wassenaar from 31 July to 4 August 1990 was the continuation of one that Charles Schmitt and I designed at Wolfenbüttel in 1985. After many years of each working on the history of modern scepticism, we felt then, that enough additional research and interpretation of sceptical materials from the Renaissance onward justified holding a conference, and putting our heads together to see where our understanding of the development of modern scepticism stood. Ezequiel de Olaso and I are the only participants of this first conference who could come to Wassenaar in 1990. Amos Funkenstein was supposed to join us, but had to call off his attendance at the last moment because of illness.

At the end of the Wolfenbüttel conference, Charles Schmitt and I felt that enough had been achieved to make it worthwhile to continue the venture by having successive conferences on other aspects of the history of modern scepticism. We felt that one subject on which much new work was being done was the role of scepticism in the transformation that took place in the seventeenth and eighteenth centuries concerning the function, merits and truth value of religion, and the place of God in understanding the world. We began planning a conference with the title of this one. The tragic death of Charles Schmitt left Constance Blackwell and myself the task of carrying on, and after many many vicissitudes in the planning, "Wassenaar" came about. This conference was the first sponsored by the new Foundation for Research in Intellectual History, based in London. In the planning of it, Manfred Walther and I conferred a few times on the possibility of having a broad conference relating modern scepticism to the areas of more practical concern, law, politics, etc. Dr Walther's input has been most helpful.

The theme, scepticism and irreligion in the 17th and 18th centuries involves us in trying to throw light on the great intellectual drama of those centuries when many western intellectuals came to challenge both the framework of thinking about God and religion, and the intellectual systems that had supported religious thinking. When I and then Charles Schmitt began writing about the rise of modern scepticism, we sought to clarify what the first modern sceptics were saying. It had been claimed in previous interpretations that Erasmus, Gianfrancesco Pico, and Montaigne, were spokespersons for an anti-Christian point of view, that included the Latin Averroists, and later flowered in the *libertins érudits* and in the scepticism of Pierre Bayle. I was struck over thirty-five years ago, and am still struck by the fideistic note that runs through sixteenth and seventeenth century avowed sceptics. They say, and they say again and again, that they are questioning dogmatic knowledge claims, and they are putting all in doubt, *in order* to base their understanding of the world on faith and revelation.

This fideism had been earlier seen as a smokescreen, a camouflage, for a secret atheism. Schmitt and I found that ancient scepticism, when revived in the Renaissance, was presented as a defense of faith, often against early Protestants, or against scholastics with rationalist tendencies. Sextus Empiricus's complete works were presented in Latin by Gentian Hervet, the secretary of the Cardinal of Lorraine, and an early opponent of Protestantism, in 1569 as the complete answer to Calvinism. Let us recall that Hervet said that he did his translation edition as relaxation after he returned from arguing at the Council of Trent, from a manuscript that was in the Cardinal's library.

The use of scepticism to undermine or attack the alleged new dogmatism of the Calvinists was developed, as I have pointed out, into a debating method, a new machine of war. The rationale for the use of scepticism in this manner was supposedly supplied by Montaigne, Father Pierre Charron, and Camus, the Bishop of Bellay, who modernized ancient Pyrrhonism as a way of criticizing all philosophical and scientific dogmatisms, while stating— whether sincere or not—that religion should be based upon faith and revelation. The position of the *nouveaux pyrrhoniens*, whether sincere or not, was reiterated by the *libertins érudits*, Naudé, Patin, La Mothe Le Vayer and Gassendi.

The possibility of applying scepticism to theology and to fundamental claims of established religion was mentioned many times by opponents of the sceptics. These opponents spelled out the irreligious conclusions and consequences that might result if one followed out a scepticism with regard to religion. Atheism became a, or the specter haunting Europe.

Whether there were or were not any actual atheists before 1650–1675 is still very much a matter of debate and investigation. The resolution very much turns on how one defines 'atheism'. One can make the question trivial by too broadly defining the term, or make the question uninteresting by too narrowly defining the term. Two different elements seem to be involved leading to two different kinds and levels of atheism: one a disbelief in, or rejection of the concept of a divine being or substance as crucial to understanding the world, and two, a disbelief in, or rejection of the framework for explaining world events presented in the Bible. The first is a mainly philosophical view, the second mainly a religious one.

Figures I have been examining in detail in the last decade, like Isaac la Peyrère and Spinoza, were accused of being sceptics about accepting the framework of explanation in the Bible, and thereby creating a basis for a most dangerous atheism. Of course, both La Peyrère and Spinoza were not atheists in the first sense, though this is compatible with Pierre Bayle's announcement that Spinoza was the first modern thinker to develop a system of atheism.

Something dramatic that greatly affected the intellectual world of the time occurred when Hobbes, La Peyrère, Spinoza and Richard Simon raised questions about the accuracy and import of Scripture. From our present vantage point one can, perhaps, say that these questions were implicit in the scepticism of Montaigne and others. Implicit in what sense? If it did not occur to the earlier sceptics, or their opponents? Implicit in a logical sense in a new framework for understanding the world that emerged in the eighteenth century? Perhaps.

When I included both La Peyrère and Spinoza in my *History of Scepticism*, some people suggested that these authors were not sceptics in any philosophical sense. La Peyrère seems to have been a believer in a special Millenarian reading of Scripture, and Spinoza a believer in the power and efficacy of reason to the extent that reasoning and reasoning alone became his answer to epistemological scepticism. Granted all of this, I think one has to recognize a kind of scepticism, most important in late seventeenth-century discussions that was produced by the writings of La Peyrère and Spinoza.

From our present vantage point the critical issues raised about the Bible by these two authors seem part of the common sense of late twentieth-century intellectuals. We lose no sleep over being told that there are contradictory or conflicting passages in Scripture, or that the text of the Bible has had a history over time. (I say, "We", though I am well aware, maybe too aware, that my country and some others are full of fundamentalists who would scream and shout at the above statement.) When we try to look at La Peyrère and Spinoza in their seventeenth-century context to ascertain what it was that they said that so alarmed and excited people then, one has to realize something strange in the setting and presentation of this kind of scepticism.

As we know, biblical exegesis was a highly developed subject, taught in universities for centuries. It had a literature going back to the early Hebrew sages and the Church Fathers. Part of the revival of learning after the invention of printing was the publication and annotation of many earlier Bible scholars. The list of such publications from the 1480s to Spinoza's day is most impressive. This vast and most detailed literature dealt with every feature of the Biblical text. Varying readings and interpretations were offered. Some of the great theological issues of the Reformation and the Counter-Reformation revolved around the texts, and even the possibility of changed texts (as in the discussion from Erasmus onward of whether there is or was any text in the New Testament stating the Doctrine of the Trinity.)

Given the concern and study of the Bible prior to La Peyrère and Spinoza, why should two unlicensed untrained savants have created such a stir, such a scandal, and such a sceptical view about the status of the Bible, and its role in explaining man and the universe? The question becomes a bit more peculiar when one adds that La Peyrère could read neither Hebrew nor Greek, that Spinoza, a dropout from a mediocre Hebrew school in Amsterdam, who knew very little of the non-Jewish literature on the matter, could make vast assertions, and *be taken seriously*. His analysis of the status of Scripture in the *Tractatus* is just a few pages, in which he makes Scripture an object of human history, to be studied contextually in human history rather than as an, or the, explanation of human history. The very point that both La Peyrère and Spinoza used as the opening wedge of their scepticism about the status of Scripture indicates how strange the case is. They both make a fuss about whether Moses could be the author of the Pentateuch, the five books of Moses, if the death of Moses is described in the Pentateuch. (This point also appears in Hobbes's *Leviathan*, and is often cited as the official beginning of modern Biblical Criticism.) The scholars and exegetes had noticed this point. Spinoza mentions Aben Ezra, a twelfth-century Spanish rabbi as having discussed this. The rabbi did not draw Spinoza's radical conclusion from this point, but rather said that there must be something special about the forty lines that deal with Moses's death and the events thereafter, something special in terms of God's message to man. Aben Ezra's commentaries were published in the late fifteenth century, and thereafter. The Jesuit, Juan Maldonado, Montaigne's friend, the first Jesuit to teach in Paris, wrote five volumes of commentary on Aben Ezra's work. Jewish students from the late middle ages onward, in usual Jewish schools learned bits and pieces of Aben Ezra's commentaries as they approached manhood. Part of them appeared in the sixteenth century Bomberg edition of the Hebrew Bible.

Spinoza assumes that he and Aben Ezra agree that the lines about Moses's death show Moses did not write the passage, *and* that the Pentateuch is a man made complitation, what La Peyrère called "a heap of copie of copie".

Aben Ezra, Spinoza's reading notwithstanding, offered one way of saving the appearances, and a still acceptable way for many readers. All sorts of other ways can and have been offered of explaining the puzzling passage, such as that God told Moses about what was going to happen, and he wrote it down, (in some versions writing the account of his own death in his own tears.)

Hobbes had made a minimal point about the death of Moses passage, namely that Moses did not write that passage, but did write all the others which are attributed to him. Hobbes's presentation of the point in *Leviathan* would have just required that one recognize a different authorship, or maybe even a different status, of a few lines of the Biblical text, and accept the rest. La Peyrère, whom I think actually preceded Hobbes on this matter, made the most of the small point, namely that the Mosaic authorship of the Pentateuch was in doubt, and Spinoza followed him in this. The questioning of the Mosaic authorship was called by Ellies-Du Pin, one of the greatest and most dangerous paradoxes presented in the seventeenth century.

Why is this such a challenging or threatening point? We are now used to the possibility that the Bible may have been, or probably was, written by many authors. We are used to this, and in being used to it, have absorbed some of the consequences of the scepticism of La Peyrère and Spinoza. Moses was the critical link between man and God. He received *the message* from God, and wrote it down. He was not an ordinary chronicler or historian, he was God's reporter, whose report was guaranteed because it came from God. Hence his report was not like a human message, but was the knowledge link with the super-natural. In the late Enlightenment Tom Paine could say, take away the Mosaic authorship, and the whole authority of the Bible tumbles, and it becomes just a collection of ancient Hebrew fables.

La Peyrère and Spinoza had no new evidence for questioning the Mosaic authorship. Neither of them studied Biblical manuscripts. But their posing of the problem had tremendous consequences, as evidenced by what happened to La Peyrère and his book; it was banned and burned all over Europe, and he was arrested and forced to apologize personally to the Pope. Spinoza personally fared better, but soon became one of the most challenged and denounced authors of the time.

The point they were making had actually appeared in quite a few wild pamphlets published in England during the Puritan Revolution by Levellers, Ranters and early Quakers, who just denied either the privileged status of the Bible or its Mosaic authorship. Some went a step further and burned their Bibles, and some wrote new ones. These people were dismissed as the lunatic fringe of the English Revolution. Only one, the Quaker Samuel Fisher, who I believe knew and influenced Spinoza, published a substantial work. But Fisher's 900-page tome caused little excitement except in erudite Quaker circles and among a few Calvinst opponents.

I should like to suggest that La Peyrère and Spinoza changed the nature and import of the discussion not by new arguments or evidence, but by changing the way of evaluating the question, thereby creating a radical and new scepticism about accepted religious knowledge. La Peyrère's title, *Prae-Adamitae*, or *Men before Adam*, could be interpreted minimally or maximally. Minimally, it could refer to some cases of humanoid beings, created by God, that preceded Adam, but are not part of present human history. A Catholic decision about the pre-Adamite theory from the early twentieth century offers this minimalist view: there were prehistoric people before Adam, but they all died off before God created Adam from whom all present members of the human race are descended. The maximalist view would be that Adam, and all the events that followed after him in Adamic history, are just a small part of human history, and have no special significance. La Peyrère did not seem to hold the maximalist position, but immediately caused people to think of it. His own Messianic views got drowned in his data about Indians and Chinese and Eskimos. There is little evidence that La Peyrère convinced many people besides Spinoza and the English Deists, but he raised the sceptical questioning of the whole Biblical framework. He said that his pre-Adamite theory did not change anything in the world. It was, he said, like the Copernican hypothesis. It was just another way of looking at the same data. However, the data when looked at in this way became a challenge to a whole previously accepted way of making sense out of the world. And, what must be part of the explanation of why this new way of looking at things made headway, it fitted in more comfortably with lots of other data from the ancient and modern worlds, data from the explorers, from other cultures, etc. Just explaining who the Eskimos or the American Indians were and where they came from became so much more simple on La Peyrère's hypothesis than on the Biblical monogenetic thesis.

Similarly Spinoza's way of explaining Biblical texts became so much simpler than that of the commentators. Menasseh ben Israel's *Concillador* attempted, in the generation before Spinoza, to account for puzzling or contradictory texts, by pointing out how they had been explained by various commentators. Spinoza, by seeing them as human texts, no longer had to offer as complex or complicated an explanation.

When Richard Simon said he accepted Spinoza's method but not his conclusions, he accepted contextualizing all information about Biblical texts. As his opponents kept pointing out: could he then avoid coming to a contextualist conclusion, that the Bible is a product of human history? If Simon wanted to insist that it could also be more, he had already provided far more evidence than Spinoza had for just accepting the historical context reading as the whole account.

Once certain alternative ways had been offered for dealing with the same data, and these ways meshed with lots of other data, and new scientific theories, then the sceptical challenge to Biblical religion became most threatening. Now that we know what happened, we can telescope the development into the Enlightenment world in a few decades and a few thinkers. Of course, it took much longer historically to reach what we now call modern results.

The same kind of development occurred with regard to the accepted philosophical theories for explicating the religious world. The Scholastic one was challenged by the Platonic, the Epicurean, the Cartesian ones, each claiming when presented in the first half of the seventeenth century, to be the right or preferred way of justifying or explaining the Judeo-Christian cosmos. Sceptical challenges to all of these theories, often generated out of the contests between the theoreticians, became a most radical sceptical undermining of the very possibility of a foundation for knowledge of God and his, or her creation, especially as developed by someone of the genius of Pierre Bayle. One can, and one has, sketched the logic of how

thinkers in the seventeenth and eighteenth centuries moved from
criticizing opponents's philosophical views to generating a scepticism about all philosophical views.

But the logic of the situation is not so clear and uniquely deter-
minative. All sorts of alterations in the premises could and have
been made that avoid the force of the opponents's deductions or
criticisms. It is part of the ingenuity of the intelligentsia that at all
times they (or we) can find adequate or satisfactory reasons for
conclusions that are supposed to be held by "reasonable" people. If
so, why do drastic changes in evaluating the merits of certain
beliefs take place? Why, in particular, were the sceptical considerations against the acceptance of the Bible and of Biblical views taken
so seriously in England, France, The Netherlands, Germany and
Italy after they were presented by La Peyrère, Spinoza and Simon?

This question is not answered by sketching out the inner intellectual life of La Peyrère, Spinoza and Simon, if we could actually
ascertain the crucial data. We may be able to understand the steps
by which these thinkers came to their views. But why did any one
else take them seriously, and later on, come to believe them?
Evidence produced by Christopher Hill and others about the views
of radical religious revolutionaries in England, 1640–1660, show
that some of these people asserted what were to become the most
extreme irreligious views: some denied that the Bible contained any
truths, that the Judeo-Christian religion was anything other than a
scam, a way of deceiving people, they denied that Adam was the
first man, or that man's soul could be immortal, plus many other
major heresies. Most of these people were not trained intellectuals,
and could not produce "good" reasons for their views. Most were
rabble-rousers, and political agitators, to be dealt with by the
authorities as a police problem, rather than a philosophical or
theological one. Even Gerard Winstanley, who made out a good
case for his views, was not taken seriously as a philosopher until
rather recently.

On the other hand, La Peyrère, who was active in the intellectual
world of Paris, of Holland and of Scandinavia, discussed his
theories with many intellectuals. Grotius wrote an answer twelve
years before La Peyrère published his book. Mersenne, Gassendi,
La Mothe Le Vayer, Rivet, Sarrau, Saumaise, Ole Worm and many
others discussed his theory with him, and even supplied him with
more evidence for it. As soon as his book was published, theologians thought they had to refute it intellectually, and shortly thereafter one finds people like Charles Blount, and Thomas Burnet in
England, the author of *L'Espion turc* in France, and Spinoza in The

Netherlands advocating the theory. So I think first we have to find adequate explanations for the transfer of such ideas. It obviously cannot be just the logic of the situation, or the over-powering force of the evidence offered, otherwise everyone would have accepted this theory. What Thomas Kuhn has called a "paradigm shift" occurred, first in a few minds, and then in many, so that the same information and reasonings could be seen entirely differently. But I think our comprehension of how this process operated then, and now, needs much more clarification. At the very time when people were becoming what we called enlightened, others, of similar intellectual background and ability, were becoming mystics, and believers in a new Millenarian Christianity that became modern fundamentalism.

Another set of problems that I have been interested in following is the effect of Jewish critiques of Christianity and Christian critiques of Judaism in the seventeenth century. Jews obviously did not accept Christianity from its outset. They were denounced for this. Their refusal to become Christians was explained by their stubbornness, their obtuseness, their spiritual weakness. Their reasons were explained in psychological and theological terms, but were not given much credence, until the sixteenth century. In the seventeenth century, especially in Amsterdam, Jewish answers to Christianity were written and circulated. Most of these were written by people who had been trained as Christians in Spanish, Portuguese, French or Italian universities, and then reverted to Judaism in Holland. They wrote in the accepted intellectual language of the Schools. Their views were taken seriously and did affect the developing critical views of English and French Deists. The Jewish arguers had not discovered any new facts, or hitherto unknown reasons for rejecting the doctrine of the Trinity or the Messianic status of Jesus. But they advanced their views in different clothes and in a changing intellectual atmosphere. Jacques Basnage, Pierre Bayle's good friend, said sadly towards the end of his very, very long *Histoire des Juifs*, that Christians should not debate with Jews about the truth of Christianity since the Christians almost always lose because they do not know the source materials as well, and do not argue as well. So, he said, Christians should leave the job of trying to convert the Jews to God. Basnage's attitude reflects, I believe, the change going on, but does not explain it.

A change on the Jewish side also took place, apparently strongly influenced by the failed Messianic expectations of seventeenth-century Judaism. In 1666, just when Spinoza was working out his Biblical criticism and his scepticism about the Bible as a framework for understanding man and nature, the Jewish world, all over the planet was transformed by the news that one Sabbatai Zevi of Smyrna was the long awaited Messiah. The letter of Henry Oldenburg to Spinoza asking if it is true that the King of the Jews has arrived shows that the sceptical irreligious world and accepted religious one met. We know that Oldenburg became a believer in Sabbatai Zevi for a while, but we do not know what Spinoza's reaction was. Almost all of the Jewish community of Amsterdam became believers. Then a year later Sabbatai Zevi converted to Islam. This caused great psychological devastation to many Jews, though a small number believed then, and even now, that only the fleshly Sabbatai converted, and that the spiritual Sabbatai would return as the long awaited Messiah, or that his conversion was part of his Messianic mission: in order to save mankind, he would have to take on the sins of mankind by committing the greatest sin of all, apostacy.

Gershom Scholem, whose biography of Sabbatai Zevi is one of the monuments of twentieth-century scholarship, has argued that the collapse of the Sabbatai Zevi movement led directly to reformed Judaism, that is Judaism no longer based on the strict Biblical framework, but rather adjustable to Enlightenment views. Another factor that may have pushed in this direction is the development of a Christian scepticism about Judaism: namely if the Jews could not tell a true Messiah from a false one, this showed that they lacked the criterion for recognizing the truth. They should then give up their views and accept Christianity.

Unhistorical, unrevealed versions of both Judaism and Christianity emerged in the course of the eighteenth century, as well as Deist religions and full-blown atheism. In the drama that led to this state of affairs, scepticism played a major role and what resulted was rechristened "scepticism"—now a doubt of all revealed religion, one of the present major meanings of the terms. The papers published here throw much light on various stages of the development of scepticism and irreligion. As we become clearer about what happened both in terms of evaluating Biblical religion, and of understanding the cosmos in non-religious terms, we may be in a better position to plunge further into understanding why it happened, and what legacy has been left to us. Perhaps we can go on from the Wassenaar conference to a future one on scepticism and its role in the nineteenth and twentieth centuries, from Kant, through various nineteenth-century involvements with scepticism, to the present concerns with the "scepticisms" of Wittgenstein and Heidegger. Examining the history of scepticism has been a fruitful way of understanding the beginning of the development of modern thought. Hopefully we can carry this on further and deeper to understand how we have gotten to the intellectual world in which we now live.

SYLVIA MURR

GASSENDI'S SCEPTICISM AS A RELIGIOUS ATTITUDE*

I. STATE OF THE QUESTION

After all that has been written on the subject, there must be some "folie des grandeurs" in attempting to say something significant about Gassendi's scepticism and its relationship to religion. I wish only to support two ideas: first that Gassendi's philosophy—and especially his particular type of scepticism—is intrinsically subordinated to his existential determination as a religious man; and second, that an international team should newly edit and translate Gassendi's work into the vernacular languages, since this is the only way to facilitate a free and open discussion of its various aspects, including the question I consider in this paper about the relationship between Gassendi's religion and his philosophy. The controversial character of the first idea is my only argument here in favour of the second.

It is now well accepted that the *cas Gassendi*—the debate about Gassendi's alleged religious scepticism—is an academic and ideological artefact that emerged from René Pintard's *Libertinage érudit* (1843),[1] which was politely but firmly criticized the following year by Henry Gouhier in the *Revue philosopique*,[2] then attacked by Bernard Rochot in 1947[3] with an article titled "Le cas de Gassendi" to which Pintard in turn replied the following year in the same journal.[4] Earlier historians of philosophy and Gassendian scholars such as Jean-Mari de Gerando (1847),[5] Felix Thomas (1889),[6]

---

* I am grateful to Richard A. Watson and Harry M. Bracken for their corrections of my English; they often amended more than only the English phrasing.

[1] Paris, 1943; Geneva, Paris: Slatkine reprint, 1983.

[2] *Revue philosopique* 1944, 65–60; Gouhier there coins the expression *le cas Gassendi*.

[3] *Revue d'histoire littéraire de la France* 1947, 298–313.

[4] "Modernisme humanisme, libertinage; petite suite sur le cas Gassendi', Ibid. 1848, 1–52.

[5] *Histoire comparée des systèmes de philosophie*, 2 vols., Paris: Librairie philosophique de Ladrange, 1847, vol. 2, 93–152.

[6] *La philosophie de Gassendi*, Paris: Felix Alcan, 1889.

Henri Berr (1898),[7] Gerhard Hess (1939),[8] Paul Pentzig (1908, 1910),[9] Jonas Cohn (1896),[10] Kurd Lasswitz (1890)[11] and George S. Brett (1908)[12] ignore the case. Even Karl Marx,[13] who depended largely on Ludwig Feuerbach's *Geschichte der neureren Philosophie von Baco v. Verulam bis B. Spinoza* (1833),[14] declares that Gassendi was a thoroughly religion-intoxicated priest who tried to veil Epicurus's genuine materialism under a "nun's dress"; and Marx discards his philosophy precisely because it is christianized Epicureanism. In a word, they take for granted that Gassendi "baptized Democritus and Lucretius as Aquinas had baptized Aristotle".[15]

There is a tradition, however, that Gassendi is the "father of modern materialism", as Friedrich Albert Lange put it in 1875[16]— but he had never read Gassendi in any text other than Bernier's digest.[17] Lange's position is refuted by the very learned and honest Bavarian scholar Franz Xavier Kiefl, whose *Doktoraldissertation* appeared in large extracts in the *Philosophisches Jahrbuch der Görres-*

---

[7] *An jure inter scepticos Gassendus numeratus fuerit*, Paris: Hachette et Cie, 1898.

[8] *Pierre Gassend; Der französische Späthumanismus und das Problem von Wissen und Glauben*, Jena-Leipzig: Wilhelm Gronau, 1939.

[9] *Pierre Gassendi's Metaphysik und ihr Verhältnis zur Scholastischen Philosophie*, Bonn: Peter Hanstein, 1908, and *Die Ethik Gassendis und ihre Quellen*, Bonn: Peter Hanstein, 1910.

[10] *Geschichte des Unendlichkeitsproblems im abendländischen Denken bis Kant*, Leipzig: Wilhelm Engelmann, 1896, 111–113, 119–120.

[11] *Geschichte der Atomistik vom Mittelalter bis Newton*, 2 vols., Hamburg-Leipzig: Leopold Voss, 1890, vol. 2, 126–187.

[12] *The Philosophy of Gassendi*, London: Macmillan and Co., 1908.

[13] Doctoral Dissertation on the difference of the philosophy of nature in Democritus and Epicurus, written in 1841 (MEGA I.1.).

[14] First edition in 1833; *Ludwig Feuerbachs Sämtliche Werke*, 10 vols., eds. W. Bolin, Fr. Jodl, Stuttgart: Friedrich Frommann, E. Hauff, 1903–1910, vol. 3 (1906), 111–127.

[15] Henry Kearney, *Science and Change, 1500–1700*, London: Weidenfeld and Nicholson, 1971, p. 170.

[16] F.A. Lange, *Geschichte des Materialismus*, 2 vols., Leipzig: Isserlohn, 1875, vol. 2.

[17] Bernier's *Abrégé de la philosophie de Gassendi* (first printed but very incompletely in 1674–1675; second edition: Lyon, Anisson et Posuel, 1678 in 8 volumes in 12°; third and final edition: Lyon, Anisson, Posuel et Rigaud, 1684, in seven volumes in 12°, containing the 1682 "Doutes" at the end of vol. 2 and the 1681 "Eclaircissemens sur le Livre de M. de La Ville" in vol. 3) definitely slants Gassendi's *Syntagma philosophicum* towards a mere rehabilitation of Democrito-Epicureanism and alters the whole spirit of Gassendi's doctrine. François Bernier (1620–1688) belongs to the generation after Gassendi. His *Traité du libre et du volontaire* (Amsterdam: Henri Desbordes, 1685) contains "Doutes" which are not in the "Morale" of his 1684 *Abrégé* (vol. 7), and show that if he had any religious faith, he did not find such easy "concordia" between it and rational thought as did Gassendi. Bayle's caricature in his *Nouvelles de la Republique des Lettres* of Dec. 1685: "La liberté des créatures seroit apparemment une des choses dont il douteroit, si la révélation d'un Enfer ne prouvoit demonstrativement, que l'homme n'est pas purement passif" (*Oeuvres*

Gesellschaft in 1893 under the title "Gassendi's Skepticismus und seine Stellung zum Materialismus";[18] but the fact that he wrote in a rather militant Roman-Catholic journal seems to have disqualified him in the eyes of scholars in the Lange tradition.

In the second half of the twentieth century, scholars have again taken for granted Gassendi's authenticity as a Roman-Catholic priest, as a Christian philosopher, as a seventeenth-century mechanist, nominalist, andidogmatist, anti-occultist, Copernican, Galilean, neo-Epicurean etc. Although some still favour Lange's position, others try to discover what led to the assumption that Gassendi professed a materialistic and antireligious philosophy without wanting to do so and even without knowing it. All of the following more or less topically or polemically discard the *cas Gassendi* as an outdated debate: Richard Popkin (1960, 1979),[19] Tullio Gregory (1961),[20] Paul Oskar Kristeller (1968),[21] John Spink (1969),[22] Olivier Bloch (1971),[23] Rainer Tack (1974), who makes a bit of a fuss about it and finally supports Pintard,[24] Wolfgang Detel (1978)[25] and Lisa T. Sarasohn (1979, 1985).[26]

Diverses de Mr. Pierre Bayle [. .], La Haye: Husson, Johnson, Gosse & al., 1727, vol. 7, p. 437b; reprint with an introduction by Elisabeth Labrousse, Hildesheim: Olms Vg., 1964, vol. 1, p. 437b) suggests either that Bernier was a fool, or, more likely, that he cryptically advocated religious scepticism with regard to the Catholic dogmas.

[18] *Philosophisches Jahrbuch. Auf Veranlassung und Unterstützung der Görres-Gesellschaft*, herausgegeben von Dr. Constant Gutberlet, 6 (1893), 23–34, 295–311, 361–373.

[19] *The History of Scepticism from Erasmus to Descartes*, Assen: Van Gorcum, 1960; enlarged version: *The History of Scepticism from Erasmus to Spinoza*, Berkeley and Los Angeles: University of California Press, 1979, 104–106 and notes 76–80, 274–275.

[20] *Scetticismo ed Empirismo. Studio su Gassendi*, Bari: Laterza, 1961, 215–216.

[21] Kristeller challenges Pintard's interpretation in his article "The Myth of Renaissance Atheism and the French Tradition of Free Thought", *Journal of the History of Philosophy* 6 (1968), 233–244. See also "Between Italian Renaissance and the French Enlightenment: Gabriel Naudé as an Editor", *Renaissance Quarterly* 32 (1979), 41–72, esp. p. 58.

[22] *French Free-Thought from Gassendi to Voltaire*, New York: Greenwood Press, 1969, 14–17.

[23] *La Philosophie de Gassendi. Nominalisme, matérialisme et métaphysique*, The Hague: Martinus Nijhoff, 1971, xiv–xvi, p. 291.

[24] *Untersuchung zum Philosophie- und Wissenschaftsbegriff bei Pierre Gassendi (1592–1655)*, Meisenheim am Glan: Anton Hain, 1974, 35–37 and 209–212.

[25] *Scientia rerum naturae occultarum. Methodologische Studien zur Physik Pierre Gassendis*, Berlin and New York: Walter de Gruyter (Quellen und Studien zur Philosophie 14), 1978, 5–6.

[26] "The Influence of Epicurean Philosophy on Seventeenth-Century Political Thought: The Moral Philosophy of Pierre Gassendi", unpublished Ph.D. Dissertation, UCLA 1979. Sarasohn ignores the problem in her 1982 and 1985 articles: "The Ethical and Political Philosophy of Pierre Gassendi", *Journal of the History of Philosophy* 20 (1982), 239–261; "Motion, and Morality: Pierre Gassendi,

Eventually—with the remarkable exceptions of Margaret Osler (1983, 1985)[27] and Lynn Sumida Joy (1987), who provides and excellent analysis and bibliography of the whole controversy[28]—specialized Gassendian scholars in the last decade[29] hardly mention it, as can be observed in Marco Messeri (1985),[30] Barry Brundell (1987),[31] Antonina Alberti (1988)[32] and Gianni Paganini (1990).[33]

Yet the two traditions are still there, one in favour of Gassendi the spiritualist and one for Gassendi the materialist; for the non-specialist, Gassendi remains on the whole a poor philosopher, because the dominant opinion is that his work lacks logic systematicity. This view is dominant because it has been propagated not only by the Cartesians, by Leibniz[34] and by platonically-oriented historians of science such as Alexandre Koyré, but also by the very best of Gassendian scholars Tullio Gregory and Olivier Bloch. This—and the French pro-Cartesian prejudice which leads practising philosophers to identify themselves with *"mens"* rather than

----

Thomas Hobbes and the Mechanical World-View", *Journal of the History of Ideas* 46 (1985), 363–379.

[27] "Providence and divine will in Gassendi's views on scientific knowledge", *Journal of the History of Ideas* 44 (1983), 459–551, and "Baptizing Epicurean atomism: Pierre Gassendi on the immortality of the soul", in *Religion, Science and Worldview* eds. Margaret J. Osler and Paul Lawrence Farber, Cambridge: Cambridge University Press, 1985, pp. 163–183.

[28] *Gassendi the Atomist: Advocate of History in an Age of Science*, Cambridge: Cambridge University Press, 1987, 16–18, 236–237.

[29] I should also include non-specialized authors whose own research led them to acquire distinguished expertise in Gassendian studies, such as Karl Schuhmann ("Zehn Jahre Gassendi Forschung", *Philosophische Rundschau* 29 (1982), 271–279, and "Zur Geschichte des neuzeitlichen Zeitbegriffs: Telesio, Patrizi, Gassendi", *Philosophia Naturalis* 25 (1988), 37–64), Rainer Specht ("Erfahrung und Hypothesen. Meinungen im Umkreis Lockes" in *Philosophisches Jahrbuch im Auftrag der Görres-Gesellschaft*, 1981, 20–49, esp. from p. 26 onwards), Konrad Moll (*Der Junge Leibniz II. Der Übergang vom Atomismus zu einem mechanistischen Aristotelismus. Der revidierte Anschluss an Pierre Gassendi*, Stuttgart: Frommann-Holzboog, 1982, who mentions Olivier Bloch's theory of Gassendi's radical "ambiguity" quite marginally, in his bibliographical survey, p. 54), Emily Michael and Fred S. Michael ("Gassendi on Sensation and Reflection: a non-Cartesian Dualism" in *History of European Ideas* 9 (1989), 583–595), David K. Glidden ("Hellenistic Background for Gassendi's Theory of Ideas", *Journal of the History of Ideas* 49 (1988), 405–424).

[30] *Causa e spiegazione. La fisica di Pierre Gassendi*, Milano: Franco Angelli, 1985.

[31] *Pierre Gassendi. From Aristotelianism to a new natural philosophy*, Dordrecht: Reidel, 1987.

[32] *Sensazione e realtà. Epicuro e Gassendi*, Firenze: Leo Olschki, 1988.

[33] "Hobbes, Gassendi e la psicologia del meccanicismo", *Hobbes oggi*, Milano: F. Angelli, 1990, 351–445.

[34] See for instance Moll, *Der junge Leibniz II*, quoting Leibniz's 1714 letter to Remond de Montmort, 73–75, where Leibniz finds Gassendi's metaphysics on the nature of the soul and on natural theology "trop chancelant"; reference edition: *Die philosophischen Schriften von G.W. Leibniz*, Carl Im. Gerhardt, ed., Berlin 1875–90: vol. III, p. 620.

with "*caro*"—may account for the neglect, in France at least, into which Gassendian studies have fallen and for the absence of a modern edition of the Corpus Gassendianum.

Whatever the case may be, the "scepticism" of Gassendi has never been questioned, it has only been qualified. Since everyone knows how Popkin characterizes Gassendi's particular brand of "constructive scepticism",[35] and after him Spink,[36] not to mention Kiefl, Berr, Gregory, Bloch and lately Brundell, it is not necessary to discuss here those places in his work where Gassendi most explicitly expresses his middle-way doctrine between the dogmatists and the Pyrrhonians, as for example in the "Praefatio" of the *Dissertationes Paradoxicae adversus Aristoteleos*[37] and in the second book of the *Logica* in the *Syntagma philosophicum* ("De Logicae fine"), where he exposes and criticizes, first, the reasons given by the dogmatists, then the various modes of the sceptical *epoche*, and finally his own definition of the kind of truth about things that is attainable, and of the type of criteria that are available for recognizing that truth.[38]

On the other hand, Gassendi's religiosity is universally attested to as an historical fact, whatever one may think of its relevance. The passages in his work where he professes his unconditional obedience to the Roman Church have been quoted repeatedly for nearly four centuries, although variously interpreted. Gassendi here con-

---

[35] Popkin, *History of Scepticism* (1979), 142–143.

[36] Spink, *French Free-Thought*, 85–93, 102.

[37] First edition 1624 under the title *Exercitationum paradoxicarum adversus Aristoteleos libri septem, in quibus praecipua totius doctrinae peripateticae atque dialecticae fundamenta excutiuntur, opiniones vero aut novae, aut ex veteribus obsoletae, stabiliuntur* Liber I: "In Doctrinam Aristoteleorum Universe", Gratianopolis (Grenoble): Verdier, 1624; of the seven books, only the second was prepared for publication in the *Opera Omnia*, and eventually Books One and Two came out in a posthumous first edition (hereafter refered to as GO followed by volume and page number plus "a" or "b" for column, and the line numbers; the edition refered to is *Petri Gassendi Diniensis Ecclesiae Praepositi, et in Academia Parisiensi Matheseos Regii Professoris Opera Omnia in sex tomos divisa [. .]*, Lugduni (Lyon): Laurent Anisson & Jean-Baptiste Devenet, 1658; GO III.97–212.

[38] GO I.67–90. Neither of the two books of the *Syntagma philosophicum*'s *Logica* are translated in the *Abrégé* of Bernier, who contented himself with the *Institutio logica* (Vol. 1 of the 1678 and 1684 editions). So did Howard Jones in his edition and translation (*Pierre Gassendi's Institutio Logica (1658)*, Assen: Van Gorcum, 1981). The only extant translation of the full *Logica* is Polish, published without the Latin text by Leszek Kołakowski, translated by Ludwik Chmaj (Pierre Gassendi, *Logika*, Krakowie: Panswowe wydawnictwo Naukowe, Biblioteka Klasyków Filozofii, 1964); the Gassendian theory of truth is on 335–361 (corresponding to GO I.79–86, "Posse aliquam Veritatem signo aliquo innotescere, & Criterio diiudicari"). See also GO III.653a, 660a (Parhelia); letters to Golius (8 March 1630) and to P. Seguier (7 July 1649), respectively GO VI.32b and 296b.

forms to the more or less stereotypical formulas used in the Church for professions of faith. Here is an example form the *Exercitationes paradoxicae* (GO III.101):[39]

> And whatever the case may be, I always entrust myself and my writings to the judgement of the Only One Holy Catholic, Apostolic and Roman Church, whose suckling I am, and for whose faith I am ready to spend my life with my blood.

II. METHODOLOGICAL PRELIMINARIES

My intent is to clarify under exactly what premise this ambiguity disappears. In the following analysis two contingent methodological axioms are assumed:

1. Gassendi is sincere; he himself believes what he says is true or *probabilior*; in other words, his writings consistently express his own thoughts.

2. It is acceptable method to try to think in Gassendi's own terms, while endeavouring to retrieve his original intentions and the meanings of his words.

On closer examination, it appears that the two axioms reinforce each other, for the first gives one an incentive to read Gassendi, and the careful perusal of Gassendi's work shows that he himself rules out insincerity. Neither the assertion nor the negation of these two axioms can be falsified. They are contingent. Strictly speaking, first, Gassendi could have been a liar, and from this starting point, whenever he says something, because he might be lying or not, we would have to decide what is the truth. In this case, the interpretation of Gassendi's philosophy would become a hazardous undertaking, an infinitely difficult and very frustrating task. Yet that alternative might be the only correct one. So to be honest, one should say that one's choice is ultimately the one that suits one best, whatever arguments one might invoke as to the probability that Gassendi was not in fact a liar. This holds true even if those arguments are approved by most historians, including Olivier Bloch, who writes:

---

[39] Sed utcumque se res habeat ... committo semper meque et mea omnia judicio Unius Sanctae, Catholicae, Apostolicae, Romanaeque Ecclesiae, cujus ego alumnus sum, et pro cujus fide sum paratus fundere vitam cum sanguine. Compare with *De Motu*, Third letter (which Gassendi also calls his "Apology" against J.-B. Morin's 1643 *Alae Telluris fractae [. .]*) to Joseph Gautier, dated Paris, 10 August 1643, (first published by Neuré and Barancy in 1649 at Lyon) in §8 and xli, GO III.527b28–32 and 563a34–40; compare with "De Proportione qua gravia decidentia accelerantur" (to father Cazré, first published in 1646), GO III.638a55–b65.

supposer que ces constructions elles-mêmes sont le fait d'une habileté
suprême reviendrait à attribuer à Gassendi un machiavélisme qui
outrepasse les limites du vraisemblable.

But Bloch remains in the realm of "vraisemblable". Because no
apodicticity can be expected, this assumption has to be taken as a
mere arbitrary axiom, and whatever is derived from it will remain
hypothetical.

Second, Gassendi may not have lied but merely erred, and then
it would be silly to say with him that it is day when it is night,
simply because he says that it is day and one has found a way to
enter his thought processes. But his own teaching advises us to
always temper the authority of an author with our own free reason
("lumen naturalis", "intuitus mentis") and experience ("prop-
riorum sensuum experientia"), and if we do follow his own example
and doctrine, we should adopt his mitigated scepticism without
renouncing our right of adhering or not to what contradicts either
our own intellectual insight, or the actual empirical evidence. This
methodological attitude amount to the Husserlian *epoche* of the
naïve *Unmittelbarkeit*.

But now there arise two final and unanswerable objections: one,
that Gassendi was not aware of his own prejudices, so he may well
have sincerely said he thought one thing, whereas he actually
thought something else. In other words, his own blindness for his
fundamental preconceptions forces him into a kind of ventrilo-
quism. Bloch seems to describe Gassendi as having such a split
philosophical personality: Epicurean-materialistic on the one side
and Christian-spiritualistic on the other.[40] As a matter of fact,
Gassendi himself objected to Descartes' naïve plan to rid himself of
all prejudices, saying that such an aim is unattainable (GO
III.279b). The second unanswerable objection is that we ourselves
are blind to our own mental structures and that these structures are
the true causes of our supposedly rational decisions, so that we are
always the victims of the delusions of a-posteriori rationalization,
or immediate "evidentia". To both objections there is but one
answer: we are bound to express what seems to us the most universally acceptable insight, neither pretending to attain to absolute
truth, nor denying others the right to show us where we may have
been misled; a point, incidentally, also taught by Gassendi.

I conclude these preliminary methodological declarations with a
final statement. The most prominent "prejudice" in Gassendi's

---

[40] Bloch, *La philosophie de Gassendi*, p. 292.

work is his assumption that the Roman-Catholic faith is in fact what in his philosophical discourses he calls abstractly and equivocally "the true religion".[41] Now this is either a pleonastic expression for the believer, since for him false religions are religions only in name and therefore not really religious at all because by necessity there can only be one true religion, or it is a badly wrought expression for the social anthropologist, because all religions are religions and as such none is truer than any other. The very fact that Gassendi is unaware of the logical equivocation of the expression "the true religion" betrays the structural nature of his faith within his mental universe. The standpoint of the phenomenologist,

---

[41] There is external evidence that Gassendi never chose to be a Roman Catholic: he was born and brought up as such. He himself knew well enough the argument of the religious sceptics (of Montaigne and La Mothe Le Vayer among others), according to which it is mere coincidence ("casus") that one is born in a particular society, and every man acquires a set of second-nature habits and prejudices through the education ("paideia") his social environment gives him: see his letter responding to Sir Edward Herbert of Cherbury's *De Veritate* (Paris 1624). Gassendi addressed the letter to Sir Edward himself, and says at the end of the printed copy that he wrote it in 1634 and gave the first copy to the "illustrissimus Baro" in 1647, having kept an unfinished copy for himself; that copy was printed in the GO III.411–419; B. Rochot made a French translation published in the *Actes du tricentenaire de Pierre Gassendi*, 1957, Paris: P.U.F., 1957, 256–285; cf. especially §12, GO III.417a48–b10, in which note the expression "nisi inter Christianos fuisses innutritus", 418a25); see also the "De libertate" in the *Syntagma Philosophicum* in which he counts the things we receive from our parents among those that are not originally in our power (GO II.844b–845a, spec. 845a3 and 59–60) but with which we are free to do what we decide. The question, whether men who have not been given a chance to choose the "true religion" could be doomed for eternity, or why divine Providence sent Christ for the salvation of man but allowed so many humans to die before having entered the Church, remains for him "altum mysterium", although he says that there will soon not remain any nation in the world to whom the Gospel has not yet be announced,—which is the only reason I could see why he should admit that those who did not adopt the "True Religion" may be said to have chosen not to do so. He does not believe it indifferent whether one belongs to this religion or that provided one practises honestly the "pietas secundum naturam"; it is clear not only from his refutation of Herbert of Cherbury's apology for deism in *De Veritate* (see specially §14, GO III.418b9–13), but also from his *Ethics* in the *Syntagma philosophicum* (GO II.840b56–60 in which he says "religion belongs to the class of things that are in our power, depending on our 'liberum arbitrium', and for that God has not decided in advance whether or not we will choose it: otherwise, one could not account for the rewards and punishments that await every individual soul after death", as stated in the *De Animorum immortalitate*, c.4 "De Statu Rationalis Animae post Mortem, ubi & de Resurrectione (in the *Syntagma Philosophicum*, GO II.650–657) and in his 1654 letter to congratulate Samuel Sorbière for his conversion from protestantism to Roman Catholicism (GO VI.328b1 ff. spec. lines 4–6: "Nempe res ejus est ponderis, cui aequipari nihil possit. De salute enim summa agitur"). So in his eyes, he is Roman Catholic because he chooses, yet he admits that he is particularly lucky to have been born in the right religious community.

which I try to adopt here, allows one, through the phenomenologic-al *epoche*, not to believe what Gassendi believed but only to take a position as though one believes, so that one can thereby understand Gassendi's point of view. This principle applies to Gassendi's religious assertions, and to the rest of his statements and demonstrations as well.

Gassendi, using the old sceptic trope of the tower seen as round from a great distance yet square when closer, shows that the only truth that is attainable is the explanation of various appearances of the same thing: *"scire tantum posse quale his aut illis appareat [res]"*.[42] In a letter to Lord Edward Herbert of Cherbury he claims that the knowledge of the thing belongs to him who makes it, therefore only to God (GO III.413b51–66). Likewise, I do not pretend to know Gassendi himself, whatever made him, but only to inquire about the variety of his appearances; and since his appearances are in fact assertions about the appearances of the world seen from his position, the phenomenal truth we are looking for consists precisely in the determination of Gassendi's standpoints with relation to every set of phenomena about which he has left his observations to us. Gassendi's dominant activity, epistemological model, and source of pleasure were his celestial observations.[43] I therefore suggest that we apply to him as the author of his own work the same method he himself used to determine the position of the stars as observed by his foreign correspondents, by using the exact determination of the time and place of the observations made; that is, we must look at the objects of Gassendi's observations in a similar fashion.

With these principles in mind, it is clear that on the supposition that he searched for satisfying and congruent solutions to all the problems which he raised, he must have written what seemed to him to be satisfactory. We can also suppose that his intellectual acumen was not necessarily inferior to ours—since we know by experience that he sometimes makes extremely intricate and subtle chains of inferences, that he was trained as a professional theolo-

---

[42] *Exercitationes paradoxicae*, II.vi. (GO III.203a). See also GO I.85a25–41 (criteria theory); also in *Disquisitio metaphysica*, GO III.279b, 281b, etc. The trope of the tower is from Sextus Empiricus's *Adv. Math.* VII.208–209.

[43] His manuscript "Observationes caelestes" (Paris, Bibliothèque Nationale, N.a.lat.1636, f° 718) shows that he used his astronomical notebook as a sort of personal diary, interspersed with the landmarks of his emotional life; for example he notes, at the bottom of the page dedicated to the 1648 moon eclipse: "discessum vitae mei car. amic. accepi"; this very dear friend could be Joseph Gautier, who died in December 1647, or more likely Mersenne, who died on 1 September 1648.

gian, and that he practised the art of philosophic even "scholastic" *Disputatio* with rare precision and clarity. Our superiority, of course, is that we have read Spinoza, Newton, Leibniz, Kant and the others, and have learned at school non-Euclidian logic and the Einsteinian theory of relativity. But if we suspend our knowledge and just follow the logic of Gassendi's thought, we can come to his own vision of the coherence of his philosophy.

III. THE HYPOTHESIS UNDER TEST

My hypothesis is this: if Gassendi's philosophy is to appear homogenous as it must have appeared to Gassendi—otherwise he would have abstained from giving it out to mislead the public[44]—one should take Gassendi's religious faith seriously and regard it as the starting point and substratum of all his choices.[45]

The hypothesis which I am putting forward provides integral answers to the following questions.

1. Why does Gassendi build his own system of metaphysics as a

---

[44] Gassendi himself condemned opportunistic and insincere conformism, when, in his vindication of Epicurus against the charge of hypocrisy and duplicity, he says that what was reasonable in a society who ignored the true religion, is no longer acceptable once the true religion has been revealed. In a passage concerning the Pythagorean attitude toward official religion and its doctrine of dual truth—that for the vulgar and that for the initiate—Gassendi rejects categorically the principle of the two truths (in *De Vita & Moribus Epicuri*, 1st ed. 1647, Lyon; also in GO V.169–236, see "De superstitiosis ritibus ab Epicuro contemptis, & de objecta simulatione", 202b41–61: ac fateor quidem veracitate, non in verbis modo, sed etiam in actionibus, nihil esse posse laudabilius: Quid facias tamen, ubi spectaris hominem extra Religionem, in qua debemus cogitatione, verbo, opere consentire?). Besides, Gassendi energetically denies the charge of insincerity brought against his second letter *De Motu impresso a motore translato* (to Puteanus, printed in 1642, especially §13 about the attitude to be adopted towards the "decretum" of the cardinals against Galilei's theory of the motion of the earth) by Jean-Baptiste Morin's *Alae Telluris fractae*, in his third letter *De motu . . .* , §6, see GO III.525–527.

[45] I am aware that there was a time when ideological prejudices interfered with historical research so much that if someone had raised such a hypothesis, he would have been suspected of clericalism, and perhaps rightly so. Even today it is difficult to test such an hypothesis, for many churchmen still appear to hesitate giving vent to their personal religious feelings and therefore tend to broaden the gap between Gassendi's secular thought and his religious life; I am referring to the interesting book by the Jesuit Father Barry Brundell (see his *Pierre Gassendi*, 1987, p. 141), who, after having very sensibly dedramatized Gassendi's attitude towards the Church in his rehabilitation of Epicurus and in his various points of opposition to the official doctrine of the Universities in scientific matters, underlines the contrast between Mersenne and Gassendi concerning the war against irreligion. He shows that Gassendi's general aloofness is due to a lack of awareness of the real danger menacing the future of the Church. See too his conclusion: 140–142.

foundation for his physics as we see him doing in the *Logica* and the
"Physicae sectio prima: De Rebus Naturae universae" of his *Syntagma philosophicum* and also as he announces as early as 1624 in the
"Praefatio" of the *Exercitationes paradoxicae* (GO III.102–103) in
order to replace the Aristotelian foundations of science? He could
have picked from ancient and modern authors what was useful to
him and have quietly lived a life of a practising astronomer, physicist and erudite like contemporaries such as Peiresc, the Du Puy
brothers and Mersenne.

2. Why did he, a doctor of theology and philosophy, take the risk
of teaching a critical—and devastating—commentary on the peri-
patetic philosophy which he was at the same time teaching *ex officio*,
while showing no intention of founding a sect or of stepping out of
the institutional church. He did not claim to be a prophet like
Giordano Bruno, he was not a heretic, he did not provoke trouble
like Valla, Campanella or even Galileo. Though Gassendi never
attacked the writings of Aquinas, he did openly discuss and refute
what he calls the "common doctrine", that is, Scholastic logic,
metaphysics, physics and ethics. Why such audacity?

3. Why did he take the trouble of contradicting Aristotelian
scientists[46] such as Robert Fludd the Rosicrucian, and in his wake
the Platonists and neo-Pythagoreans,[47] Lord Herbert of Cherbury
about the universality and power of reason,[48] Descartes and his
idealist proof for the existence of God and of the validity of rational
intuitions,[49] Jean-Baptiste Morin, and with him not only the
astrologers but also all those who confused religious truth with
scientific research,[50] etc.?

4. Why befriend free-thinkers[51] and avow as his masters noto-
rious sceptics or heterodox authors such as Lucian, Juvenal, Sextus
Empiricus, Erasmus, Vives, Ramus, Gianfrancesco Pico della
Mirandola, Montaigne and Charron?[52] And, above all, why did he

---

[46] In the "Epistolae tres de Proportione qua gravia decidentia accelerantur",
1646, GO III.564–651.

[47] *Examen Philosophiae Roberti Fluddi Medici . .* , 1630, GO III.213–270.

[48] *Epistola singularis ad Librum D. Edoardi Herberti, "De Veritate"*; cf. note 41
above.

[49] *Disquisitio metaphysica seu Dubitationes et Instantiae adversus Renati Cartesii
Metaphysicam et responsa*, 1644, GO III.271–410.

[50] See the third letter *De Motu* (GO III.625–650) already quoted above and the
refutation of astrology in *De Effectibus Siderum*, GO I.719–752, which had appeared
already in the 1649 *Animadversiones*.

[51] See Pintard, *Libertinage érudit*, 127–132, 155–156, 191–192, 326–348, and the
bibliographical notes.

[52] Letter to Henri Dufaur de Pibrac (1621), GO VI.2a5–14 and *Exercitationes
Paradoxicae*, "Praefatio" to Joseph Gautier, GO III.99.

set to the task of rehabilitating Epicurus, whom the Church Fathers had forever shown to be the greatest enemy of religion and morals? Why did he, a pastor, take the risk of being charged with the crime of introducing a wolf into the sheepfold?

5. Why did he embark on a philosophical career at all,[53] and why did he choose to be a sceptic?[54]

6. Why did he not believe in the heuristic power of mathematical language, as his venerated masters Kepler and Galileo and his friend Mersenne induced him to do? In a word, why was he reluctant towards Neoplatonism?

7. How could he seriously believe in his theory of the dual soul, "mens vegetativa" or material soul and "mens intellectiva" or immaterial and supernatural soul?[55]

8. Why did he take the findings of the ill-reputed chemist De Claves seriously in his De Varietate et Generatione Lapidum (GO II.112a–117a); and, in general, why did he mix final causes into his otherwise pure mechanical theory of natural motion?[56]

9. How could he support a Stoico-Judeo-Christian doctrine of Providence as the prime and ultimate organizer of the universe and yet acknowledge the existence of natural calamities[57] or monstrosities, the Aristotelian's "nature's mistakes" (GO II.285ff.), and whatever is felt as unnecessary evil in general?

10. How could he on the one hand advocate total submission to the Roman Catholic Church and on the other hand make war on superstition, astrology, white magic and the naïve tendency of the pious to interpret natural phenomena as interventions of supernatural powers, that is to say, as miracles or as devilish actions?[58]

11. How could he, having displayed in his polemical works an

---

[53] He studied philosophy and theology in Aix (1609–1611); in 1614 he took doctorates both in theology and in philosophy from Avignon University, and won the two competitions for the chairs of Philosophy and Theology at Aix, but chose philosophy instead of theology, as his early biographers say. For his "confessions" about his philosophical itinerary in his youth, see his 1624 letter to Joseph Gautier, "Praefatio" to the Exercitationes, GO III.99–100.

[54] See again GO III.99–100.

[55] See in the Syntagma philosophicum his Physics, II.2, especially book III De Anima and book IX De Intellectu seu Mente.

[56] See for instance in the Syntagma Philosophicum his books on the parts of animals, GO II.213a12–18, and on generation of animals, GO II.267–285.

[57] The 1629 plague in Dignes, see his Lettres familières à François Luillier pendant l'hiver 1632–1633, B. Rochot, ed., Paris: Vrin, 1944, 38–39, and his Notitia Ecclesiae Diniensis dedicated "ad clerum populumque Diniensem", GO V.672–673.

[58] See "Letter to Peiresc", in Lettres de Peiresc, Ph. Tamizey de Larroque, ed., 195–196; letter to Louis de Valois (1642), GO V.155b7–11; Syntagma Philosophicum, "De immortalitate animorum", GO II.655a–656b, Parhelia [1630], GO III.659b67–660a.

acute perception of logical looseness, expose his *Syntagma* to the
charge of contradiction, when, having stated that it is the business
of philosophy to elucidate those truths that can be attained through
mere human reason ("lumen naturae") and to abstain from interfering with theology, he introduces into his *De Anima* the notion
of that the immortal immaterial human soul adhering to a material
animal soul just as Christ was incarnated into a human being, and
into his *De Libertate* the concepts of the self-determination of the will
and of the responsibility of the immaterial soul, which added to the
even more theological concept of God's grace, have no natural
connection with the mechanistic physiology of the psyche which he
developed elsewhere?

IV. THE SOLUTION PROVIDED BY THE HYPOTHESIS

These questions can be and have been validly answered in many
different ways, but my hypothesis provides a more coherent
answer. Let us see what happens if we suppose that Gassendi's
dedication to his particular faith is of structural relevance to his
philosophical life and work. First, this supposition will have a
feedback effect on our decision to take systematically all his statements as truthful, without sorting out those that are superficial
from those that express his true deep philosophical self. Second, it
also has a feedback effect on the assumption that Gassendi's work is
coherent, because it implies that his practice is coherent with his
outspoken doctrine, something that his own doctrine demands.
Each of these conclusions involving biographical matters rests, of
course, upon our first axiom, that Gassendi does not say one thing
and think another.

   To reach the point where Gassendi's scepticism comes in, we
have to start from the origins of Gassendi's philosophical itinerary.
Can we in his life and doctrine observe a primacy of ethics over
knowledge in which doctrine reflects and justifies life? Gassendi
opens the *Syntagma Philosophicum* with a definition of "philosophy",
stating that it is "amor, studium et exercitatio sapientiae" and that
"sapientia" is "dispositio Animi ad recte sentiendum de rebus, &
recte agendum in vita". The very disposition of the soul that leads
one to judge rightly depends itself on the moral decision

> to cultivate the habit of loving, exacting and searching for the truth
> wherever it may be and covering it with kisses (GO I.1.a10–11).

This goal is reasserted at the beginning of the *Ethics* (GO II.659).
As Gassendi himself notes, there is no opposition between action

and knowledge, for all the operations of a man in search of truth are actions, and no action can be carried out without the guidance of some knowledge of its final cause as well as of the conditions determining its success.

How, then, shall we decide whether in Gassendi's theory and practice cognitive (theoretical) nature has precedence over the will (practical nature)? A passage from the *Liber Proemialis* (GO I.29–30) may provide an answer. After having denied any preference on his part for this or that philosophical school, Gassendi here asserts:

> I stick only to the sole orthodox religion, which is the one I received from my elders: the Catholic, Apostolic, Roman religion.

This statement is often considered as a typical instance of Gassendi's perfunctory or even cautious conformism. But if we read what follows directly we see it in another light:

> And as to what remains ("quod superest"), I have it this way, that I always put reason before authority.

Gassendi proceeds then to explain that from Epicurus he adopts only those points that he judges most efficient for solving problems in physics and in ethics, and that he does not follow him blindly in every one of his opinions, especially those that pertain to religion. Giving his expression "quod superest" its full weight, this means that before he begins judging freely about things, he has already decided to stick without question to the Roman Catholic Church. This text is a late echo of a similar declaration in his first work, the *Exercitationes Paradoxicae*.[59] The expression "quod superest" indicates that for Gassendi religion is a matter of decision and divine grace, free reason being ancillary to it.[60]

If we now go back to the decisive moment of Gassendi's life—and therefore of his work—we can see that it was precisely the decision to assume the religion of his mother. From then on his philosophy becomes architectonically subordinated to its essential dimension: his personal praxis as a Christian. Now, if one takes the Scriptures seriously, there is no half measure. As Philo Judaeus, one of

---

[59] "Praefatio", GO III.101: see above; this quotation is followed in the text by "[qui lecturus . .] noverit non esse me adeo pusilli tenellique animi, ut credam cujusvis esse asserere quod sit dogma, quis Fideis articulus. Ecclesiae credo: at non cuivis Sciolorum hujusmodi, qui, nisi aliunde rejicere possint quod gustus ipsorum non probat: provocant statim ad Sacram Scripturam, haeresimque esse pronunciant".

[60] See GO I.5a58–60 concerning the conditions under which philosophy is not detrimental to religion: it should be "accommodata" and "ancillans".

Gassendi's innumerable sources points out to the point of obsession, the dominant reality in a man's life is his relationship to his Creator, and the "true philosophy" in the Bible is precisely knowledge of that fact, which in philosophical terms can be expressed like this: the final cause of man's existence is to fulfill his essence, which is nothing but his Creator's will. While discussing the principle of ethics and explaining why even in religion, man's motive is always his own felicity, Gassendi says that that man's felicity is to love—and therefore to obey—the infinite, perfect, absolutely good cause of his own being, which is God.[61] Later, when he discusses the problem of man's freedom as opposed to God's omnipotence, Gassendi explains that God made man a free cause, the only one in his creation, and that man can choose to act against God's will as if God decided in his place. So from Gassendi's own perspective it is clear that the choice for a religious life is at the same time free and the most reasonable choice a man can ever make. It follows that Gassendi's philosophy as a whole is a religious performance. This notion now supports my integrated explanation of each particular theoretical choice he makes in his philosophy.

Contrary to Barry Brundell, I believe that Gassendi's philosophical work should be seen as crypto-apologetic. Where Father Mersenne engages in open apologetics, Gassendi chooses to persuade his reader under the guise of a free-thinking rationalist. This accounts for his constant reference to pagan authors to demonstrate ideas that are acceptable to a Christian philosophy, for his choice of Lucretius, for his provocative attacks on the established philosophical institutions (teaching scholastics), and for his constant assertion of his independence of judgement in all matters that do not fall under the jurisdiction of sacred dogmas (for example, his declaration about the Church's condemnation of the Copernican theory of the world in the *Syntagma philosophicum*[62]).

The other factor which essentially determines Gassendi's philosophy is his theoretical choice for what is known as his scepticism. From what has been found, we can now see why this can be understood as a religious attitude.

---

[61] See GO II.715a, where "summum bonum" is defined as heaven (abode of bliss); see also for a similar statement "pietas secundum naturam in Divinum Numen", II.710a–b. In his "psychology" (in the *De rebus terrenis viventibus seu de Animalibus* of the *Syntagma Philosophicum* and the *Animadversiones*), Gassendi establishes that one of the appetites of the rational soul is the love of God as fatherly and perfectly benevolent omnipotent power (GO II.488b55–60, "De Appetitu & Affectibus Animae").

[62] *Physica* I: *De rebus naturae universè*, Book One "De Universo & Mundo", Chapter 3 "De Systemate seu compagine Mundi", GO I.149a57–68.

Already in the *Exercitationes paradoxicae*, Gassendi reveals that his opposition to the Aristotelian idea of science has something to do with his intention of showing the impotence of secular, purely rational means for attaining absolute truth.[63] In his preface, he says that in his youth he was disappointed by the official teaching of "philosophy", so he turned to other schools but none satisfied him and so he became inclined to favour the new Academy as presented by Cicero.[64] In various places in his *Syntagma*, when he reaches the very frontier between empirically verifiable hypothesis and pure conjecture, he enhances the plurality of answers proposed by philosophers who had at their disposal only natural light; this is always the juncture where the truth as revealed by the Scriptures, that is to say, the dogmas as defined by the Church and the Ecumenical Councils, sets in. A conspicuous example is in the introduction to *De Anima* (GO II.237a44–b30). Dogma is supposed to guide reason in its choice between different rational solutions, not to contradict reason. Thus Gassendi begins his "Quis sit Anima Humana" (GO II.255a1–11) by reasserting that "Sacra Fides" is assisted only by "legitima ratio". In other cases, where dogmas give no clue as to how to solve a given enigma, Gassendi insists on the limited range of natural light, and therefore on the vanity of those who boast that reason can master knowledge of nature. Such is the case, for example, in "De usu partium in Animalibus" (GO II.226–237) with regard to the question of how congregated atoms of matter can become sensitive, or what exactly the "flos materiae" or material soul is, which he describes as organization, sensibility, adaptability, automotion, capacity to aim at final causes etc. So Gassendi's argument concerning the contradictions of the sects merges with the traditional apologetic trope concerning the contradictions of the varieties of human opinion, a trope usually connected with that of the imbecillity of human reason (which Gassendi attributes to Solomon, quoting the books of Kings and Ecclesiastes). Beyond the polemic function of these tropes, we are led to a more fundamental attitude of religious-minded scepticism: humility of the finite creature in the face of his infinite Creator. Gassendi openly admits that we should acknowledge the fact that God did not think

---

[63] There is a reference to Nicolaus Cusanus's *Docta ignorantia* and to *Quod nihil scitur* (without mention of Francisco Sanchez) in the *Exercitationes Paradoxicae*.

[64] Not all of Gassendi's readers would have failed to recognize a silent reference to Augustine's *Confessions* V.x.: "Etenim suborta est etiam mihi cogitatio prudentiores illos ceteris fuisse philosophos quos Academicos appellant, quod de omnibus dubitandum esse censerent, nec aliquid veri ab homine comprehendi posse decreverant".

it necessary for us to know things essentially.[65] He repeats this whenever he contradicts what he calls the dogmatists, that is the Aristotelians, Pythagoreans, Platonists, Fludd, Descartes, Herbert of Cherbury, Jean-Baptiste Morin.[66]

The religious aspect of this scepticism is enhanced by the fact that it calls on man to remember the weakness ("imbecillitas") of his intellect, and it is associated with a voluntarist theology: God is infinitely free, the Creator of essences and even of the logic which binds us but does not bind him, since he could create an infinity of other logics, for which he could in turn create intelligences that would be exactly and exclusively adapted to them. Our mathematics is therefore not the language in which God wrote the universe: there is no common measure between our mathematics and His.

This provides us with a clue not only to Gassendi's rejection of mathematics as having a heuristic value in the sciences of nature—because it implies that our mind is able to practise the same mathematics and logic as God's mind (something which from Gassendi's perspective is both foolish and blasphemous)—but also to his rejection of astrology (on the same grounds) and of Herbert of Cherbury's deism. Indeed, Gassendi's philosophy leads to the conclusion that whatever concerns God—the absolute, the infinite, and therefore true religion as the right way to negotiate man's relationship to God—has to transcend the limits of natural reason. This constitutes what has been called Gassendi's fideism. Gassendi

---

[65] In gnoseological contexts, he abstains from mentioning the passage of Genesis 3, 4–7 and 22 where it is said that Adam and Eve were expelled from Eden because they sought to become wise and to know as much as God; yet he refers to that passage when, in his *De Animalibus* (*Syntagma Philosophicum*, "Physica" III.2: GO II.193–658) he deals with the cognitive functions of the "anima humana" after and before the "lapsus" (the Fall).

[66] For example, Gassendi writes Lord Herbert of Cherbury: De ipsa rerum veritate, quam persuasum pene habuit ter Maximum Deum reservatam sibi voluisse . . . Et vide etiam, circa aeternam tibi tantopere commendatam foelicitatem, vide inquam, ut Deus ad illam ducere nos voluerit Revelatione solum ac Fide: illam verò naturarum intimarum notitiam abdicatam voluerit. Scilicet quasi indicarit ad statum hominis naturalem sufficere notitiam illam qualitatum externarum, & in sensus incurrentium (GO III.413a5 f.). Gassendi's reason for this is that God has given to each creature the kind and range of knowledge necessary to its nature. Thus, for our survival we need no more than the hypothetical—and to some extent efficient—knowledge that we receive through the senses and "ratiocinatio". As soon as we forget that knowledge is a vital function we begin "hubrizein": "Nempe ultra res necessarias, & sine quibus degere inclumes non possumus, appetitum protrahimus, neque ponimus limitem, aut modum . . ." (GO III.413a50–53). This is "intemperantia" (GO III.413b10), which is the philosophical and profane equivalent for the sin of pride: cf. "Proemium", *Physica*, GO I.132a4–132b6.

uses his very orthodox theory of the inadequacy of man's reason in conceiving the absolute to justify rationally the necessity that true religion be irrational, revealed by God, mysterious, and, given the historical condition of man, not universal but particular. Logically, then, this justifies the very viciousness of the circle in which reason is trapped, because God's justice is impenetrable to reason, and this is why it is necessary that we do not understand why such scandalous things happen as the fact that entire nations are denied the chance of knowing the true religion. But is this not the same trick used by the rhetoric of religious propaganda and the advocacy of the irrational in general? It works only if one wants it to work. As Pascal himself, who was hardly a hard-boiled agnostic, said: faith is a decision.

But, if I may venture a qualitative judgement: Gassendi's decision is a serene one. One does not find in it the strained, proud quality of Montaigne or Bernier, who seem to say that if God is God, He should save them but they will not surrender any of the rights and powers of human nature, least of all reason, to their relationship with God. One does not find either the somewhat wounded and desperate quality of Bayle's fideism. Perhaps the whole contents of Gassendi's works would have been the same even if he had not been a Roman Catholic, but it would definitely not have been so had he not been a deeply pious man. Connected with his fideist decision is precisely that optimistic quality found only in those who love the world in which they live, and love it systematically because they trust the Cause of causes. If his optimism could be taken to be the cause for his decision of faith, it can also be seen as an effect of that decision, for faith is a result of the constant orientation of the will towards its own submission to the will of God. Precisely that unconcerned humility explains why Gassendi did not try to give a coercive power to his speculative work: in this he stands diametrically opposed to Descartes and Hobbes. He seems more concerned with clearing the errors and obstacles away from the path to the sciences for others than in gaining immortality through a personal contribution to the progress of any particular discipline. All this has been attributed either to his intellectual weakness or to his moral pusillanimity, which are moral judgements, whereas it could well be the necessary consequence of his initial decision to put ethics before speculation, religion before philosophy, and to regard charity as a way to "voluptas".

This matter I will leave open to discussion in order to return to the methodological issue that I raised before presenting my theory about Gassendi's scepticism as a religious attitude. What exactly is the purpose of the history of philosophy: pleasure, utility, or historical truth? If we select the last as its dominant goal, then what are our ways and means to achieve it? We have only the written works of those who have gone before us. In the case of Gassendi, if we desire cumulative knowledge of his work, then it is time for us to unite our dispersed and isolated individual efforts to read him. What we need to do is read him with a kind of "period instrument", that is to say, with an instrument calibrated for a synthetic mastery of his own semantic system. This leads us to the point announced at the beginning of this paper: to suggest that an international team be formed for the purpose of providing a critical edition of Gassendi's entire works, including the correspondence, and of editing a "lexikon Gassendianum" with the assistance of modern automatic data-processing techniques. Such a project would not only be a major contribution to scholarship, it would also be wholly in the spirit of Charles Schmitt's life-long efforts to promote a scientific history of philosophy.

THEO VERBEEK

FROM "LEARNED IGNORANCE" TO SCEPTICISM DESCARTES AND CALVINIST ORTHODOXY

I

According to Descartes, Voetius's attack on him started in 1639 with the latter's disputations on atheism. Admittedly, Descartes was not named in them, but, according to Descartes, Voetius had included among the marks of atheism "those things he knew popular opinion ascribed me, wrongly for that matter".[1]

For a long time, it was virtually impossible to corroborate Descartes' statement. It is true that the disputations on atheism were reprinted in Voetius's *Disputationes theologicæ selectæ* (1648), but their text was almost certainly changed for this new edition.[2] The first three disputations of this series, however, turned up in the Saltykov-Schedrin State and Public Library of St. Petersburg.[3] They show that Descartes had a point, although his allegation that these disputations were designed *in order to* justify Voetius's later actions against him is, of course, exaggerated. Indeed, the text of the disputations shows that at the time the main object of Voetius's worries were still the Remonstrants. Nevertheless, the disputations on atheism do contain various allusions to contemporary developments that might have some bearing on Descartes. In any case, much of it was used by Voetius's friend, Martin Schoock, in *Admiranda Methodus*, one of the most violent works ever written against Descartes.

Voetius claims that there is in each man a "cognitio Dei naturalis

---

[1] "Lettre apologétique aux Magistrats d'Utrecht", in *Oeuvres de Descartes*, eds. Ch. Adam, P. Tannéry, 12 vols., Paris: Cerf, 1897–1913, vol. 8-B, 204–205; also in René Descartes/Martin Schoock, *La querelle d'Utrecht*, textes établis, traduits et annotés par Theo Verbeek, Paris: Les impressions nouvelles, 1988, 408–409.

[2] *Disputationes theologicae selectae*, vol. I, 114–226; cf. Ernst Bizer, "Die reformierte Orthodoxie und der Cartesianismus", *Zeitschrift für Theologie und Kirche* 55 (1958), 306–372; also in English in: *Journal for Theology and the Church* 2 (1965), 20–82; I have dealt myself with this problem in the introduction to *La querelle d'Utrecht*.

[3] I gratefully acknowledge the kind intervention of the International Exchange Department of the Saltykov-Schedrin State and Public Library of Leningrad, which provided a microfilm.

ingenita", a natural and inborn theology, that becomes actual as
soon as one is able to understand the meaning of the words
"God" and "exist." The truth of these notions is as evident as that
of first principles like "the whole is greater than its parts", or
"contraries cannot both be true".[4] It is impossible not to know that
God exists. Voetius is not impressed by the fact that some people
do understand the meaning of the words "God" and "exist," but
still deny God's existence. After all, there are also Sceptics who
"from sheer vanity and malice" doubt or rather pretend to doubt
the most evident principles.[5] In short, there are no speculative
atheists, that is, people who sincerely deny the existence of God.[6] In
spite of all this, Voetius is of the opinion that "nobody doubts there
are atheists".[7] He solves this paradox by introducing the categories
of "practical atheism" and of "indirect atheism." Practical atheists
are all those who disobey God's law. The practical atheist denies
God's will even if he not invariably denies His existence. Epicurus,
for example, did not deny the existence of gods, but he did say that
they have no influence on earthly matters, which is an indication of
practical atheism. Indirect atheists, on the other hand, are all those
who hold ideas that, in some way or another, *imply* atheism.
However, since the undermining of our natural notion of God is
fundamental to any kind of atheism, almost all forms of atheism,

---

[4] Nostri communiter ex Rom. 1. 18. cum 2. 15. & Iohan. I. 9. esse theologiam
innatam, hoc est statuunt κοινὰς εννοίας seu notiones innatas, latens scil.
rationis & religionis semen naturale, quod se habeat admodum habitus principiorum: qui in adultis in actum educitur, & nude actus theologicus elicitur absque
demonstratione, percepta modo terminorum apprehensione: haut aliter ac primorum principiorum veritas suo lumine radiat & in mentem nostram se infundit,
simulac enuntiationis termini percipiuntur: adeo ut nullius hominis adulti mens
ab actuali istius veritatis coruscatione & sensu ad explicationem & perceptionem
terminorum omnino [1648: omnium] possit esse libera. "De Atheismo" II, iv:
Disputationes theologicae selectae, vol. I (1648), p. 140. On natural theology in general
in this period, see John E. Platt, *Reformed Thought and Scholasticism: the Idea of God in
Dutch Theology from 1575 till 1650*, Leiden: Brill, 1982. The idea that every man has a
natural notion of God, was part of the Dutch Confession; cf. J.N. Bakhuizen van
den Brink, *De Nederlandse belijdenisgeschriften*, Amsterdam: Ton Bolland, 1976 (2nd
ed.), p. 93.
   Sed longe aliud est exterius negare axiomatis alicujus veritatem, & aliud eam
interiori mente & conscientia non sentire, aut ea non convinci. Invenias etiam
vertiginosos Scepticos qui ex mera animi vanitate & malitia: externa disputatione
in dubium trahant veritatem primo primorum principiorum: *Nihil potest simul esse
& non esse; Contradictoria non possunt simul esse vera*. "De Atheismo" II, iv: *Disputationes*, vol. I, p. 141.
[6] Speculative nulli sunt Athei, qui certo persuasi sunt non esse Deum. "De
Atheismo" II, iv: *Disputationes*, vol. I, p. 144.
[7] The Bible speaks of the fool that says in his heart "There is no God" (Ps. 14:
1). The Ephesians are described as being "without God in the world" (Eph. 2: 12).
The Gentiles "know not God" (I Thess. 4: 5).

practical or indirect, are no more than variants of scepticism. As a result, Voetius's elaborate classification of the various causes and forms of atheism is actually very simple.[8] In fact, they can be reduced to two classes, each corresponding to one of two motives for becoming a Sceptic: the one Pyrrhonian, and the other, which I propose to call "Faustian".[9]

According to Voetius, Scepticism occurs "if someone, together with ancient or modern Sceptics and Pyrrhonians, explodes, derides, or doubts the knowability of anything", or if he, "by arbitrarily embracing or rejecting any idea that is proposed", destroys man's natural desire for knowledge.[10] The Sceptic is envious of the science of others and tries to attract attention by upholding impossible views.[11] Like atheism, scepticism is primarily an act of bad

---

[8] The main cause of atheism is, according to Voetius, man himself, seduced by the Devil: "De causa principali non est quod dicamus: indubium enim esse hominem, & impulsorem diabolum" (I, iv). But there are also "causæ impellentes & adjuvantes", which can be internal or external, general or specific. To the general causes belong man's corruption and consequent aversion from God, his blindness, vanity, and arrogance; his contempt for ancients and moderns; his striving after things that are new or not easily known; his reluctance to believe things he cannot see: "Sed causæ impellentes & adjuvantes explicandæ. Quæ sunt vel internæ vel externæ. Internæ & proëgumenæ sunt, tum communiores, tum magis speciales. Illæ sunt hominis lapsi corruptio & aversio, inque ea humani ingenii cœcitas, vanitas, superbia, præsentium & antiquorum fastidium, novorum & difficillime aut minime γνωστῶν appetitus, ἀπιστία, & difficultas credendi imprimis ea quæ a sensibus remota. "De Atheismo" I, iv: *Disputationes*, vol. I, p. 125.

[9] There are only two factors which cannot be so reduced: the "scandalum" ("securitas carnalis, vita profana, imprimis derisio religionis & pietatis") and the frequent change of religion ("crebra religionis mutatio & transitus de secta in sectam"). Voetius interprets them as belonging to both the will and the intellect; cf. *Disputationes*, vol. I, p. 128.

[10] Quando quis aut cum Scepticis & Pyrrhoniis sive antiquis sive hodiernis omne scibile, omnem scientiæ certitudinem explodit, ridet, in dubium trahit aut quodlibetice quidlibet pro re nata amplectando aut repudiando, omnem naturalem veritatis conscientiam, omnem ejus amorem, omne naturale sciendi desiderium hominibus inditum (juxta Philosophum Metaph. I. c. 1) quantum in se excutit. "De Atheismo" I, iv: *Disputationes*, vol. I, p. 126; cf. Aristotle, *Metaphysica* I, i, 1, 980a22.

[11] Cujus causa est partim invidia alienæ scientiæ partim desperatio propriæ idque propter ignaviam suam aut ingenii paupertatem aut occasionis difficultatem aut defectum. Quod a suo solius ingenio expectare non possunt, ab alieno expectare nolunt; quod sua industria & labore acquirere nolunt ab aliis inventum negant: & cum tot sæculorum experientiæ ac scientiæ minimam partem assequi & discere nequeant aut per ignaviam & animi levitatem discere nolint; & tamen ex innata superbia & vanitate stet ipsis illud αἰὲν ἀριστεύειν καὶ ὑπείροχον ἔμμεναι ἄλλων: hinc est quod desperatione & tristitiâ in audaciam & imprudentiam versâ scepticum suum furorem in omnes scientias, omnia sapientum inventa, dictata, scripta; omnes Academias & honestissima studia, omnia Dei dona, omnes labores & conatus effundant. "De Atheismo" II, iv, Ibid. The Greek phrase is a quotation from Homer's *Iliad* (VI, 208; XI, 784).

faith. The "Faustian", however, gives up because eventually he cannot know all he wants to know. The kind of knowledge he tries to obtain is impossible, so that he constantly runs up against the limitations of human knowledge. His scepticism is based on frustration.[12]

One of Voetius's key concepts in this connexion is "docta ignorantia". Voetius believes that the frustration of the Faustian is caused by his not being satisfied with "learned ignorance":

> The cause of this shipwreck is that such a person was not ready to stop his intellect and subdue it, and to feed it with learned ignorance. Still, the mind should as much find its rest in learned ignorance as in science. Indeed, this, too, is to know: that we are certain that something cannot be known or must not be inquired into, for, in this way, we safely avoid the errors of others and can look down upon them.[13]

The basis of learned ignorance, therefore, is not just a refusal to know, which, according to Voetius, would be against human nature, but the insight that there are things that cannot be known, and which, therefore, one must not try to know. "Learned ignorance" functions as a warning against the "Faustian" motive, and is thus an important means to avoid scepticism.

In 1639, Descartes' fame mainly depended on the activities of two Utrecht professors, Henricus Renerius (1593–1639), a philosopher, who died few months before Voetius held his disputations on atheism,[14] and Henricus Regius (1598–1679), professor of theoretical medicine since 1638.[15] Both propagated rather exagger-

---

[12] Impatientia alicujus defectus in affectata & solide jactata πανσοφία: unde homines ad desperata consilia non raro prolabuntur. "De Atheismo" II, iv, Ibid.

[13] Causa hujus naufragii est quod noluerit alicubi ingenium suum sistere, captivare & docta ignorantia pascere. Cum tamen in docta ignorantia non minus mentis quietatio quærenda sit, quam in scientia. Est enim & hoc scire si certi simus non posse aliquid sciri aut non debere investigari: ita enim aliorum in hac parte errores tuto prætervehimur aut ex alto despicimus. "De Atheismo" II, iv, Ibid., p. 126.

[14] Ferd. Sassen, *Henricus Renerius, de eerste "cartesiaansche" hoogleeraar te Utrecht*, Amsterdam: Noord-Hollandsche Uitgeversmaatschappij, 1941 (cf. Paul Dibon, "Notes Bibliographiques sur le Cartésianisme Hollandais," in: E.J. Dijksterhuis et al., *Descartes et le Cartésianisme Néerlandais*, Amsterdam; Paris: Presses Universitaires de France; Éditions Françaises d'Amsterdam, 1950, 288–293); Paul Dibon, *L'Enseignement Philosophique aux Universités Néerlandaises à l'Époque Pré-Cartésienne (1575–1652)*, Ph.D. Diss., Leiden 1954, 197–203. Despite the rediscovery of some of Reneri's disputations in the library of the Protestant Seminary in Herborn (see Paul Dibon, *Le Fonds Néerlandais de la Bibliothèque Académique de Herborn*, Amsterdam: Noord-Hollandse Uitgeversmaatschappij, 1957, p. 106) his position remains difficult to define. See also Theo Verbeek, *Descartes and the Dutch*, Carbondale, Ill.: Southern Illinois University Press, 1992.

[15] Cf. *Querelle*, "introduction."

ated ideas about the extent of the Cartesian revolution, which, in the case of Reneri, was also amalgamated with Baconian elements. This is probably the reason why the *Disputations on Atheism* concentrated on methodological issues:

> That perverse method of divine, natural, and human wisdom by which certain people, satisfied with their own and with what they produce themselves (to use Seneca's expression), rely only on experiences of their own and try to build anew, on that basis, all knowledge of God and creatures, because they hold in suspicion all books and histories, as if they were lies and fairy tales. I take pleasure in noting that the eminently learned Mersenne, too, considers this a cause of atheism or a road to it, p. 232.[16] Aristotle is not afraid to prefer the wise who has no experience to someone who has experience but no wisdom, Metaph. I.1.[17] The same is implied in that well-known Hippocratic dictum: *Art is long, life short, the occasion rare, and experience unreliable* (or *dangerous*). Read what is said by commentators of both authors and use it as an answer to our contemporary empirics who know everything without books, without study, without education, relying only on their lazy and erratic thinking.[18]

If allowance is made for the Baconian overtones, which probably have to do with Reneri, it is clear that Voetius refers to the first three chapters of the *Discourse*, in which Descartes speaks rather disparagingly on the importance of education and erudition. Descartes' method is an easy way to obtain perfect knowledge. In fact, however, perfect knowledge is impossible, so that Cartesianism is a sure road for Scepticism.

---

[16] The reference is to Mersenne's *Quæstiones celeberrimæ in Genesim* (1621).

[17] What Voetius has in mind is probably the end of the first chapter of Book I, where Aristotle says that "the man of experience is held to be wiser than the mere possessors of any power of sensation, the artist than the man of experience, the master craftsman than the artisan; and the speculative sciences to be more learned than the productive. Thus it is clear that Wisdom is the knowledge of first principles". *Met.* I, 1. 17, 981b30–982a3 (transl. Loeb Classical Library).

[18] Perversa illa sapientiæ divinæ, naturalis, humanæ methodus, quod se solis, & in se nascentibus bonis (ut verbis Senecæ utar) contenti, tantum propriis experientiis suis innitantur, indeque omnem Dei & creaturarum cognitionem de novo fabricare velint; libris & historiis omnibus, etiam sacris diffisi, tanquam mendacii & τερατολογιῶν suspectis. Qualem fere causam seu viam Atheismi video & gaudeo etiam notatam ab eruditiss. Mersenno p. 232. Sane Aristoteles non veretur sapientem non expertum præferre experto non sapienti Metaph. I.c.I. Et hoc facit tritum illud Hippocratis: *Ars longa, vita brevis, occasio volucris, experientia fallax* (seu *periculosa*). Confer quæ habent commentatores in utrumque autorem, & ea hodiernis nostris empiricis absque libris, absque studiis, absque artibus & literis nihil non otiosâ & desultoriâ aliquâ cogitatione perspicientibus repone. "De Atheismo" I, iv, Ibid., 128–129. The use of the word "cogitatio" in this context is probably an allusion to Descartes.

II

Voetius explicitly used the concept of "learned ignorance" against the Cartesians during the Crisis of 1641. Speaking of the attack by the new philosophers on "occult qualities", he pointed out that the view of philosophers and physicians who admit the existence of this kind of causes "is more in accordance with learned ignorance". The contrary opinion, however, "which pretends to know everything and seems to promise the effortless acquisition of absolute wisdom, must be held in suspicion".[19]

But the theme was further developed during the second major Cartesian crisis (1655–1656), which resulted in the official prohibition of Cartesian philosophy by the States of Holland.[20] Although, superficially, the main issue of that debate was Copernicanism, the deeper question was scepticism. This is evident in one of the books that started it off, *De Scepticismo* (1652) by Martin Schoock.[21] According to Schoock, scepticism must be rejected, if only because we do have some definite insights in natural and revealed theology.[22] At the same time, Schoock emphasizes on almost every page the limitations of knowledge. Indeed, "inflated nitwits" and "moderns"—no doubt the Cartesians—are told that a sure road to scepticism is to strive for perfect knowledge.[23] On the other hand, even imperfect knowledge is still knowledge.[24] The best way to fight

---

[19] *Querelle*, p. 111.

[20] Cf. P.C. Molhuysen, *Bronnen tot de Geschiedenis van de Leidsche Universiteit*, 7 vols., The Hague: Nijhoff, 1913–1924, vol. 3, "Bijlagen," 55*–58*; cf. C. Louise Thijssen-Schoute, *Nederlands Cartesianisme*, Amsterdam: Noord-Hollandse Uitgeversmaatschappij, 1954 (new edition with additional bibliography by Theo Verbeek, Utrecht: HES, 1989) p. 104.

[21] *De Scepticismo Pars I*, Groningen: Ex officina Henrici Lussinck, 1652. The fact that only vol. I appeared in 1652 was due to a crisis in the paper industry. The book as it stands consists of four parts, devoted to the history of scepticism, the arguments against scepticism, the role of experience, and various particular philosophic disciplines, all belonging to the arts and to theoretical philosophy. The second volume was to be devoted to a discussion of practical philosophy and of the "higher faculties" (theology, medicine and law), and to a critical evaluation of Cartesians and Aristotelians alike ("Præfatio"; see also p. 444).

[22] *De Scepticismo* II, xiv, 136–144; for a discussion of the Cartesian proofs of God's existence, see *De Scepticismo* II, xv, 145–151.

[23] Quod nobis magno usui futurum est, non tantum contra inflatos sciolos sed & quosdam recentiores qui majorem philosophiæ quam cudere moliuntur, perfectionem præconcipiunt, quam in hominem aliquem post lapsum cadere potest. Quanquam autem hi a scepticismo alienissimi videntur, ad nihil scire tamen viam expeditissimam faciunt, dum omne scire præ suo scire nihil putant; quod tamen si penitius excutiantur ipsis ineptius deprehendetur. Sed hac de re pluribus subsequentibus libris. *De Scepticismo* II, vii, p. 107.

[24] *De Scepticismo* II, xx, 169–173.

scepticism is to keep in mind these two things.[25] Schoock explains that, although nothing is absolutely certain, some things are more certain than others. The senses, for instance, are more certain than reason. Indeed, ultimately all natural knowledge derives from the senses.[26] Reason does not have a contents of its own. It is a power to operate on given materials. It has to be subdued and, at any rate, cannot be left to itself.[27]

Schoock draws the startling conclusion that, ultimately, there are only two sources for truth, the senses and the Bible. Accordingly, he vigorously protests against the view that in astronomical and physical matters the Holy Spirit "speaks according to the mind and opinions of the erring vulgar".[28] Had the Spirit chosen to instruct the faithful "ex mente vulgi", He would have been either unable or unwilling to speak the truth, which is utterly absurd.[29] Even so, the general principles of nature remain concealed. The Bible does not reveal them, and the senses and reason are unable to attain them. Accordingly, physical explanations are essentially empirical. They are necessarily limited to the immediate causes of things and events, such as they are perceived by the senses.[30] Unfortunately, the part dealing with Cartesianism was never published.[31] Various allusions show, however, that Schoock has three reasons for accusing Cartesians of scepticism. First, because they uphold an impossible ideal of science. Second, because they reject the senses. Third, because they arrive at conclusions which contradict the Bible.[32] According to Schoock, the result of all of these is scepticism.

---

[25] Schoock had already implied as much in *Admiranda Methodus novae Philosophiae Renati des Cartes*, (Utrecht Ex officina Joannis van VVaesberge, 1643). There he criticized systematic doubt mainly for two reasons. The first is that doubt is a cheap means to achieve originality, a theme Schoock borrowed from Voetius (Sect. I, 14–59; *Querelle*, pp. 187–209); the second is that it is just another formula for the criterion of evidence (Sect. IV, ch. i, 245–254; *Querelle*, 307–311).

[26] *De Scepticismo* II, xx, p. 170.

[27] *De Scepticismo* IV, xix, p. 399 (pagination is erratic after p. 396).

[28] Utro vero modo, hoc est sive ex professo, sive incidenter de illis in ipsa Scriptura agatur, existimandum est, Spiritum Sanctum, authorem principalem, non loqui ex mente & sententia errantis vulgi sed ex rei veritate. *De Scepticismo* IV, xix, p. 401. Schoock adds that the Holy Spirit is a "spirit of truth" (John 16: 13).

[29] *De Scepticismo* IV, xix, 402–404.

[30] *De Scepticismo* IV, xx, 437–439. This is in keeping with the empirical tendency of most of Schoock's other work.

[31] There is an extensive discussion of the Cogito: *De Scepticismo* II, iv–vi, 87–102; cf. Richard H. Popkin, *The History of Scepticism*, revised edition, Assen: Van Gorcum, 1964, 201–202.

[32] See also my 'Descartes and the problems of Atheism', *Nederlands archief voor Kerkgeschiedenis/Dutch Review of Church History* 71 (1991), 211–223.

Schoock's position anticipates Voetius's contributions to the debate on Copernicanism.[33] As far as the strictly astronomical side of the problem was concerned, the case was clear. Voetius had rejected the Copernican system as early as 1639.[34] He had also affirmed that even in astronomical matters biblical testimony must be taken seriously.[35] In 1641 he had detailed his objections in the "appendix" on substantial forms.[36] "It behoves a spirit of moderation", he had said, "to suspend judgement and be satisfied with learned ignorance."[37]

In 1656 Voetius more extensively discussed the same concept. Now, he particularly insisted on the limitations of knowledge. No man is free from errors, no more than he is from misery or sin.[38] This is the very reason why the Cartesians must be distrusted:

---

[33] The disputations are all published in vol. III of the *Disputationes Theologicæ Selectæ* (1659): "De ignorantia" (3 March 1655), 632–641; "De ignorantia II", (10 March 1655), 642–652; "De ignorantia III", (21 March 1655), 652–668; "De docta ignorantia" (7 April 1655), 668–681; "De docta ignorantia II" (28 April 1655), 681–692; "De errore & hæresi" (4 July 1655), 692–703; "De errore & hæresi II" (10 July 1655), 703–713; "De errore & hæresi III" (14 July 1655), 713–721; "De errore & hæresi IV" (20 September 1656), 721–736; "De errore & hæresi V" (8 October 1656), 736–750; "De errore & hæresi VI" (22 November 1656), pp. 750–768; "De errore & hæresi VII" (6 December 1656), 768–791; "De errore & hæresi VIII" (13 December 1656), 791–809; "De fide, conscientia, theologia dubitante" (17 December 1656), 825–847. This last disputation has an "appendix on philosophic doubt", 847–869. See also Voetius' "disputatio continens aliquot positiones miscellaneas" (24 May 1656), *Disputationes*, vol. IV, 745–762. The original editions are lost. See also *Nader openinge van eenige stucken in de cartesiaensche philosophie raeckende de H. Theologie*, Leyden 1656. This pamphlet analyzed, in a not entirely satisfactory way, by Dr. A. Vos in his paper: "Voetius als reformatorisch wijsgeer", in *De onbekende Voetius. Voordrachten wetenschappelijk symposium Utrecht 3 maart 1989*, ed. J. van Oort *et al.*, Kampen: Kok, 1989, 220–241.

[34] An terra immobilis in mundi medio quiescat? Aff. cum Theologis, Physicis & Astronomis omnibus Iudæis, Arabibus, Græcis, Latinis (exceptis uno atque altero ex antiquis & omnibus hodiernis Copernici sectatoribus) innixi rationibus, ut nos putamus, solidissimis. "De creatione" V, i: *Disputationes*, vol. I, 637–638; see my paper "Voetius en Descartes", in *De onbekende Voetius*, 200–219.

[35] An in scientia astrorum speciatim in ardua quæstione de explicando systemate mundi, sacræ scripturæ ratio habenda sit? Resp. aff. Although Holy Writ is not an astronomical treatise, "tamen nullæ hypotheses sumendæ, nullæ theses defendendæ, nulla argumenta producenda quæ veritati scripturæ contradicant & authoritati ejus præjudicant. Quod si anceps pugna & disquisitio sit circa scripturæ interpretationem, præstat ἐπέχειν quam periculosas theses scandalose διαφυλάττειν, "De creatione" VI, vi: Ibid., p. 691.

[36] *Querelle*, p. 114. The texts put forward by Voetius are classical: Jos. 10, 12–14; Eccl. 1, 4–7; Ps. 19, 5–7.

[37] *Querelle*, p. 98; the passage was suppressed in the definitive version, *Querelle*, p. 100; for the details of Voetius' critique, see *Querelle*, 114–115.

[38] Post lapsum nullus hominum immunis sit ab errore: "De errore & haeresi" I, v, *Disputationes*, vol. III, p. 701; Non magis in hac vita ab omni errore immunis potest quam ab omni peccato & miseria. "De errore & haeresi" II, i, Ibid., p. 714.

One must not think that in this life "pansophy" or "quasi-pansophy"[39] are possible or a method by which to obtain easily and quickly a science of all things natural and sure and evident explanations and demonstrations. This stops those who arrogantly promise no end of wonders and who, in the name of Lull, Paracelsus, Hermes, the Brothers of the Rose-Cross, have mystified the world with this Gorgon head. The more progress the true scientist makes, the more he makes his own that confession of our former teacher Heinsius: "there is so much we do not know!"[40]

According to Voetius, ignorance as such is always reprehensible. It is a "malum triste", a regrettable evil, and even a "malum turpe", a condemnable vice.[41] According to Voetius, it was the root of all evils in the Roman Church.[42] The reason, however, why *"learned ignorance"* is good, is that it is defined as "the awareness of our ignorance and the insight that some things are unknown or cannot be known".[43] Indeed, one of the means to attain learned ignorance is to practise science, for "the more we learn, the better we become aware of our ignorance".[44]

---

[39] There is an unexplored connexion here with Comenius who used this term. This may have been because of Reneri who was a friend of John Dury (both were inmates of the "Collège Wallon"), who in turn had contacts with Comenius; cf. G.H.M. Posthumus Meyjes, *Geschiedenis van het Waalse College te Leiden, 1606–1699*, Leiden: Brill, 1975, p. 191 (see also index); G.H. Turnbull. *Hartlib, Dury and Comenius*, Farnborough, Hants: Gregg International Publishers, 1968 (original edition: Liverpool 1948); Thomas H.H. Rae, *John Dury: Reformer of Education*, Hildesheim 1972: *Studia irenica* 8, passim (see index, s.v. "Comenius").

[40] Non est somniandum in hâc vitâ πανσοφίαν aut quasi πανσοφίαν aut methodum, quâ facile & brevi omnium rerum aut saltem naturalium, scientia certa evidensque demonstratio atque explicatio haberi possit. Obstruuntur ergo hic magni hiatus promissorum qui nomine Lullii, Paracelsi, Hermetis, Fratrum roseæ crucis &c. quasi gorgone obtento hactenus mundum ludificarunt. Vere sapientes, quo ulterius progressu, eo libentius usurpabant laudatissimum illud celeberrimi Heinsii quondam Præceptoris nostri Symbolum "Quantum est quod nescimus". "De Errore et Hæresi" I, v, Ibid., 701–703 (for the final quotation, cf. *Querelle*, p. 115).

[41] "De ignorantia" II, ii, *Disputationes*, vol. III, p. 645.

[42] "De ignorantia" I, "mantissa", Ibid., p. 641.

[43] "De docta ignorantia", *Disputationes*, vol. III, p. 670. The Scriptural basis of "learned ignorance" is Rom. 12: 3 ("For I say, through the grace given unto me, to every man that is among you, not to think of himself more highly than he ought to think; but to think soberly, according as God hath dealt to every man the measure of faith") and I Cor. 4, 5 ("Therefore judge nothing before the time").

[44] Bene jactis scientiæ rerum divinarum & humanarum fundamentis, assiduo scientiam superstruere, eamque augere tum propria meditatione, tum Artificum in sua Arte & quorumvis indicio atque auxilio. Ut enim morbus per vitam & sanitatem, & tenebræ per visum percipiuntur, sic ignorantia per eruditionem: quo quis enim in hac abundantior ac solidior est, eo magis atque evidentius ignorantiam suam perspicit.

Voetius pursues by making an allusion to the Cartesians: Contra si qui inter dictos literatos, parvi aut saltem mediocris ingenii, aut exiguæ eruditionis &

The term "docta ignorantia", as it is used by Voetius, seems to be particular to him.[45] The idea on which it is based, however, is the much older doctrine of "curiositas", or "sinful curiosity".[46] Rather surprisingly perhaps, Voetius turns to Thomas Aquinas to take from him the main characteristics of "curiosity".[47] According to Thomas, the desire for knowledge ("appetitus") may be good or bad, although knowledge as such is always good. For example we are not allowed to ask demons to reveal us the future, which is a case of "superstitiosa curiositas". There is sinful curiosity, too, if we strive for knowledge about creatures without minding "debitum finem", that is, the knowledge of God. Finally, curiosity occurs when someone tries to know more than his own faculties allow him.[48]

Although Voetius is not sure that it is not already included among the variants of curiosity mentioned by Thomas, he adds one of his own. It is that of "seeking to know what cannot be known by any finite intellect or what cannot be known by human intellect during this life".[49] In fact, there is a difference. Neither Thomas nor Voetius believe that there can be a conflict between reason and

---

nullius fere, aut admodum modicæ lectionis velint esse utres & soli-ipsi; necessario aut in desperationem quidquam in scientiis præstandi, aut in morosophias, vertigines, Phaetonticos conatus prolabuntur. Est enim ἀμαθία audax & temeraria: quibus gemellis possessi, instar infantium aut ebriorum, aut ἀφρόνων, phantasticorum, phreneticorum nulla præcipitia vident, nulla pericula metuunt. "De docta ignorantia" II, 1, Ibid., p. 683.

[45] According to the *Thesaurus Latinus* the expression does occur in Augustine, but, as far as I know, it never played an important role before Cusanus (1401–1464). Voetius dissociates himself from Cusanus in "De docta ignorantia" I, i, Ibid., p. 669.

[46] For this concept, see in general: H.A. Oberman, *Contra vanam curiositatem: ein Kapitel der Theologie zwischen Seelenwinkel und Weltall*, Zürich 1974; E.P. Meijering, *Calvin wider die Neugierde: ein Beitrag zum Vergleich zwischen reformatorischem und patristischem Denken*, Nieuwkoop: De Graaf, 1980; A. Labhardt, "Curiositas: notes sur l'histoire d'un mot et d'une notion," *Museum Helveticum* 17 (1960), 206–224; A. Godin, "Érasme: <pia/ impia curiositas>", in *La curiosité à la Renaissance*, actes réunis par Jean Céard, avec la collaboration de G. Bocazzi *et al.*, Paris: SEDES/ C.D.U, 1986, 25–36 (and other papers in this volume).

[47] "De docta ignorantia," II, 2, Ibid., p. 683. Thomas is a rather unusual source in this context; cf. H.A. Oberman, *Contra vanam curiositatem*, 29–31, who concludes by saying: "Das 14. und 15. Jhdt gingen im grossen und ganzen respektvoll an dem Aquinaten vorbei. Ihre Interessen, darunter besonders die brennende Frage der curiositas, fanden sie nicht von ihm wahrgenommen", p. 31.

[48] *Summa Theologica* II, ii, qu. 167; Thomas' conclusion was: "Quanquam veritatis cognitio per se vitiosa non sit sed per accidens, quatenus videlicet eam peccatum superbiæ sequitur, appetitus tamen assequendæ cognitionis variis modis inordinatus ac vitiosus esse potest", (Ed. Leonina, vol. 10, Rome 1899, p. 346).

[49] Addi possit quintum, aut forte ad quartum reduci: 5. Cum quis studet nosse & scrutatur quæ absolute a finito intellectu aut a nullo humano ingenio in hac vita cognosci possunt. "De docta ignorantia" II, ii, Ibid., 683–684.

faith. But, whereas according to Thomas philosophy and theology virtually penetrate each other in a harmonious synthesis, the agreement between faith and reason postulated by Voetius is of a different order. This agreement can only be achieved by carefully demarcating what does, and what does not belong to the province of finite intellect. Moreover, the limits of science, must be fixed by theology and not by philosophy, because theology is of a higher order than philosophy:

> Philosophy must be accommodated to Christian Theology, not the other way round. Otherwise the maidservant would put herself, under the pretext of freedom, in the place of the mistress and dominate over her in a licentious and tyrannical way.[50]

Accordingly, philosophy is free only to the extent that it knows its own limits, that is, insofar as it is ready to submit to theology on those questions which pertain to God.[51] Voetius does not absolutely condemn philosophy. In his comments on Col. 2, 8 ("Beware lest any man spoil you through philosophy") he points out that the Apostle cannot mean "true philosophy", since he speaks of a "vain deceit". True philosophy cannot be "vain". God would be a deceiver, if it were. Vain, however, is any philosophy that is not based on the senses and on "sound reason".[52]

According to Voetius, the doctrine of learned ignorance also applies to astronomy. All astronomers confess that their discipline is difficult and that the data on which it relies are inaccurate.[53] As a result, Voetius blames the temerity of those who construct a cosmology different from that which has been revealed to the Sacred authors:

---

[50] Philosophia accommodanda ad Theologiam Christianam, non contra: alioquin ancilla prætextu libertatis substituitur dominæ, eique licentiose & tyrannice dominatur. "De errore & haeresi", Ibid., p. 741; cf. Jac. du Bois: "De Philosophie is maer een dienaresse van de Theologie/ de dienaresse nu moet swijghen daer de vrouwe spreeckt", *De naecktheyd der cartesiaansche philosophie ontbloot*, 1655, p. 10.

[51] Libertas quam vocant philosophandi, sic non est explicanda & extendenda ut impune Theologiam & Fidem grassetur ejusque fundamenta luxet aut tollat. "De errore & haeresi" V, iii, Ibid., p. 742.

[52] "De errore & haeresi" VI, i, Ibid., p. 751; Voetius also tries to prove that the philosophy which is actually meant by the Apostle, is, if anything, that of the Platonists: *Ibid.*, pp. 754–756. See also "De docta ignorantia" II, Ibid., 681–682.

[53] Astronomiæ quot sint occulta & quam imperfecta sit illa, artfices confitentur, "De docta ignorantia" I, v, Ibid., p. 679. Their opinion is corroborated by Biblical evidence: Voetius quotes Prov. 25, 3 ("The heaven for height, and the earth for depth, and the heart of kings is unsearchable") and Jer. 31, 37 ("If heaven above can be measured, and the foundations of the earth searched out beneath, I will also cast off all the seed of Israel for all that they have done, saithe the Lord").

> How great is, therefore, the temerity of those who construct their own
> world system against what was revealed by the Holy Spirit, the
> maker of it all, to Moses and to the other sacred authors; the more so
> because those who have no instruction at all and are not informed of
> all observations and measurements often are the most impertinent,
> those indeed who are not afraid to question the truth and the author-
> ity of Holy Writ, to subordinate it to their own hypothesis or require
> that it is not contradicted by it.[54]

Voetius admits that the question of the sun's movement is, in itself,
not fundamental to religion. But it certainly is a sign of "impudence
and profanity" to hold an idea that is so evidently opposed to Holy
Writ.[55] This is especially the case because, according to Voetius,
the Copernican hypothesis has not been demonstrated to provide a
true picture of the universe, and, moreover, because there is an alternative system—Tycho's—that does not disagree with Scripture.[56]
In preferring Copernicanism to the Bible, the Cartesians, therefore,
accept a blind bargain.

All participants to the debate felt there was much more at stake
than a precise astronomical problem. This was clear already in
1641, when the question was first discussed in a Cartesian context.
From the beginning, the question was not whether Copernicanism
was better as an astronomical hypothesis, but how much value
must be attached to a reconstruction of the world on the basis of
rational insights. In his disputations *De illustribus aliquot quæstionibus
physiologicis* (1641), for example, Henricus Regius (1598–1679) had
upheld the Copernican system because, he said, that system better
conforms to mechanics, "which is all but the only rule in
physics".[57] This explains why the Copernican hypothesis became a

---

[54] Unde constat quantâ temeritate systema mundi contra Spiritus Sanctus
omnium architecti revelationem Mosi aliisque scriptoribus sacris factam fabricent
nonulli; inter quos ἀμαθεῖς, omniumque observationum & mensurationum
ἄπειροι sæpe audacissimi: qui non verentur Scripturæ veritatem atque auto-
ritatem sollicitare, ut hypothesi ipsorum inserviat aut saltem non obsit. "De docta
ignorantia" I, v, Ibid., p. 679.
[55] ....errores veritati philosophicæ, etiam Scripturæ testimonio confirmatæ
oppositi, quamvis nec directe nec per primam consequentiam sint fundamentales,
ideoqie in se & per se nec hæreses sint, nec sapientes hæresin, non tamen neganda
sunt sapere profanitatem & impudentiam. . . . "De errore & haeresi" V, iii, Ibid.,
p. 741.
[56] Idem judicandum de otioso & petulanti errore circa quietem terræ & motum
solis: qui cum nulla demonstratione naturali probari possit nec tamen ob reveren-
tiam Scripturæ ab eo abstineatur, videant ne temeritatis & profanæ petulantiæ
suæ pœlnas dent & circa fidem aliquod naufragium faciant. Deus non irridetur.
"De errore & haeresi" V, iii, Ibid., p. 741.
[57] Atque hic telluris motus nobis adeo verus videtur, ut illum nullis rationibus
humanis refutari posse existimemus. Constitutio autem cœli secundum dogmata

symbol of Cartesian philosophy in general. By setting up a standard for truth that could evidently conflict with both the senses and the Bible, the Cartesians had, in fact, created a "sceptical crisis".

III

The fundamental motive behind the accusation of scepticism, therefore, was to combat "vain curiosity". Until the first half of the seventeenth century, the use of this doctrine had been limited to preventing very particular questions, such as, for example, why God elects certain people and rejects certain others.[58] In general, however, it applied to God rather than nature.[59]

This raises the question whether, in applying the idea of learned ignorance to natural knowledge, Voetius and Schoock changed its meaning. Their own idea was that they did not. According to them, God is free, so that any attempt to know His creation a priori amounts to a sacrilegious effort to penetrate into a sphere that was essentially closed to mortals, that of God's being. This, however, was exactly what the Cartesians did. Commenting on mechanist physics, Schoock points out that to subject nature to mechanics amounts to a restriction of God's actions by the rules of an essentially human craft.[60] The right way, on the other hand, is to register what it has pleased God to reveal to us, either in the Bible or through the senses, and to keep in mind that whatever we believe to know, has no more than provisional value.

Naturally, one may ask whether Aristotelianism itself is not open to the same criticism. According to Voetius and Schoock, however, Aristotelian philosophy was not one among many more or less interchangeable systems of philosophy, but the consistent development of

---

Ptolomæi & Tychonis, adversatur mechanicæ, quæ est verum & fere unicum Physicæ fundamentum. *De illustribus aliquot qæstionibus physiologicis* III, xv–xvi; see also *Querelle*, p. 90. Since the publication of *La Querelle d'Utrecht*, I unearthed a copy of this disputation in the Staatsbibliothek Preussischer Kulturbesitz (Berlin).

[58] See, for example, Abraham Heidanus, *Proeve en wederlegginghe des Remonstrantschen catechismus*, Leyden: By P.A. van Ravesteijn ende D.J. van Ilpendam, 1641, 432–438.

[59] Cf. Meijering, *Calvin wieder die Neugierde*.

[60] Inepte enim statui physicæ regulam mechanicam vel hinc manifestum, quod ars potius naturam, quam natura artem imitetur: artifex quippe & mechanicorum architectus, operum naturæ simius est, non vero omnipotens eorum conditor Deus, imitator machinarum, v.g. alicujus Archimedis. Nisi forte placeat novatoribus, Dei tum omnipotentiam, tum sapientiam in operibus creationis manifestam, circumscribere, & ad leges hujus illiusve mechanicæ adigere, *Admiranda Methodus* II, ix, p. 133; *Querelle*, p. 246.

sense experience and common sense. The division, therefore, between common sense and philosophy was not of an essential, but only of a practical nature. In adopting the Aristotelian categories of "form" and "matter" one did not commit oneself to the authority of one philosopher. Aristotelian science was not a fixed body of doctrines, but rather a collection of problems and methods which had been passed on from generation to generation.

The example of Voetius and Schoock shows that in the seventeenth century scepticism was a taboo. It belonged to a later generation to realize that scepticism of some kind was perhaps an effective weapon in upholding the sake of orthodoxy. This is clearly visible in the work of Johannes Regius (1656–1738).[61] On his taking leave as "rector magnificus" of Franeker University in 1725, his customary "oratio" took the form of a plea for scepticism.[62] Quoting lavishly from Francis Bacon, Regius insisted both on the empirical origin of all our profane knowledge and on its inherent limitations. What is given are individual things and events. General ideas are not only useless but, because of their limited corroboration, misleading. They are nothing but "entia rationis". It is nonsense to suppose that they can in any way be a true representation of things. In Regius's view, scepticism is a wholesome alternative.[63] Like a modern Sextus he reviews the achievements of the various disciplines of philosophy and science. Invariably his conclusion is that nothing is certain.[64] Like Voetius before him, Regius considers ignorance a defect. Even so, scepticism must be preferred, at least if its motives are not vicious.[65] At any rate, it is better than the

---

[61] See Ferd. Sassen, *Geschiedenis van de wijsbegeerte in Nederland tot het eind der negentiende eeuw*, Amsterdam, Brussels: Elsevier, 1959, p. 170; 173–175. For an exposition of Regius's general philosophy, see his *De beginselen der beschouwende filosofy*, Amsterdam: By Adrianus en Johannes Douci, 1735.

[62] Joannes Regius, *Oratio pro Scepticismo*, Franeker: Excudit Henricus Halma, 1725. Similar accents had been heard in a sermon on Col. 2, 8: *Nodige waerschouwinge tegen het oordeel, en meesterschap der reden over de Schriftuyre en Goddelijcke waerheden*, Franeker: By Hans Gyselaar, 1686 (Knuttel. 12542), and in *Oratio de sapientia imaginaria*, Franeker: Ex officina Francisci Halmæ, 1709.

[63] Hinc laudatus a me Scepticismus certæ veritatis amantibus, nec non errorem evitare conantibus denuo se ultro commendat. *Oratio pro Scepticismo*, p. 40.

[64] En! quid Philosophorum opinionibus, etiam pro certissimis habitis, tribuendum sit. Ibid., p. 42; Cuncta itaque hæc vaga sunt & incerta, ac proinde nulli satis nota. Ibid., p. 48; Hactenus, nihil certi compererunt. Ibid., p. 56, etc.

[65] Profecto, quamvis omnis ignorantia defectum aliquem in nobis arguat, ea, quæ est puræ negationis, illâ, quæ pravæ dispositionis est, multo existit melior; cum prior data occasione, quâ veritas quædam nobis offertur, facile emendetur; posterior nunquam, vel quam difficillime. Ibid., p. 61.

arrogance of those philosophers who pretend to know everything.[66]

Basically, Regius's position is identical with that of Voetius, but, apparently, the taboo on scepticism was lifted. Moreover, whereas Voetius and Schoock had been cautious about some kinds of philosophy only, Regius issues a warning against all philosophy. And, whereas both Voetius and Schoock had to face the impossible task of refuting what they saw as dangerous scepticism by insisting on the limitations of knowledge, Regius's task was less ambiguous. No doubt, the rise of Cartesianism and the corresponding decline of Aristotelianism had made things easier. Indeed, Regius's plea for scepticism turns out to be a plea for the rights of common sense. The concept, however, that links his position with that of Voetius and Schoock is that of "curiosity."

---

[66] Revera, intoleranda est nonnullorum philosophorum fastus, infanda arrogantia: nam nullum est problema, cum solvendo, nulla sunt in rerum natura phænomena, quibus explicandis, se pares non arbitrantur; quasi vero hujus Universi, infinita potentia conditi, incomprehensibili sapientia gubernati, ipsis paterent latifundia. Ibid., 61–62.

RICHARD A. WATSON

DESCARTES' SCEPTICISM: LOGIC VS. BIOGRAPHY

I

In a recent article, Geoffrey Scarre[1] has stated beautifully the evidence for the conclusions that René Descartes was not himself a sceptic, that he did not intend for his sceptical arguments to be taken to their limits, and that he did not believe in either the existence of or the possibility of the existence of a deceiving demon or a deceiving God. In particular, Scarre insists that Descartes presents the deceiver argument merely as a methodological device and Scarre focuses on the fact that Descartes was impatient with attempts to refute the deceiver argument, saying that it was merely "metaphysical" or "hyperbolical" and was not to be taken seriously, that is, not as an actual possibility.

Descartes' grounds for disdain of the demon, Scarre speculates, are first, a solid disbelief in the existence of witches and witchcraft and hence a modern scientist's rejection of demons and demonology, and second, a sincere belief in the existence of a benevolent God for whom deception is impossible. In other words, according to Scarre, in knowing that God exists, Descartes knows that there are no deceiving demons. And, as Scarre points out, this makes Descartes very modern, indeed, for a thousand years of Catholic tradition acknowledged that God gave Satan licence to tempt human souls through deception, and if Descartes did not believe in witches, the majority of his contemporaries did, and witches were being tortured and burned during the very years in which Descartes introduced and then retracted his deceiving demon.

Martial Gueroult argues that Descartes knows that omnipotence and deception are incompatible, and this is why Descartes qualifies his introduction of the demon by saying in Meditation II: "I am supposing that there is some deceiver who is extremely powerful

---

[1] Geoffrey Scarre, "Demons, Demonologists, and Descartes", *Heythrop Journal* 31 (1990), 3–22.

and, *if it is permissible to say* [my stress], malicious and clever",[2] knowing that it is *not* permissible to say that God is malicious or a deceiver.

Henri Gouhier says that the demon is in fact unnecessary, for the sceptical argument is complete without the demon, and the doubt is all "pretense" anyway.[3] God's existence and goodness does away with the demon (*pace* Satan), so it is foolish to make heavy going out of the rhetorical flourish that is all the demon amounts to.

II

This brings me to the historiographic issue that is the point of my paper. This issue is perhaps most explicitly broached by John Locke. Bishop Edward Stillingfleet accused Locke of being a Socinian because Locke believed in the prevalence of reason in matters of religion and in the general reasonableness of Christianity. Locke was outraged, and stated explicitly that he was *not* a Socinian.

I think we can accept the sincerity of Locke's disclaimer. Nevertheless, Stillingfleet and others discerned Socinian principles in Locke's writing, and derived from them Socinian conclusions. Locke's philosophy in fact provided aid and comfort to Socinians.

The historiographic problem here is the relation between biography and logic. There is no biographical evidence that Descartes believed that a deceiving demon is an actual possibility as opposed to a metaphysical possibility, that is, abstracted from reality, just as there is no biographical evidence that Locke was a Socinian or, even if he appeared to be, a fellow traveler. Quite the contrary, in fact, in each case.

So as historians of philosophy—at least from what I shall call the biographical school of interpretation—in giving an exposition of a philosopher's position, we are instructed to discount whatever the philosopher himself discounts. If Descartes says that the demon hypothesis is hyperbolical and rediculous, not to be taken seriously, then *we* are not warranted to take it seriously. And never mind that Locke's philosophy can be seen logically to imply Socinianism.

---

[2] Martial Gueroult, *Descartes' Philosophy Interpreted According to the Order of Reasons*, vol. 1: *The Soul and God*, Translated by Roger Ariew, Minneapolis: University of Minnesota Press, 1985, p. 286, note 30; René Descartes, *Meditationum de Prima Philosophia*, in *Oeuvres des Descartes*, publiées par Charles Adam & Paul Tannery, nouvelle présentation, Paris: Vrin, 1964, vol. 7, p. 26.

[3] Henri Gouhier, *Essais sur Descartes*, Paris: Vrin, 1949, p. 154. Discussed by Harry G. Frankfurt in his *Demons, Dreamers, and Madmen: The Defense of Reason in Descartes's Meditations*, Indianapolis and New York: Bobbs-Merrill, 1970, 85–86.

Because Locke explicitly does not intend to support Socinianism, then *we* are not licensed to see it that way.

The biographical interpretation thus opposes head on the logical interpretation.

This is a very old conflict in philosophy. It goes back at least to the opposition of Socrates to the sophists, and it remains a difference roughly between those on the one hand who take rhetoric or hermeneutics in general as the most important bases of interpretation and those on the other hand who generate their interpretations from the logical implications of a philosopher's basic principles.

Another very rough splitting of these two schools is between those who stress the historical context and the socio-intellectual milieu in trying to understand what a philosopher means, and those who claim that principles, positions, and arguments are perennial and can be examined, criticized, and evaluated independently of the cultural context in which they arise and play a role. The difference is expressed by members of what I shall call the logical school of interpretation. They *agree* that Descartes certainly did *say* that the demon is just a methodological ploy, and that he may even have believed that the demon simply could be ignored and not taken seriously, but in fact Descartes let the genie out of the bottle and can no more ignore the logical implications of the demon hypothesis than he can deny that $2 + 2 = 4$.

To begin, let me say that there is among members of the biographical school a threefold naivité—a naivité that is, I think, necessary for the sustaining of their position—about scepticism, about the interpretation of texts, and in particular about both the discernment of an author's intent and the relation of this intent to the interpretation of a text. Members of the biographical school apparently believe that sceptical arguments are like tools or instruments that can be applied or not, and they take scepticism to be an attitude that one can choose to hold or not. Thus, anyone who has a sceptical crisis is in a pathological condition. That is, someone like David Hume who really despairs about scepticism has a psychological disorder. Hume himself finds relief from sceptical doubts by wrenching himself away from study by engaging in such ordinary occupations as playing cards, conversing with friends, and eating. Hume does not, however, believe that this therapy destroys the disease of scepticism. It just relieves the symptoms. Blaise Pascal, also, relieves the symptoms of his deep sceptical depression by resorting to religious belief, but, good Jansenist, he still knows that he can never know if he is saved, and he remains terrified of the infinite immensity of space.

So those who argue that one can just ignore scepticism, and those who claim that sceptical arguments can simply be applied or not according to choice, have to hold—ingenuously perhaps—that scepticism is just a psychological attitude that can be turned on or off at will, and that one can choose to apply or not to apply sceptical arguments to a position, and, in particular, they have to claim that if the philosopher who holds or constructs the position *says* that sceptical arguments are not to be applied to it, then they do not apply and cannot be used in interpreting the position.

The second aspect of biographical school naivité is the presumption that texts are generally open to easy interpretation in context, and, in particular, that an author's intent is fairly clearly expressed in the text. Descartes' annoyance at being accused of arguing in a circle seems obvious, his impatience at being forced to respond seems clear, and his assertion that the deceiving demon is not to be taken as a serious point against his position seems to be the literal meaning of his words.

Now, supposing that this literal reading *is* the true reading, all we have is a sheer assertion, with no reason given why the demon is trivial. If it is because trust in God shows us that deception is impossible, the question is begged.

But my point here is that it is naïve to take Descartes at his literal word, and also it is naïve to take his apparent annoyance and impatience as signs that he finds the circle argument inapplicable to his position.

In a wider context, Descartes is a mathematician who understands logic. More than that, he is a natural philosopher who has virtually set God aside in his physics as nothing more than a principle of the conservation of motion and of the uniformity of the laws of nature. According to Descartes, human reason is adequate for understanding the cosmos—he disdains Pascal's pessimism—and it is perfectly clear that Descartes understands that the only real challenge to human reason is scepticism.

Now, Descartes—like Hume—may very well have thought that scepticism *should* be set aside, and perhaps—unlike Hume and Pascal—Descartes himself was tempermentally capable of choosing to set scepticism aside without any psychological disturbance or relapses. But it takes a certain kind of naivité to claim also that the logical implications of the deceiver hypothesis themselves can just be set aside, and Descartes' annoyance could just as well be interpreted as a reflection of his awareness that the logical point *does* hold, and his impatience could be interpreted as a response to the morbid concerns of Jansenists such as Arnauld who ought to take their belief in the existence of God as liberating rather than as cause for the deep religious scepticism implied in the doctrines of grace and predestination.

Descartes, after all, is an optimist. It seems pretty unlikely to him that we are being deceived by a demon. If you believe in a benevolent God, why dwell on the logical possibility of malevolence? But to take Descartes' response—as members of the biographical school do—as a claim that sceptical arguments do *not* apply against Descartes' philosophical position, is to manifest a degree of naïvité that I would not want to attribute to Descartes.

This naïvité about the logic of scepticism combines with the naïvité about the psychology of scepticism to produce a very simplistic view of an author's intent. Members of the biographical school have to hold that the author's intent is perfectly obvious and unproblematic. But this is seldom if ever the case.

As for the *Meditations*, Descartes told Father Mersenne that his true purpose in writing them was to insinuate his physics. He told Princess Elisabeth that one should spend practically no time at all thinking about metaphysical matters. These statements and many others certainly suggest that Descartes does not want us to get bogged down in metaphysical connundrums, and had he been as successful in developing a viable physics as was Sir Isaac Newton, probably we would not worry so much about his metaphysical writings as we do today. What I am saying is that Descartes viewed himself as a mathematician, a physicist, and a medical scientist, and in that context his role as metaphysician is incidental. His failure as a scientist is a major reason why we think of him primarily as a metaphysician. His intent was to provide a metaphysical grounding for his physics that the Jesuits at the Sorbonne might find acceptable. But did he really intend to say that we are warranted to reject sceptical arguments merely because we believe in a non-deceiving God? I doubt it.

But beyond the problem of discerning the author's intent (a sceptical problem, I note), there is the question of so what? So what if you know the author's true intent? Obviously it helps you get around problems of infelicities of expression, of unclarities, lacunae, and sheer mistakes in exposition. But, if you already know what an author intends to say, then the interpretation of the text in which the author attempts to say it becomes, in a sense, secondary. You do not get the meaning from the text; instead you impose the meaning on the text on the basis of knowing what the author intended to say with the text.

The danger of circularity in interpretations based on the author's intent is great. For how do you know what the author's intent is except by interpreting his text? Interpretation without knowledge of the author's intent must be done with anonymous texts and texts for which we have very little historical or biographical context in which to situate them.

Moreover, even if you do know the author's intent, there still remains the *text*. In the context of language itself, every text has to various degrees an integral content and meaning of its own. This has led the New Critics to propose that it is a fallacy to interpret a text on the basis of an author's intention—the intentional fallacy. Opposition to interpretation based on an author's intention has gone even farther in deconstructionist criticism in which the author is eliminated entirely and the text is all there is to interpret. At this extreme, textual context can be anything or nothing at all, for not only the author but also history itself can be elided as background of interpretation.

But to my more traditional point: So what if Descartes says that the deceiving demon hypothesis is to be put aside as ridiculous? And so what if Locke says his writings do not support Socinianism? The logical implications of these texts have a being, too, and the logic of the texts puts demands on us for acknowledgment during interpretation, demands, as I have already suggested, that we can no more ignore or set aside than we can deny that $2 + 2 = 4$.

The naïvité of members of the biographical school requires so much faith in our ability to know the literal meanings of texts and the intentions of their authors, and requires such blindness to logical implications of texts, that they seem to be simplistic, naïve.

Certainly, Descartes' contemporaries saw straight through his disclaimers about scepticism, and so I now turn to the logical school of interpretation—in historical context.

It cannot be said that all of Descartes' contemporaries accepted his opinion that the deceiving demon hypothesis can be set aside, but some very important ones apparently did. More precisely, three of the original six sets of objections to the *Meditations*—those of Mersenne, Arnauld, and Pierre Gassendi—specify the problem of grounding the criterion of certainty on the existence of a non-deceiving God as being circular because the argument itself is warranted only if the criterion is grounded. This Cartesian Circle is also known as Arnauld's circle because he stated it most clearly in terms reminiscent of the *Port Royal Logic*, a Cartesian logic that Arnauld wrote with Pierre Nicole.

It is an interesting point of interpretation to inquire whether or not Arnauld seems surprised at the breach of logic he records.

Obviously he is not. The language in which Arnauld states the
Cartesian Circle is so precise, dry, and brief as to betray no emotional tone at all. It is as though it is a set piece—as, indeed, the
sceptical criterion problem is—that he throws in just to be complete. And Arnauld does not comment on it, he immediately rushes
on to consider Descartes's claim that we are aware of all that is in
our mind, something that interests Arnauld much more than the
circle—something on which he has an opinion as he seems not to
have about the circle.

Similarly, Mersenne merely states the problem of the circle in a
brief paragraph and goes on without comment. And Gassendi goes
so far as to chastize Descartes for bringing up the demon, a device
he does not need. Gassendi even remarks that when faced with
geometrical proofs "the mind may very well tell the evil demon to
go hang himself".[4]

So Arnauld and Mersenne seem to set up the criterion problem
merely as stock form, and Gassendi says that the demon—and thus
the circle—should be ignored. But the circle is clearly stated.
Descartes more or less ignores the circle in his replies. He tells
Arnauld that the problem is one of remembering the argument for
God's existence. He tells Mersenne that it is merely a matter of
getting the order of reasoning right. And to Arnauld and Gassendi
he says it is merely a matter of perceiving that God exists and is not
a deceiver, and he claims that the problem of memory can be
avoided by direct perception.

Descartes, then, pays only slight and inadequate attention to the
raising of the criterion-circle-deceiving-demon problem raised by
Mersenne, Arnauld, and Gassendi. Just as their presentation seems
to be pro forma, Descartes barely makes any reply.

Only with the seventh set of objections by Father Pierre Bourdin
does Descartes become annoyed and impatient. Bourdin's exposition is sarcastic and dramatic. Unlike Mersenne and Arnauld, he
does not pass over the depth and strength of demonic doubt in a
brief formal argument, and unlike Gassendi he shows that the
demon can be taken seriously, and how catastrophic it would be if
God were a deceiver.

And now Descartes does get annoyed and impatient. But where
Bourdin uses sarcasm to present a serious possibility of demonic

---

[4] Pierre Gassendi, "Fifth Set of Objections" in *The Philosophical Writings of
Descartes*, vol. 2, translated by John Cottingham, Robert Stoothoff, and Dugald
Murdoch, Cambridge: Cambridge University Press, 1984, p. 227; "Objections
Quintae", in *Oeuvres de Descartes*, p. 327.

deception, Descartes treats the demon as a joke, suggesting that perhaps the demon has interfered with Bourdin's thought processes.[5] And as Descartes earlier reduced the issue to one of memory, here he tries to reduce it to one of simple errors, such as in counting, and he says of sceptics that their problem is that they "have never, *qua* sceptics, perceived anything clearly",[6] so it is not surprising that they don't know anything. And, again, instead of meeting Bourdin's dramatic exposition of demonic possibilities, Descartes parodies them scornfully as though *Bourdin* had originated them, as though they were *Bourdin's* invention rather than Descartes' own imaginations. This demon talk, Descartes concludes, is "childish and silly".[7]

What are we to make of this contrast between on the one hand the perfunctory presentation of the circle argument by Mersenne and Arnauld, and Descartes' virtual non reply to them, and on the other hand Bourdin's dramatic presentation and Descartes' scornful rejection of it? I suppose the answer is found in Gassendi's assertion that we can tell the demon to go hang. This—despite Mersenne and Gassendi being priests—probably is the agreed upon secular attitude to the possibility of demonic possession, and Bourdin represents the more traditional Catholic view described by Scarre that demonic possession is a real possibility and is in fact manifested in the form of witchery in their own day.

What Mersenne, Arnauld, Gassendi, and Descartes—all accomplished logicians—seem to have done is to agree about the logical possibility of demonic deception, and then to agree further that there is no practical possibility of demonic possession, so it is not to be taken seriously and can be set aside as metaphysical and hyperbolical, childish and silly.

All of this is in the context of belief in a benevolent God who is not a deceiver. Of course Malebranche said God could and does deceive us for our own good, but this benign deception also sets aside the serious sceptical doubt Bourdin dramatized. So if we want to give an interpretation of Descartes's philosophy in historical context with attention paid to the author's intentions, it would seem to be—as some interpreters of Descartes imply—*unfair* to follow out the logical implications of the deceiving demon hypothesis in giving an interpretation of Descartes' philosophy.

---

[5] René Descartes, "Seventh Set of Replies" in *The Philosophical Writings of Descartes*, vol. 2, p. 320; "Objections Septimae, Notae", in *Oeuvres de Descartes*, vol. 7, p. 475.
[6] Ibid., p. 321, 477.
[7] Ibid., p. 371, 544.

So far so good concerning what Descartes meant to say and what some of his important contemporaries took him to say. But this cannot be the end of interpretation. The fact is that there are several serious flaws in the anti-demon cohorts' reasoning. One is Descartes' own admission that God can do anything including make false what we take to be true. God can make contradictions true. So we have to accept the view that Descartes' voluntaristic non-deceiving God could deceive us.

But more than that, the reasoning that leads Descartes and his cohorts to conclude that the belief in the existence of demons is childish and silly is the same reasoning that leads to the conclusion that belief in the existence of God is childish and silly. As Hume and Immanuel Kant point out, none of the arguments for the existence of God hold. Descartes may have believed that he perceived the existence of a non-deceiving God, but he was simply deceived. He perceived the existence of a concept and his own psychological conviction, but nothing more.

And finally, in sheer secular terms, the sceptical criterion circle problem cannot be ignored. It can be dismissed on the ground that we have to start somewhere, but logically it still holds. So in terms of the logical school of interpretation, one might say that Descartes *assumes* a ground for his philosophy expressed in terms of a non-deceiving God, but that it is wrong of him and wrong of the biographical school to say that the logical problem of the ground or criterion is metaphysical and hyperbolical in the sense that it can be either dismissed or ignored as not applying to the philosophy based on the assumed ground.

Descartes, then, on the logical school interpretation becomes a mitigated sceptic, which is not surprising given his intent to be a modern scientist. And, as I remark above, if one reads only his scientific writings, one finds no claims to certainty that would be disturbed by the postulation of a deceiving demon. We do make mistakes in our trust of authority, mistakes in reasoning and memory, and mistakes in describing the natural world. But as scientists, we just keep on trying, and we do improve as the advancement of science shows. The biographical evidence that Descartes would be or was happy with this degree of certainty is distributed throughout his scientific works. But none of this means that the deceiving demon hypothesis is not a serious problem for Descartes's metaphysics, whatever Descartes and some of his important contemporaries say about it. In fact, I am suggesting that Descartes' interest in metaphysics itself is not very serious, and that when he dismisses the demon hypothesis, he is thinking more of science, as his reply to Bourdin shows, than of metaphysics, and that his own characterization of God is compatible with the *metaphysical*—as he himself says—possibility of global deception.

III

Now I want to ask just what is the relation between metaphysical and logical doubt? The linkage of "metaphysical" with "hyperbolical" suggests that Descartes wants to link the metaphysical with the extreme, and commentators have taken this to mean that taking this extreme seriously is unreasonable. But while the extreme may be improbable, it is not unreasonable. The point of the sceptical argument simply is that the extreme is still possible, and that when the stakes are very high—the stakes here being the question of God's existence and nature—the extreme *must* be taken into consideration. Again, it is just the extreme possibility that is at issue. And so while it is hyperbolical and thus improbable, and while it would be silly to conduct one's practical life as though such hyperbolical possibilities might be true, when considering such matters, say, as salvation, the hyperbolical is of real concern.

Concerning the hyperbolical, Pascal understands better than Descartes what is at issue. In the infinite immensity of the universe, anything could be the case, and we insignificant thinking reeds are surely not facing the reality of that possibility if we think that we can ignore the fact that we do not know very much, if anything, about the nature of God. And so the characterization of the deceiving demon hypothesis as hyperbolical and improbable separates it from the practical and commonplace in a way that shows us why it must be considered, not in a way that supports its being ignored.

So we are left with the metaphysical. I think that by specifying the deception hypothesis as metaphysical, Descartes may very well mean to denigrate this demonic possibility by associating it with the scholastic doctrine of occult forces and powers. Certainly the demon would have to act on our perceptual and intellectual faculties in ways that cannot be accounted for in terms of mechanical causation, which is the only form of causation allowed in Descartes' natural world. In effect, global deception or even occasional deception would be a miracle.

Of course God created the universe, and God can do anything. Descartes did have a doctrine of continual creation, and Malebranche's later occasionalism involves God in every human action. But for both Descartes and Malebranche, the universe God provides us is one in which lawful mechanical interaction is or appears to be uniform and invariable. There are no discernable outside forces or powers, not even God himself, interfering with natural mechanical causation.

A deceiving demon, then, would have to interfere with and override the laws of nature established by God, and while it is easy enough to imagine how this might be done—the demon could, for example, stimulate our sense organs in ways to make us think we are flying through the air and experiencing the revels of a witch's sabbat, when in fact we are home asleep in bed—but when one considers that these impulses on the sense organs must come from somewhere, and that they would have impacts and reactions in the local physical environment that would cause changes other than in our perceptual experiences, demonic power is seen to be diametrically opposed to and destructive of mechanical science. Indeed, demonic power is unintelligible in the context of natural philosophy. Thus, the notion of demonic power just makes no sense to Descartes, who surely lumps demonic power with the scholastic forces and powers it is a major purpose of his philosophy to deny. The deceiving demon hypothesis is thus "metaphysical" in the perjorative sense of being meaningless in a way that would warm the hearts even of twentieth century logical positivists.

As I remark above, however, such an interpretation (and I take it to be a line laid out by Scarre, although he might not wish to follow it as far as I have) of what Descartes had in mind by saying that the deceiving demon hypothesis is "metaphysical" provides also an argument, probably the major argument since Descartes' time, for concluding also that the notion of God is meaningless, or at least—and here I return to a view of Descartes supportable by concrete rather than speculative evidence—the view that concern about God is not of *practical* significance in the ordinary affairs of men. The notion of God, like that of the demon, is then metaphysical, hyperbolical, childish, and silly.

Descartes demonstrably had a limited tolerance for metaphysical speculation, whether about the metaphysical forces and powers he eliminates from his philosophy and science, or for theological discourses on God. His own tentative forays into theology got him into trouble because his notion of how to explain transubstantiation is to turn it into a problem of mechanical physics. There is nothing at all metaphysical in Descartes' two explanations of how transubstantiation takes place *except* the miracle of God's rearranging the particles of Christ's flesh and blood so that they cause us to perceive bread and wine. And note that here we have God—a deceiving God?—doing precisely just the sort of thing a demon would have to do to deceive us. Descartes does not dwell upon God's ability to make these alterations—changing the arrangement of the particles itself becomes the miracle in Descartes' exposition—because it goes without question that God has the power. But no one was satisfied with Descartes' explanations of transubstantiation. And Descartes himself probably did not take transubstantiation very seriously. Descartes seems not to have been really interested in metaphysics because it leads either to an erroneous physical science of occult forces and powers, or because it is beyond investigation by practical and scientific methods.

Thus I am convinced that Descartes surely did think the hypothesis of the deceiving demon is absurd and should be ignored. He did not believe in its practical possibility for a moment, probably because he equates the demonic power that would be required for deception with the scholastic occult forces and powers that he rejects as meaningless.

But this does not mean that he did not recognize that on the level of metaphysics where questions of God's existence and nature are considered, the possibility of God's deceiving us is real even if hyperbolical. Thus, I reject both Gueroult's view that Descartes thought God's being a deceiver is a logical contradiction, and Gouhier's view that the demon hypothesis is redundant because it merely sums up ordinary reasons for doubt. God, after all, can make contradictions real or true, and the demon hypothesis is equivalent to the God hypothesis.

My main conclusion here is that by using Descartes's arguments for rejecting scholastic forces and powers to explain Descartes's rejection of witchcraft and demonic possession, we can explain why Descartes believes that saying that the deceiving hypothesis is hyperbolical and metaphysical is reason enough for ignoring it.

But in opposition to Descartes' claim that we can ignore the demon hypothesis, I argue that a logical line of interpretation shows (and explains) how and why the demon hypothesis has been so potent in the history of Modern Philosophy. This is because the reasons for rejecting the demon turn out to be the same ones for rejecting God.

Now does this make Descartes a sceptic and an atheist? Of course not. The biographical evidence strongly supports the view that Descartes opposed scepticism and believed in God. But if we stop at that point in our interpretations—if in our interpretations of

Descartes we refuse to follow the logical implications of Descartes' philosophy because he denies them—we are not, I submit, doing the history of philosophy adequately.

Father Bourdin may have been a dogmatic ass, and he certainly raised Descartes' blood pressure, but his sly playing upon the demonic theme is crucial to a thorough understanding of Descartes' metaphysics. To ignore the bearing of the criterion-circle-deceiving-demon hypothesis on Descartes' philosophy would be childish and silly.

EZEQUIEL DE OLASO

HOBBES: RELIGION AND IDEOLOGY NOTES ON THE POLITICAL UTILIZATION OF RELIGION*

The importance of Hellenistic scepticism in the growth of modern thought is today widely acknowledged and generally accepted in the domain of theoretical philosophy[1] although little is known about its influence in practical philosophy.[2] I will refer to the political utilization of religion in Hobbes's *Leviathan*, but before doing so, I would like to make some observations about previous examples of this topic in ancient scepticism and the movement of the *libertins érudits* (henceforward simply "libertines", although on account of the frugality and insipidness of their lives, I could have called them simply "erudites"). No full study has appeared yet about the influence of the libertines on Hobbes, in spite of the fact that he was acquainted with some of them, and was even their friend.[3] The topic of the origin of religion will allow us to suggest some of the connections between Hobbes and the libertines, and also to examine those that could exist between Hobbes and ancient scepticism.

---

* I am most grateful to Richard H. Popkin, Sarah Hutton, Chris Laursen, Olivier Bloch and Manfred Walther for their comments on earlier versions of this paper. It is a pleasure to acknowledge the kindness and hospitality of Constance Blackwell and Arjo Vanderjagt.

[1] R.H. Popkin, *The History of Scepticism from Erasmus to Spinoza*, Berkeley: University of California Press, 1979 (First edition: Assen: Van Gorcum, 1960). C.B. Schmitt, *Cicero Scepticus. A Study of the Influence of the* Academica *in the Renaissance*. The Hague: Nijhoff, 1972. I have reviewed both in *Noûs* 18 (1984), 135–144, and *International Studies in Philosophy* 7 (1975), 57–68, respectively. Both books have been the main sources of the new conception of modern scepticism.

[2] Cf. R.H. Popkin, "Cudworth", forthcoming. Leaving aside matters of influence cf. J. Annas, "Doing without objective values: ancient and modern strategies" in *The Norms of Nature*, eds. M. Schofield, G. Striker, Cambridge: Cambridge University Press, 1986; and "Scepticism, old and new", forthcoming.

[3] Popkin has called my attention to recent studies by R. Tuck, especially to "Grotius, Carneades and Hobbes", *Grotiana* 4 (1983), 43–62; and to "Optics and sceptics: the philosophical foundations of Hobbes' "political thought" in *Conscience and Casuistry in Early Modern Europe*, ed. E. Leites, Cambridge: Cambridge University Press, 1988.

I am conscious of the fact that the topic of the political utilization of religion has some historical precedents which I shall to brush aside, although some of them (Sophists and Epicureans could be good examples) are relevant for the study of the problem in Hobbes's work. I will only mention here some that are specifically relevant to our subject. Thucydides, whom Hobbes studied and translated, comes to mind immediately. Also Machiavelli, not only on account of his conception of religion as a "salutary terror" and a political instrument, but especially because of his remarkable denunciation of the strategy employed by the Roman Church to keep the Italian people divided (*Discorsi*, I, 11–16 and II, 2). And, of course, Francis Bacon, whose mention is unavoidable in many aspects, both general and particular. About the relations between Bacon and scepticism and his possible influence on Hobbes, I shall have something to say later on.

I

Let us examine some important aspects of the libertines' practical philosophy, especially those regarding the origin of religion. The libertines hold that religion is an instrument of control, an artifice created in order to obtain political obedience. A symbol—not the only one—of this conception is the anonymous and clandestine work *Les trois imposteurs*.[4] According to it, the founders of the three great religions, Moses, Jesus, and Mohammed, are impostors who invented their divine missions for the sake of reaching and maintaining political power. The libertine also denies the existence of universal values and traces ethical norms and religious practices back to historical and human origins. He embraces a kind of naturalism that rejects miracles and the divine source of religions. Laws are for him the result of a struggle in which the strongest impose their interests. As a consequence of all this, an Epicureanism is developed that seeks for pleasure inside worldly limits. This attitude is usually described through the identification of its various philosophical components: Renaissance naturalism (of Aristotelian origin), Epicurean morals and certain "sceptical" traits.[5]

In *De la Sagesse*, Charron advises his readers to do what had begun to be common practice: to obey the laws and follow the ways

---

[4] Cf. in this volume Silvia Berti, "Scepticism and the *Traité des trois imposteurs*", 216–229.

[5] T. Gregory, *Etica e religione nella critica libertina*, Naples: Guida Editori, 1986.

established in the country in which each lives, not because they are just, but because they are the laws and ways of that country. It may have been this philosophical blessing of a preexistent social conduct that guaranteed the success of Charron's work. As a result, behaviour is understood to have an external, constrained and political side, and an interior one, free and ethical.

II

Let us now consider the ambiguities of scepticism, which have caused the approximation, and even identification, of the sceptic and libertine theses.

The opinions of the sceptics on the origin of the idea of gods or God are to be found in the third book of the *Outlines of Pyrrhonism* and in the first *Against the Physicists* (which is the ninth *Against the Professors*). I shall refer solely to this last text. Sextus puts it forward as an investigation, which he divides in two parts: in the first he investigates the preconception we have of gods, while in the second part the investigation is about the existence of gods. I have some ideas concerning the meaning of the sceptic *zetesis*, but this is not the moment to discuss them.[6] I shall only say that, in order to begin a *zetesis*, Sextus first tries to determine what the problem "is about". This initial knowledge, guide of the investigation, was called *prolepsis* by Epicurus (we translate it as "preconception"), and *ennoia* by the Stoics (we use "conception" for this term). Sextus employs these expressions in an interchangeable way.

So Sextus begins by examining what the preconceptions are concerning the manner in which men acquire the notion of God. The first two opinions he mentions are very close to the libertines' genealogy of religion. According to one of them, those who first governed men and considered what was more advantageous for life, as they were very intelligent, invented the fiction about gods and the belief in the fabulous tales about Hades. Here Sextus offers us a version of the state of nature: "For, since life in old times was brutish and disorderly (for, as Orpheus says, 'There was a time when ev'ry man liv'd by devouring his fellow/Cannibal-wise, and the stronger man did feast on the weaker'), purposing to check the wrongdoers they laid down laws, in the first place, for the punishing of such as were manifestly doing wrong, and after this they also invented gods as watchers of all the sinful and righteous

---

[6] E. de Olaso, "Zetesis", *Manuscrito* (Campinas, Brazil) 11:2 (1988), 7– 32.

acts of men, so that none should dare to do wrong even in secret, believing that the gods'—and here Sextus joins a verse of Hesiod and one of Homer—"'Cloaked in garments of mist all over the earth go roaming,/Watching the violent doings of men and their lawful behaviour'" (*M* ix.14–16; cf. also 54).

According to the opinion of Euhemerus the Atheist—from whose name the word "Euhemerism" was coined in order to designate collectively any doctrine about the political utilization of religion—those who governed men desired to obtain for themselves more admiration and veneration. So they invented a supra-human and divine authority and the people considered them gods (*M* ix.17; cf. also 51).

This claim can be found literally in Sextus, in many libertines, and also quite directly in chapter 12 of the *Leviathan*. But one must be careful here because Sextus mentions these explanations *to reject them*. Basically, he considers that those who charge rulers with having instilled the belief in gods into their subjects are not attacking the problem at all. The real problem consists in finding out how the leaders themselves reached a preconception of gods, since no tradition about gods existed before them (*M* ix.30–31). Here we are at the crucial point in Sextus's argument. Sextus didn't denied the political use of religion but only the assumption that politicians were the forgers of religion's concept. One could maintain that the rulers invented this concept and then transferred it to the different tribes, a fact that would explain the diversity of preconceptions about gods. But Sextus, although he could have replied to this on the basis of considering the formation of preconceptions, selects an extraordinarily dangerous answer. He adduces that there is only one common preconception (*koine prolepsis*) of gods, according to which a god is a blessed being, eternal, perfect in its happiness and incapable of doing wrong, and he believes it is irrational (*alogos*) to think men coincided in this preconception by mere chance; it seems more reasonable to him to maintain they have reached this idea in a natural way (*M* ix.33).[7]

---

[7] The only modern philosopher who follows this line of thought is Ralph Cudworth. Cudworth quotes Sextus's view of *prolepsis* about God and attacks the idea of God as a mere fictitious thing. He argues that it is inconceivable that everyone, except a few atheists agree "in one and the same arbitrarious figment", *The True Intellectual System*, 692–93 (quoted by Popkin, see note 2 above). Closer to Sextus's text, he asks how politicians should "universally jump in one and the same fictitious and arbitrarious idea". Finally he maintains that if there were no God it is not "conceivable" that the idea of God would have been formed by any one. The concept of "triangular square" is not conceivable as such although both

Sextus also criticizes the interpretation according to which the preconception of gods stems from the magnification of dream-images, like those of giants. Against Democritus and Epicurus, who shared this interpretation, he thinks that men do not reverence any gigantic beings as gods, and that their gods possess properties as specific as the ones mentioned before (*M* ix.42–44).

One is here tempted to conclude that Sextus opposes those who attribute a conventional origin to the preconception of gods, that this preconception is for him natural and, being natural and common, it must also be true. But a little later in this same treatise, Sextus states that men have a common conception (*koine ennoia*) of myths (*M* ix.66ff.). He does not argue for this opinion or reject it. But in other writings Sextus clearly pronounces himself against myths, because they contain contradictory elements. This amounts to saying that there is a common conception of myths, but they are just the same false. So the fact that a conception is common is not a criterion for the truth, but only for the naturalness of that conception.[8]

Let us consider this problem more closely. If a conception or preconception is common—there is no relevant difference here between the two terms—, then it has been acquired in a natural way. But there are conceptions acquired in a natural way that contain inconsistencies, i.e. they contradict other conceptions acquired in a natural way. But if a conception is common, it seems fair to assume that it cannot contradict another conception because, quite simply, there is no other conception to contradict. I have merely stated the problem; its elucidation is not easy at all. I shall content myself with saying that it is a testimony of the complex, sometimes incoherent character of these ideas in ancient scepticism, and with suggesting that from here stem ambiguities in modern times.

Things are simplified a lot by the profession of the sceptic most frequently cited. Sextus accepts the existence of God "in accordance with the custom of our fathers (*patria ethe*) and the laws (*nomoi*)" and does everything that contributes to his adoration and veneration (*M* ix.49; cf. *Ph* iii.2), but as regards the philosophical questions about gods, he does not commit himself hastily.

"triangle" and "square" are conceivable. Cudworth fully acknowledges Sextus as his best source of arguments on this matter, see 692–97 (also quoted by Popkin).

[8] I have suggested the case to be so in the modes of Aenesidemus, during a meeting with Popkin and Schmitt in February 1984 at the Warburg Institute. For Aenesidemus' opinions about myths cf. *PH* iii.147, 150, 154, 157, 159, 161–62.

So Sextus proposes no interpretation about the origin of the idea of God. He does not reject Euhemerism or the thesis about the magnification of oneiric giants. But then, if the only things retained from Sextus are that the sceptic accepts the customs and laws of his country and makes no consideration about their justice, and to this is added the fact that Sextus is the doxographer of the Euhemerist theses and the theories about the magnification of dreams (opinions which tend to be attributed to him, and from which he is not able to extricate himself), there are no serious obstacles left against assimilating the sceptics' position with that of the libertines.

III

Let us now concentrate our attention upon Euhemerism as a kind of "ideological thinking". In ideology we usually distinguish two aspects, the epistemic and the sociological. Ideological thinking is deceptive, but its deception has the function of concealing the interests of a social group. The ideological proposal appears to be acceptable on account of a prestigious intellectual covering that captures adherents, but what is really being enforced is an interest which it would be inconvenient to reveal, an interest not of the intellectual, but of the emotional kind, the passion for domination and power. It is then a deceptive cognitive proposal which is both prestigious and persuasive and allows a social group to attain power.

Although Euhemerism does not really fulfill these requirements of ideological thinking, it anticipates them. The passion for power does not correspond clearly to a social group, but to a founding hero (behind whom, however, it is not difficult to discern the interests he represents). The suasive element does not pretend to be intellectual, but magical-religious. Men are not told that they are going to know more, nor are they taught the truth; their ignorance and fears are exploited in order to create preconceptions and prejudices, and thus to exact more obedience in exchange for security. Or death.

Consider the case of Bacon for a moment. He is the first to point out that man is a captive of his lack of method, because he tries to investigate nature on the basis of rational preconceptions. Investigation, preconceptions: does not this remind us of our observations about the sceptics' *zetesis*? Bacon has some thing very similar to this in mind. He thinks that we start with preconceptions that are strong enough to determine our acceptance of them. These preconceptions are not useful even when employed by a genius, because "radical mistakes" cannot be destroyed (*Novum Organon*, §§26–32). If men only had these preconceptions Bacon considers that he himself would be a follower of the school of the academic scepticism, i.e. a follower of the doctrine of *akatalepsia*, one of those who affirm that nothing can be known (§§37 and 126). But he thinks there is a way of freeing ourselves from, or at least weakening the effects of, these powerful prejudices that hold us captive. Here Bacon begins to employ a word we are all familiar with: "idols" (§38). Preconceptions, idols, superstitions, prejudices, begin to be synonymous. Is it too rash to say that Hobbes learnt the lesson from Bacon and tried to describe the mechanism of concept- and prejudice-formation with greater precision?

IV

Let us examine the account of the political utilization of religion that figures in the *Leviathan*. In order to do so, I shall introduce, in a moderate way, a recent conceptualization, the so-called "ideological discourse", which, although foreign to Hobbes (and obviously to Bacon), will equip us for a better understanding of the phenomenon described and analyzed by Hobbes.[9]

Hobbes offers us an analysis which is both concrete and illuminating of the way in which an ecclesiastical power operates politically through the utilization of prestigious intellectual instruments. The libertines made the politician the actor and religious magic his instrument of persuasion. In Hobbes's analysis, delusion is forged by the priests who are high up in the ecclesiastical hierarchy, while their instrument is scholastic philosophy, some kind of philosophical magic.

Hobbes compares this ideological discourse with the true doctrine which he describes in the first chapters of the *Leviathan*. His starting-point is the sensation caused by a body we usually call object. This object acts in different ways on our sensory organs and causes diverse mental representations (appearances, images, fantasies),

---

[9] If one avoids anachronism, it is a methodology which I consider fruitful and, as such, I encourage its use in my research group on modern philosophy in Buenos Aires. After a first version of this paper was published, D.R. Kelley employed the concept of ideology for exploring some features of the French Reformation. Cf. *The Beginning of Ideology. Consciousness and Society in the French Reformation*, Cambridge: Cambridge University Press, 1983. The ancestor of my contribution to the present volume is "Hobbes y la formación del análisis del discurso ideológico", *Revista Latinoamericana de Filosofía* 6:1 (1980), 3–16.

which are only various movements in its matter. The perceived
object is one thing, and its appearance quite a different one. Only
sensation is the original fantasy of representation (chap. 2). Imagination is a "decaying sense". As time goes by, it decays more and
more; when this decadent sensation ages and passes away it is
called memory; abundant memory is experience. In chapter 12 of
the *Leviathan* Hobbes explains the mechanism of delusion.

The imaginations of those who sleep are called dreams. The
difficulty in telling the difference between dreams and sensations
was the origin of pagan religion; man creates the idea of spirits; in
the second place, as he ignores how natural and immediate causes
operate, he attributes their effects to invisible causes; thirdly, he
believes that these invisible causes are the natural and immediate
causes; fourthly, as he ignores which is the real cause, he has to
make observations and try to remember what it was that in previous times preceded the same effect, but he cannot realize that
there is a connection between cause and effect; finally, on the basis
of the same past things he expects the good or bad issue of others
which have no relation with the causes; hence spring devotion, rites
and accepting chance occurrences as a prediction.

In this spontaneous mechanism "consistheth the natural seed of
religion" and it has been exploited by the rulers of the Gentile.
Hobbes borrows from the libertines the doctrine according to
which "the religion of the Gentiles was a part of their policy", but
he makes a difference between it and true religion, established
through revelation. God has dictated religious and civil laws, "and
thereby in the kingdom of God, the policy and civil laws are part of
religion" (chap. 12). This strongly suggests that the political use of
religion in no way exhausts the meaning of religion. However the
remnant seems to be unimportant.

According to the English Protestant tradition, "there is on earth
no such universal church" (i.e. Catholic), but the church is identical with the civil and political community (chap. 39). There is then
an antagonism between the Catholic church and its supreme authority, the Pope, who has great power because he in fact acts as
arbiter in the conflicts between rulers and their subjects, as a sort of
Supreme Court of Justice. But then, if the Pope aspires to some
form of supremacy in the controversies concerning human actions,
he teaches men to disobey the civil monarch.

England rejected the debased and ignorant clergy that caused
the replacement of the Catholic religion. The political power of the
Pope was neutralized. However, in England there is no unconditional obedience to the sovereign.

Hobbes's analysis consists in pointing out the forms of prestigious discourse, which, false or senseless, are the instrument of the political interests of the bishop of Rome through certain institutions that are placed in England but are nevertheless subject to the Pope's influence. First, the universities (chap. 46): there, under a prestigious exterior of Metaphysics and speculative natural philosophy, senseless discourses are produced which give rise to endless controversy and finally sedition. Under the same cover, a moral and political philosophy is taught that, although not senseless, is subjectivistic and dissolvent.

Professors don't teach "philosophy but Aristotelity" (chap. 46). The principal terms used by the professors in their reasonings lack meaning (chap. 4) because they employ and register thoughts that the professors themselves never conceived; that is why they do not assign a constant meaning to their terms and that is why they deceive themselves (chap. 4). In Hobbes's times, the prestigious authors were Aristotle, Cicero, Suarez. Today we would think of Heidegger or Lacan. But, in any case, the prestige of the authors causes a blind admiration in the students. It is the pedants' kingdom. Among the senseless noises, Hobbes classifies neologisms and compound names. Such a misuse of words is "incident to none but those that converse in questions of matter incomprehensible, as the Schoolmen; or in questions of abstruse philosophy" (chap. 8). But without a thorough understanding of words "neither error nor nonsense can (. . .) be detected" (chap. 11).

I insist upon the self-deceiving traits of these ideologist professors.[10] If the professors do not conspire consciously, if they think, believe and teach meaningless things, then, since they are not lying they must be alienated. This indeed is Hobbes's explanation. Here is the text that follows a mention of the title of a disputation by Suárez: "When men write whole volumes of such stuff, are they not mad, or intend to make others so? (. . .) this kind of absurdity may rightly be numbered amongst the many sorts of madness; and all the time that guided by clear thoughts of their worldly lot, they forbear disputing, or writing thus, are but lucid intervals" (chap. 8).

The other form of false prestigious discourse (but not senseless) is the one of scholastic practical philosophy. Hobbes considers it the most dangerous to the value he estimates the highest, that is,

---

[10] However at the end of his analysis Hobbes speaks of "a confederacy of deceivers" (chap. 44).

the security of men. And this is not so because the papists invent
clichés in order to transmit covertly what we would now call "ideological contents" (for example, the casual name "universal church"
conceals a determination to dominate the monarchs, while the
technical term "tyrannicide" serves to justify the murder of those
not addicted to the Roman church). There is an articulated theory
and a systematic justification of sedition: each individual is entitled
to judge, according to his conscience, if the laws are legitimate or
not. Furthermore, an individual behaves sinfully if he obeys the
state before determining in his conscience the legitimate character
of the mandate. Any individual acts in a legitimate way if he kills a
tyrant.[11]

Hobbes reconstructs the chain through which these ideas de-
scend into society from the universities and their graduates.

In the last chapter of the *Leviathan*, Hobbes asks himself *cui bono?*
That is, who benefits by this doctrine of a universal church which is
superior to any terrestrial government, and for which the universities spread the venom of incessant sedition through teaching a
fantastic but "useful" philosophy.

Since the Catholic church taught that none other than itself was
the kingdom of God on earth, the Pope obtained the wordly benefit
of being the universal monarch of the whole of Christianity. England has been liberated from his power—although similar claims
are made by the Presbyterians, who maintain that they inhabit
God's kingdom. The Catholic church aspires to obtain power over
people, a power which is infallible in its public exercise, that is,
incontestable. The bishops, who derive their authority from the
Pope, can use it to inspire civil war against any state which refuses
to be governed according to their opinions and interests. The
instruments of domination are those of pagan demonology, exor-
cisms and aristotelian philosophy. The "frivolous distinctions, barbarous terms, and obscure language of the schoolmen, taught in the
universities, which have been all erected and regulated by the
Pope's authority, serve them to keep this errors from being detected, and to make men mistake the *ignis fatuus* of vain philosophy
for the light of the Gospel".

---

[11] A. Matheron is reluctant to examine this subject "car le detail en est un peu
comique", cf. "Politique et religion chez Hobbes et Spinoza" in *Anthropologie et
politique au XVIII siècle*, Paris: Vrin, 1986, p. 134. Certainly it is full of funny
features but (why "but"?) it reveals a new kind of philosophical analysis.

V

It is not rash to affirm that Hobbes's picture of alienated professors in an unreal world anticipates the setting that tempted Napoleon to use the term "idéologues" (in a pejorative sense) for the first time. Napoleon's contempt plays upon the two meanings of "idea" we have examined in this essay: idea as preconception, idea as prejudice. In spite of Hobbes's eloquence and insight, however, he has never been recognized as one of the first to contemplate the analysis of ideological discourse. I shall try to suggest why this happened.

Curiously enough, we find that Hobbes was widely read by those who practiced the analysis of ideological discourse in the eighteenth and beginning of the nineteenth century. We know that D'Holbach idolizes him and that in 1772 he translated the first part of the *Elements of Law*. This version includes the first thirteen paragraphs of Book I, which had circulated in manuscript since 1640 and were printed in 1650 under the title *Human Nature*. We also know that Destutt de Tracy, in 1814, added to his *Elements d'Idéologie* a translation of the first section of *De Corpore*.[12]

These data make our enigma seem larger. Why is it that Hobbes's constructive philosophy penetrated so deeply in France, while his denunciation of the kingdom of darkness, one of the most powerful constitutive elements of the enlightened mentality, found so small an answer?

Hobbes is the Patron Saint of Enlightenment on account of his mechanistic and antimetaphysical philosophy (also because of his social and political philosophy, the only one that Cassirer takes into account when documenting the sources of Enlightenment).[13] Concerning his denunciation of the kingdom of darkness I guess that Auguste Comte was the first to point out that "the more important critical ideas which an erroneous tradition attributes to French eighteenth-century philosophy, have Hobbes as their principal source".[14]

I believe that the greatest difficulty for the acceptance in France of Hobbes's denunciation of the ideological manoeuvres of the universities can be explained on historical grounds. The English revolution of the sixteenth century, although it broke with the Pope definitively, did not forsake the idea of establishing a national

---

[12] P. Naville, *D'Holbach et la philosophie scientifique du XVIIIe. siècle*, Paris: Gallimard, 1967, p. 218.

[13] E. Cassirer, *La filosofía de la Ilustración*, México 1950.

[14] A. Comte, *Cours de philosophie positive*, 6 vols., Paris 1830–1842, vol. 5, p. 499.

religion. Hobbes favoured this project, insofar it concentrated civil
and ecclesiastical authority in the sovereign. The French mater-
ialists, however, extended his criticisms to every religion, and on
this point they followed Spinoza rather than Hobbes. They denounced the sacred alliance between church and throne in order to
liberate political power from religion. Hobbes's solution was no
model for the situation France was in, nor did it answer to their
convictions and hopes. Furthermore, the rôle of the Catholic
church was different in each kingdom: the Pope tried to strengthen
the French monarchy, but weaken and, if possible, bring down the
English king.

ALAN GABBEY

"A DISEASE INCURABLE": SCEPTICISM AND THE CAMBRIDGE PLATONISTS

Strictly speaking, of course, perfect scepticism commits one to perfect silence, or at least to the blank pages for which Sanchez commended Socrates. Since neither silence nor the blank page appealed to the Cambridge Platonists as a polemical stratagem, we suspect straightaway that for them scepticism—at least the fully-fledged variety—will have been at most a means to an end. In this they were not alone. Even the original sceptics hoped their critical quest would lead to "quietude [ἀταραξία] in respect of matters of opinion and moderate feeling in respect of things unavoidable . . . by means of a decision regarding the disparity of the objects of sense and of thought, and being unable to effect this, they suspended judgement; and they found that quietude, as if by chance, followed upon their suspense, even as a shadow follows its substance . . ."[1] Gianfrancesco Pico della Mirandola borrowed extensively from Sextus Empiricus and, as Charles Schmitt describes it, "his choices are therapeutic rather than theoretical. Aristotle had to go because he was the chief source of secular contagion among the faithful, and Sextus was the best medicine available. Pico regarded Christianity itself as immune to sceptical infection".[2] For Descartes scepticism was the demon to be exorcized on his epistemological journey to the *cogito* and to the divinely-guaranteed certitude of clear and distinct ideas. For Glanvill in his *Vanity of dogmatizing* of 1661 scepticism signalled intellectual freedom by exposing the immodesty of dogmatic positions on matters of natural philosophy, divinity and mathematics being immune to sceptical surgery, and by exposing the pretensions of the Schoolmen, whose divinity "hath mudded the fountain of certainty with notional and ethnick admixtions". "In philosophy I'm a Seeker", Glanvill

---

[1] *Outlines of Pyrrhonism*, 1.12. Sextus Empiricus, [*Works*], trans. R.G. Bury, 4 vols., The Loeb Classical Library, London and Cambridge, Mass.: Heinemann, Harvard U.P., 1967–71, vol. 1, 19–21.
[2] Brian P. Copenhaver and Charles B. Schmitt, *Renaissance Philosophy*, Oxford: Oxford University Press, 1992, p. 246.

confessed, "yet I cannot believe, that a Sceptick in philosophy must be one in divinity".[3] Ten years later, however, he seems to have changed his mind about the value of scepticism, to judge by his ΛΟΓΟΥ ΘΡΗΣΚΕΙΑ *or, A seasonable recommendation and defence of reason, in the affairs of religion; against infidelity, scepticism, and fanaticisms of all sorts* (London 1670).[4]

In his survey of scepticism in the *Dictionary of the History of Ideas*, Popkin divides the sceptics into three broad groups. First, the "avowed sceptics", such as Montaigne, Bayle, or Hume. Second, "those who utilize sceptical materials to reach new viewpoints", such as Descartes or Hegel. Third, "those who are skeptics with regard to certain kinds of knowledge", such as Spinoza or Kant.[5] This is a useful taxonomy, except that in assigning the Cambridge Platonists to group three, I am sensible of the attendant difficulties, especially the assumption that they can in fact be treated as a group, sharing the same philosophical and theological positions. At least none of them was an avowed sceptic in Popkin's sense, and none of them utilized scepticism as a methodological instrument. Indeed I am hesitant about placing them in group three, and would prefer to describe them as "admitting to a theoretical scepticism with regard to certain kinds of knowledge, but dismissive or contemptuous of any suggestion that such a scepticism be taken seriously in the practical affairs of the mind, and especially of the Christian soul in its quest for divine knowledge and understanding". Further work would be needed to test the accuracy of this description. In this paper I make a start by surveying attitudes and responses to scepticism in the writings of major figures in the Cambridge school: Whichcote, Smith, Culverwel, Cudworth, and More.

Sceptical positions, though duly rejected, are not accorded any extended critical treatment in the writings of Benjamin Whichcote (1609–83), Fellow of Emmanuel College. This seems to be in keeping with his unadorned belief in the quasi-divine nature of human reason: "To go against Reason, is to go against God: it is the self same thing, to do that which the reason of the case doth

---

[3] Joseph Glanvill, *The vanity of dogmatizing: the three "versions"*, critical introduction by Stephen Medcalf, Hove, Sussex: The Harvester Press, 1970, 166–167, 186.

[4] See further Louis I. Bredvold, *The intellectual milieu of John Dryden. Studies in some aspects of seventeenth-century thought*, Ann Arbor: University of Michigan Press, 1956, 89–92.

[5] Richard Popkin, "Skepticism in modern thought", in *Dictionary of the History of Ideas: studies of selected pivotal ideas*, editor-in-chief, Philip P. Wiener, 4 vols. + Index, New York: Scribner's, 1968–74, vol. 4, 240–251.

require; and that which God Himself doth appoint: Reason is the Divine Governor of Man's Life; it is the very Voice of God" (Aphorism 76).[6] In the sermon on Romans 1: 18,[7] which Patrides entitles "The use of reason in matters of religion", Whichcote denies that we can be capable of faith unless we know there is a God, and this is something we know through reason: "it is as natural and proper for mind and understanding to tend towards God, as for heavy things to tend towards their center: for God is the center of immortal souls." Furthermore, reason tells us that first principles are self-evident, and "must be seen in their own light, and are perceived by an inward power of nature. For, as we say, *out of nothing comes nothing*; so, grant nothing; and nothing can be proved. Wherefore it must be within the reach of reason, to find that there is a God . . ."[8] Summing up near the end of the sermon, Whichcote passes a *moral* censure on those who pretend "the doubtfulness and uncertainty of reason, from the several opinions of incompetent persons (which is the only defence and apology, for exorbitant living, such credulous persons have;) willing to believe what their lusts lead them to."[9]

John Smith (1618–52), Fellow of Queen's College, published little, but as he himself said, "they are not alwaies the best men that blot most paper".[10] There are very few references to scepticism in the *Select Discourses* (1660), precisely because Smith sidesteps the challenge of scepticism, at least in so far as it relates to divine knowledge, by speaking of a divine life, rather than a divine science, "it being something rather to be understood by a spiritual sensation, then by an verbal description, as all things of sense & life are best known by sentient and vital faculties". So this "true method of knowing . . . is not so much by notions as actions; as religion it self consists not so much in words as things . . . he that is most practical in divine things, hath the purest and sincerest knowledge

---

[6] *The Cambridge Platonists*, ed. C.A. Patrides, London: Edward Arnold, 1969, p. 327. Whichcote's *Moral and Religious Aphorisms* were published by John Jeffery in 1703 and in a revised edition by Samuel Salter in 1753.

[7] "For the wrath of God is revealed from Heaven against all ungodliness, and unrighteousness of men, who hold the truth in unrighteousness."

[8] *The Cambridge Platonists*, ed. Patrides, p. 47. Whichcote's *Select sermons* were first published in 1698 (London) by Anthony, Third Earl of Shaftesbury.

[9] Patrides, *Cambridge Platonists*, p. 60.

[10] John Smith, *Select Discourses treating 1. Of the true way or method of attaining to divine knowledge, 2. Of superstition, 3. Of atheism, 4. Of the immortality of the soul, 5. Of the existence and nature of God . . .*, London 1660; facsimile of 1st edition of 1660, New York and London: Garland Publishing, 1978, p. 12.

of them, and not he that is most dogmatical".[11] Accordingly, Smith did not expend much energy, at least in print, on the debate between dogmatism and scepticism. Knowledge of God is not the business of the notional faculty, so sceptical claims about its weaknesses were irrelevant for Smith's purposes.

In any case, there are innate ideas and truths, "radical principles of knowledge", as Smith called them, which "are so deeply sunk into the souls of men, as that the impression cannot easily be obliterated, though it may be much darkned".[12] Just as wickedness and sensual baseness have not succeeded in extirpating from all men's souls knowledge of the immortality of the soul, or of the existence of God, or the "common principles of vertue", so neither

> is the retentive power of truth so weak and loose in all scepticks, as it was in him, who being well scourg'd in the streets till the blood ran about him, question'd when he came home, whether he had been beaten or not . . . the common notions of God and vertue imprest upon the souls of men, are more clear and perspicuous then any else . . . if they have not more certainty, yet have they more evidence, and display themselves with less difficulty to our reflexive faculty then any geometrical demonstrations.[13]

Clearly Smith had little respect for the sceptics' position. In "A short discourse of atheism" he writes that "when contentious disputes, and frothy reasonings, and contemplations informed by fleshly affections, conversant onely about the out-side of nature, begin to rise up in mens soules; they may then be in some danger of depressing all those in-bred notions of a deity, and to reason themselves out of their own sense, as the old Scepticks did . . ."[14]

Though decidedly a Cambridge man, Nathaniel Culverwel (1618?–1651?), Fellow of Emmanuel College, was not a Platonist at all, but an Aristotelian. Still, I cannot bring myself to exclude him, since he spends more pages on the challenge of scepticism, while showing more contempt for it, than any of the Cambridge Platonists proper. And that might well be because he was an Aristotelian. His *Discourse of the light of nature* (1661, written about 1646) aimed to vindicate the use of reason in matters of religion. In Chapter 9 on "The light of reason", Culverwel seems to allude to Yehuda Halevi (c. 1075–1141) in the following striking passage:

---

[11] Smith, *Select Discourses*, p. 2.
[12] Smith, *Select Discourses*, p. 13.
[13] Smith, *Select Discourses*, 13–14.
[14] Smith, *Select Discourses*, p. 50.

the Jews will by no means yield, that there is light enough in the dictates of reason, to display common notions; for they look upon it, as a various, and unsatisfactory light mix'd with much shadow, and darkness, labouring with perpetual inconstancy, and uncertainty. What are first principles become so mutable, and treacherous? Are demonstrations such fortuitous, and contingent things? Had I met with this in a fluctuating Academick, in a rowling Sceptick, in a Sextus Empiricus, in some famous Professor of Doubts, I should then have look'd upon it, as a tolerable expression of their trembling, and shivering opinion. But how come I to finde it among those divers into the depths of knowledge, who grant certainty, and yet will not grant it to reason? I would they would tell us then, where we might hope to finde it. Surely not in an Oriental tradition, in a rabbinical dream, in a dusty manuscript, in a remnant of antiquity, in a bundle of testimonies; and yet this is all you are like to get of them . . .[15]

Virtually the whole of Culverwel's Chapter 14, "The light of reason is a certain light", is an attack on scepticism and its champions, "weak and perverse beings, not fit to be honoured with the name of men", who "slight all the workings, and motions of reason, upon this account, that they are rolling, and fluctuating, that they are treacherous, and unconstant. And they look upon logick . . . as an intellectual kinde of jugling, an artificial kinde of cheating, and cozening their understanding." It wouldn't be so bad if it were only "the rude lump of the multitude" that had sunk into this degeneracy, but Culverwel has come across a famous and ancient sect of philosophers "that delight in the name of Scepticks, who by a strange kinde of hypocrisie, and in an unusual way of affectation, pretend to more ignorance then they have, nay, then they are capable of. They quarrel with all arts, and sciences, and do as much as they can to annihilate all knowledge, and certainty; and profess nothing, but a philosophical kinde of neutrality, and lukewarmness".[16]

However, Culverwel does not condemn all sceptical thinking. He describes the differences between the Academic sceptics (whom he identifies as "one sort of Academicks") and the Pyrrhonists[17] (whom he calls simply "the Skepticks"), and notes that if the

---

[15] Nathaniel Culverwel, *An elegant and learned discourse of the light of nature: with several other treatises, viz. The schism, The act of oblivion, The child's return, The panting soul, Mount Ebal, The White stone, Spiritual opticks, The worth of souls* . . ., London 1661, p. 58.
[16] Culverwel, *Light of nature*, 115–116.
[17] Culverwel describes Pyrrho not as the *originator* but as "a principal amplifier, and maintainer" of the sect of Scepticks, its "great promoter, and propagatour" (*Light of nature*, p. 119).

ἀκαταληψία of certain members of the Academic School had
signified no more than

> that the whole intelligibility of any entity could not be exhausted by
> them, that they could not perfectly, and powerfully pierce into any
> object, as to discover all, that was knowable in it; their opinion then
> was not onely tolerable, but very commendable, and undeniable . . .
> But, if their minde was this (as 'tis generally thought to be) that there
> was nothing in Being so visible, as that their understanding could
> pierce it with certainty, and satisfaction; such an errour as this was
> very derogatory to the plenitude, and exuberancy of Beings, that
> streams out in a clear cognoscibility, and 'twas very injurious to their
> own rational capacities, which were not made so strait, and narrow-
> mouth'd, as not to receive those notions, that continually drop from
> Being: but they were contriv'd, and proportion'd for the well-coming,
> and entertaining of truths, that love to spin, and thread themselves
> into a fine continuity . . .[18]

But the Pyrrhonists will tell you not to believe a word of all this,
and will bid you suspend judgement. To help you they have ten
"bridles" on assent presented by "that grand Sceptick", Sextus
Empiricus, and their "most radical, and fundamental principle, if
they may be said to have any such, [was] that all propositions were
in æquilibrio; that there was nothing could incline the balance this
way, or that . . . that there was an exact equality of reason for the
affirmation, or negation of any proposition". The result was that in
morals, ethics, and laws, all was provisional, all was "hesitancy,
and stammering opinion".[19]

As for the sceptics' ἀπορία, this was "an intellectual kinde of
continence, and virginity, to keep their minde pure and untouch'd,
whenas other understandings were ravish'd, and deflower'd with
the violence of every wanton opinion". Because of the infinite
regress in the problem of the criterion, "demonstrations did not
move these men at all". Neither did they allow themselves to
become enchained by axioms or common notions, or any first
principles ("artificial pillars, which some faint, and tired understandings have set up for themselves to lean upon"), whose use
only involves begging the question. "If you tell them", complains
Culverwell "that these common notions shine with their native
light, with their own proper beams; all, that they return, will be
this, that perhaps *you* think so, but *they* do not."[20]

---

[18] Culverwel, *Light of nature*, 116–117.
[19] Culverwel, *Light of nature*, p. 118.
[20] Culverwel, *Light of nature*, 118–119.

It is worth noting that Culverwel's wide reading included Gianfrancesco Pico della Mirandola's *Examen vanitatis doctrinae gentium* (1520). He refers to Gianfrancesco's claim that many learned men of antiquity were "deeply engaged in this sect, and some others, that did very near border upon it."[21] There was Protagoras, who thought all opinions were true, though Sextus thought that claim a touch dogmatical. And there was Anaxagoras, who argued that snow was black.

Yet the aim of the Sceptics was ἀταραξία, "a freedom from jars, and discords; from heresie, and obstinacy; to have a minde unprejudic'd, unprepossess'd". Culverwel takes a very dim view of such a philosophical purpose coming from such a source:

> A fair mark indeed! but how a roving Sceptick should ever hit it, is not easily imaginable: for what philosophy more wavering, and voluble? was there ever a more reeling, and staggering company? was there ever a more tumbling, and tossing generation? What shall I say to these old Seekers, to this wanton, and lascivious sect, that will espouse themselves to no one opinion, that they may the more securely go a whoring after all? If they be resolv'd to deny all things, (as they can do it very easily, and have seemed to do it very compendiously) truly then they have took a very sure way to prevent all such arguments, as can be brought against them . . .[22]

Culverwel then proceeds to entangle the sceptics in contradictions of their own making. They seem to grant appearances, so if Pyrrho, who used to be a painter, paints a face, would he say the face and the picture are the same thing? Would he be able to paint a non-entity, and could he paint an appearance without any foundation in reality? Do all pictures represent the same face, or are some of them false? If the latter is the case, then Pyrrho's ἀδιαφορία (indifference) must vanish. If all pictures and appearances are true, then his ἀπορία must vanish. If a thirsty Pyrrho chooses to drink rather than not, then again, what becomes of his ἀδιαφορία? And "if he be sure, that he is athirst, and if he be sure, that he seems to be athirst; what then becomes of his ἀπορία? When the dog was ready to bite him, if he was indifferent, why did he run away? If it

---

[21] Gianfrancesco Pico della Mirandola, *Examen vanitatis doctrinae gentium, et veritatis Christianae disciplinae, distinctum in libros sex, quorum tres omnem philosophorum sectam universim, reliqui Aristoteleam et Artistoteleis armis particulatim impugnant, ubicunque autem Christiana et asseritur et celebratur disciplina*, Mirandola 1520, p. f.7 *verso*. See further Charles B. Schmitt, *Gian Francesco Pico della Mirandola (1469–1533) and his critique of Aristotle*, The Hague: Nijhoff, International Archives of the History of Ideas 23, 1967.

[22] Culverwel, *Light of nature*, p. 121.

were an appearance, why did he flee from a shadow?"[23] Again, what happens to Pyrrho's ἀδιαφορία when he tries to persuade others to become sceptics, and what becomes of his ἀπορία when he does not scruple to deny certainty?

But "to scatter those empty fancies" of Pyrrho and his sect, Culverwel reveals "the true original, and foundation, the right progress, and method of all certainty":

> Now God himself, that eternal, and immutable being, that fix'd, and unshaken entity . . . must needs be the fountain of certainy, as of all other perfections . . . An atheist must needs be a sceptick; for God himself is the onely immoveable verity, upon which the soul must fix, and anchour . . . Now, that the soul may have a satisfactory enjoy-ment of its God, and that it may be accurately made according to his image, God stamps, and prints as resemblances of his other perfec-tions, so this also of certainty upon it. How else should it know the minde of its God? How should it know to please him, to believe him, to obey him? With what confidence could it approach unto him; if it had onely weak, and wavering conjectures? Now God lets the soul have some certain acquaintance with other beings for his own sake, and in order to his own glory. Nor is it a small expression of his wisdom, and power, to lay the beginnings of man's certainty so low, even as low as sense . . . 'Tis true, there is a purer, and nobler certainty in such beings, as are above sense; as appears by the certainty of angelical knowledge, and the knowledge of God himself: yet so much certainty, as is requisite for such a rational nature, as man is, may well have its rising, and springings out of sense; though it have more refinings, and purifyings from the understanding . . . his knowledge, and the certainty of his knowledge (I speak of natural knowledge) first peeps out in sense, and shines more brightly in the understanding. The first dawnings of certainty are in the sense, the noon-day-glory of it is in the intellectuals . . .[24]

Culverwel cannot excuse Plato

> for too much scorning, and slighting these outward senses, when that he trusted too much inwardly to his own fancy . . . Plato was suf-ficiently dogmatical in all his assertions; though this indeed must be granted, that some of his principles strike at certainty, and much endanger it; for being too fantastical, and poetical in his philosophy, he plac'd all his security in some uncertain, airy, and imaginary castles of his own contriving, and building, and fortifying. His con-nate ideas I mean, which Aristotle could not at all confide in, but blowed them away presently: and, perceiving the proud emptiness, the swelling frothiness of such Platonical bubbles, he was fain to search for certainty somewhere else; and casting his eye upon the

---

[23] Culverwel, *Light of nature*, p. 121.
[24] Culverwel, *Light of nature*, 122–123.

ground, he spyed the bottom of it, lying in sense, and laid there by the
wise dispensation of God himself: from thence he look'd up to the
highest top, and apex, to the πτερύγιον, and pinnacle of certainty,
plac'd in the understanding . . .[25]

As for Descartes, his mistake was to place too much assurance in
the understanding alone,

> thinking, that he thinks; why not into thinking, that he sees? and why
> may he not be deceived in that, as in any other operations? And, if
> there be such a virtue in reflecting, and reduplicating of it; then there
> will be more certainty in a super-reflection, in thinking that he thinks
> that he thinks: and so if he run *in infinitum*, according to his conceit, he
> will still have more certainty; though in reality he will have none at
> all, but will be fain to stop, and stay in scepticism; so that these
> refuges of lyes being scatter'd, first principles, and common notions,
> with those demonstrations, that stream from them, they onely remain
> as the nerves of this assurance, as the souls of natural plerophory; and
> he, that will not cast anchor upon these, condemns himself to perpe-
> tual scepticism.[26]

The chapter closes with an ironic swipe at Robert Greville's (1608–
1643) claim that "absolute contradictions may meet together".[27]

We come to Ralph Cudworth (1617–88), Fellow of Emmanuel
College, then Master successively of Clare Hall and Christ's College, and author of the unfinished yet seemingly unending *The true
intellectual system* (1678). Note that although in the dedicatory letter
to Heneage Finch Cudworth thinks it improbable "that in an age of
so much debauchery, scepticism, and infidelity, an undertaking of
this kind, should be judged by you, useless or unseasonable",[28] his
catalogue of the varieties of atheism did not include *sceptical* denials
of the validity of proofs for God's existence. One explanation is that
for Cudworth (and More) it was mechanistic materialism that
posed the greatest threat to piety and religious belief. Another is
that one can be a Pyrrhonist on the question of explanations in
natural philosophy without doubting the existence of God or the
immortal soul. Or at least one could in the seventeenth century.
Only after Brucker or possibly Bayle, it seems, do we find the

---

[25] Culverwel, *Light of nature*, 123–124.

[26] Culverwel, *Light of nature*, p. 124.

[27] Robert Greville (Second Lord Brooke), *The nature of truth, its union and unity
with the soule, which is one in its essence, faculties, acts; one with truth*, London 1641
(revision of 1640 ed.), p. 100.

[28] Ralph Cudworth, *The true intellectual system of the universe: the first part; wherein,
all the reason and philosophy of atheism is confuted; and its impossibility demonstrated*
London 1678, A2 *verso*.

widespread assumption that "scepticism" includes as a matter of
course scepticism with respect to the fundamental claims of
religion.[29]

In the appendix to chapter 4 of *The true intellectual system*, "wherein is contained a compendious confutation of all the atheistick
grounds", Cudworth argues that because God is incomprehensible
to our finite understandings, it does not follow that He is utterly
inconceivable to us, which would have the effect of making God a
non-entity, because we would then be unable to have any idea of
Him.

> For it is certain . . . that we have not such an adequate and compre-
> hensive knowledge of the essence of any substantial thing, as that we
> can perfectly master and conquer it. It was a truth, though abused by
> the sceptics, that there is ἀκατάληπτόν τι, "something incompre-
> hensible" in the essence of the lowest substances. For even body itself
> which the Atheists think themselves so well acquainted with . . . hath
> such puzzling difficulties and entanglements in the speculation of it,
> that they can never be able to extricate themselves from . . .[30]

So like More, as we shall see below, Cudworth admits the
incorrigible unknowability of the ultimate essence of things in
themselves, but that does not excuse the excesses of the sceptics.
Neither are we to be swayed by excessive inferences drawn from the
shakiness of metaphysical arguments. The "mechanic or atomic
theists", that is the Cartesians, have undercut the argument from
design, "leaving only certain metaphysical arguments for a Deity;
which, though never so good, yet by reason of their subtlety, can do
but little execution upon the minds of the generality, and even
amongst the learned do sometimes beget more of doubtful disputation and scepticism, than of clear conviction and satisfaction; the

---

[29] See Charles B. Schmitt, "The development of the historiography of scepticism: from the Renaissance to Brucker", in *Scepticism from the Renaissance to the
Enlightenment*, eds. Richard H. Popkin and Charles B. Schmitt, Wiesbaden: Har-
rassowitz, Wolfenbütteler Forschungen 35, 1987, 185–200. Constance Blackwell,
"The historiography of Renaissance philosophy and the creation of the myth of the
Renaissance eccentric genius: Cardano in Jakob Brucker's *Historia critica philosophiae* (1742–44), Brucker's predecessors, Naudé, Bayle and Buddeus and his
heirs—Buhle, Tenneman and Hegel", forthcoming in *Geronimo Cardano*, ed. Eck-
hard Kessler, in *Wolfenbüttler Forschungen* 1993, 324–357. Voetius' "De atheismo" is
an important exception to this claim: see Theo Verbeek's contribution in this
volume, 31–45.
[30] Cudworth, *True intellectual system* 1678, p. 63. *The true intellectual system . . . to
which are added the notes and dissertations of Dr J.L. Mosheim, translated by John Harrison,
M.A., with a copius general index to the whole work*, 3 vols., London 1845, vol. 2, p. 518.
In Mosheim's edition the appendix to chapter 4 (1678 edition) appears at the
beginning and as an integral part of chapter 5.

Atheists in the mean time laughing in their sleeves, and not a little triumphing, to see the cause of theism thus betrayed by its professed friends and assertors . . ."[31]

Sceptical excess must be avoided at all costs. In his discussion of "the Cartesian circle" he writes that because of it we may doubt how far Descartes succeeds in *proving* God's existence. Descartes' line of argument implies that

> we are of necessity condemned to eternal scepticism, both concerning the existence of a God, when after all our arguments and demonstrations for the same, we must at length gratifie the atheists with this confession, in the conclusion, that it is possible notwithstanding, there may be none; but also concerning all other things, the certainty whereof is supposed to depend, upon the certainty of the existence of such a God as cannot deceive.
>
> So that if we will pretend to any certainty at all, concerning the existence of a God, we must of necessity explode this new sceptical hypothesis, of the possibility of our understandings being so made, as to deceive us in all our clearest perceptions, by means whereof, we can be certain of the truth of nothing, and to use our utmost endeavour to remove the same.[32]

Which he proceeds to do by first of all attacking the Cartesian doctrine of eternal truths. Even the omnipotent God cannot make something true or false at will, otherwise the terms "true" and "false" would have no meaning. "Truth is not factitious; it is a thing which cannot be arbitrarily made, but *is*." Secondly, the truth of singular contingent propositions depends upon things themselves existing without the mind, but in the case of "the universal and abstract theorems of science . . . the measure and rule of truth concerning them . . . must be native and domestick to it, or contained with the mind it self; and therefore can be nothing but its clear and distinct perception. In these intelligible ideas of the mind, whatsoever is clearly perceived to be, *is*; or which is all one, is *true* . ."[33] So Cudworth holds firm to Descartes' criterion for distinguishing truth from falsity, while rejecting in the strongest terms the voluntarism that threatened Descartes' whole project with irremediable scepticism.

As with the other Cambridge Platonists, and Culverwel, Henry More (1614–87), Fellow of Christ's College, is a reminder that the primary purposes of the Cambridge Platonists were theological, not

---

[31] Cudworth, *True intellectual system* (1845 ed.), vol. 2, p. 613.
[32] Cudworth, *True intellectual system* (1678 ed.), p. 717.
[33] Cudworth, *True intellectual system* (1678), p. 717.

philosophical. The following passage from his letter to John Norris, dated 16 January 1686, illustrates this point (at least in his case) as well as any. Referring to Norris's *Theory and regulation of love* (of 1688), which Norris had sent to him for comment, More writes:

> I will only take notice of one place more in your ingenious Discourse, and that is, pag. 15. where I stumbled a little at your seeming severity towards the *severe Masters*, as you call them, of *spiritual mortification*. I confess some passages in them lye fair for your lash. But the high and hyperbolical expressions of holy and devout men are not be tryed by the rigid rules of logick and philosophy, but to be interpreted candidly, according to the scope they aim at. Which is a perfect exinanition [emptying] of our selves, that we may be filled with the sense of God, who worketh all in all ... And to be thus self-dead and self-annihilated, is the only sure safe passage into eternal life, peace and glory: And is the most safe and lovely condition of the soul that possibly can be attained to. All knowledge to this is but vain flattering, a feather in a mans cap tossed with the wind. Here is firm anchorage, rest, and such a peace as passes all understanding. ... This mystical death or spiritual annihilation, whereby all self-wishing is destroy'd, is the peculiar transcendency of the Christian state above that of the noblest heathen philosophers that ever were. And whoever feels it will find it so. For these are divine sensations, and lye deeper than imaginative reason and notions . . .[34]

Although the passage was written in the year before More's death, this is not the Angel of Christ's College casting the cold eye of old age on the secular philosophizing of his earlier days. This is Henry More the philosopher-theologian reiterating a conviction that he had retained from the days when as an undergraduate at Christ's he first read the neo-Platonists and the *Theologia Germanica*. In autobiographical passages of the "Praefatio generalissima" to the *Opera omnia* of 1675–79 he describes his inordinate thirst while at Cambridge for knowledge, especially of natural philosophy and metaphysics. One day his tutor at Christ's, Robert Gell, asked him why he was so obsessed with study. More replied, "that I may know". "But what is it, my boy, that you want so eagerly to know?" persisted Gell. "I am eager to know", returned More, "so that I may know". "For it seemed to me at that time", More continues,

---

[34] John Norris, *The theory and regulation of love. A moral essay, in two parts. To which are added, Letters philosophical and moral between the author and Dr. Henry More ... The second edition*, London 1694 (1st ed. 1688), 158–59. Richard Ward highlights More's "not over-valuing of speculations": *The life of the learned and pious Dr. Henry More, late Fellow of Christ's College in Cambridge, to which are annex'd divers of his useful and excellent letters. By Richard Ward, A.M., Rector of Ingoldsby in Lincolnshire*, London 1710, 62–65.

"that the supreme joy and happiness was to have knowledge [*scientia*] of things both natural and divine".[35] So there followed four years studying Aristotle, Cardano, Julius Scaliger, and others. But despite the solid arguments he found in them, there was so much that seemed either false or uncertain, or trivial and obvious, that he thought it a waste of time to read such writings. Then he turned to a close study of the principle of individuation in the Thomists and the Scotists, in the hope of finding a proof that he was an individual, and of discovering what his own self might be once he had set aside all those qualities shared by the rest of humanity. But this lead only to doubts. In particular, "I began to doubt whether I was a complete, separate being . . . or but a part of some enormous, or rather, enormously intelligent, individual . . to whom alone it is given clearly to understand what I am". And thence to a general impatience with logic and philosophy:

> . . . to speak all in a word, those almost whole four years which I spent in studies of this kind, as to what concern'd those matters which I chiefly desired to be satisfied about (for as to the existence of God, and the duties of morality, I never had the least doubt), ended in nothing, in a manner, but mere scepticism. So that . . . as a perpetual record of the thing, I compos'd that octastich entitled Ἀπορία, which can be found at the end of the second volume of philosophy . . . And these things happened to me before I had taken my degree in the University.[36]

Let us look at Ἀπορία, written about 1635, in More's own later translation:

Ἀπορία
or
The Perplexity of the Soul[37]

Nor whence, nor who I am, poor wretch! know I:
Nor, O the Blindness! whither I shall go;
But in the crooked claws of Grief I lye;
And live (I think) thus tugged to, and fro.

---

[35] *Opera omnia, tum quae Latine, tum quae Anglice scripta sunt; nunc vero Latinitate donata instigatu et impensis generissimi juvenis Johannis Cockshuti nobilis Angli*, 3 vols. London 1675–1679 vol. 1. p. vi. See also Bullough's account in *Philosophical poems of Henry More, comprising Psychozoia and minor poems*, ed. with introduction and notes by Geoffrey Bullough, Manchester: Manchester University Press, 1931, xiii–xviii, and Aharon Lichtenstein, *Henry More: the rational theology of a Cambridge Platonist*, Cambridge, Mass.: Harvard University Press, 1962, 3–8.

[36] *Opera omnia*, vol. 1, p. vii. *Philosophical poems* (1931), p. xvi: Bullough's translation (slightly modified) and that in Ward, *Life of More*, 63–64.

[37] This is the English title More provided for the translation he sent to Anne

Waking, and Dreams all one. O Father! I own
'Tis rare, we mortals live i'th clouds like Thee.
Lyes, toyes, or some hid Fate us fix, or move:
All else being dark what's Life, I only see.[38]

Writing to More in late 1670 or early 1671, Edmund Elys pointed out to him the resemblance between Ἀπορία and some lines from the poem Περὶ τῆς ἀνθρωπίνης φύσεως by the Cappadocian Father St Gregory of Nazianzus (329–89).[39] More seemed pleased that Elys had spotted the similarity, but whether or not his poem was therefore imitative of St Gregory's, as Bullough infers,[40] in neither poem is there any resonance of the *epistemological* scepticism at issue in Sextus Empiricus or Cicero's *Academica*. The poems are rather cries of the soul in search of its identity, fearful of its contingency and insecurity, and in helpless ignorance of its destiny. Accordingly, I cannot go along with Popkin's reading of Ἀπορία as descriptive of a "crise pyrrhonienne" in More's intellectual life.[41] Many doubts troubled More around 1635, but whether they fall under the rubric of strictly Pyrrhonian aporetics, despite the ostensibly allusive title of More's imitation of St Gregory, is a very moot point.

Conway probably in January 1670. Similarly, "The Extrication of the Soul" is the title he provided for Elys's translation of Εὐπορία (below in main text), also included in the same letter to Anne Conway. *Conway letters. The correspondence of Anne, Viscountess Conway, Henry More, and their friends, 1642-1684 . . .*, ed. Marjorie Hope Nicolson, London 1930, 299–300. Both Greek poems first appeared in *Philosophicall poems, by Henry More: Master of Arts, and Fellow of Christs Colledge in Cambridge*, Cambridge 1647; facsimile reprint: Menston (England): Scolar Press, 1969, p. 334. See also *Philosophical poems* (1931), p. 158.

[38] More to Edmund Elys, East Allington, Devon. Christ's College Cambridge, 12 February [1671?]. *Letters on several subjects, by the late pious Dr. Henry More. With several other letters. To which is added, by the Publisher, two letters, one to the Reverend Dr. Sherlock, Dean of St. Paul's; and the other to the Reverend Mr. Bentley. With other discourses. Published by the Reverend Mr. E. Elys*, London 1694, p. 6.

[39] "Poemata moralia", no. 14, lines 17–20: *Patrologia Graeca*, ed. J.-P. Migne, vol. 37, col. 757. Bullough mistakenly takes the English text of "The Perplexity of the Soul" to be More's translation of the tetrastich from St Gregory: *Philosophical poems* (1931), p. 238. The relevant letter from Elys to More seems to be lost, but in the reply to Elys dated 12 February [1671?] (previous note) More comments that "It's pretty you should light on a Tetrastick of Greg. Nazianzen, so like my Ἀπορία": *Letters on several subjects*, p. 6. Following this letter, Elys prints (p. 7) the Greek of St Gregory's tetrastich, together with the Latin version published in Billy's 1609 and 1630 editions of St Gregory's *Opera*. Migne includes Billy's "metrica versio" in PG, *loc.cit.*

[40] *Philosophical poems* (1931), p. 238.

[41] Richard Popkin, "The 'incurable scepticism' of Henry More, Blaise Pascal and Soren Kierkegaard" in *Scepticism from the Renaissance to the Enlightenment*, eds. Popkin and Schmitt, 165–84, at p. 171.

Certainly the resolution of More's personal crisis in the mid 1630s did not involve finding antidotes to Sextus Empiricus. After taking his B.A. degree More began to ask if natural knowledge "was really that supreme felicity of man; or something greater and more divine was; or, supposing it to be so, whether it was to be acquir'd by such an eagerness and intentness in the reading of authors, and contemplating of things; or by the purging of the mind from all sorts of vices whatsoever". He found new directions for his thinking in Plotinus, Ficino, Hermes Trismegistus, and mystical writers, "among whom there was frequent mention made of the purification of the soul, and of the purgative course that is previous to the illuminative; as if the person that expected to have his mind illuminated of God, was to endeavour after the highest purity."[42]

"But of all the writings of this kind," he then explains, "there was none, to speak the truth, so pierced and affected me, as that golden little book, with which Luther is also said to have been wonderfully taken, viz., *Theologia Germanica*".[43] Written in the mid-fourteenth century and published in 1516 and again in 1518 by Luther, the *Theologia Germanica* is a popular devotional guide advocating purgation of the self and of the will as prerequisites to the illumination of the soul and its union with the Divine.[44] "All concerns about the I, Mine, self, and things connected with them", we read in chapter 41, "must be utterly lost and surrendered, except, of course, the traits that are necessary for our existence as persons".[45] In the light of passages like this, and given the effect of the *Theologia Germanica* on More's spiritual development, it might not be inappropriate to recall that he never gave any indication that he saw the point of the *cogito* argument or appreciated its role in Descartes' philosophy.

There followed three or four years of "Holy discipline and conflict", during which "that insatiable desire and thirst of mine after the knowledge of things was wholly extinguish'd in me, as being

---

[42] *Philosophical poems* (1931), p. xvii.
[43] *Philosophical poems* (1931), p. xxxi.
[44] *The Theologia Germanica of Martin Luther*, trans., introduction and commentary by Bengt Hoffman, preface by Bengt Hägglund. (Based on Luther's 1518 edition.) (New York: Paulist Press, 1980). Bullough's "Introduction" to *Philosophical poems* (1931), pp. xxx–xxxviii. Lichtenstein, *Rational theology of a Cambridge Platonist*, 5–7, 58–60. Robert Crocker, "Mysticism and enthusiasm in Henry More", in *Henry More (1614–1687): Tercentenary studies*, ed. Sarah Hutton, biography and bibliography by Robert Crocker, Dordrecht: Kluwer Academic Publishers, 1990, 137–55, at 140–42.
[45] *Theologia Germanica* (1980), p. 127.

sollicitous now about nothing so much as a more full union with the
divine and coelestial principle, the inward flowing well-spring of
life eternal . . ." Then "there shone in upon me daily a greater
assurance than ever I could have expected, even of those things
which before I had the greatest desire to know: insomuch that
within a few years, I was got into a most joyous and lucid state of
mind; and such plainly as is ineffable", though he goes on to admit
that this did not prevent him from capturing his spiritual rebirth in
a second Greek poem Εὐπορία, "The extrication of the soul",
written about 1639 to counterpoint the Ἀπορία of the earlier period
of crisis.[46]

More's epistemology was grounded in the assumed reliability of
human reason, notwithstanding the validity of sceptical objections
to the contrary.[47] Truth is not compromised by our inability to
devise apodictic demonstrations of it. However weak might be
someone's philosophical demonstrations of God's existence, God
exists for all that, because the Bible, revelation, and the soul's
divine sagacity tell us so. It is not that weak or invalid arguments
for God's existence will make His existence doubtful, but rather, as
More notes in the preface to *An antidote against atheisme* (1653), that

---

[46] Beame of aeternall light from Heaven I came,
And, O the pleasure! unto Heaven I goe.
Now Love enfolds me in its tow'ring flame.
  I truly live, my thoughts with joy oreflow,
Farewell to Night, and dreames. The Eternall Sun
  Doth us surround of uncreated Light.
Fayth, Wisdome, Joy, free strength our race to run
  Are Life; but all thinges els are Death and Night.
This is Edmund Elys' translation, in the version More sent to Anne Conway
probably in January 1670: *Conway Letters*, p. 300. However, the text differs (apart
from variants in orthography) from that given in Elys's own autograph letter to
More of 17 December 1669: *for* "I truly live," *read* "I Feed on Truth,"; *for* "of
uncreated Light." *read* ",True, Uncreated Light,"; *for* "free strength" *read* "&
Strength". Christ's College Library, MS 21, No. 15. f. 2 *recto*. I wish to thank the
Master and Fellows of Christ's College, Cambridge, and especially Dr C.P.
Courtney, College Librarian, for permission to consult and use the unpublished
Elys-More correspondence.
[47] Trying to determine what a given writer of this or any period means by
"reason" is a semantic paperchase of unending fascination, and frustration. See
Lotte Mulligan, " 'Reason', 'right reason', and 'revelation' in mid-seventeenth-
century England", in *Occult and scientific mentalities in the Renaissance*, ed. Brian
Vickers, Cambridge; New York: Cambridge University Press, 1984, 375–401; Sarah
Hutton, "Reason and revelation in the Cambridge Platonists, and their reception of
Spinoza", in *Spinoza in der Frühzeit seiner religiösen Wirkung*, eds. Karlfried Gr
ünder and
Wilhelm Schmidt-Biggemann, Heidelberg: Lambert Schneider, 1984, 181–200, espe-
cially 184–189.

arguments that "will easily admit of evasions" only present the atheist with the excuse to reject all arguments devised for that purpose.

> Wherefore I have endeavoured to insist upon such [arguments] alone as are not only true in themselves, but are unavoidable to my adversary, unless he will cast down his shield, forsake the free use of the natural faculties of his mind, and profess himself a mere puzzled Sceptick. But if he will with us but admit of this one postulate or hypothesis, *That our faculties are true*; though I have spoke modestly in the Discourse itself, yet I think I may here, without vanity or boasting, freely profess, that I have no less then demonstrated *That there is a God . . .*[48]

At the beginning of chapter 2 More further explains:

> 1. But when I speak of demonstrating there is a God, I would not be suspected of so much vanity and ostentation as to be thought I mean to bring no arguments but such as are so convictive, that a mans understanding shall be forced to confesse that it is impossible to be otherwise then I have concluded. For, for mine own part, I am prone to believe that there is nothing at all to be so demonstrated. For it is possible that mathematical evidence itself may be but a constant undiscoverable delusion, which our nature is necessarily and perpetually obnoxious unto, and that either fatally or fortuitously there has been in the world time out of minde such a being as we call *Man*, whose essentiall property it is to be then most of all mistaken, when he conceives a thing most evidently true. And why may not this be as well as any thing else, if you will have all things fatall or casuall without a God? For there can be no curb to this wilde conceit, but by the supposing that we our selves exist from some higher principle that is absolutely good and wise, which is all one as to acknowledge *That there is a God*.
> 2. Wherefore when I say that I will demonstrate *That there is a God*, I do not promise that I will alwayes produce such arguments, that the reader shall acknowledge so strong, as he shall be forced to confesse that it is utterly unpossible that it should be otherwise: but they shall be such as shall deserve full assent, and win full assent from any unprejudic'd mind.
> For I conceive that we may give full assent to that which notwithstanding may possibly be otherwise: which I shall illustrate by severall examples . . .
> 3. And what I have said of assent is also true in dissent. For the mind of man, not craz'd nor prejudic'd, will fully and unreconcilably

[48] *An antidote against atheisme, or an appeal to the natural faculties of the minde of man, whether there be not a God . . . The third edition corrected and enlarged: with an Appendix thereunto annexed*, London 1653, 1st ed. in *A collection of several philosophical writings of Dr Henry More . . .*, London 1662, separate pagination, p. 3.

> disagree, by its own naturall sagacity, where notwithstanding the thing that it doth thus resolvedly and undoubtingly reject, no wit of man can prove impossible to be true . . .[49]

Here the argument turns on the distinction between logical and physical (im)possibility. To take More's examples, which I omitted from the above quotations, it is *logically* possible, that is there is no *contradiction* in claiming, that an altar-shaped stone found on a mountain-top and bearing a Greek or Latin inscription was formed by purely natural agents, or that Archimedes is at this moment sitting at the centre of the earth drawing geometrical figures in the dust. But only a lunatic would refuse to reject these fables as anything more than that, even though no one can show that they are absolutely impossible.

The same ideas inform *The immortality of the soul* (1659). Chapter 2 of Book 1 opens:

> 1. And to stop all creep-holes, and leave no place for the subterfuges and evasions of confused and cavilling spirits, I shall prefix some few *axiomes*, of that plainness and evidence, that no man in his wits but will be ashamed to deny them, if he will admit any thing at all to be true. But as for perfect *Scepticisme*, it is a disease incurable, and a thing rather to be pitied or laught at, then seriously opposed. For when a man is so fugitive and unsetled, that he will not stand to the verdict of his own faculties, one can no more fasten anything upon him, then he can write in the water, or tye knots of the wind. But for those that are not in such a strange despondency, but that they think they know something already and may learn more, I do not doubt, but by a seasonable recourse to these few Rules, with others I shall set down in their due place, that they will be perswaded, if not forced, to reckon this truth, of *the immortality of the soul*, amongst such as must needs appear undeniable to those that have parts and leisure enough accurately to examine, and throughly to understand what I have here written for the demonstration thereof.[50]

There is a new and significant element in this passage. Scepticism is an incurable *disease* of the mind. I do not think More's use of this description is merely figurative or polemical. Fully-fledged and seriously held scepticism, like unbridled enthusiasm, signals a mind that has gone off the rails, a mind that has become deranged. A full exploration of this topic would take us into the unfathomable

---

[49] *Antidote against atheism*, in *Collection*, separate pagination, 10–11.
[50] *The immortality of the soul, so farre forth as it is demonstrable from the knowledge of nature and the light of reason* . . ., London 1659, 1st ed. in *Collection* (1662), separate pagination, 16–17.

mysteries of Renaissance and seventeenth-century distinctions between sanity and madness. Suffice to say that if More chose to
number scepticism among the diseases of the mind, it can scarcely
have been on his list of preferred philosophical positions.

The first two of the promised axioms confirm this point. Axiom 1
says that "What ever things are in themselves, they are nothing to
us, but so far forth as they become known to our faculties or
cognitive powers", and Axiom 2, that "Whatsoever is unknown to
us, or is known but as merely possible, is not to move us or
determine us any way, or make us undetermined; but we are to rest
in the present light and plain determination of our owne faculties".
Axiom 2 follows from Axiom 1, because "the existence of that that
is merely possible is utterly unknown to us to *be*, and therefore is to
have no weight against any conclusion, unless we will condemn our
selves to eternall scepticisme".[51]

For More the choice was between the futility and epistemological
impotence of eternal scepticism, and the unmixed blessings, both
natural and divine, of "true philosophy and right reason".[52] I side
with Coudert, who has argued that although More was unable
strictly speaking to meet the sceptical challenge, nonetheless he
"had an unshakeable conviction that truth and knowledge were
obtainable"; and such certainty was not "grounded on philosophical argument, but on divine illumination".[53]

I began by suggesting that sceptical arguments were frequently
employed for non-sceptical purposes. More well understood the
role of scepticism as a critical instrument in epistemology. At least
he was in no doubt about its role in Descartes' philosophy. From
early 1650 Anne Finch, later Vicountess Conway, then 19 years
old, was lucky to have More as an extra-mural mentor, guiding her
philosophical studies and in particular taking her through at least
Parts 1–3 of Descartes' *Principia philosophiae*. The extant material
results of these philosophical "tutorials" are four letters of 1650–51,
three from More, which are replies to letters from Anne that are
lost, and one from Anne. In the first of these four letters, dated
9 September (1650), More writes:

---

[51] *Immortality of the soul*, in *Collection*, separate pagination, p. 17.

[52] *The apology of Dr Henry More, Fellow of Christ's College in Cambridge; wherein is
contained as well A more general account of the manner and scope of his writings, as A
particular explication of several passages in his Grand mystery of godliness*, in *A modest
enquiry into the mystery of iniquity . . .*, London 1664, 477–567, at p. 482.

[53] Allison Coudert, "Henry More and witchcraft", in *Henry More: Tercentenary
Studies*, ed. Hutton, 115–36, at p. 127, 128.

As for your other objection, upon the last words of the 4th Article [of Part 1], that we have no signes whereby we can discerne our sleep from waking, that this takes away all knowledge, I must first advertize you, that you are not so to understand the Mounsieur, as if he did in good earnest affirme that there is no meanes at all to distinguish waking from dreaming. But he speakes thus to heighten the difficulty of rightly philosophizing, that he may the better sett of the excellency of his Method. As is plaine from his 30th article, where I perceive you have been. For there attending to the goodnesse and truth of God, whom by this time he had found out, he is bold to assert that we are able, making right use of our [*read* the] [reason *del.*] naturall faculty He has given us, to discern what is true or false in dreames or waking . . .[54]

Something similar was true of the Cambridge Platonists as a group. Their dealings with scepticism were prompted by an awareness of the heightened difficulties of rightly theologizing at a time when the revived scepticism of the Greeks, already at odds with the intimations of the undiseased mind, also seemed cross to Daniel's prophecy that in the last days many will turn to righteousness and "knowledge shall be increased" (Daniel 12: 3–4). But unlike Descartes, the Cambridge Platonists did not use sceptical arguments to set off the excellency of their apologetic methods, which drew their strengths from other sources. Their aim was to ensure that the sceptics' bridles on the natural light of reason would not thereby become bridles also on the progress of the Christian soul towards divine knowledge and understanding.

We have been reading the poet Henry More, so I close by quoting the opening lines of *Religio laici* (1682) of John Dryden, who described himself in the Preface as being "naturally inclined to scepticism in philosophy". Perhaps these lines, conceived in a different Christian spirit, evoke a more authentic scepticism than we are likely to encounter in the writings of the Platonists—or Aristotelians—of Cambridge.

> Dim as the borrowed beams of moon and stars
> To lonely, weary, wandering travellers,
> Is reason to the soul; and, as on high
> Those rolling fires discover but the sky,
> Not light us here, so reason's glimmering ray
> Was lent, not to assure our doubtful way,
> But guide us upward to a better day.

---

[54] Alan Gabbey, "Anne Conway et Henry More: lettres sur Descartes (1650–1651)", *Archives de philosophie* 40 (1977): 379–404, at 384–385.

And as those nightly tapers disappear,
When day's bright lord ascends our hemisphere;
So pale grows reason at religion's sight;
So dies, and so dissolves in supernatural light.[55]

---

[55] *The Oxford Authors: John Dryden*, ed. Keith Walker, Oxford and New York: Oxford University Press, 1987, p. 219, 228. On Dryden's intellectual orientations see Bredvold, *Intellectual milieu of John Dryden*.

SUSANNA ÅKERMAN

THE ANSWER TO SCEPTICISM OF QUEEN CHRISTINA'S ACADEMY (1656)

Thirty-four years ago, Sven Stolpe defended a thesis on the religious development of Queen Christina of Sweden (1626–1689) entitled *From Stoicism to Mysticism* drawing on René Pintard's evidence in *Le libertinage érudit* to show that after her abdication and journey to Rome the Swedish Queen embraced a sincere, but "modernistic" Catholic position. Although it has many merits, especially in showing Christina's late acceptance of Molinos's quietism, Stolpe's work does not describe her early existential turn in enough detail to locate her decision. Nor does it definitively decide whether her conversion was sincere or whether it should be regarded as a classic example of dissimulation and disbelief.[1] In this paper, I shall briefly discuss two events that are particularly relevant to evaluating the issue: Christina's sanction of an attempted refutation of the Sceptics in her Roman academy, and then a report on her beliefs made up some months before her abdication.

Queen Christina's conversion to Catholicism, first privately at Brussels and then publicly at Innsbruck, was planned to be a massive propaganda victory for the Vatican. For six months after her arrival in Rome, she was permitted to hold academies twice a month in which speakers elaborated on topics chosen by herself. On 24 June 1656, shortly before her unexpected departure to Paris, Christina held the closing meeting of her *Academia Regia della Laeta di Svezia* (MS Urbinato Lat. 1692, ff. 45–52). It staged a refutation of the Pyrrhonian sectarians, the syndicate of *philosophanti*, who along with Arcesilaus had set "in dubio ogni cosa", believing all questions to be undecidable. The contents of this refutation would

---

[1] Sven Stolpe, *Fran Stoicism till Mystik—studier i Drottning Kristina maximer*, Stockholm: Bonniers, 1959; René Pintard, *Le libertinage érudit de la premier moitié de la dixseptième siècle*, Paris: Boivin, 1943; also my *Queen Christina of Sweden and her Circle. The transformation of a Seventeenth-Century Philosophical Libertine*, Leiden: Brill, 1991. The standard edition of letters is Johan Arckenholtz, *Mémoires concernant Christine, reine de Suède, pour servir d' éclaircissement à l'histoire de son règne . . . suivis de deux ouvrages de cette princesse*, 4 vols., Amsterdam, Leipzig 1751–60.

have escaped us, had not the moment in which it was delivered been crucially conditioned by the critical stage of millenarian expectation—the renewal of Noah's covenant, thought to have been instituted in the year 1656 before Christ that was now to be repeated. The full import and utility of these expectations had grown all the more clearer to European politicians and especially to Christina through her discussions with Isaac La Peyrère at Antwerp during her year of anticipation in Belgium in 1654–55, after which La Peyrère's *Systema Theologicum ex hypotesi Prae-Adamitae* was speedily but anonymously published. Now, in the middle of the crucial year 1656, the speaker in Christina's Roman academy, Girolamo Mazzoni, a priest also known for his astrology, declared that he was prepared to answer the Pyrrhonian arguments. He first of all made clear that the scepticism of the Pyrrhonists frequently induced an obstinate opposition to authority, but that it does so in a dispersed staccato fashion that can lead to no systematic insight. His critical point was that the principle of Pyrrhonic exaggerated doubt cannot be formulated in language, seemingly to indicate that Pyrrhonism can be no more that a continual negation of positive assertions. Mazzoni tries to persuade his audience that the Sceptic's state of doubt can be replaced by an heroic virtue whose rays shall govern the intellectual like a natural diadem. An indecisive mind will be relieved when the soul is agitated with this fury, producing an enduring mental state that goes beyond any assurance founded on a great probability or consensus of opinion. Dante's *Commedia* shows us the glory of this certitude. Plutarch's *Moralia* and its descriptions of the ancient thinkers assure us that the irresolution produced by sceptical philosophy never held a place in great nations. Thus, Mazzoni appeals solely to an internal experience of certitude, known in the creative act.

It may be helpful to recall that Arcesilaus, the leader of the Middle Academy and the first to introduce the notion of *epoché* into Pyrrhonism, in his time criticized the Stoics and their belief that there are *phantasia kataleptikè*, i.e. certain perceptions so distinct from all others and so evidently true that no doubt was possible concerning them. Mazzoni's position thus may be seen as a restatement of the stoic belief to which Arcesilaus originally addressed his doubts. Arcesilaus's point had been that there is no criterion for distinguishing these special notions from the ordinary uncertain ones. He had defied the Stoics to produce one single example of an apprehension that could not be false. Mazzoni claims that there is a tradition in which these characteristics are enshrined. The lights of certitude are set out in detail in the ancient tradition, i.e. in the books on the Deiform City of antiquity, such as in Iamblichus's *On the Egyptian Mysteries*, the writings of Mercurius Trismegistus and the *Pimander*. When he goes on to describe these writings he points to their presentation of the ancient heroes in the practical realm—how they inhabit the purest part of air, where they delight on dew, and where they do not suffer from ordinary turbulence and tempests. They excel through exercise of heroic habits, just as Aristotle affirmed that heroic virtue "supra nos est".[2]

Then Queen Christina is offered some elitist mythology. The noble and well-born, by following the example of Aristotle, Caesar and Darius, can through an heroic exercise of moral habits be transformed into Gods. They become the "demi-dieux" often referred to in monarchial panegyric—for instance, in Urbain Chevreau's ballet *Les liberalitez des Dieux*, danced in Stockholm in 1652, where Christina was eulogized three times: "elle est de la race de demi-dieux". This achieved, they shine with the splendour of the sun and outshine other inhabitants of the Zodiac. Poets like Vergil have sung of how since the days of Troy the heroism of Achilles has reigned in Italy. While the Italian reign and the Empire is no more, its self-same spirit is deposited in the Great Mother of Christ, the Church of the Catholic Apostolic faith. Mazzoni's discourse on the heroic heritage is thus crafted to fit not only those on the fringes of conformity—speculative astrologers, natural historians or the mere enthusiasts—but even the mainstream Church could now adopt the language of pure inspiration. Thus, in Christina's academy a rhetorical affirmation of a superior experience was seen as sufficient to end the threat posed by the sceptical crisis. To Arcesilaus's doubts they had produced a counterexample: the self-same nature of the illuminated mind over all times. Rational objectivity was not even the goal of this programme; it was instead to convey the shortest practical road to heroic action.

Christina could set sail for Marseille full of confidence and a triumphant journey by way of Lyon and Dijon brought her to Paris in September 1656, where Gallic messianism had now gained a wide influence. At the *Académie française* she was promptly hailed with a phrase that encapsulated providential rhetoric: "Fecit te

---

[2] On Arcesilaus's criticism of Zeno's "apprehensive presentations" see Pierre Couissin, "The Stoicism of the New Academy" in *The Sceptical Tradition*, ed. Myles Burnyeat, Berkeley; Los Angeles: University of California Press, 1983, 31–62. Also relevant is Plotinus's commentary on Aristotle's *Nichomachean Ethics* IV 3:16, 1124a at *Ennead* IV ii:21; here the soul is described as "the crowning of the virtues", a"Bund aller Tugenden".

Suecia Christinam, Roma Christianam, fecit te Gallia Christianissimam".[3] This was the glory that had long been planned, and perhaps the Parisian reception best illustrates how an answer to the Sceptics could seek a foundation in a heightened emotivism. Currents of providentialism had joined with millenarianism to produce an imagery of certitude rather distant from the wisdom that emanates from Christina's own sceptical *Maxim*: "One cannot believe anything, before one has dared to doubt".[4]

The turns of Christina's intellectual journey are worth contemplating. In 1655, her friend and librarian, the Dutch Greek scholar Isaac Vossius had been denied a passport to Italy because the Vatican had been warned of his heretical interests. Through several clandestine pamphlets the word had spread that the ex-Queen's religious beliefs might not be entirely sincere. These pamphlets, for instance, the *Brieve relation de la vie de la reyne Christine* (published clandestinely in the Netherlands in 1655 and signed by the initials of one A.H. Saint-Maurice), state that Christina had cast doubt on the immortality of the soul, on the incarnation, on Providence—which she with the Stoics preferred to call mere fate, on Hell and Heaven, and on the existence of demons. The mysterious companion piece *La genie de la reyne Christine* (1655) had argued in more detail that the Swedish Queen, along with regarding the incarnation of the Lord a mere fable, upheld five irreligious principles. These were: 1) that one should love God, not fear Him, but that one must fear the vile men and real demons on whom common people have such faith, 2) that one should act without repentance or pardon, 3) that religion at present is but a poor illusion, and one cannot be obligated to believe that which one cannot understand, 4) that no argument can refute Plato's doctrine of a universal soul and that after death the soul returns to its principle—Plato's "*l'Ame Universelle du Monde*", and finally 5) the tract contends that Christina regarded Moses as an impostor.[5] The powerful counterimage

---

[3] Paris, September 1656, Azzolino collection X, Riksarkivet, Stockholm. On this theme also my "Queen Christina and Messianic Thought" in *Sceptics, Millenarians and Jews*, eds. David S. Katz, Jonathan I. Israel, Leiden: Brill, 1990, 142–160, and "Il momento profetico nell'abdicazione della regina Cristina" in *Cristina di Svezia. Scienza ed Alchimia nella Roma Barocca*, eds. Wilma di Palma, Tina Bovi, Bari: Nuova Biblioteca Dedalo 99, 1990, 207–243.

[4] Christina's maxim may be an adaptation of Descartes's *Principles of Philosophy*, paragraph 1, as Ernst Cassirer has remarked in his *Descartes: Lehre. Persönlichkeit. Wirkung*, Stockholm: Behmann-Fischer Verlag, 1939, p. 202.

[5] *Le genie de la reyne Christine* in an important respect relates Averroist doctrines that occur in the famous document *De tribus impostoribus*, sought after by Christina

produced in these pamphlets may have been an attempt by writers who wanted to propagate their own libertine views to a wider audience by attributing them to a major character in the changing political events. But it may also be true that at the time of her public conversion Christina's understanding of the tradition of Hermetic illumination and the concept of the World Soul did not lead necessarily to either the orthodox or the heretical path.

In a memoir of his visit to the Stockholm court in 1653, the French courtier Sebastien Boudon de La Salle describes how he had heard Queen Christina argue for three or four hours on the Divine Essence and on Providence with libertine arguments. She had also called the incarnation a fable.[6] A more detailed description of another of her intellectual debates was recorded in November 1653, when the Venetian ambassador to Russia, Alberto Vimina, stopped by in Stockholm and was given an audience by the Queen.[7] Vimina relates how the Queen indignantly dismissed his questions on a proposed marriage to the German Emperor. Vimina claimed that Christina had as little regard for posterity as she had for the succession. She had made fun of ordinary beliefs about posthumous life and refused both the marital yoke and any belief in immortality. She had argued that the Soul, the form of man, is no different from the material soul of animals and thus that is was both corruptible and mortal. She had claimed that the notion of the immortality of the Soul is founded only on faith or the demands of conventional decency. Any argument that would separate the soul from the body stems rather from deceit than from knowledge. Vimina was convinced that some people must have informed her royal genious with godless doctrines and sophistic arguments. He

---

and her atheist doctor Bourdelot. Since *Le genie* draws a parallel between Christina and the divine impostorship of Numa Pompilius, it may be seen as an Averroist-libertine percursor of the French manuscripts, first published in 1719 in the Netherlands as *Le traité des trois imposteurs*; see my article "Johan Adler Salvius's questions to Baruch de Castro on 'De tribus impostoribus' in 1635", to be published in the proceedings of the Leiden seminar on "The Three Impostors" by Richard H. Popkin and F. Charles-Daubert.

[6] The Queen's knowledge of the discussions on Providence is attested to by many sources. It is typical that on 16 March 1654, Johan Micraelis from Stettin sent her a review of a work written by the Jesuit Kedinman, *Schedisasmata Romanensis . . . adversus Joh. Bergius theologia in articulo de Predestinatione & Cognata materiis*; this is a reply to Johan Bergius's anti-Lutheran review *Der Wille Gottes aller Menschen Seeligkeit* (1653): "Skrivelser till Kungl. Majt., no. 6459, Riksarkivet, Stockholm.

[7] Reported in a manuscript now in the Vatican Library as Ottoboni Lat. 2485, ff. 246–273, it is entitled "A History of the Cossack Raids in the Kingdom of Poland".

was appalled that she even denied the existence of both Heaven and Hell.

The language Vimina uses to describe the soul as a form not separable from matter may be taken to indicate an Averroistic Aristotelianism, but it may possibly also be a misrepresentation of an Epicurean position. As early as 1650, Christina had had contact with Pierre Gassendi. She had by then read his life of Lucretius as well as Michel de Marolles's new edition of *De rerum natura*. However, in a review of René Pintard's image of the Queen as a "libertine érudite", the Swedish historian Curt Weibull took seriously the official Jesuit claim that events such as her conversation with the Venetian ambassador were cases of simulated atheism which she used to protect herself against the suspicion of being Catholic in protestant Sweden.[8] He urges us to see the connection between the Queen's refusal to marry and the discussion of the posthumous life of the soul. Weibull believes that her denial of the existence of Heaven and Hell was directed against Lutheranism, when we know that even late in life Christina could regard herself a Catholic without believing in Purgatory. Since she conceals from Vimina that she has arranged for Charles Gustavus to be her Crown heir, one could and should cast doubt also on what she told him about her philosophical opinion with regard to the soul.

The question of whether Christina was indeed simulating doubt is complicated, however, by the fact that she was influenced by French atheism as late as two years after her discussions with the Jesuits (especially during the chairmanship of the famous atheist Pierre Bourdelot in her Stockholm academy in 1652–53). The final development towards sanctioning Mazzoni's refutation of scepticism in 1656 thus took a complex path. To see this in some detail we must go to Isaac Vossius's conceptbook of his correspondence with Stockholm in 1649 and 1650.[9] Vossius's view of Descartes's

---

[8] Curt Weibull, "Drottning Kristinas onvändelse till Katolicismen", *Scandia* 28 (1962), p. 241, n. 5. A source that substantiates the dissimulation thesis is the conversation in Antwerp in November 1654 recorded by the Habsburg General Raimondo Montecuccoli edited by A. Gimorri in *I viaggi . . . 1655*, Torino: Einaudi, 1942, p. 68; Christina here says that she has to continue her attempt to be regarded an atheist. But as the anonymous pamphlet *Le genie* amply demonstrates, her pronouncements of libertine doctrine did have a good deal of effect in the clandestine culture of the time.

[9] Isaac Vossius's conceptbook: Amsterdam, University Library, No. 8, VI, F28. This is cited in part in letter No. 63 of D.J.H. ter Horst, *Isaac Vossius en Salmasius. Een episode uit de zeventiende-eeuwsche geleerden geschiedenis*, The Hague:

philosophy may be related to Mazzoni's account of the Sceptics. In January 1650, Vossius wrote the historian Claude de Saumaise that scepticism only gains strength by being pitted against Platonism. He relates how the Queen had told Descartes that she had already read his doctrines in Plato, Sextus Empiricus "aliisque". To this Descartes had replied that she should only be happy that the same ideas had sprung up in his and in those other thinkers' minds as well. Vossius was pleased to conclude that no one was better suited to refute Descartes than the Queen. His ironic point was that the philosopher's brisk reply included a tacit appeal to Platonism and its doctrine of eternal ideas.

The learned polymath Saumaise agreed with Vossius's and Christina's complaint that Descartes knew nothing of the ancient philosophers.[10] He wrote that Descartes tried only to prove what other people already believe. Finally, Vossius tells us that the Queen held in low esteem Descartes's *Les passions de l'âme* (1648), regarding it as a "mediocre" work. Descartes's emphasis on stoic morality was easily available anyway in a more imaginative form in Johan Gerdes's *Kebes güldene Tafel und Epiktetus ädleste Handbuchlein*, printed at Stockholm in 1649.

In Stockholm, many regarded Descartes's *Principles of Philosophy* as just another formulation of stoic natural philosophy. Thus the military engineer Petrus Hoffwenius wrote to his friend Georg Stiernhielm that Descartes's ideas lacked utility, and he ironically concluded that it was a good thing that Descartes "had discovered the fiery nature of the sun". Stiernhielm, who was working on a synthesis of neo-Platonic and neo-stoic thought in his impressive manuscript entitled *Peplum Minervae Arctoae*—the cloak of Minerva unveiled—of 1653, claimed that Descartes's philosophy was simply "philosophare sine mente"; earlier he had called Plato's system founded on "luce sine mente", while Aristotle's was founded on "mente sine luce".[11] Stiernhielm instead was aiming to work out

---

Nijhoff, 1938. In October 1649, Vossius records that along with his father's great classical library, there arrived at Pierre Chanut's residence at Stockholm some French "Sceptici". These men were Descartes and his companions, perhaps among them the courtier La Voyette, who attended Descartes on his deathbed and who took care of Descartes *Traité de l'homme*. He later lent it to Pierre Chanut, who, without giving La Voyette his due recognition, published it with Clerselier in 1644. La Voyette bitterly complained about this to Urbain Chevreau: *Chevreauana* 2, Paris 1702.

[10] See his exchange of letters Christina now preserved in London, British Library, MS Egerton 28.

[11] Georg Stiernhielm's notes in "the blue book", p. 63, Kungliga Biblioteket,

the tradition of Comenius and Jean d'Espagnet, that postulates a third element to mediate between matter and mind—the Hermetic-appearing notion of "Lux".

When Vossius had first arrived on the Stockholm scene in the Spring of 1649, he had brought with him a presentation copy of Jean de Laet's edition of Vitruvius's work on architecture. With Dutch help, plans were soon made for the remodelling of the library into a temple of Apollo and the Muses. To this end, Vossius asked Pierre Bidal in Paris for a description of the Villa Adriani. An Alexanderplatz was planned outside the castle with equestrian statues and a mausoleum for Gustavus Adolphus. Thus in the period from 1650 to 1652, parallel to her secret conversations with the Jesuits, Christina was reading classical texts to the point that she began to call this reading her "jeu de échec". Inspired by Vossius, she sent emissaries to Paris, Rome and Florence to obtain copies of Platonic manuscripts: Porphyry's commentaries on Plato's *Phaedo* and *Parmenides*, the neo-Platonic commentaries of Hermias and Olympiodorus, Proclus's *In Alcibiadem* and *In Parmenidem*. Vain attempts were also made to recover the manuscript of the lost 15 books of Porphyry against the Christians, that Vossius's father claimed to have seen bound together with a copy of Xenophon's *Milesiaca* in the stacks of the Florentine Bibliotecas Laurenziana.[12] When Christian finally put her hands on a manuscript copy of Iamblichus's *De mysteriis Babyloniaca*, Vossius could relate how she trembled with joy. Towards the end of 1652, the Italian follower of Cremonini, Fortunio Liceto, would dedicate to the Queen his *De lucernis Antiquorum reconditus*, writing of Stockholm as "Holmiae Platonicae Republica Felix".[13]

In that same year, Christina importantly commissioned a work on the Pythagoreans which was finally brought to an end in 1664 with the publication at Uppsala by Johannes Scheffer of his *De philosophia et constitutione Pythagoricae*. This book influenced both Constantin Grimaldi's Neapolitanean history of philosophy and Ralph Cudworth's descriptions in his *True Intellectual System*.

Stockholm: J.N. box 6; cf. note 12. Petrus Hoffwenius later developed a Cartesian mechanics that was censored in 1664: MS U 33, Uppsala UB.

[12] Johan Nordström's unpublished notes for the opening chapters: "Isaac Vossius och Kristina" and "Hercule de Lacguer" for a projected volume "Kristinatidens lärde", deposited in 1967 at the Carolina Rediviva, Uppsala UB, boxes 7–12; here especially box 10.

[13] Fortunio Liceto, *Hieroglyphica, sive antiqua schemate gemmarum annularium*, Pavia 1653, p. 400.

Scheffer's volume reflects a lively interest in Sweden for these doctrines and it is particularly clear on the doctrine of metempsychosis, on the identification of Moses with Mosche the Phoenician—the atomist predecessor of Democritus—and on the fact that the Pythagoreans allowed even women to take part in discussing the esoteric doctrines of their academies. Scheffer's identification of the Swedes with the lost tribe of the Hyperboreans of antiquity, the presentation of the Gothic philosopher Zamolxes, and his idea of Pythagorean elements in northern Druidism,—these were mostly ignored when the book reached an international audience. This atmosphere probably inspired Christina's acquaintance Gilles Ménage in Paris to write the double volume dedicated in 1690 to the French Latinist Anne Dacier, the *De historia mulierum philopharum* and the *Commentarius Italiciis in VII sonettum Franciscii Petrarchae*, which portrays the Swedish Queen as the most learned of female minds. Similarly, after leaving Stockholm for The Hague in 1655, Isaac Vossius was inspired to republish the study of his father *De natura et constitutione philosophorum sectis* (1658).[14]

The character of the Queen's philosophical beliefs is also transmitted into the notes of G.W. Leibniz. On 2 December 1676 when Leibniz was planning a dialogue between Descartes and the Swedish Queen, he chose as a topic the nature of the soul; ten days later this idea was turned into a planned dialogue which turns on the Pythagorean view of metempsychosis and on Descartes's view of animal souls as insensitive automata.[15] Later, Leibniz thought he could identify Christina's views by setting her in a tradition flowing from Gabriel Naudé's reading of Cremonini's Paduan Averroism in a tradition described in his essay *On the Doctrine of a Singel Universal Spirit* (1704). Averroes's denial of individual immortality, his distinctions between a passive and an active intellect, found an Italian and a French audience through the works of Contarini and Gabriel Naudé. Leibniz also attributes this view to Spinoza and to the neo-Cartesians, who affirm the universal spirit "seemingly unawares". Leibniz argues that the operations of the universal spirit are catalogued among the modern chemists and that it can be found in the works of complex neo-Platonist figures such as Henry More. He believed, however, that the idea of the World Soul

---

[14] See Chapter V of my *Queen Christina of Sweden*. Also, Christian Callmer, *Königin Christina. Ihre Bibliothekare und Ihre Handschriften*, Stockholm: Acta Bibliothecae Regiae Stockholmensis 30, 1977.

[15] G.W. Leibniz, *Philosophische Schriften*, Berlin: Akademie Verlag, 1980, vol. 3, pp. 399, 582.

reduces God to a mere composite of individual spirits. Its appeal is simply based on a likeness to a musical organ, animated by a wind that plays on each pipe differently, but which still in essence remains the same. He declared that one must identify the individual spirits which merge into the universal soul with the small vital kernels found in all organic life. Thus the Paracelsians tended to see the elements in the World Soul as alive, operative principles while the neo-Platonists regard them as abstract, perhaps active ideas included in the Mind of God. Perhaps most interesting for the concerns of Christina's later academies is the fact that Leibniz's essay also describes the cessation of mental activity practised among the many Roman followers of the Spanish Quietist Molinos, which was based on a similar idea of an inclusion in a unitary God. The Quietist aim was to perceive their unity with the Divine through a continuing mental inspection, until they reached in Leibniz's words "that Sabbath or repose of souls in God".

Leibniz's 1704 essay incorporated developments first taking place towards the end of the seventeenth century. As early as 1656, the ramifications of the doctrine were not yet as clear, as one can easily see from Christina's own description of her position, which she revealed to the Hermetic writer of royalist alchemy C.B. de Morisot on her way to Paris.[16] She was asked what was really her religion. Christina replied that it was that of the philosophers—and she added: "this philosophy is indeterminate and its limits are uncertain, but it is best represented in Lucretius's *De rerum natura*". Her reading of Lucretius fell within the illuminist tradition of attempts at experiencing the Soul of the World—the Platonist *Nous*, the Averroist "Active Intellect", or the Stoic "Living Intelligence" expounded by Cicero's Balbus in his *De natura deorum*, from which, time and again, Christina quoted the phrase "while all religions might be false, only one of them can be true".[17]

---

[16] F.U. Wrangel, *Drottning Kristinas resa fran Rom till Franska hovet 1656*, Stockholm: Norstedts, 1923. Pintard, *Le libertinage érudit*, pp. 399, 638, n. 399.

[17] Cicero, *De natura deorum* II, 29, I:5.

Sarah Hutton

SCIENCE, PHILOSOPHY, AND ATHEISM
EDWARD STILLINGFLEET'S DEFENCE OF RELIGION

I

Edward Stillingfleet's name, or perhaps his title, Bishop of Worcester, is chiefly remembered, if at all, nowadays for his having taken issue with John Locke in 1697. Their debate started with Stillingfleet's *A Discourse in Vindication of the Trinity* (1696), written in answer to John Toland's *Christianity not Mysterious* (1697). His friendly relations with Locke, notwithstanding, Stillingfleet perceived Toland's book as an example of the kind of religious scepticism and irreligion to which Locke's *Essay Concerning Human Understanding* could lead. Locke took exception to Stillingfleet's views, and there ensued a very public exchange of letters, interrupted by Stillingfleet's death in 1699. Unfortunately for Stillingfleet, history has regarded him as the loser in this controversy. In spite of the fact that, as Locke scholars concede, he showed up some serious problems in Locke's argument and pushed Locke into giving the fullest explanation of his views that there is,[1] Stillingfleet has gone down in the history of philosophy as the man who did not understand Locke. This rather dubious and very unfair reputation—unfair, because Stillingfleet in fact understood Locke's drift very well, and that is what worried him—viewed *sub specie Lockei* Stillingfleet's own intellectual endeavours have been overlooked. While it is recognized that he was one of the most learned men of late seventeenth-century England,[2] it is not always ac-

---

[1] See, for example, R.I. Aaron, *John Locke*, Oxford: Oxford University Press, 1955 (2nd edn.), pp. 145ff.; J. Yolton, *John Locke and the Way of Ideas*, Oxford: Oxford University Press, 1956, pp. 136, 144; more grudgingly, M. Cranston, *John Locke*, Oxford: Oxford University Press, 1985 (1st edn. 1957), pp. 413ff.

[2] Locke himself acknowledged this in his *Reply to the Bishop of Worcester's Answer* in Locke, *Works*, London 1823, reprinted Aalen, 1963, vol. 4, p. 125. Testimony to his scholarliness, is Stillingfleet's vast library, bought by Narcissus Marsh after his death and still preserved intact with Marsh's other books in Dublin. Stillingfleet's manuscripts were bought by Sir Robert Harley, so contributing substantially to the Harleian collection of manuscripts now in the British Library.

knowledged that his erudition extended beyond scholarly humanism to engagement with the philosophical scientific developments
of his own day.[3] He produced an intelligent, if bookish critique of
Cartesianism.[4] He was well acquainted with the writings of Boyle,
Newton and others, and he had connections with scientific circles
through such figures as his friend, Sir Mathew Hale, and Richard
Bentley, Anglican popularizer of Newtonianism, who lived as a
member of his household for fourteen years.[5] Stillingfleet's bookish-
ness and his cautious response to new developments in
seventeenth-century philosophy do not diminish his importance in
the intellectual history of the period. On the contrary, like Henry
More before him, his dialogue with his contemporaries is revealing.

When Stillingfleet took up his pen against Locke, he had make
his mark as an Anglican apologist and champion of the Church of
England against Socinians, Deists and James II's attempts to
impose a measure of religious toleration in 1688. His opposition to
James was rewarded by William III with his elevation to the see of
Worcester in 1689. From his early career Stillingfleet was associated with the broad church movement that has been dubbed latitudinarianism. At Cambridge he knew More, Simon Patrick and
others who were later to become leading latitudinarians. His first
book, *Irenicum, a Weapon-salve for the Churches Wounds* (1659) was, as
the title suggests, eirenic in spirit and clear evidence of his latitudinarian sympathies. Nonetheless, to my mind, a measure of
theological conservatism can be detected in Stillingfleet even at this
stage in his career. Soon afterwards, he accepted an invitation to
write a defence of Archbishop Laud in 1664: Stillingfleet's *A Rational Account of the Grounds of the Protestant Religion* is a continuation of
the Laud-Fisher Debate of the 1639, a riposte to the Catholic

---

[3] Notable exceptions to the rule of ignoring Stillingfleet's part in the intellectual
debate of his time are R.H. Popkin, "The Philosophy of Bishop Stillingfleet,"
Journal of the History of Philosophy 9 (1971), 303–319, and R.T. Carroll, *The Common
Sense Philosophy of Religion of Bishop Edward Stillingfleet*, The Hague: Nijhoff, 1975.

[4] *Origines sacrae*, London 1702, book 1, chapter 2. Referred to hereafter as
Origines (2nd version).

[5] On Bentley as popularizer of Newtonianism, see M.C. Jacob, *The Newtonians
and the English Revolution, 1689–1720*, Ithaca: Cornell University Press, 1976; J.J.
Dahm, "Science and Apologetics in the Early Boyle Lectures," *Church History* 39
(1970), 172–186. also M. Hunter, *Science and Society in Restoration England*, Cambridge: Cambridge University Press 1981, 184–5. Although, to my knowledge,
there is no evidence of Stillingfleet's having been actively engaged in science, his
son, Edward (1660–1708), became Gresham Professor of Physic and was elected
Fellow of the Royal Society. His grandson, Benjamin (1702–1771), was a botanist
of some note and a disciple of Linnaeus.

polemicist, "T.C." whose *Labyrinthus Cantuarensis* (Paris 1663) had
answered Laud's reply to Fisher. Subsequently his acceptance into
the Anglican establishment was assured: he became dean of
St Paul's in 1678 and was appointed chaplain to Charles II. He
devoted his scholarly energies to a hefty history of the church in
Britain, his *Origines Britannicae* of 1685.

Stillingfleet was commissioned to write his defence of Laud on
the strength of his major defence of Christianity, his *Origines sacrae*
of 1662,[6] which attracted the attention of many prominent Anglicans, among them, Bishop Sanderson, later Archbishop. This book
is of an age with some of the most important philosophical works of
those other mid-century apologists, the Cambridge Platonists, with
whom Stillingfleet shares much common ground: in its display of
classical erudition in defence of Christianity, *Origines sacrae* is very
like Cudworth's *True Intellectual System* and Stillingfleet places himself in the same apologetic tradition when he names Du Plessis
Mornay and Grotius, as his forbears.[7] Nonetheless, one striking
thing about *Origines Sacrae* is the discrete but nonetheless emphatic
shift of position away from that of the Cambridge Platonists, especially Henry More.[8]

According to Stillingfleet's first biographer, this immensely erudite work was reckoned one of the best defences of religion in
general and of Christianity in particular.

> It having always been justly esteemed one of the best Defences of
> Religion that ever was extant in our own or any other Language; and
> would but our Modern Deists heartily and impartially apply them-
> selves to study it . . . they would find it an effective Antidote for their
> Scepticism and Infidelity.[9]

Stillingfleet does not refer to deism as such in this work, but his
concern with the problem of deism increases as his ecclesiastical

---

[6] *Origines sacrae: or a Rational Account of the Grounds of the Christian Faith, as to the
Truth and Divine Authority of the Scriptures, and the Matters therein contained*, London
1662. Referred to hereafter as *Origines* (1rst version).

[7] *Origines* (1st version), vol. 1, p. xii.

[8] *Origines sacrae* (1st version) was published in the same year as Henry More's,
A Collection of Several Philosophical Writings and six years before Cudworth's *True
Intellectual System of the Universe*. Stillingfleet's critique of Henry More is the subject
of another paper of mine, "Edward Stillingfleet, Henry More and the Decline of
Moses atticus" in *Philosophy, Science, and Religion in England, 1640–1700*, ed. R. Kroll,
Cambridge: Cambridge University Press, 1992.

[9] See *The Life and Character of that Eminent and Learned Prelate Dr. Edward Stilling-
fleet, Lord Bishop of Worcester* London 1710, also printed in *The Works of . . . Dr.
Edward Stillingfleet*, London 1707–10, 1–46. The author was probably Timothy
Godwin.

career advances.[10] In his *Discourse in Vindication of the Doctrine of the Trinity* (1697), Stillingfleet describes deism as covert Atheism: although there are, he says, "no open professed schools of Atheism", atheism operates "under some shew of Religion" setting up "natural Religion in opposition to Revealed" so as to "by degrees to loosen and unhinge the Faith of Men".[11]

This increasing concern with the problem of deism probably explains why, late in life, Stillingfleet embarked on a new version of *Origines Sacrae*. This was never completed, probably because his controversy with Locke supervened. First published posthumously in 1702,[12] it consists of the first two chapters and a list of the projected contents, a mere fragment of the projected whole. Nonetheless, as I have argued elsewhere,[13] there is enough to form the basis of a comparison between the two works. Both versions show Stillingfleet firmly believed that Christianity could and should be defensible by reason, that is, defensible in terms which rational unbelievers could understand. In the preface to the 1662 edition, he underscores its claims as rational theology when he describes it as a response to the need for a fuller and more rational defence of religion than anything written hitherto, in order to suit the philosophical temper of the age.[14] The implication is that his readership is of sceptical disposition, though in the 1662 version he does not mention scepticism as such. He does, however, express reservations about the extent and reliability of human reason in its capacity to grasp revealed truth. In the later version of the book he expressed the more anxious view that men of his time were notoriously given to scepticism and atheism, noting the "too great prevalency of scepticism and infidelity".[15] This is echoed in his

---

[10] See his *A Letter to a Deist*, London 1677.

[11] Op. cit., p. xlvi. The work from which this comes is the one which links John Locke with John Toland, so sparking the Locke-Stillingfleet controversy which occupied Stillingfleet's last years. Both in the *Discourse* and in his answers to Locke, Stillingfleet dubs as scepticism this covert atheism, or loosening of religious faith. As is well known, Stillingfleet's charge against Locke is that his epistemology promotes scepticism: "My great Prejudice against it [the way of Ideas]" he tells Locke, "is, that it leads to *Scepticism*, or at least, that I could find not way to attain to Certainty in it upon your own grounds." Furthermore, Stillingfleet's answers to Locke contains what is, to my knowledge, his only historical account of sceptical philosophy (other than materialism).

[12] Reprinted in Stillingfleet, *Works*, vol. 2, London 1709.

[13] See above at note 8.

[14] *Origines* (1st version), vol. 1, p. xii.

[15] *Origines* (2nd version), vol. 1, p. 247. Early in the seventeenth century English theologians commonly used terms such as "unbelief," "misbelief" or "irreligion," rather than "scepticism" to denote heterodoxy of belief, as in the work by Thomas

observation in his controversy with Locke, by his statement that theirs is "an age wherein the *Mysteries of Faith* are much exposed by the Promoters of Scepticism and Infidelity".[16] Scepticism was not new to Stillingfleet in his old age. As R.H. Popkin has shown, he was himself a practitioner of mitigated scepticism in his own rational defence of religion.[17] Stillingfleet's identification of scepticism as the enemy of religious belief occurs at a time when his concern about deism becomes acute enough for him to feel it necessary to reframe his anti-deist arguments. Stillingfleet's *Discourse in Vindication of the Doctrine of the Trinity* (1697) was presented as a strengthening of the case he had made in his sermon *The Mysteries of the Christian Faith Asserted and Vindicated* (1691). The same can be said, *mutatis mutandis*, in respect of his two versions of *Origines sacrae*.

While Stillingfleet's apology for religion remains true to his conviction that religion could be defended by rational means, by comparing the two versions of *Origines sacrae*, it can be shown that he re-worked his apologetic strategy, giving greater contemporary emphasis and reducing the space devoted to ancient opinion. He appears to be attempting to tighten up his arguments by incorporating contemporary philosophical debate and developments in science in order to face what he saw as the challenge of rational atheism. The second version of *Origines sacrae* contains a thoroughgoing critique of seventeenth-century philosophy which goes hand in hand with a remarkable receptivity towards seventeenth-century science. This adjustment of his arguments to prove the existence of God also entailed some adjustment in the requirements of belief. For in the second version of *Origines sacrae* Stillingfleet extends the minimum articles of true theism to include belief in Providence as part of belief in a Deity. It is with Stillingfleet's reworking of his apologetic strategy that the rest of this paper is concerned.

Jackson (1579–1640), *The Origin of Unbelief, Misbelief or Mispersuasions Concerning the Verity, Unity and Attributes of the Deity*, London 1625. At the end of the century, Stillingfleet uses the term, "scepticism" in a specifically religious context. This usage was not new with him, but, to judge by the reference to scepticism as a "New mill'd" word, in the Locke-Stillingfleet controversy, the term was relatively novel. It is also appears that Stillingfleet does not quote Sextus Empiricus in his magnum opus of 1662, *Origines sacrae*, but in the fragment of a reworking of this, written in the 1690's, he quotes Sextus at least six times.

[16] *The Bishop of Worcester's Answer to Mr. Locke's Letter*, London 1697, 37–8. Referred to hereafter as *Answer* (1).

[17] Popkin, "The Philosophy of Bishop Stillingfleet", cf. note 3.

II

The focus of *Origines sacrae* (1st version) is very much the *past*. Stillingfleet's method is in many ways that of an historian or lawyer weighing evidence and deciding what, among competing testimonies, is to be taken as admissible. In several hefty books he sets out to prove the primacy of scripture by demonstrating its authenticity when compared with other types of evidence, particularly with events claimed to be contemporary with or equivalent to the events recorded in the Bible. The sources he uses are thus chiefly historical and date chiefly from antiquity. There are four sections. The first argues that Bible story is more reliable than pagan history. The second sets out to prove the dependability of God's witnesses, the prophets, especially Moses. The third defends the claims of revelation, arguing for the superiority of the Mosaic account of creation over anything heathen philosophy can offer on the origin of the world and the nature of providence. The fourth discusses the origin of nations, arguing for the Hebrew origin of all the peoples of the world. Stillingfleets's tactic is to discredit all non-biblical testimony, whether philosophical, historical or religious. To that extent he echoes Tertullian's "What has Athens to do with Jerusalem?" On the other hand, for his classical learning he may be compared with Clement of Alexandria. His argument owes much to seventeenth-century hebraising syncretism according to which all the peoples of the earth were believed to have descended from the Hebrews and all pagan writings are corruptions of the original biblical account. It is an interpretation of history which enjoyed fairly wide currency in this period and was shared by, among others, Isaac Newton.[18] Stillingfleet's defence of Scripture centres largely on the Pentateuch, treating pagan testimony as negative confirmation of original truth contained in the Bible.

---

[18] See F.E. Manuel, *Isaac Newton, Historian*, Cambridge: Cambridge University Press, 1963 and R.H. Popkin, "The Crisis of Polytheism and the Answers of Vossius, Cudworth and Newton," in J.E. Force and R.H. Popkin, *Essays on the Context, Nature, and Influence of Isaac Newton's Theology*, Dordrecht: Kluwer Academic Publishers, 1990. Besides Newton and Vossius, other seventeenth-century hebraisers include Theophilus Gale whose *The Court of the Gentiles* was published in 1669–78, and Samuel Bochart whose *Geographiae Sacrae, seu Phaleg et Canaan* appeared in 1646. The latter was used by Stillingfleet. The former draws on Stillingfleet.

> Wherein we shall observe the same method, which Thales took in taking the height of the pyramids, by measuring the length of their shadow; so shall we the height and antiquity of truth from the extent of the fabulous corruptions of it.[19]

Stillingfleet does acknowledge that some pagans entertained "sublimer notions concerning God and soul of man" and explains this as a "wonderful discovery of Divine Providence" to prepare the gentiles for the gospel. However, he entertains strong doubts about the value of this since, without the help of revelation, the ancient heathens were misled into idolatry and superstition by their groping reason.

Although Stillingfleet sounds a note of caution about the use of Platonism as the handmaid of philosophy,[20] he does not completely reject the learning of the heathens. On the contrary: a grounding in natural philosophy is a sign of reliability among those whose opinions are biblically orthodox. Indeed he commends the early fathers for pointing out parallels between pagan philosophy and Christian doctrine in order to demonstrate, "that Christianity did not rase out, but only build upon those common foundations, which were entertained by all who had any name for reason".[21] Furthermore, it is to Moses's credit that he was highly educated and conversant with those subjects in which the Egyptians, for all their superstitious practices in religion, lead the world: as, for instance, astronomy, mathematics, medicine. Indeed, philosophers like Thales whose opinions on the origin of

---

[19] *Origines* (1st version), vol. 1, p. 17. All quotations are from the two-volume nineteenth-century edition, *Origines Sacrae or, a Rational Account of Natural and Revealed Religion*, Oxford 1836 (editor unknown), which prints both versions.

[20] It is here that he departs from the well-worn Renaissance model for reconciling philosophy and theology, the *interpretatio christiana* of Neoplatonism embodied in the so-called *prisca theologia*. He dispenses with any idea of a secret or hidden transmission of revealed truth, as also with the view that Moses was the key transmitter of revelation to the pagan philosophers. These, instead of being the best preservers of these snippets of revelation, were the worst corrupters of it. This is the point where Stillingfleet's dissociation from Henry More is clear to see, although he does not mention More by name. The details he gives of the Mosaic succession, especially the dismissive reference to literal, moral and philosophical cabalas, point to More's *Conjectura cabbalistica*, especially to the Appendix to the *Defence of the Philosophick Cabbala* published in More's *Collection of Several Philosophical Writings* in 1662. In place of a specific and identifiable line of transmission of Biblical truth to the pagans, Stillingfleet posits a general and universal tradition by which revealed but reasonable truth was derived either from the ancient Hebrews or from earliest times, and disseminated in a multiplicity of ways. See my paper, cited above at note 8.

[21] *Origines* (1st version), vol. 1, p. 11.

the world approximate to the biblical account of creation, have their learnedness to recommend them as well as their groping after orthodoxy. Ultimately, however, the credit is due not to Thales' great natural wisdom, but to his attempt to be true to what ancient tradition, deriving from Genesis, had taught him about the origins of the world. In other words, Thales was the beneficiary of indirect revelation, not of superior reason.[22] However, it is often the case that natural philosophy features in Stillingfleet's argument in the context of unreliable evidence. That is not to say that he thought all natural philosophy was discreditable, but that he thought that some ancient natural philosophy was. For this reason he attacks aspects of Greek natural philosophy: in the third book of *Origines sacrae* where he discusses the origins of the universe, he singles out Epicurus and Democritus for attack when defending creation against theories of the eternity of the world. And it is in this context that he refers to the philosophy of his own day, especially natural philosophy and particularly atomism. He mentions Descartes, Boyle and Harvey when confuting Gassendi's defence of Epicurus. Like Henry More he opts for the view that although Cartesian mechanism gives the best account of "the most noted phenomena of the world" it cannot explain the existence of matter and motion without a deity.[23] Stillingfleet's discussion of Descartes owes much to Henry More, whom he cites frequently. He concedes that Descartes has been abused "by persons atheistically disposed, because of his ascribing so much to the power of matter", and he vindicates him from charges of atheism, insisting that Descartes demonstrated the existence of God and the immortality of the soul. Belief in God and in the immortality of the soul are, for Stillingfleet writing in 1662, the twin foundation of religious belief.[24]

III

In the context of the whole work, Stillingfleet's use of seventeenth-century philosophy makes up a tiny proportion of the 1662

---

[22] Ibid., vol. 2, pp. 4–8.

[23] *Origines* (1st version), 1, 59–60.

[24] This remains his view in the 1666 revised edition of *Origines Sacrae*. Six years after that, he has not altered his position, for he writes in a sermon preached in 1672, that the basic foundation of religion, both natural and Christian, is "belief of a Deity and the Immortality of the Soul."

Origines sacrae. However, the second version, although far from complete, suggests some interesting changes in the use of philosophy. From the contents list, one can see that this second version was designed to cover much of the same ground as the first, including books on "the credibility of the Scriptures compared with other Account", "the Authority of the Writings of Moses", and "the Authority of the Prophetical Writings". Besides, the fundamentals of religion, as conceived by Stillingfleet, are the same as in the first version, namely belief in the existence of God, and in the immortality of the soul. While there is clearly far more contemporary emphasis, the past is still there, represented by the ancient philosophers and philosopher-theologians, including Aristotle, Plato, Pythagoras, Orpheus and Hermes Trismegistus. These Stillingfleet discusses in the first chapter, and to that extent his argument is still historically based, still relying on *consensus gentium* arguments. After all, if you are arguing for the naturalness of religion to all mankind, how much more universal can that consent be than that "from all antiquity"?[25] In general terms, his discussion of these figures takes further the critique of the ancient theologians evident in the first version.

Aside from this, major changes are apparent. To judge by the contents list and the first two extant chapters the projected second version of *Origines sacrae* entailed a radical re-organisation of Stillingfleet's material as a result of a re-thinking of his apologetic strategy. Stillingfleet's stated aim was much the same as in the first version, namely a "vindication of the truth and authority of the holy Scriptures". But instead of starting with a comparative account of pagan and biblical historical testimony, he begins with "A General Discourse in Vindication of the Principles of Natural and Revealed Religion, with an Answer to the Objection of Atheists and Deists". Where the first version reserves arguments of natural religion till the third book, this version *commences* with a reasoned defence of religion, progressing from natural to revealed religion. Furthermore, the work specifically addresses the claims of what he calls "modern atheistical hypotheses": that fear is the root of religion, that final causes are irrelevant and that religions are political inventions. The arguments deployed by Stillingfleet are the most fully developed section of the extant second version of *Origines sacrae*. The atheistical moderns whom he has in mind are Hobbes, Descartes and Spinoza. These three

---

[25] *Origines* (2nd version), vol. 2, p. 267.

figure as *philosophers* who undermine the generally received proofs of the existence of God and Providence and "attribute too much to the mechanical powers of matter and motion". As this suggests, the focus of this fragment is on Stillingfleet's own time, the end of the seventeenth-century. But it also makes plain that Stillingfleet perceived the hydra of atheism and unbelief to be philosophical in origin, and that its roots were not the corrosive effects of sceptical arguments but mistaken doctrines produced by supposedly rational minds.

In addition to this emphasis on new philosophy, the second version of *Origines sacrae* is striking for its attention to seventeenth-century scientific sources.[26] Whereas the philosophers are the object of attack as the aiders and abbettors of atheism, the natural philosophers are regarded as the allies of revealed religion. In combatting atheistic arguments, Stillingfleet makes extensive use of the design argument to counter old atheistic claims such as that the world came into being by chance. He cites at length Harvey, Ray, Boyle, Swammerdam, Malpighi, Leeuwenhoek, Redi, Hooke and Goedaart to illustrate the workings of providence in the constitution of animals, insects and human beings. He opposes to Descartes' rejection of final causes, the authority of "a very learned and Judicious Mathematician of our own", Isaac Newton, whose gravitational theory lent support to the idea of providential design because gravity was "not inherent and essential to matter, but by a force given and directed by Divine Power and Wisdom". Apart from Newton, and those like Boyle and Harvey who were mentioned in the first version, the scientists who figure in Stillingfleet's line-up of authorities all share an interest in the advances of microscopy—even (perhaps especially) the entomologists and parasitologists, whose recent observations were, after all, dependent on the advance in microscope technology. Part of the

---

[26] Stillingfleet's list of contemporary scientific authorities is strikingly similar to that used by Richard Bentley in the first series of Boyle lectures, his *Confutation of Atheism*, London 1692. Stillingfleet's use of these authorities is much more extensive and more detailed than Bentley's, so inviting the view that the credit for preparing Bentley to give the Boyle lectures should lie with Stillingfleet. Even though Bentley corresponded with Newton in order to check some details, it is likely that Stillingfleet was the moving spirit behind his application of science to religion: not only is Bentley's apologetic stance strikingly similar to Stillingfleet's, but it was Stillingfleet who recommended him as the lecturer to the trustees of the lectureship. See Dahm, "Science and Apologetics". Such a conclusion entails considerable modification of Margaret Jacob's suggestion that it was Newton who selected and schooled Bentley for the task of Boyle lecturer; cf. Jacob, *The Newtonians*, 151–7.

attraction of this particular branch of science must surely have
been that it laid bare hidden secrets of nature, literally revealed
the depth and detail of the organisation of nature. At all events,
Stillingfleet states clearly that he is persuaded of the value of
experimental science.

> It cannot be denied by any ingenuous Man, that in our Age a great
> improvement hath been made in *Natural* and *Experimental Philoso-*
> *phy*.[27]

Indeed, he goes on to recommend experimental science as superior to other philosophies, Mechanism and Aristotelianism in particular,
which attempted to give an account of the truth of nature:

> But there is a great difference to be made between those who have
> proceeded in the way of *Experiments* which do great service as they
> go, and such as have form'd *Mechanical Theories* of the System of the
> Universe; and have undertaken to give an Account how the World
> was fram'd, and what the immediate Causes are of those things
> which appear in the World. . . . . And I confess that the *Particular*
> *Histories* and *Experiments* relating to things of Nature, as to the *Bodies*
> of *Animals*, and the *Vegetation* of *Plants* and *Particular* qualities, tend
> much more to the true knowledge of Nature, than the mere nice
> and dry Speculations about Forms and Qualities [to be found in
> Aristotle's books].[28]

The inclusion of so much scientific authority is not the only
novelty of the second *Origines sacrae*, impressive though the scale
of these new additions is. But, in so far as he had already cited
Boyle and Harvey in the first version, Stillingfleet's inclusion of
this material constitutes an extension of the argument from
design rather than an innovation. And, as already observed, for
all the re-organisation of material in the fragment, the past is still
there, represented by figures such as Aristotle, Orpheus, Socrates
and Anaximander. It is notable that in his use of the new science
and ancient philosophy Stillingfleet does not take sides in the then
topical dispute over the relative merits of the ancients and the moderns:

> I do not go about to dispute, whether many things are not better
> resolv'd by the *New* than by the *Old Philosophy*; I am not concerned in
> the Doctrines of *Antiperistasis, Fuga vacui, Occult Qualities, Intentional*
> *Species*, and such like.

On the one hand Stillingfleet uses seventeenth-century science to
combat ancient science. The evidence of the researches of Redi,

---

[27] *Origines* (2nd version), vol. 2, p. 446.
[28] Ibid.

Malpighi and others is ranged against the materialism of the atheist Diodorus Siculus and ancient belief in spontaneous generation. The occasional comment by Stillingfleet, suggests that even if he was no more than an interested layman in scientific matters, he had a fair grasp of experimental method. For instance he derides the Egyptian belief in spontaneous generation, by noting how careless they were about verifying their supposition that the creatures of the Nile were generated from of its mud. To observe these animals from a distance

> ... is a very imperfect way of making experiments. Did any of the Egyptians take and dissect any of these perfect animals, and shew how it was possible in the formation of them, for one part of them to be nothing but mud, when the rest had all the organs belonging to such animals?[29]

Almost simultaneously, the same kind of evidence is used to combat the atheistical features of seventeenth-century philosophy, to emphasize the need for a providential dimension to arguments demonstrating the existence of God. Stillingfleet had in fact argued in *Origines sacrae* (1st version), that to deny providence is to contradict belief in God. But at that time the argument was levelled against Epicurus. Now it is directed against Descartes, a critique of whose philosophy occupies the major part of the second chapter. Stillingfleet argues that Descartes' rejection final causes is a dangerous flaw in his arguments for proving the existence of God. It is in fact contradictory to argue for the existence of God without including divine providence in the argument. Rejection of final causes

> ... must overthrow the argument to prove a Deity from the wisdom and contrivance in the works of creation, which according to them [the Cartesians] are only occasions of our meditation and praise. But how can men of sense satisfy themselves with this answer? For how can we give thanks to God for the use of our senses, without knowing that God gave us eyes to see with, with such admirable contrivance for that purpose; ... Otherwise all we have to do, is to thank God for putting matter into motion, and for establishing those laws of mechanism from whence these organs resulted. ... So that all natural religion, according to this hypothesis, comes to no more than an acknowledgement of God to be the efficient Cause of the world, although we have no reason from his works to conclude him to be so.[30]

---

[29] *Origines* (2nd version), vol. 2, p. 278.
[30] Ibid., vol. 2, 408–9.

Stillingfleet still accepts that Descartes was not atheistical in intention, and speaks of his "great and deserved reputation". But in
Origines sacrae (2nd version) he is not so easily satisfied with
Descartes's arguments and seems to have revised his view of
Cartesianism quite considerably.[31] He attacks Descartes for not
discussing the immortality of the soul and condemns Cartesian
natural philosophy for being too abstract and self-contradictory,
and as little better than Epicureanism.[32] Stillingfleet now regards
Descartes' concept of matter as a kind of Frankenstein's monster
over which the creator has no power. The ontological argument is
criticised for being too abstruse for ordinary minds. Furthermore, why should the idea of God as a being absolutely perfect not
include among His perfections his care for his creatures. Even
Aristotle was superior to Descartes in this respect. Besides, if even
the "Caffirs' of Southern African entertain a confused notion of
the Deity which admits God's providential care for His creation,
should not the clear and distinct idea of God entail the idea of
divine providence?[33]

Thus the argument from design takes on special importance
for Stillingfleet. And this, it seems to me, accounts, at least in part,
for the modern scientifically based arguments employed by Stillingfleet. They are part, not simply of an up-dated argument
from design, but of an *extended* use of that kind of argument. In
this respect Stillingfleet's apology for religion is consistent with
that of John Ray, whose *Wisdom of God in the Works of Creation*
(1691) is the *locus classicus* of the use of a scientifically-authenticated
argument from design which can be traced back to Henry More.
Stillingfleet refers approvingly to Ray in the second *Origines
sacrae*. (Ray had, in his turn, cited *Origines sacrae* (1st version) with
approval!)

Moreover, the attractiveness of Newtonianism for Stillingfleet,
is that it appeared to him to fit so neatly into the design argument,
because it presupposed a providential creator.

> But as it falls out in this case, we have this Theory of *Gravitation* fully
> demonstrated by a very learned and Judicious Mathematician of
> our own, to whom I refer the Reader, who hath given a *Mathematical*

---

[31] In this more extended and more negative assessment of Cartesianism,
Stillingfleet still draws on Henry More (chiefly his letters to Descartes). But he
has clearly read widely in the literature of Cartesianism, culling many points
from figures like Regius, Du Hamel, Huet, Rohault and Mersenne.
[32] *Origines* (2nd version), vol. 2, 455–6, 471.
[33] Ibid., p. 410.

Account of the *Coelestial Bodies*; not only of the *Sun and Stars, but of Comets and the Moon form the Principle of Gravitation*; not inherent and essential to Matter, but by a force given and directed by Divine Power and Wisdom.[34]

It is also clear, from the context of this statement, that the value of Newtonianism to the apologists for religion was that Newton had authority as a mathematician to be counterposed to Descartes' famed expertise in that field. In Stillingfleet's view, it was partly in the claim to mathematical certitude that the appeal of Cartesianism lay:

> The opinion of *Descartes* his great skill in *Geometry* hath gone much farther towards persuading the World of the truth of his Theory, than any evidences that appear'd in his Principle themselves. For men who are not deeply skill'd in those matters, are very apt to be sway'd by the Authority of those that are.

Against the mathematically attractive mechanism, therefore, Stillingfleet pits the mathematically respectable principle of gravitation,

> Which being granted, we have no reason to be displeas'd with the clearest Account can be given in a Mathematical manner, of the chief phaenomena of the Universe. And the same person [Newton] saith, *He hath many Reasons to suspect that the rest may depend upon some secret Powers, by which the particles of matter do either cohere or fly from each other; for want of the knowledge whereof, Philosophers have hitherto blunder'd in Natural Philosophy.*[35]

By the time he came to re-draft *Origines sacrae* Stillingfleet seems, like Henry More before him, to have perceived the new philosophies of the latter half of the seventeenth century as the enemies of religious belief. In the new science he also seems to have seen (more clearly than More) a means whereby to combat this philosophical atheism. That Stillingfleet saw Newton as the answer to Descartes, and that final causes were a key issue in that opposition, can be illustrated from another instance of Stillingfleet's intermingling of ancient and modern philosophy: in the second version of *Origines sacrae* he cites Anaxagoras to contest the (Hobbesian) claim that ignorance and fear are the seedbed of religion. The significance of Anaxagoras for this purpose is that his belief in God was, "not for want of understanding natural causes . . . but it was his skill in philosophy which brought him to

---

[34] Ibid., p. 476.
[35] Ibid., p. 477. Margin reference to *Principia*.

it". For instance, he declined to give a supernatural explanation of meteors, giving instead a natural explanation, thereby removing ignorant superstition and demonstrating the "effects of Divine Providence, which ordered the affairs of mankind for the best, as well as the meteors in the air".[36] In this account Anaxagoras is represented as an anti-Cartesian Newtonian, who rejected vortices but believed in gravitation as well as believing in God.

IV

On the strength of this rather fragmentary evidence, this second version of *Origines sacrae* can be seen as a straightforward updating of his previous argument to suit the changing intellectual climate. In view of the progress of atheism under the umbrella of Cartesianism, promoted by Hobbes and Spinoza, new strategies were required for facing the challenge of the new philosophies. After all, even in 1662, Stillingfleet had felt that the seventeenth century was a particularly philosophical age. And even then he argued for care in selection of arguments in defence of religion. "Every distinct kind of being hath its peculiar way of argument", he wrote.[37] For instance, it is no good using Euclid for proving that the Indies exist.

> Many times arguments may be good in their order, but they are misplaced: some may prove the thing rational, which may not prove it true; some may show the absurdities of the adversaries rejecting the thing, which may not be sufficient to prove it.[38]

And, as I have argued elsewhere, one aspect Stillingfleet's modification of his philosophical defence of religion was his rejection of the *prisca theologia*.[39] Problems of dating notwithstanding, this was, after all an anachronism in the seventeenth century when ancient philosophy no longer commanded undisputed esteem. The other change in his apologetic was the greater emphasis put upon contemporary natural philosophy.

In his use of scientific authorities, Stillingfleet bears out the contention made by Simon Patrick in 1662 in his defence of the Latitudinarians that the new science goes hand in hand with sound theology:

---

[36] Ibid., p. 328.
[37] Ibid., vol. 1, p. 470.
[38] Ibid., p. 467.
[39] See above at note 20.

... it must be the Office of Philosophy to find out the Process of this Divine Art in the great automaton of the world, by observing how one part moves another, and how those motions are varied by the several magnitudes . . .[40]

Referring to the advances made by Galileo, Tycho, Gilbert, Bacon and Harvey, Patrick goes on

nor is there any cause to doubt but the *Mechanick* [philosophy] will be faithful to her [sound Divinity], no less against the open violence of *Atheisme*, then the secret treachery of *Enthusiasm* and *Superstition*.[41]

This same view is echoed thirty-six years later by the Boyle lecturer for 1698, John Harris: lamenting the misuse of "the mechanical Philosophy" by atheists, Harris asserts:

And thus when it is rightly considered and thoroughly understood, the atomical or mechanical Philosophy is so far from being any way instrumental to the leading Men into Atheism, that there is none other, that doeth truly distinguish between Matter and incorporeal Beings; none that renders the Operations and Qualities of Bodies so intelligible, and none that prepares so clear, natural and easy a Way for the Demonstration of immaterial Substances as this kind of Philosophy doth.[42]

As with so many of the Boyle lecturers, there is no particular mention of Newtonianism. Rather, the references to corpuscularian atomism indicate Boyle is Harris's chief scientific mentor. He also acknowledges his debt to Cudworth, Bentley and Ray. And, significantly, he stresses the importance of second causes and, with them, the argument from design:

... there are no Men so ignorant of second Causes, nor any that give so poor and trifling Accounts of the Phaenomena of Nature, as these Atheistical Philosophers do. And therefore Ignorance ought rather to be reckoned among the Causes of Atheism and Infidelity, than of the Idea of God and Religion; for I am well assured, that a thorough Insight into the Works of Nature and a serious Contemplation of that admirable Wisdom, excellent Order, and that useful Aptitude and Relation that the several Parts of the World have to each other, must needs convince any one, that they are the Products of a Divinity and Almighty Power.[43]

---

[40] *A Brief Account of the New Sect of Latitude-men*, London 1662, p. 19.
[41] Ibid., p. 24.
[42] J. Harris, *Eight Sermons*, the Boyle Lectures for 1698, published in *A Defence of Natural and Revealed Religion: Being a Collection of Sermons Preached at the Lectures Founded by the Honourable Robert Boyle Esg*, eds. Sampson Letsome and John Nicholl, London 1739, vol. 1, p. 395.
[43] Ibid., p. 380.

Harris does not mention Stillingfleet specifically (in any case
Origines sacrae (2nd version) had not been published when he
wrote this). But the tenor of the passage, with its emphasis on the
design argument and its insistence that religion is rooted not in
ignorance but knowledge, including knowledge of the workings
of the universe recall Stillingfleet as much as anyone.

Stress on the argument from design increased in response to
seventeenth-century philosophical views, which, in the eyes of the
Anglicans, by leaving out providence, opened the door to atheism.[44] The evidence of natural philosophers, whether Redi,
Hooke, or Newton, could be put to good use to defend religious
belief against rational sceptics and atheists. Indeed, arguably, the
Anglican apologists used Newton in the same way that they used
Malpighi or Swammerdam, the chief difference being that Newton was much handier for conducting apologetics on a cosmolog-
ical scale, for confuting the atheistical progeny of Descartes.
Above all, he had authority as a *mathematician* to counter that of
Descartes, but he combined it with an acceptable view of the
important role of providence in ordering the workings of the
universe.

Far from being a closed mind, Stillingfleet was extraordinarily
receptive to new currents of thought. His controversy with Locke
is itself testimony to the fact that he engaged actively with new
ideas, even in old age. As Professor Popkin long ago pointed out,[45]
he was not trying to resist new developments by putting his finger
in the dyke to hold back the flood of new ideas, but actually sought
to come to terms with them, or at least to defend religion in the
changing intellectual and religious climate of the later seventeenth century. There are more parallels between the second
version of *Origines sacrae* and the critique of Locke than the fact
that Stillingfleet cites Sextus Empiricus in both.[46] In the second
Origines, as in the *Discourse in Vindication of the Trinity*, Stillingfleet
notes the perniciousness of atheism masquerading as theism

---

[44] While I do not wish to down play the importance of social and political
history for intellectual history, it seems to me unnecessary to explain the
Latitudinarian adoption of Newtonianism on the grounds that it was first and
foremost a dogma re-assuring to their socially and politically conservative views.
See M.C. Jacob, op. cit. supra, note 5. There is, it seems to me, a perfectly good
internal element in explaining the importance of providence in late seventeenth-
century apologetics.

[45] Popkin, "The Philosophy of Bishop Stillingfleet", cf. note 3.

[46] See note 15 above.

> . . . the safest way of instilling atheism, is by writing contradictions, that is by seeming at times to own a God, but by the whole series of the discourse to overthrow his being.[47]

As in both versions of *Origines sacrae*, Stillingfleet professes himself no enemy of philosophy. Rather, he projects himself as an apologist who makes it his business to keep up to date with the latest trends in contemporary thought:

> I am very far from being an Enemy to any free enquiries into the *Nature* and *Reasons* of Things, and would be glad to find any real Discussions that way. And I can easily bear the putting of Philosophical Notions into a modern and fashionable dress.[48]

Nonetheless, here, as in the second version of *Origines sacrae*, there are limits even to fashion. "The World hath been strangely amazed with *Ideas* of late",[49] Stillingfleet notes in his famous confusion of Lockean with Cartesian epistemology. But, he observes,

> None are so bold in attacking the *Mysteries of the Christian Faith* as Smatterers in *Ideas*, and new Terms of Philosophy, without any true Understanding of them. For these *Ideas* are become but another sort of Canting with such men; and they would reason as well upon *Genus* and *Species*, or upon *Occult Qualities*, and *Substantial Forms*, but only that they are *Terms out of* Fashion.[50]

It is this new way of ideas which is used "by ill men to promote *Scepticism* and *Infidelity* and to overthrow the *Mysteries of our Faith*".[51] Stillingfleet makes clear that he does not impute atheism to the purveyors of idealist—as he sees them—philosophies. As in the second version of *Origines*, it is not so much the inherent scepticism of the philosophies in question, but the sceptical application to which they are put by the enemies of religion that primarily concerns Stillingfleet. Cartesianism in the hands of a Spinoza or Locke's *Essay* in the hands of a Toland are recipes for atheism. But it is also apparent to Stillingfleet that Cartesianism and Lockean epistemology are inherently predisposed towards this kind of misuse. He argues that they lend themselves to sceptical application in a way that the theories of Boyle or Newton, or the observations of Robert

---

[47] *Origines* (2nd version), vol. 2, 371–2.
[48] *Answer* (1), 132.
[49] Ibid., p. 93.
[50] *Discourse*, p. 273.
[51] *Answer* (1), p. 23.
[52] Stillingfleet is at pains to try to argue that they are predisposed towards scepticism, because neither can in fact deliver the certainty of knowledge

Hooke do not.[52] By contrast, with the speculations of the meta-
physicians, the natural philosophy of men like Newton, Hooke and
Boyle, has certain foundations, demonstrated through experience.
Like the explorers who proved, by going to see for themselves, that,
contrary to the reasoning of men of ideas, the "torrid zone" was
inhabitable and inhabited.[53] Furthermore, scientific certainly is not
just founded on things as they are, but on things as they are ordered
by God. It has its roots in the providential order of God exhibited
in nature. And surely founded natural philosophy, in its turn,
exhibits the workings of providence in nature, thereby confirming
the providential character of the deity.

---

claimed. Cartesianism cannot bridge the gap between abstract speculation and
objective reality. "Thinking men" says Stillingfleet ". . . cannot conceive how an
objective reality of an idea in the mind can prove the real existence of that object
out of the mind." (*Origines* (2), vol. 2, p. 411. This is also a charge Stillingfleet lays
at Locke's door, as well as the further charge that there is no certainty to be had
from knowledge derived from sensory experience.
   [53] Ibid., p. 424.

ERNESTINE VAN DER WALL

ORTHODOXY AND SCEPTICISM IN THE EARLY DUTCH ENLIGHTENMENT

Cartesianism—scepticism—atheism: these are the keywords of the philosophico-theological conflict waged by the Dutch Calvinists during the early years of the Enlightenment. Central to this dispute was the application of Cartesian tenets to theology, an issue which gave rise to a vehement discussion about scepticism and atheism. In the Dutch Reformed church the debate on scepticism in the late seventeenth and early eighteenth centuries thus took place within the conflict over the reception of the "new philosophy".

Another term should also be mentioned here: Cocceianism. Since Cartesianism found such a ready acceptance among those orthodox Reformed theologians who followed the theology of Johannes Cocceius, the Dutch discussion about scepticism was closely connected with this group of liberal divines, who constituted one of the main parties within the Dutch Reformed church. It was the Cocceian theologians, or at least many of them, who, in the second half of the seventeenth century, developed a kind of Cartesian theology, in which—among other Cartesian tenets—universal doubt played an important role. Their view on the application of Cartesianism to theology became a controversial topic: it was one of the major factors in the religious war with their Calvinist brothers, the Voetians, which broke out in the late 1650s and would continue well into the eighteenth century. In this paper I shall deal with the way in which Cartesianism was received among Dutch Calvinist divines in the early Enlightenment by focusing upon one particular issue which came to occupy a prominent place in Dutch religious polemics in the course of the seventeenth century: the question of universal doubt, or, more specifically, doubt about God's existence.

DUTCH REFORMED ORTHODOXY AND ATHEISM IN
THE EARLY ENLIGHTENMENT

By the late seventeenth century Dutch Reformed orthodoxy had
developed into a complex entity.[1] The formularies of unity as laid
down by the national Synod of Dort (1618–1619) formed its basis.
This common ground, however, did not prevent the emergence
of a variety of theological and political ideas within the orthodox
boundaries. It was this diversity which in due course gave rise to
discussions about toleration. Thus one of the main issues raised in
the latter part of the seventeenth century was the question of
whether those members of the church who taught that every
human being should raise doubts—even if only once in his life—
about God's existence ought to be tolerated. Might such a dangerous, irreligious throng not seduce others into treading upon the
path leading first to that perilous phenomenon, scepticism, and
then inevitably to that devilish monster: atheism?

Fear of a steady expansion of atheism is one of the characteristics of religious literature in the early Enlightenment.[2] What
exactly the term "atheism" means in early modern times is hard to
define.[3] The concept was seldom intended to include genuine
disbelievers, but, mainly because of polemics, it was used to depict

---

[1] Cf. Paul Dibon, "Scepticisme et orthodoxie reformée dans la Hollande du
Siècle d'Or" in *Scepticism from the Renaissance to the Enlightenment*, eds. Richard H.
Popkin, Charles B. Schmitt, Wiesbaden: Wolfenbüttler Forschungen 35, 1987,
55–81: p. 55.

[2] For an illuminating treatment of the concept the early Enlightenment, see
the "Introduction" by Alan Charles Kors to a volume of essays on this topic:
Anticipations of the Enlightenment in England, France and Germany, eds. Alan
Charles Kors and Paul J. Korshin, Philadelphia: University of Pennsylvania
Press, 1987, pp. 1–6. See also Margaret C. Jacob, "The Crisis of the European
Mind: Hazard Revisited" in: *Politics and Culture in Early Modern Europe: Essays in
Honor of H.G. Koenigsberger*, eds. Phyllis Mack, Margaret C. Jacob, Cambridge:
Cambridge University Press, 1986, 251–271.

[3] For the notion of "atheism" in early modern times, see Wolfgang Philipp,
Das Werden der Aufklärung in theologiegeschichtlicher Sicht, Göttingen: Vanden-
hoeck und Ruprecht 1957; Hans-Martin Barth, *Atheismus und Orthodoxie.
Analysen und Modelle christlicher Apologetik im 17. Jahrhundert*, Göttingen: Vanden-
hoeck und Ruprecht, 1974; Hans Leube, "Die Bekämpfung des Atheismus in
der deutschen lutherischen Kirche des 17. Jahrhunderts" in Hans Leube,
Orthodoxie und Pietismus. Gesammelte Studien, Bielefeld: Arbeiten zur Geschichte
des Pietismus 13, 1975, 75–88; John Redwood, *Reason, Ridicule and Religion. The
Age of Enlightenment in England, 1660–1750*, London: Thames and Hudson,
1976; Michael J. Buckley, *At the Origins of Modern Atheism*, New Haven: Yale
University Press, 1987; David Berman, *A History of Atheism in Britain: From Hobbes
to Russell*, London: Croom Helm, 1988; Alan Charles Kors, *Atheism in France,
1650–1729*, Princeton: Princeton University Press, 1990.

a wide variety of supposedly irreligious views which were inextricably linked to a loose moral life.[4]

Whether or not the atheistic threat was as real as the popularity of apologetic literature against all sorts of "atheists" might seem to indicate, there was undoubtedly a genuine fear of the theological implications of the works by Isaac La Peyrère, Thomas Hobbes, Louis Meyer, Benedictus Spinoza, and Richard Simon. Their views were thought, not without reason, to endanger the status of revealed religion. The attack on miracles and prophecies, such essential proofs of the truth of the Christian religion; questions about the Mosaic authorship of the Pentateuch; the value of biblical chronology; the role of reason in explaining Scripture—were all regarded as casting doubt upon the divine authority of the Bible and the belief in a providential God. They paved the way first to deism, then to scepticism, and finally to atheism.

It was certainly people like La Peyrère, Hobbes and Spinoza whom orthodox Calvinist divines had in mind when they looked for the most prominent representatives of irreligion and anti-Christianity, but there was also another phenomenon which they held responsible for the creation of an atheistic climate: Cartesianism. This new philosophy, more than anything else (even more than Spinozism, since this was considered to be the illegitimate offspring of Cartesianism), dominated the debate on irreligion among Dutch Reformed divines in the early Enlightenment. It was Cartesianism, together with Cocceianism, that almost led to a rift within the Reformed church comparable to the schism of 1619 between Remonstrants and Contraremonstrants. How had this religious war come about?

In the early 1640s an anti-Cartesian party had come into being within the Dutch Reformed church which abhorred the "dangerous novelties" spread by the French Roman Catholic immigrant Descartes. Gisbertus Voetius, professor of theology and the pillar of Calvinist orthodoxy, was its leader. From his base in Utrecht, the anti-Cartesian bastion, Voetius planned a careful strategy to combat Descartes and his "atheistic" ideas.[5] Then in the 1650s,

---

[4] It was commonly believed that "speculative" atheists did not exist, but only "practical" atheists.

[5] On Gisbertus Voetius (1589–1676) and his struggle against atheism and Cartesianism, see René Descartes-Martin Schoock, *La Querelle d'Utrecht*, textes établis, traduits et annotés par Theo Verbeek, Paris: Les impressions nouvelles, 1988, Th.M.M. Verbeek, "Voetius en Descartes" in *De onbekende Voetius*.

within the Reformed church, there emerged what we may call a pro-Cartesian party which embraced the new philosophy, although mainly with moderation. These divines were associated with the theology of Johannes Cocceius who, from 1650 till his death in 1669, lectured at Leiden university, for some time regarded as the centre of Cartesianism.[6]

From then on the Dutch Reformed church was divided between these two camps and it seemed as if the times of the Remonstrants and Contraremonstrants had returned, a fact which was not lost on contemporaries. The Voetians loved to call the Cocceians the lawful heirs of Arminius: to strengthen their case the classis Goes went even so far as to draw up five articles in which Cocceian doctrines were condemned. Like their own forefathers, the Contraremonstrants, they wanted to have these new Arminians condemned at a national synod and expelled from the church. In the 1690s they made a request to the stadholder, King William III (whom they looked upon as the "author pietatis", "defensor fidei" and "impiorum severus hostis") to convoke a national synod in order to achieve this, but he refused, and with this defeat the Voetians entered into decline while the Cocceians became dominant. Not all Reformed divines sided with one or other party: some, such as Samuel Maresius, Balthasar Bekker, and Herman Witsius, did not belong, or at any rate did not want to belong, to either but chose to go their own way, although they did take part in the controversy.

The whole of Dutch Calvinist orthodoxy was involved in this religious war, in which theological, philosophical, political and social factors intervened. What had begun as a dispute between Voetius and Descartes extended into a national conflict between the members of the Reformed church. While Voetius might at first have cherished the illusion that he was fighting against a

---

Voordrachten wetenschappelijk symposium Utrecht 3 maart 1989, eds. J. van Oort et al., Kampen: kok, 1989, 200–219; Th. Verbeek, "Descartes and Atheism: the Utrecht Crisis", *Nederlands Archief voor Kerkgeschiedenis / Dutch Review of Church History* 71/2 (1991), 211–233. Th. Verbeek, *Descartes and the Dutch. Early reactions to Cartesian Philosophy 1637–1650*, Carbondale and Edwardsville: Southern Illinois University Press, 1992, ch. 2.

[6] For Johannes Cocceius (1603–1669), see Gottlob Schrenk, *Gottesreich und Bund im älteren Protestantismus vornehmlich bei Johannes Coccejus*, Gütersloh: Bertelsmann, 1923 (reprint Giessen: Brunnen-Verlag, 1985); Heiner Faulenbach, *Weg und Ziel der Erkenntnis Christi. Eine Untersuchung zur Theologie des Johannes Coccejus*, Neukirchen-Vluyn: Neukirchener Verlag, 1973; W.J. van Asselt, *Amicitia Dei. Een onderzoek naar de structuur van de theologie van Johannes Coccejus (1603–1669)*, Ede: ADC, 1988.

popish enemy, an alien in the Protestant church, he and his followers soon became acutely aware that the enemy had crept into their church and had even won many adherents—and a more intensive anti-Cartesian campaign began.[7] Not only were academic institutions deeply engaged in it (apart from Leiden, Franeker was an important Cartesian-Cocceian centre), but learned ministers in towns and villages in the country also played a conspicuous part in the quarrel. It was a debate, moreover, carried on among the common people, who were neatly informed about the developments via public sermons. In one of the provinces they even went so far as to replace the usual Sunday afternoon sermon on the Heidelberg Catechism by sermons on the Cocceian-Voetian dispute. Many pamphlets were published in Dutch, so their contents were generally accessible.[8]

A glance at the "catalogues of errors" drawn up by Voetians gives an idea of the main issues. One of them was the "theologia prophetica", which was intensely pursued by Cocceian and Cartesian theologians. Like Henry More, Isaac Newton and others, Cocceian and Cartesian theologians such as Salomon van Til, Johannes van der Waeyen, Frans Burman, Henricus Groenewegen, Abraham Gulich, Taco Hajo van den Honert and his son Johan van den Honert immersed themselves in the study of the books of Daniel and Revelation in order to discover the key with which to understand the past, the present and the future. Their prophetic

---

[7] On the reception of Cartesianism in the Netherlands, see the standard work by C. Louise Thijssen-Schoute, *Nederlands Cartesianisme. Avec sommaire et table des matières en français*, Amsterdam: Noord-Hollandsche Uitgevers Maatschappij, 1954 (repr. with additional bibliography, edited by Th. Verbeek, Utrecht: HES Uitgevers, 1989); C. Louise Thijssen-Schoute, "Le cartésianisme aux Pays-Bas" in *Descartes et le cartésianisme hollandais*, eds. E.J. Dijksterhuis et al., Paris: Presses Universitaires de France, 1950; Ernst Bizer, "Die reformierte Orthodoxie und der Cartesianismus", *Zeitschrift für Theologie und Kirche* 55 (1958), 306–372; Th.A. McGahagan, *Cartesianism in the Netherlands, 1639–1676. The New Science and the Calvinist Counter-Reformation*, Ann Arbor: University Micro-films, 1976. See also J.A. Cramer, *Abraham Heidanus en zijn Cartesianisme*, Utrecht: Van Druten, 1889; Josef Bohatec, *Die cartesianische Scholastik in der Philosophie und reformierten Dogmatik des 17. Jahrhunderts* I, Leipzig: Deichert, 1912; Klaus Scholder, *Ursprünge und Probleme der Bibelkritik im 17. Jahrhundert. Ein Beitrag zur Entstehung der historisch-kritischen Theologie*, München: Kaiser-Verlag 1966; Pieter Swagerman, *Ratio en revelatio. Een theologisch critisch onderzoek naar het Godsbewijs en de Godsleer uit de menselijke ratio en de verhouding van de natuurlijke theologie tot de geopenbaarde theologie bij enige Nederlandse hoogleraren in de theologie of in de filosofie van 1650 tot 1750*, Groningen: Faculteit der godgeleerdheid, 1967; Verbeek, *Descartes and the Dutch*.

[8] See the preface to the *Bedenckinge van Timotheus Verinus . . . waerin getoont wort hoe ongefondeert de E. Broederen sommige geleerde theologanten heterodoxien en nieuwigheden te laste leggen*, Leiden 1674.

theology was intended to serve as an apologetic instrument to
ward off the sceptical and atheist assault on Scripture: the accom-
plishment of biblical prophecies proved the divine authority of
the Scriptures. This form of apologetics became as popular as
another contemporary beloved apologetic means: physicothe-
ology, and both were simultaneously put forward in the defence
of Christianity.[9]

One of the interesting things about the Cocceians is that while
on the one hand they embraced Cartesianism, on the other they
developed this "prophetic theology". For the Voetians the reason
of this association was clear: the Cocceians discovered the same
harmony and order in the biblical prophecies as they loved in
Descartes' philosophy. Although this apologetic genre did not
flourish among the Voetians, we cannot deny that (semi-)millenarian
notions were also cherished by many followers of Voetius.
Furthermore, both camps had a pietistic strain in their theology,
the Voetians being the exponents of the so-called "Further Reformation" ("Nadere Reformatie"), while the pietistic Cocceians
were labelled as "serious" Cocceians. Thanks to those pietists on
both sides the Voetians and Cocceians would be reconciled in the
course of the eighteenth century.

In the late seventeenth century, however, there were sufficient
points of debate left to keep these Calvinist brothers at a hostile
distance from one another. One of the dominant themes was the
relationship between theology and philosophy, so inextricably
linked that changes in the one would directly affect the other: new
philosophy would bring in new divinity.[10] This was not lost on the
Voetians, who clung to Aristotelian-scholastic philosophy, being,

---

[9] On the "theologia prophetica" of the Cocceians, see Grete Möller, "Födera-
lismus und Geschichtsbetrachtung im XVII. und XVIII. Jahrhundert", Zeitschrift für Kirchengeschichte 50 (1931), 393–440. See also Ernestine van der Wall,
"'Antichrist Stormed': The Glorious Revolution and the Dutch Prophetic Tradition", in The World of William and Mary, eds. M. Feingold, D. Hoak forthcom-
ing. On the scholarly interest in Bible prophecies in 17th-century England, see
Richard H. Popkin, "The Third Force in Seventeenth Century Philosophy:
Scepticism, Science and Biblical Prophecy", Nouvelles de la Republique des Lettres 1
(1983), 35–64; Richard H. Popkin, "The 'Incurable Scepticism' of Henry More,
Blaise Pascal and Sören Kierkegaard", in Scepticism from the Renaissance to the
Enlightenment, 169–184: esp. 170–175; both reprinted in Richard H. Popkin, The
Third Force in Seventeenth-Century Thought, Leiden: Brill, 1992.
[10] See the remark by Simon Patrick, A Brief Account of the New Sect of Latitude
Men, London 1662, p. 22: "philosophy and divinity are so interwoven by the
schoolmen, that it cannot be safe to separate them; new philosophy will bring in
new divinity" (quoted in: B.C. Southgate, "Forgotten and Lost': Some Reactions

however, first of all eclectics.[11] Although he was not a pure anti-scholastic, Cocceius strove only to make use of scriptural terms in theology[12] and was thus not much concerned with the old philosophy—or any philosophy whatsoever, Cartesianism included. He always displayed a certain caution when asked about his views on Cartesianism, and when it was pointed out to him that some of his theological ideas were similar to those of Descartes he merely remarked that he had come to those conclusions long before Descartes.[13] Nevertheless, he seems not to have been unfavourable to Cartesianism. A polemical writer would call him "un double Descartes".[14]

Most of Cocceius's followers were less cautious about their views on the new philosophy, and contemporaries were struck by the fact that Cocceianism and Cartesianism often went hand in hand: like Samson's foxes they were turned tail to tail, putting a firebrand in the Reformed church between two tails (Judges 15:4, 5). It was said that nobody could be a good Cocceian without being a Cartesian—an observation which was denied by Heidanus.[15] Apparently this alliance was not of a merely external nature, as has been asserted, both then and later, but was based on philosophico-theological grounds.[16] At any rate, a Cartesian way of

---

to Autonomous Science in the Seventeenth Century", *Journal of the History of Ideas* 50 (1989), 249–268: p. 253).

[11] The eclecticism of the Voetians is emphasized by Jacobus Koelman, who refers to the inaugural oration delivered by the Voetian professor of theology in Leiden, Johannes Hoornbeek. In this respect there may also be some affinity with the Cocceians, since these divines were eclectics too.

[12] See also p. 132.

[13] Thus Cocceius wrote to his son-in-law Willem Anslaar, a learned Cocceian-Cartesian minister: "Ego professor fui, antequam Cartesius nominaretur: et non putavi ad me pertinere, scire, quid is sentiat. Et ut rem dicam, ipsius sententiam adhuc ignoro; aut, si scivi, oblitus sum. Ignoro etiam qui Theologi sententiam ejus rejecerint; neque id inquiro" (*Opera omnia* VI, Ep. 170). On Cocceius's view of the relation between theology and philosophy, see Van Asselt, *Amicitia Dei*, ch. 3; Cramer, *Abraham Heidanus*, 3–7; Thijssen-Schoute, *Nederlands cartesianisme*, 30–35.

[14] See Pierre de Joncourt, *Entretiens sur les differentes méthodes d'expliquer l'Ecriture et de prêcher de ceux qu'on appelle Coccéiens et Voetiens dans les Provinces-Unies. Ou l'on voit quel temperament on doit apporter dans l'explication des types, des allegories, des periodes, des propheties, et d'autres choses de ce genre . . .*, Amsterdam 1707, p. 22.

[15] Abraham Heidanus, *Consideratien over eenige saecken onlanghs voorgevallen in de universiteyt binnen Leyden*, Leiden 1676, 17.

[16] The alliance between Cocceianism and Cartesianism caused astonishment in the 17th century as well as in later times. Thus Jacques Basnage wrote in his *Annales des Provinces-Unies* I, The Hague 1726, p. 456: "Ce parti [the Cocceians], foible dans sa naissance, s'apuia des Cartésiens, malgré l'incompatibilité de leurs

thinking was introduced by the Cocceians into theology, on which
it was to exert a deep and prolonged influence. While the Cocceians expected many good things for religion from the new
philosophy for religion—it was a perfect means to combat
atheism—, the Voetians considered Cartesianism a threat to
Christianity which would lead immediately to atheism. The latter
found themselves confirmed in their sombre expectations by
radical expressions of "Cartesian theology" which came to the
fore in the 1660s.

One of the incisive events in the religious conflict was the
publication of Louis Meyer's *Philosophia Sanctae Scripturae interpres*. The year of its publication, 1666, might be regarded as the
starting point of a new phase in the history of Dutch Cartesianism.
To some contemporaries, such as the Scottish theologian and
millenarian John Durie, it was no coincidence that this was the
year both of the curious events around the Jewish pseudo-
Messiah Sabbatai Sevi and the publication of Meyer's book: it was
God's will that Christians should now reach agreement among
themselves about a firm and infallible rule for the exegesis of
Scripture. That rule could be presented to the Jews in the hope
that they would also accept it unanimously. Thus Meyer's work
opened the door to the unity between Christians and Jews thereby
hastening the coming of Christ's millenial kingdom.[17] However

---

principes, puisque l'un adopte sans peine un sens mystique, qui dépend de la
vivacité de l'esprit, et du feu de l'imagination des Interprètes, et que l'autre a bâti
son système sur cette maxime, qu'on ne doit croire que les choses, dont on a des
Idées évidentes, claires et distinctes". J.A. Cramer (*Abraham Heidanus*, 4–13, 156)
declares that the alliance was a purely external one. Schrenk (*Gottesreich und
Bund*, 20–21) says that this might be true in Heidanus's case, but that one may
wonder whether it can be maintained as a general thesis, adding: "Dies ver-
möchte nur eine eingehende Geschichte des Cocceianismus herausstellen"
(p. 22, note 1). Since such a history still has to be written, it is difficult to make any
more specific comment. Thijssen-Schoute is of the opinion that, besides external
factors, there are also internal motives for the alliance, see *Nederlands Cartesianisme*, 34–35, and "Le cartésianisme aux Pays-Bas", p. 241 ("Avouons du moins
que les thèmes cartésiens et les thèmes coccéjens se sont trop intimement
pénétrés pour que l'on puisse affirmer avec Cramer, que les liens qui les
rattachent ont toujours été des liens purement extérieurs). McGahagan goes on
in the same line, pointing to the concept of "fides implicita" as the binding factor
of the otherwise mysterious association of Cartesianism and Cocceianism"
(*Cartesianism in the Netherlands*, p. 364 ff.). Van Asselt, however, returns to
Cramer's view that only external factors brought them together (*Amicitia Dei*,
p. 36).

[17] See John Durie's letter to Johann Heinrich Hottinger and Johann Heidegger,
30 January 1667, Thes. Hott. 30 F83, f. 253 r/v (Zentralbibliothek
Zürich).

this may be, it was Meyer's work, with its thesis that Cartesian philosophy provided the one and only perfect method of interpreting Scripture, that showed to shocked contemporaries what the theological implications of Cartesianism really could be. Although Meyer's views on the relationship between philosophy and theology were fiercely attacked, it suddenly became apparent to what extent the new philosophy posed a serious threat to traditional Christianity. In 1673 the *Philosophia S. Scripturae interpres* was banned by the States of Holland and Westfriesland, while a year later it was forbidden by the Court of Holland (together with Spinoza's *Tractatus theologico-politicus*, Hobbes's *Leviathan* and the Socinian *Bibliotheca Fratrum Polonorum*).[18]

After Meyer's work had caused so much excitement in religious and philosophical circles, the subsequent debate on Cartesianism was marked by a series of episodes. The political events of 1672 (the fall of De Witt and the States' party and the rise of William III and the Orangist party) occasioned a change in the relations between Voetians and Cocceians, the star of the first quickly rising, while the latter were pushed back into a less favourable position. The Cocceians were accused of being pro-French: so fond of the philosophy of a papist Frenchman, why would they not betray to the French enemy their country as well? The Voetians, with William III as their protector, felt sufficiently secure to reinforce their assault on the "innovators" and "rationalists" who paved the way to "impious atheism" within the Reformed church.

The year 1676 thus saw the dismissal of the grand old man of Cartesianism, the nearly 80-year old Leiden professor Abraham Heidanus, while in the same year, through the intervention of William III, two Cocceian-Cartesian ministers, Willem Momma and Johannes van der Waeyen, were dismissed from their Middelburg (Zeeland) posts.[19] Although 1676 is sometimes considered the culmination of the history of Cartesianism in the Dutch Republic,

---

[18] In 1669 the Theological Faculty of Leiden expressed its very unfavourable opinion of Meyer's book. Its advice was signed by Heidanus and Cocceius.

[19] After his dismissal from Middelburg Johannes van der Waeyen was appointed professor of theology at Franeker. The more liberal Frisian court felt some rivalry towards William III and sometimes supported the appointment of scholars who were out of favour with William III. Van der Waeyen was one of the beloved targets of the Voetians, since he had been a staunch Voetian before he had gone over to Cocceianism around 1670. During his Voetian period Van der Waeyen had attacked the Cartesians, accusing them of scepticism and atheism. After he had joined the Cocceians the Voetians liked to confront him time and again with his earlier anti-Cartesian observations.

the story certainly did not end there. In the early 1680s an episode concerning the Frisian minister David Flud van Giffen gave rise to a prolonged national discussion on Cartesianism and Cocceianism in which many prominent theologians took part.[20] The Van Giffen affair was soon followed by the case of Herman Alexander Röell, professor in Franeker, whose brand of Cartesian theology would be labelled as dangerous "Röellianism", causing dismay within Calvinist orthodoxy well into the eighteenth century.[21] Then, in the early 1690s, Balthasar Bekker published his *Betoverde Weereld* ("The Enchanted World"), the propositions of which were clearly inspired by Cartesianism.[22] In the first decade of the eighteenth century the Walloon preacher Pierre de Joncourt rekindled the flames by publishing some satirical dialogues between Cocceians and Voetians.[23] Several years later a fierce dispute arose on Cartesianism and Spinozism between the two Franeker professors Ruardus Andala and Johannes Regius.[24] Eighteenth-century Calvinist theologians continued to write that Cartesianism had constituted the hot-bed of all libertinisms, including "bastard-Cartesianism" or Spinozism, which flourished in their time.[25] So Descartes was able to engage people's—polemical—energy in the Dutch Republic until nearly a century after he had come to live there.

All this is familiar to the historian of Dutch Cartesianism. However, the theological aspects of the Dutch debate on Cartesianism have not yet received due attention. A thorough examination of Cocceian theology will throw more light upon the exact nature of the alliance between Cocceianism and Cartesian theology, and may thus show how this complex of theological and philosophical ideas contributed to the moderate Enlightenment so typical of Dutch culture.

---

[20] On the Van Giffen affair, see Ernestine van der Wall "Profetie en providentie: de coccejanen en de Verlichting" in *Kerk en Verlichting*, eds. P. Bange et al., Zwolle: Stichting Windesheim 600, 1990, 29–37.

[21] See J. van Sluis, *Herman Alexander Röell*, Leeuwarden: Fryske Academy, 1989.

[22] See W.P.C. Knuttel, *Balthasar Bekker. De bestrijder van het bijgeloof*, The Hague: Nijhoff, 1906 (reprint Groningen: Bouma, 1979).

[23] See Pierre de Joncourt, *Entretiens* (see note 20).

[24] On the dispute between Ruardus Andala and Johannes Regius, see Thijssen-Schoute, *Nederlands cartesianisme*, p. 520. In 1725 Regius delivered an inaugural address *Pro scepticismo*.

[25] Thus the Zeeland minister and polemicist Carolus Tuinman, *Korte afschetzing der ysselykheden welke van de Spinozistische vrijgeesten uitdrukkelyk worden geleert . . .*, Rotterdam 1719, pp. 8, 9.

The Cocceian-Voetian Debate on Cartesian and Sceptical Doubt

Let us now turn to one of the contemporary issues that dominated the late seventeenth-century Dutch debate on Cartesian theology: universal doubt and its application to divine matters. In an earlier stage Cartesian doubt had not been as dominant as it would become later on, because at first Cartesian theologians did not lay much stress on this point and were cautious in handling it. However, with the development of Cartesian theology, and especially since more radical expressions of it had been put forward by men such as Louis Meyer, Louis Wolzogen, and Lambert van Velthuysen, doubt became one of the major themes in the Cocceian-Voetian dispute. Was it permissible to apply the Cartesian method of doubt to theology? Would methodical doubt not lead inevitably to sceptical doubt, and this in its turn to a denial of God? Should we accept religious propositions only insofar as they are clear and distinct to us? Might God be called a deceiver? Such matters were hotly debated by Dutch divines and led to a seemingly interminable stream of tracts and sermons dealing with the effects of Cartesian philosophy upon Calvinist theology.

The Cocceians expressed a variety of views on Cartesian doubt. For Cocceius's own opinion we are always referred to a passage in his *Considerationes de ultimis Mosis* (1650), in which he spoke derogatively about doubt as that "nova pullulans pestis". Doubt prevented man from attaining true knowledge of God. In a letter of 19 March 1661 Cocceius declared that, when writing this passage, he had had the sceptics in mind, not the Cartesians:

> Quum ultima Mosis scriberem, multa audiebam garrire de dubitatione. Putabam Scepticismum reduci. Et multi sic loquebantur. Non habebam tunc Cartesii libros; & illum quoque non nominavi. Eadem illa dubitatio nobis, dum hic fui, turbas dedit. Semper judicavi, Cartesium, dum Aristotelice locutus est de dubitatione, infeliciter locutum esse. Incipiunt, ni fallor, etiam magistri videre . . . Caeteroquin Cartesius non vult, de omnibus esse dubitandum, sed, quae distincte & clare cognoscimus, ea nobis affirmanda & tenenda judicat.[26]

When, in 1668, a new edition of the *Considerationes* was being prepared, Frans Burman suggested to Cocceius that he either leave

---

[26] See Cocceius, *Opera anecdota*, Ep. 489. See also Thijssen-Schoute, *Nederlands Cartesianisme*, p. 33; Van Asselt, *Amicitia Dei*, p. 34.

this passage out or rewrite it and give it a more favourable turn. Cocceius replied that he did not think Descartes had made a fortunate choice with the word "dubitatio". It was a pity that he had not chosen a scriptural term:

> Scriptura non commendat dubitationem, sed συνεον, νόησιν, προσοχήν ζήτησιν & imprimis studium ἀγαθῆς συνείδησεως. Ideoque non tam (quod bona tua venia dicam) propendeo ad tollendum eum paragraphum, quam etiam, si nondum satisfeci, explicandum amplius".[27]

Among Cocceius's friends and followers we meet with moderate as well as with more radical views. Prominent Cocceians and Cartesians such as Christoph Wittich, Abraham Heidanus and his son-in-law Frans Burman (who taught in the Voetian stronghold of Utrecht) were convinced that doubt was permissible as an instrument with which arrive at the truth. Heidanus, however, regarded "the injurious opinions of Academicians and Pyrrhonists" as one of the causes of atheism.[28] Burman observed that it was never permissible to be uncertain about God's existence. We should, however, only assent to this truth on the most solid grounds. Such a doubt was not so much doubt about God's existence as about man's notion of God's existence.

This view was shared by someone like the prominent Cocceian-Cartesian minister of Enkhuizen, Henricus Groenewegen, who interpreted doubt about God's existence as doubt about man himself; about whether he took sufficient note of the reasons which showed him the perfection and necessity of the divine being. According to these men, therefore, doubt about God's existence had to be regarded as subjective rather than as objective.[29] Salomon van Til, pointing to the dangers of atheism, quoted the French apologist David Derodon in order to show that the most dangerous of the irreligious are those who subtly lead others to raise doubts about divine matters.[30]

Timotheus Verinus gave the following explanation of Cartesian doubt. If it were really true that some theologians taught that we should doubt whether God exists it would be the most horrible heresy. But nobody taught such a doctrine. Verinus explained that

---

[27] Cocceius, *Opera anecdota*, Ep. 441.

[28] Abraham Heidanus, *De origine erroris libri octo*, Amsterdam 1678, 224–240 (quoted by Cramer, *Abraham Heidanus*, p. 48).

[29] Frans Burman, *Synopsis*, 1. 1, c. 14, §27.

[30] Salomon van Til, *Het voorhof der heidenen voor alle ongeloovigen geopent*, Dordrecht 1694, 4–5.

Descartes, when involved in a dialogue with a sceptic, wanted to convince him on his own grounds. Descartes had declared he had done this as a philosopher who seeks certitude and truth in nature, and that doubt was to be equated with suspension of judgement. So the crux of the matter was whether a philosopher might examine the reasons in nature for accepting something as true, and whether he might thus prove that there is a God and through examination discover the grounds of this truth, all for the purpose of convincing atheists.[31]

One of the main participants in the Cocceian-Voetian debate on Cartesianism and scepticism was Petrus Allinga, a learned minister in a small village in Noord-Holland.[32] Allinga, who has hitherto remained somewhat obscure, is an eminent representative of those religious and philosophical thoughts characterized by notions of both Cocceianism and Cartesianism. In philosophical matters he embraced the concepts of Descartes, while in theology he was attracted to the ideas of Cocceius. He declared that the thought of these two men might be extremely useful in order to confirm the doctrine of the Reformed church.[33] As to the alliance between Cocceianism and Cartesianism Allinga observed that among the Cocceians and Cartesians there reigned a "unio animorum". The causes of this union were manifest—"consensus in fundamentalibus, libertas in philosophicis, veritatum mutua amicitia, unionis necessitas ob communes veritatis hostes".[34]

Allinga emphasized that he did not follow Descartes in every respect. He therefore thought it unfair to derive arguments from Descartes' works in order to attack people like himself. Descartes had not been a member of the Dutch Reformed church and thus could not be presented as a proclaimer of novelties within it,

---

[31] See *Bedenckinge van Timotheus Verinus*, 50.

[32] For Petrus Allinga (16?–1692), see *Nieuw Nederlandsch Biografisch Woordenboek* (NNBW) 4, 37–38; *Biographisch Woordenboek van protestantsche godgeleerden in Nederland* (BWPGN) 1, 85–91; Thijssen-Schoute, *Nederlands cartesianisme*, 40, 41, 43–48, 525; McGahagan, *Cartesianism in the Netherlands*, passim. Scholder, *Ursprünge und Probleme*, p. 146, reckons Allinga, like Balthasar Bekker, among what he calls "the Cartesian middleparty". Allinga was befriended by Bekker who, in a laudatory poem on one of Allinga's works, depicted Wijdenes, the village where Allinga lived, as "the Noordholland Nazareth".

[33] Something resembling an autobiographical sketch of Allinga is to be found in the Preface to his *Zedige verhandeling van de voornaemste verschil-stukken tusschen de leeraren van de gereformeerde kerk en die haer noemen leeraren van de Augsburgsche Belijdenis, ingesteld door- ---*, Leeuwarden 1679.

[34] Petrus Allinga, *Fax dissidii extincta seu exercitationes pacificae ad nonnullas quaestiones problematicas, quae hodie in Belgio potissimum moventur*, Amsterdam 1682, Preface.

Allinga insisted—otherwise all the horrible doctrines of the papist scholastics, whose philosophy was so highly esteemed by many Reformed divines, should also be reckoned among the sins of the church. Allinga only wanted to regard as followers of Cartesianism those who belonged to the Reformed church. Other Cartesians, he said, were irrelevant to the debate.[35]

It was the discussion between Allinga and Herman Witsius, caused by the latter's famous *Twist des Heeren met sijn wijngaert* (1669) that started the debate between the Cartesian theologians and the anti-Cartesians, in which the question of complete doubt played such a major part. In the tracts which appeared during this debate, and which led in their turn to fierce discussions with prominent Voetians such as Melchior Leydekker and Leonardus Rijssenius, Allinga defended the Cartesian method of doubt. As the first of ten "special examples of miraculous and strange novelties" Witsius advanced the proposition that man, in order to attain the truth, should raise doubts about anything, even about God's existence. As the second "strange novelty" he mentioned the proposition that "God might deceive if He wanted to". According to Witsius doubt was not only the suspension of judgement but also regarding matters as false until one was convinced of their truth. This might lead to the abominable conclusion that during this period of doubt we had denied God's existence.[36]

In his reply Allinga laid much stress on the interpretation of the term "dubitatio". In true Cartesian fashion he insisted that "dubitare" meant "to suspend judgement until we have found solid grounds for embracing the truth".[37] Interestingly enough—and more in the Cocceian tradition—he declared that he himself never used the term "dubitare" in order not to offend his Reformed brothers.[38] As he pointed out, however, all learned philosophers interpreted "dubitatio" as "suspension of judgement". He referred

---

[35] Petrus Allinga, *Verdeediging van de eer en leer der voornaamste leeraren van Nederland*, 1672, p. 229; *Seker oudt in waerheydt bevestight en in liefde gesuyvert van de kladde van aenstootelyk nieuw*, Amsterdam 1673, 20–21, 26.

[36] Herman Witsius, *Twist des Heeren met sijn wijngaert*, 1669. On Witsius, see J. van Genderen, *Herman Witsius. Bijdrage tot de kennis der gereformeerde theologie*, The Hague: De Bres, 1953.

[37] Allinga, *Verdeediging*, 15–17; *Seker oudt*, p. 17.

[38] Allinga, *Fax dissidii*, p. 5: "Non male ante anneos aliquot observavit prudentissimus Theologus cl. Coccejus, subtilissimum Cartesium infeliciter fuisse usum vocabulo *dubitationis* (. . .) Quamvis vocabulum illud nunqum meum fecerim, ne fratribus essem offensioni, malevolis occasioni detorquendi vocem innocuam, ac pacificis dolori, attamen de voce ea nonnulla dicam, ut palam fiat, quis sit verus hujus controversiae status".

to Frans Burman and Christophorus Wittichius who agreed with him; but they were not the only ones: Cocceius's son-in-law Willem Anslaar, who, under the pseudonym Philalethius Elieser, wrote an interesting tract on Cocceianism and Cartesianism, defended this view strongly.[39] Furthermore, Allinga emphasized that Descartes had made a distinction between "doubt" and "falsehood" and had certainly not equated those notions.[40]

As to the charge of scepticism, Allinga pointed out that Descartes had distinguished between "to doubt" and "to persist in doubt", the latter being utterly rejected by the French philosopher. The sceptics, Allinga insisted, did not search for the truth by suspending their judgement; on the contrary, they gave their assent to what they thought was true not on the basis of solid grounds, but rather loosely. This unfounded assent was the cause of sceptical doubt, an incurable fluctuation which tore the sceptical mind apart. Without a well-based assent there would be no true religiosity, no comfort and certainty for man's soul.[41]

According to Allinga, then, Cartesianism was a perfect means to combat scepticism and atheism. Among the most important causes of atheism was the fact that man did not search for the fundamental and evident proofs given by nature of the truth of God's existence from their childhood onwards. Atheism had free play if this truth was not embraced upon solid grounds but merely as some vague rumour heard from one's parents. Man should only assent to the truth of God's existence on solid grounds, suspending his judgement until he can see those grounds.[42] "What should we do in order to assent to a proposition?", Allinga asked. Was it enough for it to be true in itself, although we do not see it as such? Or should we give our assent because we see that it is true? The first view was nonsensical. If, however, the second proposition was correct, it meant that we should not assent to the truth of God's existence without good reason.[43] Allinga was convinced that those who did not embrace their religion after a thorough investigation of its fundamental truths would fall into atheism at its first blow. That was why the Cartesian method was so important: it showed the way to certitude.

---

[39] Philalethius Elieser, *Ontdeckinge van de quade trouw en 't onverstand van Irenaeus Philalethius in sijn bittere antwoord op de vrage: Wat is Cocceanerye?*, Amsterdam 1674, 10–11.

[40] Allinga, *Seker oudt*, p. 23.

[41] Allinga, *Seker oudt*, p. 27.

[42] Allinga, *Seker oudt*, 15–17.

[43] Allinga, *Seker oudt*, 18–19.

It was as a consequence of the Fall, Allinga maintained, that man raised doubts as to whether God existed. Due to his spiritual blindness he did not see the grounds of this truth as clearly and distinctly as he did before the Fall. Whoever saw those grounds clearly, could be in no doubt any longer. How might one save oneself from this doubt? By embracing the truth of God's existence without any reason? This would not cure doubts, but only feed them. Man could only be helped by searching for solid grounds in order to assent to the truth of God's existence with a sagacious judgement.[44]

To the Voetian charge that he and others taught men to doubt whether there is a God, Allinga replied that it was the Voetians who did that, since they denied that man possessed an innate idea of God and the concept of a perfect Being. Such doctrines led to doubt and atheism, Allinga declared.[45]

Universal doubt was thus one of the central issues advanced in the Cocceian-Voetian debate. The view that man had to raise doubts about God's existence was hotly debated by Dutch divines. Doubt about God's existence implied doubt about divine revelation, since that revelation presupposed the existence of a Revealer. This in its turn implied doubt about those revealed truths such as the Trinity, Christ's mediatorial function, and so on. All this, moreover, would lead to doubt about divine laws and prescriptions, finally undermining worship and piety.[46]

In one of his replies to Allinga, entitled *Het aenstootelijcke nieuw in waerheyt en liefde ontdeckt* ("Exceptionable Novelties in Truth and Love Discovered"), Witsius dealt extensively with doubt about God's existence. Quoting from Descartes' works he referred, like many Voetians, to the fact that this philosopher had dared to call doubt about God's existence pious and respectable. For Witsius it was clear that Descartes' doubt was to be equated with "being uncertain" and "persisting in doubt", despite the passage quoted by him in which Descartes rejected such an attitude. To doubt was not only "to suspend judgement", as Allinga insisted, but it was also "to be unsure about something" and "to consider anything as false so long as one is in doubt". If we could make a person believe that "dubitatio" meant "suspension of judgement", we might also

---

[44] Allinga, *Seker oudt*, p. 19.
[45] Allinga, *Seker oudt*, p. 29; cf. the Preface to his *Zedige verhandeling*.
[46] See, for example, Petrus van Mastricht, *Novitatum cartesianarum gangraena . . . seu theologia cartesiana detecta*, Amsterdam 1677, Preface.

teach men to eat hay. Or had the Cartesians not only invented a new philosophy but a new language as well . . .?[47] If "dubitare" really meant this, however, why not just say that we should not assent to important matters, let alone divine matters, without any good reason? In that case I would agree immediately and our conflict would be solved, Witsius declared.[48] Allinga replied that Witsius had hit the nail on the head: this was exactly what he meant by "dubitatio". He regarded Witsius's interpretation of the term as proof of the fact that he had sided with Allinga and his friends.[49] Witsius's remark indeed indicated a common ground on which Calvinist and Cartesian rationalism could meet.

Witsius wondered why Descartes so often emphasized that such doubt as he proposed might not be extended to matters of faith? Why all that talk about casting doubt upon matters evident to all? Don't think, reader, Witsius declared in an attempt to ridicule the frightening aspects of sceptical doubts, that those people doubt whether they have hands or feet, head or brains, and so on as a joke—no, they are quite serious about it. Maybe you will think it absurd that a sensible man say to himself "there are no human beings in the world, no bakers, no brewers, no bread, wine, ghosts, etc.; all I have seen, heard, felt, tasted, smelled up hitherto has only been a dream, fruits of my imagination, so I have to consider these things as false". Ridiculous as this might be, Witsius proceeded, it was not impious as long as we did not apply such doubt to God. However, Descartes had not hesitated to do exactly that, saying that as long as man was in doubt about God's existence he should regard this truth as false, as a mere fable, and assert that there is no God. Of course such propositions were detested by Witsius, who approvingly quoted Cocceius's words that it was never permissible, under any circumstances whatever, to doubt whether there is a God.[50]

A systematic treatment of universal doubt is given by one of Allinga's other opponents, the Voetian minister Leonardus Rijssenius in his tract *De oude rechtsinnige waerheyt verdonckert en bedeckt door Descartes, Coccejus, Wittich, Burman, Wolzogen, Perizon, Groenewegen, Allinga etc. en nu weder opgeheldert door Leonardus Rijssenius* ("The Old

[47] Herman Witsius, *Het aenstootelijcke nieuw in waerheyt en liefde ontdeckt*, Amsterdam 1673, 13–15, 18, 26, 27.

[48] Witsius, *Het aenstootelijcke nieuw*, p. 26.

[49] Allinga, *Seker oudt*, p. 29.

[50] Witsius, *Het aenstootelijcke nieuw*, 15–17, 25, also referring to Gassendi's critique on Descartes. Witsius quotes from Cocceius' *Summa Theologiae* c. 8, §25.

Orthodox Truth Darkened and Covered by Descartes etc. and Now Rediscovered by ----").[51] Rijssenius's method is first to give a Cartesian proposition and then his own reply to it. In the 42 propositions on doubt, which are to be found in the first chapter significantly entitled "Cartesian doubt paves the way to atheism", Rijssenius gives quotations from works by Descartes, Bassecour, Clauberg, Wittichius, Groenewegen, Burman, and above all Allinga.

The first proposition concerns the observation that he who seeks the truth should cast doubt upon anything once in his life. Rijssenius denies that the method of doubt is necessary to gain the truth: we can have sure knowledge about matters which we never call into question. Doubt is the opposite of faith: they have nothing to do with each other. Rijssenius also denies that we should be in doubt in order to clear our mind of any prejudices and false opinions: false opinions should certainly be rejected, but does this mean that we should reject everything? Should we also be in doubt about true opinions? Is this not rooting up the wheat with the tares (Matthew 13: 29)? The proposition that we should raise doubts in order to prevent errors is countered by the observation that if we are in doubt, we are in error.[52]

The major part of this chapter on Cartesian doubt is devoted to doubt about God's existence. Naturally Rijssenius denies that such doubt is permissible. Man does well if he believes that there is one God (James 2: 19), and badly if he questions it. Doubt can be equated with unbelief. He who is in doubt whether there is a God is without God and a Saviour during that time. (Eph. 2:12; 3:12, 17). Rijssenius is shocked by the proposition advanced by Burman and Allinga that we should embrace the truth of God's existence only on the most solid grounds. This is a flagrant attack on God's authority, for according to these theologians we are not allowed to say that there is a God on the basis of God's Word: they proclaim that we should first investigate whether God's Word is true. The Cartesian theologians who believe that such a truth might only be accepted because man sees a reason to do so imply, as Rijssenius points out, that children and simple folk who are unable to undertake such an investigation are not allowed to embrace the truth, and that they may not be told by others what to believe. Now this is

---

[51] For Leonardus Rijssenius (ca. 1636–ca. 1696), see *NNBW* 4, 1190; Cramer, *Heidanus*, pp. 128, 137–138; Thijssen-Schoute, *Nederlands cartesianisme*, pp. 40, 41, 447. In this tract, which is dedicated to the Grand Pensionary Gaspar Fagel, he counted 383 Cartesian and 176 Cocceian errors.

[52] Rijssenius, *De oude rechtsinnige waerheyt verdonckert*, pp. 1, 2.

sheer nonsense. Rijssenius declares, insisting that belief does not require any proofs from nature. Belief precedes all investigation. Finally, Allinga's suggestion that it is not permissible to be in doubt within the boundaries of the church but only where one seeks the truth, leads Rijssenius to declare that, if this were so, a philosopher or a doubter could not be a member of the church and that such people might be excommunicated. This was exactly what Rijssenius wanted: to have the Cocceian-Cartesian divines driven away from the Reformed church.[53]

As for the interpretation by Clauberg and Allinga of "dubitare" as suspension of judgement, Rijssenius insisted that even if to doubt might be explained in this way, it was still sinful, because it implied first lack of belief, and secondly that one did not have knowledge of God, which is a sin (1 Cor. 15: 34). Allinga himself had declared that man's doubts about God were the consequence of the Fall. Well then, they were sinful, Rijssenius concluded, adding that such a suspension of judgement also suspended the works of love, fear and obedience to God and thus turned man into a practical atheist.[54]

Rijssenius returned to an issue which was also advanced by Witsius and other anti-Cartesians about the equation of doubt and falsehood: if we considered the issue about which we doubted false during the time we doubt, the truth of God's existence might also be regarded as false during that period. How long could this doubt last? Wittichius, Groenewegen, and Allinga had replied: until we are fully assured. Rijssenius concluded that the Jews consequently did not sin when they did not embrace Jesus as their Saviour so long as they saw no reason for doing so. Allinga had declared that a Jew should not simply believe that Jesus was the true Messiah, but should suspend his judgement until he saw solid grounds for assenting to this truth. Rijssenius insisted, however, that during this suspension the Jews remained the property of the devil. This way of reasoning, he added, also implied that the Socinians did not sin when they did not accept the Trinity and the resurrection of the flesh and so on, and that they were not doomed for not accepting those truths.[55]

Rijssenius's attack on Allinga and other Cocceians and Cartesians was soon followed by assaults by Melchior Leydekker and

---

[53] Rijssenius, *De oude rechtsinnige waerheyt verdonckert*, 3–10.
[54] Rijssenius, *De oude rechtsinnige waerheyt verdonckert*, p. 4.
[55] Rijssenius, *De oude rechtsinnige waerheyt verdonckert*, pp. 5, 7. Allinga's remarks about the Jews and the suspension of judgement are repeated by Van Mastricht, who tells that he read these remarks filled with horror (see *Gangraena*, 32–33).

Voetius's successor, Petrus van Mastricht. Leydekker accused the "innovators" of "Scepticismus, Atheismus, Apostasia a fide Reformatae Ecclesiae".[56] Due to the influence of Cocceian theology and Cartesian philosophy the greatest mysteries of the faith had been so forged on the anvil of novelty as not to bear the faintest resemblance to the Confession of faith any more. Leydekker implored the States General to put an end to the spread of this cancer.[57] Allinga in his turn accused Leydekker of ignorance, since he did not seem to know that "dubitatio" was in itself an innocent word, which had always been used with caution by philosophers. Its meaning had been distorted by those who did not love the truth. To the inexpert it might mean an "ambigua fluctuatio mentis inter quaedam extrema", but to those "studiosi" who sought the truth, it meant a suspension of judgement and a close scrutiny of the truth.[58] Van Mastricht's *Novitatum Cartesianarum Gangraena . . . seu theologia cartesiana detecta* (despite its title a moderate and lucid, systematic treatment of Cartesian and Cocceian matters) started with an extensive attack on Cartesian doubt in which he advanced more or less the same arguments which had been put forward by his fellow Voetians.[59]

Thus the pattern set by Voetius to equate Cartesianism with atheism was enthusiastically upheld by his followers who, more than an earlier generation of anti-Cartesians, stressed the atheistic implications of Cartesian doubt.

CONCLUSION

The Cocceian-Voetian conflict offers an instructive insight into the reception of Cartesianism in the orthodox Calvinist world of the

---

[56] Melchior Leydekker, *Fax veritatis seu exercitationes ad nonnullas controversias, quae hodie in Belgio potissimum moventur, multa ex parte theologico-philosophicae. Praefixa est praefatio de statu Belgicae Ecclesiae et suffixa dissertatio de providentia Dei*, Leiden 1677. This tract is dedicated to William III. For Melchior Leydekker (1642–1721), see *NNBW* 4, 910–913; *BWPGN* 5, 775–785; Bizer, "Die reformierte Orthodoxie", 363–371; Scholder, *Ursprünge und Probleme*, pp. 141, note 39, 145; Thijssen-Schoute, *Nederlands cartesianisme*, 450–451. Leydekker regarded David Joris, Spinoza and Hobbes as the three impostors.

[57] See the preface to his *De verborgentheid des geloofs eenmaal den heiligen overgelevert*, Rotterdam 1709.

[58] Allinga, *Fax dissidii extincta*, pp. 5, 6.

[59] Petrus van Mastricht, *Novitatum Cartesianorum Gangraena*, Amsterdam 1677. This work is dedicated to William III. For Van Mastricht (1630–1706), see *NNBW* 10, cc. 591–592; Bizer, "Die reformierte Orthodoxie", 357–362; Scholder, *Ursprünge und Probleme*, pp. 46, note 56, 136, 141, 145. Thijssen-Schoute, *Nederlands cartesianisme*, pp. 450, 489.

early Enlightenment. By focusing on Cartesian doubt as one of the major issues in this debate, we can see how it made seventeenth- and eighteenth-century Calvinist divines acutely aware of the danger of irreligion. Both parties, Voetians as well as Cocceians, were deeply engaged in the struggle against irreligion. Each interpreted this phenomenon in their own way, however, and attempted to find a convincing means of defending Christianity. The Voetians feared that "Cartesian theology" as developed by the Cocceians would undermine Calvinist orthodoxy. Perhaps they saw the dangers of the sceptical challenge to orthodox theology more clearly than the Cocceians.

The Cocceians were convinced that the certainty offered by Cartesianism would reinforce the Christian religion and thus convince the atheists of the truth of Christianity. Uncertainty, caused by lack of independent investigation of fundamental religious truths, was seen by these divines as a major factor contributing to the growth of atheism. According to them the only way out of this crisis was to apply the Cartesian method of doubt to theology. They thus brought about a severe crisis within Calvinist orthodoxy itself, a crisis that changed the face of Dutch Reformed orthodoxy for good. By their attempt to create a synthesis between Calvinism and Cartesianism the Cocceians made a considerable contribution to the development of the rationalistic supranaturalism of the Calvinist Dutch Enlightenment. Besides Cartesianism the Cocceians provided another way out of the religious crisis of their day by developing a "prophetic theology". In this respect they can be seen as the Dutch representatives of international scholarly interest in the "studium propheticum" which captured so many minds in the age of the Enlightenment.

So when the French Calvinist Pierre Bayle emerged on the Dutch scene and prepared his *Dictionnaire historique et critique* there were vehement discussions going on among Dutch Calvinists about scepticism. It was this Cocceian-Voetian debate on Cartesianism (its bastard, Spinozism, included) that constituted a major part of the Dutch historical background against which Bayle's discussion of the subject must be seen.[60]

---

[60] Cf. Elisabeth Labrousse, *Pierre Bayle* II: *Héterodoxie et rigorisme*, The Hague: Nijhoff, 1964, ix–x; Jacob, "Hazard revisited", 260 f.

DAVID S. KATZ

ISAAC VOSSIUS AND THE ENGLISH BIBLICAL CRITICS 1670–1689

The English translation of Richard Simon's *Critical History of the Old Testament* was published in 1682, and carried a manufacturer's warning like any dangerous modern medicine:

> If notwithstanding what I have already said, there shall be any who, at the first sight, shall be scandaliz'd with this Author's free way of handling the Holy Scriptures, I give this caution to all such persons, either to let it alone and not concern themselves with it, or else to reade it clear through, by which time I doubt not but they will be satisfy'd of their too nice scruples.[1]

In a sense, much the same thing might have been said about the biblical criticism of Isaac Vossius (1618–1689), "of virtuous Father virtuous Son", as Milton could have put it.[2] Indeed, Vossius did more than most to undermine the sufficiency of the biblical text, the rock-bottom foundation of Protestantism in all its myriad varieties. After Vossius and Simon, it became increasingly difficult to accept that the biblical word might have miraculously escaped the misfortunes of all other ancient manuscripts which were being examined by scholars across Europe since the early days of the Renaissance. But as King Charles II remarked, Isaac Vossius would believe anything, if only it were not in the Bible.[3] Even his old friend Saint-Évremond recalled that he had "a foolish credulity in every thing extraordinary, fabulous, or exceeding belief".[4] Nevertheless, as we shall see, Vossius's very wide-ranging textual studies ironi-

---

[1] Richard Simon, *A Critical History of the Old Testament*, London 1682, sig. A2v. The French edn appeared in 1678.

[2] Milton, of course, was referring to Henry and Edward Lawrence, father and son.

[3] "Le Roi *Charles II* connoissoit bien son caractere; car l'entendant un jour debiter des choses incroyables de ce Pays [China], il se tourna vers quelques Seigneurs qui étoient avec lui & leur dit: *ce sçavant Theologien est un étrange homme, il croit tout hors la Bible*"; Jean-Pierre Nicéron, *Memoires pour servir a l'histoire des hommes illustres dans la republique des lettres*, Paris 1727–45, vol. 13, p. 133.

[4] Saint-Évremond to François, Maréchal de Créqui, [1671] in *The Works of*

cally in the long run would have the effect of strengthening the authority of the Bible, making him a pioneer of biblical criticism, while at the same time bringing him into conflict with English scholars who were as yet unwilling to have their faith tested by a cantankerous Dutchman who spent the last two decades of his life at Windsor.[5]

I

It is inevitable, and advantageous to the reputation of Isaac Vossius, that any discussion of his life must begin with an account of his father, G.J. Vossius (1577–1649), classical scholar, philologist, and theologian.[6] The elder Vossius was actually born near Heidelberg, but of Dutch parents, and became one of the key figures among that group of Dutch Arminians led by Grotius, who sought to escape the alternate extremes of the Reformation and the Counter-Reformation and to return to the conciliatory traditions of Erasmianism. These hopes were dashed at the Synod of Dordt (1618–19), which drove out all such liberalizing tendencies from Dutch Protestantism, and established predestination as the only official religious creed. Grotius himself, a great international hero, was imprisoned for life but soon escaped, and his friend Oldenbarnevelt, the leading political figure in the country, was executed on an absurd charge of treason.[7]

Monsieur de Saint-Evremond, 3 vols., ed. P. des Maizeaux, London 1728 (2nd edn.), vol. 2, p. 68. Cf. *Oeuvres de Monsieur de Saint-Evremond . . . avec la vie de l'auteur*, ed. P. des Maizeaux, Amsterdam 1726, p. 216.

[5] No full-scale biography of Isaac Vossius has been written. Meanwhile, see: Nicéron, *Memoires*, vol. 13, 127–44; Jaques George de Chaufepié, *Nouveau dictionnaire historique et critique*, Amsterdam & The Hague 1750–6, vol. 4, 614–31; *Gentlemans Magazine* 66: 2 (Sept. 1796), 717; Louis Moréri, *Le Grand dictionnaire historique*, (Paris, 1759), vol. 10, p. 705; Joannis Francisci Foppens, *Bibliotheca Belgica* Brussels 1739, vol. 2, 777–9; A.J. van der Aa, *Biographisch Woordenboek*, Haarlem 1852–1878, vol. 19, 416–18. For contemporary excerpts from his works, see Brit. Lib., Add. MS. 3861, fos. 19, 24, 30–48; and cf. Add. MS. 4933, fos. 24, 86; 4936, f. 141.

[6] Generally on G.J. Vossius and his family, see: Niceron, *Memoires*, vol. 13, 89–127; Foppens, *Bibliotheca Belgica*, and Aa, *Biographisch Woordenboek*; for entries on the entire family; M. Pattison, *Isaac Casaubon*, London 1892 (2nd edn.), p. 256, 339, 363, 397; C.S.M. Rademaker, *Life and Work of Gerardus Joannes Vossius (1577–1649)*, Assen: Van Gorcum, 1981.

[7] On Arminianism and the Synod of Dordt, see esp. N. Tyacke, *Anti-Calvinists*, Oxford: Clarendon, 1987, chap. 4; C. Bangs, *Arminius: A Study in the Dutch Reformation*, Nashville: Abingdon, 1971; idem, "Arminius and the Reformation", *Church History* 30 (1961); R.L. Colie, *Light and Enlightenment: A Study of the Cambridge Platonists and the Dutch Arminians*, Cambridge: Cambridge University Press, 1957;

It was Isaac Vossius's fate, then, to be born in the very year that
genuine religious dialogue became impossible in Holland. He and
his famous father stayed in England until 1633, when the religious
climate had changed sufficiently to allow the elder Vossius to be
appointed to the chair of history at the university of Amsterdam.
Isaac and his brothers (all of whom became scholars) were educated in part by their father, and in part by private tuition. It had
always been clear that Isaac would follow in his father's academic
footsteps, certainly from 1639 when at the age of twenty-one he
published an edition of the *Periplus*, a geographical description of
Asia and Africa attributed to Scylax of Caryanda, the Greek ex-
plorer in the service of King Darius of Persia who crossed the
Indian Ocean to the Red Sea. In his editing and translating into
Latin of a Greek manuscript about the East, Isaac Vossius emble-
matically pointed to his future work in the Republic of Letters. In
1642, Vossius made his obligatory journey to Rome, where despite
the numerous problems involved, he managed to begin the research
which would form the basis of his first major scholarly achievement, an edition of the epistles of St Ignatius.[8]

St Ignatius (c. 35-c. 107) was the bishop of Antioch, who en
route to Rome and the lions of the Colosseum wrote seven letters to
various churches which were the subject of academic dispute until
this century. The letters were published at the end of the fifteenth
century along with four spurious ones, but generally it may be said
that Catholic scholars championed the testimony of Ignatius as
being a useful near-apostolic support of the episcopal church, while
Protestants tended to reject the entire body of documents as false.[8]
In 1644, Archbishop James Ussher of Armagh attacked the problem from a new direction, and with remarkable detective work was
able to restore the letters to their original purity.[9] Two years later,

---

A.W. Harrison, *The Beginnings of Arminianism to the Synod of Dort*, London: London
University Press, 1926; idem, *Arminianism* London: Duckworth, 1937; R.T. Ken-
dall, *Calvin and English Calvinism to 1649*, Oxford: Oxford University Press, 1979;
P. White, "The Rise of Arminianism Reconsidered", *Past and Present* 101, (1983).

[8] Isaac Vossius, *Periplvs Scylacis Caryandensis, cum tralatione & castigationibus*,
Amsterdam 1639. Selden's copy (Bodl. Lib., 4° S 39 Art. Seld.) seems to have been
unread. On Vossius's journey to Rome: Y.H. Rogge, "De Reis van Isaac Vossius
(1641–1645)", *Oud-Holland* 18 (1900), 3–20. According to Richard Parr, *The Life of
. . . James Usher*, London 1686, p. 52, this work was done by "the learned Dr. *Is.
Vossius*, from the *Greek* Manuscript in the *Medicean* Library, which the Lord
Primate had some years before given him notice of, and also obtained the Great
Duke's leave to Copy it."

[9] See, generally, J.B. Lightfoot, *The Apostolic Fathers*, Part II, London: Macmillan, 1885. Also, M.P. Brown, *The Authentic Writings of Ignatius: A Study of Linguistic*

Isaac Vossius edited the Greek text of the letters, and helped reduce scholarly doubt about their authenticity, despite the inconvenient message contained therein.[10] Here too, as we shall see, Vossius's championship of an eccentric classical text with important religious meaning served as an omen of his later work.

Isaac Vossius's early contact with the celebrated Archbishop Ussher was hardly surprising, given his father's relationship with the Irish prelate. G.J. Vossius had in 1618, on the eve of the Synod of Dordt, published a history of Pelagianism in order to erode further the Calvinist emphasis on predestination. Ussher responded with a study of a ninth-century Benedictine martyr who challenged the Pelagians and promoted a sort of proto-predestinarianism. Ussher dedicated the work to the elder Vossius, and despite their theological differences tried to bring his academic adversary to Ireland to serve as his dean.[11] "He is stirring up a controversy with Vossius", wrote Grotius in February 1632, and Ussher's Calvinist supporters hoped that the archbishop might cause Vossius to think again.[12] Ussher even sent the Arminian Laud a copy of his work, knowing full well that the then bishop of London would be displeased with it. So when Isaac Vossius corresponded with his Father's old sparring partner, beginning in the late 1640s, he was carrying on a family tradition.[13]

But despite such prodigious beginnings, it was only when Isaac Vossius's star crossed with that of Queen Christina of Sweden that his career was made, and we need to look closely at Vossius's Swedish period in order to understand his English phase. The

---

Criteria, Durham, NC: Duke University Press, 1963; V. Corwin, *St. Ignatius and Christianity in Antioch*, New Haven: Yale University Press, 1960. See also, *Polycarpi et Ignatii Epistolae*, ed. John Ussher, London 1644.

[10] *Epistolae genuinae S. Ignatii martyris*, ed. Isaac Vossius, Amsterdam 1646.

[11] For relations between Ussher and G.J. Vossius see Sir Henry Bourchier to Ussher, 4 Dec. 1629: repr. James Ussher, *The Whole Works*, ed. C.R. Elrington, Dublin 1847–64, vol. 15, 454–5; William Laud, then bishop of London, to Ussher, 23 Feb. 1629–30: Ibid., 477–9; Ussher to Dr Samuel Ward, 15 Mar. 1629–30: Ibid., 480–3; Bourchier to Ussher, 21 Jan. 1629–30: Ibid., 461–2; Ward to Ussher, 16 May 1628; Ibid., 402–5. For actual correspondence between them, see Ussher to G.J. Vossius, 4 Jun. 1632: Ibid., 555–8; same to same, 13 Aug. 1647: Ibid., vol. 16, 96–7; same to same, 17 Apr. 1649; Ibid., p. 134; G.J. Vossius to Ussher, Jan. 1648: Ibid., 119–20. See also, C.R. Elrington, "The Life of James Ussher", in Ibid., vol. 1, 113, 123. Ussher's work, dedicated to G.J. Vossius, was *Gotteschalci, et Praedestinatianae Controversiae*, Dublin 1631, repr. Ibid., vol. 4, 1–233. Elrington notes (i. 123) that the "Life, like many of his other works, is given almost entirely in the language of others, the different extracts being merely connected together by a sentence or two."

[12] Ward to Ussher, 16 May 1628: Ibid., vol. 14, 402–5.

[13] Ussher to Isaac Vossius, 18/28 Feb. 1647–8: Ibid., vol. 16, p. 116; Isaac Vossius to Ussher, 5 Oct. 1650, from Stockholm: Ibid., 160–1.

decision of her slain father Gustavus Adolphus that Christina
would receive a prince's education had the unfortunate side effect of
causing her to despair that she would ever realize her ambitions in
cold and isolated Sweden. The end of the Thirty Years War,
however, seemed to promise a brighter future even in the distant
north. For at the end of 1648, the legendary treasures of the
Hradcany Palace in Prague began to arrive in Stockholm, having
been stolen for the queen by her victorious troops. Almost over-
night, Christina and her intellectual companions received an injec-
tion of almost six hundred paintings, sculptures, embroideries,
books, manuscripts, and scientific instruments. Unique medieval
manuscripts and Renaissance treasures mingled with gilt furniture
and luxurious Spanish leather in the bleak palaces and town houses
of the Swedish sovereign and her nobility.[14]

Chief among Christina's projects was the establishment of a first-
rate library in Sweden, and to this end she engaged Isaac Vossius.
He came to Stockholm in March 1649, aged thirty-one, and soon
succeeded Johannes Caspar Freinshemius in the task of arranging
the books and manuscripts liberated in the Thirty Years War, as
well as the specimens acquired more legitimately in the Low Countries and France. Isaac's more famous father G.J. Vossius died on
17 March, so Isaac had his nephew pack up the family books and
send the entire lot to Sweden. The books were shipped out of the
Low Countries on 17 August 1649, on the very same boat that
carried Descartes himself to Queen Christina. Descartes would
succumb within six months to the effects of early-morning philosophical tutorials in the queen's icy library, but the Vossius family
books remained, and formed the nucleus of the royal collection.
Apart from producing a proper catalogue, Isaac Vossius had the
opportunity of working closely with his friend Nicholas Heinsius,
who had been brought to Stockholm on his recommendation during the autumn of 1649. Nicholas, like his better-known father
Daniel, was a Dutch classical philologist, and one of the top Latin-
ists of his age. Heinsius the younger became Vossius's roving
literary purchaser, journeying through Europe in search of worthy

---

[14] Christina still awaits a comprehensive biography in English. In any case, all
biographies must be based on the massive collection of documents in the work of
four folio volumes by C. Arckenholtz, *Memoires concernant Christine, reine de Suede*,
4 vols., Amsterdam; Leipzig 1751–50. Meanwhile, see Sven Stolpe, *Christina of
Sweden*, London, 1966, G. Masson, *Queen Christina*, London: Secker and Warburg,
1968, and S. Åkerman, *Queen Christina of Sweden and her Circle. The Transformation of a
Seventeenth-Century Philosophical Libertine*, Leiden: Brill, 1991.

additions to the royal library, carrying with him Christina's promise of a virtually limitless budget.[15]

It was during Vossius's tenure as Swedish royal librarian that Menasseh ben Israel attempted to join the growing band of international scholars that catered to the intellectual tastes of the young queen. Between 10 January 1651 and 8 February 1655, Menasseh wrote four letters that we know of to Isaac Vossius in the hope of being asked to join the team.[16] At first, Menasseh suggested that he might serve as a procurer of Hebrew books. This plan soon escalated to become a project for the publication of an entire collection of Hebrew and Jewish texts, so that Menasseh's utopian *Bibliotheca Rabbinica* could be used for the catalogue. By the beginning of 1652, Menasseh had already sent a sweetener of choice Hebrew volumes, for which he had not yet been paid, but now was asking his friend Vossius to obtain an appointment for him as the Jewish counterpart of Heinsius: "I have the idea of seeing Germany and Italy, and of going even to Venice", Menasseh wrote,

---

[15] R. Stephan, "A Note on Christina and her Academies", in *Queen Christina of Sweden: Documents and Studies*, ed. M. von Platen, Stockholm: Nationalmusei skriftserie, 1966, 365–71; C. Callmer, "Queen Christina's Library of Printed Books in Rome", in Ibid., 59–73; C. Elton, "Christina of Sweden and Her Books", *Bibliographica* 1 (1895), 5–30; Masson, *Christina*, 111–12, 127–32. See Vossius's letters to Heinsius, 1650–63: Brit. Lib., Add. MS. 5158.

[16] All four letters were originally in the collection of the Remonstrants' Library in Amsterdam but are now deposited at the University of Amsterdam: Menasseh ben Israel to Isaac Vossius (at Stockholm), 10 Jan. 1651: Amsterdam Univ. Lib., MS III E 9[31]: cf. the copy in Leiden Univ. Lib., Bur F 11 (I. 250[r-v]); same to same (addressed to Stockholm), 10 Mar. 1651: Adam. Univ. Lib., MS III E 9[37]: Leiden copy, Bur F 11 (I. 254–5); same to same (addressed to Stockholm, and sporting the remnant of Menasseh's wax seal), 2 Feb. 1652: Adam. Univ. Lib., MS III E 9[76]: Leiden copy Bur F 11 ((I. 292[v]); same to same (addressed to Brussels, "en casa de su Magestad la Reyna de Suedia"), 8 Feb. 1655: Adam. Univ. Lib., MS III E 9[193]: Leiden copy Bur F 11 (I. 362[v]). A Dutch trans. of the full text of the first two letters was published by J.M. Hillesum in *Amsterdamsch Jaarboekje* 2 (1899), 46–52; and the Spanish text of the second two letters was printed with a French translation by Cardozo de Bethencourt in *Revue des Etudes Juives* 49 (1904), 106–8, including a detailed summary of the letters printed by Hillesum. Interestingly, a MS. note on the Leiden copy testifies that these four letters from Menasseh to Vossius were seen by Prof. Dr. H.J. Schoeps in April 1951, but he does not seem to have published the texts. Although Menasseh claimed to have been a prolific letter writer, only seven further letters of his survive. Generally, see D.S. Katz, "Menasseh ben Israel's Mission to Queen Christina of Sweden, 1651–1655", *Jewish Social Studies* 45 (1983), 57–72, and the sources cited therein; and on the letters themselves, see A.K. Offenberg, "Some Remarks Regarding Six Autograph Letters by Menasseh ben Israel in the Amsterdam University Library", in *Menasseh ben Israel and his World*, eds. Y. Kaplan, H. Méchoulan, R.H. Popkin, Leiden: Brill, 1989, pp. 191–8.

so that the work will not be incomplete, and to become acquainted with more books. Consequently, I would value some sort of commission from her Most Serene Queen, in order to buy rarities for her that I will be able to obtain for her at a good price. With the favor that you have always shown me, I am asking you to recommend me to Her Majesty, may God protect her.[17]

Unfortunately for Menasseh and Vossius both, by the time Menasseh was hatching these grandiose plans, something had gone seriously wrong at the Swedish court. Isaac Vossius had fallen into disfavour for some reason, apparently because he crossed the leading foreign scholar in Christina's service, Claude de Saumaise. Vossius obtained leave in January 1652 to visit his family in the Netherlands, but this was only a face-saving device designed to allow him to withdraw from the court with a measure of dignity. The queen's library was left without a proper supervisor, although Samuel Bochart, the famous Orientalist and Hebraist, helped to fill the gap to some degree. One of Bochart's jobs was to work with the Oriental manuscripts that Christina had bought from Cardinal Mazarin's library when it was dispersed during the Frondes. Indeed, the disturbances in France soon brought Mazarin's librarian, Gabriel Naudé, to Sweden as Vossius's successor in September 1652 at three thousand rixdollars per annum. Naudé was probably the foremost librarian of his generation, so the loss of Vossius was not as great as it might have been for Christina's collection. For Vossius, the fall from grace meant the end of one employment and the beginning of another.[18]

But not quite. For although Vossius left Sweden, he remained in contact with the other scholars he left behind, and through them with the queen as well, which leads one to suspect that his withdrawal from Saumaise was tactical rather than emotional. Gabriel Naudé, Christina's new librarian, also left Sweden, in June 1653, in the company of Pierre-Hector Chanut, Louis XIV's representative at the Swedish court; Bochart; and a young man named Pierre-Daniel Huet, classicist and Hebraist, later bishop of Avranches. Huet had come to Sweden with Bochart in order to study a rare manuscript of Origen, and now on his return home with that distinguished company, stopped over in Amsterdam, where the entire party, fortified by Isaac Vossius and David Blondel the French Protestant

---

[17] Menasseh to Vossius, 2 Feb. 1652: my translation.
[18] Nicéron, *Memoires*, vol. 13, 135–6; D.J.H. Ter Horst, *Isaac Vossius en Salmasius: Eeen episode uit de 17de-eeuwsche geleerdengeschiedenis*, The Hague: Nijhoff, 1938.

theologian, paid a visit to the synagogue of Menasseh ben Israel to see the Jews at prayer. Huet described the events of that evening at length, and for Naudé it must have been one of his last memories, for he died en route to France on 4 August 1653.[19]

Vossius, meanwhile, seems to have been restored to Christina's favour, and was soon making preparations to return to her service in Sweden. By now the Swedish queen had made up her mind to abdicate, and she needed Vossius and Heinsius to help her decide which books and manuscripts she would take to accompany her on her long exile. The situation was dire. In November 1652, Bochart had written an exasperated and heartfelt letter to ex-royal librarian Isaac Vossius describing what he had had to put up with:

> J'avois travaillé plus de deux mois depuis le grant matin jusqu'au soir tout tard a ranger la bibliotheque. Et elle estoit en fort bon ordre quant M. Naudé arriva. Mais la Reine ayant eu affaire des chambres qu'elle occupoit, on la remeslee tout d'un coup et mis tous les livres l'un sur l'autre en une grand' chambre. Et quand on a affaire d'un livre, il le faut chercher quatres jours.[20]

In other words, in order to find accommodation for a number of her ladies, Queen Christina destroyed the entire order of her library that had been in progress of organization for a long time. Vossius at this moment was trying to retrieve his own books from the disorder, and even though he himself returned to Sweden in August 1653 and could supervise the search personally, nevertheless he was forced to receive other works in compensation, and shipped them back to Amsterdam in the spring of the following year.[21]

The situation at court during that autumn was very confused while Christina made preparations for her departure. The queen gave Vossius specific instructions regarding which books to include in his special list. Heinsius arrived in October, but for some reason was denied admission to her library and thus did not play any part in the selection of the exiled books. Christina herself abdicated on 6 June 1654 in the Great Hall of Uppsala Castle, and after some romantic adventures arrived by 3 July in Hamburg. Her stay there was short: she reached Antwerp by 5 August, and Vossius met her there eleven days later. Christina's selection of books followed at

---

[19] Katz, "Christina", 63–4. For more on David Blondel, see Nicéron, *Memoires*, vol. 13, 49–54.

[20] Bochart to Vossius, 2 Nov. 1652: Amsterdam Univ. Lib., III E 9, No. 122; same to same, 1 Feb. 1653, No. 140; same to same, 24 Nov. 1652, No. 126.

[21] E.F. Blok, *Contributions to the History of Isaac Vossius's Library*, Amsterdam: North-Holland Publishing, 1974, 20–6.

the end of the year, and were arranged in the upper gallery of the
Antwerp Bourse, which had been reserved for this purpose. Here
Vossius worked on the inventory of the royal library which would
become known as the Antwerp Catalogue, including about 5,200
printed books and 650 manuscripts. Just as the books were beginning to arrive in Antwerp, however, Christina's affairs carried her
to Brussels, where she stayed for about nine months until 22
September 1655 when she left for Rome, arriving there at the end of
December.[22]

By the beginning of 1656, then, the Swedish episode in Isaac
Vossius's life had come to a close. Vossius said his goodbyes to
Christina in Brussels, and when she went off to Rome, he travelled
to the Hague. Between February and May 1656 he sorted out the
collection of books which Christina had given him in compensation
for the irretrievable assimilation of his own library with hers.
Heinsius had written to him earlier to say that the rumour had it in
Stockholm that Vossius had plundered the royal library. Vossius
replied indignantly that the collection he had gained was far inferior to that which he had lost, and that he would soon be publishing an inventory from which the public could judge the real
situation for themselves. What Vossius did not say was that this
so-called inventory would be in actual fact an auction catalogue,
and that he would be selling off an overflow of 2500 books that he
did not require. Since his own library was based on the nucleus of
his father's books, Isaac Vossius hit on the commercial idea of
selling the volumes as "Librorum Gerardi Ioannis Vossii". In a
sense, then, Isaac Vossius sold his father's library twice: to Queen
Christina for 20,000 guilders in 1649, and to the general public on
4 October 1656 in a public auction.[23]

II

Vossius, then, had not only succeeded in ending his commercial
association with Queen Christina without taking a loss—a rare

---

[22] Katz, "Christina", 64–5. Cf. the catalogue Vossius made of Christina's
MSS. in 1650–1: *Catalogus Codicum Manu Scriptorum Bibliothecae Regiae Holmien-
sis*, ed. C. Callmer, Stockholm: Panorstedt-Söner, 1971 (*Acta Bibliothecæ Regiæ
Stockholmiensis* 11).
[23] Blok, *Contributions*, passim. Five copies of the auction catalogue have survived: 1) Netherlands Book Trade Assoc., Amsterdam (Nv 4a); 2) Royal Library,
The Hague (234 F. 30[5]); 3) Royal Library, Copenhagen (79[II] 39[IV]), which has
many prices entered in by hand; 4) Amiens; 5) All Souls College, Oxford.

turn of fortune, as Menasseh ben Israel discovered to his dismay—
but as things worked out, without remaining at loose ends. Vossius
now turned once again to academic controversy, and sought to
carry on the work of Archbishop Ussher, who died in 1656.
Ussher's greatest achievement was to have improved the system of
chronology devised by Scaliger, the inventor of the "Julian
Period", a cycle of 7980 years within which no day was in exactly
the same position according to three parallel systems of measure-
ment: the solar cycle of nineteen years, the lunar cycle of twenty-
eight years, and the Roman civil cycle of fifteen years. Scaliger had
managed to bridge the gap between recorded history and the Old
Testament, and thereby to calculate the day of Creation as Sunday,
25 October 3950 BC. Ussher, however, pointed out that Scaliger
had missed the crucial fact that Terah was twice married and that
Abraham's mother was his *second* wife. Furthermore, even assuming
that the sun readjusted itself after standing still for Joshua and
moving backwards for Hezekiah, recalculating the entire calendar
pushed the date of Creation back to 4004 BC: Sunday, 23 October,
to be precise. Scaliger, Ussher complained to his friend John Selden, "intending higher matters, did not heed so much his ordinary
arithmetic".[24]

The systems of Ussher and Scaliger were marvels of exactitude
which enabled the Christian world to assimilate the histories of the
gentile nations to the biblical plan, and to provide a comforting
framework within which to accommodate all known historical
facts. Ussher pinpointed not only the Creation, but all other key
dates, such as the Flood (2349 BC), and the Exodus (1492 BC).
Gibbon described the effect that the study of chronology had on his
schoolboy mind:

> from Strauchius I imbibed the elements of chronology: the tables of
> Helvicus and Anderson, the annals of Usher and Prideaux distin-
> guished the connection of events, and I engraved the multitude of
> names and dates in a clear and indelible series. But in the discussion
> of the first ages I overleaped the bounds of modesty and use. In my
> childish balance I presumed to weigh the systems of Scaliger and
> Petavius, of Marsham and Newton, which I could seldom study in

---

[24] Ussher to Selden, 2 Nov. 1627: Ussher, *Works*, vol. 15, 383–4. On chronology
generally, see A.T. Grafton, "Joseph Scaliger and Historical Chronology: The
Rise and Fall of a Discipline", *History and Theory* 14 (1975), 156–85; idem, "Scaliger's Chronology", *Journal of the Warburg and Courtauld Institutes* 48 (1985), H.
Trevor-Roper, "James Ussher, Archbishop of Armagh", in his *Catholics, Anglicans
and Puritans*, London: Secker and Warburg, 1987, chap. 3; F.E. Manuel, *Isaac
Newton, Historian*, Cambridge, Mass.: Harvard University Press, chaps. 2–5.

the originals; the dynasties of Assyria and Egypt were my top and cricket-ball; and my sleep has been disturbed by the difficulty of reconciling the Septuagint with the Hebrew computation.[25]

Even more recently, Professor Hugh Trevor-Roper described the pleasure he had as a boy derived from the labours of Archbishop Ussher:

> When I was a child I was taken regularly, on Sundays, to our local parish church, from whose formal proceedings I fear that my attention was inclined to wander. Happily, it found a rival attraction still within the holy circle of orthodoxy. The prayer books supplied in the pews contained a series of tables which, I now realize, came ultimately from the Archbishop: tables of fascinating complexity which enabled the reader to work out, via the Epact and the Golden Year, the date of Easter in any year, past or future. I never discovered what the Epact and the Golden Year were, but many a mechanical litany, many a dull sermon, formed a comfortable continuo while I conjured with these fascinating tables, checking that they worked and applying them to random years in the past and the future.[26]

Both Gibbon in the eighteenth century and Dacre two hundred years later give us a sense of the comforting quality in chronology whose claims brought strength to the faith of the devout Christian and fascinated even the doubting near non-believer. The problem, however, with an exact science is that one needs to be exact: even the differences between Scaliger and Ussher, so much in agreement about the generalities, would in the long run undermine the whole. As Paul Hazard pointed out fifty years ago, when the chronologists finished their task, and concluded their hair-splitting arguments, "they will have sown more seeds of unrest in quiet minds, and done more to undermine faith in history, than all your open scoffers and anti-religious fanatics ever succeeded in doing."[27] Paradoxically, the reason for this was the very fact that they were believers rather than sceptics. It was into this world of metaphysical accounts that Isaac Vossius cast his net.

One of the main problems faced by the chronologists was the reconciliation of the traditional Masoretic Hebrew version of Scripture with the Septuagint, the translation produced by Greek-speaking Egyptian Jews for their own use between the third and

---

[25] Edward Gibbon, *Memoirs of My Life*, Harmondsworth: Penguin, 1984, 72–3.
[26] Trevor-Roper, "Ussher", p. 159.
[27] P. Hazard, *The European Mind, 1680–1715*, transl. J. Lewis May, Harmondsworth: Penguin, 1973 (1st French edn. 1935), p. 60.

first centuries BC. Apart from the Septuagint's celebrated translation of the Hebrew עַלְמָה ("young woman") as "virgin" in the
key prophetic passage in Isaiah 7, 14, most of the differences
between the Hebrew and the Greek are textual. For chronologists,
however, it meant a world of difference which text was to form the
basis of calculation, since in the Septuagint the lives of the Patriarchs are longer, and in general and in toto, budgeted a further
fifteen centuries, and thereby increased the length of world history
by over 37-per cent. In this manner, the rival chronological claims
of the ancient Egyptians, for example, could be accommodated
with relative ease. This radical change of calendar was one of the
factors that attracted Isaac Vossius to the Greek text, and in 1659
he published his first really controversial work, defending the Septuagint scheme against the more acceptable Masoretic Hebrew
framework.[28]

Reaction to Vossius's dabbling in chronology was fierce, and
largely negative. Most significantly, apart from the arithmetical
wranglings of the participants, the most serious accusation against
Vossius was that he was a sort of chronological fifth columnist
trying to undermine the field rather than contribute to it. Even at
the end of the century, this is how he would be remembered: John
Milner, the non-juring fellow of St John's College, Cambridge, was
"tempted to question whether *Vossius* consulted the Arch-Bishop,
thõ he pretends to confute him".[29] Similarly, Samuel Bochart, the
Huguenot philologist, wrote to Vossius, laying stress not on the
mathematics of chronology, but on the various alternative sources
of the text which might throw light on the truth of the word of
God.[30]

Certainly there was a sense that in basing his chronology on the
Septuagint rather than on the Hebrew Bible, Vossius was moving
the goal-posts in an unsportsmanlike manner. Vossius himself
found it necessary to reply to his critics in a further work on the
subject published the following year, which in turn provoked a
number of responses. After Vossius, a number of other more
orthodox scholars would also adopt the Septuagint. In 1687, the

---

[28] Trevor-Roper, "Ussher", 156–61; Grafton, "Joseph Scaliger", 181–5.
[29] John Milner, *A Defence of Arch-Bishop Usher against . . . Dr Isaac Vossius*, Cambridge 1694, 32–4, 99, 115. Cf. Anthony Wood, *Athenae Oxonienses*, ed. P. Bliss,
Oxford 1813–20, vol. 4, p. 244.
[30] Bochart to Vossius, 10 July 1659: repr. Chaufepié, *Nouveau dictionnaire*, vol. 4,
623–4n.

Cistercian monk Paul Pezron would argue in favour of the Septuagint system,[31] as would the great Bossuet.[32] Vossius published
two further works on chronology during the 1660s, but by then he
had already expanded his interests to take in some of the wider
implications of his subject.

III

There is a temptation to see Vossius's life in the 1660s as a prelude
to his invitation to come to England at the end of the decade. One
can easily see the transition from one sphere of interest to another.
Queen Christina continued to stay in correspondence with Isaac
Vossius during the 'sixties, but the letters are inconsequential and
somewhat formal.[33] At the same time, his fame was spreading to
England in such a way that he was becoming more of a living
personality rather than a literary abstraction. John Evelyn the
celebrated diarist wrote an impassioned letter to Lord Chancellor
Clarendon on 27 November 1666 using Isaac Vossius as an example of the sort of scholar who by his very excellence was causing a
drain on the English economy. Evelyn wanted Clarendon to encourage the production of "immaculate copies of such books as,
being vended in great proportions, do, for want of good editions
amongst us, export extraordinary sums of money, to our no less
detriment than shame." Evelyn noted that it was "about thirty
years since Justin was corrected by Isaac Vossius, in many hun-
dreds of places most material to sense and elegancy; and has since
been frequently reprinted in Holland after the purer copy, but with
us, still according to the old reading".[34] At the same time, Vossius
stayed in touch with the world of francophone scholars, and spent
a considerable portion of the early 'sixties in Paris and Geneva.
Indeed, in 1663 Vossius received through Colbert a gift from Louis

---

[31] Isaac Vossius, *De Septuaginta Interpretibus*, The Hague 1661–3; cf. seventeenth-
or eighteenth-century notes on this work, now Brit. Lib., Add. MS. 4238, fos.
70–2; 4365, f. 186. Paul Pezron, *L'Antiquite des temps retablie*, 1687; Hazard, *European
Mind*, p. 62, 246–7. Moréri writes in his *Dictionnaire* that Vossius "avoit promis une
novelle édition des Septantes qu'il n'a point donnée".
[32] Cf. Hazard, *European Mind*, p. 62, 246–7.
[33] Christina to Vossius, 3 Nov. 1666, from Hamburg: Leiden Univ. Lib., BPL
1886; same to same, 30 Aug. 1667: Ibid.; same to same, 31 Dec. 1661, from
Hamburg: Amsterdam Univ. Lib., 103 C 4.
[34] John Evelyn to Clarendon, 27 Nov. 1666: *Diary and Correspondence*, ed.
W. Bray, London 1883 (new edn.), vol. 3, 189–90.

XIV, which may be some indication of his status in that world.[35]

But when Isaac Vossius became personally acquainted with Saint-Évremond, he reached a new plane of celebration. Charles de Saint-Évremond, the famous sceptic, soldier, poet and man of society who was buried in Westminster Abbey, had made contact early in life with the Great Condé, and fought for him in the Thirty Years War in the 1640s, just as he would serve Mazarin in the following decade. All the while he was active in literary society, writing essays, poems, and satires, which alternately won him praise and disgrace at the hands of his patrons. One of these works indeed brought an end to his career in France. In 1659 he accompanied Mazarin on the diplomatic mission which resulted in the Peace of the Pyrenees with Spain, and he secretly and bitterly reported on the meetings to the marquis de Créqui, the manuscript of which eventually fell into Colbert's hands. By the end of 1661, Saint-Évremond was in Holland, having fled France and certain imprisonment. Earlier that year he had paid a visit to England as part of the delegation sent to congratulate Charles II after the Restoration, and now returned there to universal celebration among the smart set, including Hobbes, Abraham Cowley, and Edmund Waller, the fact that he never learned English not being any obstacle at all. Saint-Évremond returned to the Continent between 1664 and 1670, living in Holland and hoping for a reprieve to come to Paris. But by then it was clear to him that his popularity was highest in London, and when Sir William Temple, the English ambassador at the Hague, invited him in the name of Lord Arlington to return, he accepted with alacrity, and received a royal pension of three hundred pounds per annum as well.[36]

While living in the Netherlands in the later 1660s, records his contemporary biographer Pierre Desmaizeaux, "M. de St. Evremond took likewise a pleasure in visiting some Learned Men, and celebrated Philosophers, who were then at the Hague, particularly Messieurs Heinsius, Vossius, and Spinoza."[37] Saint-Évremond's opinion of Isaac Vossius was very high. In 1668, Saint-Évremond wrote to the marquis de Lionne, one of the negotiators of the Treaty

---

[35] Nicéron, *Memoires*, vol. 13, p. 128.

[36] See generally W.M. Daniels, *Saint-Évremond en Angleterre*, Versailles: thèse Paris, 1907; Q.M. Hope, *Saint-Evremond: The Honnête Homme as Critic*, Bloomington: Indiana University Press, 1962.

[37] *The Works of Monsieur de Saint-Evremond*, ed., P. Desmaizeaux, vol. 1, lvi–lvii. Desmaizeaux includes here Saint-Évremond's description of Spinoza, and a reference to Stouppe's testimony of Spinoza's pantheism.

of the Pyrenees, "transmitting to you the Pieces that are now transcribing. I address one of them to Monsieur Vossius, my literary friend, and with whom there's more to be learn'd, than with any man I ever saw in my life." The reference was to Saint-Évremond's *Observations on Sallust and Tacitus* which was dedicated in the title itself "To Monsieur Vossius". In this same letter, Saint-Évremond excitedly reported that "I am just now going to receive a Visit from Monsieur Vossius, to whom I shall talk of the War in Flanders."[38] So too in a letter to Corneille, another member of the Condé set, Saint-Évremond cited "Monsieur Vossius, the greatest Admirer of Greece, who cannot bear the least comparison between the Grecians and the Latins, does yet prefer you before Sophocles and Euripides." (One wonders the purpose of such grotesque flattery.)[39] Saint-Évremond praised Vossius to Anne d'Hervart, son of a high French official, and protector of La Fontaine, yet another Condé protégé. Saint-Évremond told an amusing story about a debate between Jean Claude the Huguenot and Antoine Arnauld the Jansenist, whose book *La Perpétuité de la Foi* he intended to present to Vossius: "he is an admirer of Monsieur *Claude*", Saint-Évremond noted, "although he thinks that he should have confined himself to the first four centuries".[40]

Yet the most telling letter of all was Saint-Évremond's in 1671 to François, maréchal de Créqui, the celebrated general to whom was confided that devastating evaluation of the Treaty of the Pyrenees in 1659. By now both Saint-Évremond and Isaac Vossius were living in England, and the French libertine had the leisure for reflecting on the character of the Dutchman he had known for a number of years: "I have convers'd with a Man of the brightest natural parts in the world", he wrote,

> who being sometimes weary of the happy facility of his Genius, engag'd in arguments of Science and Religion, in which he betray'd a ridiculous ignorance. I know one of the most learned men in Europe, of whom one may learn a thousand things, curious or profound; in whom, nevertheless, you will find a foolish credulity in every thing extraordinary, fabulous, or exceeding belief.

---

[38] Saint-Évremond to Hugues, marquis de Lionne [1668]: Ibid., vol. 1, 220–1. The *Observations* are printed in vol. 1, 224–32. For further notes on these letters, see *The Letters of Saint Evremond*, ed. J. Hayward, London: Routledge, 1930.

[39] Saint-Évremond to Pierre Corneille [1668]: *Works*, ed. Desmaizeaux, vol. 2, p. 29.

[40] Saint-Évremond to Monsieur Anne d'Hervart, 24 Mar. [1669]: *Letters*, ed. Hayward, 88–90: not in Desmaizeaux's edition.

Who the first man described is, is not known; but it is enlightening that Saint-Évremond should chose to group them together, Vossius and the ignorant genius. Indeed, so as not to cause any confusion whatsoever, Desmaizeaux provided a footnote after the word "Europe", revealing the learned man as "Dr. Isaac Vossius".[41]

So when Isaac Vossius arrived in England in 1670, he found congenial if not entirely uncritical companionship waiting for him in the form of the notorious Saint-Évremond. Vossius spent the remaining nineteen years of his life in his company, as the two foreigners regaled an excited English intellectual public with Continental wisdom. Vossius came to England as the protégé of John Pearson, defender of St Ignatius and his letters, master of Trinity and later bishop of Chester.[42] King Charles II himself was said to have greeted him on his arrival, and presented him to a prebend in the royal chapel of Windsor.[43] Isaac Vossius, like his father during Charles I's reign, also found Anglicanism to be an agreeable *via media* very convenient for a man with no fixed religious address. Oxford in return showered Isaac Vossius with honours, "after he had been with great humanity and friendship entertained by some of the chief heads of colleges, as his father had been before, in 1629", and created him D.C.L. on 16 September 1670.[44]

A sense of Vossius's reception in English society can be gleaned from his appearance in the diary of John Evelyn, who as we have seen had already praised the Dutchman a number of years before. "I dind at my L: *Arlingtons*", recorded Evelyn on 16 March 1673,

---

[41] Saint-Évremond to François, mareschal de Créqui [1671]: *Works*, ed. Desmaizeaux, vol. 2, p. 68.

[42] *Dict. Nat. Biog.* Pearson shared with Vossius the championship of the authenticity of the Eusebian epistles of Ignatius, and the opposition to Saumaise, who had denied them. Vossius also did the appendix for Pearson's vindication of Ignatius, published at Cambridge in 1672: *Vindiciæ*, Oxford 1852, ii. 489, 620 ff. See also Vossius to Sir E. Sherburne, 1670 (Latin copy): Brit. Lib., MS. App. 72, f. 5; same to same, 26 Jan. 1670: Brit. Lib., Add. MS. 6487, f. 5.

[43] *Dict. Nat. Biog.* Vossius to Charles II (copy), n.d.: Amsterdam Univ. Lib.: copy in Uppsala Univ. Lib., Nordstrom Collection. Vossius was installed on 12 May 1673, in place of Thomas Viner: "Mandamus for Isaac Vossius, D.C.L. on death of Thomas Vyner, D.D. 25 April 1673.": *The Manuscripts of St George's Chapel, Windsor Castle*, ed. J.N. Dalton, Windsor 1957, p. 79; John Le Neve, *Fasti Ecclesiae Anglicanae*, London 1716, p. 387; J. Pote, *The History and Antiquities of Windsor Castle*, Eton 1749, p. 413; Anthony Wood, *Fasti Oxonienses*, ed. P. Bliss, London 1815–20 (3rd edn.), vol. 2, 190, 323. Vossius was well acquainted there with the Royalist theologian Thomas Browne, also a canon of Windsor, since 1639: Vossius was his sole executor, and provided Browne at his own expense with a fine gravestone and a Latin inscription: Wood, *Athenae*, vol. 3, 1003–4, and see n. 57 below.

[44] Wood, *Fasti*, vol. 2, 323. The future William III came to Oxford to receive the same honour on 20 Dec. 1670.

"with the *Duke*, & *Dutchesse* of *Monmoth* who is certainly one of the wisest & craftiest of her sex; she has much witt: here was likewise the learned *Isaac Vossius*".[45] That Vossius should have been invited to dine with Arlington was surely no surprise: it was Arlington who had brought him to England, and (after dinner) Vossius published a work on poetry and music dedicated to his host.[46] Exactly two years later, Evelyn noted a meeting of the Royal Society, "where was read a paper from Monsieur *Isa: Vossius* concerning an appearance in ☾, & *Archimedes's Speculum Ustorium*:" In fact, two separate discourses by Isaac Vossius were read on that day's meeting, one indeed about the legendary burning glass of Archimedes, and the other covering the spots observed on the moon's surface.[47] In October of that same year, on his birthday, Evelyn met Vossius at the home of the Lord Chamberlain, in a splendid dinner to which were invited "divers persons of quality", including the earls of Northampton (constable of the Tower) and Westmorland, not to mention the envoy extraordinary of the Elector Palatine.[48] Similarly, in April 1676, Evelyn supped at the home of John Dolben, "*Bish: of Rochesters* with *Isa: Vossius*".[49]

But despite these conquests of court society, it was only when the duchess of Mazarin came to London at the end of 1675 that Isaac Vossius really rediscovered the sort of intellectual centre that he had found in the company of Queen Christina and the circle of the prince of Condé. The duchess was the niece of the cardinal, and her presence in London was not unconnected with the fact that King

---

[45] John Evelyn, *Diary*, ed. E.S. de Beer, Oxford: Oxford University Press, 1955, vol. 4, p. 6: entry for 16 Mar. 1673. N.B. that it was Lord Arlington who invited Saint-Évremond to England as well.

[46] [Isaac Vossius], *De Poematum cantu et viribus rythmi*, Oxford 1673. Cf. response by Roger North in Brit. Lib., Add. MS 32531, f. 53.

[47] Evelyn, *Diary*, ed. de Beer, vol. 4, p. 54: entry for 4 Mar. 1675. Vossius's work on moon spots is probably his paper repr. in his *Variarum observationum liber*, London 1685, 195–200. Cf. Thomas Birch, *The History of the Royal Society*, London 1756–7, vol. 3, 192–3.

[48] Evelyn, *Diary*, ed. de Beer, vol. 4, p. 78: entry for 31 Oct. 1675. The envoy was Ezechiel Spanheim (1629–1710), the son of Friedrich Spanheim the elder (1600–49), theologian.

[49] Ibid., vol. 4, p. 89: entry for 28 Apr. 1676. From August 1677 until his death on 19 Nov. 1677, Isaac Vossius entertained at his house near Windsor his maternal uncle Franciscus Junius the younger, the famous philologist. Junius "went upon the earnest invitation of his nephew Dr. Isaac Vossius to Windsor, and continued for a time in good health and chearfulness there, and at Dr. Vossius's house near it. At length being overtaken with a fever, died of it in his said nephew's house near Windsor". Junius was buried in the chapel at Windsor Castle: Wood, *Athenae*, vol. 3, p. 1143; idem, *Fasti*, vol. 2, 357–8.

Charles II was not above responding to the influence of women. For the next twenty-four years until her death in 1699, Saint-Évremond attended her almost daily, either at Windsor or at St James's in London, or alternatively at her house in Chelsea. So too did Vossius become attached to this pseudo-court of glittering francophone foreigners, who looked upon the learned and somewhat boring Dutchman with a mixture of admiration and a feeling almost akin to pity: Desmaizeaux described the scene as it stood in about 1680:

> Mr. de St. Evremond passoit les étés à Windsor avec la Cour, & y voyoit souvent Mr. Vossius, que le Roi avoit fait Chanoine de Windsor en 1673. Madamme Mazarin se plaisoit beaucop à la conversation de ce savant homme: il mangeoit souvent chez elle, & elle lui faisoit des questions sur toutes sortes de sujets. Voici quelque traits du caractere de Vossius. Il entendoit presque toutes les Langues de l'Europe, & n'en parloit bien aucune. Il connoissoit à fond le génie & les coûtumes des Anciens, il ignoroit les manieres de son siecle. Son impolitesse se répandoit jusques sur ses expressions. Il s'exprimoit dans la conversation, comme il auroit fait dans un Commentaire sur Juvenal, ou sur Pétrone.[50]

Vossius thus provided an interesting foil to the more worldly and dashing figure of Saint-Évremond, of whom Christopher Pitt famously wrote, less elegantly than Desmaizeaux of Vossius, that

> Old Evremond, renown'd for wit and dirt,
> Would change his living oft'ner than his shirt,
> Roar with the rakes of state a month, and come
> To starve another in his hole at home.[51]

Isaac Vossius and Saint-Évremond must have been the oddest couple of Restoration London.

IV

It was in these congenial and simultaneously English and foreign surroundings that Isaac Vossius settled down in the last two decades of his life to produce some of his most interesting work, and that which in the long run would provide his greatest contribution to scholarship. His first English subject of research and controversy

---

[50] Desmaizeaux, *La Vie de Messire Charles de Saint-Denis, Sieur de Saint Evremond*, Amsterdam 1726, 214–15.
[51] Christopher Pitt, "A Dialogue between a Poet and his Servant", in *The Poetical Works of Christopher Pitt*, London 1807, p. 28.

was the thorny question of the Sibylline Oracles. We know today a good deal more about them than was possible in the seventeenth century. The Sibylline literature derives from the myth of a prophetess who delivers her predictions spontaneously, unlike other oracles who first need to be consulted. The image of a single individual woman living for a thousand years evolved into a group of such figures, residing in different countries. One of the Sibyls, Sambethe or Sabbe, was said to be the Babylonian wife of Noah's son. Aristophanes mentions a Sibylline literature in Greece in the fifth century BC. These prophetic verses were installed on the Capitol in Rome, guarded over by a college of officials, who permitted them to be studied but not consulted except by express order of the state. Five years after the buildings on the Capitol were destroyed by fire in 81 BC, a commission was ordered to obtain copies of genuine Sibylline verses in Italy and abroad. Augustus had these oracles copied in 17 BC, and five years later had those outside the canon destroyed.

Two different collections of the *Oracula Sibyllina* have survived, designated as books I–VIII and XI–XIV respectively, although this numbering does not refer to any order in the text. The first group of oracles was compiled by Christians at the beginning of the sixth century, but it includes much older material, the earliest of which is certainly of Jewish origin, with Greek and even Babylonian materials. The first published edition of the Sybilline Oracles was that of Betuleius, who edited the first eight books in 1545 from a manuscript then at Augsburg. The eighth book was not complete in this version, and further editions followed in 1555 and 1599. It was this third version, produced by Johannes Koch (Opsopoeus) that formed the basis of Isaac Vossius's discussion.

The question of the standing of the Sibylline Oracles, however, was more than a mere classical connundrum. Their eternalized presence in Michelangelo's Sistine Chapel immediately suggests this. For the Sibyls were seen in the post-Christian era as pagans who foretold the coming of Christ, his miracles, his death and his resurrection. Indeed, this came to be seen as their primary historical function, and Christian apologists who cited their poetry claimed that they were silent after the birth of Christ. Having completed their task, they were pensioned off. The Church Fathers may have had some lingering doubts about their authority, but they agreed with Augustine that the Sibyls could be used to confound the heathen. Justin Martyr, Tertullian and St Clement of Alexandria all quote from the Sibyls, and Origen defended their authenticity. Even St Jerome attributed them with divine inspiration. In sum, then, the Sibylline Oracles joined with Josephus in providing the necessary bridge between the Old and New Testaments, between classical and eastern civilizations and the Christian world. In many respects, one could hardly do without them.[52]

In the seventeenth century, there were basically three revisionist positions one could take on the Sibylline Oracles as an alternative to those which either accepted them as completely authoritative, or at the very least somewhat inspired and useful in polemics against pagans. Firstly, there was the view of Johannes Marckius, doctor in theology at Groningen, according to which the oracles were the work of the early Christians. Secondly, there was the far more radical approach of Antony van Dale, Dutch physician, who argued that not only were the Sibylline Oracles complete forgeries, but that they did not cease with the coming of Christ. Isaac Vossius's view, put forward in a book published at Oxford in 1679, was that the Sibylline Oracles were of Jewish origin. As we have seen, in a sense, all three of these alternative theories were partially correct. We know that in about 160 BC an Alexandrian Jew began to rewrite parts of the oracles using Jewish elements, and that the early Christians started retouching the texts as early as the first century AD, without denying the reality of the Sibyls's inspiration. In any case, it is clear that Vossius tried to anchor the Sibylline Oracles in the accepted progression of divine history from Jews to Christians, and save them as an acceptable source of religious data.[53]

The reaction to Vossius's Jewish theory of origin for the Sibylline Oracles was predictably intense, from both sides of the spectrum. One of the best defences of the independent authenticity of the oracles came only after Vossius's death, from Sir John Floyer, the Litchfield physician who was the first to measure the pulse rate.[54] Dr Samuel Johnson remembered "the celebrated Sir John Floyer" as the man who sent him to be touched by Queen Anne.[55] Floyer's

---

[52] For the original Greek text, see *Sibyllinische Weissagungen: Urtext und Übersetzung*, ed. A. Kurfess, Berlin 1951; *Oracula Sibyllina*, ed. A. Rzach, Prague 1891. Generally, see H.W. Parke, *Sibyls and Sibylline Prophecy in Classical Antiquity*, London 1988; H.N. Bate, *The Sibylline Oracles Books III–V*, London: SPCK, 1918; M.S. Terry, *The Sibylline Oracles*, London: Hunt and Eaton, 1890; Y. Am[ir], "Sibyl and Sibylline Oracles", *Ency. Jud.*, vol. 14, 1489–91. Cf. S.A. Hirsch, *A Book of Essays*, London: Jewish Historical Society, 1905, 219–59.

[53] Isaac Vossius, *De Sibyllinis aliisque quae Christi natalem præcessere Oraculis*, Oxford 1679 (repr. Leiden 1680), dedicated to Thomas Browne.

[54] On Sir John Floyer (1649–1734), see *Dict. Nat. Biog.*

[55] James Boswell, *Life of Johnson*, Oxford: Oxford University Press 1983, p. 32.

aim, as he declared in his dedication of the book to John Hough, bishop of Litchfield and Coventry,[56] was to follow in the footsteps of "the learned Fathers of the Christian Church, whose Opinion I have here undertaken to defend, That the *Sibylline Oracles* are true Prophecies". Floyer's general thesis, however, in declared opposition to the views of Isaac Vossius, demonstrates quite clearly the reason why Vossius had to write as he did, proclaiming the oracles the work of the Jews. "I here present to you in these Oracles", Floyer announced,

> the old *Antediluvian Religion*, and all the Moral Precepts communicated to *Japhet's* Family, which also contain many Prophesies concerning the Changes which would happen in the Kingdoms of *Japhet's* Posterity; so that we do not wholly derive all our Religion and Learning from the *Jews*, who convers'd formerly very rarely with the *Gentiles*, among whom they were but little known before their Captivity. When the *Chaldeans, Ægyptians* and *Greeks* had corrupted the *Noachic* Traditions of Religion, by applying their Sacrifices and Prayers to the Sun, Moon, and Heroes, which were appointed for God's Service, it pleas'd God to inspire the *Sibyls*, that they might restore the true ancient Worship to God alone, and correct all the errors from the old moral Precepts by these *Oracles*: The *Jewish* Men-Prophets, near the same thing, reform'd the Corruptions which Idolatry had introduc'd among them; but Woman-Prophetesses were sent to the *Gentiles*, because they used Women in their Heathen Oracles; and they could be least suspected by them for setting up any new Sect in Philosophy, or Religion.

In other words, the Sibylline Oracles provided the Christian with a means of bypassing the Jewish monopoly on the divine message, and moving one step closer to the very original communication God had with man in the halcyon days of the Garden of Eden when Adam named the animals and had perfect and complete knowledge. Claiming that mankind was originally monotheistic and had only afterwards degenerated into idolatry was an early-modern commonplace, championed by Isaac Newton and many others. But what Floyer and his supporters attempted to do was to remove the Jews entirely from the chain of command, to discount their tradi-

---

[56] John Hough won the bishopric of Oxford after the Glorious Revolution as a reward for his stand in his disputed election to the presidency of Magdalen College, Oxford. He was translated to Litchfield and Coventry in 1699, and afterwards to Worcester in 1717. Interestingly, he was acquainted with and the employer of the famous Isaac Abendana, the professional Jew of the English universities at the end of the seventeenth century: see D.S. Katz, "The Abendana Brothers and the Christian Hebraists of Seventeenth-Century England", *Journal of Ecclesiastical History* 39 (1989), p. 45.

tions and their learning, even at the expense of downgrading the authority of the Bible itself, and to construct an alternate channel of divine knowledge. Floyer noted that the Christian Fathers supported the Sibylline Oracles, and pointed out that since "we believe the same Fathers Testimony concerning the Canon of Scriptures, we cannot disbelieve 'em, when they unanimously say, that these Oracles had a divine Inspiration". This was certainly true, but it was a far cry from Augustine, who found the Oracles useful in confirming Scripture and in debates with pagans, to Floyer, who gave them an independent standing apart from the biblical text itself.[57]

Interestingly, Floyer's recommendation that Dr Johnson the boy seek medical help at the divine touch of Queen Anne is in some ways indicative of the old-fashioned and traditional nature of his approach to other problems. For at the same time that he championed the Sibylline Oracles as a divine source, thereby seeking to derail the importance of Jewish influence, he held very conventional mid-seventeenth-century millenarian views about the role the Jews would play at the end of days. At that time, "the *Jews* shall return to their own Country, and live in Peace and Plenty, and Thunder from Heaven shall destroy their Enemies". Once in Palestine, the Jews will "build their Temple, and use their old Ceremonies, till this signal coming of Christ to destroy the *Turks*, his appearing in the Air shall convert 'em:" Floyer even found support for this view in his recent research into the Sibylline Oracles:

> He that will read these Quotations from the *old Prophets*, *Esdras*, *Revelations*, and *Sibyls*, will acknowledg the *Jews* must return into their Country to build their City and Temple, and there will be besieg'd by *Gog*, who will there be destroy'd by Thunder: Then the *Jews*, and many *Gentiles*, shall be converted to *Christianity* . . . then shall Christ come with all his Saints, be King over the Earth, and all Nations shall come up to worship him

"In short", Floyer wrote, "the *Oracles* describe the chief Histories to which the Visions in the *Revelations* belong, and by understanding these, we can determine to what Histories they relate, and thereby avoid applying improper Histories to them". So much, Floyer concluded, for the view of "*Isaac Vossius*, That they were writ by the *Jews*".[58]

William Whiston the "honest Newtonian" was very kind about

---

[57] Sir John Floyer, *The Sibylline Oracles*, London 1713, sigs. A2r–A3r.
[58] Ibid., xvi, 314–15, 320, xvi–i, 249, 256.

Sir John Floyer in his own vindication of the Sibylline Oracles, and was not entirely negative about Isaac Vossius either. "Lest the Reader should be tempted to go into *Isaac Vossius's* Hypothesis", Whiston warned,

> which is the only one that is not Intolerable, *viz.* That the *Jews* had impos'd upon the Heathens, and made several Oracles compos'd by some among themselves to pass with them for really *Sibvlline*, and so to be admitted even into the Second *Capitoline* Copy it self, I shall desire him to observe, that this is meer Hypothesis, destitute of all Evidence in the World

Like Floyer, so too did Whiston conclude that

> It appears therefore, that tho' God gave positive Laws, or an Institution of religious Worship, only to the *Jews*, and intrusted them only with those *Divine Oracles* that related to the same, yet that he did not wholly confine Divine Inspiration to that Nation; but supported the Law and Religion of Nature, and the right Worship of himself, as the One true God, among the Heathen also, all along by these Oracles even till the Light of the Christian Revelation was spread over the World.

Whiston followed his remarks with the Greek and English texts of the Sibylline Oracles, taken out of Floyer's earlier book.[59]

But of course, Isaac Vossius's major opponent was Bernard Le Bovier, sieur de Fontenelle (1657–1757), whose *Histoire des oracles* created such a sensation in 1687. Fontenelle openly admits that his own book was merely a literary reworking of the research of Antony van Dale, but his outright rejection of the Sibylline Oracles seems also to have been designed to cast doubt on all established religion. An English translation by the proto-feminist Aphra Behn appeared in 1688, while Vossius was still alive, and must have caused him considerable anguish. Fontenelle summarized his objectives on the first page of his work: "My design is not to give you directly an History of *Oracles*", he wrote, "I only intend to argue against that common Opinion which attributes 'em to *Dæmons*, and will have 'em to cease at the coming of *Jesus Christ*". From Fontenelle's point of view, it was really irrelevant who began this pious fraud, for the Sibylline Oracles were nothing more than the product of a wish to deceive.[60]

---

[59] William Whiston, *A Vindication of the Sibylline Oracles*, London 1715, p. 36, 78, 83: the book is dedicated to Richard Bentley. For more on Whiston, see J.E. Force, *William Whiston: Honest Newtonian*, Cambridge: Cambridge University Press, 1984.

[60] Fontenelle, *The History of Oracles and the Cheats of the Pagan Priests*, London 1688.

The question of the authenticity of the Sibylline Oracles was not the first scholarly controversy with which Isaac Vossius was involved, but now in the last ten years of his life, throughout the 1680s, there was definitely a feeling that somewhere between the Septuagint and the Sibyllines he had become a full-blown sceptic and a danger to established religion. Such an image was really quite ironic in view of the fact that in the first case he was trying to rescue traditional chronology, and in the second he was attempting to bring all pre-Christian revelation within the Jewish sphere of influence. His close association with Saint-Évremond and the pseudo-court of the duchess of Mazarin only reinforced that popular conception. Dr Narcissus Marsh, provost of the College of Dublin and later Ussher's successor in the archbishopric of Armagh, put the Vossius problem very nicely:

> whatsoever Dr. *Vossius* says, because his Name is *Vossius, ipse dixit*, is enough to make it believed; which seems to me the more insufferable, because they cannot, or else will not make any Distinction between *Gerard* and *Isaac Vossius*, nor consider, which Way a Man's Talent lies, and whether he deals in a Subject, which he can master, or in one that masters him: If they would do but thus much, I believe, *ipse dixit*, would quickly stand for nothing, and that *Isaac* would not long pride himself with the Plumes, wherewith *Gerard*'s Fame has adorned him.[61]

Marsh was writing on this occasion to Dr Edward Pococke, the Regius professor of Hebrew and Laudian professor of Arabic, one of the most celebrated Orientalists of his day. It was Vossius's misfortune to cross him.

Edward Pococke (1604–91) is so well-known a figure in the history of early modern English scholarship that he hardly requires an introduction. Pococke took his MA at Oxford in 1626, and then proceeded to study Arabic with William Bedwell, England's leading Arabist. Pococke was appointed chaplain to the English merchants at Aleppo in 1629, and arrived there in October 1630, remaining for over five years, and mastering the oriental tongues while at the same time purchasing valuable books and manuscripts. Pococke returned to England to take up Archbishop Laud's offer of a new chair in Arabic at Oxford. Although he spent the years 1637–1640 in Constantinople at Laud's insistence, most of his later career was devoted to Oxford and to Christ Church College,

---

[61] Marsh to Pococke, 29 Apr. 1680: repr. Edward Pocock, *The Theological Works*, ed. L. Twells, London 1740, vol. 1, p. 75 (from "The Life", 1–84).

especially after his appointment to the Regius professorship of Hebrew as well in 1648, and more especially after the Restoration.[62]

John Locke said of Pococke that his "Name, which was in great Esteem beyond Sea, and that deservedly, drew on him Visits from all Foreigners of Learning, who came to Oxford to see that University. They never fail'd to be highly satisfy'd with his great Knowledge and Civility".[63] Significantly, one of the first famous foreigners who befriended the young Pococke was Isaac Vossius's more celebrated father, who was told about Pococke's preliminary Orientalist steps by John Rous, Bodley's librarian, when the Dutchman lived in England. The elder Vossius took a great interest in Pococke's work, and advised him on its publication. Leonard Twells, Pococke's eighteenth-century biographer, noted with regard to Gerhard Vossius that "indeed, that most learned Man entertain'd on this Occasion, such a Value for Mr. *Pocock*, that, tho' he was thirty Years older, and a Sort of *Dictator* in the Commonwealth of Learning, he treated him ever after with all the Kindness and Familiarity of a Friend".[64]

This early friendship between the elder Vossius and the much younger Pococke did not prevent the English Hebraist from standing his ground against what he regarded as Isaac Vossius's challenge to the very foundation of religion. In February 1679–80, Pococke finally delivered his verdict on Vossius's scholarly production: "I look not abroad among the new Books"; wrote Pococke to his friend Dr Narcissus Marsh in Dublin,

> I have not so much as seen *Vossius*'s Tract of his Sibyls, and such others as are with it; but I am told, that he speaks therein Things that are derogatory to Rabbinical Learning (but that matters not much, as for other Things) and particularly (which is *magis dolendum*) to bring Disrespect and Contempt on the *Hebrew* Bible; and all authoritative, without good Proof or Reason: And I hear, that by some at Coffee-Meetings, it is cried up. It may be suspected, that the Intention is to bring it into Doubt, whether we have any such Thing, as a true Bible at all, which we may confide in, as God's Word. It is, I see, by some wished, that the Verity of the Original Text might be vindicated from such sceptical Arguments, by some of Learning and Vigour, such as yourself. However, I doubt not, but that, by God's Providence, as the *Hebrew* Text hath hitherto stood firm, so it will

---

[62] For Pococke's life, see Ibid.; and Wood, *Athenae*, vol. 4, 318–23.

[63] Locke to Humfry Smith, 23 July 1703: John Locke, *The Correspondence*, ed. E.S. de Beer, Oxford, 1976– , vol. 8, 37–42: cf. Pocock, *Works*, ed. Twells, vol. 1, p. 24, where the letter is printed with many mistakes.

[64] Ibid., vol. 1, 3–4.

stand on its own Bottom to wear out all Assaults against it, and be, what it always was, received as the undoubted Word of God, when all the Arguments and Objections against it are vanish'd into Smoke.[65]

From where Pococke stood, Isaac Vossius looked like a dangerous sceptic because he cast doubt on the Masoretic monopoly of the Hebrew Bible and dared to suggest that other classical texts such as the Septuagint and the Sibylline Oracles might enhance the meaning of Scripture.

Dr Marsh in Dublin, the future archbishop of Armagh, Ussher's successor, agreed with Pococke completely, and if anything was even more emphatic. "I am very much grieved", he replied to his English colleague, "at what you say concerning some Mens Design to invalidate the Authority of the *Hebrew* Text, and thereby of all the Old Testament".[66] Vossius now became in Marsh's mind the leader of a sceptical conspiracy which by suggesting alternate routes to divine knowledge secretly took aim at the very heart of Protestantism itself. Marsh hoped that Pococke would take up the challenge, and denounce the son of his old patron in public. A fortnight later, Marsh wrote again to Pococke, pressing him to consider entering the fray:

> I find, Dr. *Vossius*'s last, as well as former Books, have not done much Good (I wish they have not done the contrary) here: We have not many, that can judge of the Original; but I hope to breed up good Store that Way, since we have an *Hebrew* Professor's Place lately settled on the College, to which Lecture I make all the Bachelors of Arts attend, and be examined thrice every Week, and they are likewise to be publickly examined in *Hebrew*, before they can take their Degree of Master in Arts, which I sometimes do myself. I say, I think, we have not many in the whole Kingdom, that can judge of the Original *Hebrew*.

This was the chief reason, Marsh claimed, that Isaac Vossius was able to get away with such gross theological improprieties. Marsh prayed "that God will raise up some able Man to vindicate (I may say) his own Cause: But I must add, that all Mens Eyes are fixt upon you; and I dare say, none will have the Confidence to think of putting Pen to Paper on such a Design, whilst you live."[67]

The panic expressed by Narcissus Marsh and others like him is quite understandable in view of the substantial academic

---

[65] Ibid., vol. 1, p. 74.
[66] Marsh to Pococke, 17 Apr. 1680: repr. Ibid., vol. 1, p. 75.
[67] Same to same, 29 Apr. 1680: repr. Ibid.

investment that they had made in understanding the Hebrew verity. Indeed, Marsh achieved immortality largely through this work, by means of the establishment of Marsh's Library in Dublin, the first free public library in Ireland. The collection is brimming over with Hebrew, Aramaic, Syriac, Arabic and Turkish books and manuscripts, as well as a vast amount of additional material in other Oriental languages. Marsh managed to purchase the entire library of Edward Stillingfleet, the latitudinarian bishop of Worcester who died in 1699, and to place it among his own collection. Although Marsh had a crisis of confidence in Irish Oriental learning and its future which prompted him to dispatch nearly a thousand Hebrew and Syriac codices to his friend Pococke at the Bodleian, Marsh's Library remained the centre of Hebrew learning in Ireland.[68] In fact, it was here that James Joyce warned Stephen Daedelus that beauty was not to be found "in the stagnant bay of Marsh's library where you read the fading prophecies of Joachim Abbas".[69] Champions of the Septuagint and the Sibylline Oracles would not find it easy to get readers' tickets in Marsh's Library.

But Edward Pococke disappointed Marsh, and would not attack Isaac Vossius directly. In his reply sent to Dublin and dated 1 September 1680, Pococke discussed various matters of rabbinical interpretation, Marsh's exposition of James 5, 12, and the state of religion and learning in Ireland, everything except Isaac Vossius and the hopes of the learned world that Oxford's leading Hebraist would take up the challenge offered to him. Leonard Twells, Pococke's eighteenth-century biographer, was also hard pressed to find a suitable explanation for his subject's reticence. "After what has been said", he admitted,

> of Dr. *Pocock*'s and his Friends Indignation against the above-mentioned Piece of *Isaac Vossius*, and the Expectation of Mankind, that the Professor, being the first Man in the World for Knowledge in these Matters, would appear an Advocate for the *Hebrew* Text, against the confident Assaults of that Writer, it may seem wonderful, that he neither undertook the Service, nor excused himself to his Friends, who modestly incited him thereto, but at the same Time earnestly wished to see him engaged in the Controversy

---

[68] On Marsh's Library, see L. Hyman, *The Jews of Ireland*, Shannon: Irish University Press, 1972, 229–30; G.T. Stokes, *Some Worthies of the Irish Church*, London: Hodder and Stoughton, 1900, 112–41.

[69] James Joyce, *Ulysses*, New York 1961, p. 39. Joyce himself visited Marsh's Library only twice, on 22 and 23 October 1902, to read the prophetic books of Joachim Abbas, the *Vaticinia*, Venice 1589; Hyman, *Ireland*, p. 349.

On the one hand, Twells reminded his readers, it should be remembered that Pococke was by then close to eighty years old, and anxious to finish his commentary on Hosea. Furthermore, *"Isaac Vossius*, though very learned in his Way, was a Man of strong Passions, and not over-patient of Contradiction". Pococke also entertained respect for the son of his first patron, demonstrated by the fact that when his own eldest son had visited Leiden, "he had his Father's express Commands to wait on Dr. *Vossius* there".[70]

Yet Twell's final excuse was the most telling, and points to the importance of the major issues at stake here: "the Controversy itself," he recalled,

> through the Prejudices and Passions of Men, on both Sides, became of so delicate a Nature, that it was difficult even for a Man of Judgment and Temper to enter into it, without displeasing all Parties. On the one hand, the Men of *Vossius*'s Sentiments could be satisfied with nothing short of giving up the *Hebrew* Text, as corrupt, and setting up the *Septuagint* Translation, as the only pure Canon of the Old Testament Scripture; which it appears, Dr. *Pocock* could by no Means approve of, having declared against it, as an Hypothesis, that would destroy the Certainty of the *Jewish* Scriptures.

But there was another school of thought as well:

> On the other Hand, the Partisans for the *Hebrew Verity* were not to be satisfied with a Defence of the *Hebrew* Text, in a reasonable Sort, as to all its Essentials: To please them, even the Accents in the *Masoretick* Text must be insisted on, as of Divine Appointment, and coæval with the Text itself; whilst the *Greek* of the LXX was to have no Mercy nor Quarter, but to be deemed a Translation originally bad, and, by frequent Transcribing, became so corrupted, as to be of no Certainty nor Use.

Both of these views were extremes at each end of the scriptural spectrum, and it was difficult to agree on any common meeting points.[71]

Pococke's problem was to find an appropriate way to get involved in order to save the original Hebrew text on which *sola scriptura* was based. "But our Author was not disposed to give into either of these Points;" Twells testifies,

> he rightly judged it, therefore, most expedient not directly to ingage in a Dispute, wherein, after infinite Disquiet to himself, he found no Way to please either Side; and yet, as we shall find anon, he took a Course to apprize the World of his Sentiments in the main Parts of

---

[70] Pocock, *Works*, ed. Twells, vol. 1, 75–6.
[71] Ibid., vol. 1, p. 76

this Controversy, and to convince *Vossius* and his Adherents, if they were not hardened against all Conviction, that the *Hebrew* Text was fairly defensible, and not at so great a Distance from their favourite *Greek* Translation, as they were wont to imagine.

Pococke did this by discussing and reconciling the differences between the Masoretic Hebrew and the Greek Septuagint in the course of his commentaries on Hosea and Joel. Yet throughout those works, Twells correctly observes, "Dr *Pocock*'s Zeal for the Purity of the present *Hebrew* Text, even when most stirr'd by the intemperate Opposition of *Isaac Vossius*, never provoked him to depreciate the *Septuagint*, to which that learned Man showed so violent a Partiality."[72]

By the time Twells was writing, in the early eighteenth-century, biblical criticism was already becoming an established discipline, if as yet its focus was more on the New Testament than on the Old. Twells therefore was at pains to try to understand Pococke's position:

> Some may think our Author went too far, in supposing, that the *Hebrew* Text was always, and in every Particular, read as it is at present; but if he err'd in this, he certainly err'd on the right Side, it being safer to suppose the Original *Hebrew* utterly uncorrupt, than to call its Purity in Question so oft as *Capellus* and *Vossius* did.

In the England of Pococke's day, no tampering with the Masoretic text was thought to be permissible. The Hebrew Bible was a unitary structure and an innocent-looking biblical brick could prove to be the keystone upon which the entire edifice depended. "To this we may add," Twells concluded,

> that the Knowledge of Biblical *Hebrew* being that Part of Literature, in which Dr. *Pocock* chiefly excelled, and in which he most delighted, it is the less to be wondered at, if he was prejudiced in Favour of it, especially, considering likewise, that *Hebrew Verity* was the prevailing Opinion of the Times, in which he was educated, and was then thought by most Protestants, essential to the Interests of the Reformation. But after all, perhaps he needs no Apology in this Respect.[73]

Collation of existing manuscripts, comparisons of translations, weighing of alternate readings: all of these were the Renaissance and Roman Catholic tools of textual analysis which were beginning to be applied on the Continent to the sacred text and with great result. But in England, such studies seemed to strike at the heart of

---

[72] Ibid., vol. 1, p. 76, 78.
[73] Ibid., vol. 1, p. 78.

the Protestant religion itself, and it was not until the 1750s, when Benjamin Kennicott began to collate medieval manuscripts of the Hebrew Old Testament, that biblical criticism can be said to have become almost respectable in England.[74]

This, at least, is how Pococke's stand appeared to Leonard Twells at the beginning of the eighteenth century, and this explanation is in many ways equally appealing today. A more careful examination of Pococke's other biblical research, however, renders Twells's "all-or-nothing-at-all" explanation somewhat more implausible. For Edward Pococke was also one of the first English Hebraists to recognize the potential importance of the Samaritan Pentateuch, and to encourage the acquisition of a copy of this important document. It was the Italian traveller Pietro della Valle who first obtained copies of the Samaritan Pentateuch. In 1616, Pietro visited Palestine and Damascus, and in the latter city purchased two manuscripts from a Samaritan there. One of these he gave to the French ambassador in Constantinople; the second he kept for himself, and thereby provided the first Samaritan Pentateuch to arrive in Europe.[75] Scholars soon discovered that the Pentateuch used by the Samaritans, a Jewish sect established in about the fourth century BC and still surviving today, is not an independent version, but rather a particular form of the Hebrew text written in a different script. Although the Samaritan Pentateuch differs from the Masoretic text in as many as 6000 places, most of these are unimportant, and the others are pleonastic, apart from a number of alterations designed to further the interests of the sect itself.[76]

The introduction of the Samaritan Pentateuch into the European biblical arena was bound to create a good deal of disturbance. As we have seen, scholars had long disputed over the relative value of the Masoretic text and the Septuagint, but this was a new problem. The fact that the Samaritan Pentateuch agreed with the Septuagint in about one-third of the variant readings led it to be aligned with the Greek text in seventeenth-century biblical discussion. Roman Catholic scholars defended the use of the Septuagint, as well as

---

[74] On Kennicott and his work, see D.S. Katz, "The Chinese Jews and the Problem of Biblical Authority in Eighteenth- and Nineteenth-Century England", *English Historical Review* 105 (1990), 893–919.

[75] Pietro della Valle, *Viaggi*, Bologna 1672, vol. 1, 406–8, 424: selections in R. Röhricht, *Bibliotheca Geographica Palaestinae*, Jerusalem 1963, p. 947.

[76] Generally, see J.D. Purvis, *The Samaritan Pentateuch and the Origins of the Samaritan Sect*, Cambridge, Mass.: Harvard University Press, 1968; O. Eissfeldt, *The Old Testament: An Introduction*, transl. P. Ackroyd, Oxford: Blackwell, 1965, 694–5, 782.

Jerome's Latin Vulgate (c. 400 AD): they recognized the authority of the Church as the final religious arbiter, and were not tied to the biblical word alone. Catholic biblical authorities such as J. Morinus, J.H. Hottinger, and of course Richard Simon therefore promoted the usefulness of the Samaritan Pentateuch in supplying alternate readings. Protestants, on the other hand, were generally unable to cast any doubt whatsoever on the Masoretic text of the Old Testament, without risking the breakdown of *sola fide* along with *sola scriptura*, and despite the inclusion of a Samaritan text in Brian Walton's Polyglot Bible, tended to reject the Samaritan Pentateuch outright: it was not until Benjamin Kennicott wrote in its defence in eighteenth-century Oxford that Protestants gradually came to see that its use was not necessarily an act of gross atheism.[77]

From our point of view, what is interesting is how involved Pococke the Protestant was in the discovery and exploitation of this rival text to that of the Masoretic Hebrew Bible, a source which might prove even more revisionist than the Greek Septuagint chronology or the Sibylline Oracles. Pococke and his circle even went one step further than had been done previously by actually making contact with the Samaritans living in contemporary Nablus. Scaliger in 1589 had been the first Westerner to have persuaded the Samaritans to answer direct written queries. He sent them letters from Cairo and Nablus, and received a reply in Hebrew the following year.[78] But now the man on the spot was Pococke's successor as the minister to the English factory at Aleppo, Robert Huntington. In 1672, the Samaritans sent Huntington at Jerusalem a Pentateuch for the Jews of England, with a cover letter to them written from Nablus by Merchib-Ben-Jacob. Huntington was also encouraged in his work by Job Ludolf the German Orientalist, who himself reached the Samaritans in the 1680s through the agency of a local Jew from Hebron named Jacob Levy. Pococke was very involved in all this exciting activity, and corresponded with Huntington, Ludolf and others in an attempt to see what revelation the Samaritan traditions and texts could offer.[79]

---

[77] Purvis, *Samaritan Pentateuch*, 74–5; *The Bible in its Ancient and English Versions*, ed. H. Wheeler Robinson, Oxford: Oxford University Press, 1940, chaps. 2 and 4.
[78] N. Shor, [Reports of Samaritans in the Writings of Western Christian Travellers from the 14th until the end of the 18th Centuries] (Hebrew), *Cathedra* 13 (1979), 185n.; H. Adams, *The History of the Jews*, London 1818, 499–500. The answer in Hebrew which Scaliger received in 1590 is trans. into Latin in Silvestre de Sacy, *Mémoire sur l'etát actuel des Samaritains*, Paris 1812, 16–23.
[79] Shor, "Reports", p. 186; Adams, *History*, 500–2. Ludolf's answers from the

On the face of it, one would have thought that a man like Edward Pococke, who was so opposed to Isaac Vossius's use of the Septuagint and the Sibylline Oracles as alternate non-Masoretic routes to divine wisdom, would also shrink from using the Samaritan Pentateuch, whose textual message was often at variance with that of the Masorites. But not so. Even Robert Huntington himself, the searcher of the Samaritans, opposed Isaac Vossius and argued that he had gone too far. In a letter from Aleppo dated 24 May 1681, Huntington wrote to Pococke with reference to reports of Vossius's work that had been sent halfway across the world to Syria. "I have not seen *Vossius de Sibyllis*;" Huntington confessed to Pococke,

> but to decry the *Hebrew* Text has long been his Design and Practice: And it is a great while since *Hulsius* and *Horn* have taken Notice of it; but I am no Judge of the Controversy. Whilst Men speak and fight too not for Truth, but Victory, we may well expect heterodox Opinions and seditious Actions.[80]

In other words, Huntington saw no contradiction between championing the Samaritan Pentateuch and the Hebrew Masoretic text at one and the same time, but denied Vossius's right to cast his net even further and include the Septuagint chronology and the Sibylline Oracles.

By the same token, in a reverse application of the identical principle, one would have expected Richard Simon to have offered Isaac Vossius some measure of support. Like many others, Twells also condemned

> Particularly Father *Simon*, who, whether from secret Scepticism, or a Design of reducing us to a Necessity of admitting the Authority of his Church, as the Basis of revealed Religion, made free with all the Originals of the Bible in their Turn, the authorized *Latin* Version not excepted, and opposed the Translation of the Seventy, without defending the *Hebrew* Text from any other, save wilful Corruption.[81]

Samaritans are repr. in J. Morinus, *Antiquitates Ecclesiae Orientalis*, London 1682. Their last letter was dated 1689, and reached him in 1691. Huntington sent the material he received from the Samaritans to Thomas Marshal of Oxford, who kept up the correspondence until his death in 1685: Adams, *History*, 500–3, from material in l'Abbé Gregoire, *Histoire des sectes réligieuses*, Paris 1810.

[80] Pocock, *Works*, ed. Twells, vol. 1, p. 75. But cf. the report in the *Journal de Trévoux* 17 (1706), 1818–19: "Cependant ayant fait de nouvelles recherches, j'ay enfin découvert que ce refus de communier étoit chimerique. On ne le lui proposa pas seulement. Il étoit trop éloigné de la situation d'esprit qu'il faut pour faire une action aussi sainte & aussi religieuse que celle-là."

[81] Pocock, *Works*, ed. Twells, vol. 1, p. 76.

But Richard Simon thought Vossius was as appalling as Pococke did, and wrote his "animadversions upon a small treatise of Dr I.V. concerning the Oracles of the Sibylls".[82] As far as Simon was concerned, the entire Hebrew Bible was too insecure a foundation on which to build massive chronologies, and generally he saw Vossius as far too credulous to make a first-rate biblical critic.

Attacked for using the Septuagint chronology and the Sibylline Oracles by Pococke, who himself exploited the Samaritan Pentateuch; charged with the same offence by Simon, who enjoyed pointing out the insufficiency of the Hebrew Bible, where then did Isaac Vossius stand on the important issue of biblical authority? Was he simply a disruptive sceptic as many believed, a man who allegedly read Ovid during divine service without resigning his canonry of Windsor? Desmaizeaux recalled that "il témoignoit par ses entretiens particuliers, qu'il ne croyoit point de Révélation. La maniere peu édifiante dont il est mort ne nous permet pas de douter de ses sentimens." This became a famous story, denied by some contemporaries, but told first by Desmaizeaux:

> Le Dr. Hascard, Doyen de Windsor, l'étant allé visiter avec le Dr. Wickart un des Chanoines, ne pût jamais l'engager à communier, comme c'est usage de l'Eglise Anglicane, quelque fortement qu'il l'en pressât, jusqu'à lui dire que *s'il ne le vouloit pas faire pour l'amour de Dieu, qu'il le fît du moins pour l'honneur du Chapitre.*

Hascard visited Vossius as the end drew near in February 1689, broaching once again the subject of taking Anglican communion, to which Vossius replied, "apprenez-moi comment je pourrai obliger mes fermiers à me payer ce qu'ils me doivent. Voila ce que je voudrais que vous fissiez."[83] "Other anecdotes of a like tendency", remarked T. Seccombe, Vossius's nineteenth-century biographer, "even if we cannot accept them literally, seem to indicate that he was very near to being a complete sceptic".[84]

A sceptic, however, is not a non-believer. Even Sir Thomas Browne, an uncompromising man, recognized this. "That Villain and Secretary of Hell", he wrote characteristically, "that composed that miscreant piece *Of the Three Impostors*, though divided from all Religions, and was neither Jew, Turk, nor Christian, was not a

---

[82] Richard Simon, *Critical Enquiries into the various Editions of the Bible*, London 1684; idem, *Opuscula Critica adversus Isaacum Vossium*, Edinburgh 1685.

[83] Desmaizeaux, *Saint-Evremond*, 214–17 and n. Isaac Vossius was succeeded in his prebendary by John Mesnard: Wood, *Fasti*, vol. 2, p. 408; idem, *Life and Times*, ed. A. Clark, Oxford Historical Society 1891–1900, vol. 3, p. 304.

[84] T. Seccombe, *Dict. Nat. Biog.*

positive Atheist".[85] Indeed, it should now be clear that far from being an atheist, or even a sceptic, Isaac Vossius was a critic, an important forerunner of the kind of biblical critic who would become commonplace only after the work of Benjamin Kennicott at Oxford in the mid-eighteenth-century. Kennicott was also a champion of the Samaritan Pentateuch, like Pococke, and his famous defence of this ancient text provoked a mass of hostile reaction. But by the time he wrote, a good deal was already known about their religion and customs, and sixteen Samaritan manuscripts existed in England, including seven copies of the Pentateuch deposited at Oxford, Cambridge, and the British Museum. By Kennicott's day, the Jews of India and even the Chinese Jews were being canvassed for manuscripts that might throw light on the original Hebrew verity which had been clouded by time. This sort of scriptural exploration had been pioneered by the Jesuits who first reached China in the late sixteenth century, but such a multi-textual approach was new among Protestants: Isaac Vossius stood at the genesis of this tradition.[86]

It is not surprising, then, to find that Isaac Vossius was even more strongly opposed in the 1680s than Kennicott would be in the 1750s, when biblical criticism was becoming a fact of life in Germany, and after Richard Bentley in England had already applied the same tools to an analysis of the less controversial Greek New Testament. Nevertheless, even in Vossius's day, other scholars had cast doubt on the Masoretic text. Archbishop Ussher himself admitted privately that the Hebrew Bible must have suffered the same fate as any other ancient manuscript, and was very actively involved in bringing copies of the Samaritan Pentateuch to England.[87] But he simultaneously argued that the Septuagint was in many respects a forgery.[88] Newton had doubts about the literal purity of the Old Testament, yet had a naive belief in the truth of biblical data.[89] But Ussher and Newton sought extra-Masoretic

---

[85] Sir Thomas Browne, *The Religio Medici*, London: Everyman, 1906 (first pub. 1642), p. 24. Interestingly, Browne also notes that "I cannot but wonder with what exception the Samaritans could confine their belief to the Pentateuch, or five Books of Moses." (p. 29).

[86] Katz, "Chinese Jews". Vossius's obsession with China was famous: Nicéron, *Mémoires*, vol. 13, 132–3, 141.

[87] Ussher to Selden, 2 Nov. 1627: Ussher, *Works*, vol. 15, 380–7; Ussher to Louis Cappel (Cappellus) the Huguenot Hebraist, n.d. (before 1652): Ibid., vol. 7, 589–609; Trevor-Roper, "Ussher", p. 158.

[88] Ussher, *Works*, vol. 1, 269–70; Parr, *Ussher*, p. 52, 95.

[89] Newton admitted that the Masoretic text had already been corrupted by

evidence in order to demonstrate the truth of the Hebrew Old Testament; Vossius sought to open alternative Jewish supernatural routes to divine wisdom and like Giordano Bruno and the Egyptian Hermeticists found that there were limits to critical experimentation.[90] Isaac Vossius's contribution in this pre-history of Protestant biblical criticism was to draw the borders while standing on the outside: Benjamin Kennicott would "build a fence around the biblical law", as the Talmud puts it, while standing well within.

V

All of this learned controversy, if it had any effect at all on Vossius's life in the company of Saint-Évremond and the duchess of Mazarin, it was to enhance his popularity: "Vous, M. Vossius, vous qui lisez toute sorte de bons livres, hormis la Bible, vous pouvez bien nous éclaircir', disait souvent Madame Mazarin quand les questions difficiles surgissaient."[91] Another contemporary describes Isaac Vossius as "a Person of vast Industry" with "a close retired manner, generally studying in the Night Time".[92] Letters to Vossius continued to stream in from all parts of England and the rest of the learned world. Well over a thousand of these letters have survived, and only when they are catalogued, or at least read, will we begin to have a picture of his intellectual contacts.[93] The Council of the Royal Society wrote to Vossius on 10 December 1674 for his opinion on Hooke's new quadrant for making remote observa-

---

scribes before codification, and therefore preferred the Septuagint because it was older and therefore closer to the truth: Manuel, *Isaac Newton*, p. 61, 148.

[90] See especially, M. Bernal, *Black Athena*, vol. 1, New Brunswick, NJ: Rutgers University Press, 1987, 167–169, 191–192.

[91] Saint-Évremond, *Oeuvres* (1739); *Vie*, p. 214. Cf. *Réponse aux questions d'un Provincial*, vol. 1, chap. 21 etc.

[92] Laurence Échard, *The History of England*, London 1717–18, vol. 3, p. 943.

[93] Copies and drafts of letters *from* Isaac Vossius are now in the Amsterdam University Library (having been transferred from the Remonstrants's Library), esp. RK Cod. VI F 28 (copy book of letters sent from Sweden) and RK Cod. VI F 29–30 (other letters). The originals, of course, remained with the recipients.

The originals of the letters sent *to* Isaac Vossius are now also in the Amsterdam University Library: about 1,000 letters to Vossius have survived. A contemporary set of copies can be found at the Leiden University Library, BUR F 11, but not all of the Amsterdam originals are represented. See also a volume of letters to G.J. Vossius in Brit. Lib., MS. Harl. 7012, which includes some to Isaac Vossius as well.

In 1805, the Bodleian Library spent £1,025 to purchase the MSS. of James Philip D'Orville, a classical scholar who died in Amsterdam on 14 Sept. 1751, leaving behind an ambiguous will which suggested to the University of Leiden that the rightful possession was theirs: among these MSS. were copies of letters *to* Isaac Vossius, now Bodl. Lib., MS D'Orville 468–71: 468–70 are the Latin letters

tions with great exactness.[94] Ralph Cudworth wrote to Vossius out of the blue, being personally unaquainted with him, but "becaus I value your Judgment in matters of Antiquity as much as any 's. I therfore presume at this time to request a Favour of you", being a bit of scholarly advice.[95] This was the way many scholars turned to Vossius.[96] Indeed, in a letter of 22 September 1685, John Evelyn recounted to Samuel Pepys, as one diary writer to another, the sort of unexpected subjects that were apt to come up when chatting with Vossius: "he has many learned observations about Navigation, particularly that of sailing to several parts opposite to one another by the same wind", Evelyn wrote,

> and it was (you may remember) on this hint that I informed you Vossius had by him a treatise . . . I inquired of him (when last I was at Windsor) whether he would publish it; to which he gave me but an uncertain answer. In the meantime you will not be displeased at what he tells us of a certain harmony produced by the snapping of carters' whips, used of old at the feasts of Bacchus and Cybele; and that the Tartars have to this day no other trumpets, and are so adroit as at once to make the whip give three distinct claps, and that so loud as to be heard very far off; and then speaks of a coachman at Maestricht, who plays several tunes with his lash. To a lover of music and harmony I could not omit this scrap, though I know you will laugh at me for it, and pay me with the tongs and gridiron.[97]

---

arranged in chronological order, 1637–89; 471 is a collection of letters written in other languages: W.D. Macray, *Annals of the Bodleian Library Oxford*, Oxford 1890 (2nd edn.), p. 282.

The Bodleian Library also spent over three centuries looking for the "thirteen boxes of Letters" of Isaac Vossius which had been received by Richard Allestree (1619–81), provost of Eton, and Regius professor of Divinity. An examination of the receipt written by Allestree, dated 28 Apr. 1679, reveals that although he received "from d^r Vossius thirteen boxes of Letters", what had been sent was moveable type rather than correspondence: Bodl. Lib., Add. MS. C 78, f. 30^r: cf. Macray's concern over the missing "letters" in his *Annals*, p. 243.

It may be that these sets of contemporary copies were made with an unfulfilled view to publishing Vossius's collected works. Locke, in a letter to N. Thoynard, 4 Aug. 1691 speaks of such a project afoot in Amsterdam: G. Bonno, *Les Relations intellectuelles de Locke avec la France*, Berkeley, Los Angeles: University of California Press 1955, p. 130.

[94] Thomas Birch, *The History of the Royal Society*, London 1756–7, vol. 2, p. 160; J. Elmes, *Sir Christopher Wren and His Times*, London 1852, p. 272. Cf. Isaac Vossius to the Royal Society: Brit. Lib., Add. MS. 4162, f. 229.

[95] Ralph Cudworth to Isaac Vossius, 26 Mar. 1681: Amsterdam Univ. Lib., MS III E 10^77; copy in Leiden Univ. Lib., BUR F 11, II. 83.

[96] E.g. W. Asaph to Vossius, 13 Aug. 1684: Ibid., BUR F 11, f. 102v = Ep. 686: not in Amsterdam Univ. Lib., although this is a copy; Vossius to I. Barrow, 1676: French copy with English trans: Brit. Lib., Add. MS. 4293, f. 149.

[97] Saint-Evremond, *Works*, ed. Desmaizeaux, vol. ii. 68: see n. 41 above. See, for example, a discussion of one of Vossius's favourite subjects in de Souligné, *London Bigger than Old Rome . . . against . . . Vossius*, London 1701.

Perhaps this is what Saint-Évremond meant when he said that Vossius exhibited "a foolish credulity in every thing extraordinary, fabulous, or exceeding belief".[98]

Apart from Vossius's views on musical whips, what interested all English scholars in the last years of the great Dutchman's life were his books and manuscripts, which were reputed (Wood reports) to form "the best private library, as it was then supposed, in the whole world", even after the self-proclaimed depletions he suffered in the service of Queen Christina. According to the terms of his will, made a fortnight before his death, Vossius left his "library of bookes and all other my goods, chattels, and estate whatsoever" to be equally divided between his nephew Gerard John Vossius, a councillor of Flanders, and his niece Attia Vossius.[99] In the end, after Vossius's death at Windsor on 21 February 1688–9, his nephew and niece spurned Oxford's offer of £3,000 and packed up in thirty-four cases their uncle's printed books and his 762 manuscripts, and with the connivance of the Dutch ambassador shipped them by warship for the Low Countries, a mercenary act that caused outrage among learned circles in England.[100]

Even the advantages of hindsight little avail us in trying to apportion blame for Oxford's failure. Vossius scholars have overlooked the fact that Oxford's agent in this affair was the equally

---

[98] Evelyn to Pepys, 23 Sept. 1685, in *Diary*, ed. Bray, vol. 2, p. 278.

[99] Wood, *Fasti*, vol. 2, p. 323; Isaac Vossius's will, dated 8 Feb. 1688–9 and proved 2 Mar. 1688–9: *Wills from Doctors' Commons . . . proved in the Prerogative Court of Canterbury*, ed. J.G. Nichols & J. Bruce: Camden Soc., 83 (1863), p. 149. See generally P.C. Molhuysen in *Tijdschrift voor Boek- en Bibliotheekwezen* 2 (1904), 95–100, summarized by W.R.B. Prideaux, "Isaac Vossius's Library", *Notes and Queries*, 10th ser., vol. 2 (1904), 361–2, who notes that Leiden professors Spanheim, Gronovius, and Trigland, who evaluated the Vossius collection once it arrived in Holland, were very disappointed that most of the MSS. had already been published.

[100] Vossius's heirs probably never had any intention of selling their uncle's library to the Bodleian, but merely used the Oxford scholars in order to obtain an estimate of the market value of the books and manuscripts. A catalogue of Vossius's manuscripts was drawn up by Paul Colomiès, who had known Vossius in Holland and who came over to England on Vossius's invitation in about 1681: Nicéron, *Mémoires*, vol. 7, p. 196, 203–4. Cf. a seventeenth-century catalogue of Isaac Vossius's MSS. in Brit. Lib., MS. Eger. 2260, fos. 142^r–180^v; and Add. MS. 1783, fos. 17–53. According to C. Wordsworth, *The Correspondence of Richard Bentley, D.D.*, London, 1842, p. 724, a catalogue of the Vossius MSS. was made for Archbishop Sancroft and is deposited as Bodl. Lib., MS. Bibl. Angl. II, i, p. 57: I have not been able to locate this copy. Vossius assimilated into his collection the rent roll of all the lands belonging to the dean and chapter of Windsor, which his nephew still had in 1709 in Voorburg, near the Hague: *Manuscripts of St George's Chapel*, ed. Dalton, p. 2.

celebrated and detested Richard Bentley himself. A number of letters which he wrote in the New Year 1689–90 to Edward Bernard the Oxford Orientalist reveal how wrong Bentley was in his assessment of the situation. Bentley was employed to treat with the notorious libertine Adrian Beverland, Isaac Vossius's executor, but the going was very difficult. "I can give no news about M^r V:", Bentley informed his friend Bernard,

> who hath not seen me nor any of my acquaintance this forthnight: I believe he sits in some corner
> Ipse suum cor edens, hominum vestigia vitans. If I be not mistaken, this is no fear of any body of our own nation opposing us in this Bargain. But however methinks you should have hindered the University from falling so in their price for I suppose you & I are of ye same mind to get ye Books as cheap as possibly we can, but rather than loose them, even to overbuy them for ye Reasons y^t you & I discoursed of. Which I here keep as ye greatest secret; as I beg of you to let no person who was not then present know what commission I have; for it y^t should reach Vossius's ear, there'l be no bidding any thing less, then my highest. I am informed y^t Mr Benot ye D. of Brandenburg's Envoy is treating with Vossius, & has desired a Catalogue & a price to be sent to ye University of Leyden You know they are but poor, & bid nothing for Golius's MSS, y^t are yet unsold even at their own home. Nay all Holland is in such circumstances, y^t a Person I know got but 100^{li} this last year our of an estate of 400^{lii} per annum. Add y^t this will be some months a doing, if they should negotiate about it: so y^t I have no fearful apprehensions from Leyden.

Bentley's misinformation is almost comical in light of later events.[101]

The following week, Bentley was once again in contact with Bernard, rather more pessimistic, and worrying that "we must always want that pleasure, which I so much expected, of seing Dr Vossius's Library in the Bodley". This was especially annoying, as Bentley had been informed as for a fact by Henry Godolphin of

---

[101] Bentley to Bernard, "Thursday 20th" [?19/20 December 1689]: Bodl. Lib., MS. Smith 45, f. 155^r. The dating of these three letters from Bentley to Bernard is very uncertain. We know that they date from Dec. 1689 because the letter of 28 Dec. 1689 still retains the postmark. They are ordered somewhat differently than presented here (although undated) in Bentley, *Correspondence*, ed. Wordsworth: this letter is printed pp. 9–10 (letter IV), where the editor notes that Bernard went to Holland in 1695–6 to attend the sale of Golius's library, and bought many of the Leiden Orientalist's books, which went to Narcissus Marsh, who later gave them to Oxford. Cf. J.H. Monk, *The Life of Richard Bentley, D.D.*, London 1833 (2nd edn.) vol. 1, 21–2. Other biographies of Bentley include R.C. Jebb, *Bentley*, London: Macmillan, 1882; and R.J. White, *Dr Bentley. A study in academic scarlet*, London: Spottiswoode, 1965.

Eton College, that "to his certain knowledge Matt: Voss would be glad of 2,500 for it". Bentley now saw this rather low figure "for a dutch trick to raise the price of it". Yet Bentley remained confident that he might still purchase Vossius's books and manuscripts, since it was unlikely that Vossius's heirs would "run the Hazard of removing them; when we weekly here of such losses by the French Privateers". A good sign, meanwhile, was that Beverland was inquiring for Bentley's lodgings, saying that "the Books cannot be disposed without his consent being Executor, & y^t Oxon shall have them 500 cheaper than any Booksellers." In this same letter, Bentley makes allusion to the fact that "the 3 Deans have managed this affair", a reference, presumably, to the heads of Oxford colleges who were involved as well.[102]

A short time later, Bentley was in even a more cheerful mood. "I heartily wish y^t you may come to an agreement with Mr Voss", he wrote to Bernard,

> Beverland is 7. miles out of town, but I saw a letter of his in a friends hand, mentioning how the Duke of Wolfenbuttel, whose fathers famous library is so celebrated by Conringius, employs some Dutch man to bid mony for ye Lib: Credat Judæus Apella. I hear y^t several of D^r V: manusc. are lent beyond seas to several learned men; If it be true (as it is very likely) you ought to enquire for ye catalogue of them, & buy the Right of recovering them. I cannot now so suddenly learn ye author of y^r report of a Transcript of ye Etymol: Neither will it be tanti if ye Originable be so legible, as you said. Only y^t ye Univery may suffer damage by an impression of ye booke out of such a concealed Transcript; which may be prevented in ye Bargain with Mr Voss. But in publica commoda pecces if you should break with Voss upon these considerations; they may serve to beat down the price.[103]

This was the last Bentley had to say about Vossius's books and manuscripts, apart from a laconic note to Bernard in a longer letter of 26 January 1691–2, that the "1st rate are Vossius's own MS, now at Leyden".[104]

---

[102] Bentley to Bernard, "Saturday night" (postmarked 28 Dec. 1689, a Saturday): Bodl. Lib., MS. Smith 45, fos. 157^r–159^r (Bentley, *Correspondence*, ed. Wordsworth, pp. 6–7: letter II). This letter also contains a reference to the recent death of a Dr Slade on 20 Dec. 1689.

[103] Bentley to Bernard, "Tuesday night" [?7 Jan. 1689–90]: Bodl. Lib., MS. Smith 45, f. 149^r (Bentley, *Correspondence*, ed. Wordsworth, 8–9: letter III). Bentley's remarks are mildly ironic in view of the claim by Archbishop Ussher's chaplain Richard Parr (*Life of . . . Ussher*, p. 99) that "divers Volumes" of the primate's manuscript notes "were borrowed by Dr. *Bernard*, and never restored by him".

[104] Bentley to Bernard, 26 Jan. 1691–2: Bodl. Lib., MS. Smith 45, f. 161^r (Bentley, *Correspondence*, ed. Wordsworth, 35–7: letter XVII).

John Evelyn was especially incensed about Oxford's missed opportunity, and wrote to Pepys that the Bodleian Library was

> so poor in manuscripts that they were ashamed to publish their catalogue with that of the *impressorum*, but which might have been equally enriched with any perhaps in Europe, had they purchased what was lately offered them by the executors of Isaac Vossius, though indeed at a great price, who have since carried them back into Holland, where they expect a quicker market. I wished with all my heart some brave and noble Mæcenas would have made a present of them to Trinity College in Cambridge, where that sumptuous structure (designed for a library) would have been the fittest repository for such a treasure. Where are our Suissets, Bodleys, Lauds, Sheldons, bishops, and opulent chancellors? Will the *Nepotismo* never be satisfied.

Apparently one thing Isaac Vossius taught his niece and nephew was how to trade in books and to drive a very hard bargain. Evelyn indeed went into great detail over England's loss: "I have already mentioned what Isaac Vossius brought over", he wrote to Pepys,

> that had been his learned father's, and many other manuscripts which Isaac had himself brought from Queen Christina out of Sweden in recompense of his honorary, whilst he was invited thither with Salmasius, Des Cartes, Blundel, and others, by the heroic and royal errant. But those birds, as I said, have taken their flight, and are gone.[105]

Even two decades after the event, on 21 September 1710, Oxford bibliophile Thomas Hearne recorded in his diary that

> 3,000 libs. offer'd by the University of Oxford for Vossius's Noble Library; but 'twas refus'd & the Books carry'd over Seas, to our no small Disgrace. We should have purchas'd them, & not stood in such a Case upon Punctilio & Niceties, when we are so lavish of our Money upon Trifles, that bring dishonour upon the University.[106]

---

[105] Evelyn to Pepys, [?] 12 Aug. 1689: *Diary*, ed. Bray, vol. 3, 305–6, 308–9: either the accepted date of Evelyn's letter is wrong, or he was possessed with a clairvoyant capacity hitherto unnoticed by historians, since in August 1689 the Vossius library was still in England. Fortunately, one bird which remained in Oxford was the so-called Codex Vossianus, a tenth-century Latin psalter "written in Anglo-Saxon characters, with an interlinear translation, and decorated with grotesque initial letters." As it had been in the possession of his uncle, it is now catalogued as Bodl. Lib., MS. Junius 27: Macray, *Annals*, p. 472.

[106] Thomas Hearne, *Remarks and Collections*, ed. C.E. Doble, vol. 3 (Oxf. Hist. Soc., xiii, 1888), p. 51: Hearne's entry has misled most scholars into thinking that the books were sold only in 1710, when in fact they were all in Leiden as early as October 1690: Prideaux, "Library". Cf. p. 262 for some criticism of Vossius's views; Chaufepié, iv, p. 631. For Vossius's books, see *Bibliotheca Vossiana*, The Hague

Ironically, Vossius's niece and nephew would have done better to
have accepted the Bodleian's offer: only much later, in May 1705,
and only after the intervention of the courts, did they finally receive
from the University of Leiden the sum agreed upon sixteen years
before, which came to 33,000 florins, an amount very close to
Oxford's original £3,000.[107]

VI

"Mr. St. Evremond died renouncing the Christian religion", reported Francis Atterbury, future bishop of Rochester, to a friend,
"Yet the Church of Westminster thought fit, in honour to his
memory, to give his body room in the Abbey, and to allow him to
be buried there gratis".[108] Isaac Vossius held religious views which
were much less extreme and far less uncompromising than those of
Saint-Évremond, but whether it was due to his humorless personality or risible credulity, he seems to have been less successful in his
death. Perhaps it was the equivocal nature of his alleged scepticism. Bayle, who knew about scepticism, declined to give him an
entry in his *Dictionnaire*, "à cause du peu de feuilles qui me
restent".[109] But he spoke about Isaac Vossius at length on other
occasions: "Comme il étoit fils d'un homme qui n'étoit pas moins
bon Chrétien que savant", Bayle mused, "nous devons croire qu'il
fut très-bien élevé dans les Véritez d l'Evangile, & qu'il en fut
très-persuadé plusiers années". About Vossius's later opinions,
however, Bayle was less sure, but was inclined to give him the
benefit of the doubt, as it were, before branding him a complete
sceptic.[110] John Milner thought that Vossius's views were never
completely understood:

1740, a sale catalogue for 19 Apr. 1740, with prices noted on the Bodleian Library
copy, shelfmark 2592 e. 4.
  [107] Prideaux, "Library". The sale price is usually incorrectly cited as 36,000
florins: see e.g. Francis Atterbury to Sir Jonathan Trelawny, then bishop of
Exeter, 18 Sept. 1703: *The Miscellaneous Works of Bishop Atterbury*, ed. J. Nichols,
London 1789–98, #cxviii, vol. 1, 247–8; Niceron, *Memoires*, vol. 13, p. 134.
  [108] Atterbury to Trelawny: see note 107 above.
  [109] Pierre Bayle, *Dictionnaire Historique et Critique*, Rotterdam 1720 (3rd edn.), 4,
p. 2846.
  [110] Idem, *Réponse aux questions d'un provincial* (Rotterdam 1703), vol. 3, chap. 13:
quoted in Chaufepié, *Nouveaux dictionnaire* 4, p. 631. For a similarly charitable view
of Isaac Vossius's piety, see Adrien Baillet, *Jugemens des savans sur les principaux
ouvrages des auteurs*, Paris 1722, vol. 1, 481–3.

The consideration of this uncertainty might also have prevented the scuffles between *Is. Vossius* and his Countrymen that set themselves so fiercely against him. Add hereto that if this uncertainty had been duly considered, the World would not have been burthen'd with many tedious and voluminous writings[111]

Perhaps Isaac Vossius's problem was one of communication. Vossius lacked the institutional backing of a Kennicott or the likable personality of at Saint-Évremond which were essential ingredients for promoting radical scholarly religious views. His championship of the Septuagint chronology and the Jewish origins of the Sibylline Oracles were not in themselves so entirely eccentric that he should have been the victim of such severe attacks. Isaac Vossius was himself aware of the problem, and discussed it at length after only seven years in England. "I am so far from believing that most of you will be favourable and kind to me", he told his English hosts,

> that I am even perswaded that at present there are some, who under colour of honour and good will, do secretly lye in wait for my writings, whetting already their venemous Teeth, that with the breath of a pestiferous and pysonous beast, they may either kill, or render hateful and maimed all the births of my diligence, even before they see the light. It may be you expect that with a great Train I should march out against such, and revenge my self of so great an injury: but if you think so you are much mistaken, for I take it not to be my concern to set upon those who declare War, not against me, but truth it self. If I be not misinformed by some friends, there live in some Colleges a certain kind of Men, who have mutually combined by oath, to admit of no truth which comes from my hands. And although they dissent amongst themselves in opinion, yet they agree to brand the most part of my writings (though they understand them not) with the name of erroneous and meer impostures. Should I not deserve to be laughed at, if I coveted revenge of such men, who by plucking out their own eyes court a voluntary blindness? Truly if out of hatred to me they hate truth it self; I wish them no worse, nor my self no better, than that they may enjoy their own humour, and continue still to persecute me with the greatest hatred.[112]

Domenico Caracciolo, the eighteenth-century Sicilian diplomat, observed that in "England there are sixty different religions, and

---

[111] Milner, *Defence*, p. 33.

[112] Isaac Vossius, *A Treatise Concerning the Motion of the Seas and Winds*, London 1677, sig. a2v. Cf. Vossius's much earlier work, *De lucis natura et proprietate*, Amsterdam 1662, and seventeenth-century notes on it, now Brit. Lib., Add. MS. 4394, f. 420.

only one sauce".[113] But what Isaac Vossius failed to realize was that in England, as in most Protestant countries, that sauce was the infallible Hebrew Bible as the sole channel of divine inspiration, the repository of a sanctity even greater than that of the gospels, and to challenge its authority was to give a lasting reputation of being a complete sceptic to a man who by rights should be remembered as a founding father of biblical criticism in England.

---

[113] *Notes and Queries*, Dec. 1968: repr. *The Concise Oxford Dictionary of Quotations*, Oxford 1981 (2nd edn.), p. 61.

ALAN CHARLES KORS

SKEPTICISM AND THE PROBLEM OF ATHEISM IN EARLY-MODERN FRANCE

The early-modern Christian, and, especially, Catholic learned world possessed a complex and ambivalent set of attitudes towards philosophical skepticism. It was not only that the various schools of Christian philosophy responded quite differently to formal issues of certainty and the limits of human knowledge, but that the same schools and individuals could respond quite diversely depending upon the context in which these issues were raised and the perceived nature and purposes of the interlocutors. Two tendencies coexisted uneasily within a Catholic learned world whose education and traditions linked it both to the mystery of revealed faith and to the philosophical systems of the Greeks. On the one hand, it believed that it possessed a creed whose superior truth and wisdom would be foolish to the profane world and whose salvific characteristics were categorically beyond the fruits of natural learning; on the other, it believed that its doctors and educated believers could prevail in philosophical and theological disputations with the sages of all the nations. From the first tendency, it could be deeply moved by the humbling of natural human reason and natural *scientia*; philosophical skepticism was a wondrous means of achieving that end. From the other, it could be deeply offended and threatened by claims that natural certainty was not among the gifts of philosophy; philosophical skepticism was an arrogant and insidious means of making such claims. Piety admired humility and sought *ataraxia*, and it feared the pride and concupiscence of natural mind; learned theology gloried in disputation and demonstration, and it feared the anarchy of a natural reason that suspended judgment where philosophers offered compelling proofs. The educated Christian world, of course, contained so many minds that were simultaneously pious and learnedly philosophical. It is no wonder that the motifs of philosophical skepticism were so multivalent within that world's reflections and debates. As Mersenne had noted in his *Questions harmoniques* (1633):

One and the same sword can serve an evil man to commit an infamous homicide and can be the instrument of a heroic action in the hands of a virtuous man. He who puts divine things under the scrutiny of Pyrrhonism is as blameworthy as another man is estimable for having formed ideas that represent to him the greatest worldly wisdom as a kind of folly before God, and all human science as dependent upon a night's dream. . . .[1]

"Atheism" *as a concept* functioned with at least as much complexity as philosophical skepticism in the learned world of early-modern France. On the one hand, it was a commonplace to state that no mind sincerely could deny the existence of God, that in the presence of a remarkable variety of proofs of His being, both moral and demonstrative, fitted to the unlearned or to the most learned, only wickedness in search of impunity could will the appearance of disbelief. Atheism, the culture taught, only could be the product of depraved will, not of mind.[2] On the other hand, the culture sought precisely to prove God against the often very complex imagined arguments of the heuristically useful "atheist", generating difficult "objections" and "doubts" to belief in God that learned theology had to overcome, and addressing an inordinate number of works to "atheists" whom it claimed did not exist.[3]

If we examine responses to philosophical skepticism in the context of the early-modern French encounter with the problem of atheism, the tensions inherent in the learned world's attitudes toward skepticism emerge in bolder relief. These tensions are not always apparent when one focuses solely on explicit and seemingly settled discussions of skepticism in the formal treatises of thinkers still deemed to be major figures in the history of philosophy. If we look at the contemporaneously respected professors, theologians, apologists and critics of early-modern France, however, in more than one context, we find a more problematic and unstable set of relationships to skepticism than otherwise might appear. The problem of "atheism" is an excellent foil to the problem of philosophical skepticism.

*   *   *

---

[1] Marin Mersenne, Minim, *Questions harmoniques*. . . ., Paris 1633, 161–163.

[2] Alan Charles Kors, *Atheism in France, 1650–1729*, Volume I: *The Orthodox Sources of Disbelief*, Princeton: Princeton University Press, 1990, 17–43 ("Atheists Without Atheism").

[3] Ibid., 44–109 ("Thinking About the Unthinkable" and "Atheism Without Atheists").

Let us begin with an event. In the summer of 1700, the Oratory in Vendôme upheld a doctoral thesis in theology that pertained to the role of faith in belief in the existence of God. In the presence of the bishop of Blois, to whom the thesis was dedicated, the candidate successfully defended the proposition that "The existence of God does not pertain to faith, *nor can it pertain to faith* [*Existentia Dei ad fidem nec attinet, nec attinere potest*]. So St Thomas judged". Against vigorous opposition from a theology student from Paris who attended the session, the candidate, to the approval of his Oratorian professors, committed himself formally to three additional propositions that he deemed to be entailed by his primary proposition: (1) "The existence of God is not revealed, nor can it be revealed by God"; (2) "No one can elicit an act of faith about the existence of God"; (3) "The Church does not require a positive act of faith about the existence of God".[4] For the Vendôme Oratory, thus, skeptical philosophy had best not stake its claims near this most essential preamble of the faith, since theology did not, indeed, could not receive its belief in God from Revelation or its consequences.

The Parisian student, Becquereau, who was to defend his own doctoral thesis at the Sorbonne later in that year, was scandalized by the thesis and its defense, and he sought unsuccessfully to have it condemned by the bishop of Blois. One contemporary account reported that the affair caused "much stir in the city" [of Vendôme].[5] De Becquereau, upon his return to Paris, showed the propositions to a large number of theologians at the Faculty of Theology and found about forty—many of them identified with Jansenism—willing to draft and sign a censure of them. The censure, relying heavily on Saint Augustine's views of faith and reason, granted that there was nothing the least wrong with believing in God by means of reason, "on the assumption that faith would suffice if reason had not been explored". It simply was fact, however, the censure observed, that without faith many since the Fall had become "doubtful about His existence", from which the indispensability of faith was evident. Further, a purely rational belief in God was "without [salvific] merit [*meritoria non est*]". Indeed, the censure insisted, sound doctrine "damns those who might not believe that God exists through faith unless they were to ascertain it by reason".[6]

---

[4] Bibliothèque Nationale MSS.: Fonds français 19312, 1r.-2r.
[5] Ibid. and *Nouvelles de la République des Lettres*, avril 1701, 476–477 (a letter from a correspondent in France, among the "Extraits des Diverses Lettres").
[6] Bibliothèque Nationale MSS.: Fonds français 19312, 2v.-9v.

While the outcome at the Sorbonne was clear enough in this particular case, its details reveal the ambiguities inherent in any early-modern attempt to define appropriate boundaries between the realms of natural philosophy and faith. On the surface, if the censure were theologically correct, philosophical skepticism posed no threat to the sequence of belief. Without reason or demonstration, faith could lead one from belief in God to belief in the Revelation of that God. Beneath the surface, however, the matter was not so clear. First, Becquereau had worried about achieving the censure if the names and affiliations of the persons censured were known, and he presented the propositions to the Sorbonne theologians "*in abstracto*"; the objects of the censure were not identified until after it had been achieved in that form. Second, despite such a ringing censure, the archbishop of Paris was so outraged by Becquereau's action that he "forbade him from performing any function in his diocese, even saying the mass". Third, even after being informed of the condemnation, the bishop of Blois declared himself "greatly shocked by this censure".[7] Who might be offended by the censure? Why were not all theologians, even when the issues were clearly drawn, willing to grant an essential role to faith in securing belief in the existence of God?

It depended on context, and, we shall see, it depended on context even for many of the signatories of the censure itself. If the issue appeared to be the explicit and bold claim that natural proof of God was a necessary *precondition* of faith, that seemed to go too far. Indeed, that could seem a damnable threat to the rights of faith. If the issue appeared to be the logical sequence of belief, however, considered without reference to piety, then many orthodox voices reached conclusions that made the claims of philosophical skepticism dangerous ones indeed. To understand why some saw skepticism, even fideistic skepticism, as an abyss that led to atheism itself, which is to understand the theological confidence of the Vendôme Oratory in its thesis, let us turn to early-modern considerations of the proper sequence of educated belief.

*   *   *

In the catechisms by which the Church taught children and the uneducated, the issue of the proper sequence of belief never was raised. The creed commanded assent in all of its details, the young

---

[7] Ibid., 1r.-2r; and *Nouvelles de la République des Lettres, loc.cit.*

and unlearned were taught, because it came from God's own infallible Word and Church.[8] The educated Catholic had no problem whatsoever with the central assumption in this, namely, that what God indeed revealed commanded unequivocal assent.

The logical sequence of belief, however, posed a problem of its own. Believing the articles of faith because one believed that there was a God who had revealed them and who could not err made perfect sense. For most of the learned, however, trained in the analysis and classification of arguments, fallacies and demonstrations, it was self-evidently circular to believe in the existence of God because of the creed and in the creed because it came from God. There was no problem with such a phenomenon as *a mode of faith*, and one did not have to emphasize or even raise the issue of philosophical demonstration for those who would not understand such matters. There was an essential problem with such a phenomenon as *a natural argument*, however, for it clearly involved a *pétition de principe*, that is, it presupposed the very object it set out to prove. Given the learned community's belief that it possessed a treasury of compelling demonstrations of God's existence, this fideistic sequence of belief involved an utterly unnecessary paralogism for them, and they saw no need to defend it in the abstract, let alone to unbelievers real or imagined.

What was divine in origin commanded assent, but as Aquinas had noted about the logical sequence of belief when he had addressed "the gentiles":

> We must set down in the beginning that whereby His existence is demonstrated, as the necessary foundation of the whole work. For *if we do not demonstrate that God exists, all consideration of divine things is necessarily suppressed.*[9]

Considered in terms of sequence, belief in God was not an article of the faith, but a preamble to those articles.

Certainly, there always had been and in the seventeenth century there still were those who questioned not only the validity, but even

---

[8] See the catechisms from the seventeenth century in the Bibliothèque Nationale *Imprimés*, "D" listings.

[9] Thomas Aquinas, O.P., *Summa Contra Gentiles*, l.I. c.9. par.5 (vol. 13 of the seventeenth-century edition by Jean Nicolai, O.P. et al., *Sancti Thomae Aquinatis . . . Opera Omnia. . . .* 23 vols., Paris 1660)). I am using the translation of ed. and transl. Anton C. Pegis, Saint Thomas Aquinas, *S.C.G., Book One: God*, Notre Dame and London 1975, p. 85. On the problems of assessing the place of demonstration in Aquinas's thought, see the exceptionally encyclopedic and thoughtful work of Fernand van Steenberghen, *Le problème de l'existence de Dieu dans les écrits de S. Thomas d'Aquin*, Louvain-la-Neuve 1980.

the whole theological and moral status of efforts to demonstrate philosophically the existence of God, "fideists" of diverse stripes, who, wishing to stress either the incapacity of fallen human reason or the virtue of faith (or, indeed, both) argued that belief in God was a matter of faith alone. Almost every scholastic theologian who addressed the question of God's existence felt obliged to deal with such opinions, "*de opinione dicentium quod Deum esse demonstrari non potest, sed sola fide tenetur*", as the commonplace formulation put it. Faced not with those who minimized the role of faith, however, but with such fideists who seemed to concede the philosophical terrain to the unbeliever, the Church maintained a supreme confidence in the rational and evidential demonstrability of this most fundamental preamble or foundation of its belief. Aquinas, whose re-edited works were enjoying a vast revival of readership in the seventeenth century, had believed that "what led some persons to hold this [fideistic] view was the weakness of the arguments which had been brought forth by others to prove that God exists", a problem that he thought resolved by demonstrative proofs.[10]

In his *Quaestiones de Veritate*, Aquinas had explained it quite simply:

> That God exists is not an article of faith but a preamble to an article of faith, unless we understand something else along with God's existence, for example, that He has a unity of essence with a trinity of persons and other similar things.[11]

In his commentary on Boethius, St Thomas had taught that while sacred doctrine went far beyond philosophy, it was consistent with and related to natural knowledge, since philosophy "contains . . . certain resemblances to what belongs to faith, and *certain preambles to faith*". Proof of the preambles was philosophy's foremost use to theology:

> First, we can use it [philosophy] to demonstrate the preambles of the faith, *which are necessary to the science of faith as being those things that are proven of God by natural arguments, for example, that God exists*, that God is one, or similar propositions concerning God or created beings *that faith presupposes as having been proven in philosophy*.[12]

---

[10] Aquinas, *Summa Contra Gentiles*, 1.I. c.12. (Pegis's translation).

[11] Aquinas, *Quaestiones disputatae . . . de Veritate*, q. 10, art. 12. (vol. 11 of the Nicolai, O.P. edn.). I have used the translation in Bernardino M. Bonansea, *God and Atheism. A Philosophical Approach to the Problem of God*, Washington 1979, p. 172.

[12] Aquinas, *Expositio in Librum Boetii de Trinitate*, q. 2, art. 3. (vol. 20 of the Nicolai, O.P. edn.). I have borrowed, loosely, the translation by Anton C. Pegis, offered in his general introduction to the *S.C.G.*.

Aquinas had not argued that philosophical demonstration of the existence of God was necessary to any act of faith, but simply to the *scientia* of sacred things, that is, to the science of theology. If one wished the latter, however, then philosophical demonstration of the existence of God was a presupposition of such a science. Thus, in the *Summa Theologiae*, Saint Thomas explained both the essential relationship of philosophical demonstration to theological *scientia* and the unessential nature of such preambles to any other valid sort of faith:

> The truths about God which St Paul says we can know by our natural powers of reasoning—that God exists, for example—are not numbered among the articles of faith, *but are presupposed to them. For faith presupposes natural knowledge* just as grace does nature and all perfections that which they perfect. However, there is nothing to stop a man accepting on faith some truth which he personally cannot demonstrate, even if that truth in itself is such that demonstration could make it evident.[13]

By the seventeenth century, when the claims of *évidence* in Christian philosophical theology were great indeed, even a philosophical skeptic such as La Mothe Le Vayer could accept what he took to be Aquinas's distinctions: "Saint Thomas resolved very well [*a fort bien determiné*] that our belief on this matter in not an article of the Faith". La Mothe Le Vayer's fideism, which informed so much of his submission to specific articles of the creed, did not extend to belief in this essential preamble. An article of faith, he explained, "concerns only things that are not evident and never manifest truths, which are, like this one [the existence of God], plain [*notoires*] to everyone".[14] Pierre Bayle himself had approved of this thesis while teaching at Sedan:

> It is imprudent, to say the least, to testify with certain individuals that one would not believe that there is a God if one had not learned it from Holy Scripture. For if we give faith to Holy Scripture, it is because we believe that it is the word of God. Now, before believing that a thing is the word of God, one must believe that there is a God . . . The knowledge of divine existence thus precedes the knowledge of this Revelation, *and is presupposed by it, from which it follows that it comes from natural light* [*Cognitio ergo existentiae divinae prior est cognotione revelationis et av ea supponitur, atque adeo fluit a lumine naturali*].[15]

---

[13] *Summa Theologica S. Thomae Aquinatis* . . ., ed. Jean Nicolai, Paris 1663, in-folio, Ia. q.2, art.2.

[14] François La Mothe le Vayer, *Oeuvres*. 15 vols., new edn. aug. (3rd edn.), Paris 1684, vol. 11, 408–409.

[15] Pierre Bayle, *Theses philosophiques*, xii, in Bayle, *Oeuvres diverses*, 4 vols., 2nd edn., The Hague [Trévoux] 1737, vol. 4, p. 143.

In this, they merely were repeating what Saint Thomas's respected seventeenth-century editor and commentator, the Domini-
can educator and scholar Jean Nicolai, had noted in his edition of
the *Summa Theologia*: faith pertained only to that which was inevident,
but the existence of God was manifest by demonstrative proofs.[16] It
was the almost universal understanding of the eighth session of the
Fifth Lateran Council (1513) that it was now an article of faith that
knowledge of the existence of God was philosophically demonstrable.[17] The widely admired Minim monk and teacher Emmanuel Maignan, mathematician, philosopher and theologian, termed
any opposition to this view to be, at best, an absolute "theological
error", but, most probably, an actual heresy, "entirely and expressly against the faith".[18] There were potentially embarrassing depar-
tures from such assurance to be found among admired medieval
theologians, but well before the seventeenth century, the issue was
"officially" settled, and not only by the Lateran Council. In
France, the Faculty of Theology at Paris explicitly had condemned
any fideistic claims that God could not be proven by natural
reason.[19] Why not? For most theologians, the exhilaration of their
enterprise began with the investigation of the revealed attributes
and will of God, with the Trinity, and with Christian knowledge of
the relationship of God to man. Let the philosophers or philosophically minded have the pleasure of reminding mankind, with Romans 1:19–21, that the atheist was "without excuse" for disbelief in
God even without benefit of Revelation or particular grace.

For the pious Jansenist Louis Ellies-Du Pin, theologian and royal
professor of philosophy, the utility of philosophy to theology became clear when one considered the sequence of belief. "The
certitude of the truths of religion", he explained in his *Traité de la
doctrine chrétienne et orthodoxe* . . . (1703), depended upon the reasonableness of submitting our reason to truths divinely revealed.
What made that submission reasonable, however, was the certainty
that "God cannot deceive men by revealing falsities as truths",

---

[16] *Summa Theologica S. Thomae Aquinatis*, Ia q.2, art. 2, Nicolai's note "P".

[17] *Histoire des Conciles d'après les documents originaux*, ed. Ch.-J. Hefele, continuée
par J. Cardinal Hergenroether, vol. 8, Paris: Letouzey, 1917, part 1, 420–422.

[18] Emmanuel Maignan, Minim, *Philosophia Sacra, sive entis tum supernaturalis, tum
increati, ubi de iis quae Theologia habet seu quoad Substantiam, seu quoad modum Physica, vel
similia Physicis; tum circa Deum secundum se, eiusque ut Unius ac Trini perfectiones* . . .,
Paris and Toulouse 1661, in-fol., 85–86. There would be a second edition of the
Philosophia Sacra, Lyon 1672.

[19] *Chartularium Universitatis Parisiensis*, ed. Henri Denifle, 4 vols., Paris: Delalain
1889–1897, vol. 2, pièce 1124, 576ff.

which we knew *not* by faith (which would be circular), but by "natural reason". Knowledge by natural light that there was a God who was "supremely perfect . . . convinces us in an evident manner of His veracity". Such knowledge of the existence of God, by the same logic, could not be from Revelation, but, rather, was "known by the lights of nature, and provable by reason". The necessity of natural truth in the sequence of reasonable belief in Christian doctrine, then, made it "permissible, useful, *and even necessary to join Reason to Faith in order to establish them*".[20]

Thus, the English Catholic Henry Holden's examination of faith, *De Fide*, published in Paris with the approbation of a leading theologian of the Sorbonne, began with the observation that "It is evident that in the question which I undertake to discuss [faith], *diverse things are to be supposed as demonstrated elsewhere*", first among which was "That there is a God".[21] Discussing *De Fide* two generations later in his *Bibliothèque des auteurs ecclésiastiques*, Du Pin paraphrased that simple introduction as follows:

> With regard to the existence of God, he [Holden] believes it *a preamble necessary to the Faith, rather than an Article of Faith*, because it is impossible to believe any Article on the basis of the authority of God who revealed it, unless one presupposes the existence of God: *and he does not believe that one can give one's consent to this proposition, 'God exists,' because God revealed it.*[22]

Aquinas surely had not said *that*, but there was the argument stated plainly enough, by an anti-Thomist Jansenist, no less, that the Faith itself, and assent to its foundation, required an anterior demonstration of God's existence. If that were the case, then even the most piously motivated skeptical challenge to the demonstrability of the preambles was a serious business indeed.

To the counter-argument that a proper Christian *philosophy* should *begin* with unquestioning belief in the existence of God, France's leading Aristotelian philosopher of the latter half of the seventeenth century, Pierre Barbay, replied that it should not. Barbay, whose courses in Aristotelian philosophy at the University of Paris helped to shape the thinking of a generation, acknowledged that some wanted the proposition "God exists [*Deus est*]" to be a "first principle of Metaphysics" that must be adhered to "indisputably [*sine*

---

[20] Louis Ellies-Du Pin, *Traité de la doctrine chrétienne et orthodoxe* . . ., Paris 1703, 3–10, 552–556.

[21] Henry Holden, *An Analysis of the Divine Faith*, W.G., transl., Paris 1658, 1–2.

[22] Louis Ellies-Du Pin, *Bibliothèque des auteurs ecclésiastiques du dix-septième siècle.* 7 vols., Paris 1708, vol. 2, p. 166.

controversia]". He explicitly and vigorously rejected this claim, however, insisting that the *only* indisputable first principle was that "it is impossible for something to be and not to be at the same time", from which one was obliged to demonstrate other truths, including the existence of God.[23] Indeed, only after that demonstration could natural philosophy then address the issue of divine attributes, such as His veracity, upon which knowledge of the truth of Revelation logically depended.[24]

Maignan, in his influential courses on philosophy and theology at the University of Toulouse, explained to his students that while philosophy dealt with natural and theology with supernatural things, theology could rely upon natural light to create a "sacred philosophy", the object of which would be to demonstrate the existence of God, to understand God's works in nature, and to establish the foundations of religion. The fruit of this, his *Philosophia Sacra* (1661), was published with an unusually large number of approbations from the superiors of his Minim order, from Minim professors of theology at Toulouse, from a *professeur-régent* of theology at Toulouse, and from several Carmelite theologians. For Maignan, while theologians legitimately could presuppose the existence of God as the "first principle of the faith [*primum fidei principium*]", they obviously could *not* prove it to the unbeliever from Revelation, and needed to appeal to natural philosophy to establish that principle when challenged. For the Christian, Maignan insisted, gentile disbelief in God's existence was "inexcusable" not because it violated "Scripture", which the gentile could not know, or "probability", or "hypothesis", but precisely because it violated indubitable philosophical knowledge, that is to say, natural *"scientia"*.[25]

The theologian Jean-Claude Sommier, protonotary apostolic and soon to be a cardinal, in a work dedicated to Pope Clement XI and published with approbations from Oratorian *and* Jesuit theologians, from professors at the collège royal and the collège d'Epinal, and with the *imprimatur* of the count-bishop of Toul, wrote in 1708 that reason was absolutely "necessary" to the faith. Without rational foundations, he insisted, even faith would fall, since faith was obeyed voluntarily, which meant "on the basis of a full hearing

---

[23] Pierre Barbay, *Commentarius in Aristotelis Metaphysicam*. 2nd edn., rev., Paris 1676, 24–29. The first edition of Barbay's In *Aristotelis Metaphysicam* was 1674. His *In universam Aristotelis philosophiam introductio* was in a fifth edition by 1707.

[24] Pierre Barbay, *in Aristotelis Metaphysicam*, 361–372.

[25] Emmanuel Maignan, Minim, *Philosophia Sacra*, 57–104. The discussion of the *primum fidei principium* is found on 59–60.

of the evidence [*avec connoissance de cause*]": "one never could believe sincerely what one did not see and perceive, if one were not truly persuaded [by reason] that one must believe it. . . . *Without true reason, and without evident knowledge, there cannot be true religion*". It was above all because of this that "it would be a heresy to say that one cannot know the existence of God without faith".[26]

As François Feu, doctor of theology from the Sorbonne, reminded his readers, proof of the existence of God was essential not only because the faith must be armed "against various temptations" offered by the atheists, but because it was the obvious *precondition* of all theology.[27] The preface of John Ray's work on the existence of God, translated into French in 1714, put the matter quite simply. Theology, like all sciences, properly could assume rather than prove the existence of its object of inquiry, but that created an essential need for a natural philosophical proof of God's being:

> Since the principle foundation of religion is the belief in and fear of God, and since one could not love Him nor serve Him without knowing Him, and without being fully persuaded of His existence, it is absolutely necessary to establish firmly this first principle.[28]

Those concerned explicitly with fideistic claims felt obliged to make this point quite strongly. When Descartes imagined the atheist faced only by a philosophical skeptic, he found the consequences unacceptable. In the dedication of his *Meditations*, Descartes urged that proof of God and proof of the immortal soul were "the principal [questions] that should be demonstrated rather by the arguments of philosophy than of theology". While it was "sufficient" for "us others who are faithful to believe by faith [*par la foi*] that there is a God", he advised, "certainly it does not seem possible ever to persuade the unfaithful of any religion, nor scarcely of any moral virtue, *if in the first place one does not prove these two things [the existence of God and the immortality of the soul] by natural reason [si premièrement on ne leur prouve ces deux choses par raison naturelle]*".[29]

---

[26] Jean-Claude Sommier, *Histoire dogmatique de la religion; ou La religion prouvée par l'authorité divine et humaine, et par les lumières de la raison*. 3 vols., Paris 1708–1711, vol. 1, i-ii.

[27] François Feu, *Theologici Tractatus ex Sacris Codicibus, et Sanctorum Patrum Monumentis Excerpti*. 2 vols., Paris 1692–1695 vol. 1, p. 2.

[28] John Ray, *L'existence et la sagesse de Dieu, manifestées dans les oeuvres de la création*, transl. G. Broedelet, Utrecht 1714, *Préface*.

[29] René Descartes, [Dedication] "To Messieurs the deans and doctors of the Sacred Faculty of Theology of Paris", in *Meditationes de Prima Philosophia in qua Dei existentia et animae immortalitas demonstratur*, Paris 1641.

In 1661, Jean de Silhon, in his effort to warn the faithful of the incompatibility of skeptical philosophy and faith, despite fideistic claims to the contrary, insisted that "three constant and indubitable truths" were the foundation of Christianity, and that if they were rendered dubious by natural philosophy, the faith itself could not stand: first, "that there is some Sovereign Being to whom all nature is subject, and who . . . can be neither deceived Himself in His knowledge nor want to deceive others"; secondly, that His signs to our senses cannot be imaginary or illusory (as the skeptics would claim); and third, that His signs could only be from Him. Before one could accept the faith one had to accept the existence of the God who revealed the faith, and before one could know the existence of that God, the certainty of knowledge had to be secured against skeptical philosophy. Only "*evidence*", a certainty beyond opinion and probability, made possible that "science" on which the truths essential to the establishment of the faith depended.[30]

In 1675, faced with the skeptical academic philosophy of canon Simon Foucher, the Benedictine monk and philosopher Dom Robert Desgabets declared himself wholly unimpressed by "the Academics [skeptical philosophers] who make a profession of piety [and] say that Faith suffices for us. . . ." While he did not question Foucher's piety or sincerity, he observed that "one is right to say to them [the fideists] that it is not an inconsiderable evil [*mal*] to reverse as much as they do the natural order *which requires that one be convinced by reason of the immortality of the soul and of the existence of God before one proposes our mysteries to the unbelievers [l'ordre naturel qui veut que l'on soit convaincu par raison . . . de l'existence de Dieu auparavant qu'on propose de sa part aux infidelles nos mystères]. . . .*"[31] In 1696, his fellow Benedictine, the philosopher Dom François Lamy, seeking to refute Spinoza rather than the skeptics, put the matter bluntly indeed. Metaphysical certainty was a matter of paramount importance, Lamy wrote, for on the basis of its conclusions "one will be persuaded that there is a God, or that there is not; that He is free and intelligent, or that He is not; that He has a providence full of light and wisdom, or that He has not; that He is just, veracious, omnipo-

---

[30] Jean de Silhon, *De la certitude des connoissances humaines*, Paris 1661, 6–7, 60–68, 546–554.

[31] Dom Robert Desgabets, O.S.B., *Critique de la Critique de la Recherche de la vérité, où l'on découvre le chemin qui conduit aux connaissances solides. Pour servir de réponse à la Lettre d'un académicien*, Paris 1675, 7–11. In his discussion of skepticism and God, Ibid., 57–71, Desgabets warned that without a principle of certainty, "we would not be assured that there is a real world, a religion, a God, etc". (*nous ne serions pas assurés qu'il y a un vray monde, une Religion, un Dieu, etc.*).

tent, [and] the true cause of everything that has being, or that He is not". Obviously, Lamy noted, "all our ethics and our religion must vary extremely according to the diversity of these alternatives". That being the case, *"nothing is more important to man than the knowledge of a science ["metaphysics"] which alone can give him the means of sorting out the best parts of all that."* In short, he advised:

> [R]eligion and the certitude of the faith themselves depend in some fashion on metaphysics, in that it is necessary for it [metaphysical philosophy] to prove for them at least that there is a God; that this God is not a deceiver; and that His testimony is infallible.[32]

Far from being a marginal work, Lamy's text was published with the approbation of Fénelon himself, and with further approbations from the powerful Hideux, theologian, doctor of the Sorbonne and *curé des Saints Innocents* and from Coulau, the influential director of the Bibliothèque Mazarine.[33] Ten years later, in his *Premier élémens des sciences*, Lamy reiterated these same themes: reason first must establish the existence of God before faith in His word can occur; to believe by faith that God exists would be to accept the word of a being whom you did not yet know to exist, which would be absurd.[34]

No less a theologian and philosopher than Malebranche himself completed the equation of "preamble" with an essential obligation to prove God by reason prior to real faith. In his *Conversations chrétiennes*, first published in 1676, one of his interlocutors, Aristarque, declares himself "convinced [of the existence of God] by faith; but I confess that I am not fully convinced of it by reason". Malebranche's Théodore replied:

> If you say things as you think them, you are convinced of it neither by reason nor by faith. For do you not see that the certitude of the faith comes from the authority of a God who speaks, and who can not be a deceiver. *If, therefore, you are not convinced by reason that there is a God, how will you be convinced that He has spoken?* Can you know that He has spoken, without knowing [first] that He is?[35]

---

[32] Dom François Lamy, O.S.B., *Le nouvel athéisme renversé, ou réfutation du sistême de Spinosa. Tirée pour la plupart de la conaissance de la nature de l'homme*, Paris 1696, 5–8.

[33] Ibid. The approbations *follow* the *Avertissement*.

[34] Dom François Lamy, O.S.B., *Les premiers élémens des sciences, ou Entrée aux connoissances solides, en divers entretiens, proportionnés à la portée des commerçans, et suivis d'un essay de logique*, Paris 1706, 68–94.

[35] Malebranche, Oratory, *Conversations chrétiennes* [1677] in *Oeuvres complètes de Malebranche*, ed. André Robinet, 21 vols., Paris 1958–1970, vol. 4, p. 14 The *Conversations chrétiennes* enjoyed seven editions.

If that were the case, then demonstration of God was, to say the least, no simple logical exercise, and to whatever extent one accepted Malebranche's view, to that extent one's belief in God depended in one's own mind precisely upon philosophical demonstration. For Malebranche, this posed no problem, since "everything proves God".[36] Nonetheless, it clearly raised the stakes of the struggle against philosophical skepticism dramatically.

*   *   *

If any group of thinkers should have been on guard against such claims of the indispensability of philosophical certainty to faith, surely it would have been the signatories of the censure of the Oratory of Vendôme, but an examination of that list reveals how critical was the *context* of the denunciation of such views. An explicit appeal to, above all, Jansenizing theologians had produced a condemnation of a theoretical use of St Thomas to support the view that natural proof of the existence of God was essential as a real *precondition* of faith. Recall Malebranche's rhetorical question, urged on behalf of the view that faith in God's existence, absent rational conviction to that effect, was illogical: "If . . . you are not convinced by reason that there is a God, how will you be convinced that He has spoken?" Among the signatories of the censure, however, was Malebranche's editor and frequent approbator, Blampignon. Recall the Benedictine François Lamy's thesis that "religion and the certitude of the faith" *depended* on metaphysical proof of God, but among the signatories of the censure was Hideux, who gave warm approbation to the very work in which Lamy made such an argument. When eight years after the censure, Sommier, soon to be made a cardinal, repeated and, in effect, extended the most extreme implications of Lamy's and Malebranche's argument, making sincere religious belief entirely dependent upon prior rational and natural conviction of the existence of God, he received the approbation of Pissonat, another signatory of the censure.[37]

Much depended, then, upon the circumstances of the question. If the issue were explicitly the status of faith, then these figures could censure such an elevation of philosophical demonstration. If the

---

[36] Malebranche, *De la recherche de la vérité*, in Ibid., vol. 2, p. 19, 103–104 (where he urges that in fact, nothing has more proofs than God's existence).

[37] Bibliothèque Nationale MSS.: Fonds français 19312, 1r.-9v. See the *Approbations* in the cited works.

issue were philosophical skepticism or actual disbelief, however, the same censurers could find nothing unsound, threatening or exceptional in the claim of reason's indispensability to faith, or, more precisely, in the argument that faith required anterior philosophical demonstration of God's existence.[38] They could be moved, depending on context, by both their sense of the need for faith since the fall *and* their sense of the divine illumination of the rational mind. The censure of 1701, a defense of the rights of faith, had little audience. The works of Malebranche, François Lamy and Jean-Claude Sommier had, by comparison, a very large one. Philosophically confident, such proponents of the necessity of natural demonstration of the preambles of the faith succeeded in making the issue of philosophical skepticism one that could not be separated from the issue of atheism.

* * *

If the logical sequence of belief were from demonstration of God to acceptance of His Revelation, then a criterion of truth by means of which God's existence could be proven was indispensable to sound theology. Villemandy's well-received *Scepticismus debellatus* (1697) saw the Cartesian "circle" as far more than a paralogism. By making entailed demonstration dependent on God's will, Villemandy argued, Descartes had removed the ability to prove God. If, as Descartes believed, God could have willed that the whole were less than its parts, then there was no escape from Pyrrhonism, which led ineluctably, Villemandy feared, to atheism.[39] Reviewing

---

[38] The study of approbations is exceptionally helpful in the analysis of the patterns and alliances of the theological community (although, as with current peer review, there was much that fell through the cracks of cursory readings). A full examination of the early-modern approbation would allow us to identify the theological and religious sympathies (and learn much about the strategies) of large numbers of doctors of theology throughout France. This is especially important given the intensity of divisions among Catholic schools of thought (each with eminent defenders). Even in times requiring the greatest prudence, authors knew where to turn for needed approbations, and there were not only distinct groups of Thomist, Molinist and Jansenist censors and superiors who could be counted on to grant permissions to works that competing schools found both essentially dangerous to the faith and often libelous of other theologians, but there were similar camps of Aristotelian, Cartesian, Malebranchist and fideistic censors. Usually, censors simply noted that a work "contained nothing contrary to the faith", a criterion that allowed a great deal of *philosophical* latitude. Occasionally, as in the first editions of Pascal's *Pensées*, they used their approbations for their own polemical purposes, offering an extended defense of an author's work.

[39] Pierre de Villemandy, *Scepticismus debellatus . . .*, Leiden 1697.

the work, the *Histoire des Ouvrages des Savans*, in that same year, found it deplorable that Pyrrhonism flourished in times of great learning rather than in times of dark ignorance, and commended Villemandy for "waging war against Pyrrhonism . . . this dangerous and harmful sect . . . that deprives [mankind] of the certitude of knowledge".[40]

Over ten years later, the *Histoire des Ouvrages des Savans* praised the late Jacquelot for having observed "that Pyrrhonism, or skeptical philosophy, had infected many minds, and that if they [its adherents] did not formally deny the existence of God, they placed it in doubt, and made it problematic".[41] To criticize reason, the *Nouvelles de la République des Lettres* had observed in 1707, "tends directly to Pyrrhonism, that is to say, to the total extinction of Reason". It termed such Pyrrhonism "the most extravagant and indefensible" of opinions, and insisted that "a Pyrrhonist is a true atheist, and the most incurable of all atheists".[42]

These were common objections to philosophical skepticism. As Jean de Silhon had argued in 1661, the Academic principle that "there are no indubitable [propositions]" clearly entailed that "the existence of God, for example, is a truth of which one can doubt", and that the great issue of his being could not be decided with certainty.[43] In his *Theologia naturalis*, the eminent Jesuit Théophile Raynaud argued that skeptical philosophy, by eliminating the possibility of demonstrative proof, led, if unrefuted, to atheistic conclusions.[44] If one did not abandon Academic philosophy after its critical forays, in order to establish positive proof of God, a Jesuit reviewer of a French translation of Cicero's *De natura deorum* observed, such philosophy "appears to lead gradually [*insensibilement*] to Atheism".[45] Buddeus's celebrated *Theses theologicae de atheismo et superstitione variis*, first published in 1717 and translated into French by the Sorbonniste Louis Philon in 1740, identified skepti-

---

[40] *Histoire des Ouvrages des Savans*, fév. 1697, 240–250.
[41] Ibid., déc. 1708, 528–29.
[42] *Nouvelles de la République des Lettres*, juillet 1707, p. 45.
[43] de Silhon, *De la certitude . . .*, 1–5.
[44] Théophile Raynaud, S.J., *Opera omnia . . .*, 19 vols. (in folio!), Lyon 1665, vol. 5, 205–17, 292–298.
[45] Johann Franz von Buddeus, *Theses theologicae de atheismo et superstitione variis . . .*, Jena 1717 (3rd Latin edn., Jena 1737). Translated as Jean-François Buddeus, *Traité de l'athéisme et de la superstition, par feu Mr. Jean-François Buddeus, Docteur & Professeur en Théologie. Avec des remarques historiques et philosophiques*, transl. Louis Philon, ed. Jean-Chrétien Fischer, Amsterdam 1740, 17–20. See especially n.2 on 18 and n.1 on 19.

cism as one of the two explicit schools of philosophical atheism. "It is certainly *the same thing*", he wrote, "to affirm without exception that there is nothing certain and to deny the existence of God".[46]

The Pyrrhonism explicated by Sextus Empiricus, then, striking against the notion of a criterion of certainty, was presented frequently and diversely as incompatible with the theistic preamble of any coherent faith. The anonymous translator of Sextus into French, writing in 1727, insisted that he saw no such problems in the *Hypotyposes*. The work, he noted, simply shared Sextus's "great knowledge of the opinions of the ancient philosophers". Many great philosophers and, indeed, great Christian theologians "have been Pyrrhonians", he observed, and without danger, since far from ever asserting that he could disprove God, Sextus merely had identified the problems with purely philosophical discussions of Divinity. While he himself was "not strong enough" to overcome skepticism, the translator noted, he was certain that there were those who were.[47]

Reviewing this edition, the Jesuit *Journal de Trévoux* refused to allow its readers to find any such comfort. The reviewer noted "with indignation" the danger of Sextus's work having been "brought onstage" so often for so long, "sometimes in Greek, sometimes in Latin, and now in French". All skeptics, the *Journal* opined, "want one to doubt . . . if there is a Providence [and] if there is a God". Such skeptics claimed that their doubt was pure humility", but they could not state this "in good faith". The translator had noted that Christian faith was wholly sheltered from skeptical discussion; the Jesuit journal disagreed, because if one granted even the Pyrrhonian theoretical criticism of a *criterium* of truth (that the criterion's truth itself would depend on a prior criterion, ad infinitum), not even faith could save Christian belief. If, as Sextus claimed, natural human reason and the natural senses could not attain or provide a means to attain certainty, then "how save the idea of God from this general wreckage of ideas?" The reviewer was not thinking about the religious priority of faith over philosophy, a perspective that might have informed a review of an excessively naturalist or rationalist work, but about the implications of skepticism for a sequence of belief that should culminate in

---

[46] The *Hypotyposes* was translated anonymously into French as *Les Hipotiposes, ou Institutions pirroniennes de Sextus Empiricus, en trois livres, traduites du grec, avec des notes.* (S.l., 1725), *Préface* (unpaginated, xxii pp.) and *Réflexions* . . ., 277–284. The translation was reprinted, London [?] 1735.

[47] *Journal de Trévoux*, jan. 1727, 36–62; *Hipotiposes*, 277–284.

acceptance of the Christian creed. His argument, to the journal's large and diverse audience, showed again how critical the issue of rational proof of the "preamble" of the faith could be made to appear. His use of the term "I" placed the Christian, and not the unbeliever, into the sequence that must begin with *philosophical* certainty:

> How will I believe that there is a God if I must distrust my *reason* which tells me it, the wonders of nature which announce it to me, geometrical truths which are even more suited to my intelligence, and more sensibly evident? [If] I have no *Criterium*, no discernment, no rule of truth or certainty, what will assure me thus of the existence of this God? . . . for it is to these blasphemies that one comes by reasoning consequentially [from philosophical skepticism].[48]

*   *   *

The problem, however, was that there always had been and were deeply Christian voices who saw no dependency of their faith upon the philosophers and the schools of natural *scientia*. Jerusalem, for them, was not indebted to Athens; it had liberated the human soul from Athens. Fideism presented as the only route to knowledge of the existence of God may have been condemned, but it never could be suppressed. In 1665, the Dominicans of the Faubourg Saint Germain produced a French edition of John Tauler's fifteenth-century treatise on spiritual knowledge of things divine, *Les Institutions divines*. There, the Christian could encounter an attitude toward natural knowledge that was of powerful attraction to the pious of both, perhaps all, centuries. Suffering, humiliation, penitence and Christ, for Tauler, as, indeed, for Pascal, were the only routes to God. "One must know", Tauler had written, "that the instinct or the light of nature that appears in the understanding incites us and leads us only to phantasms and to illusions, and to the search for and possession of [concupiscent] pleasure, enjoyment, and praise of ourselves."[49] Christian belief had as its goal *not* anything related to philosophy, but "faith completely naked and completely pure, without any other knowledge".[50] Indeed, for Tauler, "our faith being confirmed by no experience whatsoever becomes more pure, more . . . sincere, more . . . useful, and more

---

[48] *Journal de Trévoux*, loc. cit. The lengthy quotation is found on 53–54.
[49] John Tauler, O.P., *Les Institutions de Thaulere . . . Traduction nouvelle*, Paris 1665, p. 49.
[50] Ibid., 81–82.

meritorious".[51] In an *Avertissement*, Tauler's translators warned that to be understood, the work should be read in a spirit of abasement and humility, which they thought would be difficult for "persons accustomed to the reasonings of a base and human Philosophy".[52]

Philosophical Christians might insist on the necessity of a criterion of truth to the faith, but as Baker's *Reflections upon Learning . . .*, translated with ecclesiastical approbation into French as the *Traité de l'Incertitude* (1714), noted, philosophers led us to the darkest obscurity not only because they disagreed among themselves on every basic question, but precisely because they could not agree even upon "the first *criterium* of truth". Cartesians refute the schoolmen; the schoolmen refute Descartes. In human philosophy, every position not only can be but has been effectively opposed.[53] It might depend on how the issues were framed, but many Christian sensibilities would have agreed with Pascal in the *Entretien de . . . Pascal et . . . de Sacy* published by Desmolets: without knowing God first, one cannot know truth of any kind.[54] As Guéret put it in 1671, addressing the philosophers, "For almost six thousand years, you have been searching for the truth, and not one of you has discovered it? One would say that it hides itself expressly to maintain the disputes that give you your livelihood." It was not in philosophy that one would find the route to certainty.[55]

The sieur de Balzac's passionate *Le Socrate Chrétien* insisted that Christ had ruined not merely idolatry and the demons, but human wisdom and philosophy as well. Christ had refuted all philosophers. Without Christ, we never should know God or the divine origin of the world. The early fathers and doctors of the Church may have stooped to use the language of philosophy to convert those born into such systems, but now it was better to be "in pure ignorance" than to speak philosophically of things divine.[56] Piety, not philosophical theology, was the only route to God.[57]

Saint-Évremond's fideism may have pleased some by its wit, but

---

[51] Ibid., 376–377.

[52] Ibid., *Avertissement* (unpaginated, xvii pp.).

[53] Thomas Baker, *Traité de l'incertitude des sciences*, Paris 1714, 1–8, 332–347 and passim.

[54] Pierre-Nicolas Desmolets, Oratory, *Continuation des Mémoires de littérature et d'histoire*, vol. 5, part 2, Paris 1728, 313–317.

[55] Gabriel Guéret, *La Guerre des autheurs anciens et modernes*, The Hague 1671, 77–79.

[56] Jean Louis Guez, sieur de Balzac, *Socrate Chrestien . . . et autres oeuvres . . .*, Arnhem 1675, 6–9, 27–41.

[57] Ibid., p. 54.

surely it pleased other Catholic minds for the piety of its sense of faith's domain. The more important a question is for us, he observed, he more obscure it is as a question of natural knowledge. Thus, "Unless faith subjugates our reason, we pass our lives in believing and in not believing, in wanting to convince ourselves, and in not being able to convince ourselves."[58] Theology should teach "docility and submission" in all domains, he pleaded; instead, it insists upon disputations and proofs. "We burn to death a man so miserable as not to believe in God", he wrote in 1662, "and nevertheless, we publicly ask, in the Schools, *if He exists* [*On brûle un homme assez malheuruex pour ne pas croire en Dieu; et cependant on demande publiquement, dans les écoles, s'il y en a un* { emphasis his }]".[59] For Canon Simon Foucher, philosophers gave us so many grounds for considering the antitheses of all of our beliefs, that *without* skepticism, the habit of *suspending* belief, we ran the serious risk of honest doubts becoming actual disbelief. "We are so accustomed in the world to judge", he noted, urging a healthy skeptical philosophy as an alternative to this dilemma, "that we don't fail to support the negative of a proposition as soon as we cease supporting its affirmative".[60] What Foucher understood was that Christian philosophical disputation and mutual refutation themselves could produce such essential doubt, thus concluding that a refuge from philosophy was in some sense necessary. As we now shall see, it was ironically the very attempt to provide faith with its "preamble" that led to some of the most intense philosophical contestations of early-modern France, and, thus, to a growing appeal of skeptical fideism.

* * *

As I have argued elsewhere, the second half of the seventeenth century in France witnessed a great "fratricide" among Christian philosophical theologians, as Cartesian, Aristotelian-scholastic, and then Malebranchist Catholics (and Huguenots) warred for the privilege, honor, prestige and rewards, spiritual and material, of being the philosophical voice of their faith. Since the foremost

---

[58] Charles de Saint-Évremond, *Oeuvres mêlées de Mr. de Saint-Evremond, publiées sur les manuscrits de l'auteur,* new edn., rev., corr and aug. 5 vols., Amsterdam 1706, vol. 1, 135–136.
[59] Ibid., 184–185.
[60] Simon Foucher, *Dissertation sur la Recherche de la vérité, contenant l'Apologie des académiciens. Où l'on fait voir que leur manière de philosopher est la plus utile pour la religion, et le plus conforme au bon sens . . .*, Paris 1687, p. 21.

function of that voice was to provide the creed with its most
essential preamble, natural demonstration of the existence of God,
much of their mutual contestations centered upon each other's
proofs of God. All camps believing, on the whole, that there could
be only one victor among them, they sought in their polemics to
deliver to *coup de grâce* to their rivals. For two generations, in
university and seminary, and before the ever-growing reading public, in textbooks, learned tomes, polemical treatises, the pages of the
learned journals, satires, replies, replies to replies, and replies to
replies to replies, they undertook to demonstrate that their philosophical opponents, mistaken epistemologically, ontologically and
logically, were incapable of proving the existence of God. While
each camp proclaimed the efficacy of its own demonstrations, the
effect of this was that every extant proof of God was "refuted", in
works of impeccable orthodoxy, published with ecclesiastical *imprimatur* and learned approbation.[61] The assault upon Cartesian
proofs by Aristotelian and Thomists became a general critique of
all efforts at a priori proof.[62] The assault upon Aristotelian and
Thomist proofs by Cartesians and Malebranchists became a general critique of all attempts at a posteriori proofs.[63] The assault upon
the most particular of Malebranchist proofs, that what we termed
"the idea of God" could only be direct apperception of Perfect
Being itself, led to a firestorm that raised serious charges of atheism
against those who sought so fervently to prove God by direct
intellectual experience of Him.[64] It would be both the skeptical
fideists and the first atheists who were there to pick up the pieces.

Even some of the most fervent participants in these debates
moved towards fideism, something which is not, upon reflection,
surprising. François de La Pillonnière, who as a Cartesian and then
Malebranchist Jesuit had withstood awhile his Society's most intense pressures to abandon his philosophical commitment, decided,
by the end, that he had come to worship "a chimerical God", and
that the debates of the philosophers established nothing. Belief in
God, he concluded, was an utterly supernatural gift, achieved by
"faith", not natural lights.[65]

Such fideism, we have seen, was in theory not an acceptable

---

[61] Kors, *Atheism in France*, vol. 1, 263–379.
[62] Ibid., 297–322.
[63] Ibid., 323–356.
[64] Ibid., 357–379.
[65] François de La Pillonnière, *L'Athéisme découvert par le R.P. Hardouin. . . .*
S.l.n.d. [1715], which was reprinted in Thémiseul de Saint-Hyacinthe, *Mémoires*

philosophical conclusion for Catholic theology, and La Pillonnière would convert to Protestantism after leaving the Jesuits. As Sommier had warned, "it would be heresy to say that one cannot know the existence of God without faith".[66] Nonetheless, the appeal of fideism clearly grew throughout the late seventeenth and early eighteenth centuries, and with it, the reputation of Pascal, who had written, in the *Pensées*, that it was generally in vain that we looked for proof of God in nature or in our reason, when He was only truly known in the heart and through the grace of Christ.[67] Such a position was far more an attitude toward the priority of faith and religious experience over philosophy than a formal embrace of any philosophical position towards demonstration of the existence of God, but it was a far cry from the attitude towards *praembulae fidei* being taught elsewhere. Nonetheless, it is more than interesting to note its appeal in a culture that professed to believe that atheism was an act of will whose madness was made manifest by the luminous evidence of God to the natural mind and that professed to believe the logical sequence of belief to be natural proof of the God to whose Revelation one then logically submitted one's mind.

La Pillonnière was not the only direct participant in these contestations to move towards fideistic skepticism. One of the Aristotelian Jesuits' favorite critiques of Cartesian proof of God had been the celebrated *Censure* by Pierre-Daniel Huet, who later became a priest and bishop. The posthumous publication of Huet's treatise on "the weakness of the human mind" surprised and intrigued those who thought they knew him. In his *Préface*, addressed to "My friends the philosophers", Huet explained that he was in the end "profoundly shocked by these continual disputes of the philosophers", and that he had found his peace in philosophical skepticism, and from recognition of the weakness of the human mind, in faith as the source of his beliefs.[68] In the body of his treatise, he

---

littéraires. 2 vols., The Hague 1715, vol. 2, 403–435. See also La Pillonnière, *An Answer to Reverend Dr. Snape's Accusation . . . Containing an Account of His Behaviour and Sufferings amongst the Jesuits . . .*, London [1717] and *. . . Further Account of Himself . . . And of His Advances in His Inquiries after Truth*, London 1729.

[66] Sommier, *Histoire dogmatique de la religion*, vol. 1, "Discours préliminaire, ou Apologie de la raison et de la foy contre les pyrrhoniens et les incrédules", i-iii.

[67] Blaise Pascal, *Pensées de M. Pascal sur la religion, et sur quelques autres sujets, qui ont esté trouvées après sa mort parmy ses papiers* the so-called "port-Royal edn.", with preface by Étienne Perier, Paris 1670, 55–65, 190–193, 153. In Ibid., 190–193, Pascal argued that St. Paul did not say that God was obvious to all in nature, but merely that He was indeed there. The *Pensées* was published with an unparalleled eleven pages of approbations.

[68] Pierre-Daniel Huet, *Traité philosophique de la foiblesse de l'esprit humain*, London

applied all of the positions explicated by Sextus Empiricus against both knowledge by reason alone and knowledge derived from the senses, denying the certainty of both. He addressed scholastic critiques of Cartesian *a priorism* against the rationalists, and Cartesian critiques of scholastic sensationalism and induction against the Aristotelians. We needed "some means more useful" than our natural faculties to achieve certainty of any kind, he concluded: "Now, this means is the Faith by which, during his life, man acquires some knowledge of God and of things divine." That means, he opined, was a gift of God to those who were not presumptuous about the powers of their minds.[69] He noted, as a major objection to his position, that all schools of philosophy claim the absolute certainty of proof of the existence of God. In the final analysis, however, he argued, all human proofs were at best merely probable, and it was "clear" from the way that "clever philosophers openly have fought these principles" that even here, "in this natural knowledge that we have of God", "one does not achieve a perfect and complete certainty on all points". Each school of philosophy succeeded in putting the "first principles" of each other school into doubt, while "Faith does not depend on first principles, but presupposes them as certain. . . ." That was the better route.[70] All human belief required faith.[71]

Huet's friend and fellow member of the Académie française, the abbé d'Olivet, translator of Cicero's *de Natura Deorum*, defended his memory against the host of critics who either denied that the pious Huet could have written this or who were appalled by what they saw as his assault upon the natural certainty of the existence of God. It is a sad day, d'Olivet noted, when a man is treated like an atheist for having written that the natural human mind has "no means of achieving the knowledge of any truth" without "faith, a pure gift of God", our only "infallible" guide.[72] If one recalls the discussion of "preamble" with which we began, however, one can understand, in context, the shock.

* * *

1741, 1–10. The *Traité* was first published (posthumously) in Latin, Amsterdam, 1723. It was found among his papers in both Latin and French. As was his wont, Huet had written it first in French and then translated it into Latin.

[69] Ibid., passim. The quotation about "things divine" is found on 211.

[70] Ibid., 275–290.

[71] Ibid., 284.

[72] Abbé Joseph d'Olivet, *Histoire de l'Académie Française depuis 1652 jusqu'à 1700*, Paris 1729, *Addition*, 362–369.

Even theologians untempted by pure fideism clearly were sensitive to the ravages effected by Cartesian-scholastic-Malebranchist
debate. In 1712, the Capuchin Nicolas Anaclet du Havre noted for
his students the views of pious theologians who believed that they
could "prove that one cannot demonstrate the existence of God".
His own explication of their arguments revealed the inroads of
Aristotelian-Cartesian polemic, laying out the most essential positions of both camps against even the theoretical possibility of, on
the one hand, *a priori* and, on the other, *a posteriori* proof. The
answers to such problems, the theologian advised the teachers of
his order, was to consult the great theologians who had written on
the existence of God, and he referred them to the authorities: St
Thomas *and* Malebranche; Huet *and* François Lamy; the Jesuit
Pétau, *and* the Cartesian Thomassin *and* the fideistic Pascal. In
short, he referred them to the very problem itself.[73]

For others sensitive to these dilemmas, the task became to find
what remained standing and solid after the assaults of the diverse
theological and philosophical camps against each other's citadels.
The Capuchin Basile de Soissons, in his *Traité de l'existence de Dieu*
(1680), wished that the Church did not see fideism as "a violence
against truth", but acknowledged the need to prove God. He
apologized for having to refer to Aristotle, who, after all, he reminded his readers, believed in the eternity of the world, and he
apologized for using "several [scholastic] philosophical terms
rather barbarous in our ordinary language", but he believed that
there was *one and only one* philosophical argument that could overcome the most demanding critic: the proof from contingent
beings.[74] The Jesuit Boutauld, in *Le théologien dans les conversations
avec les sages et les grands du monde* (1683), declared it "a great abuse to
run and ask [the philosophers] if it is true that there is a God", and
denied the need for "demonstrations drawn from the books of
Aristotle or Saint Thomas". There was only *one* proof of God
beyond the certainty of faith, he concluded: the *moral* (that is to say,
persuasive but not demonstrative) proof from the order of the
world, and the certainty of faith. "[I]f you want to know [it] better

---

[73] Nicolas Anaclet Du Havre, O.F.M., Capuchin, *Sujet de conférences sur la
théologie positive . . . à l'usage des Capucins*. 3 vols., Rouen 1712, vol. 1, part 3, 48–49,
61–62, and vol. 2, 1–2.
[74] Basile de Soissons, O.F.M., Capuchin, "Traité de l'Existence de Dieu . . .
Contre les Infidelles et les Athées de notre siècle," paginated separately [45 pp.] at
the end of *Fondement inébranlable de la doctrine Chrétienne. . . . 3 vols., Paris 1680–1683,
vol. 1.

by speculations and convictions", he warned, "tomorrow you will know it no longer". In short: "Absolute God though He is, He has not had any other argument nor any demonstration than this one to make known His Divinity to men".[75]

Thus, even among those who rejected all a priori proof, there no longer was a consensus that the "five ways" of St Thomas were all invulnerable to refutation, and many theologians were conscious of the explicit toll taken by Cartesian-scholastic debate. In 1680, the abbé Armand de Gérard addressed a Christian laity that he believed to be increasingly confused and appalled by the divisions within the Catholic intellectual community. Although he favored the Thomistic arguments as *illustrations* for those who already believed, he asserted that *both* Aristotelian scholasticism and Cartesian innovation stood condemned by their manifest inabilities to prove the God known by authority. Against the Cartesians, he argued that if God is infinite and perfect, He cannot be known by our finite and imperfect ideas. Against the scholastics, he argued that if God is spirit, He cannot be known by the corporeal senses from the beings of the corporeal world. If creation, design and governance were obvious, he asked, then why did "the two greatest geniuses of antiquity", condemned to think without the grace of faith, not see it? Aristotle himself had believed the world eternal, and had denied that divine providence extended to the terrestrial world. Epicurus had believed the world the product of the fortuitous concourse of atoms, and had denied all providence entirely. It was not philosophy that taught us the existence of the true God, but *Genesis*. After a "recourse to faith", we then looked for the evident marks of the Creator in the universe and found them.[76] In brief, he had accepted the scholastic critique of Cartesianism. He had also accepted the heart of the Cartesian critique of scholastic proofs, that a-posteriori proof was only useful *after* one already knew God.

The implications of such a position were made patently (and perhaps painfully) clear to learned readers and students of philosophical theology in Nicolas L'Herminier's *Summa Theologiae*, first published in 1701–1703 and having a second edition in 1718–1719.

---

[75] Michel Boutauld, S.J., in Coton and Boutauld, *Le théologien dans les conversations avec les sages et les gens du monde*, Paris 1683, 16–47. This was in a fourth printing by 1696.

[76] Abbé Armand de Gérard, *La philosophie des gens de cour*, Paris 1680, *Epître*, *Préface*, and 1–54 (see, especially, 33–35). On his view of appropriate *a-posteriori* argument, see 116–186.

L'Herminier was a professor of theology at the Sorbonne, and a Jansenist sympathizer with little respect for either the scholastics or the Cartesians in their mutual contestations. In his *Summa*, he rejected Descartes's proofs of God (and all *a priori* demonstration by cause or "necessary conjunction") as question-begging, agreeing with scholastic critics that such demonstrations presupposed the very object of their proof. He agreed that the "formal" being of ideas as mere modes of finite human mind obviated the possibility of proof from their "objective" being, and that the very existence of atheists refuted the premises of Descartes's chain of argument.[77] When he turned to St Thomas's "five ways", however, he revealed the profound influence on his theology of the common Cartesian argument that unless an *a posteriori* proof established "a perfect being", it had failed to demonstrate the existence of God against the objections of the would-be atheist.

St Thomas's proofs from contingent being, motion, and efficient cause, he reasoned, were clearly *not* demonstrative. No one, he argued, conceivably denied that there was *a* necessary being given contingency, *a* prime mover given motion, and *a* first cause given a sequence of effects. St Thomas, however, wholly had begged the question of whether or not such entities had to be "a *perfect* being". Assume, the theologian explained, eternally existing atoms with inherent essential motion, as so many of the ancients did, and one has assigned just as plausibly to such atoms the status that St Thomas assigned to God. If the issue were whether or not *any* cause existed of the phenomena we observe, St Thomas triumphed. Atheists, alas, demanded further demonstration that such causes could be found only in a perfect being, and St Thomas merely presupposed the very issue in dispute. Turning to St Thomas's proof from degrees of perfection, L'Herminier concluded that it too begged the central issue in dispute. If there were, in fact, "degrees of perfection", St Thomas had demonstrated that such things could only have a perfect cause. The argument, however, presupposed perfection, and would wholly *inefficacious* against the thinker who believed all that we observed to be merely the result of fortuitous arrangements of atoms, and believed human judgments about the qualities of such things to be merely arbitrary pronouncements about how such things affected our physical senses and well-being. Further, he charged, the whole argument about "nega-

---

[77] Nicolas L'Herminier, *Summa Theologiae ad usum scholae accommodata*. 3 vols., Paris 1701–1703, vol. 1, 24–40, 49–55.

tions" of perfection obviously told us merely what was *not*. Only the argument from providential governance triumphed, L'Herminier concluded, for only providence demonstrated qualities— intelligence, benevolence and will, for example—that could *not* be attributed to corporeal entities.[78] As all students of skepticism know well, however, it was precisely the "problem" of providence that always had produced the most fideistic impulses of the learned Christian world.[79]

*　*　*

Debates about proof of God, and, in particular, Cartesian-scholastic mutual refutation, occupied a salient place in the popular learned journals, reaching a very wide audience among the educated public. Virtually every "refutation" of a proof of God received extended explication and review in these journals. At almost any moment during two generations, these contestations commanded attention. The remarkable recriminations of Arnauld and Malebranche, which so rent the Cartesian camp, each claiming that the other could not prove God, found their forum in what was in many ways the *least* (although chronologically the first) of these journals, the *Journal des Sçavans*, which in the four consecutive weekly issues of June 28, July 5, July 12 and July 19 of 1694, let the titans go at each other in its pages.[80] Let us stop the clock, so to speak, at the very dawn of the 18th century. In May, 1700, in the *Histoire des Ouvrages des Savans*, Jacquelot attacked a criticism of Descartes's proofs.[81] In January, 1701, the *Journal des Sçavans* let the abbé Brillon reply for the injured critic.[82] In January and February of 1701, the *Journal de Trévoux* let opposed critics join the issue.[83] For the next two years, in mutually referential and mutually cited debates across the journals, the fratricide continued. In November, 1701, the *Nouvelles de la République des Lettres* informed readers of the status of the debate and the interlocutors, cited and summarized

---

[78] Ibid., 40–63.

[79] It also produced a great outpouring of Cartesian and Malebranchist criticisms of any attempts to prove God from *a-posteriori* evidence of governance. See Kors, *Atheism in France*, vol. 1, 346–349.

[80] These, of course, were in addition to exchanges in their books. Arnauld and Malebranche both used the journals: in this case, see *Journal des Sçavans*, the issues specified in the texts.

[81] *Histoire des Ouvrages des Savans*, mai 1700, 199–222 (!).

[82] *Journal des Sçavans*, 10 jan. 1701.

[83] *Journal de Trévoux*, jan.-fév. 1701, 187–217.

what had transpired in other journals (though generally assuming that its readers had read those too), published letters from two participants, and after presenting Jacquelot against Werenfels against Jacquelot against Brillon against Dom François Lamy against La Montre (who, it claimed, "was content merely to transcribe" the view of Régis), commented, in a revealing phrase, that "Here is a dispute which is going to be in fashion [*Voilà une Dispute qui va devenir à la mode*]".[84] These and wholly new contestants had a vast field on which to set their arguments. The *Nouvelles de la République des Lettres* gave space to such mutual refutations in September and November of 1701; May, July, and September of 1702; February and August of 1703. The *Histoire des Ouvrages des Savans* did the same in May of 1700, and in February, May, and September of 1701. The *Journal de Trévoux* did so, at exceptional lengths, in January–February 1701, and in July–August and September–October of that same year, and in July and September 1702 (by which time it had moved to monthly issues). These were *not*, to say the very least, private debates.[85]

* * *

Such a climate also meant that everyone had "the atheist" (in the guise of an adversary or reader unpersuaded by one's own arguments) always looking over one's shoulder, and, perhaps, increasingly internalized as a critical presence. It was, for some, one gets the distinct impression, exhausting. No one could avoid or ignore the arguments of potential dialecticians waiting to find the arbitrary assumptions, logical fallacies and failure to anticipate objections in one's work. There were too many of them; they were all too clever; they ignored the object of one's efforts and derided one's work before the world. Perhaps some of the appeal of fideism lay there. The editors of the first edition of Pascal's *Pensées* had

---

[84] *Nouvelles de la République des Lettres*, nov. 1701, 510–515 (the quotation is found on 513).

[85] These debates preceded these exchanges and followed them, without much change in their terms, which replicated the erudite literature of mutual theological refutation. Note the length of many of them. For these debates at the dawn of the 18th century, see *Nouvelles de la République des Lettres*, sept. 1701, 317–358; nov. 1701, 483–509; mai 1702, 272–277; juillet, 1702, 31–41; sept. 1702, 293–296; fév. 1703, 188–200; août, 1703, 163–171; *Journal de Trévoux*, jan-fév. 1701, 187–217; juillet-août, 1701, 3–14, 190–191; sept.-oct. 1701, 203–207; and *Histoire des Ouvrages des Savans*, mai 1700, 199–222; mai 1701, 226–229; sept. 1701, 420–428; and fév. 1701, 43–49.

conceded that those who wanted "proofs and geometric demonstrations of the existence of God" would be disappointed, but they denied the efficacity of empirical, metaphysical and commonplace proofs. Further, they informed the reader, Pascal had written elsewhere that "'I do not feel myself strong enough'" to prove to doubters "the existence of God".[86] In 1672, a Jansenist supporter defended Pascal for this, quoting him to the effect that "one would seek in vain the traces of God in the dead works of nature".[87] In 1728, the Oratorian priest (and librarian) Desmolets published the remaining fragments of Pascal's *Pensées*, one of which reminded the reader that neither David nor Solomon, the wisest of our fathers, had sought to "prove" his God, and that this was, indeed, "an admirable thing".[88]

Perhaps, despite the outcry, many of them understood Huet's retreat only too well. At the end of a long defense of Malebranche's proof of God's existence against its critics, in a "criticism of a criticism" of a work that he loved, the Benedictine Dom Robert Desgabets took a long breath. He granted that the proof was beset by theoretical objections and difficulties, but, his rationalism suddenly less confident, he pleaded that "there being no other argument but this one that is proportioned to everyone's capacity, . . . there would be peril to disparage it and combat its solidity". Perhaps, he conceded, it convinced us only because God first had revealed Himself to us in Scripture, and perhaps "men corrupted by sin never would have taken it upon themselves to think of God . . . if God first had not made Himself known to man, and if this knowledge had not been passed down from father to son by means of instruction. . . ."[89] Gaspard Langenhert, who had retired from public philosophical dispute in the face of objections to which he felt he could not respond satisfactorily, wrote in his *Philosophus Novus* (1701–1702) that a Christian philosopher can *only* be skeptical, and should embrace neither Platonic, Epicurean, Aristotelian nor Cartesian systems. "All science", Langenhert urged, including knowledge of God's existence, "presupposes faith, which . . .

---

[86] Pascal, *Pensées* "Préface", unpaginated, but see especially what would be xlvi-xlviii.
[87] Jean Filleau de La Chaise, *Discours sur les pensées de M. Pascal . . .*, Paris 1672, 5–59 (some attribute this work to Philippe Du Bois-Goibaud).
[88] Desmolets, Oratory, *Continuation des Mémoires de littérature et d'histoire.*, vol. 5, part 2, 313–317.
[89] Dom Robert Desgabets, O.S.B., *Critique de la Critique de la Recherche de la vérité . . .*, Paris 1675, 85–89.

cannot . . . be demonstrated by the sole lights of nature." He who
wishes to know anything whatsoever of God, he specified, must first
believe "by faith" that there is a God. *All* sciences, he noted,
assumed their objects of study to exist: the mathematician cannot
"prove" points and lines to exist; the physicist cannot "prove"
bodies to exist; the theologian cannot "prove" God to exist![90]

* * *

Fideism and atheism, both rejecting natural philosophical demonstration of the preamble of the faith, though for categorically
distinct ends, were in that sense two sides of the same coin. If an
eighteenth-century manuscript that correctly described much of
the atheist Jean Meslier's life and reading is correct in its other
claims, the priest who became an atheist knew and presumably
read the work of the Jesuit philosopher Claude Buffier, read the
abbé Houtteville's treatise on Christianity, and read the Jesuit
Tournemine's unauthorized preface to Fénelon's treatise on the
existence of God.[91] Since scholars have been known to express
amazement that the "isolated" Meslier ever could have emerged
from Catholic culture without the influence of free-thought, it is not
fruitless to ask what he would have or could have encountered in
such orthodox works.[92] Buffier's and Tournemine's furious recapit-
ulations of the scholastic critiques of Cartesian and Malebranchist
proofs of God may well have disabused Meslier of any *a priori*
grounds of belief, or, as the culture liked to phrase it, replies to
objections and doubts.[93] Houtteville's treatise had praised Pascal's

---

[90] Gaspard Langenhert, *Philosophus Novus*, Paris, 1701–1702, vol. 1, 13–73. See
also, *Nouvelles de la République des Lettres*, fév. 1702, 230.
    [91] Bibliothèque de l'Arsenal, MSS.: 2558, §1, 1–5. Voltaire derived his own "life
of Meslier" by abridging either this source or, more likely, a source common to
both.
    [92] See, among many examples, Jean Fabre, "Jean Meslier, tel qu'en lui-
même . . .", in *Dix-Huitième Siècle* No. 3 (1971), 107–115, where he argued that
Meslier's reading clearly consisted primarily of Christian books that served as
"guarantors of the faith", from which he concluded that "this peasant and
self-taught curé, liberated from dogmas but not from scholasticism, cleared for
himself the path of a merciless atheism."
    [93] Claude Buffier, S.J., *Traité des premières véritez et de la source de nos jugemens, où
l'on examine le sentiment des philosophes sur les premières notions des choses*, Paris 1724,
passim, and *Elémens de métaphysique . . .*, Paris 1725, 39–79; René-Joseph Tournemine, S.J., "Réflexions . . . sur l'athéisme . . .", in Fénelon, *De l'existence de Dieu*,
Paris 1713, where he assured readers that since *a priori* proofs did not demonstrate
God, Fénelon had merely used them *ad hominem* to aid such poor reasoners in their
beliefs.

emphasis on the need for "faith" to know God, his understanding, in Houtteville's words, "that it is not by metaphysical and abstract proofs" that men should "be led to perfect conviction". Natural demonstrations, on the other hand, Houtteville insisted, inferences from nature, "depend too much on the imagination and the senses to extend to first principles, sources of all truth". It was not by means of reason or the senses, but "by the heart", that God's existence could be known.[94] Buffier, however able to direct scholastic objections against the Cartesians, was also aware of the force of rationalist criticisms of scholastic proofs. In Buffier's philosophy, one cannot "prove" with "absolute evidence" that nature even exists as we conceive of it, that we know true things from it, or that God exists. All *a-priori* proof is question-begging, and all *a-posteriori* proof lacks even the theoretical possibility of "complete demonstration", since it must (and, he believed, should) *assume* "first truths". These first truths, the Jesuit Buffier specified, are principles which are *not* demonstrable themselves, but without which no other demonstrations are possible. Barbay, you will recall, had limited "first truths" to one, Aristotle's principle of non-contradiction, confident that one could get from there to God and to science. For Buffier, these "first truths" incapable of being demonstrated only could be acquired "by way of sentiment", and they included some interesting propositions to be placed beyond possibility of proof: one's own existence; the existence of bodies; the principle that what all men know by "sentiment" and "experience" is true; and (with *a-priori* proof no longer an option), the principle that order "could not be the effect of chance". It is both impossible and malicious, Buffier insisted, to ask for "certain proof" of these "first truths", for they must be presupposed by human thought and we know they are *not* amenable to demonstration.[95]

Whatever the official condemnations of philosophical skepticism, it permeated the culture, and both fideistic and, more metaphorically, atheistic skepticism may have been nourished, paradoxically, by the very confidence in reason's role upon which so much of early-modern orthodoxy insisted.

---

[94] Abbé Claude-François Houtteville, *La religion chrétienne prouvée par les faits* . . ., Paris 1722, cliii-clviii.
[95] Buffier, S.J., *Elémens*, 79–132.

Silvia Berti

SCEPTICISM AND THE *TRAITÉ DES TROIS IMPOSTEURS**

Writing about Pierre Bayle, undoubtedly a key figure in the under-standing of seventeenth- and eighteenth-century scepticism, Pierre Jurieu noted: "Il y a bien moyen d'être Athée sans être Spinosiste. Pour Spinosiste il ne l'est point: mais il est difficile de dire ce qu'il est".[1] For my part, I have serious doubts about the theoretical possibility of being an atheist without having recourse to Spinoza. The author of the *Traité des trois imposteurs* (or *Esprit de Spinosa*) must have thought the same when he decided to base his attack on revealed religion on Spinozan and Hobbesian foundations. We will try to understand how an anthropological notion of the origin of religion, based on a doctrine of imagination and on Spinoza's biblical criticism, permitted a new and more radical use of libertine scepticism, finally released from its destiny of ambivalence.[2] On this theme it appears particularly significant that the first French translation of Shaftesbury's *Sensus communis*,[3] which contained a lengthy discussion of the new Pyrrhonism, should have been dedi-cated by its publisher Scheurleer to the Dutch diplomat Jan Vroesen (1672–1725), who was almost definitely the author of the *Traité*.[4] In presenting the volume the translator, Pierre Coste, who ten years previously had introduced French readers to Locke's

* Acknowledgement is gratefully made to Anne Russel-Roberts who translated this contribution into English.

[1] P. Jurieu, *Le philosophe de Roterdam accusé, atteint et convaincu*, Amsterdam 1706, p. 130.

[2] On the double-faced character of libertinism, well synthesized by the defini-tion "sceptical fideism", cf. R.H. Popkin, *The History of Scepticism from Erasmus to Spinoza*, Berkeley-Los Angeles University of California Press, 1979 (amplified version of his *The History of Scepticism from Erasmus to Descartes*, Assen: Van Gorcum, 1960).

[3] Cf. *Essai sur l'usage de la raillerie et de l'enjouement dans les conversations qui roulent sur les matières les plus importantes* (by A. Ashley Cooper, Earl of Shaftesbury), La Haye: H. Scheurleer, 1710.

[4] For the attribution of the *Traité* to Jan Vroesen, cf. S. Berti, "Jan Vroesen, autore del 'Traité des trois imposteurs'?", in *Rivista storica italiana* 10:2 (1991), 528–543.

Essay, wrote: "On sait confusément en France & en Hollande, qu'il y a en Angleterre des Esprits pénétrans & hardis qui parlent, & qui écrivent avec beaucoup de liberté contre les Opinions les plus généralement établies. Ils passent dès-là pour des vrais *Pyrrhoniens*. On leur donne ce tître fort communément: & bien loin de s'en choquer, ils commencent à s'en faire honneur".[5] We know, therefore, from Coste—who spoke of it with barely-concealed pride— that English freethinkers boasted of the nickname "Pyrrhonians" which was often attributed to them.

It is difficult to believe, however, that such a definition would have pleased the author of the *Esprit*, in spite of the fact that the translation of Shaftesbury's work was dedicated to him, and above all in spite of his familiarity with the texts and profound participation, shown in the *Traité*, in that intellectual tradition—a participation which would involve a radical new elaboration that would change its appearance and historical significance. It is evident in fact that a new page had been turned. We are now a long way from that type of religious indifferentism, strictly related to the scepticalPyrrhonian option, which through a historical comparison of different religions and consequent critical examination, together with doubt kept faith safe. The typically sceptical suspension of judgement and almost constant implication of subtly corrosive analyses of the historical-religious phenomenon conducted in the libertine line of thought, are completely absent in the *Esprit*. (It need not be pointed out that in that option scepticism and libertinism go hand in hand.) The characteristic sceptical oscillation between a natural faith and a rational incredulity did not apply to the author of the *Esprit*.[6] He preferred to put his trust in the most rock-like of modern philosophies, that of Spinoza, much more at ease with the truths of reason than with doubt. This is an extremely important point—for its historiographical significance too—because it signals a breaking point between the libertine tradition of incredulity and the new, radical consciousness with which the early Enlightenment saw the connection linking religious criticism to political conscience.

---

[5] *Essai sur l'usage de la raillerie, Preface du traducteur*, iii-iv. One of the issues of *Nouvelles Litteraires* by Du Sauzet published in 1720 (vol. 11, p. 208), reveals that the translator in question was Pierre Coste, the journalist friend of Desmaizeaux.

[6] The case of the *Esprit* is a brilliant confirmation of R.H. Popkin's thesis in his article "Scepticism in the Enlightenment" in *Transactions of the First International Congress on the Enlightenment* in: *Studies on Voltaire and the Eighteenth Century* 26 (1963), 1321–1345, where he maintains the Enlightenment's substantial extraneousness from Pyrrhonian thematic principles.

Contrary to *areligious* libertinism, and therefore at the most incredulous, the *Traité* proposes a decidedly antichristian and *irreligious* option which denies even the idea of revelation and creation. To this end, as I have shown elsewhere,[7] it makes use of those pages of the *Ethica* which, going back to the definition of God as *causa sui* and necessity whose essence implies existence, constructed an implacable criticism of the theory of final causes and of the prejudice towards an anthropomorphic conception of God. Using the Spinozan analysis of the confusion between imagination and intellect, in which efficient causes are often mistaken for final causes, the *Esprit* demolishes the misunderstanding according to which man was created to worship God.[8] On the contrary, if the correction of the inversion thus produced confirms that it was man who created God, then religion itself is fraud. Ignorance, fear and prejudice are, together with the Spinozan analysis of the imagination, at the origins of religion. But the clear individuation of the mind's self-deception is not only, according to the author of the *Esprit*, a theoretical acquisition: it delegitimizes the presumed sacredness of the foundations of civil and ecclesiastic authority. In this way the text denounces abuse by priests and politicians, who take advantage of the imposture to affirm and ably consolidate their dominion. At least one passage, representative of what has been said up to this point, deserves to be quoted: "Ceux qui ignorent les Causes physiques ont une Crainte naturelle, qui procéde du doute où ils sont, s'il est une Puissance capable de leur nuire, où de les ayder . . . Cette crainte chimérique des Puissances invisibles est la semence des *Religions*, que chacun se forme à sa mode" (II, 4–19). Up to this point the text translates to the letter certain of Hobbes's passages in

---

[7] Cf. S. Berti, "La Vie et l'Esprit de Spinosa (1719) e la prima traduzione francese dell'Ethica", *Rivista storica italiana* 98:1 (1986), 5–46. For an English version of this essay, enriched and brought up to date, cf. "The First Edition of the 'Traité des trois imposteurs', and its debt to Spinoza's 'Ethics'" in *Atheism from the Reformation to the Enlightenment*, eds. M. Hunter, D. Wootton, Oxford: Clarendon Press, 1992.

[8] I refer, naturally, to the *Appendix* to the first part of the *Ethica*. Regarding, more specifically, the passage on the misunderstanding which causes men to maintain that God made everything with man in view, and man himself to be worshipped (G, II, 78, 2–6), this is the translation provided by the *Esprit*: "La source des Dieux étant trouvée, les Hommes ont cru qu'ils leur ressembloient, & que, comme eux, ils faisoient toutes choses pour quelque fin. Car ils disent unanimement, que Dieu n'a rien fait que pour l'Homme, & réciproquement, que l'Homme n'est fait que pour Dieu" (II, 25–29). The reference in brackets, like those which follow, refers to the chapter and lateral numeration of the text of my French-Italian edition of the *Trattato dei tre impostori. La vita e lo spirito del Signor Benedetto de Spinoza*, Torino: Einaudi, forthcoming.

Leviathan XI, enouncing the theme of the chapter.[9] Immediately afterwards, as an introduction to the very long fragment extracted from the *Appendix* to the first book of the *Ethica*, one reads: "Les Politiques, auxquels il importoit que le Peuple fût imbu de semblables frayeurs, ont fait de la créance des Dieux vengeurs des Loyx divines & humaines violées, une Loy fondamentale de leurs Etats, & par l'appréhension d'un terrible Avenir, ils ont porté leurs Sujets à leur obéir aveuglément" (II, 19–24). The reference to the Hobbesian "ignorance of natural causes", recorded above, with which the *Esprit* opens in that first chapter which, in homage to the *Ethica* is entitled "De Dieu", unites harmoniously with Spinoza's observation that "tous les Hommes sont nez dans une ignorance profonde à l'égard des Causes des Choses" (II, 38–39).

As can be seen, the author is very skilled at linking two different philosophies, underlining the points where they agree and passing over those where they differ.[10] This passage constitutes the general basis of the argument, and opens the way to the use of the antifinalistic theme which would serve as a foundation to Hobbes's subsequent treatment of the religious theme (concentrated in Chapter IV). A continuance of sceptical echoes can be found in that sort of pessimism which inevitably emanates from the consideration of human psychology, which in its darkest depths entertains feelings of fear and chasms of most primitive ignorance. In effect, always according to Spinoza, superstition and prejudice, which enslave men, are derived from the imagination, a structure which cannot be eliminated from the mind any more than can the intellect which liberates it; in strictly Spinozan terms, therefore, an "attack"

---

[9] Cf. Hobbes, *Leviathan* XI: "And they that make little, or no enquiry into the naturall causes of things, yet from the feare that proceeds from the ignorance it selfe, of what it is that hath the power to do them much good or harm, are enclined to suppose, and feign unto themselves, severall kinds of Powers Invisible . . . And this Feare of things invisible, is the naturall Seed of that, which every one in himself calleth Religion".

[10] Historiography has debated for a long time on what type of connection exists between the philosophies of Hobbes and Spinoza, a connection which is made by acquisition in the *Esprit*. One of the most interesting contributions is that of A. Pacchi, "'Leviathan' and Spinoza's 'Tractatus' on Revelation: some elements for a comparison", *History of European Ideas* 10 (1989), 577–593. See also M.A. Bertman, "Hobbes' and Spinoza's Politics", in *Spinoza nel 350° anniversario della nascita*, ed. E. Giancotti, Napoli: Bibliopolis, 1985, 321–331, as well as the monographic issue of the *Revue Philosophique de la France et de l'Etranger* 2 (1985). Among the classic studies cf. F. Tönnies, *Studien zur Philosophie und Gesellschaftslehre im 17. Jahrhundert*, hrsg. von E.G. Jacoby, Stuttgart-Bad Canstatt: Fromann-Holzboog, 1975, 293–313 and L. Strauss, *Spinoza's Critique of Religion*, New York: Schocken Books, 1965.

on superstition cannot be conceived. However the *Traité* gives a radical political sense to the discourse on the "préjugez de la naissance" (I, 11), which render people easy prey to "Personnes payées pour soûtenir les Opinions recües". People would shake off "le joug de ces Ames vénales" (I, 25–26), if only they were aware of the abyss in which they are constrained by ignorance. "Il n'auroit pour cela qu'à se servir de sa Raison"—continues the text—"il est impossible qu'en la laissant agir, il ne découvre la *Vérité*" (I, 27–29). Thus the shadow of scepticism noted above is dissipated by this omnipotent and unfolded reason, capable of total emendation and ready to attain truth. Once again the significance of this affirmation has an eminently practical character: following the light of *droite raison*, forcing oneself to correct false reasoning and destroy prejudice, it would be seen that people are "susceptible de *Vérité*" (I, 46). A unitarian and, it should almost be said, symbiotic reading of Hobbes and Spinoza is consolidated by a forcedly materialistic interpretation of the Spinozan concept of substance, which would further strengthen the connections between the two thinkers, permitting, amongst other things, the subsequent utilization of those Hobbesian passages in which the contradictoriness of the "Spirit incorporeal" formulation is maintained.[11] With a freely tendentious translation of the Def. 6, in which God is defined as "un Etre absolument infini, dont l'un des Attributs est d'être une Substance éternelle, et infinie" (III, 5–6), the text turns substance into an attribute, which is far from Spinoza's intentions. It would not, evidently, be permitted, according to the *Ethica*, to omit a reference to the other infinite, constitutive attribute of substance: Thought. This "forgetfulness" allows the author of the text to affirm God's materiality: if, in fact, substance is material and infinite, since outside God there can be no substance, then God too is material.[12]

As can be seen, if one substitutes the theory of imposture as a misinterpretation and obscuration of reason, for the theory—dear

---

[11] I refer to this passage of our text: ". . . bien que les *Corps* & les Esprits ne soyent en effet qu'une même chose, & qu'ils ne différent entre eux que du plus au moins; puis qu'être *Esprit & incorporel* est une chose incompréhensible (IV, 47–50). Cf. *Leviathan* XII, 170–71. It is scarcely the moment to recall Hobbes's conception which identifies substance with the body (on the basis of which, therefore, even spirits are material): one of its consequences is that the definition of the spirit as incorporeal implies a clear contradiction.

[12] Even on this issue there seem to be traces of what Hobbes wrote of himself in the third person: "Affirmat quidem Deum esse corpus" (*Opera Latina*, vol. 3, p. 561).

to the libertines—that imposture is a deception original to legislators, the sceptical issue remains excluded. On the contrary, the chapters from I to IV, which are the carrying structure of the entire text, through a materialistic reading of Spinozan onthology, lead to multiple certainties of a theoretical and practical order, drawing a vigorous attack on the foundations of absolutism. However, we should ask how the conspicuous presence of libertine passages can harmonize with the rest of the text. The explanation lies, in my opinion, in the fact that from the sceptical-libertine tradition he deals only with that which is univocally interpretable and capable of being inserted within the Spinozan conceptual framework. In doing this, the author demonstrates an acute sensibility and trained historiographical consciousness, reinvigorated and integrated by the publishers (Charles Levier and probably Thomas Johnson) who brought out the first edition of the *Esprit* in 1719.[13]

The familiarity and dexterity with which the author of this extraordinary collage of texts—which constitute almost all of the *Esprit*—makes use of Vanini's *De arcanis*, is an ideal illustration of what has been stated up to now. It is extremely significant, in fact, that the first appearance in this work of a passage by Vanini should be in a fully Spinozan context, more precisely within that chapter III (*Ce que c'est que Dieu*) in which we have read of the materialistic transformation of Spinoza's doctrine and its connection with Hobbesian thought. It is even more significant that the passage in question should be about the identification of God and Nature. After having defined the Bible as "un tissu de Fragmens cousus ensemble en divers tems, & donnez au Public à la fantaisie des *Rabbins*" (III, 87–88),[14] he continues by saying that Christians prefer to worship this unreliable book rather than listening to "la Loy naturelle, que Dieu, c'est à dire la Nature, entant qu'elle est le principe du Mouvement, a écritte dans le coeur des Hommes" (III, 97–99). Thus, translating this passage of the dialogue *De Deo* from

---

[13] On the editorial undertaking, cf. Berti, "The first edition of the 'Traité des trois imposteurs'", 193–200.

[14] The author of the *Esprit* based this impudently libertine affirmation of his on this explanatory note: "Le *Talmud* porte, que les *Rabbins*, balancérent, s'ils ôteroient le Livre des *Proverbes* & celui de l'*Ecclésiaste* du nombre des Livres de la Bible. Ce qui les empêcha de le faire, fut, qu'ils y trouvérent quelques endroits, où il est parlé avec éloge de la Loy de Moyse. Ils en eussent fait autant des Prophéties d'Ezechiel, si un certain Chananias n'eût eu l'habileté de les concilier avec la même Loy" (III, 104–109). The fragment is constructed of an incredible *collage* of passages extracted from chapters II and X of Spinoza's *TTP* (G, III, 142, 6–10 and G, III, 29–35). It is however perfectly endowed with autonomy of sense and enables the author to give a Vaninian feeling to an improbable Spinozan mosaic.

the *De arcanis*,[15] Vanini is assimilated with Spinoza through the ideal passage operated by the *Deus sive Natura*. The process of philosophical homologation has come about in this way: first the text gives a materialistic version of Spinoza; then Vanini, through his own naturalism, on which a materialistic hue is conferred, comes to be assimilated with Spinoza. The extract from the *Esprit* proceeds, still guided by Vanini, to describe the Bible as "un Livre dont l'Original ne se trouve nulle part" (III, 115), full of "choses surnaturelles, c'est à dire impossibles" (III, 118), in which trials and rewards are only of concern in a future life, "de peur que la fraude ne se découvre dans celle-cy" (III, 121). At the end of this key chapter we find ourselves confronted with a masterpiece of *pastiche*. Here the author manages to blend together Vanini's theme of the *rusticana plebecula* constrained to obedience by the fear of God, and Spinoza's theme of the dialectic between *spes* and *metus*. Not content with this, he does not hesitate to recall the antifinalistic theme of the *Appendix* to the first part of the *Ethica* (already used at the end of the previous chapter): this reappears in the consideration that men are kept obedient by the idea that God's real aim was human destiny (III, 124–129).[16] As well as for reasons intrinsic to the text, this assimilation of Vanini with Spinoza, which occurs both in the Baylian sense, through the symbolic figure of the virtuous atheist, and in the philosophical identification of naturalism and pantheism, is also of notable importance because once again, as had already happened in the Hobbes-Spinoza connection, it anticipates[17] and synthesizes a cultural tendency which was to

---

[15] Cf. G.C. Vanini, *De admirandis Naturae reginae deaeque mortalium arcanis*, Dialogus L, *De Deo*: "In unica Naturae Lege, quam ipsa Natura, quae Deus est (est enim principium motus) in omnium gentium animis inscripsit", printed in *Le opere di Giulio Cesare Vanini e le loro fonti*, ed. L. Corvaglia, 2 vols., Milan, Genoa, Rome, Naples 1934, vol. 2, p. 276.

[16] This is the passage in question: "Ainsi le Peuple, toûjours flottant entre l'Espérance & la Crainte, est retenu dans son Devoir par l'Opinion qu'il a, que Dieu n'a fait les Hommes, que pour les rendre éternellement heureux ou malheureux. C'est cette Opinion, qu'ont fait naître l'Espérance & la Crainte, qui a donné lieu à une infinité de *Religions*, dont nous allons parler." On the connection between hope and fear, from which can be traced the origins of superstition, cf. also *TTP, Praef.* (G, III, 5, 6), and *ETH*, III, P 50 S (G, II, 177–8). The text of the *Esprit*—a difference which is not unimportant—speaks of religions and not, like Spinoza, of superstitions. For the Spinozan distinction between religion and superstition cf. *Ep.* LXXVIII to Oldenburg (G, IV, 307, 18–308).

[17] The text can, in my opinion, be dated between 1702 and 1711 (with a slight margin of possibility that it can be extended backwards chronologically to the very last years of the seventeenth century); on this cf. Berti, "Jan Vroesen, autore del 'Traité des trois imposteurs'?", 534–543.

become ever more widespread in the first two decades of the eighteenth century, especially in Protestant *milieux*.[18] Naturally Bayle is at the origin of this renewed interest in Vanini. I am not only referring to the celebrated passages of the *Pensées diverses*, but also to what can be read in the *Eclaircissement sur les athées* added to the end of the second edition of the *Dictionnaire* (1702), where Bayle distinguishes between the "profanes", considered "francs athées" by Père Garasse, but really, according to his judgement, mere "athées de pratique", people who live "sans nulle crainte de Dieu, mais non pas sans aucune persuasion de son existence", from the "athées de theorie, comme Diagoras par exemple, Vanini, Spinoza & c. gens dont l'atheïsme est attesté ou par les historiens, ou par leurs écrits".[19] A distinction of great finesse and interpretative subtlety, not always equalled by the later, much more sophisticated historiography. The Vanini-Spinoza association came about, therefore, in Bayle and in the *Esprit*—more or less contemporary texts— and it is understandable that the ideal place for their propagation should be within the Huguenot culture exiled in Holland. It is interesting that even in German academic and erudite circles which gave birth to the many dissertations by Deutsche, Apel, and above all Schramm,[20] by far the most significant text was by Peter Friederich Arpe (1682–1740), one of the most interesting and many-sided figures of the first generation of the German Enlightenment, who lived in Holland from 1712 to 1714, and had contact with Prosper Marchand. His *Apologia pro Julio Caesare Vanino, Neapolitano*, published in Rotterdam in 1712 (but with the suggestive indication: Cosmopoli, Typis Philaletheis) is an original defence of Vanini against accusations of atheism made mainly by the Jesuits and Père Garasse, set out in a complex, eighteen point construction. Arpe was linked in various ways to the history of the *Traité*:[21] one of the pieces of evidence which enables us to attribute the work

---

[18] Cf. in general on this theme L. Bianchi, *Tradizione libertina e critica storica. Da Naudé a Bayle*, Milan: Franco Angeli, 1988, 183–209.

[19] Cf. P. Bayle, *Dictionnaire historique et critique*, Seconde edition. Revue, corrigée & augmentée par l'Auteur, Rotterdam: R. Leers, 1702, vol. 3, p. 3139.

[20] Cf. J.W. Apel, *De vita et fatis Julii Caesaris Vanini, dissertatio prior*, Jenae 1708; J. Deutsche, *Dissertatio posterior de Vanini scriptis et opinionibus*, Jenae 1708; J.M. Schramm, *De vita et scriptis famosi Athei Julii Caesaris Vanini tractatus singularis*, Cüstrini 1709.

[21] Cf. the contribution, on this specific theme, of M. Mulsow, "Freethinking in Early 18th-Century Protestant Germany: Peter Friedrich Arpe and the 'Traité des trois Imposteurs'" in *Heterodoxy, Spinozism and Free-Thought. The "Traité des trois imposteurs" in the European Culture of the Early Enlightenment*, eds. S. Berti, F. Charles-Daubert, R.H. Popkin, Dordrecht: Kluwer, Forthcoming.

to Jan Vroesen comes from him;[22] for a long time the authorship of Jean Rousset de Missy's *Réponse* was erroneously attributed to him.

It would be useful at this point to look more closely, only apparently deviating from our main theme, at the case of David Durand (1680–1763), a Protestant minister who originally came from Languedoc.[23] He moved first to Basle and then to Rotterdam, where in 1717 he published, thanks to Caspar Fritsch, an intimate friend of Marchand, *La Vie et les sentimens de Lucilio Vanini*, a complex and argumentative work which is of notable importance to the understanding of Vanini's success in the sixteenth century, in which Durand proposed to demolish the apologetic intentions and arguments variously used in respect of the Italian freethinker. It is of interest to examine it here to ascertain whether and in what sense the Spinoza-Vanini coupling is present in this text and whether echoes of the *Esprit* are to be found in its pages. Turning directly to Basnage de Beauval in the autobiographical *Avertissement* prefixing his work, Durand informs us of the fact that in 1710 he should have assumed the direction of the *Histoire des ouvrages des savans*.[24] During the preparatory work to the *Journal* he had published an extract of Schramm's book on Vanini, but he soon wanted a direct acquaintance with "le fort & le foible de Vanini . . . par la Lecture entiere des ses ouvrages".[25] Durand found all those impious writings in the library of Basnage de Beauval himself, who was "ravi de me les prêter"[26] (and I do not think one can find a qualitatively more significant proof than this of the circulation of Vanini's texts in Huguenot circles). But what is the philosophical judgement formulated by Durand on Vanini? "D'abord on ne sauroit nier", writes Durand on the subject of the *De arcanis*, "qu'il n'y soit *Matérialiste*, qui est ce qu'on apèle aujourdhui Spinosiste".[27] A confirmation which is almost embarrassingly apt of what has been said before on the Vanini-Spinoza synthesis in the *Esprit*: given by acquisition that Spinoza is a materialist, it easily follows that to the naturalist-materialist Vanini can be assigned, without too much perturbation,

---

[22] For the text of this piece of evidence cf. Berti, "Jan Vroesen", p. 541.

[23] On his life cf. S. Beuzeville, "Préface sur la vie et les ouvrages de l'auteur", in D. Durand, *La vie de J.F. Ostervald, pasteur de Neufchâtel en Suisse*, London 1778, i-xiv and Eug. Em. Haag, *La France protestante ou vies des protestants français*, 10 vols., Paris, 1846–1859, vol. 4, 485–7.

[24] Cf. the "Avertissement" in D. Durand, *La Vie et les sentimens de Lucilio Vanini*, Rotterdam: Fritsch, 1717, i.

[25] Ibid., ii.

[26] Ibid.

[27] Ibid., 120–121.

the definition of Spinozist. It is difficult to imagine that Durand was unaware of the text of the *Esprit*. Moreover, a few pages later, Durand transcribed in notes (in Latin) the same passage utilized in the *Esprit*, providing his own French translation within the text with several identical passages (for example: "que des illusions forgées", III, 115[28]). In continuing to look through Durand's short work we come across a phrase which renders our hypothesis almost certain: "Il court un Mss. en Hollande entre les mains des curieux où ces mêmes paroles sont répetées plus d'une fois, tant elles ont ébloüi les Esprits superficiels".[29] The contents of the manuscript, and the period of its circulation, lead us back, unequivocally to the *Esprit*. We know, amongst other things, that Durand had finished writing his text in August 1714.[30] Before publishing it, his publisher Fritsch, requested an opinion from Prosper Marchand,[31] (who seems to constantly reappear like a ghost in every event relative to free thought in Holland in the early eighteenth century). Fritsch himself possessed, still in 1740, a copy of a manuscript of the *Esprit* belonging to Benjamin Furly, which Levier copied in a great hurry in 1711.[32] On the other hand, it can not have been too difficult to obtain this kind of manuscript during those years and in those circles.[33]

Turning once again our attention directly to the text of the *Esprit*, we see how passages extracted from the dialogue *De Deo* from Vanini's *De arcanis* constitute the central framework of the chapters

---

[28] Ibid., 125–126.

[29] Ibid., p. 128.

[30] Cf. "Avertissement", ix. The book remained "au fond d'un coffre jusqu'en 1716".

[31] Fritsch, in fact, wrote to Marchand from the Hague on 24 (21?) August 1716 (Leiden, UB, March. 2): "Avéz vous leu la vie de Vanini de Mons. Durand? en cas que si, dites moy S.V.p. ce que vous en pensés", confessing that he had not "le tems de la parcourir". A proof that publishers are not always acquainted with what they publish.

[32] Cf. the letter from Fritsch to Marchand of 17 January 1740 (Leiden, UB, March. 2): "Vous vous souvenés peut estre que c'etoit mon Frere qui nous en apporta le Mspt a la maison, appartenant à M.r Furly, Levier le copia fort précipitament. Je la garde encore cette copie", and again "Levier la copia en 1711, cette sorte de livres étoint sa marotte" (Leiden, UB, March. 2, letter from Fritsch to Marchand on 7 November 1737).

[33] Just to give an example, Marchand spoke of a manuscript kept "dans le Cabinet d'un des Ministres de l'Eglise Wallonne" of the Hague. Cf. "Impostoribus (Liber de Tribus)" in Marchand, *Dictionnaire historique*, The Hague: Pierre de Hondt, 1758, vol. 1, p. 323. Marchand himself knew only too well how to acquire clandestine manuscripts if we are to give credit to a letter written to him by Durey de Morsan, in which the latter offers him "des mss. français copiés furtivement sur ceux de la bibliothèque du Roi ou ceux de la bibliothèque de l'abbé Bignon" (Leiden, UB, March. 2, 18 December 1753).

dedicated to Moses and Jesus Christ (with an important extract
from dialogue LVII in the section dedicated to Mohammed). The
choice of Vanini for this part of the work is easily explained: the
author of the *Traité* must have searched Spinoza's works in vain for
texts which were aggressive against Christ. Spinoza always showed
a profound respect for the human figure of Christ, in whom God's
wisdom manifested itself so plainly. The idea of using Vanini, who
was among the first in European culture to express a radical
underestimation and disdain not only for Christ's divinity (a theory
held with some liberality among the anti-Trinitarians through
Bodin, to Spinoza, to name but a few), but also for his human
presence, showed an unequivocal choice on the part of the author of
the *Esprit*. When, several years later, the publishers of *La Vie et
l'Esprit de Spinosa* (1719) wanted to reinforce the radicalism of the
text by including the chapter which contested Christ's divinity,
they had, of necessity, to refer once again to Spinoza: his conception of God, which with definitive rigour frustrated every creation-
ist hypothesis, was the best adapted to provide solid arguments
against belief in the divinity of Christ. As someone with a good
knowledge of Spinoza, Levier[34] made use, in this context, of a
passage which was less well-known but of great argumentative
strength, taken from a letter from Spinoza to Oldenburg (*Ep.*
LXXIII), in which he equates the idea that God made himself into
a man with the contradictory hypothesis that a circle could assume
the nature of a square.[35] For all that Levier was certainly, as
Marchand wrote, "extrêmement infatué du Système de Spinosa",[36]
his interest in libertine thought was also conspicuous. As we know,
while preparing the edition, he and his collaborator Johnson,
added six chapters to the text of the *Esprit* (from XII to XVII)
extracted from Charron's *Les trois Véritez* and *De la Sagesse* and from
Naudé's *Considérations politiques sur les Coups d'Estat*.[37] We will try to
understand what their intention and awareness was.

---

[34] On Levier's Spinozism cf. Berti, "The First Edition of the 'Traité des trois
imposteurs'", 195–196. Levier owned both the Latin and the Dutch editions of
Spinoza's *Opera Posthuma*, two copies of the *Tractatus Theologico-Politicus*, and the
1663 edition of the *Cogitata Metaphysica*. Cf. the auction catalogue of his private
library, *Catalogus Librorum Bibliopoli Caroli Levier*, Hagae Comitum: Apud Viduam
Caroli Levier, 1735, 94–95.

[35] This is the passage: "Mais, d'ailleurs, si Jésus-Christ étoit Dieu, il s'ensuiver-
oit, comme le dit St. Jean, que Dieu *auroit été fait chair*, & auroit pris la Nature
humaine, ce qui renferme une aussi grande contradiction, que si l'on disoit, que le
Cercle a pris la Nature du Quarré, ou que le Tout est devenu Partie" (X, 55–59).

[36] Cf. "Impostoribus (Liber de Tribus)" in Marchand, *Dictionnaire*, p. 325.

[37] Ibid., p. 324.

In introducing the section dedicated to the "deux célébres modernes" our publishers give us a passage which is an explicit declaration of intent: "Quoi qu'*Ecclésiastiques* l'un & l'autre, & par conséquent obligez à garder des mesures avec la *Superstition,* on ne laissera pas néanmoins d'apercevoir au travers de leurs ménagemens, & de leur *stile Catholique,* qu'ils disent des choses aussi libres & aussi fortes que nous" (XI, 118–122). This extract demonstrates in a surprising way the historical-critical capacity and sense of perspective of Levier and his collaborator, who are capable of identifying the intellectually subversive significance of several parts of Charron and Naudé's work. In this way, linking the solid Spinozan-Hobbesian structure to the sceptical elaborations of libertinism, they constructed their own irreligious tradition, and together gave form to their own path to incredulity. I will limit myself here to considering Charron's case in which the sceptical theme is central.[38] Concerning the use made of *De la sagesse,* it should be said first of all that the publishers of the *Esprit* chose to use several particularly radical passages which Charron had inserted in the first edition (1601), but which had not been published again either in the following edition (1604), which had been revised and purged by the author, nor in the posthumous one (1607). This was the case with the well-known extract which begins: "C'est premierement chose effroyable, de la grande diversité des *Religions* . . . c'est merveille que l'entendement humain aye pû estre si fort abesty & enyvré d'impostures?" (*Sagesse,* II, 5; *Esprit,* XIII, 2–97).[39] This contains an implicitly antichristian argumentation: religions resemble each other not only in their dogma and in foundations such as faith in God the creator, in providence and in the immortality of the soul—this can be read in the other editions—but also in miracles, sacred mysteries and in the false prophets necessary for the affirmation of religious faiths. If Charron's sceptical relativism led to a substantial devaluation of the cognitive

---

[38] On Charron the contributions of A.M. Battista and Tullio Gregory remain fundamental. Of the latter I point out in particular "La saggezza scettica di Pierre Charron" *De Homine* 21 (1967), 163–182 and "Il 'libro scandaloso' di Pierre Charron" in *Etica e religione nella critica libertina,* Napoli: Guida Editori, 1986, 71–109. Cf. also the collective volume *La saggezza moderna. Temi e problemi dell'opera di Pierre Charron,* Napoli: Edizioni Scientifiche Italiane, 1987, which has an exhaustive bibliography. For an examination of the resumption of sceptical themes in the Renaissance, cf. Ch.B. Schmitt, "The Recovery and Assimilation of Ancient Scepticism in the Renaissance", in *Rivista critica di storia della filosofia* 27 (1972), 363–384.
[39] The same passage is also quoted by Marchand. Cf. "Impostoribus (Liber de Tribus)" in Marchand, *Dictionnaire,* p. 317.

capacities of reason, with a consequent invitation to the fideistic acceptance of the revelation,[40] the publisher of the Hague gave priority to the critical aspect, expunging the passages in favour of Christianity. All Charron's texts are subjected, in the *Esprit*, to a most peculiar treatment: each extract in which praise of the Christian religion appears is suppressed. An example, still from Chapter XIII: the violent Charronian *excursus* on the terrible cruelties common to different religions ends with a phrase which is not reproduced in the *Esprit*: "mais tout cela a esté aboly par le christianisme" (p. 125). The same thing happens to the passage immediately following, which confers a charter of truth and superiority to the Christian religion: "Mais l'on n'est point en doubte ny en peine de scavoir quelle est la vraye, ayant la Chrestienne tant d'avantages et de privileges si hauts et si authentiques par dessus les autres" (p. 125–26). An identical method is followed in regard to *Les Trois Veritez* (which takes up the whole of chapters XII and XIV), and which completely loses the flavour of a Catholic apologetical treatise, essentially conceived in order to annul the arguments of the "schismatiques". Charron's work is thus denuded of its proper idealogical clothing, according to which, in order to better affirm the truth of the Catholic religion, the author considered himself obliged to give space to the most radical objections of the *esprits forts*. It was evident to anyone who read the text with the eyes of a free-thinker that the work's construction, much more than the mere "technical" manifestation of a confutative procedure, actually revealed the existence of a "double truth". This allowed Levier to isolate and reproduce (Chapter XIV) out of context several of Charron's pages which were certainly among the most irreducible ever written against the Christian religion. I refer to the third of the *Trois Veritez*, the one which fascinated Pierre Bayle. Levier's choice was without doubt mindful of, and probably dependent on, Bayle's observations contained in the voice of *Charron* in the *Dictionnaire*, of which Levier could not have been ignorant. Bayle, in fact, as an authentic assertor of the *tolérance des religions*—to quote the title of a work by his friend Henri Basnage de Beauval—reproduced the same section of the *Trois Veritez* in his pages[41] (referred to in the *Esprit* XIV, 33–85). For these specific reasons, and more generally for the use

---

[40] On this specific aspect of Charron's relativistic attitude cf. in particular Popkin, *The History of Scepticism*, 55–62; cf. also his "Charron and Descartes: the fruits of Systematic Doubt", *The Journal of Philosophy* 51 (1954), 831–837.

[41] Cf. Bayle, *Dictionnaire*, entry "Charron", rem. (P), 147–48.

which is made of the sceptical tradition, the first edition of the *Esprit de Spinosa* must be considered a post-Baylian text. Thus, by leaving out the more orthodox and static side of the sceptical-libertine tradition, and saving only its corrosive antireligious ferments, the first edition of the *Esprit* presented itself as a Spinozan mini-Bayle, on the threshold of the Enlightenment.

Ruth Whelan

THE WISDOM OF SIMONIDES:
BAYLE AND LA MOTHE LE VAYER

Souvenez-vous, je vous supplie, de la pieuse modestie de Simonide, qui n'aiant demandé au Roy Hieron qu'un jour, pour traitter devant luy de l'essence divine, luy en demanda deux, & puis trois en suite, protestant que plus il y pensoit, plus il y trouvoit de difficultez à s'acquitter de sa promesse. Pour moi je ne doute point que cette humble profession d'ignorance n'ait esté beaucoup plus agreable au souverain Estre, tout Payen qu'estoit Simonide, que l'insolence d'un Eunomius, & de cette espece d'Arriens ses sectateurs, qui se vantoient de connoistre Dieu aussi exactement qu'il se pouvoit comprendre luy-mesme.

François de La Mothe Le Vayer[1]

Hieron Tyran de Sicile pria ce Poëte de lui dire ce que c'est que Dieu. Le Poëte lui répondit que cette Question n'étoit pas de celles que l'on explique sur le champ, & qu'il avoit besoin d'une journée pour l'éxaminer. Quand ce terme fut passé, Hieron demanda Réponse; mais Simonide le pria de lui accorder encore deux jours. [. . .] Le Tyran surpris de cette conduite en voulut sçavoir la cause. J'en use ainsi, lui répondit Simonide, parce que plus j'éxamine cette matiere, plus elle me semble obscure.

Pierre Bayle[2]

The historian of ideas attempting to compare the thought of Bayle and La Mothe Le Vayer—two of the most elusive thinkers in seventeenth-century France—might be better advised to imitate the wise silence of the poet Simonides. For there is as yet no consensus concerning the import either of their Pyrrhonist critique of religion or their fideistic solution to the dilemmas created by critical reason. Almost fifty years after the publication of his study on the *libertins érudits*, René Pintard is still convinced that La Mothe Le Vayer's Pyrrhonism is destructive of religious belief and that his fideism is insincere, a prudent disguise for unbelief.[3] In the mean-

---

[1] François de La Mothe Le Vayer, Lettre cxvi: "Paralleles historiques", *Oeuvres*, 2 vols., Paris 1662, vol. 2, 931–32. Simonides is also used in the La Mothe Le Vayer's dialogue "De la divinité" to illustrate the incomprehensibility of the divinity. I have used a modern reprint of the *Dialogues faits à l'imitation des anciens*, Paris: Fayard, 1988, p. 314.

[2] Pierre Bayle, "Simonide", footnote F, *Dictionnaire historique et critique*, 4 vols., Rotterdam 1720, (all references are to this edition). Later in the same footnote (at marginal note 44), Bayle quotes the passage from La Mothe Le Vayer given above.

[3] R. Pintard, *Le libertinage érudit dans la première moitié du XVIIe siècle*, Genève-

time, Richard Popkin suggested that La Mothe Le Vayer's Pyrrhonism is directed against Calvinism rather than religion in general and that his fideism is "compatible with Catholicism" and with the "simple Christianity" he may have professed.[4] Bayle's critical profile is just as contradictory. Elisabeth Labrousse's view of Bayle as a heterodox thinker who criticizes all institutionalized religion in the name of a more idealistic Christianity, and as a moral rigorist who repudiates the social conformity of the sceptics, is accepted by all who see Bayle as a confessional and intellectual misfit.[5] But ideology is not confused by these critics with religious belief and few are willing to pronounce on the sincerity of his professed fideism.[6] Italian critics, however, have been more categorical. To them, Bayle's use of religious ideologies suggests no latent religious belief, in their view he is either a sceptic, an atheist, or a deist.[7] Implicitly, these conflicting views point up the difficulty of interpreting fideistic thinkers. As Popkin put it, "the problem becomes one of finding adequate standards for determining sincerity or intent".[8] The difficulties are even greater when we compare the two thinkers.

All critics agree that Bayle was quite deeply influenced by La Mothe Le Vayer[9] but opinions differ as to the nature of that

---

Paris: Bovin, 1943 140–47, 505–38 and "Les problèmes de l'histoire du libertinage, notes et réflexions", *XVIIᵉ siècle* 127 (1980), p. 154 (this article has been reprinted as a preface to the 1983 reprint of *Le libertinage*, the remark concerning La Mothe Le Vayer is on p. xxxvi)

[4] R.H. Popkin, *The History of Scepticism from Erasmus to Spinoza*, Berkeley, Los Angeles, London: University of California Press, 1979, p. 96.

[5] See E. Labrousse, *Pierre Bayle*, vol. 1: *Du pays de Foix à la cité d'Erasme*; vol. 2: *Hétérodoxie et rigorisme*, The Hague: Nijhoff, 1963–1964; W. Rex, *Essays on Pierre Bayle and Religious Controversy*, The Hague: Nijhoff, 1965; J. Solé, *Le débat entre protestants et catholiques français de 1598 à 1685*, 4 vols., Paris: Aux Amateurs de Paris, 1985, and R. Whelan, *The Anatomy of Superstition: a study of the historical theory and practice of Pierre Bayle*, Oxford: The Voltaire Foundation, 1989 (Studies on Voltaire and the eighteenth century, p. 259).

[6] J. Solé is perhaps the exception. In his article "Religion et conception du monde dans le *Dictionnaire* de Bayle", *Bulletin de la Société de l'histoire du protestantisme français* 118 (1972), p. 96, he maintains that Bayle is a rigid Calvinist: "naïf et pieux produit d'un village protestant des Pyrénées".

[7] See G. Cantelli, *Teologia e ateismo: saggio sul pensiero filosofico e religioso di Pierre Bayle*, Firenze: La nuova Italia, 1969; C. Senofonte, *Pierre Bayle dal Calvinismo all'Illuminismo*, Napoli: Edizioni Scientifiche Italiane, 1978; G. Paganini, *Analisi della fede e critica della ragione nella filosofia di Pierre Bayle*, Firenze: La nuova Italia, 1980; L. Bianchi, *Tradizione libertina e critica storica da Naudé a Bayle*, Milano: Franco Angelli, 1988; G. Mori, *Tra Descartes e Bayle, Poiret e la teodicea*, Bologna: Il Mulino, 1990.

[8] Popkin, *The History of Scepticism*, p. 95.

[9] See P. Rétat, "Libertinage et hétérodoxie: Pierre Bayle", *XVIIᵉ siècle* 127 (1980), p. 200; and Bianchi, *Tradizione libertina*, passim.

influence. Ruth Cowdrick presented Bayle's reading of the *libertins* while a student as crucial to his own "penchant toward scepticism in philosophy".[10] Pintard goes further, arguing that Bayle's views on history and religion are often drawn from Naudé and La Mothe Le Vayer and that he also adopts the tactics and "l'art des subterfuges libertins".[11] However, Richard Popkin contends that Bayle "did not learn his doubts from Naudé or Sorbière or La Mothe Le Vayer"; instead "he had to develop his pyrrhonism from within himself".[12] On another note, Walter Rex remarked on the libertine tone Bayle adopts in the *Pensées diverses sur la comète*, demonstrating that this is partly a disguise for a work of controversy "on the Protestant side".[13] I myself have sought to show the importance of both Naudé and La Mothe Le Vayer for Bayle's view of history, maintaining, nonetheless, that his use of the *libertins* is absorbed into first a Calvinist and later a humanist methodology.[14] Finally, Elisabeth Labrousse warns against confusing Bayle's admiration for La Mothe Le Vayer with an inclination to impiety.[15] In her view, the Huguenot and the libertine world-views had much in common: they shared a hostility to superstition and popular error. In fact, the Huguenots welcomed the *libertins* as allies in their controversy with the Church of Rome. Clearly, then, not only is our view of these authors, to quote Popkin again, "dependent on a prior guess as to how to interpret them"[16] but our assessment of the influence of La Mothe Le Vayer on Bayle also depends on our prior interpretation of each writer.

In my opinion, no conclusive interpretation of the religious belief

---

[10] R.E. Cowdrick, *The Early Reading of Pierre Bayle*, Scottdale: Mennonite Publishing House, 1939, 66–80.

[11] Pintard, *Le libertinage*, 573–575. Bianchi's *Tradizione libertina* offers a more detailed discussion within the same line of interpretation.

[12] R.H. Popkin, "Pierre Bayle's place in seventeenth-century scepticism" in, *Pierre Bayle, le philosophe de Rotterdam*, ed. P. Dibon, Amsterdam: Maison Descartes, 1959, p. 3. C. Borghero, *La certezza e la storia: cartesianismo, pirronismo e conoscenza storica*, Milano: Franco Angelli, 1983, p. 8 makes a similar point.

[13] Rex, *Essays on Pierre Bayle*, 3–74, especially p. 62 and 72.

[14] Whelan, *The Anatomy*, passim and "Un travail d'Hercule: critique et histoire chez Gabriel Naudé (1600–50)" in *Pratiques et concepts de l'histoire en Europe: XVIe— XVIIIe siècles*, eds. C. Grell, J.M. Dufays, Paris: Presses de l'Université de Paris-Sorbonne, 1990, 59–71.

[15] Labrousse, *Pierre Bayle*, vol. 1, 127–28n., for a discussion of La Mothe Le Vayer's early influence on Bayle. A complete edition of Bayle's correspondence is currently being prepared by an international team of scholars under the direction of E. Labrousse for publication by the Voltaire Foundation in Oxford. The first volume, which will add considerably to our understanding of Bayle's early reading, is scheduled for publication in 1994.

[16] Popkin, *The History of Scepticism*, p. 95.

of these authors can ever be offered by the historian. For by definition, the historian "must stand on the written record"[17] and, in these cases, it is precisely the written record which it is so difficult to interpret. The problem is surely one of method: what method or methods should the historian use to elucidate the thought of fideistic writers? Pintard recommends a combination of the sociological and the psychological approaches and praises Elisabeth Labrousse for her judicious use of both in elucidating Bayle's work.[18] While this method has yielded studies of the most extraordinary analytical finesse, it has, nonetheless, two major drawbacks. In the first place, as the history of interpretation of these authors indicates, contextualization is a reversible criterion. It is possible to demonstrate both the religious and libertine affinities of both authors and to draw conclusions accordingly.[19] In the second place—and Pintard's study is the more vulnerable here— the argument from contextualization leads to conclusions of guilt (if the author is a libertine) or innocence (if the author is a believer) by association.[20] Thus, while the sociological approach succeeds in establishing an author's historical importance, it proves inadequate to assess the intent of these peculiarly equivocal authors. Of course, "intent", understood as private belief, is not the domain of the

---

[17] P.O. Kristeller, "The myth of Renaissance atheism and the French tradition of free thought", *Journal of the History of Philosophy* 6 (1968), p. 243.

[18] Pintard, "Les problèmes de l'histoire du libertinage", p. 162 (and in *Le libertinage*, p. xlii).

[19] M. Heyd's review of Cantelli's study (see n. 7 above) is an interesting case in point. Heyd writes "Cantelli has performed a valuable service by showing systematically the affinities between Bayle and his Catholic and libertine contemporaries, but, in my opinion, he did not draw the appropriate conclusions from this evidence" ("A disguised atheist or a sincere Christian? The enigma of Pierre Bayle", *Bibliothèque d'humanisme et de renaissance* 39 (1977), p. 165). In Heyd's view, the "appropriate conclusions" are that Bayle is to be understood within the socio-cultural context of the Huguenot diaspora in Holland, as Labrousse has so masterfully demonstrated. While I too find Labrousse's interpretation more convincing, it seems to me that Heyd (and undoubtedly I myself) cannot elude the critical dilemma posed by Popkin, namely that this conclusion is based on a prior guess as to how to interpret Bayle.

[20] Kristeller (see n. 16 above) argued the case of Pomponazzi most convincingly against Pintard. At one point in his argument, his reductionist summary of Pintard's thesis could be applied, *mutatis mutandis*, to interpretations of either La Mothe Le Vayer or Bayle: "The theory of the double truth is considered as an insincere device for covering secret disbelief. The jokes are taken to reveal the author's true anti-theological theories and opinions. The charges made by his theological opponents are accepted as confirming the impious implications of his thought" ("The myth of Renaissance atheism", p. 237). This is not to argue the futility of the sociological method, merely to suggest I think, a more judicious application of it, such as in the article by R. Zuber, "Libertinage et humanisme: une rencontre difficile", *XVIIe siècle* 127 (1980), 163–79. It must be said, however,

historian, but in authors who flaunt fideism as a solution to intellectual dilemmas, "intent" is in fact part of the public argument. To
fail to evaluate intent, understood in this way, is to fail in our
historical assessment of these writers. This leaves only one solution
to the problem of method, which does not replace but may enrich
the sociological approach. We must study the fideistic discourse
itself and place it in the context of the author's other attitudes to
religious belief,[21] considering not only what the author says he
believes but also what he does in situations where belief seems a
possible response. If we can study this discourse in two authors,
often associated in the history of ideas, so much the better. The
object of the comparison cannot be to provide a definitive interpretation of these writers, nor will it establish a spurious
coherence[22] between their views or within their respective systems
of thought. As I hope to demonstrate, while there is in fact a
significant continuity between their positions, there is a major
difference between their respective understanding of the relationship between faith and reason.

It has often been noted that Bayle had a long and deep acquaintance with the works of La Mothe Le Vayer who is undoubtedly,
along with Plutarch and Montaigne, one of his favorite authors.
References to the writer he would later call the "French Plutarch"[23]
are scattered throughout his correspondence and published work
and, taken as a whole, they fall into an observable pattern. As a
general rule, Bayle cites the works of La Mothe Le Vayer more for
purposes of erudition than for reasons of shared convictions. This

---

that Zuber is open to the same charge as Pintard. To decide La Mothe Le Vayer's
beliefs partly on the basis of what contemporaries like Balzac thought of him (see
p. 172) is a method which begs the question: it fails to challenge the presuppositions of the contemporary critics. If such a method were used for Bayle the debate
would close on the assumption that he was an atheist or freethinker, given that the
majority of his contemporaries (affected by the presuppositions of Cartesian
rationalism) saw him in this light.

[21] P. Rétat's article, "Libertinage et hétérodoxie: Pierre Bayle", *XVIIe siècle* 127
(1980), 197–211 is perhaps the most sensitive analysis to date of Bayle's fideistic
discourse and its heterodox implications.

[22] It is interesting to note that both Pintard (*Le libertinage*, 518–20) and Cantelli
(see Heyd, "A disguised atheist", p. 164) are concerned to present La Mothe Le
Vayer and Bayle respectively as coherent thinkers. Although Pintard concludes
that La Mothe Le Vayer is incoherent (p. 520), he seeks throughout his analysis to
harmonize the positions adopted by La Mothe Le Vayer in the *Dialogues d'Orasius
Tubero* with the rest of his published work. However, it might be more
appropriate—certainly in the case of Bayle—to speak, as Rétat puts it, "en termes
de conjonction et de tension des contraires" (Rétat, "Libertinage et hétérodoxie",
p. 210).

[23] Bayle, "Vayer", footnote K, this title was often given to La Mothe Le Vayer
in the seventeenth century.

pattern substantiates Labrousse's findings with respect to Bayle's early correspondence, namely, that he and his family endured the libertinism of these writers for the sake of their learning.[24] But it is not just Bayle's curiosity which prompts him to read La Mothe Le Vayer, there is also a profound harmony between their literary tastes. Undoubtedly as a result as much of his intellectual temperament as of the circumstances of his early life—his provincial upbringing and dependence on the libraries of his father and his father's generation—Bayle prefers the literature of the age of Louis XIII and the sixteenth-century to that of his own generation.[25] It is the aesthetic of variety, an aesthetic he seeks to imitate in his own work, which appeals to him: the easy movement from Rabelaisian humour to reflections on Greek and Roman antiquity, from prurient curiosity to a fine point of erudition. This affinity is not without relevance to the present discussion. Pintard conflates La Mothe Le Vayer's obscenity with impiety,[26] forgetting to take account of the robust taste of that generation; Bayle defended himself against a similar charge, which was partly inspired by his contemporaries' preference for the classical aesthetic.[27] If we take account of the presuppositions of their critics, it seems safer to conclude that the profane sense of humour of these writers does not imply either a secret or a shared profanity. The fact is, the argument

---

[24] Labrousse, *Pierre Bayle*, vol. 1, p. 128n. As she so wryly observes, this attitude is the opposite of twentieth-century appreciation of the *libertins*: we endure the turgid erudition for the sake of the impious asides.

[25] It is interesting to note that Bayle laments that La Mothe Le Vayer is no longer fashionable in the late seventeenth-century, concerned as it is with *politesse* and court literature ("Vayer", footnote K, a remark added to the second edition in 1702).

[26] Pintard, *Le libertinage*, 143–44.

[27] See Bayle, "Eclaircissement sur les obscénitez", published for the first time with the second edition of the *Dictionnaire* (1702) and included in all subsequent editions. I realize, of course, that the issue of the obscenity of the *Dictionnaire* is more complex than I imply. Nonetheless, I think it is fair to question the literary presuppositions of those who make the accusation. It is quite clear, when reading Bayle's work, that his literary tastes are very old-fashioned and his sense of humour is very much in tune with that of the satirical writers of the sixteenth-century, to whom obscenity is no stranger. Significantly, one of Bayle's favorite contemporary authors is Molière, whose own failure to observe the unity of tone demanded by the classical aesthetic and contempt for the restrictions dictated by *préciosité* brought him into difficulties with his critics. That Bayle himself is impatient with *préciosité* becomes clear in the course of the "Eclaircissement", where he argues that insistence on polite terminology is an impoverishment of the language. The consistency of these arguments with his own literary style and preferences must surely work in favour of our taking them seriously. Labrousse, *Pierre Bayle*, vol. 1, p. 127n., has remarked on the fact that Bayle recommends Le Vayer's *Hexaméron rustique*—one of the latter's more obscene works—to his brother Jacob, a Reformed minister, and she warns against the anachronism which would lead us to see this as a sign of impiety. Bayle considers the accusations of obscenity

that La Mothe Le Vayer inspired Bayle's libertinism would be more convincing if based on another group of Bayle's references to La Mothe Le Vayer. These references, which are in a minority, occur at telling points in the miscellaneous works and in key articles on heterodox or fideistic thinkers in the *Dictionnaire*. They indicate that, despite his condemnation of the religious views of the *libertins* in his early correspondence,[28] Bayle later came to see himself as in some way conditioned by, or at least in sympathy with intellectual libertinage. I shall question the extent to which Bayle's thought is in fact continuous with this tradition. The question has been asked before,[29] but more recent research on seventeenth-century Pyrrhoism and on Bayle himself may lead to modified conclusions.

It is no surprise to find that La Mothe Le Vayer, Bayle and other like-minded thinkers are often associated with what has been called a "conspiracy theory" of intellectual history, that is to say, with the view that certain writers knowingly conspired to undermine traditional religious values. As Pintard so admirably demonstrates, the *libertins* formed a jealously guarded coterie, a learned club, whose principle rules were free thought and free speech. This sociological exclusivity has intellectual consequences and is also expressed stylistically in their writings. It is inseparable from their contempt for popular error—the term is wide-ranging in their usage[30]—and inspires La Mothe Le Vayer to create a conspirational *mise en scène* in

---

brought against La Mothe Le Vayer in "Vayer", footnote D. The assumption that he identifies with La Mothe Le Vayer on this (as on other counts) is reinforced by the fact that he gives a cross-reference to this footnote in the "Eclaircissement sur les obscénitez" (at marginal note 19). The two references to La Mothe Le Vayer's work which occur in this "Eclaircissement" (at marginal notes 63 and 87) are erudite borrowings.

[28] Labrousse, *Pierre Bayle*, vol. 1, 127–28n. gives the essential texts. In these early letters Bayle pronounces on the *libertins'* lack of piety, a judgement he is no longer prepared to make in the articles on heterodox thinkers in the *Dictionnaire*. Rétat is right, I think, to argue that in these articles Bayle is writing an indirect apologia for his own heterodoxy and fideism (see "Libertinage et hétérodoxie", p. 210). However, Pintard is misguided, in my view, when he sets the earlier against the later judgement and concludes—always in pursuit of coherence—that the later judgement is hypocritical (*Le libertinage*, p. 574): it is surely more interesting to ask why Bayle changed his mind. The answer to this question will certainly reveal the progression in Bayle's own religious views and the way in which he incorporates La Mothe Le Vayer into his own maturing thought.

[29] Popkin, "Pierre Bayle's place in seventeenth-century scepticism".

[30] See La Mothe Le Vayer, "De la divinité", *Dialogues*, p. 303: "J'ay une telle antipathie contre tout ce qui est populaire (vous sçavez combien nous estendons loing la signification de ce mot) [. . .]". For Naudé, see Whelan "Un travail d'Hercule", p. 67. See also J.-P. Beaujot, "Du syntagme 'erreur populaire' et de ses ambiguïtés chez Pierre Bayle" in *Beiträge zur Analyse des sozialen wortschatzes*, ed. U. Ricken, Halle 1975/1977, 59–70.

his writings.[31] There can be no doubt that Bayle absorbed this mentality when he encountered it in the 1670s, at a time when he was himself in search of an intellectual style. If fitted well with the Huguenot self-image of a beleaguered minority holding to Reformed dogma while threatened by Roman superstition. It also provided a sociological model—the free exchange of ideas—which Bayle and his friends Basnage and Minutoli tried to imitate during their shared years in Geneva and later in their correspondence.[32] Bayle's published work, and particularly the *Pensées diverses*, is continuous with this early influence: the conspiratorial air, the critique of popular superstition, the significant quotations from La Mothe Le Vayer, all speak for themselves.[33] But the most important feature of this shared attitude is the intellectual antimony which is common to both thinkers: sociological and stylistic elitism are merely the setting for an unremitting critique of the criterion of universal consent. They both use two sets of arguments to undermine the validity of this supposed criterion of truth. The first is the tireless demonstration—drawing on centuries of popular religious beliefs—that the multitude tends to embrace folly more easily than truth, a demonstration which suggests that general consent is a criterion of error.[34] The second is the lethal updating of the tenth

---

[31] La Mothe Le Vayer is of course inspired by the literary models of Greek and Roman Antiquity: the dialogue, the banquet, the letter to the disciple or friend are all well-tried stylistic forms. Nonetheless, he injects them with an air of shared secrets and conspiracy (For example, "De la divinité", *Dialogues*, p. 313).

[32] I anticipate here on the sociological and intellectual framework of Bayle's early correspondence. As the publication of the entire extant correspondence prior to Bayle's departure for Sedan (i.e. volume 1 of the edition, see n. 15 above) will demonstrate, Bayle and his friends created a coterie of their own, whose purpose was to read papers and discuss ideas. Their club did not have the same conspiratorial air, nor were the *libertins* their only sociological model, but their letters do betray their awareness of a shared culture, shared presuppositions and a certain exclusivity; cf. R. Whelan, "Republique des Lettres et littérature: le jeune Bayle épistolier", *XVIIᵉ siècle* 178 (1993), 655–70.

[33] See Rex, *Essays on Pierre Bayle*, 30–74, especially p. 62; Whelan, *The Anatomy*, 122–34 and 144. I have attempted to trace the stylistic expression in Bayle's work of this notion of the learned coterie, see Whelan, "Le *Dictionnaire* de Bayle: un cénacle livresque?", *Littérales* 1 (1986), 37–51.

[34] It would be pedantic to attempt to give all the references in the work of La Mothe Le Vayer and Bayle relevant to this demonstration. Bayle's arguments have been more than adequately discussed by Rex, *Essays on Pierre Bayle*, 30–74. Le Vayer returns obsessively to this theme, but some of his more readily available discussions are to be found in the *Dialogues faits à l'imitation des anciens*: "De la philosophie sceptique", "Le banquet sceptique" and "De la divinité". I think it important to note that one of Bayle's references to La Mothe Le Vayer in the *Pensées diverses* incorporates him into Bayle's own critique of pagan and Roman catholic superstition (see *PD* §xxxi, *Oeuvres diverses* (=*OD*), 4 vols, The Hague 1737, vol. 3, p. 25b; all references are to this edition and to section, volume, page and column).

trope of those attributed by Sextus to Aenesidemus, which, in La
Mothe Le Vayer's view, subsumes all the others, namely, the
infinite variation in human customs, moral behaviour, religious
practices and philosophical conclusions which both writers use—to
a greater or lesser extent—to render universal consent a meaningless concept.[35] Moreover, to the infinite folly of the multitude Bayle
and La Mothe Le Vayer both oppose the wisdom of an enlightened
minority, whose critical acumen enables them to avoid the contagion of popular error.[36] It is this opposition and its application to
religious phenomena which lends credence to the "conspiracy
theory" of their work. And, on the face of it, conspiracy there is.

Although Euhemerism[37] is by no means an index of libertinage,[38]
La Mothe Le Vayer and Bayle's use of it to undermine the possibility of natural knowledge of God appears suspect in a time when
rationalist apologetics were in vogue.[39] To their mind religion

---

[35] See Sextus Empiricus, *Outlines of Pyrrhonism* I.xiv, 145–63; La Mothe Le
Vayer, makes this claim for the tenth trope in "De la philosophie sceptique",
Dialogues, p. 29 and 59; on La Mothe Le Vayer's obsessional use of this argument,
see Popkin, *The History of Scepticism*, 90–93. Bayle remarks on it and on La Mothe
Le Vayer's use of voyage literature for his information in "Vayer", footnote K and
in the *Réponse aux questions d'un provincial* (= *RQP*) §xcvi, *OD*, vol. 3, p. 694b. As
Labrousse, *Pierre Bayle*, vol. 2, 257–89, has pointed out, Bayle does not follow La
Mothe Le Vayer or the sceptics in their moral relativism. However, he does use
the argument of the infinite variety of world religions and views of God in the
Continuation des pensées diverses (= *CPD*) and in the *RQP* to undermine the use of the
argument from general consent as a proof of the existence of God in contemporary
Christian and, more precisely, rationalist protestant apologetics. There are some
significant quotations of La Mothe Le Vayer in these works, made to substantiate
Bayle's own arguments (for example, *CPD* §iv, *OD*, vol. 3, p. 194b, where
reference is made to Le Vayer's refutation of the maxims in support of general
consent and *RQP* §xcvi, *OD*, vol. 3, p. 694b, where one of La Mothe Le Vayer's
examples of variation in moral customs is alleged against the criterion of general
consent). The critique of general consent is, of course, part of the wider discussion
of the *reality* of human knowledge.
[36] On this dichotomy in Bayle, and its implications for intellectual history, see
Whelan, *The Anatomy*, 27–30 and 119–4; on his "libertine" inspiration, see Pintard,
Le libertinage, 505–42; La Mothe Le Vayer's ideal Sage is not only a sceptic, he is
also one who "abomine les violentes contraintes d'une multitude" and who fears
"la contagion en cette derniere presse [. . .] comme celuy qui croit l'epidemie
spirituelle beaucoup plus dangereuse que toute autre" ("De la divinité", *Dialogues*,
p. 303). For a similar attitude in the thought of Gabriel Naudé, who also uses these
morbid metaphors, see Whelan, "Un travail d'Hercule". 59–71.
[37] I use the term in its traditional sense, namely the theory that the deities of
Hellenic and Roman mythology were deified men and women.
[38] The theory is a feature both of the Patristic critique of pagan superstition and
of seventeenth-century Christian apologetics. On this see, F. Laplanche, *L'Évidence
du Dieu chrétien: religion, culture et société dans l'apologétique protestante de la France
classique (1576–1670)*, Strasbourg: Faculté de théologie protestante, 1983.
[39] Zuber, "Libertinage et humanisme", argues that as a result of Garasse's
campaign against the *libertins*, "C'est dans une philosophie de la certitude que

seems to have more to do with human psychology than with knowledge of the divinity. Generally speaking—and without any originality—they attribute the development of religion to four causes. Firstly, the dominance of the imagination in human knowing partly explains the creation of powerful illusions concerning the existence of gods who are interested in human affairs. In the second place, illusion is fortified by fear: people deified natural and paranormal phenomena which they could not explain. Thirdly, national heroes and heroines, and "les choses utiles à la vie" were given divine status by primitive peoples. Finally, legislators and priests encouraged these human tendencies either for purposes of social control or personal profit.[40] If this analysis were confined to primitive paganism, then neither La Mothe Le Vayer nor Bayle could be accused of libertinage. In fact, both of them introduce comparatist discussions of Old Testament figures, biblical miracles and contemporary Christian religious practices,[41] which may be designed to suggest that the Judeo-Christian tradition is also an expression of the same psychological or political motivations detected in paganism. Furthermore, La Mothe Le Vayer's oblique criticism is not limited to Calvinism, nor is Bayle's directed exclusively against

l'adhésion au christianisme devait trouver son fondement intellectuel: l'aristotélisme redevenait obligatoire" (p. 171) In Bayle's case the prevailing philosophy of certitude was Cartesianism which provides a philosophical basis for natural knowledge of God. In fact both authors allow a limited natural knowledge of the *existence* of God, but use the variety and, in their view, the extravagance of world religions to illustrate human inability to know the *nature* of God (see La Mothe Le Vayer, Lettre cii, "Du culte divin", *Oeuvres* vol. 2, 859–60 and *Prose chagrine*, *Oeuvres*, vol. 2, 1134–35; and Bayle, "Anaxagoras", footnote G, §viii. See the discussion of this in E.D. James, "Scepticism and fideism in Bayle's *Dictionnaire*", *French Studies* 16 (1962), p. 318.

[40] See La Mothe Le Vayer, "De la divinité", *Dialogues*, 318–20, the short quotation is from La Mothe Le Vayer; Bayle (in the order of the argument): "Nestorius", footnote N, "Junon", footnote M; "Hélène", footnote Y, *CPD* §xix, *OD*, vol. 3, p. 213a–b; *PD* §§cv, xxviii, lxxxi, cviii, *OD*, vol. 3, p. 72a, 24a, 52a–53a, 73a, *CPD* §§xv, lxxi, *OD*, vol. 3, p. 207b, 292a–293b; "Macédoine", footnote F; "Dejotarus", footnote I, "Escope", footnote H, "Critias", footnote H, *PD* §§lxxx, cix, *OD*, vol. 3, p. 51b–52a, 73b–74a, and *CPD* §xlix, *OD*, vol. 3, p. 255a. It is possible that these arguments figured among those which shocked Bayle when he first read the *Dialogues d'Orasius Tubero* (see Labrousse, *Pierre Bayle*, vol. 1, 127–28n). His adoption of them himself is, however, not necessarily an indication of impiety. For what I consider to be the wider context of these views in his thought see Whelan, "La religion à l'envers: Bayle et l'histoire du paganisme antique", in *Les religions du paganisme antique dans l'Europe chrétienne XVIᵉ—XVIIIᵉ siècle*, Paris: Presses de l'Université de Paris-Sorbonne, 1987, 115–28.

[41] For example: see La Mothe Le Vayer, Lettre xciii, "Rapports de l'histoire profane à la sainte", *Oeuvres*, vol. 2, 796–800; See also *De la vertue des païens*, *Oeuvres*, vol. 1, p. 566, 573 etc.; and *Prose chagrine*, *Oeuvres*, vol. 2, 1133–34. For Bayle, see "Rimini", footnote B and "Jonas", footnote B, also Whelan, "La religion à l'envers", p. 121.

Roman catholicism, so the argument that their sly analogies are stimulated by essentially inter-confessional considerations is not applicable.[42] Finally, both of them are aware of the dangers of comparatism.[43] They both declare that the biblical revelation is true and the pagan analogies are but vile imitations, inspired by the devil,[44] but critics are hardly to be blamed for seeing this as a sleight-of-hand. The creation of analogies between pagan myths and biblical stories, as Bayle and La Mothe Le Vayer appear to realize, can be used to reduce the revealed tradition to the level of a mythology.[45]

The challenge to traditional belief offered by these thinkers does not stop, however, with their libertine critique of religious phenomena. Although Popkin is right, generally speaking, to distinguish between their Pyrrhonist critique of the grounds of human knowing—arguing that while La Mothe Le Vayer casts doubt on "the reliability of sense information", Bayle seeks to undermine "the reliability of reason"[46]—La Mothe Le Vayer's discussion of the proofs of immortality, and Bayle's later use of that discussion, is indicative of a deeper unity of thought and purpose than Popkin perhaps appreciated.[47] The immortality of the soul is one of two philosophical issues (the other is the existence of God) on which

---

[42] For example: La Mothe Le Vayer, *Prose chagrine*, *Oeuvres*, vol 2, p. 1115 and 1134f and *Hexameron rustique ou les six journées passées à la campagne entre des personnes studieuses*, Cologne 1671, 12° in 8's and 4's, "VIe journée", 137–51.

[43] For example: La Mothe Le Vayer, Lettre xciii, "Rapports de l'histoire profane à la sainte", *Oeuvres*, vol. 2, p. 796, 799–80; and Bayle, "Phaselis", footnote B, see Labrousse, *Pierre Bayle*, vol. 2, p. 309n.

[44] For example: La Mothe Le Vayer, Lettre xciii, "Rapports de l'histoire profane à la sainte", *Oeuvres*, vol. 2, p. 799; and Bayle "Abaris", footnote B and "Xenophanes", footnote E. Footnote to complete.

[45] For the moment I leave in suspension my own and other critics efforts to read these analogies—certainly in Bayle's case—in the context of an ethno-centrism, which takes for granted that pagan myths are falsehoods and Judeo-Christian "myths", historical fact or revealed truth. The validity of this socio-historical interpretation of Bayle's thought—and, indeed La Mothe Le Vayer's—is precisely what is here at issue.

[46] Popkin, "Pierre Bayle's place in seventeenth-century scepticism", p. 3.

[47] There are three quotations from La Mothe Le Vayer in the footnotes to the article "Pomponace", at footnote B, marginal notes 13 and 19 and footnote E, marginal note 48. The first (a reference to "De la divinité", *Dialogues*, p. 322) refutes La Mothe Le Vayer's reading of Pomponace as a duplicitous thinker, who has recourse to faith only to hide his unbelief, alleging instead that his rejection of philosophical proof (in this case Aristotelianism) was accompanied by a sincere acceptance of the revealed doctrine of immortality. The second and third (references to La Mothe Le Vayer's *Petit discours chrestien de l'immortalité de l'ame*) quote La Mothe Le Vayer's treatise, on the one hand, on a point of erudition and, on the other, to substantiate Bayle's own argument that there is no impiety in the

both authors admit—albeit with qualification—the validity of proofs drawn from natural reasoning. Bayle, however, is a little more categorical than his predecessor. La Mothe Le Vayer agrees that the thinker must not neglect anything "de ce qu'on peut tirer d'avantageux par le discours de cette mesme raison, pour la justice d'une si bonne cause", whereas Bayle admits that he personally finds Cartesian dualism a convincing proof of the immateriality and hence the immortality of the soul.[48] However, both thinkers point to the variety of philosophical positions on the question of immortality, and particularly to the materialist implications of Aristotelianism, in order to demonstrate that certain proofs of immortality might be convincing to some but they must not be taken to mean that immortality is a self-evident or necessary truth.[49] In fact, if we are to believe La Mothe Le Vayer and Bayle, the proofs of the immortality of the soul are, in fact, rather weak.[50] Both thinkers are aware of the heterodox implications of this position and, indeed, their critics have not failed to use this, together with the continuity with the thought of Pomponazzi implied—in La Mothe Le Vayer's case—and stated—in Bayle's—as an indication

---

assertion that the mortality of the soul is a consequence of Aristotelian philosophy. Two further points must be made concerning the use of La Mothe Le Vayer in this article. Firstly, the articles "Pomponace", "Perrot", "Charron" and the footnote M to the article "Dicéarque", all interconnected by Bayle through a series of cross-references, were all added to the second edition of the *Dictionnaire* (1702). Many of the articles added to this edition are part of an indirect apologia for those of Bayle's views which had been challenged after the publication of the first edition. (Indeed, this dimension to the article "Pomponace" has been noted by James, "Scepticism and fideism", p. 319; and Rétat, "Libertinage et hétérodoxie", p. 210). Secondly, if this series of articles is read together with La Mothe Le Vayer's treatise on immortality, it is clear that Bayle's quotations from this work are but the tip of his real use of La Mothe Le Vayer. Bayle is inspired quite directly—*mutatis mutandis*—by his predecessor, applying to Cartesianism the kind of arguments Le Vayer uses to undermine the philosophical orthodoxy of his own day. In fact, I have every reason to believe that Bayle read or re-read La Mothe Le Vayer's treatise as he prepared these additional articles. The pattern fits with his practice elsewhere (see Whelan *The Anatomy*, 172–73).

[48] La Mothe Le Vayer, *Petit discours chrestien de l'immortalité de l'ame, Oeuvres*, vol. 1, p. 492; Bayle "Pomponace", footnote F.

[49] La Mothe Le Vayer, *Petit discours chrestien de l'immortalité de l'ame, Oeuvres*, vol. 1, p. 513–15. Bayle, "Pomponace", footnote F: he refers to Gassendi's critique of Descartes to prove that the Cartesian argument for the immortality of the soul is not a self-evident truth, given that it does not appear so to another philosopher. I think that the article "Rorarius" (1697, with some considerable additions in 1702) with its discussion of the souls of animals must be interpreted as part of Bayle's technique of setting one philosophy against another (here the Aristotelian and Cartesian positions) in order to encourage either a suspension of judgement, and/or suggest the bankruptcy of human reason.

[50] La Mothe Le Vayer, *Petit discours chrestien de l'immortalité de l'ame, Oeuvres*, vol. 1, p. 513. Bayle, "Charron", footnote O (1702).

of their respective incredulity.[51] The conclusion is not without foundation. If, in an area where both authors allow the use of natural reason, compelling proof is wanting, then what of those areas of belief where proof is more difficult to estáblish? And in effect, La Mothe Le Vayer suggests obliquely and Bayle argues mercilessly that in the area of Christian theodicy, for example, the burden of proof is against rather than in favour of traditional belief.[52] Thus, it would seem that the mentality shared by these two thinkers (of course, in their view, they figure prominently among the critical minority) and the questioning of generally accepted beliefs it entails, has led them to the kind of radical doubt often seen as typical of their thought.[53] Nonetheless, both La Mothe Le Vayer and Bayle argue obsessionally that, properly understood, their destructive critique of religious belief is not just compatible with religious truth, it is also actively conducive to faith.[54] It is time to consider the grounds for what is, in effect, a declaration of intent:

---

[51] La Mothe Le Vayer spends quite a lot of energy justifying those who agree to the materialist implications of Aristotelian philosophy against the charge of impiety, which seems to suggest an awareness of the problem (indeed his earlier treatment of Pomponazzi—see note 51 above—implies that he is aware of the heterodoxy of the position). The same can be said (and has been, see note 50 above) of Bayle's defense of Pomponazzi in the article of that name. Pintard argues that Bayle's defense of Pomponazzi and his use of La Mothe Le Vayer in the course of the argument are to be taken as indications of Bayle's own libertinage (*Le libertinage*, 517–20 and 574). For the view that Pomponazzi influenced the development of intellectual libertinage, see H. Busson, *Le rationalisme dans la littérature française de la Renaissance (1533–1601)*, Paris: Vrin, 1957 (nouvelle édition, revue et augmentée).

[52] See La Mothe Le Vayer, Lettre cii, "Du culte divin", *Oeuvres*, vol. 2, p. 863 and *Prose chagrine*, *Oeuvres*, vol. 2, p. 1114 and Bayle "Manichées", "Pauliciens" etc. The problem of Bayle's discussion of Manicheism has been the subject of much critical debate. It is one of the points where he departs from Le Vayer's more cautious critique of religious dogma, but the arguments are so well known that I prefer not to raise them here.

[53] Indeed, Le Vayer warns against precisely this danger of Pyrrhonism: "Car les doutes du Pyrrhonisme tout pur, qui n'est pas circoncis comme nous l'avons dit, ni d'ailleurs soûmis à la Foy, donnent de grands avantages parfois sur les plus Sçavans, par ses dix moiens de l'Epoche, qui sont comme autant de testes de Gorgone. Mais il pourroit arriver à la longue, que dans cette habitude à mettre tout en doute indifferemment, l'on s'aveugleroit enfin malheureusement contre les lumieres du Ciel; ce qui feroit perir l'ame sans remission' (*Prose chagrine*, *Oeuvres*, vol. 2, p. 1136).

[54] The respective texts are too well known to warrant citation, for a discussion of this issue, see Popkin, "Pierre Bayle's place in seventeenth-century scepticism". It is when he claims that the pyrrhonist suspension of judgement is conducive to faith that Bayle identifies most strongly with La Mothe Le Vayer. He not only quotes at length from his predecessor (see "Pyrrhon", footnote C), he also refers his readers back to "Pyrrhon", footnote C in "Eclaircissement sur les pyrrhoniens" §5, *Dictionnaire*, vol. 4, p. 3004, as containing his own views on the issue of the relation between reason and faith.

on it hangs our interpretation of their respective religious beliefs.

Although La Mothe Le Vayer and Bayle come at if from somewhat different angles, their critique of popular error, their rejection
of general consent as a criterion, and their shared conviction that
the immortality of the soul is not a necessary truth are part of their
common preoccupation with the problem of the criterion of truth
and, more especially, with the nature of proof. The difference
between them in this, as in the other issues, is one of degree rather
than kind. La Mothe Le Vayer may prefer to use the tenth trope,
Bayle may prefer to set reason at loggerheads with itself, but both
are intent on questioning the truth claims of the Dogmatists.
Moreover, for both of them, although more intensely in Bayle's
case, it is the criterion of *évidence* and the truth claim of Cartesian
rationalism—regarded by both thinkers as a new dogmatism—
which is particularly under fire. Herein lies the key to their respective attitudes on the problem of the immortality of the soul. Neither
of them accepts that immortality is demonstrable, because demonstrability and self-evidence are seen by both of them as typical of
mathematical proof: neither of them will accept that mathematical
reasoning can ever be a proof of real existence.[55] Moreover, Bayle is
also convinced that even if the Cartesian proof is self-evident to
him, the fact that it is not self-evident to all is a proof—not of the
relativity of the criterion[56]—but of the limitation of the human
mind.[57] The position taken by both authors on the issue of immor-

---

[55] La Mothe Le Vayer, *Petit discours chrestien de l'immortalité de l'ame*, *Oeuvres*,
vol. 1, p. 514; *évidence* cannot be the criterion of truth in this instance because: "il
n'est pas juste de demander ici de ces demonstrations invincibles, & qui semblent
estre au dessus de toute dispute, quoique peut-estre il y en ait par tout. Car comme
Aristote dit luy-mesme en ce dernier chapitre du second livre de sa Metaphysique
que nous avons déja allegué, & qui ne peut estre trop consideré veu son excellence,
il ne faut pas exiger en toutes choses des preuves semblables á celles qu'on donne
dans les pures Mathematiques, pource que ce seroit vouloir forcer la Nature, qui
ne permet pas qu'on en puisse apporter toûjours de si concluantes, quand il se
trouve de la repugnance de la part du subject." That this critique of *évidence* is
associated in La Mothe Le Vayer with a critique of Cartesianism is implied in his
Prose chagrine, *Oeuvres*, vol. 2, p. 1109: "*Ceux de ce temps* n'ont gueres degeneré pour
ce regard, & l'on peut prononcer sans mécompte de la pluspart de *nos Novateurs*, la
mesme chose qu'Aristote impute à d'autres au dernier chapitre du premier livre de
sa Metaphysique, qu'ils ont voulu faire des belles Mathematiques une fort laide &
fort mauvaise Philosophie. Car comme il adjouste si bien à la fin du second livre,
les evidences & les certitudes de la Mathematique ne doivent estre exigées qu'aux
choses qui sont dépouïllées de toute matiere" (italics mine).
[56] This is the argument James put forward in his early article "Scepticism and
fideism", (1962) and which he revised in his later "Pierre Bayle on belief and
évidence", *French Studies* 27 (1973), 395–404.
[57] This is how I interpret the entire thrust of Bayle's Pyrrhonist critique of
knowledge and belief in the *Dictionnaire*. It fits with the discussion of the primary/
secondary quality distinction and of the definition of matter as extension in the

tality is paradigmatic of their understanding of all human knowing.[58] La Mothe Le Vayer maintains, undogmatically[59] and in line with the Pyrrhonian tradition, that people can only know how things seem ("le vrai-semblable") rather than how they are.[60] Bayle is a mitigated Cartesian: he allows that some but not all propositions are self-evident, an argument which allows him to retain the criterion but limit its application. In other words, like Arnauld and Nicole, who influenced him, Bayle distinguishes between orders of knowledge.[61] In his view, "le Christianisme est d'un ordre surnaturel",[62] consequently the criterion of natural reasoning, namely that of self-evidence, is by definition not applicable to the order of knowing to which immortality belongs.[63] This is not to argue, however, that Christian doctrines are uncertain; as we shall see, Bayle attempts to provide this order of knowledge with a certitude applicable to it. But let us first consider the implications for religious knowledge of these similar attitudes to rational criteria.

It follows from the distinction between truth and appearance in La Mothe Le Vayer and from the limitations that Bayle imposes on the criterion of self-evidence that if God is truth, then, on the one hand, human beings—limited to the world of appearances—cannot know him and, on the other, that arguments for his existence based on the criterion of self-evidence cannot prove his real existence. And, indeed, even if man could find out God, how could he be sure

---

article "Zenon"; with the setting at loggerheads of theological propositions and self-evident, common notions in "Pyrrhon"; with the discussion of the immortality of the soul in "Pomponace" and the related articles; and of the souls of animals in "Rorarius", namely that mathematical definitions cannot be proven to have anything but an ideal existence (and therefore are invalid as proofs of real existence), and that the self-styled *évidence* of certain proposition is neither self-evident to all nor applicable to certain kinds of truth.

[58] The problem of the immortality of the soul is raised by Bayle in the "Eclaircissement sur les pyrrhoniens" as a paradigm of human knowing (§5, *Dictionnaire*, vol. 4, 3004–05).

[59] La Mothe Le Vayer, "De la philosophie sceptique", *Dialogues*, p. 27: "quand nous disons qu'il n'y a rien de vray ny de certain, cette voix n'est pas simplement ny absolument affirmative, mais contient tacitement une exception de soi mesme".

[60] La Mothe Le Vayer, *Opuscule ou petit traité sceptique sur cette commune façon de parler, "n'avoir pas le sens commun"*, *Oeuvres*, vol. 2, pp. 382, 391–92; *Prose chagrine*, *Oeuvres*, vol. 2, p. 1133, 1162.

[61] See Arnauld and Nicole, *La logique ou l'art de penser*, ed. L. Marin, Paris: Flammarion, 1970, Part IV, 359–431 and the discussion of this in Borghero, *La Certezza e la storia*, 106–24. Like so many of his contemporaries, Bayle was deeply interested in this work. The extent of its influence on him has not yet been properly assessed.

[62] Bayle, "Eclaircissement sur les Pyrrhoniens" §i, *Dictionnaire*, vol. 4, p. 3001.

[63] My position is similar to that taken by James in his "Pierre Bayle on belief and *évidence*" and to the more extensive argument in C.B. Brush, *Montaigne and Bayle: variations on the theme of skepticism*, The Hague: Nijhoff, 1966.

it was God, if his criterion of truth is not applicable to "non-self-evident phenomena"? Reason, then, for both writers is a critical and not a creative tool,[64] it can tell what truth is not, but is hard pressed to establish what truth is. In fact, La Mothe Le Vayer and Bayle both point to the variations in theological propositions within Christendom as an indication of man's inability to find out God. Moreover, the diversity of theologies makes the charge they both bring against primitive paganism—that religion is a projection of human illusion—applicable to Christianity. "C'est ainsi", writes La Mothe Le Vayer, "que chacun rend le Ciel partisan de ses interests, & que l'homme ne pouvant connoistre quels sont les sentimens de Dieu (je m'explique ainsi, puisque nous ne pouvons parler qu'improprement de luy) aime mieux luy attribuer les siens propres, que d'avoüer son ignorance".[65] Theology itself, in this analysis, becomes a form of approximate thinking which, certainly in Bayle's view, makes it analogous to popular error.[66] Thus, the only option for the Sage, or even for the theologian, is to imitate the wisdom of Simonides. To quote Bayle: "Nos plus grans Théologiens, s'ils agissoient comme Simonide, c'est-à-dire, s'ils ne vouloient assûrer sur la nature de Dieu que ce qui par les lumieres de la Raison leur paroîtroit incontestable, évident, & à l'épreuve de toute difficulté, demanderoient incessamment de nouveaux délais à tous les Hierons".[67] Why? *Because God is past all finding out.* For both authors, Simonides is a paradigm of the search for understanding of God: it ends in ignorance and in silence. Let us not hastily conclude that both authors are surreptitiously advancing the preambles of atheism. This may be what their respective thought will later become but, in and of themselves, they see their position as continuous with the tradition of the *theologia negativa* which, as Bayle points out, has a long—if at times suspect—tradition in the history of Christian belief.[68] They may both lack the tremulous mysticism often associated with the tradition, but this is not sufficient to cast doubt on the sincerity of their negative theology,[69] which is, after all, consistent with their understanding of religious belief.

---

[64] La Mothe Le Vayer, *Opuscule ou petit traité sceptique, Oeuvres*, vol. 2, p. 381; Bayle, "Acosta", footnote G.

[65] La Mothe Le Vayer, *Opuscule ou petit traité sceptique, Oeuvres*, vol. 2, p. 390; see Bayle, "Simonides", footnote F. Significantly, this article was added to the second edition of the *Dictionnaire* (1702).

[66] Bayle, "Simonide", footnote F and *CPD* §§20 and 21, *OD*, vol. 3, 213b–217b; La Mothe Le Vayer, *Prose chagrine, Oeuvres*, vol. 2, p. 1162.

[67] Bayle, "Simonide", footnote F.

[68] Bayle, "Simonide", footnote F.

[69] Rétat, "Libertinage et hétérodoxie", 205–06 makes a similar point.

Indeed, far from providing the preambles to atheism, both authors present their doubt concerning the possibility of knowing God
as an indispensable preamble to faith. In La Mothe Le Vayer's
view, the conviction that reason is a blind guide purges the seeker
of all dogmatic self-sufficiency[70] and, according to Bayle, leads him
to "renoncer à ce guide, & d'en demander un meilleur à la cause de
toutes choses. C'est un grand pas vers la Religion Chrétienne; car
elle veut que nous attendions de Dieu la conoissance de ce que nous
devons croire, & de ce que nous devons faire: elle veut que nous
captivions notre entendement à l'obéïssance de la Foi".[71] If reason
is taken to mean Dogmatic or Cartesian reason,[72] faith is seen by
both authors to be the absolute antithesis of a rational
apprehension of God. In their view, God is apprehended only if he
takes the initiative, making himself available to the seeker whose
reason has proven inadequate to detect him. Thus, both of them
appeal to the Pauline epistles to point up the "folly" of Christianity
and the gratuitous nature of faith, which they present as a "don de
Dieu".[73] In fact, La Mothe Le Vayer offers a voluntarist view of
faith: "C'est pourquoy, au lieu que dans les sciences nous acquies-
çons facilement à l'evidence des principes connus par nostre intellect, dans nostre Theologie nous consentons à ses principes divins
par le seul commandement de nostre volonté, qui se rend obeïs-
sante à Dieu aux choses qu'elle ne voit et ne comprend pas, en quoy
consiste le merite de la foy Chrestienne, 'fides non consentit per
evidentiam objecti, sed ex imperio voluntatis', dit S. Thomas",[74]
which Bayle echoes in his attribution of faith to the influence of
grace (= "foi justifiante"), education or temperament (= "foi
historique").[75] While both of them imply that divine authority is
the basis of faith, there is, nonetheless, an important distinction

---

[70] La Mothe Le Vayer, "De la divinité", *Dialogues*, p. 308 and 312; *Prose
chagrine*, *Oeuvres*, vol. 2, p. 1133.
[71] Bayle, "Pyrrhon", footnote C.
[72] For a wider discussion of this important distinction see A. McKenna, "*Deus
absconditus*: quelques réflexions sur la crise du rationalisme chrétien entre 1670 et
1740", in *Apologétique 1680–1740: sauvetage ou naufrage de la théologie?*, Genève: Labor
et Fides, 1991, 13–28 Bayle does not always mean "Cartesian reason" when he
speaks of the relationship of reason to faith. While he stresses the incompatibility
of Cartesian reason and faith, he does not, in my view, make reason, understood as
human intelligence, inoperative in the act of faith.
[73] See La Mothe Le Vayer, "De la divinité", *Dialogues*, 307–08, *Prose chagrine*,
Oeuvres, vol. 2, 1132–33; Bayle, "Simonide", footnote F; "Eclaircissement sur les
pyrrhoniens" and "Eclaircissement sur les manichéens".
[74] La Mothe Le Vayer, "De la divinité", *Dialogues*, p. 306.
[75] Bayle, "Pyrrhon", footnote B.

between their respective view of the human response to that authority. For La Mothe Le Vayer, faith is blind; it is the will's assent to God, an acceptance of things *unseen* ("qu'elle ne voit pas") and *not understood* ("[qu'elle] ne comprend pas"). For Bayle, however, while it may be voluntarist, faith is not completely blind. He describes it elsewhere as an "acte de l'entendement",[76] implying that it involves some form of cognition. The mind is captured in obedience to faith but it is not compeletely inoperative: it receives from God "*la connaissance* de ce que nous devons croire". Propositional and/or Cartesian theology may be impossible, then, but even the simple believer must accept the tenets of his cathecism.[77] Nonetheless, although these views are consistent with their respective authors' negative theology, they do not answer the nagging question of their intent. Their appeal to faith as the natural exit from the bankruptcy of reason could be a mere sleight-of-hand, designed to distract their critics. However, one more question remains which, I believe, will enable us to evaluate their intent.

Both authors, as we have seen, make the divine initiative and authority the grounds of faith, but for this to be a valid proposition they must also tell us wherein that authority is vested and how it may be apprehended by the seeker. It is at this point that their thought diverges; we will consider each of them in turn, looking first at La Mothe Le Vayer. To his mind, although doubt is all around, the believer can be certain in his faith, because he bases it on "veritez revelées", that is on "des Oracles divins que l'Eglise a receus".[78] This is a logical conclusion for a Christian Pyrrhonist, outwardly—at least—a Roman Catholic. Religious truth is revealed to the seeker and received by him through the medium of the church, which also guarantees the validity of that revelation. Nonetheless, there are two problems with this position, if we consider it from the point of view of La Mothe Le Vayer's intent. The first is the status of revelation in his thought, which is consistent with his negative theology. In his view, revelation is not conceived as God-speaking, or even, as in the thought of Pascal, as God-hiding, instead, revelation is for La Mothe Le Vayer, God-unknowable:

> Nous ne disons en cela que ce qui est conforme à la meilleure Theologie, puisque celle de Sainct Denys n'enseigne rien plus expressément que la foiblesse de nostre esprit, & son ignorance à

---

[76] Bayle, "Eclaircissement sur les Pyrrohoniens" §v, *Dictionnaire*, vol. 4, p. 3004.
[77] Bayle, "Simonide", footnote F.
[78] La Mothe Le Vayer, *Prose chagrine, Oeuvres*, vol. 2, p. 1133 and 1134.

l'egard sur tout des choses Divines. C'est ainsi que ce grand Docteur
explique ce que Dieu mesme a prononcé par la bouche de ses
Prophetes, qui a establi sa retraitte dans les tenebres. Car cela estant,
nous ne sçaurions nous approcher de luy, que nous n'entrions dans
ces mysterieuses tenerbres; d'où nous tirons cette importante leçon,
qu'il ne se peut connoistre qu'obscurément, couvert d'enigmes ou de
nuages, & selon que dit l'Eschole, en l'ignorant.[79]

Considered in context, there is nothing surprising in this assertion:
the obscurity of the Bible was one of the major polemical arguments of the Counter-Reformation, which sought to drive the protestants to seek refuge in the authority of the church. Although, La
Mothe Le Vayer seems to be making a similar argument, his own
unremitting critique of the criterion of general consent actually
undermines the validity of the church's authority. For, as the
protestants never tire of demonstrating: what is the tradition of the
church but universal consent under a different guise? We cannot
know if La Mothe Le Vayer intended us to draw this consequence
from his thought, but even if he did not, we have no reason, given
his stated view of revelation, to argue that his acceptance of divine
authority mediated through the church is any different from the
external social conformity of the Sceptic. In other words, if the
revealed God is God-unknowable, then, revelation is emptied of its
content. Consequently, there is nothing to distinguish acceptance
of the authority of the depositary of this revelation from compliance
with a set of customs. Of course—chronology aside—if La Mothe
Le Vayer's position is compared to that of Pascal, for whom "la
coutume est notre nature. Qui s'accoutume à la foi la croit [. . .]",[80]
then we may argue that La Mothe Le Vayer's fideistic discourse is
open to interpretation as a serious profession of faith. In my own
view, however, the evidence of the available documents concerning
La Mothe Le Vayer's belief is inconclusive.

    In contrast to this, Bayle's quirky attitude to the grounds of faith
has nothing of the characteristics of a mere external conformity to
custom. Indeed, his life-long discussion of the criterion of religious
truth seems to suggest that, while it may have been an intellectual
problem for him, he was nonetheless concerned to articulate some
grounds for his essentially irrational view of the act of faith. As a
Calvinist, he cannot and would not wish to have recourse to the

---

[79] La Mothe Le Vayer, *De la vertu des païens*, "De Pyrrhon et de la secte
sceptique", *Oeuvres*, vol. 1, p. 665. The passage is quoted by Bayle in "Pyrrhon",
footnote C.
    [80] Pascal, *Pensées*, ed. La Lafuma, Paris: Seuil 1963, §419. I am grateful to A.
McKenna (Université de St-Étienne) for drawing my attention to this *pensée*.

authority of the church to validate his belief. In his view, divine authority is expressed in the "Véritéz révélées", a statement which raises the further question as to how these revealed truths are known. The issue, then, becomes that of "la Divinité de l'Ecriture", that is to say, whether or not revelation is to be equated with the Bible. This question, "si l'Ecriture a été composée par des Auteurs inspirez de Dieu", is according to Bayle, a "question de fait".[81] In other words, an apparently theological question is conflated by him with the question of *historical* proof. To his mind, although factual questions are not capable of mathematical proof, they are susceptible of a "démonstration morale", which yields either "une grande probabilité" or "une tres-grande probabilité".[82] Although he never offered a coherent moral demonstration of the inspiration of Scripture, three moral proofs, common in protestant apologetics of the day, may be extrapolated from his work. The first one, which he applies to history, but which is offered in the context of Biblical inspiration, takes the form of a syllogism. The major premise is: "impossible tot homines tot saeculis convenire ad mentiendum" and the minor "hoc dicunt tot homines tot saeculis".[83] In other words, general consent makes a rather surprising reappearance to validate the claim that the Bible *is* divine truth. This is not a suspect use of the criterion, I believe, since it is also the validation of historical knowing, a domain in which Bayle's commitment to the possibility of truth cannot be questioned. In the second place, he appeals to the internal consistency of the Bible, claiming that there is in Scripture "quelque chose de surnaturel dans l'enchaînement [des] faits".[84] Finally, he uses a somewhat backhanded version of the proof of the divinity of Scripture from the majesty of its style.[85] Of course, none of these moral proofs conclusively establishes either the divinity of Scripture or Bayle's acceptance of it as the basis of his own religious views. Bayle could even allude to the

---

[81] Bayle, "Eclaircissement sur les pyrrhoniens" §i, *Dictionnaire*, vol. 4, 3001–02.

[82] Bayle, "Beaulieu", footnote F. The section of the text giving rise to footnote E and F, with the notes themselves, was added to the second edition (1702). In his more sanguine moments he goes so far as to argue that factual questions are more certain than mathematical demonstrations since they are not subject to doubt concerning their real existence ("Dissertation contenant le projet" §ix, *Dictionnaire*, vol. 4, p. 2983.

[83] Bayle, "Beaulieu", footnote F (1702). See the discussion of this in James, "Scepticism and fideism", 313–14 and "Pierre Bayle on belief and *évidence*", p. 400.

[84] Baye, "Simonide", footnote F (1702), see James, "Pierre Bayle on belief and *évidence*", p. 400.

[85] See Whelan, *The Anatomy of superstition*, 163–65.

moral proofs and believe that, as moral proofs, they are convincing without himself being convinced by them. What further evidence— if any—is there that he intended his arguments to be interpreted as serious grounds for faith?

At this point in the argument, Bayle's general attitude to Scripture and practice of it must be invoked. As I have sought to demonstrate elsewhere, while his use of the Bible indicates that its truth claims are problematical to him, he nonetheless seems unwilling to take the final step of rejecting its truth claims altogether. There are two areas of problems for Bayle, the first are textual and the second are moral. While he is sympathetic to Richard Simon's textual criticism, at crucial points in his own exegesis of certain passages he deliberately refuses to implement it. Why? To do so would be to undermine a theology of the Bible which, for all its difficulties, Bayle appears unwilling to jettison. He would seem to hold to a propositional view of revelation, as the communication of 'truths unavailable to reason by means beyond the ordinary course of nature'[86] and to accept the verbal inspiration of the Bible, which we have seen he equates with revelation. In other words, Bayle's practice of Scripture in the *Dictionnaire* suggest that, unlike La Mothe Le Vayer, he equates divine speaking with the biblical text. The second set of problems, however, conflicts with this view. For Bayle is obsessed by the immorality and violence of the Old Testament, which naturally undermine its divinity. Considered with care, however, it is quite clear that Bayle appeals to a traditional Calvinist exegesis to drive a wedge between this behaviour and the God of the Bible. That is to say, he condemns the patriarchs' actions, not sneeringly as Voltaire will later do, but in order to save the Bible from condemnation by association.[87] However, given the potentially reversible nature of the passages in Bayle's work on which my argument is based,[88] we cannot conclude that Bayle was a pious Calvinist. We do, however, have *some* reason to believe that when he proposes to the seeker (or is it the doubter?) that he look to God for "*la connoissance* de ce que nous devons croire", he is proposing a not unproblematical acceptance of revelation, which he con-

---

[86] This is the summary of the propositional definition of revelation by W.J. Abraham, *Divine revelation and the limits of historical criticism*, Oxford, New York, Toronto & Melbourne: Oxford University Press, 1982.

[87] See Whelan, *The Anatomy of Superstition*, 146–79.

[88] H.T. Mason, "Pierre Bayle's religious views", *French Studies* 17 (1963), 205–17 provides an alternative to my interpretation.

flates with the Bible. The religious knowing which the Scripture offers is, of course, not *rational*,[89] in the sense of self-evident: doctrines such as the Trinity, the Incarnation, the Resurrection, and the afterlife, like God himself, are essentially incomprehensible.[90] But because the Bible is a historical text, the order of knowledge to which these truths belong is capable of moral proof, yielding moral certitude.[91] Thus, in the final analysis, it is the consistency of the arguments on the nature of truth and proof which convinces me of the sincerity of Bayle's intent. This cannot prove, to use his own distinction, that he had a *foi divine* or *justifiante*—such proof is outside the domain of the historian—but it does suggest that he held at least to a fairly damaged version of the *foi historique*.

The comparison of the religious thought of La Mothe Le Vayer and Pierre Bayle has not, then, been a futile exercise. We have discovered that Bayle's repeated references to La Mothe Le Vayer's published work originates in a close self-identification and also in a significant affiliation with La Mothe Le Vayer's ideas. We have

---

[89] I must disagree here with James, who, it seems to me, uses "rational" in two senses in his two articles (for references see n.60 above). The first I agree to, namely the use of "rational" to describe that which complies with the criterion of *évidence*. To extend this, as he does, to include Bayle's conception of the truth-status of the Bible is—in my view—not allowable! He argues: "So far we have seen the points at which Bayle eludes the charge of fideism. First, he claims the inspiration of the Scriptures to be rationally demonstrable—which means he has a rational justification for his faith as a whole" ("Scepticism and fideism", p. 318; a claim repeated in "Pierre Bayle on belief and *évidence*", p. 400). I agree that in "Beaulieu", footnote F, Bayle argues that the syllogism "impossible tot homines" yields an axiomatic rather than a moral proof, but it is axiomatic within the second rather than the first (self-evident) order of truth. Thus, it seems to me that to argue that Bayle has a "rational" basis for his view of Scripture is to confuse the issue, and is certainly not sufficient grounds on which to claim that he is not a fideist. His arguments are, in his view, morally certain but they are not "rational", since morally certain proofs suffer contradiction. If he holds in matters of faith to a set of proofs that suffer contradiction, then he is still, to some degree at least (and most certainly from the point of view of the Cartesian) a fideist.

[90] These are the doctrines proposed by Bayle in "Perrot", footnote L as the Christian mysteries.

[91] H.M. Bracken, "Bayle not a sceptic?", *Journal of the History of Ideas* 25 (1964), 169–80, criticized James's view that there is an idea of morally certain proof in Bayle. While I agree with many of the points Bracken makes in that article, I think he underestimates the place of moral proof in Bayle's thought. James may have based his argument mainly on the article "Beaulieu" (see Bracken, p. 171), but the position taken by Bayle there is consistent with his view of historical truth and with his practice of history throughout his life. It is possible that James's own confused use of the term "rational" and his unwarranted assertion that Bayle's religious views were in some way "rational" set the Bracken-James debate on the wrong footing. In my view, the failure of these two critics to distinguish between orders of knowledge in Bayle leads to much misunderstanding both of Bayle and between their respective views of Bayle.

also appreciated that although, as Popkin argued, La Mothe Le Vayer is part of the Montaignian tradition, he himself had conceptualized his reaction to Cartesianism sufficiently to provide a precedent and possibly an inspiration for Bayle's own critique of the application to religious knowing of the criterion of self-evidence. The important difference between their respective attitudes to the grounds of belief must alert us, however, to the need for caution in assessing La Mothe Le Vayer's real influence on the thought of his successor. While La Mothe Le Vayer was a favorite author, he was only *one* author in the vast kaleidoscope of Bayle's reading and intellectual affinities. Until we know more about the genesis and evolution of Bayle's thought it would be unwise to attempt to estimate more exactly either in what way or to what degree La Mothe Le Vayer was a catalyst in Bayle's development. All the more so, since there is another major difference between the two thinkers' cultivation of doubt. La Mothe Le Vayer uses the tenth trope, and other sceptical modes, as a means to an end. Like Sextus, he sees *epoche*, or suspension of judgement, as the means to a moral goal, which is *ataraxia*[92]. *Ataraxia*, to his mind, is freedom from either intellectual or moral disquiet. It is the mark of the Sage, distinguishing him from the fickle multitude, which allows him to avoid the contagion of popular error and/or behaviour. In other words, it is a form of social and intellectual elitism.[93] Bayle, as we have seen, has enough of the vanity of the intellectual to share, to a

---

[92] For this distinction, see D. Sedley, "The motivation of Greek scepticism" in *The Skeptical Tradition*, ed. M. Burnyeat, Berkeley, Los Angeles, London: University of California Press, 1983, p. 21.

[93] La Mothe Le Vayer, "Dela philosophie sceptique", *Dialogues* 60–61: "je me trouvay incontinent au milieu d'une egalité de raisons, la balance du discours demeurant en equilibre, à cause que tout pesant egalement, elle ne sçavoit de quel costé incliner. C'est ce que nostre famille appelle ἰσοσθενή διαφωνίαν; laquelle n'eust pas plustost jetté racine dans mon esprit, y produisit cette excellente ἐποχή, ou suspension à ne rien prononcer temerairement; et ce fut lors que me croyant encores fort esloigné, je me trouvay comme insensiblement au bout de la carriere. Car l'ombre ne suit point si inseparablement le corps, que l'Epoche est aussi tost atteinte de ces deux divines compagnes, l'ἀταραξία en ce qui regarde les opinions (qui est un estat ou assiette d'esprit hors de tout trouble et agitation) et la ὑετριοπαθεία aux passions, qu'elle modere et regit selon les loix et prescriptions de la droitte raison. [. . .] en cette suspension d'esprit consistoit le celebre εὑεστώ de Democrite, je veux dire le plus haut degré de la beatitude humaine". Also, "De la divinité", *Dialogues*, p. 304: "Mais pource qu'il n'y a rien de plus opposé à nostre heureuse suspension d'esprit que la tyrannique opiniastreté des opinions communes, j'ay tousjours pensé que c'estoit contre ce torrent de la multitude que nous devions employer nos principales forces, et qu'ayant dompté ce monstre du peuple, nous viendrions facilement à bout du reste".

large degree, in this attitude. Nevertheless, his pursuit of *epoche* is socially committed rather than socially detached.

> si l'on convient d'un côté que l'on ne sauroit donner de bonnes preuves que Dieu révele clairement l'éxistence de ses mysteres dans sa parole, on a grand tort de prétendre qu'un homme qui ne les croit pas mérite de perdre ses biens, sa liberté, sa patrie: car il a pour lui les lumieres de la Raison, & vous ne sauriez nier qu'il n'agisse raison-nablement, lors qu'il refuse de renoncer à ses lumieres, à moins qu'il ne paroisse qu'elles sont évidemment combattues par le témoignage de Dieu. [. . .] Tout ce donc que la raison & la charité éxigent de vous, c'est de prier Dieu pour lui, & de faire en sorte par les voies d'une instruction modérée, qu'il trouve moins de probabilité dans ses opinions que dans les vôtres.[94]

His critique of the criterion of self-evidence, and his notion that moral rather than demonstrable proof is proper to religious know-ing, is motivated, then, by his concern for religious and civil toleration.[95] *Epoche* in Bayle's thought is therefore the basis of an *ataraxia* of quite a different kind. *Ataraxia* is not an absence of disquiet but an acceptance of the limitation of human knowing; it is also an undogmatic state of mind which pre-empts intolerance and fosters not the intellectual's contempt (as in La Mothe Le Vayer's case) but the refugee's respect for the otherness of the other. This is a profound difference in the intellectual profiles of the two authors. It is a final indication that the mentality of late Renaissance thought has been transformed into the social consciousness of early modern Europe.

---

[94] Bayle, "Nicolle", footnote C (1697).

[95] There is potential in La Mothe Le Vayer's thought for tolerance. In "De la divinité", *Dialogues*, p. 307, he sees the pyrrhonist suspension of judgement as pre-emptive of heresy and controversy, which is presumably what led Popkin to believe that La Mothe Le Vayer's arguments are essentially directed against the Calvinists. I hope I have demonstrated that it is difficult to reduce La Mothe Le Vayer's thought in this way. The potential in favour of toleration of his argument is, however, never exploited. In fact, for political reasons he is opposed to tolera-tion and in favour of some form of constraint (we must remember he was writing at the time of Richelieu, during the period when absolutism was being elaborated).

HARRY M. BRACKEN

BAYLE'S ATTACK ON NATURAL THEOLOGY
THE CASE OF CHRISTIAN PYRRHONISM*

Popkin[1] has shown that Bayle's use of the arguments of the Pyrrhonians is very different from that employed by other seventeenth-century philosophers. I want first to examine those uses of scepticism from another vantage point and to suggest that Bayle's real goal, e.g. in *Dictionnaire* article "Pyrrho", is to *attack* Christian [Catholic] Pyrrhonism. Then I propose to see how sceptical style arguments are otherwise employed both in the seventeenth-century and in our own time. Bishop Pierre-Daniel Huet,[2] to take a distinguished seventeenth-century representative of the Catholic Pyrrhonist (fideist) tradition, uses sceptical arguments to prepare us for revelation. All rational claims and presuppositions are swept away in order to clean our mental slate so that it may be, as it were, written upon by Holy Authority. That, I take it, is the standard position among the Christian Pyrrhonists.

Bayle seems to take a different tack. In Remarks B and C of "Pyrrho", Popkin finds Bayle demolishing reason in order to replace it with faith. But perhaps that is not the whole story. Certainly Bayle's demolition appears to be total: propositions which possess "evidence", the criterion of truth, are shown to be "false" when compared with the religious truths expressed in the doctrines of the Trinity, Incarnation, Transubstantiation, etc. Moreover, it is a much stronger claim than Christian Pyrrhonists ever made.

---

* Richard Popkin introduced me to Bayle almost immediately upon my arrival as a graduate student at Iowa in 1954. As he notes in the article cited at note 1, Bayle has occasioned for us many "lively discussions"—a process that I expect will continue. In addition to that general indebtedness, in preparing this paper I have greatly benefited from discussions with Elly van Gelderen and F.R.J. Knetsch.
[1] Richard H. Popkin, "Pierre Bayle's Place in 17th-Century Scepticism", in *Pierre Bayle: Le philosophe de Rotterdam*, ed. Paul Dibon, Amsterdam: Elsevier, 1959, pp. 1–19.
[2] See his *Traité philosophique de la foiblesse de l'esprit humain*, London: Jean Nourse, 1741. It circulated in Latin manuscript form as early as about 1690. In reference to Huet, cf. Léon Tolmer. *Pierre-Daniel Huet (1630–1721): Humaniste-Physicien*, Bayeux: Colas, 1949.

Second, Popkin finds another line—mainly in Bayle's other writings: this time Bayle seems to argue that the choice of faith over reason "is based on a metaphysical axiom that is as evident as 'the whole is greater than the part'". (p. 11) Summarizing Bayle's argument, Popkin writes that for Bayle there is nothing "more reasonable than believing God rather than the natural light". (p. 11)

Popkin asks: "what status this proof of fideism has", and he answers: "As far as I can tell, Bayle does not make clear what special status certain axioms and proofs of reason have which exempt them from the sceptical difficulties which beset the rational world". (p. 11) So the radical scepticism which Bayle articulates in "Pyrrho", that is, his apparent attack on all principles of reason, Popkin takes to conflict with Bayle's claims that his religious fideism is grounded on principles of reason. Popkin also notes that one of Bayle's targets is the Socinian movement. Bayle feels that the Socinians are intent on introducing rational considerations into all aspects of religion and hence of seeking to dissolve the faith/reason distinction. By subjecting the Christian mysteries to philosophical inquiry, the Socinians guarantee that we shall be immersed in controversy *ad infinitum*.

However, I maintain that in "Pyrrho" Bayle uses scepticism to undermine it—almost as a set of variations on Descartes' use of scepticism in the *Meditations*. I contend that "Pyrrho" is an attack on Christian Pyrrhonism. It is *primarily* directed at Catholics, specifically at those Catholics who defend the notion of "natural theology". Catholic theologians generally maintain that natural reason, human reason unaided by any revelation, can discover certain truths relevant to religion, e.g. the existence of God. Thomas Aquinas, for example, called such "naturally" discovered truths "preambles" to the faith. With the Reformation and the reappearance and wide dissemination by Catholics of the writings of Sextus Empiricus,[3] a new form of natural theology arises in the course of the development of the Counter-Reformation. Thus in Montaigne or Huet, sceptical arguments are employed to destroy intellectual pride and rational pretense, so that one finally becomes totally humble. Once one's mind is a blank tablet, God may choose to write His revealed truths upon it.

In this fashion, Pyrrhonism paradoxically becomes a part of

---

[3] Cf. Richard H. Popkin, *The History of Scepticism from Erasmus to Spinoza*, Berkeley: University of California Press, 1979.

natural theology. Natural reason in the guise of Pyrrhonism is
given a role in preparing one to receive religious truth. Thus the
tropes of Sextus Empiricus emerge as sixteenth-century versions of
Thomas's preambles to the faith, albeit with this difference: Thomas took his arguments in natural theology to be constructive
preparations for faith. Moreover, natural theology has always been
one element in the Church's general claim to be the world's preemi-
nent Teacher and the custodian of the human means which may
facilitate the action of the divinity. It is in this context that Christian Pyrrhonists offer a sort of "negative" natural theology. They do
not wish to be any more committed to the "truth" of the Pyrrhonian claims than Sextus had been, but like him, they appreciate
that the tropes nevertheless have an effect on our psyches. A
(negative) natural theology, while not giving us a human means to
acquire a religion, nevertheless may facilitate its acquisition. By purely natural means, we are put in a state of mind which is more
receptive to the acceptance of God's Word. Such natural and human
means do not coerce the action of God, but they do humanly prepare
us for that divine intervention. This use of scepticism as a preparation for faith may fit well within the Catholic tradition, but it is not
acceptable to those Calvinists who seek to remain true to Calvin's
principles. The problem can be seen in the case of Kierkegaard. He
also seems to find that scepticism can play a role in a person's
understanding what it is to become and to be a Christian.

From Bayle's Calvinist point of view it is *totally* inappropriate to
assert that one human can help another in this matter. For example, precisely because scepticism seems to function in Kierkegaard
as a kind of natural theology, some commentators think he is
ultimately a Catholic thinker. Once one suggests that a species of
natural theology can "help" us, one is setting our course towards
Rome. It is a slippery slope from Teacher to Mediator to Infallible
Guide. Calvin knew those risks. In the religiously charged atmosphere in which Bayle writes, the role of a natural theology is
well-understood. That is why Bayle appreciates that sceptical arguments function as preambles to the faith among the Catholic
fideists he opposes. But *prima facie*, it would appear that because of
the absolute rejection of natural theology which stands at the core
of Reformation Calvinism, Calvinist uses of Pyrrhonism are likely
to be different. That is, those Calvinists do not say that by means of
Pyrrhonian arguments faith becomes more accessible. Such a
potential enhancement of the role of human teachers threatens both
the Protestant "way of examination" and the connected doctrine of
the inviolable conscience. For those Calvinists, there is simply no

room for spiritual directors who might guide us on the road to faith.

Thus far I am claiming that article "Pyrrho" is primarily aimed at Catholic fideists. Bayle does not say that the doctrine of the Trinity is true in theology and false in philosophy. Rather, he is challenging Catholic natural theology by forcing Catholics to grant (a) that the doctrine of the Trinity (for example) is true and *hence* (b) evident principles of arithmetic are *false*. Not only is Bayle rejecting the so-called "two-fold doctrine of truth", he is advancing a most un-Pyrrhonian (i.e. a dogmatic) conclusion. There are two consequences: Catholic defenders of natural theology find themselves in an awkward position because if they admit that "evident" proposition can be false they are then deprived of any sort of traditional (e.g. Thomist) natural theology.

But Bayle's real target, the (Catholic) Christian Pyrrhonists— i.e. those who employ Pyrrhonism as a sort of natural theology— fail in their claim to undermine all the certitudes of human reason, and thereby to make us humble before God. They fail because the uses of "natural reason" which Pyrrhonian theology prescribes to prepare us to accept the Christian mysteries, have the unwanted and paradoxical consequence that far from making us humble, they now seem to equip us with such dogmatic and intellectually arrogant claims as the demonstrable—thanks to theology—falsity of arithmetic principles, as well as perhaps the principles such demonstrations themselves require.

The argument in "Pyrrho" is thus double-edged: the Catholic Pyrrhonists either fail to engender humility, as just noted, or they are obliged to admit that the Pyrrhonian arguments they advance are themselves undermined by the Christian mysteries. Hence the Catholics have no grounds for Pyrrhonism as a useful theological tool and the Calvinist case against natural theology is sustained. The Socinians, on the other hand, having exalted reason over faith in the mysteries, are left with nothing but their natural theology. All hitherto religious discourse becomes philosophical and open to endless dispute. None of these options is acceptable to those Calvinists who (like Bayle) remain committed to the original ideas of the Reformation.

What is new and exciting in Bayle's analysis is his treatment of Christian Pyrrhonism as a piece of natural theology. As for the Socinians, they suffer from the opposite problem. If Pyrrhonism as well as all other forms of natural theology stand defeated before the Christian mysteries for the Catholics, the Socinians must accept the disasterous consequences of the absorption of religion by philosophy.

So in brief, I contend that in "Pyrrho" Bayle is not offering sceptical arguments on his own behalf. But there are passages in other parts of Bayle, for example in the *Réponse aux questions d'un provincial*, the *Dictionnaire* article "Bunel", remark E, and *Entretiens de Maxime et de Thémiste*, which seem to provide the basis for Popkin's contention that central features of Bayle's thought are irreconcilable. The problem is that Bayle says there are truths and axioms which are not subject to sceptical attack and which provide a basis for saying that there is nothing more reasonable than believing what God, rather than the natural light, says. If my interpretation of "Pyrrho" is correct, there is nothing incoherent in Bayle's not subjecting these axioms to sceptical attack. There is nothing incoherent because the argument in "Pyrrho" is an *attack* on Pyrrhonism when Pyrrhonism is employed by Catholics as a natural theology.

In the *Réponse*, Bayle is trying to counter a misreading of his position by some liberal theologians. They accuse him of erecting faith on the ruins of reason. In effect, at least if I am correct, they do not see that Bayle is attacking a Catholic position. As for the question of whether he is presenting a range of axioms not subject to sceptical attack, two points: (1) Bayle's "Pyrrho" does not commit him to presenting "sceptic-proof" principles, for the reason I have given. (2) the principles he does advance as evident and certain may indeed be challenged, but Bayle does not provide the challenge. So the worry that Bayle's position in this regard contains irreconcilable elements may not be warranted.[4]

However, if Bayle argues that there are fundamental principles which are evident and certain and upon which one found one's faith, isn't Bayle himself slipping into the natural theology quagmire? There are at least two questions: (1) what role do these principles of natural reason play in his dispute with the theological liberals? (2) how are philosophical truths related to religious ones?

In aswering (1) Bayle seems to have two concerns. He wants to establish that by introducing philosophical reasoning into discussions about the Christian mysteries, the Socinians threaten the Christian religion. He does not believe that one is entitled to impose rational criteria for our acceptance of, for example, the

---

[4] In this connection see Walter Rex, *Essays on Pierre Bayle and Religious Controversy*, The Hague: Nijhoff, 1965, pp. 156 f, where the issue of axiomatic principles is discussed in the context of conscience. Cf. *Commentaire philosophique*, I, 1. (*Oeuvres diverses*, II, 367b–368).

Biblical text. There are Christian mysteries which we cannot understand or which may *appear* to be contrary to reason, but it does not follow, as the liberals say, that we are then entitled to reject them or to say that they are opposed to reason. That is the line he also pursues in "Eclaircissment III" at the end of the *Dictionnaire*. There is nothing more reasonable than believing what God says.

It is (2) which raises puzzles. It may appear that Bayle is somehow relating philosophy and theology. Certainly Bayle believes that much of theology *is* philosophical. As he notes in his *Commentaire philosophique*, theologians of necessity accord priority to philosophy, their disputations being argumentative. But this is not to say that any of the principles given special status in his arguments with the liberals help us on the road to faith.[5] Once we have faith, we may say that it is founded on God not being a deceiver, but being able to prove, by principles of natural reason, that God is not a deceiver, is totally irrelevant to generating faith. In the most crucial sense, philosophy (reason) and faith are radically disparate domains. My impression is that Bayle is a traditional conservative (in the historical sense) Calvinist when it comes to receiving Scripturally based faith. Our intellects must be illuminated and, depending on the details of the particular Calvinist theology, our wills may also need to be acted upon—a point brilliantly explained by Rex.[6] So there is no question of the natural light, common notions, axioms of reason, etc., standing as stepping stones to faith. Nothing counts but the "folly of preaching". James[7] once argued that Bayle's apparent sceptical/fideistic position should be seen as standing within the traditional Protestant framework. I now think that is partly correct. But when James writes: "the role of reasoned apologetic is to increase for the unbeliever the *probability* of the apologist's beliefs", (p. 312) he is giving philosophy a (natural

---

[5] Bayle *Dictionnaire*, S.V. "Beaulieu" contains a delightful account of some of Bayle's views about purely philosophical reasoning. I have used the third edition of the *Dictionnaire*, Rotterdam: Michel Bohm, 1720. See also *Pierre Bayle: Historical and Critical Dictionary: Selections*, ed. and transl. Richard H. Popkin. Indianapolis: Hackett, 1991 (2nd ed.). The definitive study of Bayle is Elisabeth Labrousse, *Pierre Bayle*, 2 vols. The Hague: Nijhoff, 1963–64. See also Gianni Paganini, *Analisi della fede e critical della ragione nella filosofia di Pierre Bayle*, Florence: La Nuova Italia, 1980.

[6] Rex, *Essays on Pierre Bayle*, esp. chap. 1.

[7] E.D. James, "Scepticism and Fideism in Bayle's *Dictionnaire*", *French Studies* 16 (1962), 307–324. See also my "Bayle not a sceptic?", *Journal of the History of Ideas* 25 (1964), 169–180.

theology) role in reference to faith. There is no doubt that philosophical elements—in this context primarily scholastic—seeped
into Protestant theology and weakened the conceptual bulwark
Calvin had erected against natural theology. Nevertheless, I contend that Bayle remained true to Calvin's principle. As a footnote, I
might add that at least when it comes to natural theology, Karl
Barth's extended criticism of natural theology in his *Church
Dogmatics*,[8] appears to express opinions close to Bayle's.

It has often been observed that in many parts of his writings
Bayle accepts what might be called a natural law position with
respect to universal moral principles. When it comes to matters of
"pure" philosophy, the influence of both Descartes and Malebranche on his thinking is evident. The sceptical inclinations which
often surface in Bayle's writings are on occasion conjoined with
positions which he does not challenge on sceptical grounds. So it is
not as if there are no "rational" positions to which Bayle sub-
scribes. Nor is there any shortage of places, among others in the
Réponse, where he attacks Christian Pyrrhonists and Socinians.
They both suffer ultimately from the same conceptual error—they
systematically blur the distinction between faith and reason. This is
at least a part of what Popkin means when he says that Bayle does
not stand in the same tradition as his Catholic predecessors. I want
to suggest that Bayle never adopts a thoroughgoing sceptical position, which is to say that he stands in a different tradition. This is of
some interest to me because I want to see how sceptical arguments
have been used. Finally, it is important to notice that even in his
Entretien, Bayle appeals to *theological* ideas which he continues—
aside from Jurieu's apocalyptic theory—to share with Pierre
Jurieu. I think Knetsch[9] is correct in arguing that the Bayle-Jurieu
disagreements are primarily rooted in their profoundly different
political views, rather than in their theology.

The Church used Sextus because he provided what seemed like
the perfect manual for the analysis of the criterion problem generated by the Protestant Reformation. A Latin translation of the
Outlines of Pyrrhonism, by Henry Estienne, appeared in 1562. Gen-

---

[8] Karl Barth, *Church Dogmatics*, transl. G.W. Bromily and T.F. Torrance,
Edinburgh: T & T Clark, 1960, vol. 2, pt. 1. In this connection see also Alvin
Plantinga, "The Reformed Objection to Natural Theology", in *Rationality in the
Calvinian Tradition*, eds. Hendrik Hart, Johan van der Hoeven, Nicholas Wolter-
storff. Boston: University Press of America, 1983.

[9] Cf. F.R.J. Knetsch, *Pierre Jurieu: Theoloog en politikus der Refuge*, Kampen: Kok,
1967. On this point see also Rex, *Essays on Pierre Bayle*, 189–193.

tian Hervet's edition of 1569 includes Estienne's translation of the *Outlines* plus his own of the *Adversus mathematicos*. As Popkin[10] notes, Hervet remarks in his letter of dedication to his patron, Charles Guise, Cardinal of Lorraine, that he had found the manuscript in the Cardinal's library and that because he thought it would prove useful in countering the Calvinists, he prepared the translation. Thus if the Calvinists could be interpreted as appealing to reason in religious matters, they could be neatly subverted.

Montaigne's *Apology for Raimond Sebond* gives much wider diffusion to the arguments of Sextus. He spells out the usefulness to the Church of the criterion and other sceptical arguments. For example, to choose another religion ought to require that one *know* that the new group is the true Church. But that requires a criterion, etc. Lacking the satisfactory formulation of a criterion, he appeals to "inertia", and urges that one stay with one's traditional religion. Of course, neither Montaigne nor Hervet try to prove that Catholicism is true, only that if the Reformers are understood as making truth-claims these can be cast into doubt by sceptical arguments.

In the hands of Hervet, Montaigne, and a bit later, Bishop Huet, Christian Pyrrhonism hopes to achieve a "rational" destruction of reason and recourse to blind faith. In all three, the operative point is that there are no grounds for a successful challenge to the hegemony of the Church. Thus there are two steps: first destroy all rational claims; second, submit to the imposition of papal authority. On the other side we have the position which Calvin advances. Each person can have direct access both to the Holy Scripture and to God. There is no natural theology. There is no Church as mediator. There is no Church as Teacher and sole interpreter of Scripture. Christ's message is not filtered through the hands of any organization. No one group has a right to The Keys. It was said that Calvin had made every peasant a pope. Certainly he claims that the idea of God is innate and accessible for all of us. Note that once one tries to ground the idea of God in empirical data in the scholastic fashion, then Teachers and Mediators can acquire privileged positions. Calvin's position generates what may appear to be an excessively individualistic model, but it paves the way for two important features of Protestantism: the Way of Examination and the closely related primacy, privacy, and inviolability of Conscience. In brief, a structure impervious to sceptical attack develops, one which is still very much alive in Bayle.

---

[10] Popkin, *History of Scepticism*, p. 19 f.

Descartes' position often appears to be Calvinist. Perhaps it is only that he, like the Calvinists, was influenced by Augustine. The ultimate touchstone Descartes seeks to locate in the course of his *Meditations* is intended to be exempt from sceptical challenge and to give us access to truths which are grounded in innate structures. The intellectual motivation for relying on innate ideas is not simply epistemological. It is true that by means of innate ideas common to every human Descartes hopes to guarantee the objectivity of our knowledge, but it is also true that Descartes aims to provide us with access in our minds to a bedrock which is exempt from all and any sort of demonic or other authoritarian influence. Descartes' model does not demean reason. On the contrary, it exalts our capacity to withstand the forces of political (i.e. clerical) power. The Church was right to put Descartes on the Index!

So far I have been contending that scepticism has, on occasion, been useful to those in authority. Scepticism enables authorities to undermine their opposition's rational claims. I think that is the role it played in the sixteenth century and one can see signs of similar influences in the twentieth. Recall this very Cartesian-like line from Orwell's *1984*: "Freedom is the freedom to say that two plus two make four. If that is granted, all else follows".[11] The sceptical crisis Orwell faced, and against which he hoped this "important axiom" would provide a buckler, was that generated by Nazism. "Nazi theory", he writes in *Homage to Catalonia*, "indeed specifically denies that such a thing as 'the truth' exists".[12]

Descartes in his *Meditations* and Orwell in *1984* see clearly the forces that are arrayed against them. "In the end", Orwell's Winston says, "the Party would announce that two and two make five, and you would have to believe it. It was inevitable that they should make that claim sooner or later: the logic of their position demanded it". (p. 68) Both Descartes and Orwell see that nothing short of total control of our minds will satisfy. And the test is always the same. People must be forced to believe what the authorities actually think is false. Nothing short of that suffices. It is the ultimate "power trip". It not only tests loyalty but also the effectiveness of the propaganda and terror machines. As we realize only too well, even a Cartesian-style reflection upon an independent object of

---

[11] George Orwell, *1984*, Harmondsworth: Penguin, 1954, p. 68.

[12] George Orwell, *Homage to Catalonia*, Harmondsworth: Penguin, 1966, p. 236. See also my "Descartes-Orwell-Chomsky: Three Philosophers of the Demonic", ch. 6 in my *Mind and Language: Essays on Descartes and Chomsky*, Dordrecht: FORIS, 1984.

knowledge may not provide an absolute defense against the systematic application of state or clerical power.

Philosophers were available in the 1930s to advance arguments
to make the Nazi attack on "the truth" philosophically respectable.
This brings us to what Chomsky[13] calls Orwell's problem: "how
can we know so little, given that we have so much evidence". What
are the factors that block our understanding of a situation and so
enhance the plausibility of, e.g. Nazism or Stalinism? One important factor is propaganda. Another is the role intellectuals play in
our cultures as well as the theories some philosophers devise which
help render intellectual criticism totally impotent.[14]

Heidegger, and those who follow in his wake, apply to the
traditional (as well as the Cartesian) doctrine of truth the sort of
attack which had been mounted in the sixteenth and seventeenth
centuries by the Counter-Reformation Christian Pyrrhonists. Just
as Sextus Empiricus's assault on truth is first used by the counter-
reformers as a means for generating a sceptical crisis whereby the
Catholics might defeat the Reformers intellectually, so with
Heidegger and his followers we are given a method for attacking
the notion of truth (although the means employed are not those of
Sextus). As a consequence a new sceptical crisis arises. Once again
it is created in order to facilitate an expansion of political power.
But notice that the philosophical position which sought to be secure
against the sixteenth-century sceptical crisis emerges as the particular target of those who were seeking to create a similar crisis in
our own century. From Heidegger to our own "End of Philosophy"
philosophers, Descartes has been a primary target. So perhaps it
should not surprise us that someone on the other side, like Orwell,
should present his account of the necessity for our preserving truth
in a spectacularly Cartesian form.

The sceptical crisis which began in the 1930s expands in the
years after World War II. From Heidegger to De Man and Wittgenstein, Rorty and Derrida, the aim is to destroy both Cartesian
and Kantian style epistemology. Sometimes this is achieved by
what is now called hermeneutics—the infinite unravelling of a text,
although the process appears not to have been infinite for the
Rabbis. Beneath all the commentaries, there was for them a real

---

[13] Noam Chomsky, *Knowledge of Language*, New York: Praeger, 1986, p. xxv.
[14] Chomsky has written often on this topic, but see his (with Edward S.
Herman) *Manufacturing Consent: The Political Economy of the Mass Media*, New York:
Pantheon, 1988.

text. The more unconstrained unravelling work of Fr. Richard Simon, perhaps the first post-Reformation practitioner of the art, earned him the active displeasure of his Church, and his books were placed on the Index. He had opened up a potential internal challenge to Church legitimacy which could not be countenanced. Some post-World War II philosophers prefer to destroy epistemology with non-theories about philosophy of language and the nature of meaning. Such non-theories are intended to reveal that talk about any sort of independent and universally valid standpoint is a product of conceptual confusion. There are no Platonic meanings, there are only linguistic parlor games which we are trained in childhood to play and in which various "forms of life" are reflected. Rhetoric finally displaces logic.[15]

In his contribution ("Overcoming Epistemology") to a well-known collection of essays entitled *After Philosophy: End or Transformation?*,[16] Charles Taylor says that the epistemological tradition to be "overcome" holds that "knowledge is to be seen as correct representation of an independent reality" (p. 466). He names as major critics of this tradition: Hegel, Heidegger, Merleau-Ponty, and Wittgenstein. He maintains that the decisive shift in focus is that from trying to locate an independent foundation of knowledge to a recognition that we are always agents in the world and hence that the total "disengagement" from it is impossible.[17] In the same volume, Rorty, agreeing with a passage from Sartre writes:

---

[15] There is an extremely interesting Preface, by Newton Garver, to Jacques Derrida, *Speech and Phenomena*, Evanston: Northwestern University Press, 1973, transl. David Allison. Garver discusses not only the primacy of rhetoric over logic for Derrida and Wittgenstein but also a number of other affinities and parallels between them.

[16] Ed. by K. Baynes, J. Bohman, and T. McCarthy, Cambridge: MIT Press, 1987.

[17] Writing in *McGill News* (Spring 1990) "Quebec Focus", Taylor blames the "hyper-Cartesian visions" of Trudeau and Levesque for undermining the old (colonial?) Canadian "two-nation" ideology and hence with contributing to the current Canadian constitutional crisis with the attendant threat of Quebec independence. I would have thought it a good thing if Cartesianism helped dissolve the xenophobia and racism which, not unsurprisingly, usually characterize the notion of a (blood-based) nation. My suspicion is that Taylor's frequently expressed hostility towards "Cartesianism" more likely rests not only on his view (noted in the text) about "overcoming epistemology" but also on his belief that rights inhere in the community rather than in the individual. It often appears that in this as in certain other cases, a philosopher's "nationalism" drives his anti-epistemological, anti-Cartesian approach to philosophy and not the other way round. (I take "identity" talk, especially in its "ethnic" forms, to be a highfalutin way of expressing nationalist sentiment).

This hard saying brings out what ties Dewey and Foucault, James and Nietzsche, together—the sense that there is nothing deep down inside us except what we have put there ourselves, no criterion that we have not created in the course of creating a practice, no standard of rationality that is not an appeal to such a criterion, no rigorous argumentation that is not obedience to our own conventions. (p. 60)

Our own period has been increasingly dominated by movements which, for whatever reasons, agree that epistemology, theories of knowledge, and in particular, the Cartesian outlook, must be displaced. With the acceptance of the death of truth, various options are recommended to us: for example, relativism, contextualism, and linguistic behaviourism. Even pragmatism has been resurrected, a sure sign that our suspicion that truth has been displaced by power is warranted. Orwell saw the point that the death of truth creates an open field for rhetoric and the exercise of power. He saw that a theoretical movement was afoot in Spain which would contribute to making propaganda virtually irrefutable. Participants in this movement understood how to employ rhetoric, the glorification of the irrational, and the demeaning of intelligence, as foundations for constructing fascism. And that is also why Orwell has his Winston talk like a Cartesian—there must be some critical standpoint from which the falsity of the claims of power can be understood.

When the grounds of reason are dissolved into fantasy, we are usually given new options, as Popkin has so eloquently demonstrated: fideism, for example, becomes a common sixteenth-and-seventeenth-century escape from the sceptical crisis. And although the Church has always claimed to be uncomfortable with fideism, and declared it a heresy, the author of a most fideistic work (and a severe critic of Descartes), Bishop Huet, prospered within the Church and was not placed on the Index. Ryle, Wittgenstein and Heidegger also devote much effort to showing Descartes' philosophical errors. Descartes and, for that matter, Chomsky, argue for innate ideas and for non-vacuous accounts of human nature. Rorty, on the other hand, represents the modern age when, as noted, he says that "there is nothing deep down inside us". My contention is that the real goal of the anti-Cartesians is to convince us that we are ultimately "blank tablets" and thus suitable objects of control in a world they try to show is truth-free. I do not think the moderns are very different from their predecessors in this regard, and both understand the usefulness of sceptical-type arguments.

In the course of this paper I have tried to focus on the uses to which sceptical crises have been put. I began with the employment of the arguments of Sextus Empiricus by the Catholics with their aim of destroying any rationally based claims which the Protestants might employ. The appropriate response to the ensuing irrationalism was Catholic faith. I then discussed Bayle and sought to show that his discussion in "Pyrrho" should perhaps not be read as a statement of his sceptical opinions but rather as a radical attack on those Catholics for whom Pyrrhonism functions as a form of natural theology. As for religious truth, he sees it as a gift from God without the benefit of any proofs, arguments, or other human interventions. Descartes was briefly discussed because he, perhaps setting a pattern for Bayle, seeks to drive through the sceptical difficulties and emerge with access to an independent and directly accessible truth. I then turned to some twentieth-century thinkers whose scepticism or, if you prefer, nihilism, has had a very similar goal to the sixteenth-/seventeenth-century versions. Namely, the destruction of reason in order to make room for political power. Finally, I called attention to their anti-Cartesianism and suggested that the undermining of theories of human nature has on several notable occassions made easier the task of those seeking unlimited power.

LOTHAR KREIMENDAHL

DAS THEODIZEEPROBLEM UND BAYLES FIDEISTISCHER LÖSUNGSVERSUCH

Der von Leibniz geprägte Terminus "Theodizee" bedeutet soviel wie Rechtfertigung Gottes. Die Vernunft verspürt das Bedürfnis danach angesichts der Existenz des Übels in der Welt, die als von Gott abhängig gedacht wird. In der klassischen, auf Epikur zuruckgehenden Formulierung handelt es sich bei dem Theodizeeproblem näherhin um folgendes Trilemma: "Will Gott das Übel vermeiden und kann er nicht? Dann ist er nicht allmächtig. Kann Gott das Übel vermedien und will er nicht? Dann ist er nicht allgütig. Wenn er es aber vermeiden will und auch kann, woher kommt dann das Übel?"

Schon aus dieser knappen Exposition geht hervor, daß sich das Theodizeeproblem nur unter bestimmten Voraussetzungen stellt. Auf der Seite Gottes ist an ein Wesen zu denken, dem zumindest die folgenden vier Prädikate zukommen. Es muß erstens ein personales Wesen sein, das ein bleibendes Interesse an seinen Produkten hat. Es muß zweitens ein intelligentes, allwissendes Wesen sein, das nicht blindlings schafft, sondern mit Verstand zu Werke geht und sämtliche Konsequenzen seines Tuns überblickt. Drittens muß ihm Allmacht zukommen, denn nur so ist gewährleistet, daß es kann, was es will. Und viertens schließlich muß es allgütig sein, denn nur unter dieser Voraussetzung besteht überhaupt Anlaß, sich über das Vorhandensein des Übels zu wundern. Da in der christlichen Religion Gott diese Prädikate beigelegt werden, stellt sich das Theodizeeproblem hier in seiner ganzen Schärfe. Auf Seiten des Übels hingegen ist keine weitere Voraussetzung erforderlich. Gleichgültig in welcher Gestalt es sich präsentiert, ob – um Leibnizens Einteilung zu übernehmen – als metaphysisches, moralisches oder physisches Übel; es bedarf hier nur der Anerkennung seiner Faktizität in der Welt, wie wir sie erfahren.

Damit sind zugleich die drei grundsätzlichen Lösungsmöglichkeiten des Problems angesprochen. Erstens kann man die Existenz Gottes schlechthin leugnen, also einen streng atheistischen Standpunkt beziehen. Dann entfällt wegen des Fehlens eines Angeklagten der ganze Prozeß. Oder man streicht aus der oben genannten

Liste zumindest eins seiner Prädikate oder schränkt es auf den Bereich des Endlichen ein; welches, mag gegenwärtig dahingestellt sein. Zweitens kann man die Existenz des Übels als eines wirklich solchen leugnen, indem man das so Erfahrene als nicht zu eliminierende Einschränkung selbst des Kompossiblen erklärt oder als vom Schöpfer zur Erreichung höherer Zwecke absichtlich in den Weltenlauf eingestreute Begebenheiten auffaßt bzw. zeine Anstößigkeit auf andere Weise zu minimieren sucht. Auf die sich im Rahmen dieser zwei grundsätzlichen Möglichkeiten bewegenden Antworten, die also entweder auf eine Depotenzierung der göttlichen Eigenschaften oder der Negativität des Übels hinauslaufen – und von denen bis zum Ende des 18. Jahrhunderts schon eine ganze Reihe gegeben worden sindsowie auf die Konsequenzen, die sie je nach sich ziehen, gehe ich jetzt nicht näher ein, sondern stelle nun eine Variante der dritten grundsätzlichen Möglichkeit vor, die das Theodizeeproblem ohne jede Abmilderung des in ihm gedachten Widerspruchs zu lösen sucht: die fideistische Position.

Der Fideismus bezeichnet die Auffassung, wonach das menschliche Selbst- und Weltverständnis letztlich nicht auf Vernunfteinsichten gegründet bzw. auf solche zurückführbar ist und anhand intersubjektiv gültiger Evidenzkriterien ausweisbar wäre, sondern in einem Glauben wurzelt. Dieser Glaube muß nicht religiös gefärbt sein, wie man etwa bei Hume sehen kann. Die Annahme der persistierenden Existenz aktual nicht wahrgenommener Gegenstände oder der realen Existenz einer Außenwelt kann seines Erachtens nicht auf Vernunfteinsichten gegründet werden, sondern ist ein "natural belief", ein natürlicher Glaube, der vom religiösen Glauben, dem "faith", im Englischen auch terminologisch unterschieden wird. Der religiöse Fideismus, demzufolge die Wahrheiten der Religion allein auf den Glauben gegründet sind, ist somit der Sonderfall einer auf ein bestimmtes Gebiet restringierten nicht-rationalen Weltsicht. Daß in ihm eine "Lösung" des Theodizeeproblems möglich wird, liegt auf der Hand, denn er bestreitet die Kompetenz der Vernunft, hierüber zu urteilen und entzieht dem Problem damit den Boden. Die Schwierigkeiten, die sich – um in der Sprache Kants zu sprechen – bei der Verhandlung der Sache vor dem Gerichtshof der Venunft auftun, sind sämtlich hinfällig, wenn sie mit dem Auge des Glaubens betrachtet wird, weil die vorausgesetzte höchste Weisheit der Gottheit eben nicht nach den Maßstäben der endlichen Vernunft beurteilt werden kann.

Was den Fideismus nun philosophisch interessant werden läßt ist der Umstand, daß es Versuche gibt, ihn unbeschadet seiner

nicht-rationalen Struktur mit rationalen Argumenten als die einzig
mögliche Weltsicht zu erweisen. Den m.W. anspruchsvollsten,
wenngleich nicht ersten dieser Versuche hat Pierre Bayle in seinem
Dictionnaire historique et critique von 1697 vorgelegt. Die Probleme, die
der fideistische Lösungsversuch mit sich bringt, treten hier besonders klar hervor, klarer jedenfalls als bei Montaigne oder Charron,
die Bayle in gleicher Absicht vorangegangen waren – und klarer
auch als bei Kierkegaard, für den ja der Sprung in den Glauben
keinerlei Rechtfertigung erfahren kann, weil damit Voraussetzungen verknüpft sind, über die noch nicht entschieden ist.

Bayle empfiehlt nicht nur den Sprung in den Glauben, sondern
will ihn als unbedingt notwendig erweisen. Das geschieht durch
den Nachweis der völligen Inkompetenz der Vernunft im Felde
theoretischer Erkenntnis. Dazu dient ihm der Skeptizismus, der
von Bayle also nicht als Selbstzweck vorgetragen wird, sondern als
Mittel dient. In mitunter geradezu poetischen Bildern äußert er
sich wiederholt über die völlige Unzulänglichkeit der theoretischen
Vernunft. Bayle präsentiert sich als Skeptiker, jedoch nur als ein
partieller, denn er nimmt das Gebiet der Moralphilosophie und der
Geschichte von seinen Zweifeln aus. Was gut und böse ist, lehrt
eine universalgültige – weil in der Vernunft selbst begründete Ethik
–, und daß ein Individuum namens Cicero gelebt hat, ist gewisser
als daß es die Gegenstände der Mathematik gibt. Die partielle
Skepsis aber vertritt Bayle in ihrer absoluten Form, und zwar
sowohl hinsichtlich der Aussagen der theoretischen Vernunft als
auch dieses Vermögens selbst. Folglich ist auch sein mit diesem
Mittel errichteter Fideismus nur ein partieller – er erstreckt sich
lediglich auf das Gebiet vorgeblich theoretischer Vernunfteinsichten – als solcher aber ein absoluter. Die Möglichkeit, daß eine
natürliche Religion als "praeambula fidei" den höheren Glaubens-
wahrheiten voraufgeht und auf diese vorbereitet, ist damit ausgeschlossen, und erst recht kann keine Rede davon sein, daß die
Glaubenssätze selbst mit der Vernunft faßbar oder auch nur durch
sie gegen Einwände verteidigt werden könnten, wie Leibniz meinte.
Da sich die Vernunft schon auf ihrem eigentlichen, angestammten
Gebiet in Widersprüche und Antinomien verstrickt, vermag sie im
Felde der Glaubenssätze erst recht nichts zu entscheiden.

Reduziert man Bayles Ausführungen, mit denen er den Fideismus inthronisieren möchte, auf ihr argumentationslogisches Minimum, so beruhen sie auf zwei Prämissen und einer daraus
gezogenen Folgerung. Man könnte sie versuchsweise wie folgt re-
konstruieren:

1. Prämisse: Der Mensch bedarf der Wahrheit.
2. Prämisse: Die Vernunft ist ein zur Wahrheitsfindung untaugliches Instrument.
3. Schluß: Folglich ist Zuflucht zum Glauben zu nehmen.

Die erste Prämisse, wonach der Mensch ohne eine Antwort auf die letzten Fragen nicht zu leben vermag, findet sich bei Bayle nicht explizit formuliert. In ihr drückt sich das ganz selbstverständliche Lebensgefühl einer Zeit aus, in der die Menschen von der Sorge um ihr Seelenheil umgetrieben wurden, wie es für eine weithin säkularisierte Gesellschaft kaum noch nachvollziehbar ist. Es überrascht insofern nicht, daß Bayle diese Voraussetzung nicht ausdrücklich nennt oder sie gar mit Gründen stützt.

Seine ganze Aufmerksamkeit gilt der zweiten Prämisse, die er dem oben Gesagten zufolge auf zwei Wegen zu verifizieren sucht. Was die Bestreitung des Wahrheitsanspruchs der *Aussagen* der Vernunft betrifft, so kann man der mangelnden Systematik Bayles, mit der er an oft überraschenden Stellen des *Dictionnaire* die ihm interessant erscheinenden philosophischen Lehren prüft, dadurch abhelfen, daß man seinen rhapsodischen Widerlegungen die Intention unterstellt, die Unzulänglichkeiten aller Philosopheme in der seit Descartes geläufigen Trias metaphysischer Fragen nach Gott, der Welt und der Seele aufzuweisen. Gelingt ihm dies, dann ist seine These zwar immer noch nicht verifiziert – denn möglicherweise gibt es eine Lösung des jeweils behandelten Problems, die bislang nur noch nicht gefunden oder von ihm, Bayle, unberücksichtigt geblieben ist – doch hätte er immerhin auf diesem aposteriorischen Wege gezeigt, was auf diese Weise zu zeigen möglich war. Bevor ich aber auf Bayles Aushebelung aller rationalen Theologie, Kosmologie und Psychologie näher eingehe, muß der erste, apriorische Weg, in dem die Verderbtheit der Vernunft selbst erwiesen wird und der folglich die ganze Last des Beweises trägt, näher beleuchtet werden.

Bayle führt den Nachweis der antinomischen Beschaffenheit der Vernunft in dem Artikel über Zeno und besonders dem über Pyrrho. Der letztere gilt deshalb zu Recht als der zentrale Artikel des *Dictionnaire*. Was er hier vorbringt, läuft auf die Aufhebung der Evidenz als Wahrheitskriterium hinaus. Dazu geht Bayle so vor, daß er unmittelbar einleuchtende Vernunftsätze mit Glaubenssätzen konfrontiert, die durch die Offenbarung verbürgt sind und die jenen widersprechen.

Hierfür nun einige Beispiele. Bayle setzt der Lehre von der Dreieinigkeit den Satz der Logik entgegen, wonach zwei Dinge, die einem dritten gleich sind, auch untereinander gleich sind. Er wird indes durch die Offenbarung Lügen gestraft und ist also, obwohl von höchster philosophischer Evidenz, dennoch falsch. Es ist ferner evident, daß es keinen Unterschied zwischen Individuum, Person und Wesen gibt. Gleichwohl lehrt das Trinitätsdogma, daß die Personen unbeschadet der Einfachheit von Individuum und Wesen vermehrt werden können.

Die Abendmahlslehre bietet dem Skeptiker besonders reichliche Gelegenheit, philosophisch evidente Sätze in ihrem Licht als falsch erscheinen zu lassen. Zunächst widerspricht sie dem Grundsatz, daß ein Körper nicht zur gleichen Zeit an verschiedenen Orten sein kann. Ist das aber, wie sie lehrt, dennoch möglich, so hat das Konsequenzen für unsere Identität; denn woher sollen wir jetzt noch Gewißheit haben, von anderen Menschen unterschieden und nicht zur gleichen Zeit in verschiedenen Zustandsweisen an mehreren Plätzen dieser Welt zu sein? Und warum sollte Gott, der doch stets auf die einfachste Weise handelt, mehrere Menschen geschaffen haben, da nach der Abendmahlslehre ein Mensch ausreichen würde, der je nach Erfordernis der Lage an verschiedenen Orten in verschiedener Gestalt auftreten könnte? Letztendlich käme man gar mit der Annahme eines einzigen Geschöpfs zur Erklärung der ganzen Mannigfaltigkeit der Welt aus! – Der Satz der Identität wird durch die Abendmahlslehre gleichfalls aufgehoben, denn man weiß nicht mehr, ob zwei Körper, die als voneinander verschieden wahrgenommen werden, tatsächlich nur einer sind, und damit fällt auch die angeblich so evidente Wissenschaft der Mathematik. Ferner sind Geist und Materie nicht mehr unterscheidbar, weil der Voraussetzung nach zwei Körper an demselben Ort sein können. Die Materie ist also nicht länger undurchdringlich und verliert ihre wesentliche Qualität der Ausdehnung Infolgedessen kann sie jetzt Eigenschaften eines geistigen Wesens wie Empfindungsfähigkeit, Willen, und Vernunft annehmen, kann also auch denken. Doch damit nicht genug. Bayle weist überdies darauf hin, daß der Transsubstantiationslehre zufolge, nach der sich Wein und Brot in Blut und Leib Christi verwandeln, die Akzidentien losgelöst von ihren Substanzen bestehen können, was philosophischer Einsicht widerspricht.

Aber nicht nur im Bereich eher spekulativer theologischer Thematik, sondern auch im Gebiet der Sittlichkeit führt die Konfrontation von evidenten Sätzen der Vernunft mit den Lehren des Christentums zur Aufhebung aller Evidenz. Bayle zeigt das zunächst an seinem Lieblingsthema der Theodizee auf. Es ist evident, daß man das Böse verhindern muß, wo man nur kann, und daß man sündigt, wenn man es dennoch zuläßt. Gleichwohl ist dieser Satz falsch, denn die Theologie lehrt, daß Gott nichts tut, was seiner Vollkommenheit zuwider wäre, wenn er all die Übel in der Welt zuläßt, die er kraft seiner Allmacht leicht verhindern könnte. Es ist ferner nach den Maßstäben unserer Vernunft evident, daß ein Geschöpf, das noch nicht existiert, keine moralische Verfehlung begangen haben kann und daß es gerechterweise nicht dafür bestraft werden darf, doch erweist die Lehre von der Erbsünde unsere Gewißheit als irrig. Schließlich führt Bayle es als einen evidenten Satz der praktischen Vernunft an, daß die sittliche Wohlanständigkeit stets der Nützlichkeit vorzuziehen sei, und zwar nach Maßgabe der Heiligkeit des Handelnden um so entschiedener. Gleichwohl sagt die Theologie, Gott habe dieser Welt, in der Sünde und Unordnung dominieren, gegenüber einer vollkommenen, tugendhaften und wohleingerichteten Welt aus Gründen seines höheren Ruhmes den Vorzug gegeben. Bayle warnt immer wieder davor, mit dem Argument der Undurchschaubarkeit der göttlichen Pläne und Absichten zu operieren, denn damit läuft man den Skeptikern geradewegs in die Arme und begibt sich zugleich der einzigen Möglichkeit, die reale Existenz der Körper sicherzustellen. Denn man räumt damit ein, daß unsere Begriffe nicht Gottes Begriffe sind und ihn unser Begriff von Wahrhaftigkeit folglich nicht hindern müßte, uns die Existenz einer gegenständlichen Welt nur vorzutäuschen.

Am Ende der Gegenüberstellung von Vernunft- und Glaubenssätzen zieht Bayle sein Fazit: Wenn es ein Kriterium gäbe, durch das die Wahrheit mit Gewißheit erkannt werden könnte, so wäre das die Evidenz. Die Evidenz ist aber kein solches Kriterium, weil sie auch falschen Sätzen zukommt, folglich kann die Wahrheit nicht erkannt werden.

Nun liegt es auf der Hand, daß dieses Fazit auch ganz anders hätte ausfallen können. Wenn Bayle durch die Konfrontation von klaren Vernunfteinsichten mit dunklen Glaubenssätzen letztlich die Paralyse der Vernunft betreiben will, um derart die philosophische Skepsis als notwendige Vorbedingung des Glaubens zu erweisen, so mochte mancher Leser, wenn er dem Satz des Widerspruchs mehr vertraute als etwa dem Trinitätsdogma, zu ganz anderen Schlußfolgerungen als den ausdrücklich von Bayle gezogenen kommen. Bayles wiederholtes Bekenntnis zum Fideismus konnte als Ausdruck einer perfiden Unterwanderungsstrategie des Glaubens aufgefaßt werden. Zudem wurden die Einwände der Vernunft ja nicht eigentlich widerlegt, sondern vielmehr durch die Macht des Glaubens niedergeschlagen. Ein solches Verfahren konnte aber bestenfalls den überzeugen, der von der Wahrheit der Glaubenssätze bereits überzeugt war.

Damit ist die Frage nach der Aufrichtigkeit von Bayles Bekenntnis zum Fideismus gestellt. War er persönlich ernstgemeint, so daß diejenigen Leser, welche die Konsequenzen der Bayleschen Argumente dort zu Ende dachten, wo er sie in den Glauben abbog, und die dabei zu deistischen, wenn nicht atheistischen Positionen gelangten, diese zu unrecht als die wahrhaft von ihm vertretenen Ansichten ausgeben? Oder war Bayle in Wirklichkeit ein Kryptoatheist, der sich nur darum wiederholt zum Fideismus bekannte, weil er in seinem Schutz frei philosophieren und häretische Auffassungen vor dem Leser ausbreiten konnte, was er ungetarnt nicht hätte wagen dürfen? Diese Frage ist in der Bayle-Forschung heftig umstritten, und für beide Auffassungen lassen sich gute Gründe anführen. Allein die Natur der Sache scheint eine endgültige Entscheidung für eine der beiden Alternativen nicht zuzulassen. Die Antithese "Fideismus oder Atheismus" verliert jedoch an Bedeutung und wird letztlich sogar obsolet, wenn man den Fideismus nicht als das – vermeintliche oder tatsächliche – Ziel, sondern, wie den Skeptizismus auch, lediglich als ein Mittel zur Ermöglichung von Toleranz versteht. Denn Bayles gesamtes Schaffen und so auch das *Historische und Kritische Wörterbuch* ist ein einziges großes Plädoyer für religiöse Toleranz. Bayle braucht dazu eine Sittlichkeit, die ihre Normen nicht aus einer Offenbarung ableitet und empfiehlt dennoch die Unterwerfung unter den Glauben. Das erscheint paradox, erweist sich jedoch bei näherem Hinsehen als konsequent. Denn die Empfehlung des Glaubens geht Hand in Hand mit dem Erweis seiner Bedeutungslosigkeit für das Handeln des Menschen. Immer wieder zeigt Bayle an den verschiedensten Inhalten des Glaubens seine rationale Unfaßbarkeit auf. Er steht quer zur Vernunft, die nicht das Geringste von ihm begreifen, ja nicht einmal die bloße Existenz Gottes sicherstellen kann. Fragen nach dem sich in der Eucharistie vollziehenden Geschehen, nach der Erbsünde und der Trinität entziehen sich ihr vollkommen. Gleichwohl beruht die Attraktivität des Glaubens auf den Mysterien, wie es beispielsweise in den Artikeln über Socin und Ariosto heißt. Aber, wie Bayle in Übertragung eines Wortes von Sokrates betont, "quod supra nos, nihil ad nos"; was über uns ist, geht uns nichts an. Wie sollen wir praktizieren, was wir nicht verstehen? Denn "alle Zwecke der Religion finden sich besser in den Gegenständen, die man nicht begreift: sie flößen mehr Bewunderung, mehr Ehrerbietung, mehr Furcht, mehr Vertrauen ein" (*F. Socin*, H). Zudem ". . . inkommodieren die spekulativen Geheimnisse der

Religion das Volk nicht sehr'' (ebd.). Der Glaube, den Bayle empfiehlt, wird in seiner praktischen Bedeutung ausgehöhlt und rückt schließlich in so weite Ferne, daß er als Handlungs- und Orientierungsmaßstab völlig wirkungslos wird. Zur Erreichung dieses Zieles dient Bayle der Skeptizismus, und der Fideismus selbst erweist sich als die lediglich notwendige Voraussetzung für die Möglichkeit von Toleranz. Was von der Substanz des Glaubens übrigbleibt, reicht keinesfalls aus, um sittliche Forderungen daraus abzuleiten und sie als allgemeinverbindlich vorzuschreiben. Die Frage nach der persönlichen Aufrichtigkeit des Bayleschen Fideismus ist für die Sache der Toleranz also ohne Belang, denn wenn er ehrlich gemeint war, so war der Möglichkeit einer auf die Offenbarung gegründeten Ethik dennoch der Boden entzogen, und wenn Bayle, wie viele seiner Leser im 18. Jahrhundert meinten, in Wahrheit radikaler Deist oder gar Atheist war, dann schied eine theonome Sittlichkeit von vornherein für ihn aus. Beide Lesarten führen zum gewünschten Ziel. Da also auch bei Zugrundelegung der weniger radikalen Position das übergeordnete Argumentationsziel erreicht wird, ist es nicht erforderlich, Bayle gegen den Wortlaut der Texte und das Zeugnis weiterer Dokumente zu lesen, die seinen Fideismus als persönlich ernstgemeint erscheinen lassen.

So dient der Skeptizismus zur Begründung des Fideismus, der seinerseits die unmittelbare Voraussetzung für religiöse Toleranz ist, indem er mit der Aufhebung der theonomen Ethik den Sumpf austrocknet, der in Bayles Analyse die Intoleranz hervorbringt. Die damit geschaffene Lücke schließt Bayle mit einer rationalen Ethik, die gleichursprünglich mit der Vernunft ist und deshalb universal gilt. Sie ist auch, wie der *Commentaire philosophique* bereits gelehrt hatte, Maßstab für die Interpretation der Bibel; an ihren Vorschriften muß sich das Verhalten selbst der heiligen Männer als tatsächlich sittlich erweisen. Steht es im Widerspruch dazu, besteht Anlaß zu Tadel, den Bayle selbst einer so angesehenen biblischen Gestalt wie dem König David zur Empörung vieler seiner Zeitgenossen nicht erspart (*David*, G; *Sara*, K). Bayle schließt nicht mehr aus der vorausgesetzten Heiligkeit einer Person blindlings auf die Sittlichkeit ihrer Taten – die es dann angesichts der tatsächlich begangenen Verfehlungen durch mitunter halsbrecherische Konstruktionen zu erweisen galt –, sondern er setzt in gut aufklärerischer Manier die praktische Vernunft und ihre Vorschriften als das alle Menschen zu allen Zeiten Verbindende voraus. Von Skepsis findet sich hier keine Spur, was ebenfalls den nur instrumentellen Charakter des Bayleschen Zweifels im Gebiet der theoretischen Vernunft belegt. Gleichwohl ist Bayle hier unverhältnismäßig weniger ausführlich. Er entwickelt weder eine theologiefreie Theorie der Sittlichkeit, noch sind seine sporadischen Ausführungen hierzu immer miteinander verträglich; ein philosophisch konstruktiver Kopf war Bayle nicht. Hier ließ er eine Lücke offen, um deren Schließung sich das 18. Jahrhundert intensiv bemühen sollte. Seine Stärke liegt ganz in der Kritik, wie Bayle selbst wußte. Dem Abbé de Polignac gegenüber bezeichnete er sich einmal als ein guter Protestant im wahrsten Sinne des Wortes, denn er protestiere aus vollem Herzen gegen alles, was jemand auch sage oder tue.

Die Vernunft, so hat sich gezeigt, ist also ein völlig untaugliches Erkenntnisinstrument. Sie "hat eine zerstörende, keine bauende Kraft: Sie ist zu nichts geschickt, als Zweifel zu erregen und sich nach rechts und links zu wenden, um einen Streit zu verewigen" (*Manichäer*; D). Doch Bayle beläßt es nicht bei diesem ganz allgemeinen und gleichsam a priori geführten Nachweis. Er schildert darüber hinaus anhand vieler Beispiele den Kampf der konstruktiven mit der destruktiven Vernunft und den Sieg der letzteren. Betrachten wir nun diesen aposteriorischen Weg, auf dem Bayle die Unzulänglichkeit der Vernunft als Instrument zur Wahrheitsfindung erweisen will. Es wird sich zeigen, daß sämtliche der geprüften philosophischen Antworten auf die Fragen nach Gott, der Welt und der Seele unzulänglich sind und deshalb ebenso viele Argumente für die Notwendigkeit des Sprunges in den Glauben abgeben.

Herausragendes Thema in der *rationalen Psychologie* ist neben der Vernünftigkeit der Tiere die Frage nach der Unsterblichkeit der Seele. Hinsichtlich des ersten Problems führt alles philosophische Räsonieren auf folgendes Dilemma: Entweder man billigt auch den Tieren eine vernunftbegabte Seele und folglich die Unsterblichkeit zu, oder man hält sie für bloße, selbstgesteuerte Automaten. Beides, so Bayle, ist gleichermaßen absurd. Was die Unsterblichkeit der menschlichen Seele betrifft, so ist sie auf philosophischem Wege nicht sicherzustellen. Das wußten auch Charron, Perrot und Pomponazzi, die deshalb Zuflucht bei der offenbarten Lehre nahmen und von Bayle als Vorläufer seines Fideismus in dieser Frage angeführt werden. Die Prinzipien des Aristoteles führen zur Lehre von der Sterblichkeit der Seele, denn die Voraussetzung ihrer Unsterblichkeit ist ihre Immaterialität. Diese kann Aristoteles jedoch nicht zeigen, da nach seiner Meinung die Tierseele auch mit dem Empfindungs-, Erkenntnis- und Begehrungsvermögen ausgestattet und dennoch materiell ist (*Pomponatius*, F; *Charron*, O). Bis zu Descartes hat keine einzige Philosophenschule einen tüchtigen

Beweis der Unsterblichkeit vorgelegt, doch auch die Cartesianer tun gut daran, ihre Leser auf das Zeugnis der Schrift als letzter Gewißheitsquelle in diesem Punkt zu verweisen. Denn der Beweis, wonach alles, was denkt, von der Materie verschieden und unsere Seele also ein Geist oder eine einfache, unteilbare und folglich unsterbliche Substanz sei, erscheint nicht jedermann so überzeugend wie ihnen. Hätte sonst wohl, so fragt Bayle, ein so gelehrter Mann wie Gassendi so starke Einwände gegen ihn erhoben? Auf der anderen Seite aber ist auch die Sterblichkeit der Seele nicht zu vindizieren, wie Bayle dem entsprechenden Beweisversuch Dikaearchs entgegenhält. Denn die wesentliche Voraussetzung dafür – die Materialität der Seele – ist nicht abzusichern, weil es unbegreiflich bleibt, wie aus einem bloßen Arrangement von Materie Denken hervorgehen sollte. Behauptet man dies dennoch, muß man konsequenterweise aller Materie das Denken zubilligen, was für Bayle absurd ist.

Erfolglos bleiben die Bemühungen der Vernunft auch in der *rationalen Kosmologie*. Es gelingt ihr nicht, eine konsistente Theorie über das Weltganze aufzustellen. Die konsequenteste antike Kosmologie – diejenige des Epikur – ist falsch, weil deren grundlegende Prämisse, wonach die Materie ihre Existenz von sich selbst habe, von der Offenbarung als irrig erwiesen wird. Aber auch die modernen, von Descartes, Spinoza, Malebranche und Leibniz entwickelten Lösungen des Weltproblems scheitern sämtlich. Die Prüfung dieser kosmologischen Systeme und Entwürfe gibt Bayle Gelegenheit, die Berechtigung der Einführung des Gottesbegriffs in naturwissenschaftliche Fragestellungen zu behandeln sowie den Erklärungswert von Zweckursachen zu beurteilen. Bayle schätzt diesen nicht so hoch ein wie die Naturwissenschaftler seiner Zeit. Denn er glaubt, daß ihre Einführung neue Probleme nach sich zieht: Wie nämlich soll eine finalistische Erkenntnis und Beurteilung der Dinge möglich sein, wo uns die göttlichen Zwecke und Absichten doch weithin verborgen sind?

Die eigentliche Domäne der Bayleschen Kritik ist aber die *rationale Theologie* und hier besonders die Bestreitung einer jeden rationalen Lösungsmöglichkeit des Theodizeeproblems. Auf die Frage, woher das Übel stamme, wenn es einen Gott gibt, der zumindest die oben genannten vier Eigenschaften auf sich vereinigt, vermag die Vernunft keine schlüssige Auskunft zu geben. Sämtliche Antworten, die im Laufe der Jahrhunderte in dieser Absicht gegeben worden sind, überzeugen nicht, wie Bayle an ausgesuchten Beiträgen der Theologiegeschichte nachweist.

Nach der gängigen Auffassung kam das Übel durch den Mißbrauch des freien Willens in die Welt, den Gott dem Menschen schenkte. Allein aufgrund seiner Allwissenheit muß Gott den bösen Gebrauch vorausgesehen haben, den die Menschen davon machen. Es widerspricht aber einem wahrhaft gütigen Wesen, Geschenke zu geben, deren Mißbrauch es voraussieht. Gott hätte das Geschenk zurücknehmen oder den üblen Folgen vorbeugen müssen, was ihm kraft seiner Allmacht möglich ist. Und dies wäre um so mehr zu erwarten gewesen, als er die nach der Sünde fällige Bestrafung seiner Geschöpfe ebenfalls voraussah. Er hätte nicht nur eine Welt ohne Übel, sondern den Menschen auch ohne Neigung zur Sünde schaffen können. Dazu hätte er ihm die Freiheit nicht einmal nehmen müssen; eine kleine Änderung in der Disposition seines Willens oder eine Abmilderung der Attraktivität des Übels würde dazu ausgereicht haben. Kurz, Gott hätte die Randbedingungen so gestalten können, daß ein Mißbrauch dieses größten Geschenks ausgeschlossen bliebe.

Vielleicht läßt Gott die Sünde zu, so eine andere Antwort, damit sich seine Weisheit vor dem Hintergrund der durch die Sünde in die Welt gekommenen Unordnung besser abhebt und um so heller erstrahlt? Das hieße, so Bayle, Gott mit einem Vater vergleichen, der seinen Kindern die Beine bricht, um hinterher der ganzen Stadt seine Geschicklichkeit in der Heilung von Knochenbrüchen zu zeigen. Daß es aber, so eine dritte Antwort, freie Wesen zur freiwilligen Liebe und Verehrung Gottes geben müsse, ist ganz unplausibel, denn der intendierte Zweck wird durch den vorausgesehenen Mißbrauch der Freiheit aufgehoben. Auch kann Gott – viertens – das Übel nicht nur zugelassen haben, denn die bloße Zulassung erklärt streng genommen nicht, daß er es gewiß vorhersah. Er muß das Übel positiv gewollt haben, obwohl er es hätte so leicht verhindern können. Um diese Konsequenzen zu vermeiden, haben einige die Auffassung vertreten, Gott habe den Sündenfall gar nicht vorhergesehen. Allein damit ist nichts gewonnen, denn sie macht nur Gottes Regierung der Welt verächtlich, löst das Problem aber nicht. Denn zumindest wußte Gott, daß Adam in der Versuchung stand, zu sündigen. Weder seine Güte noch seine Heiligkeit konnten es darauf ankommen lassen, ob Adam der Versuchung widerstehen würde. Bayle erläutert dies durch ein Beispiel: Eine Mutter, die ihre Töchter auf einen Ball gehen läßt, obwohl sie die große Gefahr, die deren Ehre dort droht, gewiß voraussieht, zeigt damit deutlich, daß sie weder ihre Töchter noch die Keuschheit liebt. Und wenn die Mutter über ein unfehlbares Mittel zur Abwehr aller Versuchungen verfügt und es den Töchtern gleichwohl nicht gibt, so liegt ihre Strafbarkeit am Tage.

Doch wenn die Mutter gar durch ein Fenster beobachtet, wie ihre Tochter unmittelbar vor dem Verlust ihrer Ehre steht und dennoch nicht einschreitet, obwohl sie kann – eine solche Mutter würde diese Bezeichnung nicht verdienen.

Die christliche Theologie kann die Existenz des Übels in der Welt also nicht erklären. Der Manichäismus hingegen vermag das, denn er geht von der Erfahrungswelt aus, in der sich eben neben dem Übermaß von Übel und Leid auch Spuren des Guten und Sittlichen finden. Er wird diesem Mischcharakter des Erfahrenen durch die Annahme zweier Prinzipien, eines guten und eines bösen, gerecht, die beide an der Hervorbringung des Menschen beteiligt waren (*Manichäer*, D). Bayle wird nicht müde, die "Abscheulichkeit" dieser Lehre zu betonen, denn sie steht im Gegensatz zur biblischen Lehre, aber ebenso oft stellt er ihren hohen Erklärungswert und die Schwierigkeit heraus, sie zu widerlegen. Der Manichäismus ist von seinen Anhängern nicht immer so gut vertreten worden, wie es möglich ist; Bayle holt das nach und zieht sich damit den Vorwurf zu, er wolle diese alte und kirchlicherseits verurteilte Lehre zu neuem Leben erwecken. Ein jedes System muß nämlich zweierlei Bedingungen erfüllen. Zunächst muß es auf klare Begriffe gestützt und in sich konsequent sein. Dann aber muß es auch den Phänomenen gerecht werden und sie erklären können. Nun überzeugen uns die deutlichsten und gewissesten Begriffe davon, daß ein durch sich selbst existierendes Wesen notwendigerweise Einheit, Ewigkeit, Unendlichkeit, Allmacht besitzen und mit aller Vollkommenheit, darunter auch Güte, ausgestattet sein muß. Schließen wir derart a priori, d.h. in der vorkantischen Terminologie von der Ursache aus, so trägt diese dem Christentum zugrundeliegende Theorie den Sieg davon und schlägt den Manichäismus aus dem Felde. Dieser gleicht den Mangel an konzeptioneller Einheit und begrifflicher Konsistenz – es gehen z.B. die Prädikate der Unendlichkeit und Allmacht verloren – durch den Vorteil aus, daß er die Phänomene erklären kann, was die monistische, christliche Theorie nicht vermochte. Schließt man also a posteriori, d.h. von der Wirkung – also der Welt her, – so behält der Manichäismus die Oberhand, oder, wie Bayle an anderer Stelle sagt: Die Erklärungen des Christentums siegen, wenn sie offensiv vorgetragen werden; sie unterliegen aber, wenn sie mit Einwänden konfrontiert werden.

Soviel zu Bayles Beweis der zweiten Prämisse, die da hieß: Die Vernunft ist ein zur Wahrheitsfindung untaugliches Instrument. Es ist jetzt zu prüfen, ob sich aus den beiden Prämissen – einmal unterstellt, sie wären wirklich zufriedenstellend abgesichert – der

Fideismus tatsächlich als die einzig mögliche Weltsicht zwingend ergibt, wovon Bayle selbst im Laufe der Jahre immer überzeugter wurde.

Zunächst fällt auf, daß die Lösung des Theodizeeproblems im Rahmen einer umfassenden fideistischen Weltsicht erfolgt. Deren Kristallisationskern ist zweifellos die Theodizeefrage, doch ist diese nun in jener aufgehoben. Eine solche Lösungsstrategie erscheint einerseits philosophisch klug, denn hätte Bayle nur die Leistung der Vernunft auf dem engen Feld der Theodizee geleugnet, so hätte er mit dem Vorwurf rechnen müssen, dies sei eine aus durchsichtigen Gründen gemachte Ad hoc-Annahme. M.a.W.: Bayle hätte diese sehr partielle Skepsis legitimieren müssen, und das dürfte, gerade auch angesichts der Folgelasten, kaum zu bewältigen sein. So entschließt sich Bayle, die Vernunft als Erkenntnis- und Wahrheitsquelle völlig zu verwerfen und Vernunft und Glauben in möglichst großen Gegensatz zu bringen, um auch den letzten Anschein zu tilgen, der Glaube könne eine rationale Struktur haben, die mit den Mitteln der Philosophie erfaßbar sei.

Allein dieser Lösungsversuch macht gleich auf eine erste Schwierigkeit aufmerksam. Denn konsequenterweise ist nun auch die Erkenntnis in den Wissenschaften, die im 17. Jh. einen enormen Aufschwung erlebten, nicht von den Bemühungen der forschenden Vernunft, sondern von der Offenbarung abhängig, und Bayle spricht das auch offen aus. Für diese verblüffende Einschätzung, die freilich ganz in der Konsequenz seines Ansatzes liegt, dürften zwei Umstände verantwortlich sein: zum einen, daß Bayle kein Mathematiker oder Naturwissenschaftler war; zum anderen, daß er bei den wissenschaftlichen Fragen wohl hauptsächlich an die theologisch relevanten wie etwa der nach der raumzeitlichen Begrenztheit oder Unbegrenztheit des Weltganzen dachte, an denen sich Zeno ja schon abgearbeitet hatte.

Zweitens. Zur Zurückweisung jedweder Erkenntnisleistung der Vernunft dient Bayle der Skeptizismus. Die von ihm eingesetzten Argumente sind allesamt bekannt; er arrangiert sie lediglich neu und lenkt ihre Stoßkraft in eine Richtung, durch die das ursprüngliche Anliegen, aus dem heraus die Skepsis entwickelt wurde – die Zurückweisung jedes objektiven Erkenntnisanspruchs – ins Gegenteil verkehrt wird. Denn Bayle will mit ihr gerade eine positive Aussage begründen, nämlich den Glauben als die einzige Wahrheitsquelle rechtfertigen. Man kann Bayle deshalb nicht im strengen Sinne des Wortes als Skeptiker bezeichnen, denn an zumindest zwei Annahmen hält er unbeirrt fest: an der Wahrheit der christlichen Religion und der Inkompetenz der Vernunft sowie ihrer Aussagen. Diese in der zweiten Prämisse formulierte Annahme ist für sein Beweisziel unverzichtbar, allein je evidenter sie feststeht, desto weiter entfernt sich Bayle damit vom pyrrhonischen Skeptizismus, und desto näher kommt er einem negativen Dogmatismus. Mit der Skepsis läßt sich eben keine objektive Erkenntnis begründen, wenngleich auch Descartes und andere vor Bayle bereits diesem Irrtum erlegen waren.

Das führt auf einen dritten, grundsätzlichen Einwand. Die Vernunft verwickelt sich stets in Widersprüche und ist aufgrund ihrer antinomischen Beschaffenheit prinzipiell nicht in der Lage, auch nur eine einzige Erkenntnisleistung zu erbringen – bis auf den einen Fall freilich, wo aus der Inkompetenz der Vernunft auf die Notwendigkeit des Sprunges in den Glauben geschlossen werden soll. Aber dieser Schluß stellt natürlich auch eine Vernunftleistung dar, und so gelangt Bayle zu seiner fideistischen Konklusion durch einen impliziten Widerspruch.

Viertens ließe sich fragen, ob die dem Schluß zugrundeliegende Disjunktion, wonach entweder die Vernunft oder der Glaube die Quelle der Wahrheitsfindung und Lebensorientierung ist, wirklich erschöpfend sei, so daß durch die Falsifizierung der einen eo ipso die Verifizierung der anderen gegeben wäre. Hier lassen sich leicht andere Alternativen denken, die Bayle nicht diskutiert; so etwa die Sinnstiftung durch Traditionen und Kultur, also durch Geschichte im weiteren Sinne.

Konkurrierende Angebote gibt es fünftens aber auch bei der Frage, welchem Glauben sich die Vernunft unterwerfen solle. Schon Gottsched, der Herausgeber der 1741–1744 erschienenen deutschen Übersetzung des *Dictionnaire*, hielt Bayle entgegen, daß nach seinen Prinzipien hier eine Lehre um so willkommener erscheint, je widervernünftiger sie ist. Aber selbst dann, wenn die christliche Religion calvinistischer Prägung inthronisiert ist, an die Bayle denkt, ohne dies hinlänglich klar zu machen, kann auf die Leistungen der Vernunft nicht völlig verzichtet werden. Denn die Bibel als grundlegende Richtschnur des Glaubens und des Handelns ist, wie Bayle weiß, nicht völlig zuverlässig. Es gibt Unstimmigkeiten in ihr, die ein wortwörtliches Verständnis verbieten – zumal wenn man bedenkt, daß sich auch nach Bayles Ansicht die Propheten der Fassungskraft des Volkes anpassen mußten. Die Bibel bedarf also der interpretierenden Exegese, die jedoch nur mittels der "trügerischen" Vernunft erfolgen kann.

Aus diesen Gründen, so scheint mir, muß Bayles Versuch, den Fideismus mit den Mitteln der Skepsis zu errichten, als gescheitert beurteilt werden. Eine Lösung des Theodizeeproblems ist durch die Verbindung von christlicher Religion und philosophischer Skepsis nicht zu erreichen.

Mit diesem Ergebnis will ich durchaus nicht zu verstehen geben, daß ich jede philosophische Behandlung des Theodizeeproblems für zum Scheitern verurteilt halte. Ebensowenig freilich scheint mir eine philosophisch befriedigende Lösung in Sicht zu sein. Wenn man jedoch – nicht zuletzt von und durch Bayle – gelernt hat, vermeintlich endgültigen philosophischen Lösungen mit einer gewissen Zurückhaltung zu begegnen, dann mag die Frage, welcher Ansatz der weiterführende sein mag, sich vor die alte Frage nach Erfolg oder "Misslingen" der philosophischen Versuche in der Theodizee stellen. Der Leibnizsche Zugang erscheint bei aller Kritik, die ihn nicht erspart werden kann, in dieser Hinsicht in der Tat als der perspektivenreichere. Doch weshalb er das ist und aus welchen Gründen auch er gleichwohl zurückgewiesen werden muß, das gäbe Stoff genug für wenigstens einen weiteren Aufsatz.

James E. Force

BIBLICAL INTERPRETATION, NEWTON, AND ENGLISH DEISM

Defining the essence of English deism between the Glorious Revolution and, say, Newton's death in 1727, is a most formidable, if not insuperable, task. As with "priestcraft", "atheism", or "freethinking", "deism" is one of the dirty words of the age. Besides the confusions resulting from the pejorative stigmatization of the deists by their many Christian opponents,[1] the term is hard to define because of the claim on the part of some deists that they are in fact Christian,[2] and, most importantly, because of the still widespread influence of Sir Leslie Stephen's century-old view that, because the deists share so many fundamental, rational suppositions with their orthodox opponents, such as, for example, Archbishop John Tillotson, it is practically impossible to distinguish between them. Sir Leslie Stephen emphasizes the rational

---

[1] One problem in the use of the term is that "deists" are often directly equated with "atheists" in polemics against them. In sharp contrast to the older view, best presented by G.E. Aylmer, that real atheists did not exist in the seventeenth century, David Berman has recently argued that the many seventeenth-century denials of the very possibility of atheism is reason enough to believe actual atheists really existed. See David Berman. *A History of Atheism in Britain: From Hobbes to Russell*, London: Croom Helm, 1988. Cf. G.E. Alymer, "Unbelief in Seventeenth-Century England", in *Puritans and Revolutionaries. Essays in Seventeenth-Century History Presented to Christopher Hill*, eds. Donald Pennington and Keith Thomas, Oxford: Clarendon Press, 1978, 22–46.

[2] Günter Gawlick emphasizes that *some* deists claim to be sincerely Christian. See his article in *Historisches Wörterbuch der Philosophie*, 4 vols., ed. J. Ritter, Basel: Schwabe, 1971, vol. 1, s.v. "Deismus". The most famous of those who declared themselves to be "Christian deists", as well as the most learned and intellectual defender of deism, is Matthew Tindal, (ca. 1657–1733.) Tindal was a student of law first at Lincoln College, Oxford, and later at Exeter College. In 1678, he was elected to a Law Fellowship. In 1679, he received the B.A. degree and the B.C.L. degree. In 1685, he received the D.C.L degree and was admitted as an advocate at Doctor's Commons, a society of ecclesiastical lawyers, with a pension of 200 pounds per year for life. Tindal died in 1730 maintaining that he had always been a "Christian deist". However, even if such protestations of Christianity are sincere with Tindal, which is not clear, I maintain that truly "Christian deists" are a minority and that the characteristic element of mainstream deism is a negative rejection of revealed truth, *especially* as the century progresses.

common ground between the deists and the orthodox Anglican divines, who eventually triumph over them, when he writes that:

> The unconsciousness with which men like Tillotson put forward arguments capable of being turned against themselves explains one secret of their strength. If Protestantism was unintentionally acting as a screen for rationalism, rationalism naturally expressed itself in terms of Protestantism. Whatever, that is, was gained by reason was gained by Protestants. The intellect, though it had broken the old barriers, was still, to a great degree, running in old channels.[3]

Difficult though it may be to provide a thoroughly comprehensive, essentialist definition of deism, the term is nevertheless a meaningful one because deism is *not* all things to all men in the early eighteenth century. Finally, too many men of letters of the time agree about the essential nature of English deism for modern scholars to ignore the simple fact that what sets the deists apart from even their most latitudinarian Christian contemporaries is their simple desire to lay aside scriptural revelation as rationally incomprehensible and,

---

[3] Sir Leslie Stephen, *History of English Thought in the Eighteenth Century*, 2 vols., New York: Peter Smith, 1949, vol. 1, p. 79. This book was first published in 1876. As recently as 1980, Henning Graf Reventlow hesitates to separate the deists from their latitudinarian contemporaries within the established church. See his *The Authority of the Bible and the Rise of the Modern World*, trans. John Bowden, Philadelphia: Fortress Press, 1985, 290–1, where Reventlow writes that "Deism was an extreme but by no means isolated phenomenon; even its orthodox opponents shared a series of its fundamental presuppositions. It was precisely that which made it so difficult to challenge the Deistic arguments successfully, though as a rule these were presented by mediocre thinkers and not with any brilliance. Some Deists apparently went only a little way beyond already familiar standpoints (in small steps, often arguing on adjacent territory and also differing among one another). That is evident from the purely external fact that a number of English Deists felt themselves to be Christian writers, in contrast to the Libertines of France, and this is indicated by the titles of their writings; their attitude seems only gradually to become distinct from that of the Latitudinarians". James O'Higgins makes the standard identification of rational deists and rational, orthodox clergy when he writes that "The Latitudinarians recognised the inadequacy of natural religion unaided by Revelation, but their religion seemed suspiciously similar to it". See James O'Higgins, S.J., *Anthony Collins. The Man and His Works*, The Hague: Martinus Nijhoff, 1970, p. 46. See, also, Ernest Campbell Mossner, who, in his discussion of Tindal's *Christianity as Old as the Creation*, writes: "Citation from the rationalistic orthodoxy of such latitudinarians as Archbishop Tillotson, Samuel Clarke, and Thomas Sherlock, a deceptive device frequently employed by the deists, provides some indication of how close in thought rationalistic orthodoxy and rationalistic deism actually were". See Mossner's article in *Encyclopedia of Philosophy*, s.v. "Tindal, Matthew".

On the face of it, quotations or brief references drawn from orthodox divines, even rationalistic ones, which are intended as "deceptive devices" by the deists seem an unpromising sort of evidence for demonstrating "closeness" between members of deistic and orthodox camps. Thus, Archbishop Tillotson, whose

hence, useless, if not detrimental to human society and to religion. While there may possibly be exceptions, such as Matthew Tindal (if we are to believe him), many, if not most deists, especially as the eighteenth century wears on, agree that revealed scripture is nothing but a joke or "well-invented flam".[4]

The rejection of Scripture on rational grounds by the deists is noted repeatedly throughout the first half of the century. John Leland squarely states that the negative rejection of revealed Scripture is *the* characteristic element of deism in his historical and analytical account of the movement, a view further codified by such authorities as Ephraim Chambers and Samuel Johnson.[5]

---

orthodoxy is never doubted, is briefly quoted by John Toland (in *Christianity Not Mysterious*), Anthony Collins (in *A Discourse of Freethinking*), and David Hume (in the essay "Of Miracles"), and yet their intention in their works is vastly different from Tillotson's intention as it is comprehensively expressed in the whole body of his writing and not just in isolated snippets used to introduce deistic arguments for the setting aside of revelation.

One modern scholar who understands the need to re-think deism outside of the constraints of Sir Leslie Stephen's time-honored perspective is Peter Gay: see *Deism: An Anthology*, ed. Peter Gay, Princeton: D. Van Nostrand Company, Inc., 1968, p. 12. However, I differ with Gay about what must be revised in Sir Leslie Stephen's interpretation. Gay wishes to emphasize *both* the genuine differences between the deists and their Anglican critics *and* also to ignore what I regard as Sir Leslie Stephen's most astute distinction between "positive" and "negative" deism. I agree that the main point of concern with the deists is their difference and not their similarity with their Anglican opponents, but my self-consciously essentialist definition of deism boils down to Sir Leslie's "negative" categorization because that is what was understood at the time as the essence of deism.

John Redwood emphasizes the negative rejection of scripture as the primary point of differentiation between deists and mainstream churchmen. See John Redwood, *Reason, Ridicule and Revolt. The Age of Enlightenment in England, 1660–1750*, London: Thames and Hudson, 1976.

Gerard Reedy has also challenged Sir Leslie Stephen's view that late seventeenth-century orthodox Anglican theology is thoroughly rationalistic, a challenge which inevitably must contribute to the differentiation between the deists, who are thoroughly rationalistic in their call for the rejection of *any* reliance upon revelation, and the orthodox theologians of the Anglican church. See Gerard Reedy, S.J. *The Bible and Reason. Anglicans and Scripture in Late Seventeenth-Century England*, Philadelphia: University of Pennsylvania Press, 1985.

[4] The entire doggerel depicting Thomas Burnet's deism (which may possibly account for why he never became Archbishop of Canterbury) is cited in the *Dictionary of National Biography* s.v. "Burnet, Thomas" who, according to the rhyme, believes:

> That all the books of Moses Were nothing but supposes,
> That as for Father Adam and Mrs. Eve, his Madame,
> And what the devil spoke, Sir,
> 'Twas nothing but a joke, Sir,
> And will-invented flam.

[5] John Leland underscores the negative anti-scripturalism of the deists when he

A typical example of the contemporary chorus of writers in the first half of the eighteenth century who define the essence of deism as simply the setting aside of revelation is the Anglican country parson and Whig propagandist, William Stephens Rector of Sutton.[6] "DEISM", writes Stephens, is "a denial of all reveal'd Religion".[7] Indeed, his stated purpose in writing his pamphlet, *An Account of the Growth of Deism*, is simply "To collect and put together those Motives whereby some had been induced to lay aside all *Revelation*".[8]

In the eighteenth century, Newtonian natural philosophy is often identified as a contributing cause of deism. William Whiston claims that it is the very success of Newtonian natural philosophy in underpinning the design argument which has caused the deistic denial of, and scorn for, revealed religion. Whiston writes:

> . . . as to *Deism*, or the Denial of the Scripture, and of Divine Revelation, it is really Ill mens *last Refuge*, and taken up of late, not by honest Enquirers, impartially searching after Truth and discovering upon Evidence, that all Revealed Religion is false; but that it is chiefly fallen into of late, by some Irreligious Persons, in the Distress of their Affairs, and upon that surprizing and overbearing Light, which Sir *Isaac Newton's* wonderful discoveries have afforded; whereby they have perceived that Natural Religion, with its Foundations,

---

describes their most basic goal in his *A View of the Principal Deistical Writers that Have Appeared in England in the Last and present Century; With Observations upon them, and Some Account of the Answers that have been published against them. In several Letters to a Friend*, 3rd ed., 2 vols., London 1757, 1, p. ii.

> *viz.*, to set aside revelation, and to substitute mere natural religion, or, which seems to have been the intention of some of them, no religion at all, in its room.

In his famous *Cyclopaedia*, 2 vols., London 1737, vol. 1, s.v. "Deists", Ephraim Chambers gives an equally essentialist definition:

> The appellation *Deist* is more particularly given to such as are not altogether without religion, but reject all revelation as an imposition, and believe no more than what natural light discovers to them. . . .

Samuel Johnson, the codifier of English usage in his time, in his great *A Dictionary of the English Language*, 2 vols., London 1755, vol. 1, s.v. "DEISM", defines the essential nature of the term as:

> The opinion of those that only acknowledge one God, without the reception of any revealed religion.

[6] See James E. Force, "Introduction" to *William Stephens, An Account of the Growth of Deism in England (London, 1696)*, The Augustan Reprint Society, Berkeley and Los Angeles: University of California Press, 1990.

[7] William Stephens, *An Account of the Growth of Deism in England*, London 1696, p. 4.

[8] Ibid. I have emphasized Stephens' phrase, "lay aside".

were now become too certain to bear any farther Opposition. That this is true, I appeal to a certain Club of Persons, not over-religiously dispos'd, who being soberly asked, after Dr. *Bentley's* remarkable Sermons at Mr. Boyle's Lectures, built upon Sir *Isaac Newton's* Discoveries, and level'd against the prevailing Atheism of the Age, *What they had to say in their own Vindication against the Evidence produc'd by* Dr. Bentley? The Answer was, *That truly they did not well know what to say against it, upon the Head of Atheism: But what, say they, is this to the fable of Jesus Christ?* And in Confirmation of this Account, it may, I believe, be justly observ'd, the present gross *Deism*, or the Opposition that has of late so evidently and barefacedly appear'd against Divine Revelation, and the Holy scriptures, has taken its Date in some Measure from that time.[9]

The idea that Newtonian natural philosophy is a dangerous tool in the hands of deistic opponents of revelation is a common one then and continues in our own time.[10]

But not until the nineteenth and twentieth centuries is Newton *himself* identified as a deist.[11] The immensely erudite and subtle

---

[9] William Whiston, *Astronomical Principles of Religion, Natural and Reveal'd*, London 1717, 242–3. The high-church, non-juring Bishop, George Hickes, writes to his fellow high-churchman, the layman, Roger North, that "It is their Newtonian philosophy wch hath Made Not onely so many Arians but Theists, and that Not onely among ye laity but I fear among our devines". George Hickes to Roger North, 23 May 1713. B.M. Add. MSS 32551, f. 34.

[10] John Redwood, *Reason, Ridicule and Religion. The Age of Enlightenment in England. 1669–1750*, Cambridge, Mass.: Harvard University Press, 1976, p. 169.

[11] For Blake, Newton is the supreme spokesman of pernicious materialism based upon the evidence of the "Five Senses". Thus, in "Europa, a Prophecy", Blake writes

A Mighty Spirit leap'd from the land of Albion
Nam'd Newton: he seized the Trump & blow'd the enormous blast!
Yellow as leaves of Autumn, the myriads of Angelic hosts
Fell thro' the wintry skies seeking their graves,
Rattling their hollow bones in howling lamentation.
[From *The Complete Writings of William Blake. With All the Variant Readings*, ed. Geoffrey Keynes, London: The Nonesuch Press, 1957, p. 243.]

Blake concludes the second chapter of his "Jerusalem" with a section entitled "To the Deists". Newton is not specifically mentioned here, although Voltaire, Rousseau, Gibbon, and Hume are. Blake describes the nature of deistic religion:

Deism, is the Worship of the God of this World by the means of what you call natural Religion and Natural Philosophy, and of Natural Morality or Self-Righteousness, the Selfish Virtues of the Natural Heart. This was the Religion of the Pharisees who murder'd Jesus. Deism is the same & ends in the same. (See *The Complete Writings*, p. 682.)

Accordingly, I think Paul J. Korshin is correct when he writes that, for Blake, "The Deists of history—Locke, Newton, Voltaire, Rousseau, Gibbon, and their ilk—are the Pharisees and hypocrites responsible for human suffering". See Paul J. Korshin, *Typologies in England, 1650–1820*, Princeton: Princeton University Press, 1982, p. 351.

voice of Richard S. Westfall has joined this chorus in a most important paper from 1982 entitled "Isaac Newton's *Theologiae Gentilis Origines Philosophicae*". Westfall's analysis of this significant unpublished manuscript—which he dates[12] from "the period soon after late 1683"—is the clearest and most powerful argument ever made to show that Newton holds "a frankly deistic position".[13] While specifically acknowledging that the "essentially negative spirit" of the later deists does "not belong to Newton", Westfall, in the light of his comprehensive reading of Newton's theological manuscripts, concludes that despite the differences between Newton and the deists, Newton arrives rationally "at conclusions remarkably similar to theirs".[14]

Westfall's exposition of this holograph manuscript is exact and

---

For a twentieth-century interpretation that Newton is himself a deist because, "In effect, Newton ignored the claims of revelation and pointed in a direction which many eighteenth-century thinkers would willingly follow", see Gerald R. Cragg, *Reason and Authority in the Eighteenth Century*, Cambridge: Cambridge University Press, 1964, p. 13.

[12] Richard S. Westfall, "Isaac Newton's *Theologiae Gentilis Origines Philosophicae*", in *The Secular Mind. Essays Presented to Franklin L. Baumer*, ed. Warren Wagar, New York: Holmes & Meier Publishers, 1982, p. 15.

[13] Ibid., p. 31. In a brief descriptive catalog of books prepared recently in conjunction with a library exhibition, Westfall makes an exceptionally brief and clear statement of his argument that Newton is a deist. Describing the context and nature of Matthew Tindal's *Christianity as old as the Creation*, Westfall writes that:

Matthew Tindal was another of the prominent Deists. The title of his book suggests its central argument, that true Christianity consists solely of the natural religion known to all men by their natural reason from the beginning of the world, that the Gospels only republished the religion of nature, and that all the rest of Christianity during the previous fifteen hundred years, was a packet of superstitions foisted onto believers by priests serving their own self interest.

Newton's published works contain the argument from design for the existence of God, an argument so similar to a thousand other arguments common in his age that commentators have assumed his orthodoxy. His extensive theological papers, however, which he kept very private during his own life and which have become available to scholars only recently, indicate a much more religiously troubled man, who believed that the ground was shifting under the traditional structure of Christianity and that it was necessary to rethink some of its teachings. He rejected the doctrine of the Trinity as irrational. He pursued the themes of natural religion, and in one manuscript treatise composed shortly before the *Principia* and thus long before Tindal even thought of his book, he adopted a position on what he called the one true religion that was very close to the position Tindal expressed nearly half a century later. Newton manifestly considered this treatise important; he continued to draw upon it for the rest of his life. (See *Newton and the Scientific Revolution. An exhibition prepared and described by Richard S. Westfall*, Bloomington: The Lilly Library, Indiana University, 1987, 66–7.)

[14] Westfall, "Newton's *Theologiae Gentilis*", p. 31.

scholarly. He traces Newton's development, in this work, of three major themes. The first two themes, acknowledges Westfall, are in the mainstream of seventeenth-century scholarship and thus not in the least deistic. The third theme, in Westfall's view, transcends the boundaries of mainstream seventeenth-century historical comparative religion and prefigures the main "conclusion", but especially the method, of such a deist as Tindal.

The first theme which Newton is concerned to show—as Westfall analyzes this manuscript—is that the ancient theologians, especially the Egyptians, developed a rational monotheistic religion based on astronomical observations of the heavens which teach them that the earth moves around the central fire of the sun. Newton maintains that the content of this religion is esoterically symbolized by Egyptian priests in both hieroglyphs and in such Egyptian religious rituals as the annual procession of the priests in which the singular importance of scientific observations of the heavens to their theology is symbolized by the order of precedence in ancient Egyptian religious processions.[15]

---

[15] Ibid., 18–9. Westfall here cites the basic manuscript which alone is entitled "Theologiae Gentilis Origines Philosophicae", which is now known as Yahuda MS 16, and which is a sizeable and nearly complete Latin treatise in five chapters. Westfall rightly suggests that this manuscript is the basis for Newton's treatise entitled "The System of the World." Newton wrote "The System of the World" sometime before the fall of 1685. An English translation was first published in 1728. The title of this work is the same as the title of Bk. III of the *Principia*. This separate treatise was intended to be the second book in Newton's original conception of the *Principia* in two books. When he decided in the summer of 1685 to expand the *Principia* to three books he also decided to change the nature of Book III and to shift it from the open accessibility of his original "System of the World" to a treatise for mathematicians. He therefore wrote an entirely new Bk. III at this time and entitled it "System of the World (In Mathematical Treatment.)" His original treatise was copied in part by his amanuensis, Humphrey Newton, and deposited in the University Library. Originally composed by Newton in Latin, this work was published in English in 1728 by an anonymous translator. This translation was followed into print by the original Latin text which was published by John Conduitt who changed the title from Newton's original, *De motu corporum (Liber secundus)*, which no longer made any sense, to *De mundi systemate*. A modernized English translation was published by Florian Cajori along with his updated edition of the *Principia*. Newton is most clear in this statement of his view about the nature of ancient rational theology:

> It was the ancient opinion of not a few, in the earliest ages of philosophy, that the fixed stars stood immovable in the highest parts of the world; that under the fixed stars the planets were carried about the sun; that the earth, as one of the planets, described an annual course about the sun, while by diurnal motion it was in the meantime revolved about its own axis; and that the sun, as the common fire which served to warm the whole, was fixed in the centre of the universe.

Newton's second goal in this manuscript is to interpret the heroes and demi-gods of pagan antiquity to illustrate how *all* of these "gods" must be identified with Noah and Noah's descendants and also how these men are first idolized by their people as gods and ultimately identified with stars, planets, terrestrial elements, and mythological creatures recognized through various symbols, e.g., Saturn's scythe. The genealogy of the gods of these gentiles also becomes for Newton, just as for other seventeenth-century euhemerists,[16] the political history of the kingdoms of the Egyptians, the Babylonians, and the Assyrians. Westfall deftly traces the glibness with which the historian, Isaac Newton, here identifies Noah with Saturn and the three sons of Noah with the

---

This was the philosophy taught of old by *Philolaus, Aristarchus* of *Samos, Plato* in his riper years, and the whole sect of the *Pythagoreans*; and this was the judgment of *Anaximander*, more ancient still; and of that wise king of the *Romans, Numa Pompilius*, who as a symbol of the figure of the world with the sun in the centre, erected a round temple in honor of *Vesta*, and ordained perpetual fire to be kept in the middle of it.

The *Egyptians* were early observers of the heavens; and from them, probably, this philosophy was spread abroad among other nations; for from them it was, and the nations about them, that the *Greeks*, a people more addicted to the study of philology than of Nature, derived their first, as well as soundest, notions of philosophy; and in the Vestal ceremonies we may yet trace the ancient spirit of the *Egyptians*; for it was their mysteries, that is, their philosophy of things above the common way of thinking, under the veil of religious rites and hieroglyphic symbols. See *Sir Isaac Newton's Mathematical Principles of Natural Philosophy and his System of the World*, Translated into English by Andrew Motte in 1729, the translations revised by Florian Cajori, 2 vols., Berkeley and Los Angeles: University of California Press, 1934, 2, p. 549.

Just as Newton's "Theologiae Gentilis" serves as the Ur-source for the above text, it also serves as the spring for what are now known as the "classical scholia". These scholia were composed by Newton in the 1960s when he was considering a second edition of the *Principia* in which these "classical scholia" would be additions to Propositions IV through IX of Book III. This contemplated second edition was never published. In these "classical scholia", Newton tries to show that important elements of his natural philosophy—atomism, gravity, the inverse square law, and the cause of gravity by a "certain infinite spirit", an "*anima mundi*", which "pervades all space into infinity, and contains and vivifies the entire world"—were known by ancient philosophers. On these scholia, see the original groundbreaking article by J.E. McGuire and P.M. Rattansi, "Newton and the 'Pipes of Pan'", *Notes and Records of the Royal Society of London* 21:2 (Dec. 1966), 108–43. McGuire and Rattansi's study must now be examined in the light of Paolo Casini's more recent essay entitled "Newton: The Classical Scholia", *History of Science* 22 (1984), 1–57.

[16] About 300 B.C., Euhemerus of Messene wrote *The Sacred History* in which he theorized that the traditional deities were merely earthly rulers deified and worshipped by their subjects. See Jean Seznec, *The Survival of the Pagan Gods. The Mythological Tradition and Its Place in Renaissance Humanism and Art*, trans. Barbara F. Sessions, New York: Harper Torchbooks, 1953, 11–36.

three sons of Saturn. The most important of these sons, as Newton sees ancient religious history, is the outcast, Ham, who becomes the original of the god (and the planet) Jupiter. Ham had four sons— Cush, Mizraim, Phut, and Canaan. Newton identifies these men as the originals for the gods Hercules, Osiris, Anateus, and Busiris, respectively. Osiris/Mizraim had three children, including the bastard son Thoth (known much later to the Greeks as Mercury.) Thoth succeeded his father (Osiris/Mizraim) as the ruler of Egypt and became the founder of idolatrous gentile theology, first, by naming the planets after his forebears (Saturn after Noah, Jupiter after Ham, etc.) and, second, by combining astronomical learning (especially the heliocentric theory) with religious rites and, third, by encoding these esoteric doctrines in hieroglyphic symbols. With the Egyptian conquest of her neighbors, including the Jews, these now idolatrous hieroglyphic symbols were taken as the cause of the polytheistic worship of the gods, as symbolized in this language system, by the conquered peoples.[17]

Newton traces a similar pattern of polytheistic and, therefore, idolatrous accretions to an original rational monotheism in his account of the historical origins of the Babylonian and Assyrian dynasties and religions. Just as Ham's son, Osiris/Mizraim, is the founder of the Egyptian dynasty and of Egyptian theology, Ham's son Cush (later known as Hercules), a mighty warrior, conquers Babylonia. Cush's son, Nimrod, later proceeds to the conquest of Assyria.[18] In both these empires, a similar idolatrous deification of their own kings occurs.[19]

Westfall is in agreement with Manuel that this euhemeristic and syncretistic project of tracing all ancient history back to Noah and Noah's offspring and then explaining the polytheistic and idolatrous religions of these gentile nations as the result of the posthumous deification of their leaders and heroes is a common project among seventeenth-century historians. Westfall cites the development of similar themes in writers well known to Newton, especially Samuel Bochart, Sir John Marsham, and Gerard Vossius.[20] West-

---

[17] Newton, *The Chronology of Ancient Kingdoms Amended*, London, 1728, 225–6. Newton's basic project in this massive work is to apply a version of what Whiston calls the "third way" to the chronological data of scripture and "to make Chronology suit with the course of Nature, with Astronomy, with Sacred History, with Herodotus . . . and with itself". Cited in Derek Gjertsen, *The Newton Handbook*, London: Routledge & Kegan Paul, 1986, p. 565.
[18] Westfall, "Newton's *Theologiae Gentilis*", 19–21.
[19] Ibid., p. 20.
[20] Ibid., 23–4. Cf. Frank E. Manuel, *Isaac Newton, Historian*, Cambridge, Mass.:

fall clearly recognizes that these two themes in the "Origines" manuscript (i.e., the rational knowledge of God from the "frame of nature" rationally possessed by the gentiles subsequent to, but independent of, scriptural revelation and the progressive corruption of this rational monotheism into idolatrous polytheism) are the direct result an intellectual orientation which Newton shares with writers such as Vossius. Newton's speculations in this area, though recognizable as the sort of treatment a natural philosopher might give "of themes well established in the learned community of the day",[21] is in no sense deistic anymore than it is original.

Nevertheless, Westfall reads Newton as a deist for two basic reasons. First, in Westfall's interpretation, Newton, in his method for arriving at the true interpretation of scripture, goes well beyond the euhemerism of Vossius, Bochart, and Marsham—all of whom claim that their goal is to defend Christianity—and places such ancient historical sources as Berossus the Babylonian and Sanchuniathon the Phoenician on an equal plane of authority with such Biblical historical accounts as that of Moses. In the "Origines", claims Westfall, these ancient pagan sources appear "as independent authorities on the period after the Flood, authorities as reliable as Moses and frequently more useful".[22] Newton is a deist, for Westfall, primarily because of the epistemological status of the Bible. Newton plainly rejects the view that the Bible is, in every passage, true and divine and he attempts to utilize other ancient historical sources, as well as aids from natural philosophy, to help in correcting our understanding of it.

Second, Westfall categorizes Newton as a deist because, through Newton's methodological use of a variety of sources including

Belknap Press of Harvard University Press, 1963, p. 104, and Manuel, *The Eighteenth Century Confronts the Gods*, Cambridge, Mass.: Harvard University Press, 1959, 103–25.

[21] Westfall, "Newton's *Theologiae Gentilis*", pp. 18 and 22. In a recent article, Danton B. Sailor shows how Newton's keen interest in both the rational religious knowledge of the gentiles of antiquity and its progressively idolatrous subversion through ancestor, hero, and kingly deification is influenced by Newton's reading of his long-time Cambridge colleague, Ralph Cudworth. Sailor has carefully analyzed Newton's notes on Cudworth's *True Intellectual System of the Universe*, London, 1678, which are contained in four pages of folio holograph manuscript by Newton entitled "Out of Cudworth" and in the possession of the William Andrews Clark Memorial Library in Los Angeles. Newton is interested in Cudworth, therefore, in precisely the same way that he is interested in the works of Bochart, Marsham, and Vossius. See Danton B. Sailor, "Newton's Debt to Cudworth", *Journal of the History of Ideas* 49 (1988), 511–8.

[22] Westfall, "Newton's *Theologiae Gentilis*", p. 24.

ancient pagans as well as the results of his own natural philosophy, Newton arrives finally, according to Westfall, at a deistic "conclusion" similar to that later held by Tindal. This deistic "conclusion" consists of a "hatred of superstition and mystery"; a rationally deduced concept of an immutable monotheistic god known to these ancients through reason alone on the basis of the design argument; and, finally, a recognition of the subsequent corruption of this original and rational monotheism into a decadent and corrupt polytheism. Thus, Westfall writes:

> Newton's religion of Noah was identical to Tindal's Christianity, as Old as the Creation. Both insisted on the two basic precepts to love God and to love one's neighbor, and both argued that Christ came, not to deliver a new religion, but to restore the original pure one.[23]

In response to Westfall's first point of emphasis regarding the independent authority of pagan historians and, seemingly, the demotion in status and authority of holy scripture, several related points must be made.

Newton does indeed consider Berossus a more reliable historical source than Moses for historical details of events between the creation and the flood (e.g., Nimrod's conquest of Assyria), but he never questions the divine origin and the reliability, when interpreted by the best method, of the prophecies concerning the messiah (which he believes are fulfilled in the person of Jesus, God's deputed "vice-regent" though neither co-substantial nor co-eternal with God the Father) or of those prophecies in Daniel and Revelation which predict the events leading to the apocalypse.[24] For Newton, the Bible, though corrupt and unreliable in parts, contains a core of prophetic truth revealed to man by God.

As I note at the start of this paper, "English Deism" is notoriously difficult to define universally given the wide range of "deists" in England. Even so, one element to which most, if not absolutely all, deists subscribe at the turn of the seventeenth and well into the eighteenth century is not so much any positive doctrine of a monotheistic god accessible purely to reason, especially through the design argument, as it is an adherence to some form of the design argument of natural religion *coupled* with the rejection of any use of the scripture whatever. By the middle of the 18th century, John Leland underscores this essentially defining, negative, anti-

---

[23] Ibid., p. 29.
[24] Ibid., 22–3.

scriptural aspect of deism when he describes the most basic deistic goal:

> *viz.*, to set aside revelation, and to substitute mere natural religion, or, which seems to have been the intention of some of them, no religion at all, in its room.[25]

For most deists, including Tindal, the religion of reason is complete in itself and contains all that is true and knowable to humanity concerning god.[26] Tindal goes on to argue that, because of the rational nature of man, God cannot "reveal" to him any truth save by "shewing its Agreement with those self-evident Notions, which are the Tests by which we are to judge of everything, even the Being of a God and natural Religion".[27]

Perhaps the most telling remarks about the nature of deism at this time come from Samuel Clarke who goes to great lengths in his 1705 Boyle Lectures to categorize four types of deists. The first three sorts of deists all believe incorrect doctrines on the basis of their independent reason which has led them astray; they have made mistakes in their rational theorizing about god's nature; they logically reduce to atheists. Deists in Clarke's fourth category, who equate with Dante's virtuous pagans in limbo, believe all the right doctrines about God, also on the basis of their independent reason, and would have been worth the trouble of converting (presumably, one would only have had to show them the Bible and, perhaps, the *Principia*) save that none in this category exist any longer in Clarke's time when both the Bible and the *Principia* are widely available.[28]

---

[25] John Leland, *A View of the Principal Deistical Writers that Have Appeared in England in the Last and present Century; With Observations upon them, and Some Account of the Answers that have been published against them. In several Letters to a Friend.* 3rd ed., improved. 2 vols., London 1757, vol. 1, p. ii.

[26] Tindal, *Christianity as Old as the Creation*, p. 163.

[27] Ibid., p. 184.

[28] In his Boyle Lectures for 1705, Clarke taxonomizes the deists into four categories. The first category of deist believes that God is "an Eternal, Infinite, Independent, Intelligent Being" who "made the World" but "does *not at all concern* himself in the *government* of the World nor has any regard to, or care of, what is done therein". See Samuel Clarke, *A Discourse Concerning the Unchangeable Obligations of Natural Religion, and the Truth and Certainty of the Christian Revelation. Being Eight Sermons Preach'd at the Cathedral-Church of St. Paul, in the Year 1705, at the Lecture Founded by the Honourable Robert Boyle Esq.*, London 1706, p. 19. For Clarke, the notion of an absconding creator must logically lead to "*downright Atheism*". (Ibid., p. 20)

Clarke's second category of deist believes in a Supreme Being and in the attribute of divine providence but restricts the operation of God's providential "Power" to the sphere of "every *natural* thing that is done in the world". Thus, for

Newton shows his distaste for the crucially important deistic project of setting aside scripture in favor of reason early in the 1680s. In an important letter to Newton, Thomas Burnet deistically argues that the Mosaic account is neither a physically accurate description of what happened nor a scientifically adequate account and, hence, unnecessary. A bit of doggerel verse from the time summarizes Burnet's attitude and explains why he did not advance far in the Church. A popular ballad of the 1680s has the character "Burnet" singing:

---

deists of this second sort, God "takes no notice of the morally good or evil Actions of Men: these things depending, as they imagine, merely on the arbitrary constitution of Humane Laws". (Ibid., 26–7) Once again, Clarke sees this sort of deism leading inevitably to atheism. (Ibid., p. 28)

Clarke defines deists of the third category as those who believe in a deity of total dominion whose all-powerful providential government of the world extends into both the natural and moral realms which he rules in accord with his infinite attributes of justice, truth, and goodness. Deists of this third sort go on to deny any future state for mankind, however. (Ibid., p. 32) These deists, too, reduce themselves to atheism because, though they acknowledge the *Moral Attributes* of God in words, in fact, these very *Moral Attributes* are "entirely taken away" by these deist-atheists just because they do not recognize the wholly *Transcendental* character of such aspects of God's moral nature as Goodness and Justice. In their use of human language to describe these aspects of God's nature they "mean nothing". (Ibid., p. 34)

Those in Clarke's fourth category of deists have all the correct theories about the nature and attributes of God. Such deists correctly believe that God is "One, Eternal, Infinite, Intelligent, All-Powerful, and Wise"; that God is a "Being of Infinite Justice, Goodness, and Truth, and all other moral as well as natural perfections"; that God made the world "for the manifestation of his Power and Wisdom, and to communicate his Goodness and Happiness to his Creatures"; that God preserves the world by his "continual All-Wise Providence, and governs it according to the eternal Rules of Infinite Justice, Equity, Goodness, Mercy and Truth"; and that man has moral duties and obligations on which turn his reward or punishment in a future state. [*Ibid.*, p. 32.] The only difference between deists in this fourth category and Christian theists such as Clarke (or Newton or Whiston) is one of epistemological method. These fourth-category deists "*pretend to believe* only so far, as it is discoverable by the Light of Nature alone; without believing any Divine Revelation". (Ibid., p. 37) Deists who hold these views about the nature and attributes of God solely on the basis of rational inquiry and analysis (rather than on the basis of *both* scriptural authority *and* rational analysis of all other possible sources including the book of nature and the ancient theological tradition) and then go on to live according to them, are "very close to the Kingdom of God" and worth engaging in dialogue "in order to convince them of the Reasonableness, Truth, and Certainty of the *Christian Revelation*". (Ibid.) Alas for Clarke "there are very few or none *such Deists* as These, among our modern deniers of Revelation." (Ibid.) With Whiston, Clarke assails modern deists, i.e., those in the first three categories who operate exclusively with their independent rational faculties and independently of Biblical revelation, for "their Trivial and vain Cavils, their bantering and ridiculing, without and before examination; their directing the whole stress of their Objections, against particular Customs, or particular and perhaps uncertain Opinions or Explications of Opinions, without

That all the books of Moses Were nothing but supposes.
That as for Father Adam and Mrs. Eve, his Madame,
And what the devil spoke, Sir,
'Twas nothing but a joke, Sir,
And well-invented flam.

In a letter to Newton, Burnet writes that the Mosaic story is only "ideall, or if you will, morall",[29] and that its purpose is only to impress the vulgar understanding of the followers of Moses. Newton takes issue with Burnet's deistic attempt to set aside the books of Moses in his most significant reply in which he outlines briefly his methodological approach to the scriptures. Newton agrees that the Mosaic account of creation is *not* "philosophical", but neither is it "feigned".[30] Newton writes that for Burnet to declare that Moses described events "when there was no such thing done neither in reality nor in appearance . . . is something hard".[31] Rather, in Newton's view, Moses describes actual historical events at the creation in the language of what a witness would have seen "had he lived & seen ye whole series of w^t Moses describes". Newton prefers natural mechanical explanations for such events (such as Whiston's later theory of the cometary origins of the earth and the flood) but concludes that "I doe not think them alone sufficient for the creation".[32] And just as he utilizes gentile historians to elaborate on the details of human history after the creation about which Moses is silent, so, too, Newton observes that other ancient historians provide a kind of negative corroboration of his own rational understanding of Gen. 1:1. Newton conjectures that "one may suppose that all ye planets about our Sun were created together, there being in no history any mention of new ones appearing or old ones ceasing".[33]

Newton's remarks to Burnet in this letter are given a lengthy

---

at all considering the main Body of Religion; their loose, vain, and frothy Discourses; and above all, their vitious and immoral Lives. . . . If they were truly in earnest such *Deists* as they pretend and would sometimes be thought to be; those Principles . . . would unavoidable lead them to *Christianity*". (Ibid., 41–2) As with Whiston (see citation no. 9), the negative element had come to overshadow any positive, systematic theory about the nature of God derived from reason alone by the early eighteenth century.

[29] Burnet to Newton, 13 January 1680/1, in *The Correspondence of Isaac Newton*, Vol. 2, 1676–1687, ed. H.W. Turnbull, Cambridge: Cambridge University Press, 1966, p. 324.

[30] Ibid., p. 332.

[31] Ibid., p. 331.

[32] Ibid., p. 334.

[33] Ibid., p. 332.

elaboration in Whiston's 1696 work, a *New Theory of the Earth*, which is prefaced with a ninety-five page "Introductory Discourse Concerning the Nature, Stile, and Extent of the Mosaick History of the Creation". It is in this "Introductory Discourse" that Whiston develops his Newtonian "third way" between simple-minded literalists and scoffing deists who, in their characteristic preference for the design argument of natural religion, laugh at the idea that revelation may be utilized as a serious source of knowledge about God. Whiston describes his "third way", which is, literally, a METHOD for rightly interpreting scripture,[34] in this fashion:

> 'Tis hard to say whether those dishonour God most who embrace Doctrines, suppos'd deducible from Scripture, tho' plainly absurd and unreasonable in themselves; or those who venture to deny or at least wrest and prevaricate with the obvious meaning of such Texts whence those Doctrines us'd to be infer'd. Both these methods of procedure are bold and dangerous; Effects of our own Pride, and too high an opinion of our proper apprehensions and abilities, and of sad consequence to our selves, to others, and to Divine Revelation. There is a third or middle way, which, tho' an instance of real self-denial, we both may and ought to take.[35]

---

[34] As Henry Guerlac has noted, the term "method" seems to have been a coinage by Plato who used it first in the *Phaedrus* where Socrates advocates an art or technique of rhetoric in contrast to the trickery of the Sophists. The word itself is derived from *meta* and *odos* in Greek and suggests a movement along a road passing through or between. A method, then, is literally a way through and, as we shall see, for Whiston his "third way" is a method which takes him between the Scylla of the literalists and the Charybdis of the deists. See Henry Guerlac, "Newton and the Method of Analysis", in *Essays and Papers in the History of Modern Science*, Baltimore: The Johns Hopkins University Press, 1977, p. 195.

[35] William Whiston, *A New Theory of the Earth, From its Original, to the Consummation of all Things. Wherein The Creation of the World in Six Days, The Universal Deluge, and the General Conflagration, As laid down in the Holy Scriptures, Are shewn to be perfectly agreeable to Reason and Philosophy. With a large Introductory Discourse concerning the Genuine Nature, Stile, and Extent of the "Mosaick" History of the Creation*, London, 1696, in the separately paginated "Introductory Discourse", 72–3. Whiston's public attempt to provide a "third way" of Biblical interpretation provoked the wrath both of uncritical, fideistic "literalists" as well as that of scoffing, negative deists. The criticism of the literalists is most interesting for Whiston, despite his attempts to distance himself from the deists, is lumped in with them. When Whiston publishes his *Memoirs* in 1749, they are immediately answered by an obviously orthodox, but anonymous, pamphleteer who asserts that Whiston's "third way" has only served to put his work "exactly upon a footing" with the deistic positions of Matthew Tindal and William Wollaston. Addressing Whiston, this anonymous writer, in a stunning refutation of Whiston's lifelong attempt to refute the deists (Cf. Note 9), asserts that:

> Your friend *Wollaston* indeed says, that such truth may be come at by reasoning, but he might as well have said, that two and two are five; for if eternal truth may be come at by reasoning, then every degree of probability

It is important to appreciate how Whiston, as a Newtonian exegete, elaborates Newton's privately communicated thoughts on method (in his letter to Burnet.) Fully to understand scripture and nature, according to Whiston, one must be as learned in the "true and demonstrative Principles of [natural] Philosophy as one is in the "History of Nature." Science is combined with historical interpretation of scripture to counteract the scoffing ridicule of such deists as Charles Blount who echoes the more deistic strains in Thomas Burnet. Whiston urges that genuinely wise men, i.e., Newtonian scientists who are also Biblical critics,

> would rather set themselves carefully to compare Nature with Scripture, and make a free Enquiry into the certain *Phaenomena* of the one, and the genuine Sense of the other; which if Expositors would do, 'twere not hard to demonstrate in several such cases, that the latter is so far from opposing the truths deducible from the former . . . that 'tis in the greatest harmony therewith. . . .[36]

Whiston's and Newton's chief concern in comparing the two divinely authored volumes of scripture and nature is to interpret the Biblical account of a natural phenomenon in a fashion which "shall at once keep sufficiently close to the Letter of *Moses*, and yet be far from allowing what contradicts Divine Wisdom, Common Reason, or Philosophick Deduction".[37] While the natural history of the phenomena of the first six days of creation relating to the

---

(of which reasoning consists) must be an argument for the truth in question; but every argument for the truth in question can only stand against an objection which must have existed before that argument could be made; therefore such reasoning must ever leave eternal truth just where it was. Hence it appears, that eternal truth being self-evident only by the negation of error, whenever it is revealed, it must reveal itself. Hence it is, that God must work in us both to will and to do, because the utmost that we can do of ourselves is only to depart from error and probability. Hence it is, that treatises of morality, and defenses of Christianity, have had so little effect upon the world; we say it is because people do not attend to them, but the true state of the case is, they cannot prove any one single proposition that they pretend to; when they talk of morality, they constantly, like *Tindal* . . . refer to a knowledge we have not, else should we not want their morality; and when they pretend like you [Whiston], to defend Christianity, behold they come off with probabilities concerning the truth of the *New Testament*. And hence it is . . . that mankind are in deeper ignorance, than ever they were since the creation. It is . . . because they think, that, by reasoning, and reading such books as yours, and *Tindal's*, and *Wollaston's*, they can come at it; whereas, by beginning there, they cannot take a more effectual way to keep themselves in error. (Anonymous, *A Letter to the Revd. William Whiston A.M. Occasioned by his Publication of the Memoirs of His Own Life*, London 1750, 37–8)

[36] "Introductory Discourse", p. 64.
[37] Ibid., p. 2.

Noachian deluge as described by Moses in Genesis is not a "Nice and Philosophical account of the Origin of All Things",[38] neither is it, as the "loose" Deists such as Burnet insist, "a meer Popular, Parabolick, or Mythological relation".[39]

Though Whiston and Newton have their differences over the interpretations of particular Biblical prophecies—one sore point is their split over the prophecy of the seventy weeks in Daniel—there is no evidence that they ever differed on the crucial question of the ultimate harmony between at least some parts of scripture, natural history, human history, and future events. The Bible in large part is for both a document capable of scientific exegesis. Even the most obscure texts regarding the history of the transformation of the earth over the first six "days" of its existence are, Whiston argues, perfectly reconcilable with "true and demonstrable principles of philosophy", though not with "ingenious and precarious *Hypotheses*".[40] If only critics would follow this procedure, Whiston claims that it

> would more contribute to the recovery of the Ancient Honour, and due Esteem of the Sacred Scriptures, then all the most Zealous and general Harangues from some popular Topicks, either for them or against their Contemners, the loose *Deists* and pretended *Socinians* of this Age.[41]

Whiston labels this method, in which he compares scripture texts of historical events with other historical records and/or with the "Principles" of Newtonian natural philosophy, as the "third or middle way". With this method, he—and Newton—seek to avoid the "Erroneous Extremes"[42] both of absolute literalists who accept every word of scripture uncritically and who suppose that it is a "real and Philosophical relation to the proper creation of things"[43] and of the "loose" deists who, in sharp opposition, assert the primacy of reason over revelation and go so far as to assert that reason betrays revelation "no more to be accounted for or believ'd, than the fabulous representations of *Aesop*".[44]

Newton, in all his private theological papers, including the highly significant "Theologiae Gentilis Origines Philosophicae", al-

---

[38] Ibid., p. 3.
[39] Ibid., p. 2.
[40] Ibid., p. 65.
[41] Ibid., p. 64.
[42] Ibid., p. 75.
[43] Ibid., p. 31.
[44] Ibid., p. 2.

ways adheres to the Postulates later published by Whiston in his
"Introductory Discourse" as the summary of what Whiston calls
"the third way" and which he summarizes in three "Postulates":

I.   The Obvious or Literal Sense of Scripture is the True and
        Real one, where no evident Reason can be given to the
        contrary.

II.   That which is clearly accountable in a natural way, is not
        without reason to be ascrib'd to a Miraculous Power.

And, most importantly, given Westfall's argument that it is the
demotion of the Bible (from the one source of all that is true to one
source among many each of which must be checked against the
others) which finally leads Newton to a deistic conclusion, Whiston's third Postulate:

III.   What Ancient Tradition asserts of the constitution of Nature,
        or of the World, is to be allow'd for True, where 'tis fully
        agreeable to Scripture, Reason, and Philosophy.[45]

The following text from Newton is, therefore, highly significant
regarding Newton's own METHOD of interpreting scripture:

> So then the first religion was the most rational of all others till the
> nations corrupted it. For there is no way (wthout revelation) to come
> to ye knowledge of a Deity but by the frame of nature.[46]

Westfall observes that the parenthetical phrase in this text,
"wthout revelation", is inserted in the manuscript "as an
afterthought"[47] and discounts its importance. I am inclined to
interpret this significant phrase in an opposite manner. Given
Newton's happy circumstance of being born after the delivery of
revelation along with Newton's lifelong commitment to the study of
how properly to understand Mosaic history and the fulfillment of
divine prophecies in history in the light of ancient religious tradition and modern natural philosophy, I believe that we have good
reason to acknowledge the importance of such revelation as a
source of religious knowledge for Newton. The phrase may have
been an afterthought, but its *addition* seems to me to show that, for
Newton, the Bible remains still a pathway to true knowledge about
the nature of God and, especially, about prophetic history, past
and future. Newton always believes in the divine origin of a core

---

[45] Ibid., p. 95.
[46] Newton, Yahuda MS 41. ff. 9–10. Cited by Westfall, "Newton's *Theologiae
Gentilis*", p. 25.
[47] Ibid.

element of revealed prophetic scripture which must be properly interpreted. Finally, Newton is no deist because he believes always that the Bible contains a prophetic core of divine truth accessible to properly guided reason.

As for the arrogance of the deists, with their smug assurance that human reason is the measure of all things, including God, Newton constantly warns against feigning hypotheses and urges instead a cautious empiricism through which he recognizes the power of God to effect changes even in created natural law. Newton's epistemological caution is legendary. It is reflected in his advice to interpreters of prophecy not to attempt to necessitate God almighty by predicting in advance when or how God will choose to fulfill his prophetic promises.[48] It is reflected in his fourth Rule of Reasoning in which

---

[48] Newton is adamantly cautious in his treatment of prophecies. One must never attempt to predict exactly how, where, and when God will fulfill his prophetic promises. Such an ability exceeds our rational power. God gives us such prophecies not to gratify human curiosity but so "that *after* they were fulfilled they might be interpreted by the Event, and his own Providence, not the Interpreters be manifested thereby to the world". (Newton, *Observations upon the Prophecies*, p. 251) It is this circumspect and fallibilistic method of interpreting unfulfilled future prophecies which makes Newton's method of Biblical interpretation explicitly analogous to his scientific method of analysis and synthesis. (Cf. Note 49.) In the method of analysis and synthesis, Newton *begins* from *certain* experiments and observations. This certain data is analyzed by induction to provide *probable* "Principles" which, though they are "the best way of arguing which the Nature of Things admits of", are not themselves absolutely certain. These "Principles" become the best possible basis, even though they are not certain, for deductive future predictions regarding natural phenomena. In analyzing historical prophecies, Newton, as abundant MSS. testimony suggests, begins with what he regards as indubitable testimony whether derived from Moses or Berossus. Such testimony, when analyzed, suggests *possible* future outcomes, *but* until predicted outcomes actually materialize in the empirical world, they have the same probable status as his inductively derived "Principles". Consequently, as Newton insists in this text, we must await future observations in order to KNOW. "Interpreters" or "Scientists", after all are not God.

In contrast, to Newton's explicit voluntarism, Tindal, again, argues that, because of the rational nature of man, God cannot "reveal" to him any truth save by "shewing its Agreement with those self-evident Notions, which are the Facts by which we are to judge of everything, even the Being of a God and natural religion" (Tindal, *Christianity as Old as the Creation*, p. 184) Tindal here echoes Ralph Cudworth who adopts this position to argue against the voluntarism of Descartes. In Cudworth's view, God is unable to do anything repugnant to human reason and urges that "*Conception* and knowledge are hereby made to be the *Measure* of all *Power*; even *Omnipotence*" (Cudworth, *The True Intellectual System of the Universe*, London 1678, p. 719) Newton, by contrast to both Cudworth and Tindal, adopts a voluntarism akin to that of Descartes and emphasizes God's omnipotence over the constraints of human rationality. Similarly, Whiston writes that "We depend on God Almighty as to what we *know*, as well as what we *have*, or what we *are*". (Whiston, "Introductory Discourse", p. 77) Of course, in his agreement with Tindal on the point of the constraints on God's power by the limits of human

he makes experience, not *a priori* hypotheses, the great guide of common life and in other methodological pronouncements regarding the priority of experience and observation as the basis for an induction regarding first "Principles" induced by the initial "method of analysis".[49] It is reflected in his analysis of the repeated pattern of the corruption of true monotheism in the hands of

---

understanding, Cudworth sounds more like a deist than Newton who adamantly maintains the totality of God's power and dominion over creation.

[49] Newton's metaphysical conception of God's dominion and power is not divorced from the empiricist epistemology which he adopts in his empirically grounded scientific method but is entirely consonant with it. Newton's single methodological procedure for obtaining "knowledge" begins with "Analysis" (*resolutio*) and then moves to "Synthesis" (*compositio*.) For Newton, in contrast to Descartes, the initial path of "Analysis" is identified with empirical experiments and observations. On the basis of this empirical starting point, Newton inductively derives probationary "Principles" such as the Inverse Square Law. The second part of his method is the synthetic deduction of future phenomena on the basis of these "Principles". Newton's clearest statement of his two-pronged method is in the famous passage Query 31 of the second English edition of the Opticks:

> As in Mathematicks, so in Natural Philosophy, the Investigation of difficult Things by the Method of Analysis, ought ever to precede the Method of Composition. *This Analysis consists in making Experiments and Observations*, and in drawing general Conclusions from them by *Induction*, and admitting of no Objections against the Conclusions; yet *it is the best way of arguing which the Nature of Things admits of*, and may be looked upon as so much the stronger, by how much the Induction is more general. And *if no Exception occur from Phaenomena, the Conclusion may be pronounced generally.* But *if at any time afterwards any Exception shall occur from Experiments, it may then begin to be pronounced with such Exceptions* as occur. By this way of Analysis we may proceed from Compounds to Ingredients, and from particular causes to more general ones, till the Argument end in the most general. This is the Method of Analysis: And the *Synthesis consists in assuming the Causes discover'd and establish'd as Principles, and by them explaining the Phaenomena proceeding from them*, and proving the Explanations. See Sir Isaac Newton, *Opticks or A Treatise of the Reflections, Refractions, Inflections & Colours of Light*, based on the 4th London edition, 1730: New York: Dover, 1952, Query 31, 404–5. An abbreviated version of this Query was published in the Latin edition of 1706 as Query 23. In the above citation, I have added the italics.

Clearly, for Newton, experiments and observations which admit of "no exception" are "certain" even though the "Principles" inductively derived from them are only probable and that, even so, such "Principles" are initially "the best way of arguing which the Nature of Things admits of". It is also the case, for Newton, that a single, well-chosen *experimentum crucis* may be the basis for the firm induction of a "Principle" or Law which governs the current natural order. Nevertheless, even the best scientific knowledge which Newton's version of the *probatio duplex* can provide is limited to the current "Nature of Things" which, in turn, is utterly dependent, both for its being and its continued operation, upon the absolute will and power of the Lord God of supreme dominion described in the "General Scholium". Because of God's sovereign nature as "Lord God", the laws of nature are, in an important sense, *both* necessary and contingent. They are necessary— and thus knowable by the double method—*only* while God, who created them,

self-serving schemers such as Thoth in ancient times and Athanasius in the fourth century. Newton's cautious empiricism and the
underlying mistrust of human reason in the face of both the power
of God and what history reveals about the natural tendency towards idolatry, upon which his epistemology is based, is also
reflected in his heterodox disciple, Samuel Clarke, who writes:

> Indeed in the original uncorrupted State of Humane Nature, before
> the Mind of Man was depraved with prejudicate Opinions, corrupt
> Affections, and vitious Inclinations, Customs and Habits; right
> Reason may justly supposed to have been a sufficient Guide, and a
> Principle powerful enough to preserve Men in the constant Practice
> of their Duty. But in the present Circumstances and Condition of

---

maintains them in operation. Newton is no enthusiast and he labors mightily to
separate the few cases of genuine historical (often catastrophic) miracles from the
many cases of idolatrous and false ones. (Newton, "Paradoxical questions concerning ye morals & actions of Athanasius & his followers", William Andrews
Clark Memorial Library MS) Nevertheless, Newton accepts the reality of direct
divine intervention in nature through miraculous—"specially provident"—acts of
will (which are simultaneously supremely acts of power) which interrupt the
ordinary coursing of nature and nature's generally provident laws and his reading
of prophecy leads him to expect a "new heaven and a new earth" when the laws
and principles of the current system may no longer apply. For Newton, the
primacy of God's power results in a distinctive contingency in the natural order
even while Newton acknowledges the virtual necessity of that order in its
ordinary—"generally provident"—current operation and provides a unique
methodology, the *probatio duplex*, for studying its operation. For Newton, the whole
of creation is "subordinate to [God], and subservient to his Will". (Newton,
Opticks, Query 31, p. 403) This is the theological and metaphysical background to
Newton's most famous methodological statement in his fourth "Rule" of
reasoning:

> *In experimental philosophy we are to look upon propositions inferred by general induction
> from phenomena as accurately or very nearly true, notwithstanding any contrary hypotheses
> that may be imagined, till such time as other phenomena occur, by which they may either be
> made more accurate, or liable to exceptions.*
>   This rule we must follow, that the argument of induction may not be
> evaded by hypotheses. (*Sir Isaac Newton's Mathematical Principles of Natural
> Philosophy*, 2, p. 400) This rule is not added to the

Principia until the second edition of 1713. Newton's view about the contingency
of human knowledge, in the light of God's absolute power and dominion over
every aspect of creation, parallels that of Robert Boyle who writes that

> in this very phenomenal world of partial regularity, at any moment all our
> science may be upset by the elimination, or change of regularity through the
> operation of Him who is the guider of its concourse. For the most optimistic
> investigator must acknowledge that if God be the author of the universe, and
> the free establisher of the laws of motion, whose general concourse is neces-
> sary to the conservation and efficacy of every particular physical agent, God
> can certainly invalidate all experimentalism by withholding His concourse, or
> changing those laws of motion, which depend perfectly upon His will, and
> could thus vitiate the value of most, if not all the axioms and theorems of

Mankind, the wisest and most sensible of the Philosophers them-selves have not been backward to complain, that they found the *Understandings* of Men so *dark and cloudy*, their *Wills* so *byassed and inclined to Evil*, their *Passions* so *outragious and rebelling against Reason*; that they look upon the Rules and Laws of right Reason, as very hardly practicable, and which they had very little Hopes of being able to persuade the World to submit to: In a Word, they confessed that Humane Nature was strangely *corrupted*; and acknowledged this *Corruption* to be a Disease whereof they knew not the true *Cause*, and could not find out a sufficient Remedy. So that the great Duties of Religion, were laid down by them as Matters of *speculation and dispute*, rather than as the *Rules of Action.* . . . To remedy all these Disorders, and conquer all these Corruptions; there was plainly wanting some extraordinary and supernatural *Assistance*; which was above the reach of bare Reason and Philosophy to procure . . .[50]

One final point must be made about how, on the basis of his method of Biblical interpretation, Newton actually does go well beyond the results of such writers as Vossius and Cudworth and comes to view Jesus Christ as neither co-substantial nor co-eternal with God. This Arian position is definitely unorthodox, even heret-ical, but it is clearly not deistic. Even in his Arianism, Newton takes the Bible seriously. Nor is Newton's Arianism paradoxical as Westfall claims when he writes that "the *Origines* appears to be incompatible with Arianism, to go beyond its recognition of the special status of Christ, who was more than a man even if he was not wholly divine, and to verge on a frankly deistic position".[51] I

---

natural philosophy. Therefore reason operating in the mechanical world is constantly limited by the possibility that there is not final regularity in that world, and that existential regularity may readily be destroyed at any mo-ment by the God upon whom it depends. (Robert Boyle, *Reconcilableness of Reason and Religion*, in *The Works of the Honourable Robert Boyle*, 6 vols., ed. Thomas Birch, London 1772: 4, p. 161)

Fifty years prior to Hume's *Treatise of Human Nature*, Newton, from a vastly different metaphysical and theological starting point, is telling us that the future need not resemble the past and that, consequently, we must mark ALL the consequences of this fact in regulating our expectations of what sort of human knowledge scientific empiricism can provide.

[50] Clarke, *A Discourse Concerning the Unchangeable Obligations of Natural Religion*, 239–40. In his "Newton's *Theologiae Gentilis*", p. 30, Westfall cites this text as evidence that Newton's "deism" goes well beyond the slightly more orthodox theology of his disciple, Samuel Clarke. For the reasons which I give, I take this text to represent Newton's own position and to be the reason why he utilizes the evidence of scripture in contrast to a deist such as Tindal whose chief desire is simply to proscribe the use of scripture totally. Newton shares with Clarke an acute awareness of the cyclical rise and fall of purely rational religions. They also share the same view about the Lord God sharing his dominion with Jesus Christ. See Clarke, *The Scripture-Doctrine of the Trinity*, London 1712, 332–3.

[51] Westfall, "Newton's *Theologiae Gentilis*", p. 29.

maintain that Newton's view about Jesus is a natural consequence of his taking the Bible to be a serious source of religious knowledge. In Newton's view, though not of the same substance as God and though not co-existent with God from eternity, Jesus, as God's deputed vice-regent has had his moments of glory in the divine cosmic drama. Jesus dominates both the Old and the New Testaments in a startling and crucially important fashion in Newton's scripturally based Arian Christology. Among other things, God deputes his vice-regent, Jesus Christ, in the Old Testament, to walk in the Garden of Eden with Adam, to appear as an angel to Abraham, to fight with Jacob, to give the prophecies to the prophets, and, ultimately, in the New Testament, to preach again the pure and uncorrupted religion of Noah to Jew and Gentile alike. Newton's understanding of Christ's final mission of recalling fallen humanity to the true religion of Noah, though a radical departure from traditional and orthodox interpretations of Christ's life, is perfectly consistent with heterodox Christian theism, but it is totally inconsistent with both orthodox Christianity and the scoffing dismissal of "the fables of Jesus Christ" by the deistic natural theologians.

Finally, while Westfall may be correct in his second point that the ultimate payoff of all of Newton's comparative textual analysis between the Bible, the "ancient theology", and modern natural philosophy leads Newton to a conclusion about the nature of God which one may argue is roughly similar to some particular forms of deism (i.e., a God as old as creation who insists from mankind only that we love Him and one another), his means of getting to that conclusion make him a "differing Christian" rather than a true deist. Newton simply does not fit the definition of "*Deist*" as given in Chambers' *Cyclopaedia*:

> The appelation *Deist* is more particularly given to such as are not altogether without religion, but reject all revelation as an imposition, and believe no more than what natural light discovers to them. . . .[52]

Perhaps my argument may seem to be far too "essentialist" and universalist given the tremendous variations in the use of the terms "deist" and "deism" in the first half of the eighteenth century. Nevertheless, while Newton may very well share rationalistic ele-

---

[52] E. Chambers, *Cyclopaedia*, 2 vols., London 1738, s.v. "Deists". Cf. Samuel Johnson's more succinct definition: "The opinion of those that only acknowledge one God, without the reception of any revealed religion." Samuel Johnson, *A Dictionary of the English Language*, 2 vols., London 1755, Vol. 1, s.v. "DEISM".

ments with the "positive" deists, he is never a radical, "negative", religiously sceptical deist because he always believes that the Bible contains a core of divine truth accessible to reason following a proper interpretative method. Furthermore, Newton is finally no deist because he ultimately believes, with Robert Boyle, that some divine truths exceed the grasp of human reason and must remain forever "above reason".

OLIVIER BLOCH

SCEPTICISME ET RELIGION DANS LA *REPONSE A UN THEOLOGIEN* DU MEDECIN GAULTIER ET SA POSTERITE CLANDESTINE

Le texte dont j'ai choisi de traiter est plus connu, du moins des spécialistes de la littérature clandestine, sous le titre de *Parité de la Vie et de la Mort*. Il s'agit d'un des traités à mes yeux les plus intéressants, philosophiquement parlant, de cet ensemble – il serait du reste mal venu de ma part de dire le contraire, puisque j'en prépare l'édition pour un avenir proche.

Le titre que je viens de mentionner est celui que porte la version qui en est imprimée, sans lieu ni date, dans un recueil de *Pièces philosophiques*, aux côtés des *Dialogues sur l'âme* et du *Jordanus Redivivus*, le frontispice propre de chacune de ces deux dernières pièces portant la date de 1771.

Le titre de cette version imprimée reproduisait celui d'un des deux extraits manuscrits dont elle est tirée, extrait qu'on trouve dans le recueil Ms 1192 de la Bibliothèque Mazarine. L'autre extrait, un peu plus étendu, et qui représente de toute évidence une version antérieure du texte, bien que, comme c'est le cas de l'autre manuscrit, le filigrane du papier porte la date de 1742, est inclus dans le recueil Ms 2239 de la Bibliothèque de l'Arsenal; son titre justifierait déjà que l'on en parle dans notre réunion, puisque il s'agit cette fois d'une *Nouvelle Philosophie Sceptique*.

Mais c'est avant tout l'original, dont sont tirées directement ou indirectement ces versions successives, et qui formera le centre de ma prochaine édition, qui justifie mon entreprise présente, puisqu'il s'agit d'une

> Reponse en forme de dissertation à un theologien qui demande ce que veulent dire les Sceptiques, qui cherchent la verité par tout dans la Nature, comme dans les écrits des Philosophes; lors qu'ils pensent que la Vie & la Mort sont la même chose. *Où l'on voit que la Vie & la Mort des Minéraux, des Métaux, des Plantes & des Animaux, avec tous leurs attributs, ne sont que des façons d'être de la même substance, à laquelle ces modifications n'ajoûtent & n'ôtent rien.*

Cette *Réponse* constitue un petit volume in 12° de 208 pages, dont le frontispice donne le nom de l'auteur : "le sieur Gaultier, médecin à Nyort", – l'éditeur : Jean Elies, à Niort également, – et la date : 1714. Les pages liminaires qui suivent contiennent un "Avis" de l'auteur, puis deux approbations de théologiens et un permis d'imprimer. Publication d'allure tout à fait officielle donc, ce qui paraît assurément étrange, étant donnés le contenu et l'orientation dominante de l'ouvrage, et aussi ce que l'on sait par ailleurs de la personnalité des protagonistes, de l'auteur à l'éditeur en passant par le signataire du permis d'imprimer. Toutefois, si cette étrangeté peut, sans que d'ailleurs j'aie pu établir quoi que ce soit de sûr dans un sens ni dans l'autre, faire soupçonner qu'il s'agisse d'une supercherie, un ensemble de considérations, tirées encore du contenu de l'ouvrage, et de la biographie du médecin Gaultier, – "nouveau catholique" de Niort converti à la veille de la révocation de l'Edit de Nantes, et qui avait au début de l'année précédente été à Amsterdam coéditeur d'un éphémère *Mercure Sçavant*, aussitôt remplacé par les *Nouvelles de la République des Lettres* de Pierre Bayle, – me conduisent à penser qu'elle ne saurait être bien tardive, que le texte est, quoi qu'il en soit, bien l'œuvre d'Abraham Gaultier, et que la rédaction doit en avoir été effectivement achevée peu après 1710.

I. L'AFFABULATION DE LA *RÉPONSE*

On doit, en première analyse, s'épargner la peine de s'interroger sur l'identité des "Sceptiques" dont l'auteur prétend rapporter la doctrine : il ne s'agit pas d'une obscure secte contemporaine de l'auteur, ou d'un courant de pensée oublié, mais d'une fiction littéraire, elle-même inspirée d'une autre fiction.

La "réponse" que l'auteur est censé donner à un "théologien qui demande ce que veulent dire les sceptiques" est en effet de toute évidence une réplique de débat que met en scène la Remarque B de l'article *Pyrrhon* du *Dictionnaire* de Bayle, où un abbé philosophe expose à un autre abbé, qui ne l'est pas, la force des arguments sceptiques, le renfort que, face au dogmatisme religieux, le scepticisme ancien reçoit de la nouvelle philosophie mécaniste, cartésienne en particulier, dans la subjectivisation des qualités sensibles, et autres "modifications" de l'âme, au sens malebranchien du terme, qu'elle établit, et, exemples théologiques à l'appui, les contradictions que rencontrent les "évidences" les plus communément admises. Ce sont effectivement ces thèmes qui servent d'armature aux trois premiers articles ou paragraphes qui suivent dans la *Réponse* de Gaultier les pages d'introduction du texte.[1]

---

[1] L'ouvrage est en effet, à l'exception de ces premières pages (5 à 7), divisé en

La signature baylienne du titre est confirmée par la lecture de la suite de l'article *Pyrrhon* du *Dictionnaire*, où l'on trouvera dans la Remarque E sur l'indifférence de Pyrrhon la clef du thème de la "parité de la vie et de la mort", puisque Bayle y "rapporte" à ce propos un mot de Pyrrhon:

> Raportons encore ce petit mot. Pyrrhon soutenoit que mourir et vivre c'étoit toute la même chose. Pourquoi donc ne mourez-vous pas, lui demanda-t-on; parce, repondit-il, qu'il n'y a nulle différence entre la mort et la vie. Diogene Laërce ne fait point mention de cela; mais Stobée nous l'a conservé.

Si donc l'argument dont part l'opuscule de Gaultier est une transposition proche de la Remarque B de l'article *Pyrrhon* : un connaisseur de la philosophie des sceptiques informe de sa teneur un théologien qui n'est pas philosophe, justifiant le titre donné à l'ouvrage par son premier extracteur clandestin, – et si le thème central de la "parité de la vie et de la mort", qui fournit celui du second extrait manuscrit et de l'imprimé final, est tiré du même article en sa Remarque E, on peut dire aussi que le problème apparaît d'abord posé dans les termes bayliens, qui sont ceux de notre rencontre, puisqu'il s'agit bien, dans cet article, du rapport entre scepticisme et religion, du défi philosophique que le premier lance à la seconde, et des conséquences qui en découlent pour le fidéisme baylien :[2] l'affabulation de la *Réponse*, comme telle, dépend de cette problématique, et le titre même de son dernier article : "Que le propre de la théologie est de soumettre la philosophie à ses lois", paraît témoigner d'une adhésion à ce fidéisme.

II. L'ORIENTATION BAYLIENNE CHEZ GAULTIER

L'orientation baylienne en matière de scepticisme et de fidéisme occupe, de fait, une place non négligeable dans le texte de la

---

soixante-dix articles ou paragraphes bien individualisés par leur titre et la typographie, mais non numérotés. Les extraits manuscrits reprennent ces divisions, en leur donnant des numéros de paragraphe. Par commodité, je donne ici dans le cours de mon texte, comme je le ferai dans mon édition, aux paragraphes de la *Réponse* elle-même des numéros entre crochets carrés.

[2] Voir le début de l'article, la phrase à laquelle renvoie la Remarque B : "C'est avec raison qu'on le déteste dans les écoles de Théologie" (2e éd., p. 2430), le début de ladite Remarque, qui insiste sur cette opposition radicale, la Remarque C, qui, développant le thème amorcé à la fin de la précédente, justifie l'usage que l'on peut faire du scepticisme pour humilier la raison au profit de la foi, et le troisième éclaircissement sur le pyrrhonisme ajouté par Bayle dans la seconde édition pour répondre à l'émotion suscitée chez les réformés par l'article qui nous intéresse.

Réponse, depuis l'*Avis* de la page 3 où l'auteur se défend par avance, au nom du fidéisme, contre les attaques qu'il prévoit,³ jusque donc au paragraphe [70] et dernier, en passant par les premiers paragraphes, où il s'inspire manifestement des développements de la Remarque B où l'abbé philosophe exposait les "avantages" que le pyrrhonisme peut tirer de la philosophie cartésienne (*Réponse*, §1 : "Ce que nous raportons aux objets, n'y est point"⁴ et §2: "La connoissance que nous avons d'un objet, consiste dans le sentiment qu'il nous cause"⁵), et où il niait l'existence d'un critère de la vérité, qui devrait par excellence être celui de l'évidence (*Réponse*, §3 : "L'évidence n'est point la marque de vérité"⁶), et un certain nombre de professions de foi qui émaillent les développements sinueux du texte de l'ouvrage.⁷

---

³ "Le Philosophe qui donne au Public cette Réponse, en forme de Dissertation Physique, où il montre que la Vie & la Mort sont la même chose, ne prétend parler que des Animaux, des Plantes, & des Mineraux; n'ayant pas dessein de confondre l'Homme avec la Bête, ni dans la Vie, ni dans la Mort; ni de donner la moindre atteinte à tout ce que la Foy & la Religion enseignent de la spiritualité & de l'immortalité de l'ame. S'il donne une liberté aux Animaux, il entend une liberté naturelle, en ce qu'ils agissent d'eux-mêmes, sans violence; & si ce petit Ouvrage ne peut éviter la censure & la mauvaise humeur des Critiques, l'Auteur avertit, qu'il n'a pas eu la présomption de croire, qu'il fût au goût de tout le monde".

⁴ p. 8–12. Voir surtout le début de ce paragraphe : "Ce que nous sentons à la presence des objets, est un sentiment qui n'est point ailleurs qu'en nous; qui n'est nullement dans les objets, où nous le raportons, & qui ne leur ressemble point du tout. L'épingle qui nous pique, en est un exemple; car on ne peut dire que le sentiment qu'elle cause, soit dans l'épingle, ni qu'il luy ressemble. Il en est de même des autres sens, du goût que nous avons quand nous bûvons du Vin, ou que nous mangeons des Viandes; de nôtre odorat, quand nous respirons les fumées des corps odorans; de nôtre oüie, quand l'air ému entre dans nos oreilles; & de nôtre vûë, quand les corps colorez & lumineux agissent sur nos yeux. Ainsi les sensations & les idées qu'excitent en nous les objets exterieurs, par l'entremise de nos sens, ne sont point ailleurs qu'en nous, & ne peuvent être dans les objets, ni leur res-[9]sembler du tout. C'est sur ce principe que nos Philosophes soûtiennent ce Paradoxe : *Bien loin*, disent-ils, *que toutes les choses qui paroissent, soient existentes, rien au contraire de ce qui paroît n'existe*; voulant dire, que tout ce qui paroît, s'y [*sic*] diversifié aux yeux & aux autres sens, ne peut être qu'en nous, en tant que nous sommes capables de sentiment, & n'est point du tout dans les objets, ou dans la substance, à laquelle nous le raportons; puis qu'elle est toûjours trés-uniforme, en tout ce qu'elle a d'essenciel." (p. 8–9).

⁵ p. 12–13.

⁶ p. 13–17, en particulier le début : "C'est pour cela que les Sceptiques combatent opiniâtrement l'évidence, qui est aux Dogmatiques, la marque caracteristique de la vérité. Car ils soûtiennent que la verité ne se peut pas plus connoitre par l'évidence, que par toute [14] autre voye;" (p. 13–14), et, quelques lignes plus loin : "Pour voir donc les choses clairement, & avec évidence, il n'est pas nécessaire qu'elles soient telles qu'on les voit; puisqu'il y en a, qui avec autant de clarté les voyent & les sentent en même temps d'une maniere toute contraire." (p. 14).

⁷ Voir §25 (contre la métaphysique cartésienne) : "Aussi ce n'est point d'une raison Physique, que se doit tirer la croyance de l'immortalité & de la spiritualité

de nôtre ame; puisque cette croyance ne nous est salutaire, qu'autant que nous l'avons; [*sic*] parce que l'Eglise & la parole de Dieu l'ordonnent. L'on n'a donc que faire de chercher dans la nature ce qui n'est peut-être point de son ressort; car la raison qu'on en tireroit, pourroit jetter l'esprit dans l'illusion, sans donner l'éclaircissement qu'on cherche." (p. 75), – §41 (contre les prétendues *Méditations Métaphysiques* de Malebranche – en fait, celles de l'abbé de Lanion) : "Que pensez-vous, Monsieur, de ces Méditations? Elles ont toutes l'air d'un Roman, où l'on affecteroit le merveilleux, pour attirer d'avantage l'attention du Lecteur; car de la maniere qu'on nous y peint, nous sommes méconnoissables : Dieu luy-même, qu'on met sur la Scene, comme le seul Acteur, n'est point celuy qui a créé [120] l'Univers. Si le Pére Mallebranche y eût pensé, & qu'il fût allé le droit chemin, sans se laisser emporter à ses imaginations, qui naturellement n'ont point de bornes ni de regle, il auroit apris que la question de Dieu est comme une pilule qui devient plus amere, quand on la remache, & que cette question apartient de droit à la Théologie, & non à la Métaphysique. Il ne devoit donc point employer Dieu par tout, comme il a fait : mais puisqu'il vouloit écrire sur la Métaphysique, il auroit mieux tourné ses vûës sur les actions de la nature, les séparant de leur sujet par la pensée; & il auroit trouvé là de quoy remplir toutes ses Méditations. Par cette route, il ne se seroit jamais avisé de prendre des actions naturelles pour Dieu, de les prendre pour nôtre ame, ni pour toute autre substance spirituelle. Si donc il se fût conduit de la sorte, que la nature l'eût guidé & non son imagination, il auroit proposé les choses comme elles sont, & auroit évité les insultes & les railleries ausquelles il s'est exposé, par les consequences qui se peuvent tirer de sa Doctrine." (p. 119–120), – §43 (à propos de la liberté selon Malebranche) : "Ainsi la volonté qui tient toûjours au bout de nos penchans ou de nos inclinations, doit aussi être l'effet de quantité de causes nécessaires, & non d'une seule. Cependant, bien que nôtre ame se laisse souvent entraîner par la force des causes naturelles, & qu'elle y succombe quelque fois; cela n'empêche point qu'elle n'ait la force & la liberté de faire ou de ne pas faire les choses; puisque cette liberté est une de ses propriétez essentielles. Mais, comme cette liberté de nôtre ame est toute Théologique & Spirituelle, quand on la considere sans aucun raport au corps, ce n'est [131] point de cette espece de liberté dont je parle; je me contente de la croire, comme l'Eglise l'enseigne." (p. 130–131), – §45 (contre Spinoza) : "Si Spinoza eut esté docile, & qu'il eût eu des égards pour la Réligion, il auroit suivi des principes bien plus surs, que toutes ses speculations. Il auroit crû que l'ame de tous les hommes est spirituelle & immortelle; que Dieu est incomprehensible; qu'il est par tout par son essence; qu'il a créé l'Univers sans en faire partie, non plus qu'un Machiniste ne fait point partie de sa machine. Ainsi il auroit apris que la Nature n'est point le premier être; qu'elle ne subsiste que par les Loix qu'elle a reçû de son Créateur, & qui ont entre'elles un tel commerce & un si merveilleux raport, qu'elles en font comme un tout, & y operent toutes choses [39] immediatement, à moins que Dieu, par miracle, ne les change ou ne les arrête, quand il luy plaît; afin de faire éclater sa puissance & sa gloire. Ainsi les éfets de la Nature, dont les Physiciens récherchent si curieusement les causes, ne viennent pas de Dieu immediatement; c'est pourquoy toute leur vûê est d'en trouver les causes naturelles les plus proches de leurs éfets, sans avoir d'égard à celles qui en sont les plus éloignées; parce queelles [*sic*] ne tombent pas sous les sens. Cependant cela n'empêche point, qu'on ne référe avec raison tout à Dieu, comme à la premiere cause; quoyque les éfets soient produits immediatement par des causes naturelles." (p. 138–139), – §68 ("Nos mœurs viennent de la nature") : "Ce qu'on a dit, porte à croire, que les Mœurs de l'homme viennent de même de l'humide radical, qui fait toute la nature de son corps, comme il fait celle des Bêtes. Cet humide radical est donc le siége & la cause immediate de ses passions, le fond corrompu de son cœur, & la source du mal qu'il fait; à moins que la grace du saint Esprit, que Dieu distribuë suffisament à tous les hommes, ne le tourne tout-à-fait au bien." (p. 193).

C'est toutefois, répétons-le, le dernier paragraphe de la *Réponse*[8] qui paraît le plus imprégné de ce fidéisme, donné à la fois comme seul refuge contre l'attaque pyrrhonienne, et comme le fruit même que le croyant peut recueillir de cette attaque. C'est bien de ce pouvoir délétère du scepticisme à l'égard de la théologie que part la "réponse" finale du médecin philosophe à son interlocuteur théologien,[9] pour le rassurer aussitôt au nom de la supériorité des "raisons toutes Célestes" que la seconde peut opposer aux "démonstrations les plus évidentes" du premier,[10] supériorité qui tient à la source divine où elle puise ces raisons.[11]

On peut cependant douter, c'est le moins qu'on puisse dire, de la fidélité de Gaultier à l'orientation dont se réclame Bayle dans les passages dont s'inspire la *Réponse*, et de la sincérité du fidéisme ainsi affiché.

III. SCEPTICISME ET MATÉRIALISME

Il me paraît en effet difficile de ne pas reconnaître à ce dernier paragraphe, où la théologie est censée soumettre à sa loi "la

---

[8] p. 199–207.

[9] "[. . .] si cette même Philosophie [*scil. celle des sceptiques*], qui épluche les choses si scrupuleusement selon les seules régles de la raison naturelle; qui les tourne de tous les côtez, & les suit dans tous les récoins, sans en faire aucun jugement, s'introduisoit aux apartements de la Théologie, sur ce que ces deux Sciences ne sont point encore convenuës de leurs limites, elle y causeroit du desordre capable de boulverser ses plus assûrez fondemens." (p. 200).

[10] "Mais ne l'apréhendez pas; car quand elle a osé y paroître, & qu'elle s'est mise en devoir d'en manier les préceptes, de les embroüiller selon sa méthode, & de faire perdre la droiture des idées que nous en avons, elle n'a jamais poussé loin ses attaques ni ses vaines récherches. Car cette Divine Science les a toûjours términées avec avantage, & n'a point manqué de la réduire au silence; luy rémontrant que toutes ses raisons & ses démonstrations les plus évidentes, ne concluent rien contr'elle, & ne sont de son propre aveu même, d'aucun poids, dans l'ordre naturel où elle les débite : car quand elle les employe pour luy faire guer-[201]re, comme elle fait à toutes les autres Sciences, elle les réjette incontinent, comme raisons douteuses & incertaines; le principal de ses principes étant d'oposer à toute sorte de conclusions, une autre conclusion de même poids & d'égale consequence, dont ensuite elle ne fait plus de cas. Ainsi la Théologie luy oposant la force de ses raisons toutes Celestes & toûjours triomphantes, luy fait mettre bas les armes en le moment; la chasse de ses retranchemens avec une superiorité sans égale, & la couvre de confusion & de honte." (p. 200–201).

[11] "Mais, Monsieur, je sçay que j'écris à un Théologien qui connoît présentement mieux que je ne fais les défauts de la Philosophie Sceptique, & qui voit assez qu'elle ne sçauroit porter que de faux coups à la Théologie; puisque cette Divine Science ne tire ses raisons que de la parole de Dieu, qui engendre dans nos cœurs une persuasion & une Foy vive sans évidence; au lieu [203] que l'autre tire les siennes de la Nature seulement, qui produisent en l'esprit une persuasion à la verité; mais qui est accompagnée d'idées claires & distinctes." (p. 202–203).

philosophie'' – (et pas seulement, notons-le, la philosophie sceptique . . .), – et ce en dépit des "raisons" et "démonstrations les plus
évidentes" qui appartiennent à celle-ci (p. 200), des raisons qu'elle
tire "de la Nature seulement, qui produisent en l'esprit une persuasion à la verité; mais qui est accompagnée d'idées claires et distinctes" (p. 203), opposées à la "Foy vive sans évidence" dont se
prévaut la théologie, – de ne pas reconnaître, donc, à ce paragraphe
un caractère profondément sarcastique, à peine dissimulé sous les
méandres du développement, et les maladresses sans doute feintes
dont l'auteur prétend s'excuser.

Méandres et maladresses apparentes me paraissent en l'occurrence être le fait d'une tactique libertine éprouvée, à laquelle ressor-
tissent également les professions de foi qui ponctuent le développement, et dont le caractère conventionnel rappelle par exemple
celles sur lesquelles s'ouvrait et se fermait quelques dizaines d'années auparavant le traité d'athéisme radical qu'était le *Theophrastus
Redivivus*.

Le scepticisme exposé par Bayle et utilisé par lui au profit, au
moins apparent, d'une apologétique fidéiste, est en effet l'objet,
chez son ex-coreligionnaire, d'un gauchissement matérialiste systé-
matique. Cette inflexion se manifeste, dès le titre de la *Réponse*, dans
l'affirmation selon laquelle "la Vie & la Mort des Minéraux, des
Métaux, des Plantes & des Animaux, avec tous leurs attributs, ne
sont que des façons d'être de la même substance, à laquelle ces
modifications n'ajoûtent & n'ôtent rien", et les trois premières
pages du texte lui-même,[12] qui développent un monisme maté-

---

[12] "Pour ne pas tenir d'avantage vôtre esprit en suspend, sur les sentimens des
Philosophes Sceptiques, qui pensent comme vous le sçavez, Monsieur, que la Vie
et la Mort sont la même chose : Je vous diray d'abord que le fondement de leur
Philosophie est, qu'il n'y a dans la Nature qu'un premier principe, ou qu'une
substance, dont les attributs essentiels sont par tout semblables; que cette substance est la base & le fondement de tous les Etres qui y sont; que son essence nous
est absolument inconnuë; qu'elle est [6] étenduë, ayant ses parties les unes hors
des autres; qu'elle est imperceptible & divisible; qu'elle est impénétrable; puisqu'un pied cubique de cette substance, joint à un autre pied cubique, n'en sçauroit
jamais faire un pied cubique seulement; qu'elle est aveugle, insensible, & sans
connoissance, & non pourtant sans force ny vertu; qu'elle est indifferente à être
cecy ou cela; qu'elle est mobile & pliable en tous sens; & que, comme un Prothée,
elle est susceptible de toutes sortes de formes, n'y ayant rien, qui n'en puisse
naître; mais faisant tout nécessairement sans sçavoir ce qu'elle fait : Ses ordon-
nances, pour ainsi dire, & ses arrêts, consistant en ce qu'elle execute seulement ses
efets, après en avoir exactement établi les causes.
Ne vous semble-t'il point déjà, Monsieur, que cette substance, soit qu'elle engendre les corps, soit qu'elle les corrompe, est toûjours la même, comme de la cire que
l'on dispose differemment : car elle n'est nulle part sans ses attributs essentiels; &

rialiste, d'inspiration ou au moins d'illustration biologique. Celui-ci fait, dans les paragraphes mêmes du début qui portent le plus nettement l'empreinte baylienne, l'objet d'une sorte de juxtaposition par laquelle les conclusions qui le favorisent et les arguments qu'il suscite sont accolés à ceux que Bayle tire de la philosophie cartésienne et postcartésienne;[13] il est sans cesse rappelé comme un leitmotiv tout au long de l'ouvrage, et l'on peut y trouver le modèle du néo-spinozisme répandu à l'époque des Lumières, encore qu'il ne semble bien rien devoir à l'œuvre de Spinoza.[14]

C'est cette signification matérialiste prêtée par Gaultier au "scepticisme" qui caractérise en effet le plus nettement la longue

---

que la difference qui arrive [7] dans ses générations & dans ses corruptions, ne vient que des qualitez sensibles, qu'elle prend & qu'elle perd à succession de temps. Mais si ces qualitez sensibles, comme les Sceptiques le soûtiennent, ne sont point dans les objets, où nous les raportons, & qu'elles ne soient rien dans ces objets, que de pures illusions, il faut que la substance, qui se corrompt, soit la même que celle qui s'engendre; ainsi la substance qui est morte, ne doit point differer de celle qui est vivante; par consequent la Vie & la Mort sont une seule & même chose, ou une même substance." (p. 5–7).

[13] Cf les deux alinéas finaux du § [1] : "Si aprés être assûré par l'experience, que nos idées & nos sentimens ne sont point dans les objets, où nous les raportons, nous jettons les yeux sur l'esprit de l'homme, qui est le sujet de nos idées, nous verrons, qu'entent qu'il est une créature, il ne peut être un premier principe d'action : il ne peut donc agir que par des causes exterieures, sans quoy il est tranquille & dans l'inaction, à peu prés comme il l'est dans le someil, où il n'est point traversé de songes; ainsi l'esprit n'agissant que par des causes exterieures, & l'action de ces causes se terminant en luy-même, il en resulte des sensations & des idées qui ne peuvent se trouver ailleurs qu'en nous. Qu'on le prenne comme on voudra, soit de la part des objects, soit de la part du principe de nos sensations, les Sceptiques prouvent, ou prétendent prouver que nos [11] sensations & nos idées nous appartiennent, & qu'elles ne réprésentent point les objets tels qu'ils sont; bien que nous les raportions hors de nous, semblables à ce que nous nous les imaginons. D'où il suit, que nous ne pouvons rien sçavoir des choses de dehors; & que nous ne connoissons que les passions & les perceptions, que les objets exterieurs produisent en nous, & qui ne peuvent être ailleurs, qu'en nous. En effet nous ne sçavons point assez, si l'Homme a naturellement le cerveau fait de sorte, qu'il ne trouve pas tant, ce qui est absolument vray, que ce qui luy convient, & qui s'accomode à sa nature.

Ce qui semble confirmer leur pensée, c'est qu'ils prétendent que l'esprit ou l'ame de l'Homme, est comme son corps, une production de la nature, ou de la substance universelle, qui seule fait la réalité de tous les Etres qui sont dans le monde. Comme cette substance est originairement insensible, & qu'elle ne sçait ce qu'elle fait quand elle agit, il faut que la connoissance qui naît de ses ouvrages, [12] soit non-seulement fort incertaine; puis qu'elle vient d'une cause si variable : mais qu'elle soit encore dans le sujet qui connoît sans que ce sujet puisse dire que ses sensations où [*sic*] ses idées representent les choses précisément comme elles sont." (p. 9–11).

[14] Voir mon étude "Le médecin Gaultier, *Parité de la vie et de la mort*, et Spinoza" dans *Spinoza au XVIIIème siècle. Actes des journées d'études organisées les 6 et 13 decembre 1987 à la Sorbonne*, eds. O. Bloch, Hélène Politis, Paris : Méridiens Klincksieck 1990, 105–120.

digression philosophique qui occupe le centre de la *Réponse*. Après les trois paragraphes déjà mentionnés que l'auteur consacre pour l'essentiel à l'exposition de l'argumentation proprement sceptique, et après le développement (§§4 à 22) de la thèse de la "parité de la vie et de la mort" et de ses conséquences à partir d'exemples tirés des divers règnes de la nature, et d'un "petit traité d'anatomie", entendons d'une embryologie épigénétiste, il se lance en effet, à l'occasion de la conséquence qu'il a tirée de son exposé, à savoir que "La vie des Animaux, ou ce qui est la même chose, leur ame sensitive ne peut donc être que les fonctions qui naissent de leurs organes" (p. 66), dans une critique du cartésianisme (§§24 à 29, pp. 69–87), qui s'étend bien au-delà de la théorie de l'animal machine pour s'en prendre à l'ensemble de la métaphysique carté-sienne, puis, après un retour aux conséquences psychophysiologi-ques qu'il tire quant à lui de ses conceptions en matière d'"anato-mie" sur la question de l'origine de la conscience ou du "sentiment des Animaux" (§§30 à 36, pp. 87–106), revient à la polémique (§§37 à 56, pp. 106–168) contre ce "que nous aprennent sur ce sujet les Physiciens, tant anciens que modernes." (p. 106, au début du §37), rubrique sous laquelle il s'en prend principalement aux théories de Malebranche, à l'occasion desquelles il s'attaque aussi à Spinoza (§§39 à 46, pp. 110–144), pour finir sur une attaque livrée contre les conceptions physiques de Hartsoeker (§§51 à 56, pp. 154–168).

Au cœur de cette polémique philosophique, qui ne s'embarrasse pas de subtilité, se trouve, comme dans la vulgate de la critique libertine, puis du matérialisme des Lumières, le refus radical des preuves de l'existence de Dieu, des représentations qu'en proposent les théologies et métaphysiques anciennes et nouvelles, de celles qu'elles prétendent donner de la spiritualité et de l'immortalité de l'âme, renvoyées à la seule foi, dans des parenthèses ou incises qui, il faut bien le dire, sont très fugitives.

Plus proche, apparemment, bien que là encore il n'y ait sans doute pas de dépendance effective, des positions spinozistes de l'Appendice d'*Ethique* I et de la Préface d'*Ethique* IV, apparaît la critique des normes et valeurs traditionnelles que Gaultier parsème, en quelque sorte, à travers la *Réponse*.

On la trouve d'abord dans la première série des conséquences, relativistes ou nihilistes, que tire Gaultier de l'énoncé primitif de sa thèse, en l'occurrence dans le §[10]: "L'homme court toujours après rien", où il prend l'exemple de la *beauté* pour montrer la dépendance d'une telle valeur à la "nature" et à la "substance universelle", par l'intermédiaire des deux facteurs : "tempéra-

ment", et "habitude", entre lesquels, sous le nom d'"organisation", et d'"éducation", débattront les matérialistes du XVIIIe
siècle pour savoir à qui donner la priorité, voire l'exclusivité dans la
formation de l'homme, et donc de ses normes et valeurs.[15]

On la retrouve assez fugitivement à l'intérieur de la digression
philosophique centrale, à la fin du § [43], à propos de la question
de la liberté chez Malebranche, où Gaultier prend vigoureusement
parti pour le nécessitarisme.[16]

---

[15] "Si l'on prenoit un autre sujet que les actions & les mouvemens de l'homme,
pour confirmer que tout est vanité, & que tout n'est rien, la beauté peut en servir
d'exemple; car elle est comme tous les objets de la nature, des modes de la
substance universelle. Voyons donc ce que c'est que la beauté, qui enchante si fort
l'homme, & sçachons, si elle est autre chose que modes, & un beau rien? Nous
reconnoîtrons ce qu'elle est & ce qu'elle vaut, si par gradation nous remontons
jusqu'à son origine. La beauté dépend entierement du goût, & de l'opinion; ce
goût & cette opinion viennent de nôtre temperament, & des impressions desquelles nous sommes prévenus : ce temperament naît du climat & des alimens que
nous prenons; & ces impressions tirent leur origine d'une habitude à voir, & à
entendre toûjours les mêmes choses, enfin si l'on re-[32]monte à la source de tout
cela, l'on se trouve dans le cours admirable de la nature, & l'on est arrêté à la
substance universelle, par où tout commence, & où tout se termine. Vous connois-
sez donc par là, que tout est fait sur le même patron, & que tout vient de la même
substance : mais comme ce premier & ce dernier principe; car il est le commence-
ment & la fin des choses naturelles, fait tout aveuglement & sans connoissance : ce
qu'il y a de plus beau n'est pas plus à estimer que ce qu'il y a de plus laid; puisque
les causes en sont également réelles & nécessaires, & qu'il n'y a pas plus de peine à
la nature à faire l'un que l'autre. Les choses ne sont donc belles ou laides, que par
raport à nôtre goût & à nos opinions; & ne sont ni belles ni laides par raport à la
nature qui les produit." (p. 31–32).

[16] "La liberté naturelle que nous avons, est l'effet de quantité de causes qui se
succedent les unes aux autres, & qui concourent unanimement à le produire; à peu
prés comme un Horloge qui marque les Heures, le mouvement de la Lune, celui
du Soleil, &c. Car, si l'on suposoit que l'Horloge a du sentiment, elle peut
s'a-[120]percevoir comme nous qu'elle fait les choses sans contrainte & avec
liberté, quoyqu'elle les fasse par des causes nécessaires. Cette liberté n'exclud donc
point la nécessité des causes : d'où l'on voit que la liberté d'indifference que nous
avons, à prendre ce terme à la rigueur, n'est point une chose qui vienne de la
nature. Ce n'est pas que nous ne nous trouvions souvant dans un état, où les
causes par les raports qu'elles ont ensemble, sont indifferentes à produire un effet
plûtôt qu'un autre : mais cela n'établit point la liberté d'indifference absoluë. Car
comme la Vie est dans un contiuel [*sic*] changement, & qu'elle n'est pas un
moment dans la même assiéte, il s'ôte ou il survient toûjours quelque cause qui fait
pencher la balance qui étoit auparavant en équilibre. C'est ainsi qu'un homme qui
est dans un état nonchalant, qui ne pense à rien & qui ne sçauroit dire ce qu'il
veut, se tire de cette indifference par le vin qu'il boit avec ses amis : car il en est
égayé; il a des pensées qui ne lui seroient point venuës, & des désirs qui le portent
à faire bien des [130] choses; au lieu qu'un autre qui est fort éveillé, qui pense à
beaucoup d'affaires & se forme des desseins, perd tout cela, & n'est plus touché de
rien, que de dormir, s'il prend de l'*Opium* : D'où il est clair, que des causes
naturelles font pencher la balance, qu'elles donnent nos inclinations, quoy qu'elles
soient des causes nécessaires; il suit encore que nous devons sentir, faire les choses

Mais il faut sans doute voir encore dans cette dispersion et cette discrétion relatives la marque d'une tactique libertine, car aussi bien la critique de la "beauté" que celle du libre-arbitre sont remises en mémoire lorsque, dans les dernières sections de l'œuvre, l'auteur tire les conséquences qui s'ensuivent selon lui des positions des "Sceptiques" du point de vue de la morale (§58, "La Justice et l'Injustice, la Vertu et le Vice ne sont point des êtres réels"[17], pp. 170–172), puis, après un retour aussi abrupt qu'inopiné à son "traité d'anatomie", et avant le chapitre de conclusion déjà mentionné, énonce en cinq paragraphes (§§65 à 69, pp. 186–199) une nouvelle série de conséquences métaphysiques et morales, où il apparaît plus que jamais que, à travers la question de l' "âme sensitive des bêtes", c'est bien de l'homme et de sa raison ou ses raisons qu'il s'agit. L'on peut y voir en effet que si (§65 – où se

---

librement; quoy que nous les fassions nécessairement. Ainsi la volonté qui tient toûjours au bout de nos penchans ou de nos inclinations, doit aussi être l'effet de quantité de causes nécessaires, & non d'une seule. Cependant, bien que nôtre ame se laisse souvent entraîner par la force des causes naturelles, & qu'elle y succombe quelque fois; cela n'empêche point qu'elle n'ait la force & la liberté de faire ou de ne pas faire les choses; puisque cette liberté est une de ses propriétez essentielles. Mais, comme cette liberté de nôtre ame est toute Théologique & Spirituelle, quand on la considere sans aucun raport au corps, ce n'est [131] point de cette espece de liberté dont je parle; je me contente de la croire, comme l'Eglise l'enseigne." (p. 128–131).

[17] "Cet état d'incertitude où se trouvent les Sceptiques, les entraîne à d'autres extrémitez : Il leur semble que la Nature comprend tout, & qu'une chose n'est pas meilleure que l'autre. C'est pourquoy ils s'imaginent que la Justice & l'Injustice, la Vertu & le Vice, le Bien & le Mal sont seulement des éfets de la Nature. Ainsi ils tirent aisément de ce principe l'origine du [171] mal, que la Théologie ne découvre point sans peine. Ils prétendent donc que le Bien & le Mal, la Vertu & le Vice, la Justice & l'Injustice sont une seule & même chose, comme ils le disent de la Vie & de la Mort. Pour le prouver, ils rémontent de ces éfets par gradation jusqu'à leur origine, à peu prés comme on l'a déjà fait de la Beauté & de la Laideur; puis réconnoissant que ces choses se terminent toutes également dans le cours admirable de la Nature, ils les régardent comme ses propres fruits; puisqu'ils viennent de même source. Mais comme la Nature agît en aveugle, sans sçavoir ce qu'elle fait, & qu'ainsi on ne peut luy imputer ni bien ni mal, justice ni injustice, Vertu ni Vice, ils pensent que tout cela n'est rien que par raport à nôtre devoir, & à l'entretien de la société civile; non plus que l'ordre & le desordre qui se voyent partout dans le monde; car chàque chose est toûjours placée où la Nature l'a mise, & non ailleurs. Il n'y a donc point d'ordre ni de desordre dans la Nature que par raport à nos sens & aux jugemens que nous faisons. En éfet [172] ce que les uns voyent bien ordonné, les autre ne le voyent pas de même; une chose est un bien à celuy-cy, qui est un mal à celui-là; la justice qui s'exerce dans un lieu, est une injustice en l'autre : Il en est de même de la vertu & du vice, qui se confondent selon les lieux, les temps, les opinions & les Coûtumes. Ces choses donc, comme toutes les autres de cette trempe, ne sont rien dans la Nature, & n'y ont point d'existence particuliere; ainsi elles ne sont quelque chose, que par raport à nous, comme les jugemens vrais ou faux que nous faisons." (p. 170–172).

trouve une référence expresse au passage antérieur sur la beauté) "Les inclinations et les aversions des Bêtes sont un concours d'actions, qui se lient et se succèdent, comme par une chaîne", il est possible de produire une "Expérience qui montre sensiblement que nous pouvons prendre les inclinations des Bêtes et que l'esprit suit les penchants du corps" – (§66), que (§68) "Nos Mœurs viennent de la Nature; les Mœurs des Payens en sont une raison sensible"[18], – et qu'enfin (§69) "Les bonnes et les mauvaises habitudes sont la

---

[18] "Ce qu'on a dit, porte à croire, que les Mœurs de l'homme viennent de même de l'humide radical, qui fait toute la nature de son corps, comme il fait celle des Bêtes. Cet humide radical est donc le siége & la cause immediate de ses passions, le fond corromptu de son cœur, & la source du mal qu'il fait; à moins que la grace du saint Esprit, que Dieu distribuë suffisament à tous les hommes, ne le tourne tout-à-fait au bien. C'est ce même principe ou son tempérament qui fait pencher son esprit, & qui l'incline vers sa pente, luy faisant vouloir souvent des choses contre son devoir, contre son jugement & contre sa conscience. Saint Paul l'enseigne assez, quend il dit : *Je fais le mal que je* [194] *ne voudrois point faire, & je ne fais point le bien que je voudrais faire.* Ovide aussi l'avoit bien vû; puisqu'il fait dire à Medée, *Video meliora probóque, deteriora sequor* : D'où il est clair, que la volonté est le penchant de nôtre nature, & qu'ainsi elle est l'éfet d'une infinité de causes, & non d'une seule, comme on se l'imagine; puisque ce penchant force & entraîne l'esprit, & le soûmet tellement à ses loix, qu'il le contraint souvent bon gré malgré de le suivre contre sa propre conscience. Cela est évident, à considerer un yvrogne qui est d'ailleurs impudique; car il sçait bien que l'yvrognerie & l'impudicité sont des crimes : mais il y trouve tant d'attraits & de si grands charmes, qu'il les commet avec plaisir. D'où il suit que ce n'est pas tant la persuasion de la verité, qui le détermine à agir, que les passions présentes du cœur, le tour de sa nature & l'inclination qu'il a déja, ou qu'il aquiert par des habitudes. Si l'on en doute, je demanderois volontiers quel autre principe il peut y avoir des actions de l'homme; & pourquoy le Payen, le Juif, le Chrétien & le [195] Mahometan, dont les opinions sont si differentes sur la maniere de servir Dieu, & de vivre selon les loix de la bien-seance, se copient & se ressemblent si fort les uns les autres, qu'on diroit qu'ils sont tous de la même croyance, s'il étoit vray que leur croyance pust absolument diriger leurs mœurs & leurs actions : car ils sont tous également portez à l'avarice, à l'ambition, à l'envie, au désir de se vanger, à la haine, à la colere; en un mot à tous les vices & à toutes les Vertus qui peuvent satisfaire leurs passions. Il est donc vray-semblable, s'il n'est pas certain, que les passions & les penchans de l'homme, de quelque opinion qu'il soit imbu, viennent de son temperament, comme d'un fond propre à les produire; & que les sentimens Philosophiques & Théologiques, où il est, ne portent sur sa complexion, que peu ou point d'influance, capable de la réprimer ou de la faire aller un meilleur train. Aussi la Nature aplique ces caracteres assez également dans le cœur de l'homme, nonobstant la différence de ses opinions; & l'experience aprend qu'il les suit avec beaucoup d'acord. L'on [196] voit donc que l'opinion ne change guére les mœurs ou les tempéramens : & que ce n'est presque point son caractere de les bien ou mal diriger. En éfet, si un yvrogne ne dérobe pas, ce n'est point la crainte des jugemens de Dieu qui l'en empêche; car si cela étoit, il s'abstiendroit de boire comme de dérober. Puis donc qu'il ne le fait pas, il est à croire que s'il ne dérobe point, c'est qu'il n'y trouve pas d'attraits, & que son tempérament ne l'y porte pas, ou qu'il craint l'infamie & le suplice, à quoy il est plus sensible qu'aux douceurs qu'il tireroit du larcin." (p. 193–196).

même chose, si l'on s'en tient aux principes du Sceptisme [*sic*]"[19].

La naturalisation de l'homme dans ses actions et dans ses choix, eux-mêmes ramenés aux effets des penchants naturels, la référence au thème de la "vertu des payens", ont ici une coloration libertine peu douteuse. Il est vrai que Gaultier doit s'inspirer de l'utilisation faite par Bayle de ce dernier thème au profit de sa thèse de l'indifférence de la morale aux croyances, qui fonde chez lui celle de l'athée vertueux, et de la possibilité d'une société d'athées.[20] Mais il est clair que l'on est dans la *Réponse* plus près de la source libertine que de son utilisation baylienne, avec le relativisme radical des

---

[19] "Si donc les Mœurs & les actions de l'homme, bonnes ou mauvaises, naissent de sa Nature, & qu'elles n'ayent point d'autre origine, comme se l'imaginent les Sceptiques : il faut dire qu'elles ne sont que l'enchaînement d'une infinité de mo-[197]des, que subit l'humide radical, tant par la construction qu'il fait, des parties solides du corps, que par la Nature & le mouvement des liqueurs qu'il établit & qu'il engendre de même de sa propre substance. D'où il suit que l'humide radical, qui est ainsi le premier principe du corps de l'homme, & qui en fait les parties & les humeurs, est capable de toute sorte de flexions; puisqu'il y produit tant de choses differentes & si mêlées. Il peut donc prendre, comme il se voit clairement par les Hydrophobiques, des tours & des penchants qui deviennent les auteurs de toutes ses actions, du Vice & de la Vertu, des bonnes & des mauvaises Mœurs. C'est ainsi qu'un homme qui n'a guére bû de vin dans sa vie, contracte insensiblement l'envie de boire beaucoup, en fréquentant des yvrognes; ce qui se fait, parce que le vin luy enracine de plus en plus le désir de boire, donnant à sa nature le branle, qui l'a fait pencher de ce côté-là, & qui l'emporte sur toutes ses autres passions.

Si un homme naturellement chaste devient débauché, à voir des gens adonnez à [198] l'impudicité; c'est parce que les parties qui servent à la génération, de foibles & refroidies qu'elles étoient auparavant, deviennent plus sensibles & plus échaufées par l'exercice, & qu'elles engendrent une semence plus vive & plus abondante; donnant par là plus de sensibilité & de plaisir qu'il n'en auroit eu sans cela. Les mauvaises habitudes qu'on contracte, & qu'il est si difficile de déraciner; parce qu'elles sont enfoncées & si dominantes dans la nature de l'homme, qu'elles le ménagent entierement, viennent donc des inflections que peut subir sa nature : d'où il paroît que nos actions naissent toutes du tempérament, à moins que la grace n'y intervienne, qu'elle n'en détourne ce qu'il y a de mauvais, & qu'elle ne le range à son devoir. Les habitudes consistent donc dans le tour & le penchant de la complexion; et ce tour fait ordinairement ceder la place aux causes qui luy sont contraires, & les emporte comme un torrent, qui entraîne tout vers sa pente. Ce qui aprend que les Mœurs, les passions, les penchans & les habitudes de l'homme, viennent de la même source, du [199] même tempérament ou de la même substance, qui se modifie differament. En éfet selon les principes du Sceptisme, que les bonnes inclinations mortifient les mauvaises, ou que les mauvaises fassent éclipser les bonnes; elles ne different pas plus les unes que les autres du même sujet, que le mouvement de l'aiguïlle d'une montre, qui marque les heures bien ou mal, differe de l'aiguïlle. Ainsi les bonnes & les mauvaises Mœurs, qu'elles se succedent les unes aux autres, ou qu'elles soient éteintes par la mort, ne different qu'en aparance, & ne sont au fond qu'une seule & même chose, ou que le même corps." (p. 196–199).

[20] Voir en particulier les *Pensées diverses sur la comète* (1683[2] – la 1ère édition étant celle de la *Lettre sur les comètes* à Rotterdam en 1682 : Gaultier a pu lire l'une ou

valeurs, voire l'immoralisme, que développe au nom des "Scepti-ques" le §[69], où sont mis sur le même plan le Bien et Mal, les "bonnes" et les "mauvaises mœurs", les "vices" et les "vertus", un plan qui n'est autre que celui du mouvement, entendons le mouve-ment d'un *corps*.[21] Et cela surtout si l'on considère que, doctrinale-ment, ce paragraphe constitue la véritable fin de l'opuscule tout entier, auprès duquel le paragraphe final prend figure de pirouette sarcastique.

L'on est donc loin de l'appel à la conscience intérieure du bien et du mal que, contre leur rattachement fallacieux à la croyance religieuse, Bayle tirait quant à lui[22] des considérations dont s'ins-pire Gaultier, et bien plus près de l'amoralisme d'un La Mettrie dans l'*Antisénèque*, dans la mesure où, comme l'a montré Theo Verbeek, celui-ci dépend davantage qu'on ne le croit d'ordinaire de la tradition libertine, et de ses prolongements clandestins. Et ce dévoiement naturaliste, matérialiste, et amoraliste, que Gaultier fait subir aux orientations bayliennes me paraît caractéristique de l'ensemble de son attitude vis-à-vis du scepticisme baylien et de son rapport à la religion : d'outil proposé aux âmes religieuses pour humilier la raison métaphysique et théologique au profit d'une foi réformée libérale et d'une moralité de la conscience intérieure, le scepticisme devient le masque et l'instrument d'un matérialisme et d'un athéisme, pour qui les professions de foi et les protestations de respect pour la religion et la théologie font office à la fois de couver-ture et de sarcasme, de la part d'un ancien coreligionnaire de Bayle. Ancien coreligionnaire qui, peut-être au contact même du

---

l'autre en Hollande, où il se trouvait au moins à la fin de 1683 et au début de 1684) – voir dans les extraits des *Œuvres diverses* procurés par Alain Niderst, Paris, Ed. Sociales, 1971, p. 72 sqq., et cf. dans la *Réponse* le §[58] qui se réfère à la question de l'origine du mal, topos baylien par excellence.

[21] p. 196–199 (notons au passage que l'exemple de l'ivrogne pourrait bien lui aussi venir de Bayle *Pens. Div. Com.*, dans l'édition citée, p. 79). Pour les parallèles libertins, cf, par ex., dans le *Theophrastus Redivivus*, le Traité VI sur la vie selon la nature, où l'on trouve au centre du chapitre I l'idée que "il n'y a rien qui soit par nature un mal, rien d'illicite, rien de malhonnête" (p. 794, éd. Canziani.-Paganini, Florence, 1981 – et cf. p. 796–7 et 800), et qui insiste très fortement sur l'absence de différence entre l'homme et l'animal (cf. ib. p. 803–804), d'où le chapitre II qui porte tout entier sur cette "egalité et communauté entre tous les êtres animés", sans différence autre que d'espèce entre l'homme et tous les autres animaux, – et le chapitre III sur cette égalité naturelle elle-même (contre les conventions de la loi . . .) – thèmes libertins par excellence, qui justifient dans le chapitre IV et dernier (portrait du sage : *Icon sapientis*) la défense d'une sagesse amoraliste et individualiste, du type de celle qu'illustraient les sonnets amœbées de des Yveteaux et des Barreaux.

[22] Cf. *loc. cit.* p. 75.

scepticisme de ce dernier, avait, à en croire ce que laissait entendre en 1685 un autre de ses coreligionnaires, et non des moindres, perdu dès cette date la foi, et était peut-être d'ores et déjà passé à l'athéisme.[23]

IV. Les Extraits Clandestins

Reste à dire, dans le cadre de notre présente rencontre, quelques mots de la destinée de l'ouvrage du médecin Gaultier.

On a dit que cet ouvrage a servi de matière, à une époque et dans des conditions que je ne suis pas en mesure de préciser, mais dont rien jusqu'à présent ne semble attester le caractère précoce, à la constitution d'extraits manuscrits dont nous possédons deux specimens : l'un, correspondant sans doute à la version la plus ancienne, est reproduit dans le recueil 2239 de la Bibliothèque de l'Arsenal sous le titre de *Nouvelle Philosophie Sceptique*, l'autre se trouve dans le recueil 1192 de la Bibliothèque Mazarine sous le titre de *Parité de la Vie et de la Mort*. Ce dernier titre est repris dans une version imprimée, sans doute en 1771, que donne un recueil de *Pièces Philosophiques*, version finale qui dérive apparemment des deux versions manuscrites.

Chacune des trois versions comporte quelques traits originaux, particulièrement du point de vue qui nous occupe.

La première, qui fait au reste précéder les extraits eux-mêmes de "Reflexions sur l'attachement aux préjugés. L'immaterialité de l'ame et l'existence de Dieu" (*Nouv.Philos.Scept.*, Arsenal 2239, pp. 1–13), qui ont un caractère ouvertement athée et matérialiste, vend, si j'ose dire, d'emblée la mèche, en déclarant, dès le début de l "Avertissement" qui suit, que :

> Comme l'auteur de cet ouvrage vouloit cacher ses sentimens en developpant la philosophie sceptique et en l'adressant à un Théologien il a pris des précautions pour eviter la censure et la mauvaise

---

[23] On trouve en effet dans la copie d'une lettre de Maximilien Misson au médecin Pinet de Niort, en date du 10 novembre 1685, conservée à la Bibliothèque Municipale de Poitiers, ms 535, la phrase suivante (p. 367) où, après avoir fait mention de plusieurs nouveaux convertis, parmi lesquels son correspondant, et les avoir plaints de leur abjuration, il écrit à propos d'Abraham Gaultier: "Je crois qu'ils passent de mauvais quarts d'heure, quand ils ont la tête sur l'oreiller. Pour notre ami Gaultier, je le plains plus que tous. Que le Dieu que j'adore, me veuille garder d'un état pareil au sien", – état dans lequel, vu le contexte, on doit bien évidemment reconnaître l'état spirituel que reflètera quelque trente ans plus tard la *Réponse à un théologien*.

humeur des critiques; en avertissant qu'il ne pretend parler dans cette dissertation phisique que des animaux *etc.* [l'extracteur reproduit ici l'"Avis" de la *Réponse*] (p. 13ter)

et en terminant ledit Avertissement sur la remarque que le "systeme" de Gaultier lui-même "n'est que pur Atheisme et Materialisme" (p. 16). Après quoi, dans le style indirect qui est le propre de cette version, il épingle au passage les déclarations orthodoxes de la *Réponse* en les signalant comme de simples précautions destinées à endormir les censeurs,[24] et, à propos du paragraphe final, qu'il résume très rapidement, remarque :

> C'est ici que notre Medecin, après avoir caché ses propres sentimens sous le nom des sceptiques du systeme desquels il ne paroit donner qu'une idée sans l'adopter finit en disant que cette philosophie sceptique parle seulement de la vie et de la mort naturelle, sans pousser ses vuës jusqu'à la vie et à la mort spirituelle, qui au sortir de ce Monde, dureront éternellement pour etre la recompense de ceux qui auront fait bien ou mal.
>
> On voit aisément en lisant ce dernier chapitre que pour susciter l'aprobation des Docteurs auxquels il soumet la censure de son ouvrage, l'auteur a crû nécessaire de soumettre la philosophie aux loix de la [91] Théologie; c'est pourquoi il dit que toutes les fois que la philosophie a osé entreprendre d'en manier les precepts, de les embrouiller selon sa methode, et de faire perdre la droiture des idées que nous en avons, celle ci lui opposant la force de ses raisons toutes celestes et toujours triomphantes, l'a couverte de honte et de confusion. (p. 90–91)

C'est au reste à propos de cette dernière déclaration de l'extracteur-rédacteur de la *Nouvelle Philosophie Sceptique* que celui du *Parité de la Vie et de la Mort* manuscrit marque le plus nettement sa dépendance à son égard.

Il commence en effet, dans un style direct qui est censé reproduire le discours de Gaultier, le résumé de ce dernier paragraphe sur un désaveu exprès de cette interprétation de son prédécesseur :

> Peut être croira-t-on que j'ai caché mes propres sentimens sous le nom des sceptiques, du système desquels je viens de donner une idée. Peut être croira-t-on que, partisan de cette philosophie, je n'ai pas [102] seulement entendu parler de la vie et de la mort naturelles, mais que j'ai poussé mes vues jusqu'à la vie et la mort Spirituelles qui

---

[24] Voir par exemple, dans le paragraphe où se trouve la critique de Spinoza, la phrase suivante: "L'auteur ramene tout ensuite à la Religion en disant que si Spinosa eut eu des égards pour elle, il auroit suivi des principes plus surs, qu'il auroit crû l'ame spirituelle et immortelle, que Dieu a tout créé etc. (Ceci est pour faire passer son ouvrage à l'approbation)" (p. 66).

au sortir de ce monde doivent durer éternellement à ce que disent les Théologiens. Je ne puis empêcher les conjectures, et suis trop instruit que toutes les fois que la philosophie a osé manier les principes de la théologie, on lui a reproché de les avoir embrouillés et fait perdre la droiture des idées qui en résultent. Mais que celle-ci auroit-elle à craindre de celle-là? Ses raisonnemens celestes ne sont-ils pas toujours surs de triompher?

(*Parité de la vie et de la mort*, Maz.1192, p. 101-102).

Ce propos presque final donne le ton de toute cette version, laquelle de feint bout en bout de faire parler dans le même style direct l'auteur du texte initial, puisqu'il y reprend à son compte, voire, à l'occasion, en les accentuant quelque peu, ses protestations d'orthodoxie, que le premier extracteur tenait pour fallacieuses.

Mais on ne doit voir là bien évidemment qu'une différence purement tactique, ce second extracteur, qui réduit quelque peu l'étendue de son texte par rapport au premier, ayant en général soin de reproduire sans du tout les atténuer les passages les plus scabreux que comportait la *Réponse* de Gaultier.

A cet égard, le rédacteur de l'imprimé final prend à son tour le parti d'une hypocrisie qui ne peut tromper personne : non seulement, en effet, reprenant soigneusement les mêmes passages, il en accentue à l'occasion, dans les remaniements de détail qu'il leur fait subir, les traits matérialistes, remplaçant par exemple plus d'une fois le terme "substance", par celui de "matière", ou en adapte les développements aux besoins de la polémique anticléricale des Lumières, substituant par exemple sans vergogne à la mention (exacte) du "Reverend Pere Lamy, bénédictin",[25] celle, fantaisiste, du "P. Lamy, Jésuite"[26] . . . , – mais encore ajoute de nombreux passages de son cru qui, sans du reste apporter d'idées originales ni d'altérations substantielles à la pensée de Gaultier, tendent aux mêmes effets d'accentuation et de modernisation.

Quelle que soit la tactique utilisée – et la divergence tient à la fois à la diversité des situations réelles ou intentionnelles, celle de la clandestinité stricte, qui permet de se passer de précautions oratoires, et celle de la publication officielle ou tolérée, et aux différences qui séparent la tradition libertine de son héritage des Lumières, – il semble bien qu'aucune des versions dérivées de la *Réponse* ne trahisse la pensée et les intentions du médecin Gaultier, et que ce soit à bon droit qu'elles se servent de son œuvre au profit

---

[25] *Réponse*, p. 131 – il s'agit en effet de Dom François Lamy.
[26] *Parité de la vie et de la mort* imprimé, p. 86.

de la propagande de l'aile radicale des Lumières : la *Réponse* doit, me semble-t-il, apparaître comme un relais très significatif, et qui a sans doute effectivement joué un rôle non négligeable, dans l'histoire du scepticisme, et du rapport entre scepticisme et religion, dans la mesure où elle opère directement le passage d'un scepticisme utilisé au profit de l'apologétique religieuse, tel que Bayle le présente pour sa part, à un scepticisme qui sert de couverture à l'athéisme et au matérialisme de l'époque des Lumières.

CONSTANCE BLACKWELL

DIOGENES LAERTIUS'S "LIFE OF PYRRHO" AND THE INTERPRETATION OF ANCIENT SCEPTICISM IN THE HISTORY OF PHILOSOPHY—STANLEY THROUGH BRUCKER TO TENNEMANN[1]

Research on the recovery of ancient scepticism in the Renaissance has concentrated on the recovery and use of Sextus Empiricus and Cicero's *De Academica*.[2] Charles Schmitt's comprehensive article, "The Rediscovery of Ancient Skepticism", specifically excluded Diogenes Laertius's "Life of Pyrrho" from consideration.[3] An historian of philosophy doing research on the "fortuna" of ancient scepticism in the seventeenth and eighteenth century can not ignore the work. A reading of the writings of the mid-eighteenth century historian of philosophy, Jacob Brucker, makes it clear that Diogenes Laertius's "Life of Pyrrho" had been read carefully and had been subject to substantial controversy among historians of philosophy and philosophers during the seventeenth and eighteenth centuries.[4] The controversy was not merely over the correct

---

[1] This paper is dedicated to the memory of Charles B. Schmitt, who pioneered the subject of the recovery of ancient scepticism. I should like to thank Richard Popkin for his interest in the topic of ancient scepticism in Brucker; this paper would not have been written without his interest and help. I should also like to thank C. Ligota and P. Salman for their helpful comments, as well as R. Bock and C. Strickland.

[2] Charles B. Schmitt, *Gianfrancesco Pico della Mirandola (1469–1533) and his Critique of Aristotle*, The Hague: Nijhoff, 1967; *Cicero Scepticus. A Study of the Influence of the* Academica *in the Renaissance*, The Hague: Nijhoff, 1972; "John Wolley (ca. 1530–1596) and the first Latin translation of Sextus Empiricus *Adversus logicos I*" in *The Sceptical Mode in Modern Philosophy. Essays in Honour of Richard Popkin*, eds. R.A. Watson, J.E. Force, Dordrecht: Nijhoff, 1988, 61–70; "The Rediscovery of Ancient Scepticism in Modern Times" in *Reappraisals in Renaissance Thought*, ed. Charles Webster, London: Variorum, 1989, chap. XII, 225–251; E. de Olaso, "Las Academicas de Ciceron y la filosofia renascentista", *International Studies in Philosophy* 7 (1975). For the impact of Zeno of Elea see Antonio Lamarra, "Scepticism and the Infinite" in *L'infinito in Leibniz. Problemi e Terminologia; Das Unendliche bei Leibniz. Problem und Terminologie*, ed. A. Lamarra, Rome: Ateneo, 1990, 95–118.

[3] See Schmitt, "The Rediscovery of Ancient Scepticism", p. 247, note 48.

[4] Brucker's first work on Pyrrho was *De Pyrrhone a Scepticismi universalis macula absolvendo*, Jena 1716, which was reprinted by Brucker in *Miscellanea historiae*

reading of key words or facts, but also and more importantly, over how to read the life as a whole, how that life elucidated the true nature of ancient scepticism and what Pyrrho's response to his philosophical training tells us about the intellectual development of Greek philosophers. At this time the "Life of Pyrrho" was read by certain historians of philosophy in various ways. For some the writing of the life was a mere exercise in collecting information about scepticism uncovered by seventeenth and eighteenth century classical scholarship, but others synthesized the information about the scepticism this classical scholarship had made available and began to reflect on how certain types of reasoning developed in philosophy. Both approaches are part of the history of the reputation of Pyrrho in the history of philosophy.

Much has been written lately on the historiography of philosophy. One view by a philosopher working in contemporary philosophy is Richard Rorty's in "The Historiography of Philosophy".[5] He has identified four genres of history of philosophy: the contextualist who places philosophy in its historical context, the rationalist who wants to converse with past philosophers in the terms of current philosophy, the *Geisteshistoriker* who studies the problematics of philosophers to give plausibility to a certain image of philosophy, and the doxographer. Rorty defines their books as those that "start from Thales or Descartes and wind up with some figure roughly contemporary with the author, ticking off what various figures traditionally called "philosophers" had to say about problems traditionally called "philosophical".[6] For the doxographer Rorty has nothing positive to say, claiming that such historians of philosophy "decorticate the thinkers they discuss" because they try to have all their thinkers discuss common problems following the formula of neo-Kantian notions of the central problems of philosophy. Recent scholarship into the history of the history of philosophy reveals that, far from being a nineteenth-century creation, history of philosophy was well developed as a subject in the eighteenth.[7]

---

vindelicorum philosophicae litteriae criticae olim sparsim edita, Augsburg 1748. Brucker's second article on Pyrrho in his history of philosophy is in the *Historia critica philosophiae*, published in six volumes between 1742 and 1767 at Leipzig. I have used the second edition of Leipzig 1767, vol. 1, 1317–1332. This chapter had been published in a German version in his *Kurze Fragen*, Ulm.1731–6, vol. 2.

[5] R. Rorty, "The historiography of philosophy: four genres" in *Philosophy in History*, eds. R. Rorty, J.B. Schneewind, Q. Skinner, Cambridge: Cambridge University Press, 1984, 49–75.

[6] Ibid., 61–2.

[7] For the bibliography of the historiography of philosophy see E. Garin, *Storia*

How various historians of philosophy were influenced by each other, how contemporary philosophy influenced them, and how they influenced contemporary philosophy need to be studied.[8]

Not only is the tradition of the history of philosophy more vital and complex than Rorty would have us believe, but the historiographical and philosophical questions raised about Pyrrho have echoes in current scholarship. For example, there remain today two central problems in the study of the life of Pyrrho, one a textual one—the correct reading of the various pieces of information available—and a second philosophical one—could Pyrrho possibly have lived a life according to his own principles. The correct reading of the "Life of Pyrrho" is still being analyzed as the work by the current historians of Ancient Scepticism, Brancissi and Dal Pra, attest.[9] For both scholars the main obstacle to a reconstruction of Pyrrho's thought is the near impossibility of harmonizing and reconciling the diverse testimony transmitted from the biographical information in Diogenes Laertius, the philosophical information in Sextus Empiricus and Cicero. This problem of interpretation was identified in the seventeenth century, and differing reconstructions caused differing interpretations during the seventeenth and eighteenth centuries. The second question, can a sceptic live with his own scepticism, has been recently examined by Burnyeat.[10] This question was equally central to historians trying to retell and explain Pyrrho's life in the seventeenth and eighteenth centuries.

---

della filosofia italiana, 3 vols., Turin: Einaudi, 1966; M.A. del Torre, *Le origini moderna della storiographia filosofia*, Florence: La Nuova Italia, 1976; L. Braun, *Histoire de l'histoire de la philosophie*, Paris: Edition Ophrys, 1973; volumes edited by G. Santinello – general title *Storia delle storie generali della filosofia* – are *Delle origini rinascimentali alla "historia philosophica"*, eds. F. Bottin et al., Brescia: La Scuola, 1981; *Dall'età Cartesiana a Brucker*, eds. F. Bottin, M. Longo et al., Brescia: La Scuola, 1979; and *Il secondo illuminismo a l'età Kantiana*, 2 vols., eds. I.F. Baldo et al., Padua: Antenore, 1986; English translation ed. C.W.T. Blackwell – general title *Models of the History of Philosophy*: vol. 1, *From the Renaissance to the 'historia philosophica'*, Dordrecht: Kluwer, 1993.

[8] On the historiography of Renaissance philosophy see my "The historiography of Renaissance philosophy and the creation of the myth of the Renaissance eccentric genius – Cardano in Jacob Brucker's *Historio critica philosophiae* (1742–1744), Brucker's predecessors, Naudé, Bayle and Buddaeus—and his heirs—Buhle, Tennemann and Hegel", forthcoming in *Girolamo Cardano*, ed. E. Kessler, *Wolfenbüttler Forschungen* 1993.

[9] Aldo Brancicci, "La filosofia de Pirrone e le sue relazioni con il cinismo" in *Lo scetticismo antico*, 2 vols., ed. G. Giannatoni, Naples: Bibliopolis, 1981, vol. 1, 211–242; M. del Pra, *Lo scettismo Greco*, 2 edn., Rome: Laterza, 1975, 39–82.

[10] M.F. Burnyeat, "Can the skeptic live his skepticism?" in *The Skeptical Tradition*, ed. M. Burnyeat, Berkeley: University of California Press, 1983, 117–148.

Interest in Pyrrho's life grew out of the development of the history of philosophy in the seventeenth century, which drew on an everincreasing interest in Diogenes Laertius's *Lives of the Philosophers.*[11] which had developed since the fifteenth century. There had been three editions of the Greek and Latin texts of Diogenes Laertius in the sixteenth century, the first by Froben in 1533, the second by Estienne in 1579, reissued with notes by Isaac Casaubon in 1593, and the third by Aldobrandi in 1594. The principal editor in the seventeenth century was Giles Ménage whose edition with his extensive notes in 1664 (reissued in 1692 with notes by Aldobrandi and Casaubon) remained authoritative through the eighteenth century. The first real history of ancient philosophy was by Thomas Stanley who based his history on Diogenes Laertius.[12] Although Stanley's *History of Philosophy* claimed not to follow any one of the philosophers, the assumption of all those engaged in the study of the history of philosophy at that time was that there were some key truths to be found by studying the history of different philosophies. Stanley, an Englishman and classicist, claimed that he had been influenced by Bacon and Montaigne. He finished his work in 1655, the section on oriental philosophy was translated into Latin by Jean Le Clerc (1690) and the complete work by Olearius (1711). This Latin translation had an important influence on the continent and was still being quoted as a source by Brucker eighty years after its first publication. A German professor at Leiden. Georg Horn, wrote an *Historia philosophica* the same year that Stanley published and in 1657–8, Johannes Gerhard Vossius published his work.

PYRRHO'S CHARIOTS

From what we know at present, it appears that the "Life of Pyrrho" was not widely known and when known, not widely used before the seventeenth century. The "Life of Pyrrho" had been virtually unknown in the Middle Ages, Pyrrho was not one of the figures treated by Walter Burley in his *Liber de vita ac moribus philosophorum*. Diogenes Laertius was first translated by Ambrogio

---

[11] I. Tolomio, "Il genere 'Historia Philosophica' tra Cincquecento e Seicento", in *Storia: Dalle origini rinascimentali*, 159–163.
[12] Thomas Stanley, *History of Philosophy*, London 1655. For Stanley see L. Malusa, "Le prime storie generali della filosofia in Ingliterra e nei Paesi Bassi" in *Storia: Dalle origini rinascimentali*, 176–213.

Travesari in the 1430s and the first known quotation from it was by
Giovanni Tortelli in his *De Othographia* (1448–52).[13] Although the
De orthographia was used by Niccolò Perotti who in his *Cornucopiae*
(1489) included an extended definition of the word "scepticus",[14]
Pyrrho's name was not included by such early writers of dictio-
naries who used Tortelli and Perotti, such as Ambrogio Calepino or
Thomas Eliot, but he was included in Estienne's *Thesaurus* with an
entry which seems to owe as much to Aulus Gellius and Cicero as
to Diogenes Laertius.[15] More needs to be known about the references to Pyrrho in the sixteenth century. We do know, however,
that Diogenes Laertius's "Life of Pyrrho" was read by Talon for his
commentary on Cicero's *De Academica*,[16] but it seems that it was not
until the seventeenth century that a reading of the "Life of Pyrrho"
for evidence about the nature of scepticism itself began in earnest.
Central questions arose among the readers of the "Life of Pyrrho".
How do you assess the evidence given in the life? Is it all true? If it
is true, how could someone live in the way Pyrrho was said to have
lived? If it is not true, what should be accepted and what rejected?
The evidence selected was taken to be the truth about ancient
scepticism. How these questions were answered depended on both
the philosophical orientation of the writer and the scholarship on
ancient scepticism at hand. In the seventeenth century there were
two approaches to the text, one followed Stanley, accepted the
information in Diogenes Laertius as fact, and tried to work within
it. The second was originated by La Mothe Le Vayer in the *De La
Vertu des Payens* (1647). He read Diogenes Laertius's text critically,
interpreted the material and wrote what many in the seventeenth
and eighteenth centuries came to think was a more creditable

---

[13] Giovanni Tortelli, *De orthographia*, Venice 1471, n.p.: ". . . dicitur Elidlensis
philosophus et teste Diocle Plistarchi filius. Hunc Apollodorus prius fuisse pic-
torem dixit. Audivitque Anaxarchum a quo nihil declinare visus est: cum omnia
substinuisse illum dicant. Immo aiunt Pyrrhonem quandoque furore adeo istiga-
tum fuisse, ut sumpto cum carnibus coquum in forum usque persequeretur. Quin
et in Helide discipulorum disputationibus fatigatum: abiecto pallio alpheum
tranassel. Eratque Sophistis infestissimus, et cum primo valde pauper fuerit a suis
civibus magno deinde honore habitus: factus est pontifex. Vixitque ad annos ferme
nonaginta. Et illum puto: de quo Cicero in libro *De finibus* saepissime meminit et
Gellius in *IX Noctum Atticarum* libro capitulum speciale confecit."
[14] C.B. Schmitt, "The development of the historiography of scepticism: from
the Renaissance to Brucker" in *Reappraisals*, chap. XIV, p. 186. On Ficino's use of
the term "sceptici", see P.O. Kristeller, *Il pensiero filosofico de Marsilio Ficino*,
Florence: Biblioteca storica del Rinascimento, 1953, p. 461.
[15] H. Estienne, *Thesaurus*, Geneva 1573, vol. 4, p. 36.
[16] Schmitt, *Cicero Scepticus*, p. 89.

version of Pyrrho's life. Both these approaches were followed during these two centuries and as a result two distinct views of ancient scepticism evolved.

Stanley's approach to Diogenes Laertius's text was consistent with the fact that Stanley was primarily a neo-Latin poet and philologist. Stanley's chapter on Pyrrho was indebted not only to Diogenes Laertius's text but to an earlier edition printed in 1593 with notes by Isaac Casaubon. Casaubon's notes not only amended the Greek text, but they included references to additional information about the philosophers in Cicero and Plutarch among others and made historical correction to remarks by Diogenes Laertius, many of which Stanley incorporated directly into his work. Stanley probably took the idea of incorporating material from Sextus Empiricus at the end of the chapter from Diogenes Laertius himself, who summarized ten sceptical arguments from Sextus and five from Agrippa.

The historical comment from Casaubon which Stanley added to his text was the correction of the identification of Pyrrho with Pytho, the disciple of Plato. This note added little to the interpretation of Pyrrho's life. What was important for the future lives were the topics under which Stanley organized the material he paraphrased and translated from Diogenes Laertius. Although Stanley's "Life of Pyrrho" covered only three pages of text, the way Stanley organized Pyrrho's life gave thrust to the story and carried with it conscious or unconscious implications for the interpretation of Pyrrhonism. He divided the material into "His country, Parentage, Time and Master" and "His Institution of a Sect" and "His Manner of Life". The text under this last topic reads:

> Conformable hereunto was his manner of Life; he shunned nothing, nor took any heed, but went straight on upon everything. Chariots, if it so happened, precipices, dogs, and the like, not turning out of the way, nor having any regard to Sense: being saved, as *Antigonus* saith, by his friends that followed him. But *Aenesidemus* affirms, that though he discoursed Philosophically upon suspension, yet all his Actions were not inconsiderate.[17]

By beginning the section "Conformable was his manner of Life", a phrase Stanley took from Diogenes Laertius's text, he seemed to imply that Pyrrho had lived his scepticism. But a problem appeared at once. Stanley's text ended with the statement by Aenesidemus which implied that Pyrrho's actions had not been

---

[17] Stanley, *History of Philosophy*, London 1659, part 4, p. 2.

extreme. By merely restating the text as he found it, Stanley left the reader with contradictory information—a Pyrrho wandering around blindly—and a Pyrrho who was not inconsiderate in his actions. This English version of Pyrrho's life was printed again in 1687, in 1701 and finally in 1743. The last editor read the Pyrrho text and clearly interpreted it to mean that Pyrrho had not followed his sense perceptions—annoyed he commented:

> All the Subtilty of these Gentlemen lay in finding Reasons of Diffidence and Distrust in Matters which appeared plain and evident.[18]

A retelling of Diogenes Laertius's *Lives of the Philosophers* was written by François de Salignac de la Mothe Fénelon in his *Abrégé des vies des plus illustre philosophes avec un recueil de leurs plus belles maximes*.[19] Since it was written before his death in 1715, it is possible he had not read Stanley, whose work in English was almost unknown but which had been translated into Latin in 1711; yet in many ways it followed Stanley's method of uncritically rewriting Diogenes Laertius's text. Fénelon's chapter on Pyrrho emphasized the fact that

> He gave so little credit to the intimation of sense, that he never turned aside to avoid a rock or percipices; and would rather have suffered himself to be crushed to pieces, than stir a foot to get out of the way of a chariot. But some of his friends always accompanied him, and saved him from danger.[20]

Before this section, Fénelon had described Pyrrho as travelling extensively without telling anyone where he was going. Fénelon did not see any contradiction in the story of Pyrrho's life in the description of his travelling to India and at the same time not trusting his sense perceptions as La Mothe Le Vayer had done. Essentially all Fénelon did was to retell Diogenes Laertius's *Lives of the Philosophers* in a more elegant way without analyzing the biographical or philosophical problems inherent in the text. While this was not a very scholarly edition, it was the most singularly popular version of the *Lives of the Philosophers* available in French and English in the eighteenth and nineteenth centuries, going through twenty-one

---

[18] Stanley, *History of Philosophy*, London 1743.

[19] For Fénelon see G. Piaia, "La storiographia filosofica in Francia tra il Bayle e il Deslandes" in *Storia: Dall'età Cartestiana a Brucker*, 168–9.

[20] M. de Fénelon, *Abrégé des vies des anciens philosophes*, 2nd ed., Paris 1740, p. 407. "Il souffroit tout sans se mettre en peine de rien. Il se fait si peu à ses sens, qu'il ne se détournat ni pour rochers, ni pour précipices, ni pour aucun autre péril; il se seroit plutôt éviter la rencontre d'un chariot. Il y avoit toujours quelques-uns des ses amis qui avoient soin de le détourner dans les occasions."

French editions between 1726 and 1873 and eight English editions
between 1726 and 1840. It might be added that Fénelon's version of
Pyrrho's life was the one generally known outside the scholarly and
philosophical community.

A more interesting life of Pyrrho was written in 1737 by A.-F.
Boureau-Deslandes in his *Histoire critique de la philosophie où l'on traite
de son Origine des ses progrès, et des diverses révolutions qui lui sont arrivées
jusqu'à notre tems.*[21] Deslandes was interested in the problems Pyrrho's way of life revealed. After telling the story of Pyrrho's voyage
with Anarchus to India and his return after the death of both Anarchus and Alexander. Deslandes then described Pyrrho's "unique
life of study" and went on to define Pyrrho's philosophy: justice
and injustice were chimerical, and law and custom established
virtue and vice. Where, asked Boureau-Deslandes, did Pyrrho
think virtue and vice came from? "Mais ce bien et ce mal ne
subsistent que dans leur imaginations", it was only one's own self
which made a person happy or sad. Taking his cue from either the
Diogenes Laertius text or Stanley, he said:

> La conduite de Pyrrhon repondoit parfaitement à sa manière de
> penser. Il n'amoit rien, il ne briguoit aucune dignité. . . . il n'avoit
> aucune attention ni à son exterieur, ni à son habillement.[22]

Deslandes commented, that Pyrrho's indifference towards life and
death should be admired; however, since this indifference was
unrealistic for ordinary people, people did not have to imitate it.[23]
Yet, he thought, Pyrrho's rigorous scepticism could serve as the
basis for religion, as the realization that nothing could be understood should make us aware that man lived in profound ignorance.
"How better to make us turn to religion!" he exclaimed.[24] From
the text quoted Deslandes appears to believe that Pyrrho was

---

[21] Anonymus (A.-F. Boureau-Deslandes), *Histoire critique de la philosophie*, Amsterdam 1737, vol. 2, 365–68. For Deslandes see G. Piaia, "Storia 'critica' delle
filosofia e primo illuminismo: André-François Boureau-Deslandes" in *Storia: Dal-
l'età Cartesiana a Brucker*, 200–236.

[22] Boureau-Deslandes, *Histoire critique*, vol. 2, p. 366.

[23] Ibid., p. 367: "Cette indifférence pour la vie et pour la mort, si noblement
exprimée dans les Ouvrages des Anciens, a été la source de tant d'actions extraor-
dinaires qu'ils ont faites, et que nous admirons encore, sans les pouvoir trop
limiter."

[24] Ibid., p. 368: "Cest art est la confession la plus ingénue que nous puissions
faire et de la foiblesse de notre esprit et de cette profonde ignorance où nous
sommes tous plonges. Qui de plus propre a nous inspirer une juste defiance de nos
foibles lumières! Quoi de plus capable de tourner nos regards vers la Religion! Elle
seule ne se trompe point et ne peut tromper personne".

completely indifferent, yet his treatment of Pyrrho concluded with his version of an extract from Sextus Empiricus which defended Pyrrhonism from the charge of denying the possibility of all truth:

> Ne croyéz pas, dit Sextus, que le Pyrrhonnisme suppose la destraction de toutes les Sciences, et pour ainsi dire, un entier renoncement aux lumières de son esprit. Quel homme voudroit s'avilir de dégrader jusque'à ce point? Combien se sentiroit-il pas de repugnances et de difficultés, avant qui de rompre si durement avec lui-meme? Le véritable Pyrrhonien est donc celui qui examine les choses avec une attention scrupuleuse, qui recherche la vérité, mains qui la voit toujours suyante à ses yeux.[25]

If Deslandes admitted that Pyrrho did not pay attention to his dress, he makes it clear that Pyrrho did react to sense perceptions because he complained when he felt injury and did not hesitate to flee from danger. Unlike Stanley and Fénelon, Deslandes incorporated Pyrrhonism into his view of the history of philosophy, not as a method of thought or a stage in the development of philosophy but as the natural attitude one should cultivate towards philosophy when one saw that so many different and contradictory systems had been created by the philosophers.[26]

Walter Anderson's *The Philosophy of Ancient Greece* (1791)[27] was written to replace Stanley. Anderson (d. 1800) was a minister and a specialist in Greek and French history who was familiar with the work of David Hume, with whom he disagreed. Although Anderson acknowledged his debt to Stanley, he clearly stated that he would give space to "remarks upon the reasoning employed, of their physical, theological and moral systems".[28] While Anderson was familiar with Aldobrandi's notes on Diogenes Laertius, he either ignored or did not have the important notes by Ménage and thus

---

[25] Ibid., p. 369.

[26] Ibid., vol. 1, vi–vii: "Le principal et l'essentiel à mon avis, c'est de remonter à la source des principales pensées des hommes, d'examiner leur variété infinie, et en même-temps le rapport imperceptible, les liasons delicates qu'elles ont entr'elles; . . . c'est de rappaller les opinions des Philosophes anciens, et de montrer qu'ils ne pouvoient rien dire que ce qu'ils on dit effectivement, c'est en un mot de suivre et de démêler ce prodigieus amas de vérités et d'erreurs, qui sont parvenues jusqu'à nous, et qui jettent encore les plus éclaires dans une sort de Pyrrhonisme".

[27] Walter Anderson, *The Philosophy of Ancient Greece Investigated in its Originds and Progress to the Areas of its Greatest Celebrity in the Ionian, Italic and Athenean Schools; with Remarks on the Delineated Systems of their Founders; Some Accounts of their Lives and Character and those of their most Eminent Disciples*, Edinburgh 1791; for Anderson see F. Bottin, "La storiographia filosofica nell 'area Britannica" in *Storia: Il secondo illuminismo e l'età Kantiana*, vol. 2.

[28] Anderson, *The Philosophy of Ancient Greece*, p. vi.

was ignorant of the comments by La Mothe Le Vayer quoted here. He was, however, well versed in Cicero's *De Academica* and in Sextus Empiricus. Anderson's antipathy towards Pyrrhonism becomes apparent in his retelling of Pyrrho's life. He began with a comment on the story about Pyrrho walking around without any regard for his own physical safety. Anderson elaborated writing:

> Pyrrho soon showed himself to be of a temper fitted to personify Scepticism in its most glaring shapes. Discrediting alike the testimony of the senses, the impulse of affection, and the plainest dictates of reason, he strove to act, even in the common affairs of life, like one who had a controversy with them all. It was not his part, who believed not the reality of motion in bodies, or of their action upon one another, and to whom every bias he found in himself was equal to another, to turn aside from a precipice, or avoid the shock of a wagon or chariot that comes his way. His friends and others in pitying him, were often obliged to perform those services which he could find no reason, in theory for doing personally.[29]

It did not occur to Anderson to question Diogenes Laertius's evidence; he took it at face value and concluded Pyrrho had been intellectually dishonest. Anderson flatly did not think that anyone could live with the type of scepticism Pyrrho seemed to espouse. He noted the fact that Pyrrho did survive, and therefore Anderson concluded he must have been dishonest. Anderson explained Pyrrho's actions thus:

> He carried this behaviour for some time, and when he was not liable to be much disturbed, as far as could consist with any regard to his preservation, and not to be accounted a person altogether delirious.[30]

Most students of scepticism credited Pyrrho with the ability to question well, but not Anderson, who said Pyrrho's reasoning facility was weakly combative and gave as an example the comment:

> "You who hold life to be a matter of indifference, why do you not die? 'It is', replied Pyrrho for that very reason and because it is indifferent to me to live or die".

To Pyrrho's indifference over whether people listened to what he had to say, Anderson comments that Pyrrho

> seemed to do with nobody but himself and to resolve all the efforts of his mind into that of maintaining indecision and indifference in all human opinions and sentiments.[31]

---

29 Ibid., p. 405.
30 Ibid., p. 405.
31 Ibid., p. 406.

Anderson's lack of sympathy with Pyrrho led him to judge Pyrrho's actions on Anderson's own terms and extrapolate their implications. Anderson flatly denied that anyone could live as Pyrrho professed to do:

> Pyrrho, nor no man that acted or moved his body in the least, could consistently exhibit his hesitation and indifference in the degree he is said to have held them forth in theory.[32]

It is exactly the question of assenting to sense perceptions that was central to Anderson's attack on both Pyrrho and Sextus Empiricus. He was particularly critical of Sextus' statement:

> We yield to custom and novelty, to phantasms which meet our compliance from necessity and submission to the laws of our country, which teach us that virtuous action is a real good and vicious behaviour an evil.[33]

Anderson's lack of sympathy with Pyrrho led him to judge Pyrrho's actions in Anderson's own terms and extrapolate their implications. Anderson flatly denied that anyone could live as Pyrrho professed to do:

> "That the human mind is naturally and contingently induced to assent to the truth of propositions as the imagination to the appearance of things".[34]

All these interpretations accepted the story of Pyrrho and his chariots as true, and Stanley's editor, Deslandes and Anderson in their different ways considered scepticism to be a doctrine that man could not live by. Significantly, the more critical account, the one by Anderson, was written with the knowledge of the sceptical writings of David Hume.

Pyrrho without the Chariots

The writings of Jacob Brucker (1696–1779)[35] were as central to eighteenth and early nineteenth century interpretations of Pyrrho in the histories of philosophy as Stanley's work had been in the seventeenth and early eighteenth centuries. Charles Schmitt found

---

[32] Ibid., p. 407.
[33] Ibid., p. 408.
[34] Ibid., p. 409.
[35] Jacob Brucker, *Historia critica philosophiae*, vol. 1, 1317–1332. For Brucker see *Storia: Dall'età Cartesiana a Brucker*, 529–635, which has a complete bibliography of Brucker's reputation on 632–635.

Brucker to be the first person to introduce contemporary scepticism into the history of philosophy.[36] Not only was Brucker very interested in the questions which arose around the "Life of Pyrrho", but he himself espoused a form of historical scepticism. In sum, Brucker's view of scepticism was complex and must be studied with care so that we can understand not only his own view but also how this view influenced the characterization of scepticism by later historians of philosophy. Brucker's view of contemporary scepticism was on the whole negative, and although he found one pair of Sceptics who found refuge in religion—La Mothe Le Vayer and Huet—he did not respect their reasons for doing so, for he believed that by succumbing to scepticism, they had put themselves under the "yoke of authority" of the Roman Catholic church.[37] Brucker found other manifestations of contemporary scepticism unfriendly to religion as it denied the "certainty of all revelation and divine faith".[38]

This attitude makes us unprepared for the fact that the title of Brucker's first printed work was in defense of Pyrrho: *De Pyrrhone a Scepticismi universalis macula absolvendo* (Jena 1716). It was written against the charge of universal scepticism made by his teacher J.F. Budde. This work was republished in the *Miscellanae historiae philosophicae literariae criticae, olim sparsim edita, nunc uno fasce collecta multisque accessionibus aucta et illustrata* (Augsburg 1748). This edition was as well known to later historians of philosophy as the essay on Pyrrho in the *Historia critica philosophiae*, as Tennemann's bibliography in his *Grundriss der Geschichte der Philosophie* attests. Brucker carefully assessed earlier source material and constructed an authoritative life of Pyrrho, which he developed in greater detail in the *Historia critica philosophiae*; in turn Buhle and Tennemann drew on this. Brucker's method of procedure in his chapters on the ancient philosophers was very systematic: he first listed and evaluated previous sources of the life of the philosopher and then proceeded to construct his own version, concluding the article with a list of the philosophical doctrines to which he often added important comments. He drew on four different types of sources for his description of Pyrrho and the history of Ancient Scepticism: 1) the biographical-philosophical material from La Mothe Le Vayer and

---

[36] Schmitt, "The development of the historiography of scepticism", 185–200.

[37] Brucker, *Historia critica philosophia*, vol. 4, 547–574.

[38] Ibid., p. 601: " . . . certum tamen est, Baylium hac incertitudine, ea ipsa principia confellere aggressum, fuisse, quibus omnis revelationis et divinae fidei certitudo nititur . . ."

Bayle about the character of Pyrrho, 2) the accusations about Pyrrho in the histories of atheism by Budde and Reimmann, 3) the placement of scepticism and Pyrrho by Budde and Gentsken in the history of philosophy, and 4) the versions of the history of Ancient Scepticism by Foucher and Huet.

A study of Brucker's sources should begin with La Mothe Le Vayer. Although he did not write a history of philosophy, La Mothe Le Vayer's[39] interpretation of the life of Pyrrho in *De La vertu des Payens* was so influential to historians of philosophy, it is necessary to study it in some detail. La Mothe Le Vayer read widely in Greek and Latin and he had an original mind. His interpretation of Pyrrho could not only be found in his *De la vertu des Payens*, but his key remarks were added by Giles Ménage to his commentary on Diogenes Laertius[40] and by Bayle in his entry on Pyrrho in his *Dictionnaire historique et critique*.[41] They thus influenced generations of readers throughout Europe in the seventeenth, eighteenth and nineteenth centuries. La Mothe Le Vayer began his chapter on Pyrrho with an attack on the reliability of Diogenes Laertius's text:

> Si Pyrrho avoit esté tel que plusieurs l'on represente, je ne pense pas que personne eust voulu suivre ses sentiments, et nous serions mesmes ridicules de nous amuser à les examiner.[42]

La Mothe Le Vayer then quoted the statement by Antigouns Carystius that Pyrrho walked about without paying any attention to chariots or precipices, and contrasted them with the one by Aenesidemus who said that Pyrrho never did anything extravagant. Here La Mothe Le Vayer's superior scholarship asserted itself. He was able to identify Aenesidemus from his reading of the *Bibliotheca* by Photius published in 1601.[43] It was evident to him that Aenesidemus was a reliable witness on Pyrrho because he could identify Aenesidemus as someone who had written eight books on the Pyrrhonian sect. Thus he was more reliable than Antigonus Carystius.

> Mais pourquoy croirions nous plutôt cet Antigonus, qu'Aenesidemus, qui à escrit huit livres de la secte des Pyrrhoniens, et asseure qui leur xxx ne commit jamais aucune de ces extravagances.[44]

---

[39] La Mothe Le Vayer, *De la vertu des payens*, Paris 1642, 252–278.

[40] Diogenes Laertius, *De vitis et dogmatibus*, ed. Marcus Meibomius cum annotationibus Is. Casauboni. Th. Aldobrandi, et Mer Masauboni, Aeg. Menagi observationes, Amsterdam 1692, vol. 2, p. 426.

[41] Pierre Bayle, *Dictionnaire historique et critique*, 5th ed., Amsterdam, Leiden 1734, vol. 3, 669–674.

[42] La Mothe Le Vayer, *De la vertu des payens*, p. 206.

[43] Photius, *Bibliotheca*, Augsburg 1601.

[44] La Mothe Le Vayer, *De la vertu des payens*, p. 253.

When La Mothe Le Vayer retold Pyrrho's life, he listed incidents which proved that Pyrrho had watched where he was going: 1) he walked to India, something he could hardly have done if he had not followed directions,[45] 2) he was approved of by many great philosophers,[46] 3) he was the founder of a sect and recommended by a great many people[47] and 4) he was created a priest. This evidence made it clear, that Pyrrho was a man who in everyday life paid attention to what he was doing and who was esteemed by those who knew him. These facts gave La Mothe Le Vayer the evidence he needed to state that Carystius's testimony about Pyrrho and the chariots was false.

Pierre Bayle's entry on Pyrrho in the *Dictionnaire historique et critique*[48] owed a great deal to La Mothe Le Vayer, and while there are many interesting things to say about this entry, what we are interested in here is how Bayle rearranged the information found in Diogenes Laertius to tell a version of Pyrrho's life which he thought probable. Like La Mothe Le Vayer, Bayle felt free to question parts of Diogenes Laertius's text. One key difference between them was that La Mothe Le Vayer separated his version of the life of Pyrrho from his comments about Pyrrhonism—Bayle did not. This interweaving of the life of Pyrrho and the doctrines of scepticism will reappear in Brucker's opening statements. Bayle began by quickly sketching in the information about Pyrrho's birth, his discipleship to Anaxarchus and his travels to India. Bayle then characterized Pyrrho's scepticism by associating his beliefs with those of Arcesilaus, summarizing the sceptic doctrine of affirming nothing and denying nothing. Sceptics, said Bayle, searched all their lives for truth, but arranged their quest so as not to find it. Bayle takes the question of the sceptic's irreligion head on by stating that the sceptic was feared by the church unfairly as the sceptic's statements about inaccessibility of truth showed that man must implore God

---

[45] Ibid., p. 253: "En effet on tombe d'accord qu'il vescut prèz de quatre-vingt dix ans, et qu'il passa la meilleure partie de ce temps la dans les vayables, ayant esté trouver les Mages de Perse, et s'estant abouché dans l'Inde avec les Gymnosophistes. Est-il vray-semblable qu'un homme qui se précipitoit dans toute sorte de dangers, fust arrivé jusques à un si grand âge?"

[46] Loc. cit.: "Certes elles on si peu d'apparence, et il est si difficile de s'imaginer comment un si grand nombre de Philosophes les auroient approuvées qui je ferois conscience d'y déférer, quant elles ne seroient contredittes par personne, et que le reste de la vie de Pyrrhon ne les concaincroit point de fausseté."

[47] Loc. cit.: "Quoy qu'il en soit on le doit considerer comme Fondateur d'une grande compagnie, et par conséquant qu'il estoit sans doute recommendable en beaucoup de façons."

[48] Bayle, *Dictionnaire*, vol. 3, 669–674.

for help.[49] At this point Bayle brought in Antigonus Carystius's story of the chariots, commenting

> Il faut prendre pour de mauvases plaisanteries ou plutôt pour des imposture, les contes d'Antigonus Carystius de Pyrrhon ne préféroit rien à rien et qu'un chariot et un precipice ne l'obligeoient point à fair un pas en arrière ou à cote, et ses amis que le suivient lui sauverent fort souvent la vie. Il n'y à nulle aparence qu'il ait eté fou jusqu'à ce point-la.[50]

The two German histories of Atheism which Brucker used and answered, J.F. Budde's *Theses de atheismo et superstitione*[51] and J.F. Reimmann's *Historia universalis atheismi et atheorum falso et merito suspectorum*[52] had a completely different approach to Pyrrho. Both Budde and Reimmann argued that there were differences between ancient sceptics and modern ones, and they were more critical of Pyrrho and associated with his position, phrases in Sextus Empiricus which questioned the existence of God. For Budde what was particularly damning was what he perceived to be Pyrrho's universal scepticism, for universal scepticism questioned the existence of God itself.[53] Reimmann also claimed that sceptics were said to have a touch of atheism about them and referred the reader to Sextus Empiricus's *Outlines of Pyrrhonism* III. 1. Whether Pyrrho was an Atheist was a key question Brucker had to answer, but before he could do so, he had to establish that scepticism was a philosophical sect.

The earliest reference to scepticism in a German history of philosophy was by Brucker's teacher, Budde in his *Elementa philosophiae instrumentalis* (1703). Budde did not agree with the traditional division of philosophy between sceptics and dogmatists since he said that true sceptics should not be permitted the name of philos-

---

[49] Ibid., p. 669: "Il import peu qu'on dise que l'esprit de l'homme est trop borné pour rien découvrir dans les véritez naturelles, dans les causes qui produisent la chaleur, le froid, le flux de la mer, etc. Il nous dout suffire qu'on s'exerce à la chercher des Hypotheses probables et à receuiller des Expériences, et je suis fort assuré qu'il y a très peu de bons Physiciens dans notre Siècle, qui ne se soient convaincus que la nature est un abîme impénétrable, et que ses efforts ne sont conus qu'à celui qui les a fait, et qui les dirige. Ainsi tous ces Philosophes sont a cet regard Académiciens et Pyrrhoniens."

[50] Ibid., p. 671.

[51] J.F. Budde, *Theses theologicae de atheismo et superstitione*, ed. J. Lufus, Leiden 1767, 22–25. For Budde see M. Longo, "Le storie generali della filosofia in Germania, 1690–1750" in *Storia: Dall'età Cartesiana a Brucker*, 373–405.

[52] J.F. Reimmann, *Historia universalis atheismi et atheorum falso et merito suspectorum*, Hildesheim 1725. For Riemmann see Longo, "Filosofia in Germania", 407–412.

[53] Budde, *Theses theologicae*, p. 125.

ophers, as they did not want to admit anything about philosophy
or theology, reason or divine authority; thus for Budde sceptics
were neither a philosophical sect nor genuine philosophers, and
instead he linked them with the sophists.[54] Budde did note that
there was not merely one type of sceptic among the contemporary
sceptics: some admitted the authority of divine literature and
suspended their judgement about philosophy, some suspended
their judgement about physics, some about morals.[55] While Budde
was critical of Pyrrho, he characterized as true wise men other
philosophers who engaged in moderate scepticism: Zeno of Elea,
Heraclitus, Socrates, and the Academics. These people were not a
philosophical sect, but had a similar approach to searching out
truth.[56] It was Budde's categorical condemnation of Pyrrho as a universal sceptic that moved Brucker to write his first youthful article.
One other German history of philosophy discussed Pyrrho: F. Gentzken's *Historia philosophiae*.[57] This discussion indicated that Gentzken was influenced neither by Bayle nor by Budde. Gentzken did
not try to reconcile conflicting pieces of information in Diogenes
Laertius and said on the one hand that Pyrrho did nothing inconsiderate and on the other that Pyrrho did not watch where he was
going when chariots and dogs were passing. The question of Pyrrho's atheism did not come up for him, and he added at the end of
his entry the comment that Pyrrho had been made a priest, and
that all philosophers had been granted immunity because Pyrrho
had been so highly honoured,—evidence usually used by those who
tried to establish that Pyrrho had been a highly respected figure
and religious.

Pyrrho had been given an honoured place in two earlier histories
of scepticism which Brucker knew and rejected—Huet's *De la
foiblesse de l'esprit humain* and Foucher's *Histoire de Académiciens*.[58]
Foucher claimed that scepticism began with Socrates, went
through Plato to Arcesilaus, continued with Plotinus and ended
with Descartes, while Huet went even further and stated that the
origin of all philosophy was the sceptical method of doubting.
Brucker also rejected the statement in Diogenes Laertius that
Homer was the first sceptic:

---

[54] Budde, *Elementa philosophiae instrumentales*, 2nd ed., Halle 1706, p. 7.
[55] Loc. cit.
[56] Ibid., p. 8.
[57] F. Gentzken, *Historia philosophiae*, Hamburg 1725.
[58] D. Huet, *Traité philosophique de la foiblesse de l'esprit humain*, Amsterdam 1723,
and Foucher, *L'histoire et les principes de la philosophie des Académiciens*, Paris 1693.

For they say that in Laertius, Homer was the first to tread this path
and that later there were also seven wise men who went in that
direction, and also Archilochus and Euripides, both of whom practised that form of philosophy as well as Xenophanes and Zeno of Elea
and Democritus, all of whom were sceptics, likewise, Plato, Empedo-
cles, Heraclitus and Hippocrates. Sextus Empiricus boasts almost the
same list and he is followed at length by Huet who summons great
men and philosophers from every part of the ancient world.[59]

Brucker made it quite clear that he had a definition of scepticism
which was narrower. It was a definition based on his interpretation
of Pyrrho's life as interpreted from his analysis of the evidence in
Diogenes Laertius and Pyrrho's historical place in the development
of Greek philosophy. Brucker placed particular emphasis on the
importance of the influence of those philosophers with whom Pyrrho studied. On the one hand, he separated Pyrrho from Socrates
and some of his school who doubted, saying that modesty was
characteristic of great men

> who did not claim all wisdom for themselves but modestly recognized
> the limit of the human intellect.[60]

and on the other, unlike Budde, Brucker also did not classify
Pyrrhonian scepticism as universal doubt, since he did not claim
that Pyrrhonists denied all knowledge. Rather Brucker states that

> the Sceptics assert in Laertius that they discern things through
> feelings and passions of the soul and they know for example that it is
> day and that they are alive.[61]

This view, that the Sceptics admitted certain knowledge about
everyday things, was very different from that implied by Stanley
and Anderson.

---

[59] Brucker, *Historia critica philosophiae*, vol. 1, p. 1330: "Aiunt enim apud LAER-
TIUM: principem in ea calcanda fuisse Homerum, postea septem quoque
sapientes in ea fuisse versatos, Archilochum item et Euripidem id genus philosophiae exercuisse; Xentophantem etiam, et Zenonem Eleatem, ac Democritum
Scepticos fuisse, itemque Platonem, et Empedoclem, Heraclitum idem et Hippoc-
ratem. Eadem fere iactat SEXTUS EMPIRICUS, et prolix persequitur PETRUS
DANIEL HUETIUS. qii omnes fere veteris oris viros magnos et philosophos in
partes vocat."

[60] Ibid., p. 536: "Ignorantiam itaque hanc doctam et philosophicam merio
vocaueris, quae non omnium sibi rerum incertudinem, finem philosophandi prop-
osuit, sed prudentem et modestam terminorum, quibus circumscriptus est huma-
nus intellectus, agnitionem adhibuit ad inquirendam veritatem, et consequendam
scientiam . . . Qui itaque cum HUETIO, Socratem inter scepticismi patronos et
doctores numerant, ad haec non attendunt, nec sensum scopumque verborum
Socratis recte assequuntur."

[61] Ibid., p. 1329: "Hinc apud LAERTIUM, de affectionibus et passionibus
animae se decernere, aiunt, et sciire se v.g. quod dies sit, quod vivant etc."

Before we analyze his chapter on Pyrrho, a word should be said about Brucker's notion of how history of philosophy should be written, as it is important to understand the place scepticism had in Brucker's method of evaluating philosophical evidence. Brucker's *Historia critica philosophiae* was introduced by a "Praefatio praeliminaris" which showed the historian of philosophy how to apply criteria of historical criticism to the history of philosophy. Brucker drew up fifteen cautions in which he advocated sophisticated techniques of historical criticism, use of tests of chronology for texts, methods of studying sources, examining the various definitions of philosophical terms and the problems of weighing evidence. Brucker was not only interested in how and why systems of philosophy rose to the fore and in the interrelationship between the personalities of the philosophers and their philosophy. Thus he stressed that when the systems of the philosophers were studied, their circumstances, temperaments and methods of education should be taken into account. The personality of the philosopher and his circumstances affected his philosophy according to Brucker. This led to extensive biographical data in the *Historia critica philosophiae*, data which was quoted by later historians of philosophy until Hegel.

Despite the careful weighing of testimony about a philosopher and his philosophy, Brucker did not believe that certainty was possible in history, and he advised the historian of philosophy to submit himself to the discipline of historical scepticism as articulated by F.W. Bierling in *Commentatio de Pyrrhonismo historico*.[62] It should be noted here that Brucker did not discuss historical scepticism in his *Vorbereitung* of his *Kurze Fragen*. One work which was published between these two versions was Gilbert-Charles le Gendre's *Traité de l'opinion ou Mémoires pour sevir à l'histoire de l'esprit humain* (Paris, 1733), but whether Brucker read this work or not is not clear; he did not refer to it, nor did he mention it in the *Praefatio* of his *Historia critica philosophiae*. However, it is interesting for the history of Pyrrhonism to note that Le Gendre specifically rejected Pyrrhonism for what he called a "sceptique moderée" which was the attitude he was going to use to assess opinions of the various philosophers, scientists, medical doctors and magicians he was going to describe:

> Le point de vue de cet ouvrage est la science de doubter, non pas en Pyrrhonien, mais lorsqu'il est advantageus de suspendre son

---

[62] F.W. Bierling, *Commentatio de Pyrrhonismo historico*, Leipzig 1724. On the history of this text see C. Borghero, *La certezza e la storia, Cartesianesimo, pirronismo e conoscenza storica*, Milan: Franco Angeli, 1983, 278–288.

judement. C'est un traité des opinions qui ont regne dans le sciences prophanes, c'est l'essai d'une sceptique moderée et une route nouvelle pour former l'esprit par sa propre histoire, dont aucun auteur jusqu'ici n'a formé le projet. J'examine l'empire de l'opinion sur chaque science, afin que l'esprit s'accoutume à une sage defiance par la vie de ses erreurs. J'indique leurs source dans les sens l'imagination, les préjugés, dans les artifices des uns et la credulité des autres, dans l'amour du merveilleus et sur tout dans les passions.[63]

Brucker articulated his historical scepticism a little more precisely, and I think this should be linked with Brucker's admiration for the moderated scepticism of some of his contemporaries. Thus it was not an abberation that Brucker was attracted to Bierling. In his discussion of contemporary scepticism, we have his approval of Glanvill's use of scepticism in scientific enquiry. Some scientists

> maintained that in the field of natural science, philosophical speculation should be pursued in terms of witholding assent and checking definitions. This was because they saw that there were many secret places in it which are still hidden from us, that scholars dispute many things from the assumption of uncertain and precarious hypotheses and that most things come back to a false explanation of phenomena which scholars observe. . . . Some learned and modest men have restricted these things (disputes) to only moderate and sober limits, having drawn the conclusion from them that it was rash to make a declaration about unknown things, that hypotheses should not be embraced as clear and undoubted truths, and that progress should only be made from the known to the detection of the unknown; it was to this end Joseph Glanvil applied his Scepticism scientificam adversus dogmaticorum vanitates.[64]

The sceptical method used to identify errors and set out probable truths as a way to gather information was the correct method of proceeding in the accumulation of human knowledge according to Brucker. To use this method, the philosophical enquirer should cultivate modesty and sobriety.

---

[63] Gilbert-Charles le Gendre, *Traité de l'opinion ou Mémoires pour servir à l'histoire de l'esprit humain*, Paris 1733, vol. 1, p. 1.

[64] Brucker, *Historia critica philosophiae*, vol. 4, p. 539: "Quae licet nonnulli viri eruditi et modesti moderatis tantum sobriisque limitibus incluserunt, conclusione ex his deducta, de ignotis non temere statuendum, hypothetica non pro certis et indubitatis veritatibus amplectenda, et ex cognitis ad ignotorum detectionem progrediendum esse, quo scopo *scepsin scientificam adversus dogmaticorum vanitates* adhibuit IOSEPHUS GLANVIL . . ." On the debate about Glanvil's scepticism see B.C. Southgate, "'Cauterising the tumour of Pyrrhonis': Blackloism versus Skepticism", *Journal of the History of Ideas* 53 (1993), 631–645.

The historian of philosophy must follow the laws of historical reliability. He must allow his intellectual assent to be "altogether suspended", and he must admit "his lack if certainty".[65] Historical Pyrrhonism supplied a "sobering remedy".[66] Historical Pyrrhonism was a method of assessing uncertain facts and at the same time an attitude toward truth. For the historian to write history of philosophy, he must adopt this attitude toward information about philosophers in the past.

While Brucker did describe Pyrrho's life as a self-contained story, he also related his education and the development of his subsequent philosophy as the logical consequence of the Greek philosophy which had preceeded him. Brucker organized Greek philosophy according to sect, starting with the Ionic, then progressing through the school of Socrates, the Cyrenaics, Plato and with him the new, middle and third Academy, Aristotle, the cynics, Zeno and the stoics, then Pythagoras and his disciples. He grouped Pyrrho with the Eleatic sect, Heraclitus and the Epicureans. At the beginning of the chapter on Pyrrho in the *Kurze Fragen*, Brucker directly dealt with Budde's statement that the sceptics were not a sect by saying that if philosophy was to be understood in a narrow sense, it was not, but if it was to be understood in a wider sense—if philosophy meant the search for truth whether it arrived at its objective or not—then there was one more sect, the sceptics.[67] La Mothe Le Vayer's characterization of Pyrrhonism as a search for truth was placed at the beginning to form part of the definition of scepticism. The chapter on Pyrrho was divided into clear sub-topics: *Secta Sceptica, Nomen, Scriptores ad eius historiam facientes, Conditor sectae Pyrrho, Origines Scepticismi Pyrrhonis, Sectores Pyrrhonis, Timon Phliasius*, and *Duratio sectae exigua*. The question of whether Pyrrho was an atheist, an issue Brucker had taken up in 1716, was dealt with in an extended discussion at the end of the chapter where Brucker listed key sceptical philosophical opinions. Brucker, true to his own statement of the correct method for the historian of philosophy, opened his chapter with a detailed review complete with

---

[65] Ibid., p. 18: " . . . *Et hic omnino suspendendus intellectus assensus est, et fatenda candide incertitudo.*"

[66] Loc. cit.: "Qui pyrrhonismus historicus uti maxime sobrium in historia medicamen est, ita quoque in philosophica historia non tantum adhibendus est, ubi certum probabilitatis gradum attingere non licet, dubiusque intellectus haeret: sed muniendus eo etiam est animus, ut nihil praecipue primas verisimilitudinis rationes non prae se ferens, temere pro vero admittatur, sed eo usque suspendatur intellectus iudicium, donec adhibitis ratiocinandi regulis et accurato examine fundamenta fidei historicae rei debitae patescant."

[67] Brucker, *Kurze Fragen*, vol. 2, 705–6.

footnoted references to all the fragments and sources of Pyrrhonism known to him—from this information, Brucker gathered the various views which he could then judge as true, probable or false. He began with the sources mentioned in Diogenes Laertius, Antigonus Carystius, Pyrrho's near contemporary, and Diocles Mages, as well as Aenesidemus, to whom Brucker appended the adjective "splendid". Like La Mothe Le Vayer, Brucker noted that an epitome of Aenesidemus was to be found in Photius. Brucker then listed other lost works by Thedotius and Favorinus and then went on to praise Sextus Empiricus and his commentaries which had "enormous erudition and acquaintance with all ancient philosophy". He added also as his source Diogenes Laertius and Suidas and concluded with a list of modern authors favourable to Pyrrho: Foucher's *Dissertations sur la Recherche de la verité contenant l'histoire et les principes de la philosophie des académiciens* (Paris 1693). Huet's *De la foiblesse de l'esprit humain* and Bayle's article on Pyrrho in the *Dictionnaire*. Brucker, ever fair minded and in search of additional information, recommended that the reader interested in Pyrrho not overlook his enemies and look for information about Pyrrho in *Questiones Academicae* by St Augustine and Claudius Ptolomaeus's book *De iudicandi facultate verique et falsi regulae*.[68]

Brucker then told his own version of Pyrrho's life. What was central to Pyrrho's development for Brucker was that after Pyrrho's life as a painter, he turned to the philosophy of Democritus whose philosophy Brucker thought to be responsible for Pyrrho's scepticism. Pyrrho studied under Dryson or Bryson, son of Stilpo; as Brucker said:

> There is no doubt that Pyrrho, instructed in the weapons of dialectic, learned from him (Dryson) all about those noble battles in which the Eristics attacked all the philosophers and debated about everything on both sides of the argument.[69]

According to Brucker, Pyrrho's trip to India was equally important in leading him to scepticism, for when he went there in the train of Alexander and in the company of Anaxarchus, he heard the Brachmans and the Gymnosophists and their learning which

---

[68] Brucker, *Historia critica philosophiae*, vol. 1, 1319–20.

[69] Ibid., p. 1320: " . . . Alii primum Pyrrhonis praeceptorem Drysonem, vel Brysonsem vocant, Stilponis filium, Clinomachi discipulum, cuius supra mentio facta est. Qui cum parentis arte excellerent, dubium non est, Pyrrhonem dialecticis armis instructum egregias illas pugnas, quibus omnes adoriebantur philosophos Eristici, et de omnibus in utramque partem disputabant, ab eo didicisse."

was tailor made to confirm his mind in uncertainty to which it was in any event extremely prone.

Thus equipped, seeing dogmatists everywhere

> he stated that nothing at all could be understood and maintained, that none of the conclusions of the Dogmatists could in any way be held.[70]

Brucker went on:

> Those who have set forth a history of his life and view from ancient sources record that he said that nothing was nonourable or dishonourable, just or unjust, and so forth, indeed—that none of these things were in reality so, that men did all those things through following law and custom and that in any matter one thing was of no more importance than another.[71]

Brucker was well aware that this attitude presented a problem. As he points out, in the text, it is said that Pyrrho lived a type of life that was in accordance with the opinion that he never declined anything or avoided anything, but he met everything head on, whatever came before him, whether chariots, precipices, dogs and the like, nor yielded to his senses, while his friends followed him and saved him from disasters. To this Brucker commented:

> If however these doctrines, paradoxical in themselves and fit for overturning not only every truth but also everything that is honourable, were to be joined together, it is not without reason that people brought Pyrrho into suspicion, as being a man of disturbed mind and one raving through too much cleverness and knowledge. However, we shall regard him in a gentler light and we will with justice free the man from the reputation of insanity of this sort if we consider the course of his praiseworthy life and his deeds, praised as he was,

---

[70] Ibid., p. 1320–21: "Tum ad Anaxarchum, Metrodori Chii discipulum, delatus est, cui quoque constanter adhaesit, et cum eo, Alexandrum Magnum sequente, ad Indos profectus est, cum Brachmanibus et Gymnosophistis illius regionis congressus. Hos vero praeceptores ita audivit, ut ex illorum doctrina in sua arva derivaret, quaecunque animum ad incertitudinem valde inclinantem confirmare apta essent . . . His itaque praesidiis munitus, cum dogmaticorum subsellia ubique occupata vidisset, novam tum quidem temporis (Academia enim media nondum ea aetate florebat) philosophiam excogitavit, et nihil quicquam comprehendi posse dixit, neque omnio quicquam dogmaticorum decernendum esse statuit."

[71] Ibid., p. 1321: "Traduntque, qui vitae eius et placitorum historiam ex veteribus exposuerunt, nihil vel honestum esse dixisse, vel inhonestum, iustum vel iniustum, et sic in reliquis: nempe nihil horum reapse tale esse legem vero et consuetudine sequentes omnia ista homines facere nec in quapiam re hoc magis esse, quam illud."

according to Laertius, by the ancients, though not all of them, for his great erudition and, as seemed to many, for his decision to embark on the noble pursuit of philosophy.[72]

Brucker then took great care to characterize Pyrrho's personality, this was particularly important for Brucker, for he believed that the emotional life of a philosopher affected his ability to reason. Brucker characterized him as a man whose "spirit was altogether remote from arrogance and disdain", who did housework for his sister, who lived a solitary life, always persevering amid terrors and griefs with the same expression whether in illness or in a storm. Brucker, true to his aim of objectivity, then listed those things for which Pyrrho was criticized, pointing out that his life had not always been according to his doctrine. Brucker admitted that Pyrrho was angry when a friend did not purchase necessary goods for sacrifice, and said himself that one should strive to act according to philosophy, as far as it was possible, but that he, Pyrrho was only a man. Brucker concluded by saying;

> Who would believe that this can be true for a man who perpetually denies all use of the senses to the point of madness? Who would not detect the lie that records that friends and companions seized a man who was negligent in everything from dangers when in fact he lived a very solitary life and accomplished various journeys on his own in which no one rescued him from dogs, precipices and chariots? We can not fail to see from this that the disposition of Pyrrho which was inclined towards a lack of concern for the emotions and that his mind in every respect was immovable and undaunted by petty reasoning or scepticism, gave rise to the fable about him.[73]

Brucker then mentions Epicurus's praise for Pyrrho, which, Brucker contended, Epicurus would not have offered had Pyrrho been

---

[72] Loc. cit.: "Quae si doctrinae in se paradoxae, omnique non veritati tantum, sed et honestati evertendae aptae jungantur, non sine causa in eam suspicionem adducunt Pyrrhonem, fuisse hominem mentis emotae et nimia arte atque scientia insanientis. Mitius tamen de eo sentiemus, et ab eiusmodi insania virum merito liberabimus, veteribus tantum non omnibus ob erigegriam eruditionem, et, quod multis visum fuit, nobilissimam philosophiae excolendae viam initam, ut scribunt LAERTIUS . . ."

[73] Ibid., p. 1322: "Quis haec convenire credat viro omnem sensuum usum ad insaniam usque neganti? quis non mendacium palpet, tradens amicos comites cum omnia negligentem periculis eripuisse, cum solitariam valide vitam amaverit, et itineria quoque varia solus confecerit, in quibus nemo eum canibus, praecipitiis, curribus eripuit? Cui non manifestum ex his est, Pyrrhonis animum ad indifferentiam 'ton padon' mentemque ex utraque parte immotam et imperterritam istis Scepticismi rationis, ut postea decemus, tendentem, occasionem cudendae fabulae dedisse? Addimus his alia, quae tantis deliriis non agitatum fuisse Pyrrhonem evincunt."

insane. Equally important for Brucker was the fact that Pyrrho was selected to be a priest, for it implied that Pyrrho believed in God and therefore was not an atheist and that Pyrrho knew what he was doing when he performed religious rites.

> What sort of priest, I ask would he be who was so insane as to be ignorant, being delirious of what he was doing.[74]

At this point, Brucker made a very important point about Pyrrho's attitude toward sense perception, and, as a result, it indicates how much better than Stanley or Alexander Brucker had read Sextus Empiricus.

> We may pass by other reasons by which Pyrrho can be purged of this stain, adding however, this point, that the very doctrine of the Sceptics which did not reject the use of the senses quite clearly refuted this tale which was rejected by learned men long ago and disapproved of by the ancients and indeed by Aenesidemus. Of course the disengagement of Pyrrho did not reject an external appearance of the senses of which the rule of life of the Sceptic did not disapprove, but the definitions of dogmatic statements and an arrogance about knowledge.[75]

It is quite clear from this retelling of Pyrrho's life that Brucker was sympathetic to him. An explanation for this comes in the section "The origins of Pyrrho's scepticism". Brucker explained Pyrrho's scepticism as a logical response to the state of Greek philosophy during his time. Pyrrho had been aware of the philosophy of Democritus. As Brucker described Democritus's view, he denied that any real qualities existed in things themselves and believed that no differences lay in them. Nothing existed but atoms and the rest was opinion. Pyrrho had admired Democritus and had taken his physics as the basis for his philosophy. To these influences Brucker added Pyrrho's stay among the dialecticians where, as the result of having been subjected to attacks from their sophisms, Pyrrho learned to oppose them by maintaining that there was uncertainty in everything and by assuming indifference.

---

[74] Loc. cit.: 'Qualis quaeso vero pontifex, qui ita insanit, ut quid faciat, delirans ignoret?"

[75] Loc. cit.: "Alias rationes, quibus ab hac labe purgare potest Pyrrho, praeterimus, hoc unum adiicientes, ipsam Scepticorum doctrinam, quae in vita agenda sensuum usum non reiicit, satis evidenter refutare fabulam a viris doctis dudum reiectam et inter veteres quoque iam Aenesidemo impotatam. Scilicet ????? Pyrrhonis non externam sensuum apparentiam reiecit, quam vitae regulam non improbabant Sceptici, sed dogmaticorum definitiones rerum, et scientiae arrogantiam, cui evertendiae fundamenta rerum patere negabat . . ."

Timon, Pyrrho's disciple, congratulated him for his ability to withstand their attacks:

> I am amazed, Pyrrho, that you have been able at long last to get away from the stupid and empty Sophists, their vain self-conceit, and to untie the chains of false pretentioness.[76]

But it was not just those philosophers under whom Pyrrho studied who caused his scepticism to develop. In a long footnote in the *Kurze Fragen*,[77] Brucker recounted his own version of the history of sceptical attitudes in philosophy and their contributions to the history of philosophy and to what he identified as scepticism per se. Although Brucker found Huet's view that all the genuises of philosophy were sceptics an exaggeration, he was aware that a certain type of sceptical doubting did inform much of philosophy and be noted that many great men proclaimed their own intellectual modesty as Socrates had done. He however made the point that narrowly considered this was not scepticism. Yet Brucker acknowledged that there was much in ancient philosophy which led to scepticism: some philosophers might have had their own thoughts and opinions but because they were such bad communicators, they came across as uncertain and as not believing themselves in what they were saying. Early Greek philosophy, Brucker found to be defective in its construction of proof; he noted it often required people to rely on their faith alone instead of on reason, which led intelligent philosophers to question the thruthfulness of others. Brucker developed the subject in the *Historia critica philosophiae* in the section on the causes of scepticism. As he explained it:

> ... certain dogmas existed among the ancient philosophers which opened a very wide door to scepticism, among them with justice is to be counted the very famous dogma that everything is in a state of flux and is not the same in one moment as it had been before. The Pyrrhonists themselves saw that from this doctrine there followed the uncertainty of human condition and they admitted that Scepticism was a route to this opinion of Heraclitus. Those who stood out among the Dogmatists, Pythagoras, Plato, Democritus and Epicurus realized this and since they did not dare to deny the flux of matter in order to show that the object of science was stable, the former pair made up numbers and ideas or intelligible things while the latter pair introduced immutable atoms. However, while they put up hypotheses rather than evident truths, by this very process they strengthened

---

[76] Ibid., p. 1324: Mirror, qui tandem potuisti evadere Pyrrho Turgentes frusta, stupidos vanosque sophistas, Atque imposturae fallacis solvere vincia.

[77] Brucker, *Kurze Fragen*, vol. 2, 705ff.

rather than destroyed the opinion of the Sceptics that everything was
in a state of flux and changeable from moment to moment and that
those hypotheses did not suffice to establish for us certain
knowledge[78]

suffice to confirm for us a body of certain knowledge.[79] Despite the
fact that Brucker understood why someone might have wanted to
become a sceptic, he thought that the sceptical objections to the
dogmatists could only too easily erode into purile sophisms. This
weakness was caused by a "sluggishness in the search for truth".
Historical Pyrrhonism and scientific scepticism did not fall prey to
such weaknesses.

Brucker relegated the topic of the sceptic's atheism to the end of
both his Latin and German chapters and included it in his discussion of the tenets of scepticism. In this discussion, Brucker
answered the accusations of Reimmann and Budde that sceptics
were atheists. Brucker began his discussion by noting that Sextus
Empiricus admitted that there were Gods and that there was
Providence and that all men had a common and preconceived
notion of God and that "he was remote from death, perfect in
happiness and was a being to whom no evil could befall".[80] Yet, the
fact remained that the sceptics included in their questions one on
the existence and nature of God. They held that nothing of certainty could be maintained about God and that arguments could be
offered and refuted on both sides. Thus Sceptics built up arguments
for the existence of God and tore them down and believed that
assent about God's existence should be suspended. Thus,

---

[78] Brucker, *Historia critica philosophiae*, vol. 1, p. 1330: "Inter quae famosissimum
dogma merito numerandum est, cuncta fluere, nec uno quidem momento
idem esse, quod prius fuit. Ex hac enim doctrina incertitudinem humanae cognitionis sequi, ipse Pyrrhoni viderunt, Scepticismum viam ad hanc Heracliti opinionem esse fatentes, ipsique, qui inter dogmaticos eminuerunt, Pythagoras,
Plato, Democritus et Epicurus intellexerunt, qui cum materiae fluxum negare non
auderent, illi ut scientiae obiectum stabile exhiberent, numeros et ideas, sive
intelligibilia commento sunt, hi atomos immutabiles introduxerunt, ast dum
hypotheses magis, quam evidentes veritates supponebant, hoc ipso Scepticorum
opinionem magis firmarunt, quam destruxerunt, fluxa inque momenta mutabilia
esse omnia, nec fussicere istas hypotheses, ut certam firment scientiam."

[79] Loc. cit.

[80] Ibid., p. 1342: "Sed et hoc mordicitus tenent Sceptici, stulte obiici, legisla-
tores et duces communem de Diis notionem confinxisse, asseruntque pro indubita-
to, omnes homines communem et anticipatam de Deo notionem habere, fecundum
quam est quoddam beatum animal, et ab interitu alienum et in felicitate perfec-
tum, et in quod nullum cadere potest malum, esseque a ratione alienum, omnes
forte fortuna in easdem incidere Dei propries, non autem ad hoc moveri naturali-
ter etc. de quibus omnibus late et erudite quidem disserit SEXTUS, dignus
omnino, qui de gravissimo argumento totus legatur."

they included the doctrine concerning God among those which could possibly be, and about which however, not only the Dogmatists have decided nothing on which the mind can rely, but also the Sceptic has no means of determining or defining in taking a particular side as is clearly revealed from those things which Sextus says at great length and with great learning concerning this argument.[81]

Brucker concluded that if these facts were taken into account, the sceptics were not in any formal sense atheists, but yet they were not very pious and laid open the way to atheism.

Thus we can see that while Brucker was well aware that there had been a general scepticism among philosophers, he separated Pyrrhonism from both this and from Academic scepticism. It would appear that the reason for this was that Brucker was interested in the history of Greek philosophical sects and placed each type of scepticism with the sect out of which it grew—Pyrrhonism was placed with the Eleatics and Academic scepticism was placed after Plato. It was up to later historians of philosophy to make the connection between these types of scepticism and to think out how sceptical questioning operated in philosophy over its history.

Later treatments of Pyrrho's life all raised the question of Antigonus Carystius's chariots and precipices, but dropped all discussion of Pyrrho's atheism. Although one cannot call the *Encyclopédie* a history of philosophy, it was widely read and an important example of how Brucker's material was reworked.[82] If one had believed the chariot story, commented Diderot, one would have thought Pyrrho mad:

> Si cela est, il faut regarder Pyrrhon comme une de ces têtes qui naissent etonnées, et pour qui tout est confondu, mais il n'en rien, il raisonoit comme un insensé et se conduisoit comme tout le monde.[83]

The article began suggestively with the statement that scepticism was a method of thought. Budde had said that scepticism was not a sect, and Brucker that scepticism was a sect—in a way, but when Diderot added that it was a method of questioning, we have something new. He said:

---

[81] Loc. cit.: "Ut VII suam, si modo ulla apud Pyrrhonios datur, sententiam de Deo explicent, doctrinam de Deo inter ea referunt, quae esse forte possunt, de quibus tamen non Dogmatici tantum nihil, quo niti animus queat, statuunt, sed et Scepticus non habet, quod pro parte affirmante statuat, definiatue, ut ex iis luculenter patescit, quae fuse docteque de hoc argumento SEXTUS disserit."

[82] J. Proust. *Diderot et l'Encyclopédie*, Paris 1962, 293–315.

[83] *Encyclopédie, ou dictionnaire raisonné des sciences, des arts et des métiers, par un société de gens de lettres*, eds. D. Diderot, J. le Rond d'Alembert et al., 35 vols., Paris 1751–80, vol. 13, p. 608.

Dans les autres écoles, on avoit un système reçu, des principes avoués, on prouvoit tout, on ne doutoit de rien; dans celui-ci, on suivit une méthode de philosopher tout opposée.[84]

He seemed to imply that scepticism was an approach to philosophy as a whole. Diderot then went on to explain the tenets of scepticism—that nothing is to be demonstrated and that those who claimed it could be were liars—that the more a philosopher studied, the more uncertainty he found—that there were no fixed points to knowledge. Diderot praised Pyrrho's tranquility of spirit and added that Pyrrho had been created a priest and he concluded with a completely invented comment by Pyrrho:

C'est moi qui possede la vérité, c'est moi qui apprend à être sage; venéz messieurs, donnéz-vous la peine d'entrer: mon voisin n'est que un charlaton qui vous en imposera.[85]

There was a great interest in scepticism in Germany in the last years of the eighteenth century which developed in reaction to the philosophy of David Hume which we cannot discuss here, but one important book should be mentioned: Carl Friedrich Stäudlin's *Geschichte und Geist des Skepticismus*. The book begins with a long and important essay on the nature of scepticism and then recounts its history to philosophy. Brucker had accepted historical scepticism as a way to examine facts and scientific scepticism as an approach by which probable truth could be identified, Stäudlin saw scepticism as a natural response to philosophic dogmatism.

When one surveys, on the other side, the many different repeated attacks on the certainty of human knowledge, and the, in part very weak, defense of dogmatism, one no longer finds it strange that, after all, a system was developed that undermined the whole edifice of human knowledge which, unlike the sophists and some Megarians who debated the pros and cons of the issue for personal benefit, described everything as uncertain without personal regard.[86]

---

[84] Loc. cit.

[85] Loc. cit.

[86] C. F. Stäudlin, *Geschichte und Geist des Skepticismus*, Leipzig 1794, p. 281: "Wenn man nun von der anderen Seite die verschiedenen, immer wiederholten Angriffe auf die Gewissheit der menschlichen Erkenntnis und die zum Teil sehr schwache Verteidigung des Dogmatismus überschaut, so wird man es gar nicht befremdlich finden, dass endlich eine Kunst erfunden wurde, nicht nur etwa wie die Sophisten und mehrere Megariker aus Charlanterie und Eigenutz über Alles pro und contra zu peroriren und mit Trugschlüssen zu spielen, sondern das ganze Gebäude menschlicher Erkenntnis in allen seinen Fundamenten wanklend zu machen und alles ohne allen Unterschied als ungewiss darzustellen."

When Stäudlin retold the story of Pyrrho's life, the placed Pyrrho at the time of Aristotle and Epicurus and identified his teacher as Anaxarchus. He tells the story of Pyrrho's voyage with Anaxarchus and Alexander to India and invented the story that Pyrrho knew the tenets of the older philosophers well as he intended to dispute them all. This comment Stäudlin invented to create the image of Pyrrho as the critic of philosophy up to his time. He then attacked the story of Pyrrho and the chariots and precipices, saying that they had been made up by mockers. What sets Stäudlin's version of Pyrrho's life apart from earlier ones is his comment that scepticism led to the conclusion that all human knowledge was relative and subjective.

> He developed ten ways to question human knowledge which all led to the conclusion that all human knowledge is relative and subjective and has no inherent truths that are absolute and lasting.[87]

Finally, Stäudlin added an important historical remark—he noted that very little was known about Pyrrho's scepticism and that scepticism probably developed between the time of Pyrrho and that of Sextus Empiricus, but that we do not have the evidence of this development; as a result, he warned the reader not to believe that Pyrrho believed everything in Diogenes Laertius.

The next treatment of Pyrrho in a history of philosophy was by J.F. Buhle in *Geschichte der neueren Philosophie seit der Epoche der Wiederherstellung der Wissenschaften*.[88] Buhle placed Pyrrho after the Academic sceptics, and although he did not make any comment about what this might mean, he brought the two schools of scepticism together. Buhle continued the positive characterization of Pyrrho that Bayle had begun and that was developed by Brucker and made more positive in the article in the *Encyclopédie* and in Stäudlin's book. He told the usual story of Pyrrho's life, rejecting the chariot episode and commenting that it had been created to make Pyrrho look ridiculous. Buhle did not emphasize Pyrrho's questioning of the dogmatists, but rather his search for tranquility of spirit—a tranquility which Buhle believed belonged only to a wise man. Buhle remarked that although Pyrrho had been so indifferent,

---

[87] Ibid., p. 285: "Er ersann zehn verschiedene Arten, die menschliche Erkenntnis zweifelhaft zu machen, die alle dahin führten, dass die ganze menschliche Erkenntnis etwas bloss Relatives und Subjectives sei, und keinen innern Character der Wahrheit, nichts Absolutes und Bleibendes an sich habe."

[88] C. F. Buhle, *Geschichte der neueren Philosophie seit der Epoche der Wiederherstellung der Wissenschaften*, Göttingen 1800.

he left no philosophical writings, yet he was thought to be a philosophical genius of the rarest type and to judge from the testimonies about his life, he had been held in the highest regard by his contemporaries because of his spirit, his sentiments and the purity of his manners. Buhle ended his description with the observation that Pyrrho had been made a high priest, important evidence for Brucker and Stäudlin that Pyrrho had been held in high regard by his contemporaries and that he believed in God. Despite this positive characterization of Pyrrho, Buhle included a reference in a footnote to Stäudlin's *Geschichte und Geist des Skepticismus* which he recommended because it contained important answers to sceptical arguments.[89]

W.G. Tennemann's characterization of Pyrrho in his *Geschichte der Philosophie*[90] showed a greater sensitivity to both the historical development of scepticism in particular and philosophy in general than earlier historians and his positioning of Pyrrho in the history of philosophy dramatically shifted Pyrrho's philosophical paternity. Tennemann developed a theme introduced by Diderot and developed by Stäudlin, that scepticism was a method of philosophizing. To understand Tennemann's point of view, it is necessary to read both his *Geschichte der Philosophie* and his *Grundriss der Geschichte der Philosophie*.[91] Pyrrho was placed neither at the end of the discussion of ancient philosophy as in Brucker nor after the Academic Sceptics as in Buhle, but after Socrates, Antisthenes and the Cyrenaic and Megaric schools of philosophy and associated with Socrates. Tennemann's article on Pyrrho in the *Geschicte der Philosophie* began with a statement about the natural role of scepticism in the history of philosophy. This characterization brought in a theme still current in the work of Del Pra—Pyrrho, the follower of Socrates. Reason, as Tennemann described, had a natural distrust of speculation, and thus reason assumed the methods of scepticism and in questioning of dogmatism, it enlarged knowledge. Here scepticism seemed to be playing a role not unlike that of moderate scepticism advocated by Glanvill and recommended by Brucker. However, here the scepticism which was talked about was the type of scepticism which included Pyrrho and Sextus Empiricus. As Tennemann said:

---

[89] Ibid., 446–455.
[90] W. G. Tennemann, *Geschichte der Philosophie*, Leipzig 1799, vol. 2, 166–188.
[91] W. G. Tennemann, *Grundriss der Geschichte der Philosophie*, ed. A. Wendt, Leipzig 1820.

Reason's distrust of speculation which had been much aided by the
disunity of philosophers continued through the first period into the
second. Of course, the sceptical spirit was not as well received as the
dogmatic one and this spirit favoured that natural tendency of en-
larging knowledge.[92]

But Pyrrho and Sextus Empiricus did not have identical types of
scepticism; rather later sceptics naturally developed doubts with
far more clarity because philosophy itself had progressed.

> . . . it is likely that there must have been a progressive development
> analogous to all human inventions, systems and theories, but even
> more likely because of the following reasons: firstly, Scepticism is a
> constant companion of Dogmatism and responds almost always to
> the nature of the latter. Just as the dogmatic systems became more
> comprehensive and were arrived at more logically, so in response
> Scepticism rose to stronger and more comprehensive attacks on
> Dogmatism.[93]

Tennemann noted that it had been particularly difficult to understand exactly what Pyrrho's scepticism had been like because the
testimony by Pyrrho's successors had been distorted by the hatred
of the dogmatists and, as a result, the sceptics had been carica-
tured. This hatred, Tennemann thought, had caused the creation
of the anecdotes which portrayed Pyrrho as an eccentric rather
than a serious thinker and probably had been caused by the inability of philosophers to understand that Pyrrho's doubts might have
been limited to dogmatic assertions and had not been about custom
and ordinary judgements about sense perception. This misunderstanding could easily have caused people to characterize Pyrrho as
a man who would not avoid mad dogs and abysses. Tennemann, in
his retelling of Pyrrho's life, made subtle modifications from earlier
versions which substantially changed how scepticism and Pyrrho

---

[92] Tennemann, *Geschichte*, vol. 2, p. 166: "Das Misstrauen der Vernunft gegen
Speculationen, welches durch die Uneinigkeit der Philosophierenden so sehr
genährt wurde, pflanzte sich aus der ersten Periode auch in die zweite fort. Aber
natürlich fand der skeptische Geist nicht so viel Emphänglichkeit als der dogma-
tische, da dieser durch den natürlichen Hang zur Erweiterung der Erkenntnis
begünstigt wird."
[93] Ibid., p. 168: "Dass aber auch bei dem Skepticismus eine Fortschreitung
statt gefunden hat, ist schon durch die Analogie aller menschlichen Erfindungen,
Systeme und Theorien wahrscheinlich; noch wahrscheinlicher aber durch
folgende zwei Gründe: Erstlich der Skepticismus ist ein beständiger Gefährte des
Dogmatismus, und richtet sich fast immer nach der Beschaffenheit des letzten. So
wie die dogmatischen Systeme umfassender und mit mehr Kunst bearbeitet
werden, in dem Verhältnisse erhebt sich auch der Skepticismus zu starken und
weit greifenden Angriffen des Dogmatismus."

were perceived—it had not been the influence of Anaxarchus that had caused Pyrrho's scepticism, but both the writings of Democritus and Pyrrho's knowledge of Socrates's philosophy. Tennemann insisted boldly that Pyrrho could well have known about Socrates.

> The question of how Pyrrho could have acquired knowledge of Socrates should not embarrass us, though neither Dryson or Clinomadus had been his teacher, but Phaedo was from the same town and founded a school there.[94]

His primary proof was, however, that Pyrrho and Socrates were of a similar mind. Quoting Timon he said:

> I would only like to know how you, Pyrrho, unique in your way, can continue to live in such serenity and peace and soar above peopple like a god and honoured old man, how and where did you find the art to tear yourself away from blind worship of opinion, the empty wisdom of the sophists and to destroy the magic wall of persuasions. You are not concerned to research the air that surrounds Greece, what everything is made of and what it will dissolve into.[95]

This Tennemann described as Socratean sobriety. In particular Pyrrho was like Socrates because of his interest in ethics, his belief that speculative thinking was of no use and that man should follow his feelings in all practical dealings. Tennemann turned to Cicero's *De finibus* IV. 16 for his proof:

> In my view, therefore, while all who defined the End of Gods as the life of moral conduct are in error, some are more wrong than others. The most mistaken no doubt is Pyrrho, because his conception of virtue leaves nothing as an object of desire whatever.[96]

He then went on to use incidents from Pyrrho's life to further illustrate his contention. Pyrrho had a peaceful disposition,

---

[94] Ibid., p. 171: "Auch darf uns die Frage, auf welchem Wege er Kenntnis vom Socrates erlangen konnte, gar nicht in Verlegenheit setzen, wenn auch weder Dryson noch Klitomachus, chronologischer Schwierigkeiten wegen, seine Lehrer waren, da Phaedo aus derselben Stadt war, und daselbst auch eine Schule errichtet hatte."

[95] Ibid., p. 172: "Nur dieses, heisst es in einem, wünscht mein Geist zu wissen, wie Du, Pyrrhon, einzig in Deiner Art, noch immer mit solchen Gleichmuth, mit solcher Ruhe leben kannst, und gleich einem Gott unter den Menschen hervorragst. Und wie und wo fandest Du doch, ehrwürdiger Greis, die Kunst Dich von aller blinden Verehrung der Meinungen, von allen leeren Weisheitsdünkel der Sophisten loszureissen, und die Zaubergeister der betrügerischen Überredung zu zerstören. Dich kümmert es wenig zu erforschen, woher die Luft, welche Griechenland umgibt, oder woraus jedes Ding entstand, und in was es aufgelöst wird."

[96] Ibid., p. 175.

discharged his obligations, was morally and ethically pure, enjoyed the respect of his fellow citizens, and in only one way was different from Socrates—he did not have a high opinion of men, as his quotation from Homer attested: "We are the leaves of the tree". He went on to describe in the *Grundriss der Geschichte der Philosophie* the similarity between Socratic irony and Pyrrhonian scepticism.

> In common with Socrates (whom in some particulars he resembled) he maintained that virtue alone is desirable (Cic. *De Oratore* III. 17. *De Finibus* III. 3. *Academica* II. 62.) that everything else, even science, is useless and unprofitable. To support this last proposition which was also connected with the irony of Socrates, he alleged that the contradiction existing between the different principles supported by disputants demonstrates the incomprehensibility of things. All this, he argued, should make a philosopher withold his assent, and to endeavour to maintain an air of freedom from all impressions.

Tennemann's *Grundriss der Geschichte der Philosophie* gave a tight and clear summary of his position. There he clearly stated how scepticism functioned as an integral part of the history of philosophy. Philosophy advanced by inquiry into the nature of our faculties of cognition—into the knowledge of things, or, on the other hand, from the assumed knowledge of things to the theory of knowledge; the former Tennemann called the critical method, the latter the dogmatic. The object of scepticism was to identify errors, this activity Tennemann believed was the precursor of the critical method that led to the "science of reason".[97] Thus, for example, when Tennemann came to describe Greek philosophers, he listed two important lines of enquiry that they developed: the first gave attention to the objects of science and the second gave an introduction to method and with this method came scepticism which opposed dogmatism. The two approaches were necessary for philosophy to progress.

By the end of the eighteenth century there were two completely different views of ancient scepticism which had developed through the study and interpretation of the life of Pyrrho, one that it was a philosophy which could not be lived, and the other that it was a method of questioning. If one looks back to Budde and Brucker, the

---

[97] Tennemann, *Grundriss*, p. 35: "Der Skepticismus ist der Vorläufer der Kritischen Methode, welche durch gründliche Untersuchung des Erkenntnisvermögens, und besonders der Vernunft, nach ihren ursprünglichen Gesetzen an Zwecken das Mass, den Grad und die Beschaffenheit der Vernunftwissenschaft, in so weit sie möglich ist, so wie den Weg dazu nich willkürlich, sondern nach Grundsätzen bestimmt und also Propadautik herumtappen, das Spekulieren auf gut Glück und das erfolglose Streben verhütet wird."

line of development of the latter view is clear, although it would not have been a line of development that either would have agreed with. Budde had separated Pyrrhonian scepticism—universal scepticism as he called it—from the moderate scepticism of the wise men like Socrates. Brucker had separated historical scepticism and scientific scepticism and Socratic sceptical questioning from Pyrrhonian and Academic scepticism, and Pyrrhonian and Academic scepticism from each other. He did this because he was interested in identifying the philosophical traditions and their immediate historical sources. Historical Pyrrhonism and scientific scepticism were methods of questioning, not schools of philosophy, while ancient Pyrrhonism and Academic scepticism were. With Stäudlin and Buhle, sceptical questioning and Pyrrho's way of life began to take on a more personal tone and the subjectivism of the sceptical approach to reality was noted. Tennemann, changing the intellectual paternity of Pyrrho radically, linked him with Socrates and suddenly placed him in the tradition of the great wise men of philosophy. But equally important was Tennemann's development of Stäudlin's historical observation that scepticism developed between Pyrrho and Sextus Empiricus. Thus scepticism was described as interacting with developing dogmatism.

It is the "sayings of the philosophers", not their lives which have become the matter of philosophy and its history today. But it is salutory to note that one of the most important characters in philosophy, Pyrrho, and one of the most important movements in philosophy, scepticism, could not have been understood without the developing debate about the interrelationship between the philosopher's life and what that life implied about the possibility of living his philosophy. This timeless question is still with us. Equally important for our understanding of the development of philosophy is our evaluation of the importance of the historical Pyrrho. In working out who the historical Pyrrho was and in trying to understand Pyrrho as a philosophical human being, living in a particular time in history, the historians of philosophy of the seventeenth and eighteenth centuries raised basic questions about the development of scepticism and its relationship to other aspects of Greek philosophy at that time. This in turn raises the question for Tennemann about the relationship of scepticism as a method of questioning to the development of philosophy itself—a question which still has meaning in the history of modern philosophy. These thoughtful studies by seventeenth- and eighteenth-century historians of philosophy were far from the dry and distorting activity imputed to historians of philosophy by Richard Rorty.

INDEX OF NAMES

BRILL'S STUDIES IN INTELLECTUAL HISTORY

1. POPKIN, R.H. *Isaac la Peyrère (1596-1676)*. His Life, Work and Influence. 1987. ISBN 90 04 08157 7
2. THOMSON, A. *Barbary and Enlightenment*. European Attitudes towards the Maghreb in the 18th Century. 1987. ISBN 90 04 08273 5
3. DUHEM, P. *Prémices Philosophiques*. With an Introduction in English by S.L. Jaki. 1987. ISBN 90 04 08117 8
4. OUDEMANS, TH.C.W. & A.P.M.H. LARDINOIS. *Tragic ambiguity*. Anthropology, Philosophy and Sophocles' *Antigone*. 1987. ISBN 90 04 08417 7
5. FRIEDMAN, J.B. (ed.). *John de Foxton's Liber Cosmographiae* (1408). An Edition and Codicological Study. 1988. ISBN 90 04 08528 9
6. AKKERMAN, F. & A.J. VANDERJAGT (eds.). *Rodolphus Agricola Phrisius, 1444-1485*. Proceedings of the International Conference at the University of Groningen, 28-30 October 1985. 1988. ISBN 90 04 08599 8
7. CRAIG, W.L. *The Problem of Divine Foreknowledge and Future Contingents from Aristotle to Suarez*. 1988. ISBN 90 04 08516 5
8. STROLL, M. *The Jewish Pope*. Ideology and Politics in the Papal Schism of 1130. 1987. ISBN 90 04 08590 4
9. STANESCO, M. *Jeux d'errance du chevalier médiéval*. Aspects ludiques de la fonction guerrière dans la littérature du Moyen Age flamboyant. 1988. ISBN 90 04 08684 6
10. KATZ, D. *Sabbath and Sectarianism in Seventeenth-Century England*. 1988. ISBN 90 04 08754 0
11. LERMOND, L. *The Form of Man*. Human Essence in Spinoza's *Ethic*. 1988. ISBN 90 04 08829 6
12. JONG, M. DE. *In Samuel's Image*. Early Medieval Child Oblation. (in preparation)
13. PYENSON, L. *Empire of Reason*. Exact Sciences in Indonesia, 1840-1940. 1989. ISBN 90 04 08984 5
14. CURLEY, E. & P.-F. MOREAU (eds.). *Spinoza. Issues and Directions*. The Proceedings of the Chicago Spinoza Conference. 1990. ISBN 90 04 09334 6
15. KAPLAN, Y., H. MÉCHOULAN & R.H. POPKIN (eds.). *Menasseh Ben Israel and His World*. 1989. ISBN 90 04 09114 9
16. BOS, A.P. *Cosmic and Meta-Cosmic Theology in Aristotle's Lost Dialogues*. 1989. ISBN 90 04 09155 6
17. KATZ, D.S. & J.I. ISRAEL (eds.) *Sceptics, Millenarians and Jews*. 1990. ISBN 90 04 09160 2
18. DALES, R.C. *Medieval Discussions of the Eternity of the World*. 1990. ISBN 90 04 09215 3
19. CRAIG, W.L. *Divine Foreknowledge and Human Freedom*. The Coherence of Theism: Omniscience. 1991. ISBN 90 04 09250 1
20. OTTEN, W. *The Anthropology of Johannes Scottus Eriugena*. 1991. ISBN 90 04 09302 8
21. ÅKERMAN, S. *Queen Christina of Sweden and Her Circle*. The Transformation of a Seventeenth-Century Philosophical Libertine. 1991. ISBN 90 04 09310 9
22. POPKIN, R.H. *The Third Force in Seventeenth-Century Thought*. 1992. ISBN 90 04 09324 9
23. DALES, R.C. & O. ARGERAMI (eds.). *Medieval Latin Texts on the Eternity of the World*. 1990. ISBN 90 04 09376 1
24. STROLL, M. *Symbols as Power*. The Papacy Following the Investiture Contest. 1991. ISBN 90 04 09374 5

25. FARAGO, C.J. *Leonardo da Vinci's 'Paragone'*. A Critical Interpretation with a New Edition of the Text in the *Codex Urbinas*. 1992. ISBN 90 04 09415 6

26. JONES, R. *Learning Arabic in Renaissance Europe*. ISBN 90 04 09451 2

27. DRIJVERS, J.W. *Helena Augusta*. The Mother of Constantine the Great and the Legend of Her Finding of the True Cross. 1992. ISBN 90 04 09435 0

28. BOUCHER, W.I. *Spinoza in English*. A Bibliography from the Seventeenth-Century to the Present. 1991. ISBN 90 04 09499 7

29. McINTOSH, C. *The Rose Cross and the Age of Reason*. Eighteenth-Century Rosicrucianism in Central Europe and its Relationship to the Enlightenment. 1992. ISBN 90 04 09502 0

30. CRAVEN, K. *Jonathan Swift and the Millennium of Madness*. The Information Age in Swift's *A Tale of a Tub*. 1992. ISBN 90 04 09524 1

31. BERKVENS-STEVELINCK, C., H. BOTS, P.G. HOFTIJZER & O.S. LANKHORST (eds.). *Le Magasin de l'Univers. The Dutch Republic as the Centre of the European Book Trade*. Papers Presented at the International Colloquium, held at Wassenaar, 5-7 July 1990. 1992. ISBN 90 04 09493 8

32. GRIFFIN, JR., M.I.J. *Latitudinarianism in the Seventeenth-Century Church of England*. Annotated by R.H. Popkin. Edited by L. Freedman. 1992. ISBN 90 04 09653 1

33. WES, M.A. *Classics in Russia 1700-1855*. Between Two Bronze Horsemen. 1992. ISBN 90 04 09664 7

34. BULHOF, I.N. *The Language of Science*. A Study of the Relationship between Literature and Science in the Perspective of a Hermeneutical Ontology. With a Case Study of Darwin's *The Origin of Species*. 1992. ISBN 90 04 09644 2

35. LAURSEN, J.C. *The Politics of Skepticism in the Ancients, Montaigne, Hume, and Kant*. 1992. ISBN 90 04 09459 8

36. COHEN, E. *The Crossroads of Justice*. Law and Culture in Late Medieval France. 1993. ISBN 90 04 09569 1

37. POPKIN, R.H. & A.J. VANDERJAGT (eds.). *Scepticism and Irreligion in the Seventeenth and Eighteenth Centuries*. 1993. ISBN 90 04 09596 9

38. MAZZOCCO, A. *Linguistic Theories in Dante and the Humanists*. Studies of Language and Intellectual History in Late Medieval and Early Renaissance Italy. 1993. ISBN 90 04 09702 3

39. KROOK, D. *John Sergeant and His Circle*. A Study of Three Seventeenth-Century English Aristotelians. Edited with an Introduction by B.C. Southgate. 1993. ISBN 90 04 09756 2

40. AKKERMAN, F., G.C. HUISMAN & A.J. VANDERJAGT (eds.). *Wessel Gansfort (1419-1489) and Northern Humanism*. 1993. ISBN 90 04 09857 7

41. COLISH, M.L. *Peter Lombard*. 2 vols. 1993. ISBN 90 04 09861 5 (set)